The Special Law Governing

Public Service Corporations

The Special Law Governing

Public Service Corporations

AND ALL OTHERS ENGAGED
IN PUBLIC EMPLOYMENT

IN TWO VOLUMES
Volume 2

A LAW CLASSIC

Bruce Wyman, A.M., LL.B.
Professor of Law in Harvard University

BeardBooks
Washington, D.C.

PREFACE TO VOLUME II

I would add that as this treatise has been going through the long process of manufacture this past six months the publishers have permitted me, and the printers have co-operated with me, in adding new citations as new cases of great importance have come out. The treatise thus contains the law into 1911, and it is hoped that the time and money which have been spent in keeping the work up to date while it was in the process of manufacture will be appreciated. I have printed in an Appendix the Interstate Commerce Legislation as amended by this Congress. And I have discussed throughout this treatise the judicial decisions which have been made under the Interstate Commerce Acts. I might add that whatever slight unconventionality anyone may note in the format of this book is due to my own insistence upon clearness in the presentation. While no types are used in any part of the composition which are not distinctly moderate in size, it may be noted that the Reference Tables, through which one must search, are set one point larger than is the standard, although this adds a few pages to each volume; for I know that in the last few years particularly, I would have been very grateful to bookmakers if this had been their custom.

B. W.

CAMBRIDGE, February, 1911.

TABLE OF CONTENTS

VOLUME II

CHAPTER XXIV

DISTRIBUTION OF FACILITIES AVAILABLE

CHAPTER XXV

REGULATION OF THE SERVICE

PART VII. LIABILITY FOR DEFAULT

CHAPTER XXVI

CONDUCT OF THE UNDERTAKING

TABLE OF CONTENTS

CHAPTER XXVII

PROTECTION OWED DURING PERFORMANCE

CHAPTER XXVIII

FAILURE IN THE UNDERTAKING

[x]

TABLE OF CONTENTS

CHAPTER XXIX

LIMITATION OF LIABILITY

PART VIII.   TERMINATION OF SERVICE

CHAPTER XXX

END OF THE UNDERTAKING

BOOK IV. REGULATION OF PUBLIC SERVICE

PART IX. RESTRICTION OF CHARGES

CHAPTER XXXI

GENERAL THEORY OF RATE REGULATION

CHAPTER XXXII

PROPER BASIS OF CAPITALIZATION

[xiv]

CHAPTER XXXIII

RATE OF RETURN

CHAPTER XXXIV

OPERATING EXPENSES

CHAPTER XXXV

DETERMINATION OF PARTICULAR RATES

TABLE OF CONTENTS

CHAPTER XXXVI

CHARACTERISTICS OF THE RATE

[xviii]

PART X. PREVENTION OF DISCRIMINATION

CHAPTER XXXVII

PROHIBITION OF DISCRIMINATION

Table of Contents

CHAPTER XXXVIII

ILLEGAL DISCRIMINATION

CHAPTER XXXIX

JUSTIFIABLE DIFFERENCES

CHAPTER XL

RELATIVE DISCRIMINATION

TABLE OF CONTENTS

CHAPTER XLI

CONSTITUTIONAL SUMMARY

TABLE OF CONTENTS

APPENDIX A

THE INTERSTATE COMMERCE ACT

TABLE OF CONTENTS

APPENDIX B

THE COMMERCE COURT ACT

APPENDIX C

THE ELKINS ACT

APPENDIX D

THE EXPEDITING ACT

APPENDIX E

FORMS FOR PROCEEDINGS BEFORE COMMISSIONS

TABLE OF CONTENTS

APPENDIX F

FORMS FOR PROCEEDINGS INVOLVING COMMISSIONS

§ 1. Bill to enforce order of the Commission.
2. Abstract of answer to above complaint.
3. Bill to enjoin order of the Commission.
4. Abstract of answer to this bill.

BOOK III. CONDUCT OF PUBLIC EMPLOY-MENT

PART VI. MANAGEMENT OF THE BUSINESS—*continued*

CHAPTER XXIV

DISTRIBUTION OF FACILITIES AVAILABLE

§ 830. Proper management.

§ 830. Proper management.

It must be plain to anyone familiar with the progress of the law governing public services that the oversight of the law over the conduct of public employment is becoming constantly more searching. Doubtless as those who conduct these businesses maintain, it will be wise to leave to those responsible for their management a reasonable discretion in every respect. But this does not mean that the law should not arrive at working standards of proper management with sufficient detail to be really effective. For law should always be present to hold those who have the active management strictly accountable for any conspicuous failures in public service. And in every public business it is sufficiently plain that the modern law will require efficient management according to the highest standards of the particular business.[1] "At the same time, it must be remembered that railroads are the private property of their owners; that while from the public character of the work in which they are engaged, the public has power to prescribe rules for securing faithful and efficient service, and equality between shippers and communities, yet in no sense is the public a general manager." [2]

Topic A. *Arrangements Made for Facilities*

§ 831. Notice necessary for special requirements.

Certainly if special arrangements are desired, the proprietor is entitled to notice. If cars are needed in which to load carloads of goods, notice of that fact must be given to the carrier in advance. He cannot be expected to

---

[1] The quotation which follows is from Interstate Comm. Comm. v. Chicago Gt. W. Ry. Co., 209 U. S. 108, 52 L. ed. 705, 28 Sup. Ct. 493 (1908), affirming an elaborate opinion in 141 Fed. 1003 (1905).

[2] See Lake Shore & M. S. Ry. Co. v. Smith, 173 U. S. 684, 43 L. ed. 858, 19 Sup. Ct. 565 (1899).

provide empty cars of every sort at each station enough to meet an unexpected demand. Only after reasonable notice of the need of such a car will he be liable for delay in supplying the car.[1] This was particularly plain in a recent case [2] where a shipper, an importer, complained that the railroad company had not kept sufficient cattle cars in readiness near the wharves to take his cattle from incoming vessels, although he had apprised them generally of his contingent needs. But the court held that upon such a requisition the railroad company need not keep over a hundred cattle cars tied up at the wharf station for many days in expectation of the arrival of the designated steamers, and certainly they were under no obligation to keep in touch with the bulletins posted at the chamber of commerce for the purpose of ascertaining when vessels would be reported, so as to be prepared to furnish carriage for the transportation of their cargoes.

§ 832. Reservation of accommodations granted.

It is customary in certain services, in innkeeping and carriage particularly, to reserve accommodations upon cer-

---

[1] *Illinois.*—Chicago & A. R. R. Co. v. Erickson, 91 Ill. 613, 33 Am. Rep. 70 (1879); Illinois C. R. R. Co. v. Bundy, 97 Ill. App. 202 (1901).

Missouri.—Huston v. Wabash Ry. Co., 63 Mo. App. 671 (1895).

New York.—Tierney v. New York Central & H. R. R. R. Co., 76 N. Y. 305 (1879).

South Carolina.—P o r c h e r v. Northeastern R. R. Co., 14 Rich. Law, 181 (1867).

Wisconsin.—Ayres v. Chicago & N. W. Ry. Co., 71 Wis. 372, 37 N. W. 432, 5 Am. St. Rep. 226 (1888).

Where there is a definite contract, however, further notice is unnecessary:

Indiana.—Pittsburgh, C., C. & St. L. Ry. Co. v. Racer, 10 Ind. App. 503, 37 N. E. 280, 38 N. E. 186 (1894).

North Carolina.—McAbsher v. Richmond & D. R. R. Co., 108 N. C. 344, 12 S. E. 892 (1891).

[2] Di Giorgio Imp. & S. S. Co. v. Pennsylvania Ry. Co., 104 Md. 693, 65 Atl. 425, 8 L. R. A. (N. S.) 108 (1906). But in Maryland as elsewhere a reasonable request for cars must be honored. Baltimore & O. R. R. Co. v. Whitehill, 104 Md. 295, 64 Atl. 1033 (1906).

tain conditions for prospective patrons upon their application. But it seems that there is no obligation to institute the practice or to continue it if once adopted; for it is only to those who demand immediate service that there is a present obligation. Thus while a sleeping car company may reserve a berth and justify a refusal to give the berth later to another,[1] it is under no obligation to grant a reservation to one demanding it. This was held in a case where an applicant found all the berths occupied, but one was to be vacated at the next station; he then demanded of the conductor a ticket for this berth from that station to his destination. The conductor refused to sell him such a ticket, and the refusal was held justified.[2] It would follow that upon the berth being vacated the conductor, not having consented to reserve it, must sell it to the first applicant, whether the former applicant or another.[3] It is no excuse for a sleeping car company's breach of contract to reserve a certain berth for plaintiff that another person demanded it before plaintiff presented herself to pay for and occupy it, even if there was no other unoccupied.[4] It would follow that the company should have recourse against the intending passenger who should not take up the reservation, although it is probable that after notification the company should mitigate the damages by reselling the accommodations if possible.

[1] *United States.*—Mann Boudoir Car Co. v. Dupre, 54 Fed. 646, 21 L. R. A. 289, 4 C. C. A. 540, 13 U. S. App. 183 (1893).

Texas.—Pullman Palace Car Co. v. Cain, 15 Tex. Civ. App. 503, 40 S. W. 220 (1897); Pullman Palace Car Co. v. Nelson, 22 Tex. Civ. App. 223, 54 S. W. 624 (1899).

[2] Searles v. Mann Boudoir Car Co., 45 Fed. 330 (1891).

[3] Pullman Palace Car Co. v. Reed, 75 Ill. 125, 131, 20 Am. Rep. 232 (1874). See also Cincinnati, N. O. & T. P. Ry. Co. v. Raine, 130 Ky. 454, 113 S. W. 495, 132 Am. St. Rep. 400 (1908).

[4] Pullman Palace Car Co. v. Booth (Tex. Civ. App.), 28 S. W. 719 (1894).

§ 833. Contract obligation to supply facilities.

It is not unusual to find a special agreement for the supplying of facilities made generally in advance. Such a contract is obligatory usually as both mutual consent and consideration may be found. The railway company's undertaking to have ready a car at the time designated is matched against the shipper's undertaking to take the car. If the company does not supply the car it is liable to the shipper for his consequential damages; and if the shipper fails to take the car he is liable to the carrier for whatever loss it may incur by bringing the car to the designated point without getting the expected freight.[1] In case of a special contract of this sort the general principle applies that a party who by his own contract puts himself under obligation is bound to make his promise good notwithstanding many apparently good excuses. Thus a carrier cannot excuse its failure to furnish a car that it has contracted to provide on the ground that it does not have cars available, even if it can show that its present shortage is altogether unexpected.[2]

[1] *United States.*—Missouri Pac. Ry. Co. v. Texas & P. Ry. Co., 31 Fed. 864 (1887).

Alabama.—Baxley v. Tallahassee & M. R. R. Co., 128 Ala. 183, 29 So. 451 (1900).

Indiana.—Pittsburg, C., C. & St. L. Ry. Co. v. Racer, 5 Ind. App. 209, 31 N. E. 853 (1892).

New York.—Clark v. Ulster & D. R. R. Co., 189 N. Y. 93, 81 N. E. 766, 13 L. R. A. (N. S.) 164, 121 Am. St. Rep. 848 (1907).

Even station agents apparently have power to bind the railroad company to a contract to furnish cars. See Wood v. Chicago, M. & St. P. Ry. Co., 68 Iowa, 491, 27 N. W. 473, 56 Am. Rep. 861 (1886).

A contract of shipment made by a railroad company which contains a provision providing for carriage by a particular train or within a particular time is not discriminatory and void within the meaning of the Interstate Commerce Act. Kirby v. Chicago & A. R. Co., 146 Ill. App. 31 (1908).

[2] *Alabama.*—Baxley v. Tallahassee & M. R. R. Co., 128 Ala. 183, 29 So. 451 (1900).

Indiana.—Pittsburg, C., C. & St. L. Ry. Co. v. Racer, 10 Ind. App. 503, 37 N. E. 280, 38 N. E. 186 (1894).

Missouri.—Currell v. Hannibal & St. J. Ry. Co., 97 Mo. App. 93, 71 S. W. 113 (1902).

§ 834. New business accepted without notification.

A further point should be made here. If the proprietors of the business, with knowledge of the congestion of their business which will prevent them from fulfilling their engagements promptly (however little they may be to blame for these conditions) accept new business without notifying the customer of the conditions, they will be liable not only for any delay that they cause thereby to the business which they have accepted, but will be liable also for delaying in forwarding the business which they accepted without giving warning.[1] If this rule results in imposing liability upon the proprietors whatever way they may turn thereafter, when they might have refused the new business which is causing them the trouble, they have only themselves to blame.   In some of the carriers'

New Hampshire.—Deming v. Grand Trunk R. R. Co., 38 N. H. 455, 2 Am. Rep. 267 (1869).

North Carolina.—McAbsher v. Richmond & D. R. R. Co., 108 N. C. 344, 12 S. E. 892 (1891).

South Carolina.—Mathis v. Southern Ry. Co., 65 S. C. 271, 43 S. E. 684, 61 L. R. A. 824 (1902); Texas & P. Ry. Co. v. W. Scott & Co. (Tex. Civ. App.), 86 S. W. 1065 (1905); Southern Kansas Ry. Co. of Texas v. Morris (Tex. Civ. App.), 99 S. W. 433 (1907); Southern Kansas Ry. Co. v. Samples (Tex. Civ. App.), 109 S. W. 417 (1908); Texas & P. Ry. Co. v. Shawnee Cotton Oil Co. (Tex. Civ. App.), 118 S. W. 776 (1909).

Texas.—International & G. N. R. R. Co. v. Young (Tex. Civ. App.) 28 S. W. 819 (1894).

[1] The text represents the general law. See particularly:

United States.—H e l l i w e l l   v.

Grand Trunk Ry. Co., 7 Fed. 68 (1881); Bussey v. Memphis & L. R. R. Co., 4 McCrary, 405 (1882); Petersen v. Case, 21 Fed. 885 (1884); Thomas v. Wabash, St. L. & P. Ry. Co., 63 Fed. 200 (1894).

Missouri.—Russel Grain Co. v. Wabash R. R. Co., 114 Mo. App. 488, 89 S. W. 908 (1905).

New York.—Tierney v. New York C. & H. R. R. R. Co., 76 N. Y. 305 (1879).

North Carolina.—Patterson v. Steamship Co., 53 S. E. 224, 5 L. R. A. (N. S.) 1012, 111 Am. St. Rep. 848, 140 N. C. 412 (1906).

Utah.—Nichols v. Oregon Short Line, R. R. Co. 24 Utah, 83, 66 Pac. 768, 91 Am. St. Rep. 778 (1901).

Wisconsin.—Ayres v. Chicago & N. W. Ry. Co., 71 Wis. 372, 37 N. W. 432 (1888).

cases it is said that acceptance of goods for transportation without giving notification of the probable cause of delay is tantamount to an assurance all is well. But, whether this is a more sound statement or not, it certainly is true that when a carrier well knows of the demoralization of its traffic and accepts goods without notifying the shipper, he is liable.[1]

§ 835. Statutory definition of these obligations.

As has just been seen there is a common law obligation to bring forward proper facilities upon due notification. Besides this there are in many States remedial statutes, providing often that cars shall be furnished within a stated number of days upon request under penalty of a certain amount per day for default. These statutes receive strict interpretation because of their penal character.[2] And in accordance with general principles, they receive so far as may be interpretation in accordance with the common law, the railroad company commonly being excused for such reasons as would furnish an excuse at common law.[3]

[1] Louisville & N. R. R. Co. v. Farmers' & D. L. S. Com. Firm, 107 Ky. 53, 52 S. W. 972 (1899), holding carrier liable for not informing shipper that connection was congested.

See also Hasseltine v. Southern Ry. Co., 75 S. C. 141, 55 S. E. 142, 6 L. R. A. (N. S.) 1009 (1906), holding carrier of passengers liable for taking a passenger without notifying him that he would be prevented by quarantine restrictions from completing his journey.

[2] *North Carolina.*—Branch v. Wilmington & W. R. R. Co., 88 N. C. 570 (1883).

Texas.—Texas & P. Ry. Co. v. Barrow, 33 Tex. Civ. App. 611, 77 S. W. 643 (1903).

See further Houston, E. & W. T. Ry. Co. v. Campbell, 91 Tex. 551, 45 S. W. 2, 43 L. R. A. 225 (1898).

But see St. Louis, I. M. & S. Ry. Co. v. Wynne Hoop & Cooperage Co., 81 Ark. 373, 99 S. W. 375 (1907).

[3] *Arkansas.*—St. Louis, S. W. Ry. Co. v. Clay Ginn. Co., 77 Ark. 357, 92 S. W. 531 (1906).

Georgia.—Pennington & E. v. Douglass, A. & G. Ry. Co., 3 Ga. App. 665, 60 S. E. 485 (1907).

Illinois.—People v. Illinois & St.

[713]

§ 836. Constitutionality of legislative regulation.

Of late years there have been decisions enough to make it clear on principle how far such statutes may go in interfering with the management of a public service. The general power of regulation potentially covers all departments of the business.[1] But plainly this power of regulation by the State should not be exercised outrageously. If the company is giving proper service it ought not to be interfered with. In most cases the interposition of the State will be found to have some justification. However, the cases apparently hold that dictation as to minor matters may be unnecessarily vexatious, invading the general right of a company to conduct its own affairs in its own way.[2] A distinction should be taken however. Although without such legislation a regulating commission might hesitate to make orders in respect to the provision of facilities, with such legislation remedies may be applied. And in late years the attention of the public has been so directed to this need of the betterment of service that such statutes have become common; and by

L. R. R. & Coal Co., 122 Ill. 506, 14 N. E. 261 (1887).

North Carolina.—Hardware Co. v. Railroad Co., 150 N. C. 703, 64 S. E. 873, 22 L. R. A. (N. S.) 1200 (1909).

Texas.—B. F. Allen v. Texas & P. Ry. Co., 100 Tex. 525, 101 S. W. 792 (1907).

[1] Atlantic C. L. R. R. Co. v. North Carolina Corp. Comm., 206 U. S. 1, 51 L. ed. 933, 27 S. Ct. 585 (1907).

See also Winchester & S. R. R. Co. v. Commonwealth, 106 Va. 264, 55 S. E. 092 (1906).

[2] Lake Shore & M. S. Ry. Co. v. Smith, 173 U. S. 684, 43 L. ed. 858, 19 S. Ct. 565 (1899).

See also Beardsley v. New York, L. E. & W. R. R. Co., 162 N. Y. 230, 56 N. E. 488 (1900).

State legislation of this sort is void if it interferes with interstate transportation.

Houston & T. C. R. R. Co. v. Mayes, 201 U. S. 321, 50 L. ed. 772, 26 Sup. Ct. 491 (1906). And see McNeill v. Southern Ry. Co., 202 U. S. 543, 50 L. ed. 1142, 26 Sup. Ct. 722 (1906).

If it can be said to be only proper police it can stand.

See Allen v. Texas & P. Ry. Co., 100 Tex. 525, 101 S. W. 792 (1907). And Patterson v. Missouri Pacific Ry. Co., 77 Kan. 236, 94 Pac. 138 (1908).

these statutes much advance in the development of this duty has been accomplished.

Topic B.   Proper Priorities in Service

§ 837. Imperative need of the company itself.

In time of stress when the company involved has not sufficient facilities to meet all demands made upon it for service, it is not enough to say as matters were left in the last chapter that the company is excused from not meeting particular demands upon it. Being in public service still, it must always discharge its public duties so far as it is able, handling the business demanding its attention with proper regard to the exigencies of the whole situation. To give one example, it is sufficiently obvious that such service as the company itself needs in order to maintain its service for the benefit of all concerned has precedence over everything. Thus a railroad may give coal cars bringing its own coal supply to any point where the supply is low precedence over other shipments.[1] But if it has failed in its primary duty to provide sufficient facilities for all the business that it should have anticipated would be offered, it cannot excuse its failure to serve its patrons promptly by urging that its facilities are now being used for its own imperative business. Thus a telegraph company will not be excused for delaying a private message by showing that its lines were being used for despatching train orders at the time it was attempted to forward the message in question, unless the court is clear that the company had provided lines enough to handle with the utmost promptness all the business which should have been foreseen.[2]

[1] Louisville & N. R. R. Co. v. Queen City Coal Co., 13 Ky. Law Rep. 832 (1892).

[2] Leavell v. Western Union Telegraph Co., 116 N. C. 211 (1894). See further, Western Union Telegraph Co. v. Swoveland, 8 Ind. App. 563, 42 N. E. 161 (1895).

§ 838. Emergency calls given precedence.

In time of war troops and their equipment should be given the right of way over all other business. Probably the more efficient way of handling the situation would be to leave the experienced management in charge of moving the trains, but in case of exigency the military staff might assume complete control.[1] And indeed at any time governmental business may be given precedence over private business. For in any real emergency the usual priorities should be set aside if necessary. Thus to save life nothing else should be considered, as in the case where passengers were moved from a burning station leaving freight cars to destruction. "Had they turned their attention to plaintiff's property, neglected other duties and left helpless women and children to their fate," said the Pennsylvania court, "it is just possible they might have succeeded in getting the three cars off the siding. They were not obliged, however, to sacrifice every feeling of humanity to the preservation of plaintiff's property."[2]   In cases of public calamities it may sometimes be necessary to give relief trains precedence over all other trains. Thus at the time of the Chicago fire, supplies to relieve the homeless population were rushed to the city, even passenger trains in the way being side-

But the commission may require a railroad to count cars devoted to supplying the railroad itself with coal for its own use against a coal shipper in his commercial allotment. Interstate Commerce Commission v. Illinois Central R. R. Co., 215 U. S. 452, 30 Sup. Ct. 155 (1910).

This priority of the proprietor is confined to its needs in its public capacity. A railroad engaged in the coal business cannot prefer itself over its competitors. New York, N. H. & H. R. R. Co. v. Interstate Commerce Commission, 200 U. S. 361, 50 L. ed. 515, 26 Sup. Ct. 272 (1906).

[1] Illinois Cent. R. R. Co. v. Ashmead, 58 Ill. 487 (1871).

But only in so far as the government use interferes with its general business: Illinois Cent. R. R. Co. v. McClellan, 54 Ill. 58, 5 Am. Rep. 83 (1870).

[2] Pennsylvania R. R. Co. v. Fries, 87 Pa. St. 234 (1878).

tracked. The unusual contingency it was said by the Michigan court justified this unusual procedure.[1] Upon similar principles a water company is excused for temporarily failing to give its household customers a proper supply while the fire plugs are opened in that district to extinguish a fire.[2]

§ 839. Personal requirements.

It will usually be the case that personal service to a person waiting should be given before taking care of goods. It usually makes more difference if the passenger is kept waiting than if freight is. Thus by the general rule passenger business has priority over freight business.[3] Indeed, in proper management passenger service should be separated from freight service, and separate trains run for the passengers.[4] And a shipper cannot complain because his cattle cars are not attached to passenger trains when the line is cleared.[5] When a public supply is being used both for domestic and manufacturing purposes as, for instance, water or gas, it would seem to be evident that in time of shortage the domestic demand should be preferred to the commercial demand,[6] because the cutting off of domestic supply would involve personal hardship, an element not so strongly present in commercial use.

§ 840. Perishable freight.

By the general rule as between two offerings of freight, perishable freight should be sent ahead of other freight. Live stock constitutes the plainest example of freight which should have priority. And next in order come meats

[1] Michigan Central R. R. Co. v. Burroughs, 33 Mich. 6 (1875).

[2] Campbell v. East London Waterworks, 26 L. T. (N. S.) 475 (1872).

[3] Farnsworth v. Groot, 6 Cow. 698.

[4] People v. St. Louis, A. & T. H. Ry. Co. (Ill.), 45 N. E. 824 (1896).

[5] Briddon v. Great Northern Ry. Co., 28 L. J. Exch. 51 (1858).

[6] Mayor, etc., of Town of Boonton v. United Water Supply Co. (N. J. Law), 64 Atl. 1064 (1906).

and fish, fruit and vegetables, for the transportation of which a special equipment and a fast schedule are imperatively demanded.   In the leading New York case,[1] the court said: "The question how the carrier was employed, and how he used and employed his means of transportation during any given period when property was delayed, would always be a proper subject of inquiry, and that on this inquiry proof that his means of transportation were employed in transporting perishable property, in preference to other property received at the same time, would always be held a sufficient excuse for delay.   The judge so states the rule.   The preference as he states it is between property received at the *same time*."   Consequently in a late New York case it was held that hay not being perishable might be delayed in transit in time of stress in favor of other goods.[2]

§ 841. Business needs of the country.

Even as between the same commodities there may be

[1] Marshall v. New York C. R. R. Co., 45 Barb. (N. Y.) 502 (1866). See also Peet v. Chicago & N. W. Ry. Co., 20 Wis. 594, 91 Am. Dec. 446 (1866).

[2] Frey v. New York C. & H. R. R. R. Co., 114 App. Div. 747, 100 N. Y. Supp. 225 (1906). But see State ex rel. v. Chicago & N. W. Ry. Co. (Neb.), 120 N. W. 165 (1909).

In Swetland v. Boston & A. R. R. Co., 102 Mass. 270 (1869), it was said that the carrier is not bound to give such preference to perishable freight.   And in Central of Ga. Ry. Co. v. Augusta Brokerage Co., 122 Ga. 646, 50 S. E. 473 (1905), it was pointed out that in making arrangements for through routing and rating a railroad could prefer one commodity over another.

Where there is a press of business, perishable goods, or goods the inherent character of which is such as to render them peculiarly liable to serious injury from delay, have been considered of such exceptional character, as to authorize a reasonable preference as to expedition in hauling them, over freight not of such a character.   Southern Ry. Co. v. Atlanta Sand & Supply Co. (Ga.), 68 S. E. 807 (1910).   But this rule cannot be used as a cloak for discrimination.   State v. Chicago & N. W. Ry. Co. (Neb.), 120 N. W. 165 (1909).

priorities to be observed in emergencies. It is conceivable that in time of shortage, coal for a gas works necessary for the convenience of a whole community could be given precedence over a manufacturer. Goods of special classes which have a brief market might be preferred to staple commodities which are always salable. If the carrier forwards first those goods which are most necessary to the public, it can hardly be said that the carrier is not performing its public duty. But on the other hand it would be safe generalization that no preference is justifiable between goods of the same nature, unless some such public interest appears. Not even a Southern carrier can give King Cotton preference over lumber, as a recent case holds.[1] But it seems that where a carrier must make a choice for the time being between through business and local business, the through business may be given the preference, as it involves the meeting of connections or the disarrangement of subsequent schedules, while the delay of local business has no further consequences.[2]

§ 842. Priority of accepted business.

It should, however, be pointed out that these rules of priority which have just been considered are usually applicable only to the situation where business is being offered at the same time in competition. Business already accepted must generally be carried through in accordance

[1] Ocean Steamship Co. v. Savannah, L. W. & S. Co. (Ga.), 63 S. E. 577 (1909).

[2] Chicago, St. Louis & Pittsburg R. R. Co. v. Wolcott, 141 Ind. 267, 39 N. E. 451 (1894).

Private telegrams must give way to the transmission of intelligence of public and general interest and to communications for and from officers of justice. Western Union Telegraph Co. v. Ward, 23 Ind. 377, 85 Am. Dec. 462 (1864).

A telegraph company should make no discrimination between private dispatches and those of any other character, except messages of public and general interest and those to and from officers of justice. Western Union Tel. Co. v. Swoveland, 42 N. E. 161, 8 Ind. App. 563 (1894).

with the engagements already made without regard to its
character.[1] Thus when a railroad has already accepted
more freight than it can promptly handle, it should refuse
to receive any more. Even if the freight that has been
accepted is not perishable when the freight that is being
offered is perishable, it should still refuse. Generally
speaking, accepted business of every sort must be attended
to ahead of offerings which would have higher claim if they
were competing on an equal basis. It should be conceded, however, that in a great emergency new business
might be given precedence.[2]

Topic C. Assignment of Available Facilities

§ 843. Right to assign facilities.

As the provision of facilities is primarily a question of
management, the decision as to the assigning of accommodations should be left to those providing the services
unless they act outrageously. Thus the inn, though a
public house, does not become in any sense the house of
the guests; the innkeeper continues to be the housekeeper,
and the management of the premises remains absolutely
and at all times in his hands, subject only to the right of
the guests to receive reasonable entertainment. It follows that the innkeeper, in the course of his management,
has the absolute right to assign the guest to any proper

---

[1] *Iowa.*—Hewett v. Chicago, B.
& Quincy Ry. Co., 63 Iowa, 611, 19
N. W. 790 (1884).

Illinois.—Michigan Cent. R. R.
Co. v. Curtis, 80 Ill. 324 (1875).

Mississippi.—Heirn v. McCau-
ghan, 32 Miss. 17, 66 Am. Dec. 588
(1856).

Missouri.—State v. Young, 119
Mo. 495, 24 S. W. 1038 (1894).

New York.—S t r o u g h v. New
York Cent. & H. R. R. R. Co., 181
N. Y. 533, 73 N. E. 1133, aff'd 92

App. Div. 584, 87 N. Y. Supp.
30 (1905); Tierney v. New York C.
& H. R. R. R. Co., 76 N. Y. 305
(1879).

Texas.—Gulf, C. & S. F. Ry. Co.
v. McAulay, 26 S. W. 475 (1894).

West Virginia.—McGraw v. B. &
O. R. R. Co., 18 W. Va. 361, 41
Am. Rep. 696 (1881).

Wisconsin.—Peet v. Chicago &
N. W. Ry. Co., 20 Wis. 594, 91 Am.
Dec. 446 (1866).

[2] See §§ 837 *et seq.*, *supra.*

chamber, although the traveler has expressed a strong preference to another. "All that the law requires of him is to find for his guests reasonable and proper accommodation, if he does that he does all that is requisite." [1] So, too, a carrier in the regular conduct of his business may assign seats to his passengers. This is peculiarly true of a ferryman who wishes to keep his boat balanced. There is fundamental truth in what an Illinois court said in such a case: "The ferryman must be the Captain." [2] Upon these principles it was held in a late case that where several street cars are standing at a depot waiting for passengers from an incoming railway train, a passenger had no right to complain because he was directed to take passage in one car, instead of another, so long as there was no unreasonable discrimination shown. [3] Indeed in a recent case it was said to be the duty of a steamship company to assign berths to passengers upon their embarking without discrimination in order of application. [4]

§ 844. Separate accommodations.

As all that the law requires is that each person served shall have reasonable accommodation, no legal objection can be taken to the separation of different classes of passengers. Thus it has several times been held that a railroad

[1] *England.*—Fell v. Knight, 8 M. & W. 269, 10 L. J. Ex. 277, 5 Jur. 554 (1841); Scrivenor v. Reed, 6 W. R. 603 (1858).

Canada.—Doyle v. Walker, 26 Up. Can. (Q. B.) 502 (1867).

[2] Claypool v. McAllister, 20 Ill. 504 (1858), citing Fisher v. Clisbee, 12 Ill. 344 (1851).

[3] Dobbins v. Little Rock Ry. & El. Co., 79 Ark. 85, 95 S. W. 794 (1906).

[4] Patterson v. Steamship Co., 140 N. C. 412, 53 S. E. 224, 5 L. R. A.

(N. S.) 1012, 111 Am. St. Rep. 848 (1906).

See Texas & Pac. Ry. Co. v. Pearl, 3 Wills. 4 (1885), holding that a railroad has the power to assign seats to passengers.

It follows that the act of the conductor in requesting a passenger to go on the platform of a coach because of the crowded condition of the coach is an act done in managing the train. Central of Ga. Ry. Co. v. Brown (Ala.), 51 So. 565 (1910).

may set aside cars for women.[1] As to this a leading case [2]
says: "We think a regulation setting apart a car for ladies,
or gentlemen accompanied by ladies a reasonable regulation. A passenger may not dictate where he will sit, or
in which car he will ride. If he is furnished accommodations equal in all respects to those furnished other passengers on the same train he cannot complain." There
must be no general discrimination in assigning people to
such special cars. Thus a railroad cannot exclude colored
women from the ladies' car.[3] But in special instances the
power of the conductor to assign accommodations remains.
Thus if the other cars are crowded the conductor may in
his discretion admit such other passengers as he may
choose to the ladies' car.[4]

§ 845. Changing accommodations.

It would seem to follow from the power of the management to assign accommodations, that the facilities orig-

[1] *United States.*—Brown v. Mem-
phis & C. Ry. Co., 5 Fed. 499 (1880).
   Iowa.—McKinley v. Chicago &
N. W. Ry. Co., 44 Iowa, 314, 24
Am. Rep. 748 (1877).
   New York.—Peck v. New York
C. & H. R. R. R. Co., 70 N. Y. 587
(1877).
   Missouri.—Chilton v. St. Louis
& I. M. Ry. Co., 114 Mo. 88,
21 S. W. 457, 19 L. R. A. 269
(1892).
   [2] Memphis & C. R. R. Co. v.
Benson, 85 Tenn. 627, 4 S. W. 5, 4
Am. St. Rep. 776 (1887).
   [3] Chicago & N. W. Ry. Co. v.
Williams, 55 Ill. 185, 8 Am. Rep.
641 (1870).
   [4] Bass v. Chicago & N. W. Ry.
Co., 36 Wis. 450, 17 Am. Rep. 495
(1874).
   In Bresewitz v. St. Louis, I. &

M. & So. Ry. Co., 75 Ark. 242, 87
S. W. 127, 70 L. R. A. 212 (1905),
it was held that a passenger who
without protest to the conductor,
obeyed the directions of a porter
to ride in a smoking car, although
his ticket entitled him to first-class
passage, could not hold the carrier
liable for sickness caused by the
continuous ride in its bad atmos-
phere.
   In Southern Ry. Co. v. Wood,
114 Ga. 159, 39 S. E. 922 (1901),
it was held however that, where
plaintiff and her children were not
given the accommodations which
their tickets entitled them to have,
but were compelled by the conduct-
or to go into a dirty smoking car
and were thereby made very sick,
they were entitled to recover damages.

inally given might be changed. It is well established, for instance, that an innkeeper after having assigned a guest to one room may, at will, change his room and put him into a different one, provided the new room is also a reasonable accommodation.[1] In the analogous case of the sleeping car, the authorities are in conflict;[2] but it would seem to be the better rule that the company might change a berth once assigned if equal accommodation for the journey be given. However, it has been held that if a passenger has once settled himself in a seat the conductor should not disturb him merely for his personal convenience.[3] And in another recent case it was held that where a shipper was directed by the carrier's agent to load hogs in a car already assigned for other service, the carrier is responsible for such damages as naturally result from the removal of the hogs.[4]

§ 846. Insistence upon the unit of service.

That public service is generally conducted upon some

---

[1] *Alabama.*—Hervey v. Hart, 149 Ala. 604, 42 So. 1013, 9 L. R. A. (N. S.) 213, 123 Am. St. Rep. 67 (1906).

England.—Doyle v. Walker, 26 U. C. (Q. B.) 502 (1867).

[2] *United States.*—Duval v. Pullman P. C. Co., 62 Fed. 265, 23 U. S. App. 527, 33 L. R. A. 715, 10 C. C. A. 331 (1894), permitting change of berth. Mann Boudoir Car Co. v. Dupre, 54 Fed. 646, 13 U. S. App. 183, 4 C. C. A. 540, 21 L. R. A. 289 (1893), probably goes too far in permitting a change to be made after the passenger had retired.

Indiana.—Pullman P. C. Co. v. Taylor, 65 Ind. 153, 32 Am. Rep. 57 (1879), forbidding change of berth.

[3] McLain v. St. Louis & G. Ry. Co., 131 Mo. App. 733, 111 S. W. 835 (1908).

[4] Weisinger & Son v. Southern Ry. Co., 129 Ky. 592, 112 S. W 660 (1908).

Only the conductor can insist upon a passenger removing hand baggage from a seat which he is holding without right. See Thorpe v. New York Central & H. R. R. R. Co., 76 N. Y. 402, 32 Am. Rep. 325 (1879).

Query whether a passenger may so reserve a seat by putting his hand baggage in it that he may forcibly retake the seat from an intruder. See case cited in 57 Albany L. J. 19.

unit basis has already been remarked; and upon this unit both the proprietor and the public may insist. Thus a water company can compel a customer to take for the established period provided it is reasonable.[1] On the other hand the customer can refuse to commit himself beyond the reasonable period thus defined, for the company cannot demand that he shall take more than the established unit.[2] In innkeeping nowadays the sleeping room is the unit. A traveler cannot therefore ask the proprietor to let him sleep in an unused bed in a room already taken by a guest.[3] The case of the sleeping car is somewhat peculiar in this respect. It seems that the company offers in the alternative either the single berth or the entire section; and the traveler may probably insist upon having one or the other at his election. It seems therefore that a car company may sell a whole section to a single applicant, and justify the refusal to assign the upper berth, unused by the purchaser, to a passenger applying for it later.[4]

[1] Compare Harbison v. Knoxville Water Co., 53 S. W. 993 (1899), holding requirement that water must be taken by the quarter reasonable, with Rockland Water Co. v. Adams, 84 Me. 472, 24 Atl. 840, 30 Am. St. Rep. 368 (1892), holding requirement that water must be taken by the year unreasonable.

[2] See Wheeler v. Northern Colo. Irr. Co., 10 Colo. 582, 17 Pac. 487, 3 Am. St. Rep. 603 (1887), holding that an irrigation company cannot compel a land owner to commit himself for ten years.

But a telephone company may make its unit six months instead of three months. Buffalo County Telephone Co. v. Turner, 82 Neb. 841, 118 N. W. 1064, 19 L. R. A. (N. S.) 693, 130 Am. St. Rep. 699 (1908).

[3] See Browne v. Brandt (1902), 1 K. B. 696; Fell v. Knight, 8 M. & W. 269 (Eng.), 10 L. J. Ex. 277, 5 Jur. 554 (1841).

[4] See Searles v. Mann. Boudoir C. Co., 45 Fed. 330 (1891), holding that a whole section may be reserved in a sleeping car.

Legislation requiring the car company to give the passenger the advantage of the section at the price for the lower berth when the upper berth is unsold is unconstitutional interference. State v. Redman, 134 Wis. 89, 114 N. W. 137 (1908).

§ 847. Choice of facilities.

In many businesses alternative services are provided, such as sleeping cars and day coaches upon railway trains.[1] The more costly cars may surely be more comfortably equipped, if the less costly provide reasonable accommodation. This is true also of freight cars, there being special stock cars for the transportation of race horses much better fitted than the ordinary stock cars.[2] Where there are such alternative services, it is obvious that the customer should be given his choice; the company should not dictate without reason. Thus it would seem clear that persons belonging to a certain race could not be excluded from the superior accommodations if they wish to have them.[3] But sometimes reasons may exist for rules regulating the choice. Thus for the transportation of passengers in palace cars, certain classes of tickets for the journey may be refused.[4]

§ 848. Separation based upon race.

Considered in this light then, it would seem that there could be no question as to the legality of the provision of separate accommodation for colored persons, whether by

[1] See Pullman Palace Car Co. v. Lee, 49 Ill. App. 75 (1892).

[2] Coupland v. Housatonic R. R. Co., 61 Conn. 531, 23 Atl. 870, 15 L. R. A. 534 (1892).

[3] See Pullman Palace Car Co. v. Cain, 15 Tex. Civ. App. 503, 40 S. W. 220 (1897).

[4] Lawrence v. Pullman P. Car Co., 144 Mass. 1, 10 N. E. 723, 59 Am. Rep. 58 (1887).

In Thorpe v. New York Central & H. R. R. R. Co., 76 N. Y. 402, 32 Am. Rep. 325 (1879), it was held that where the ordinary coaches are crowded a passenger has a right to enter a parlor car operated by the same company, no regulation against this being promulgated.

But in Bass v. Chicago & N. W. Ry. Co., 36 Wis. 450, 17 Am. Rep. 495 (1874), it was held that when the ordinary coaches are full a passenger has no right to enter the ladies' car.

regulation ¹ or legislation.² The Tennessee court ³ goes
to the root of the matter when it says: "We know of no
rule that requires railroad companies to yield to the disposition of passengers to arbitrarily determine as to the
coach in which they take passage." The right to determine the question rests with the carriers as the North
Carolina ⁴ court clearly says: "Among those reasonable

¹ *United States.*—Chiles v. Chesapeake & O. Ry. Co., 218 U. S. 71,
30 Sup. Ct. 667 (1910); Houck v.
Southern Pac. Ry. Co., 38 Fed.
Rep. 226 (1888).

Alabama.—Bowie v. Birmingham
Ry. & El. Co., 125 Ala. 397, 27 So.
1016, 82 Am. St. Rep. 247, 50 L. R.
A. 632 (1899).

Arkansas.—Bradford v. St. Louis
I. M. & So. Ry. Co., 124 S. W.
516 (1910).

Kentucky.—Chiles v. Chesapeake
& O. Ry. Co., 125 Ky. 299, 101 S.
W. 386, 11 L. R. A. (N. S.) 268
(1907).

Michigan.—Day v. Owen, 5
Mich. 520, 72 Am. Dec. 62 (1858).

Mississippi.—Southern Light &
Traction Co. v. Compton, 86 Miss.
269, 38 So. 629 (1905).

Missouri.—Chilton v. St. Louis
& I. M. Ry. Co., 114 Mo. 88, 21
S. W. 458, 19 L. R. A. 269 (1893).

Pennsylvania.—West Chester &
Philadelphia R. R. Co. v. Miles, 55
Pa. St. 209, 93 Am. Dec. 744 (1867).

South Carolina.—Smith v. Chamberlain, 38 S. C. 529, 17 S. E. 371,
19 L. R. A. 710 (1892), waiting
rooms.

But see Coger v. Northwestern
Union Packet Co., 37 Iowa, 145
(1873), and see Gray v. Cincinnati
So. Ry. Co., 11 Fed. 683 (1882).

² *United States.*—Plessy v. Ferguson, 163 U. S. 537, 41 L. ed. 256,
16 Sup. Ct. 1138 (1896); Chesapeake & O. Ry. Co. v. Kentucky,
179 U. S. 388, 45 L. ed. 244, 21 S.
Ct. 101 (1900); Anderson v. Louisville & N. R. R. Co., 62 Fed. 46
(1894).

Florida.—Patterson v. Taylor,
51 Fla. 275, 40 So. 493 (1906).

Georgia.—Hillman v. Georgia R.
& Banking Co., 126 Ga. 814, 56
S. E. 68 (1906).

Louisiana.—Ex parte Plessy, 45
La. Ann. 80, 11 So. 948, 18 L. R. A.
639 (1893).

Mississippi.—Louisville, N. O.
& T. Ry. Co. v. State, 66 Miss. 662,
6 So. 203, 14 Am. St. Rep. 599
(1889).

Tennessee.—Smith v. State, 100
Tenn. 494, 46 S. W. 566, 41 L. R. A.
432 (1898).

An appreciable mixture of col-
ored blood makes a person colored.
Lee v. New Orleans Gt. No. R. R.
Co., 125 La. 236, 51 So. 182 (1910).

³ Chesapeake O. & S. Ry. Co. v.
Wells, 85 Tenn. 613, 4 S. W. 5
(1887).

⁴ Britton v. Atlanta & C. A. L.
Ry. Co., 88 N. C. 536, 43 Am. Rep.
749 (1883).

Constitutional difficulties will
arise whenever the application of

regulations which they have a right to adopt is the one of classifying their passengers and assigning them to separate, though not unequal, accommodations. This right, as regards the separation of the white and colored races in public places has been expressly and fully recognized in many of the courts, both state and national."

§ 849. No real discriminations permissible.

This right to assign is subject to the limitation strictly insisted upon that there must be no inequalities imposed by this assignment to designated facilities. Thus if the races are separated the cars must be equally equipped with proper conveniences.[1] And if such special facilities as ladies' cars or sleeping cars are available to one race they must also be to the other.[2] Legislation also must treat the races without the least discrimination as is well brought out in two recent Florida cases. In one of these cases,[3] the court had under review a State statute requiring street car companies to provide separate cars, but con-

such legislation to interstate transportation is attempted.

United States.—Hall v. Decuir, 95 U. S. 485, 24 L. ed. 547 (1877).

Kentucky.—Ohio Valley Railways Receiver v. Lander, 104 Ky. 431, 47 S. W. 344 (1898).

Maryland.—Hart v. State, 100 Md. 595, 60 Atl. 457 (1005).

New York.—Carrey v. Spencer, 36 N. Y. Supp. 886 (1895).

Texas.—Pullman Palace Car Co. v. Cain, 15 Tex. Civ. App. 503, 40 S. W. 220.

Some cases treat the separation of the races to avoid trouble as almost a duty. See Wood v. Louisville & N. Ry. Co., 101 Ky. 703, 42 S. W. 349 (1897); Quinn v. Louis-ville & N. Ry. Co., 98 Ky. 231, 32 S. W. 742 (1895).

[1] *United States.*—Houck v. Southern P. Ry. Co., 38 Fed. 226 (1888).

Texas.—Henderson v. Galveston, H. & S. A. Ry. Co. (Tex. Civ. App.), 38 S. W. 1136 (1896).

And see Coger v. North Western Union Packet Co., 37 Iowa, 145 (1873).

But see Day v. Owen, 5 Mich. 520, 72 Am. Dec. 62 (1858).

[2] *Illinois.*—Chicago & N. W. Ry. Co. v. Williams, 55 Ill. 185, 8 Am. Rep. 641 (1870).

Texas.—Pullman Palace Car Co. v. Cain, 15 Tex. Civ. App. 503, 40 S. W. 220 (1897).

[3] State v. Patterson, 50 Fla. 127, 39 So. 398 (1905).

taining a provision that the act should not apply to colored nurses having the care of white children or sick white persons. This act was held to be unconstitutional, because giving to the white race the privilege of being accompanied by negro nurses while denying to negroes the privilege of being accompanied by white nurses. In view, very probably of this holding, the council of Pensacola passed an ordinance, also requiring separate compartments for the two races but providing in general terms that it should not be construed to apply to nurses attending children or invalids of the other race. This ordinance was held in the other case,[1] to be free from the vice of the statute; with respect to the exception of nurses, it was declared that such exception was a proper and reasonable classification and did not render the ordinance invalid.

Topic D. Fair Apportionment of Service

§ 850. Duty not to discriminate.

Even when we have the case where by reason of unexpected press of business the management is excused from meeting all demands upon it, it still is not free from legal obligation in dealing with the situation. On the contrary a secondary obligation now rests upon it to deal with the

---

[1] Crooms v. Schad, 51 Fla. 168, 40 So. 497 (1906).

In Louisville & N. R. R. Co. v. Catron, 102 Ky. 323, 43 S. W. 443 (1897), it was said that even where exceptions to the color separations were made for cases of nurses and officers, this means only that such attendants may accompany their charges not that such charges may accompany attendants.

And see Wood v. Louisville &

N. R. R. Co., 101 Ky. 703, 42 S. W. 349 (1897).

In Southern Ry. Co. v. Thurman, 28 Ky. L. Rep. 699, 90 S. W. 240, 2 L. R. A. (N. S.) 1108 (1906), it was said that the railroad was not liable if in good faith it assigned a white person to the colored car.

But see Ex parte Plessy, 45 La. Ann. 80, 11 So. 948, 18 L. R. A. 639 (1892).

situation for the best interests of all concerned. It may not discriminate in this situation any more than in any other, but must perform its public duty impartially. Refusing the goods of one to take those of another certainly seems discrimination in the usual sense in which that word is used. And indeed where no justification appears for a carrier who serves one customer ahead of another, such discrimination will be held a violation of the carrier's duty.[1] Certainly where orders for cars are filed, filling an order which is later in time is plain discrimination against the earlier order passed over.[2] Two extreme cases will illustrate this. In one a railroad apparently desirous of keeping from market ties on its route furnished cars to other shippers of lumber while refusing this complainant cars for his ties.[3] In the other the railroad refused its quota of cars to a colliery because the owners would not sell their coal to a company affiliated with it.[4]

[1] The general propositions contained in the text are derived from many cases, more particularly from:

Delaware.—Truax v. Philadelphia, Wilmington & B. R. R. Co., 3 Houst. 233 (1864).

Illinois.—Great Western Ry. Co. v. Burns, 60 Ill. 284 (1871).

New York.—S t r o u g h v. New York C. & H. R. R. R. Co., 181 N. Y. 533, 73 N. E. 1133, aff'd 92 App. Div. 584, 87 N. Y. Supp. 30 (1905).

North Carolina. — Patterson v. Steamship Co., 140 N. C. 412, 53 S. E. 224, 5 L. R. A. (N. S.) 1012, 111 Am. St. Rep. 848 (1906).

[2] Cases directly on this point are:

Kentucky.—Newport News & M. V. R. R. Co. v. Reed, 10 Ky. L. Rep. 1020 (1889).

Minnesota.—Rhodes v. Northern P. R. R. Co., 34 Minn. 87, 24 N. W. 347 (1885).

Texas.—Houston & T. C. Ry. Co. v. Smith, 63 Tex. 322 (1885).

Utah.—Nichols v. Oreg. Short Line Ry. Co., 24 Utah, 83, 66 Pac. 768, 91 Am. St. Rep. 778 (1901).

[3] American Tie & Timber Co. v. Kansas City S. Ry. Co., 175 Fed. 28, 99 C. C. A. 44 (1909).

See further, State v. Chicago & N. W. Ry. Co. (Neb.), 120 N. W. 165 (1909).

[4] Loraine v. Pittsburg, J. E. & E. R. R. Co., 205 Pa. St. 132, 54 Atl. 580 (1903).

See further, Toledo & O. C. Ry. Co. v. Wren, 78 Ohio St. 137, 84 N. E. 785 (1908).

§ 851. Serving applicants in rotation.

Where the applicants for service are in the same general class the traditional rule, as has just been seen, has been to serve customers in the order of their application. Thus the law for grist mills has always been first come, first served.[1] This works well enough when each applicant wishes a small service. Indeed where the application is practically indivisible, no other rule is practicable. Thus the normal rule as to telegrams is that they shall be forwarded in order of receipt.[2] In most situations this rule of rotation will plainly govern. Plainly no other rule is applicable where the service which each applicant desires is the natural unit in the particular service. Thus a steamship company should assign berths to passengers in the order of their application.[3] As between two shippers offering two shipments either one of which will exhaust the space available, the one which first applies should be given precedence in the normal case.[4]

[1] *Alabama.*—Sadler v. Langham, 34 Ala. 311 (1859).

Georgia.—Loughbridge v. Harris, 42 Ga. 500 (1871).

Maine.—State v. Edwards, 86 Me. 102, 29 Atl. 947, 25 L. R. A. 504, 41 Am. St. Rep. 528 (1893).

Nebraska.—Getchell v. Benton, 30 Neb. 870, 47 N. W. 468 (1890).

Tennessee.—Harding v. Goodlett, 3 Yerg. 41 (1832).

West Virginia.—West v. Rawson, 40 W. Va. 480, 21 S. E. 1019 (1895).

[2] *Colorado.*—Western Union Tel. Co. v. Graham, 1 Col. 230, 9 Am. Rep. 136 (1871).

Indiana.—Western Union Tel. Co. v. Ward, 23 Ind. 377, 85 Am. Dec. 462 (1864); Bierhaus v. Western Union Tel. Co., 8 Ind. App. 246, 34 N. E. 581 (1893).

Nevada.—Western Union Tel. Co. v. Call Publishing Co., 58 Neb. 192 (1895), 78 N. W. 579 (1897); Mackay v. Western Union Tel. Co., 16 Nev. 222 (1881).

South Carolina.—Pinckney Bros. v. Western Union Tel. Co., 19 S. C. 71, 45 Am. Rep. 765 (1881).

Tennessee.—Telegraph Co. v. Munford, 87 Tenn. 190, 10 S. W. 318 (1889); Telegraph Co. v. Mellon, 96 Tenn. 66, 33 S. W. 725 (1896).

England.—Reuter v. El. T. Co., 6 E. & B. 341 (1856).

[3] Patterson v. Steamship Co., 140 N. C. 412, 53 S. E. 224, 5 L. R. A. (N. S.) 1012, 111 Am. St. Rep. 848 (1906).

[4] Ocean Steamship Co. v. Savannah L. W. & S. Co. (Ga.), 63 S. E. 577, 20 L. R. A. (N. S.) 867 (1909).

§ 852. Proration of limited supply.

There are several public services, as has been noted, where there is a natural limitation upon the amount of the supply available. Take the case of natural gas—when it is found that no more can be obtained by sinking more wells in the district, what shall be done? The actual cases which have come up in the natural gas regions have decided not merely that there should be a proration of the available supply when the demand outruns the supply, but apparently that new applicants within the same district must be received and given their share of the supply.[1] Then there is the case of the irrigation system—in a period of drought how shall the available supply be distributed? At this point the matter is complicated by the established law in those regions as to priority in water right by reason of earlier appropriation; and the general rule follows of giving full supply to an earlier taker in preference to a later one, those who are upon the same plane sharing equally.[2]

[1] Those interested in this problem should consult:

Indiana.—State ex rel. Wood v. Consumers' Gas Trust Co., 157 Ind. 345, 61 N. E. 674, 55 L. R. A. 245 (1901); Indiana N. Gas & O. Co. v. State ex rel. Armstrong, 162 Ind. 690, 71 N. E. 133 (1904).

Pennsylvania.—Thompson Glass Co. v. Fayette Fuel Gas Co., 137 Pa. St. 317, 21 Atl. 93 (1890); Black Lick Mfg. Co. v. Saltsburg Gas Co., 139 Pa. St. 448, 21 Atl. 432 (1891).

[2] Those interested in this problem should consult:

United States.—Souther v. San Diego Flume Co., 112 Fed. 228 (1901), 121 Fed. 347, 57 C. C. A. 561 (1903).

California.—Volkmar v. Volkmar, 147 Cal. 175, 81 Pac. 413 (1905); Doland v. Clark, 143 Cal. 176, 76 Pac. 958 (1904).

Colorado.—Farmers' H. L. C. & Ry. Co. v. Southworth, 13 Colo. 111, 21 Pac. 1028 (1889); Nichols v. McIntosh, 19 Colo. 22, 34 Pac. 278 (1893); Northern Colo. Irr. Co. v. Richards, 22 Colo. 450, 45 Pac. 423 (1896); White v. Highline Canal & Ry. Co., 22 Colo. 191, 43 Pac. 1028 (1886).

Oregon.—Cole v. Logan, 24 Oreg. 304, 33 Pac. 568 (1893).

§ 853. Distribution of cars to stations.

It is obviously impossible to regulate the order of accepting goods according to the time of offers for shipment over the whole line. Reasonable facilities must be provided for each station, and when the space provided for the station has been exhausted no further goods need be received there until it is possible to get more cars without depriving another station of its supply. This matter was discussed in the case of Ballentine v. North Missouri Railroad.[1] In the course of his opinion in that case Mr. Justice Fagg said: "It seems to have been the theory upon which the petition proceeded in this case, that it was the duty of the defendant to have shipped the live stock in the order of time in which it was offered with reference to the entire line of its road, and not to any particular station. This is altogether unreasonable, and in its practical operation would work great hardships upon all companies. Its duty in this respect, then, must be understood in reference to each particular station and not to the operation of the road as a whole. Whilst it may be difficult to lay down any general rule upon this subject, sufficiently accurate in its terms to cover all cases that may possibly occur, still we think it can be approximated by saying that its means of transportation must be so distributed at the various stations for receiving passengers and freight along the entire line of its road, as to afford a reasonable amount of accommodation for all." [2]

[1] 40 Mo. 491 (1867). See further, Pittsburg, C., C. & St. L. Ry. Co. v. Wood (Ind. App.), 84 N. E. 1009 (1908).

[2] Where a railroad company discriminated against a shipper who had no other means of shipment than over its line, and refused to furnish him with cars at times when it was supplying them freely to other shippers at points where it competed with other lines, it is held liable. Chicago, St. L. & P. Ry. Co. v. Wolcott, 141 Ind. 267, 39 N. E. 451, 50 Am. Rep. 320 (1895).

But in Little Rock & Ft. S. Ry. Co. v. Oppenheimer, 64 Ark. 271, 43 S. W. 150, 44 L. R. A. 353 (1897), furnishing cars first to com-

§ 854. No part of the system given preference.

All cars available should be used for the equal benefit of the whole system, no part being given preference over another. The question was considered at length in Ayres v. Chicago & Northwestern Railway.[1] In that case Mr. Justice Cassoday said: "It must be remembered that the defendant has many lines of railroad scattered through several different States. Along each and all of these different lines it has stations of more or less importance. The company owes the same duty to shippers at any one station as it does to the shippers at any other station of the same business importance. The rights of all shippers applying for such cars under the same circumstances are necessarily equal. No one station, much less any one shipper, has the right to command the entire resources of the company to the exclusion or prejudice of other stations and other shippers. Most of such suitable cars must necessarily be scattered along and upon such different lines of railroad, loaded or unloaded. Many will necessarily be at the larger centers of trade. The conditions of the market are not always the same, but are liable to fluctuations, and may be such as to create a great demand for such cars upon one or more of such lines, and very little upon others. Such cars should be distributed along the different lines of road, and the several stations on each, as near as may be in proportion to the ordinary business requirements at the time, in order that shipments may be made with reasonable celerity. The requirement of such fair and general distribution and uniform vigilance is not only mutually beneficial to producers, shippers, carriers, and purchasers, but of business and

petitive points was held not unjustifiable.

[1] 71 Wis. 372, 37 N. W. 432, 5 Am. St. Rep. 226 (1888). See also Martin v. Gt. Northern Ry. Co., 110 Minn. 118, 124 N. W. 825 (1910).

trade generally.   It is the extent of such business ordinarily done on a particular line, or at a particular station, which properly measures the carriers' obligation to furnish such transportation." [1]

§ 855. Apportionment of cars to shippers.

By the principles just established, facilities are assigned to localities not in the order of their application, but in proportion to their usual requirements, as this is regarded as fair to all concerned, upon the whole.   When it becomes a question of the assignment of facilities to applicants in the same locality there is sometimes a disposition to adhere to the simple rule of rotation in the order of application.   But upon reflection it is sufficiently plain that here too it is more fair to all concerned that there should be an apportionment of the facilities available. This law is quite modern; it was hardly worked out before State v. Chicago, Burlington & Quincy Railroad Company.[2]   The problem there arising for decision was whether

---

[1] The principle permitting that policy to be adopted which will best clear the congestion with the least injury is well illustrated by the two following decisions which are really not at all inconsistent. In Galena & C. U. R. R. Co. v. Rae, 18 Ill. 488, 68 Am. Dec. 574 (1857), it was held that a railroad might be justified, in press of business, in taking grain from wagons or boats, while grain in private warehouses was awaiting transportation. On the other hand, in Choctaw, O. & G. R. R. Co. v. State, 73 Ark. 373, 84 S. W. 502 (1904), it was held that in time of stress the railroad might handle coal cars upon private sidings when it could not furnish facilities for shippers

in its own yards which were congested with cars.

Nevertheless in State v. Chicago & N. W. Ry. Co. (Neb.), 120 N. W. 165 (1907), it seems to have been conceded that a railway would usually be justified in retaining cars until they were reloaded. Another cautious decision of this general sort is Union Pacific R. R. Co. v. Updike Grain Co., 178 Fed. 223 (1910).

[2] 71 Neb. 593, 99 N. W. 309 (1904). See also:

Arkansas.—St. Louis S. W. Ry. Co. v. Clay Ginn. Co., 77 Ark. 357, 92 S. W. 531 (1906).

Minnesota.—Martin v. Gt. Northern Ry. Co., 110 Minn. 118, 124 N. W. 825 (1910).

it was fair, in assigning the cars properly apportioned to a given station in accordance with its usual business, to pro-rate these cars among shippers in proportion to their usual business. And the court thought that it was, saying: "The question is not whether he received all the cars he wanted, but whether the cars on hand were apportioned in fairness and without unjust discrimination." [1] In a case a little later, the same court expressed its sympathy for a railroad placed in the difficult position of trying to do business with two active and jealous competitors in such a manner as to remain upon good terms with both by reciting these lines—

> "How happy could" they "be with either,
> Were t'other dear charmer away!"

§ 856. Basis of prorating cars.

It seems now well established, therefore, that it is the duty of the management when the supply is short to pro-rate cars apportioned to the station among the applicants. The law has become quite elaborate in late years as to the various elements that may enter into the consideration as to what is a fair apportionment. Thus in a recent case [2] it was said in apportioning cars: "I am of the opinion that in reaching a proper basis for the distribution of rail-

---

[1] State v. Chicago, B. & Q. R. R. Co., 72 Neb. 542, 101 N. W. 23 (1904). See further:

Kentucky.—Newport News & M. V. R. R. Co. v. Mercer, 16 Ky. Law Rep. 555, 29 S. W. 301 (1895).

Nebraska.—State v. Chicago & N. W. Ry. Co. (Neb.), 120 N. W. 165 (1909).

[2] United States v. West Virginia Northern Ry. Co., 125 Fed. 252 (1903).

Moreover an arrangement, entered into between a railroad and warehousemen along its route that cars shall be distributed to warehousemen, no notice being taken of storers as such, as it leaves possibilities of abuses in the dealings of the warehouseman, is not to be supported. United States ex rel. v. Oregon Ry. & Nav. Co., 159 Fed. 975 (1908).

road cars it is necessary that an impartial and intelligent study of the capacity of the different mines be made by competent and disinterested experts, whose duty it should be to carefully examine into the different elements that are essentially factors in the finding of the daily output of the respective mines which are to share in the allotment. Among the matters to be investigated are the following: the working places, the number of mine cars and their capacity, the switch and tipple efficiency, the number and character of the mining machines in use, the hauling system and the power used, the number of miners and other employés, the mine openings, and the miners' houses. No one of these various and essential elements can safely be said to be absolutely controlling, though likely the most important of them all are the real working places, the available points at which coal can be profitably mined." [1]

§ 857. Private facilities considered in the apportionment.

By the most recent development in this law of car distribution the private cars utilized by a particular shipper are counted as part of his allotment.[2] This is elaborately defended in one of the latest cases [3] thus: "It is a charter duty of railroads to provide cars, as well as tracks and locomotives; and in the distribution of cars by an interstate railroad company among coal mines on a percentage basis in times of shortage of cars, private cars owned by shippers or consignees, which have no right upon the company's tracks except by virtue of its charter, must be con-

[1] Every presumption will be in favor of an arrangement of car distribution which has been generally acquiesced in. United States v. Norfolk & W. Ry. Co., 109 Fed. 837 (1901).

[2] But such distributing arrangements are not necessarily conclusive

even when agreed upon between the railroad and the principal shippers. United States v. Norfolk & W. Ry. Co., 143 Fed. 266, 74 C. C. A. 404 (1906).

[3] Chicago & A. Ry. Co. v. Interstate Commerce Commission, 173 Fed. 930 (1908).

sidered as leased to it and as forming a part of its commercial equipment; and while the owner is entitled to the exclusive use of such cars, they are to be counted against the mine as a part of its percentage in the distribution." [1] This whole matter as to the regulation of the distribution of cars was threshed out in a series of cases in the United States Supreme Court within a year. [2] It was noted that the regulations established by the railroads had dealt with the car situation as though there were four classes of cars, 1, System cars, that is, cars owned by the carrier and in use for the transportation of coal; 2, company fuel cars, that is, cars belonging to the company, and used by it when necessary for the movement of coal from the mines on its own line, solely for its own fuel purposes; 3, private cars, that is, cars either owned by coal mining companies or shippers or consumers and used for the benefit of their owners in cnveying coal from the mines to designated points of delivery; 4, foreign railway fuel cars, that is, cars owned by other railroad companies and sent to mines upon other lines, the coal being intended for use as fuel by such foreign railroad companies. As Mr. Justice White pointed out in making this analysis of the problem in the leading case, [3] some systems of car distribution had excluded some of these classes from consideration in the allotment, and other systems had excluded

[1] Majestic Coal & C. Co. v. Illinois C. R. R. Co., 162 Fed. 810 (1908).

See Logan Coal Co. v. Pennsylvania Ry. Co., 154 Fed. 497 (1907), holding a division of cars based upon subtracting such special or private cars as were coming to a shipper from his capacity figures and allowing him his pro rata amount upon the balance not outrageous.

[2] See Interstate Commerce Commission v. Chicago & Alton R. R. Co., 215 U. S. 479, 30 S. Ct. 163 (1910); Baltimore & Ohio R. R. Co. v. United States ex rel., 215 U. S. 481, 30 S. Ct. 164 (1910).

[3] Interstate Commerce Commission v. Illinois Central R. R. Co., 215 U. S. 452, 30 Sup. Ct. 155 (1901).

others. Such class distinctions, he admitted, might perhaps be made by the railroads without its being personal discrimination. But, as he said in writing the opinion of the court, it was within the power of the Interstate Commerce Commission to insist that all shippers should be treated alike, regardless of what classes of cars they were utilizing in their shipments.

CHAPTER XXV

REGULATION OF THE SERVICE

§ 860. The function of regulations.

§ 860. The function of regulations.

The part which regulations play in the conduct of a public business is very considerable. Public businesses are usually carried on upon a large scale, and for their proper conduct established regulations are plainly necessary. In recognition of this fact great scope is given to regulations by the law, large discretion being given to those who are confronted with the problem of reducing to order a complicated business. As a result the rule usually followed by the courts is to hold justifiable a regulation which is made by a company in good faith and enforced by it without discrimination unless it is plainly outrageous in its general operation. Whether the court might have itself done differently, or even if it sees hardship in particular cases, is not, as will be seen, enough to induce it to set the regulation aside or hold it no justification. This discloses the real addition which the right to make regulations brings to the ordinary law of public service. Without regulations a company may refuse to accede to particular requests, but it must then show that the particular request is unreasonable. But with a general regulation a service may be refused to anyone notwithstanding his particular hardship unless the whole rule is shown to be unreasonable.

Topic A. Establishment of Regulations

§ 861. Who may make regulations.

The regulating power that is possessed by those who conduct a public employment is part of that right of management of their business which the law concedes to remain in them. Proper regulations may be made at each stage of the hierarchy of the administration by the officer in authority.[1] Thus general managers may make regulations for the whole system, and district managers additional ones for their own territory; and even minor officials such as conductors or station agents may sometimes make regulations. All such regulations take effect upon the officers or employés subordinate to the official who has made the regulations; and it follows that inferiors cannot waive the regulations of a superior or make regulations inconsistent with them.[2] Thus a railroad company is not bound by a conductor's agreement to let a passenger off at a station at which the published regulations of the company do not allow the train to stop; but a superior can of course, set aside the regulation of an inferior; and indeed the person who has made the regulations himself may do so.

§ 862. Publication of regulations.

By the general rule regulations are not binding unless there has been due notification of them.[3] This does not mean that in every individual case they must have been

[1] For authority for the text which follows, see Miller v. Georgia Ry. & B. Co., 88 Ga. 565, 18 L. R. A. 323, 15 S. E. 316, 30 Am. St. Rep. 170 (1891); and Commonwealth v. Power, 7 Met. (Mass.) 596 (1844).

[2] For authority for the text which follows, see Ohio & M. R. W. Co. v. Hatton, 60 Ind. 12 (1877); and Schiffler v. Chicago & N. W. Ry. Co., 96 Wis. 141; 71 N. W. 97, 65 Am. St. Rep. 35 (1897).

[3] *California.*—Griffith v. Cave, 22 Cal. 534, 83 Am. Dec. 82 (1863).

Indiana.—Chicago, St. L. & P. Ry. Co. v. Holdridge, 118 Ind. 287, 20 N. E. 837 (1889).

Kansas.—Brown v. Kansas City, F. S. & G. R. R. Co., 38 Kan. 634, 16 Pac. 942 (1888).

Maryland.—Western Maryland Ry. Co. v. Herold, 74 Md. 510, 22 Atl. 323, 14 L. R. A. 75 (1891).

Michigan.—Carland v. Western Union Telegraph Co., 118 Mich. 369, 76 N. W. 762, 43 L. R. A. 280, 74 Am. St. Rep. 394 (1898).

New York.—McGowan v. New York City Ry. Co., 99 N. Y. Supp. 835 (1906).

Pennsylvania.—Pennsylvania R. R. Co. v. Spicker, 105 Pa. St. 142 (1884).

Texas.—Eddy v. Rowell (Tex. Civ. App.), 26 S. W. 875 (1894).

brought home to the person who is held to be governed
by them; it simply means there must be such publication
of them as should fairly affect the patrons concerned with
knowledge of them.[1] Publication may be by notices
posted upon the premises, by provisions printed upon
tickets [2] by advertisements or handbills or in any other
way that promises sufficient publicity.[3] Private instructions given to its employés to disregard established
regulations in certain circumstances will not usually
affect patrons at all; and generally speaking regulations
governing the conduct of officials among themselves need
not be made known.[4] Indeed there are certain instances
where it is requisite that the regulations should be kept
secret.[5]

[1] *California.*—Wright v. California Central Ry. Co., 78 Cal. 360
(1889).

Georgia.—Macon & W. R. R. Co.
v. Johnson, 38 Ga. 409 (1868).

Maryland.—Baltimore City Pass.
Ry. Co. v. Wilkinson, 30 Md. 224
(1869).

Michigan.—Van Dusan v. Grand
Trunk Ry. Co., 97 Mich. 439, 37 Am.
St. Rep. 354, 56 N. W. 848 (1893).

Pennsylvania.—Whitsell v. Crane,
8 Watts & S. 369 (1845).

Tennessee.—Knoxville Traction
Co. v. Wilkerson, 117 Tenn. 482,
99 S. W. 992, 9 L. R. A. (N. S.)
579 (1906).

Texas.—Western Union Tel. Co.
v. McMillan (Tex. Civ. App.), 30
S. W. 298 (1895); Gulf C. & S. F.
Ry. Co. v. Moody (Tex. Civ. App.),
30 S. W. 574 (1895).

Virginia.—Norfolk W. Ry. Co.
v. Wysor, 82 Va. 250 (1886).

[2] *Connecticut.*—Coupland v. Housatonic R. R. Co., 23 Atl. 870, 15 L.
R. A. 534, 61 Conn. 531 (1892).

Massachusetts.—O'Neill v. Lynn
& B. Ry. Co., 155 Mass. 371, 29
N. E. 630 (1892).

New Hampshire.—Johnson v.
Concord R. R. Corp., 46 N. H. 213,
88 Am. Dec. 199 (1865).

Tennessee.—Trotlinger v. East
Tennessee, Va. & Ga. R. R. Co., 11
Lea, 533 (1883).

[3] However passengers while bound
by the conditions printed on tickets
are not necessarily bound by conditions affecting transfers of which
they are not so notified.

Pennsylvania.—Perry v. Pittsburg Union Pass. Ry. Co., 153 Pa.
St. 236, 25 Atl. 772 (1893).

West Virginia.—De Board v.
Camden Int. Ry. Co., 62 W. Va. 41,
57 S. E. 279 (1907).

[4] See also Lake & M. S. R. R.
Co. v. Brown, 123 Ill. 162, 14 N. E.
197, 5 Am. St. Rep. 510 (1887).

[5] See, however, Philadelphia, W.
& B. R. R. Co. v. Rice, 64 Md. 63
(1885), discussing a private marking system.

§ 863. Changing regulations.

The power to make regulations of course includes the power to suspend them or to modify them, to alter them or to do away with them altogether. But such suspension, modification, alteration or withdrawal must keep within the limitations of the original power. When regulations are changed there must be due notice, the same rules applying as in the publication of the original regulation.[1] Probably it will not do to go so far as to say that exactly the same steps must be taken to give publicity to the change as were taken in the establishment;[2] it is enough doubtless if equal publicity is given to the change although the same methods be not employed.

By the regulations which were posted and printed at the various stations "live animals" were "allowed as baggage men's perquisites." As no special notice of this rule was brought home to the owner, the company was held liable for loss of the dog by the baggage man. Cantling v. Han. & St. Joe R. R. Co., 54 Mo. 385 (1873).

So merely posting a notice as to the conditions governing limited tickets is not sufficient to bring these home to the passenger; the ticket itself should refer to them. Railroad Co. v. Turner, 100 Tenn. 213, 47 S. W. 223 (1898).

This case apparently goes too far to one extreme—a rule adopted by a telegraph company regulating its relations with its patrons is not binding upon them without their assent, although they have knowledge thereof. Webbe v. Western Union Telegraph Co., 169 Ill. 610, 48 N. E. 670, 61 Am. St. Rep. 207 (1897).

This case apparently goes too far to the other—a consignee of goods impliedly contracts to submit to all reasonable rules for the regulation of shipments adopted by a railroad company, and the fact the shipper was not consulted in framing such rules does not affect their validity. Pennsylvania R. R. Co. v. Midvale Steel Co., 201 Pa. St. 624, 51 Atl. 313, 88 Am. St. Rep. 836 (1902).

[1] *New Jersey.*—Consolidated Traction Co. v. Taborn, 58 N. J. L. 1, 32 Atl. 685 (1895).

New York.—Pearsall v. Western Union Telegraph Co., 124 N. Y. 256, 26 N. E. 534, 21 Am. St. Rep. 662 (1891).

Pennsylvania.—Lake Shore & M. S. R. R. Co. v. Greenwood, 79 Pa. St. 373 (1875).

Tennessee.—Knoxville Traction Co. v. Wilkerson, 117 Tenn. 482, 99 S. W. 992, 9 L. R. A. (N. S.) 579 (1906).

[2] Sears v. Eastern R. R. Co., 14 Allen (Mass.), 433. 92 Am. Dec. 780 (1867).

Even a provision in the original regulation that there may be change therein without notice, should be unavailing, as it is inconsistent with the general requirement that all patrons should be notified of anything to which they are required to conform.[1] Two allied cases which have arisen on this topic should be stated here. In one [2] it was held that if a time-table is altered and the change is not notified to all local agents, so that at one station a passenger buys a ticket under misapprehension, he may sue the company. In the other [3] it was held that where a railroad company fails to inform its conductor of a change in rules as to the sale of tickets and stoppage of trains, and such conductor, through want of such information, wrongfully refuses to carry a passenger and ejects him from the train, the company is liable therefor.

§ 864. Waiver of regulation.

Likewise regulations may be waived either expressly or by custom. Of express waiver all that it is necessary to say is that the waiver must be made by an official having at least apparent authority in the premises.[4] If it should be apparent that the agent has no such authority, his waiver is ineffectual. But where a conductor on the road informed the passenger that he could stop off at an intermediate point, and wrote on the ticket to that effect, it has been held that this waiver was effectual, although the ticket stated that no agent could modify the contract.[5]

---

[1] Geer v. Michigan Central Ry. Co., 142 Mich. 511, 106 N. W. 72 (1905).

[2] Van Camp v. Michigan Central R. R. Co., 137 Mich. 467, 100 N. W. 771 (1904).

[3] Sheets v. Ohio River Ry. Co., 39 W. Va. 475, 20 S. E. 566 (1894).

[4] *Indiana.*—Pennsylvania Co. v. Bray, 125 Ind. 229, 25 N. E. 439 (1890).

Missouri.—McGee v. Missouri Pacific Ry. Co., 92 Mo. 208, 4 S. W. 739 (1887).

[5] Oakes v. Northern Pacific Ry. Co., 20 Oreg. 392, 26 Pac. 230, 12

In the case of time-tables, however, it is generally agreed that a conductor cannot bind the company by a promise to stop when no stop is scheduled.[1] Waiver may come about also by acquiescence when those who have apparent duty to enforce it do not take steps to do so in the face of constant violation of it.[2] Thus if a street railway company has a regulation that passengers shall not ride upon the platforms, but practically at all times the conductors permit passengers so to ride without expostulation, most cases hold that the regulation is thereby waived.[3] But when a street railway company regularly permits passengers to ride on the front platform of its cars, this constitutes no waiver on its part of a rule providing that if passengers choose to ride on the front platform, they do so at their own risk.[4]

L. R. A. 318, 23 Am. St. Rep. 126 (1891). See also Sickles v. Brooklyn Heights R. R. Co., 99 N. Y. S. 953, 113 App. Div. 680 (1906).

[1] See White v. The Evansville & T. N. R. R. Co., 133 Ind. 480, 33 N. E. 273 (1892), and Schiffler v. Chicago & N. W. Ry. Co., 96 Wis. 141, 71 N. W. 97, 65 Am. St. Rep. 35 (1897). But see Texas & P. Ry. Co. v. Elliott, 22 Tex. Civ. App. 31, 54 S. W. 410 (1899).

[2] *Michigan.*—Lake Shore & M. S. Ry. Co. v. Pierce, 47 Mich. 277 (1882).

Missouri.—Burke v. Missouri Pacific Ry. Co., 51 Mo. App. 491 (1892).

Minnesota.—Jacobus v. St. Paul & C. Ry. Co., 20 Minn. 125 (1873).

New York.—Ebling v. Second Ave. Ry. Co., 69 N. Y. S. 1102, 60 App. Div. 616 (1901).

Pennsylvania.—Drake v. Penna.

Ry. Co., 137 Pa. St. 352, 20 Atl. 994, 21 Am. St. Rep. 883 (1890).

Texas.—San Antonio & A. P. Ry. Co. v. Lynch (Tex.), 55 S. W. 517 (1900).

[3] *United States.*—Nassau E. Ry. Co. v. Corliss, 126 Fed. 355 (1903).

Georgia.—Augusta Ry. & El. Co. v. Smith, 121 Ga. 29, 48 S. E. 681 (1904).

Maryland.—United Ry. & El. Co. v. Hertel 97 Md. 382, 55 Atl. 428 (1903).

Massachusetts.—Stevens v. Boston Elev. Ry. Co., 184 Mass. 476, 69 N. E. 338.

Washington.—Graham v. McNeill, 20 Wash. 466, 55 P. 631, 43 L. R. A. 300, 72 Am. St. Rep. 121 (1899).

[4] McDonough v. Boston Elevated Ry. Co., 191 Mass. 509, 78 N. E. 141 (1906).

§ 865. Essential elements of valid regulations.

The fundamental principles governing regulations are simple. Regulations which are in promotion of public service are valid.[1] Regulations which are inconsistent with public duty are void.[2] This was stated in one of the earliest American cases on the subject as a matter of course in dealing with the somewhat complicated regulations of a canal company, as to the order of passage of boats at locks.[3] "The defendants, as owners, had the right to prescribe such reasonable rules and regulations for the government of vessels passing along their canal,

---

[1] *United States.*—Gray v. Cincinnati Southern Ry. Co., 11 Fed. 683 (1882).

Alabama.—Armstrong, Admx., v. Montgomery St. Ry. Co., 123 Ala. 233, 26 So. 349 (1898).

Illinois.—Chicago & N. W. Ry. Co. v. Williams, 55 Ill. 185, 8 Am. Rep. 641 (1870).

Indiana.—Chicago, St. L. & P. R. R. Co. v. Graham, 3 Ind. App. 28, 29 N. E. 170, 50 Am. St. Rep. 256 (1891).

Iowa.—Phelan v. Boone Gas Co., 125 N. W. 208 (1910).

Kansas.—Atchison, T. & S. F. R. R. Co. v. Gants, 38 Kan. 608, 17 Pac. 54, 5 Am. St. Rep. 780 (1888).

New York.—Montgomery v. Buffalo Ry. Co., 165 N. Y. 139, 59 N. E. 1126 (1900).

North Carolina.—McRae v. Wilmington & W. R. R. Co., 88 N. C. 526, 43 Am. Rep. 745 (1883).

Pennsylvania.—McMillian v. Federal St. & P. V. Pass. Ry. Co., 172 Pa. St. 523, 33 Atl. 560 (1896).

Washington.—State v. Independent Telephone Co., 109 Pac. 366 (1910).

Wisconsin.—Plott v. Chicago & N. W. Ry. Co., 63 Wis. 511, 23 N. W. 412 (1885).

[2] *Florida.*—So. Florida R. R. Co. v. Rhodes, 25 Fla. 40, 5 So. 633, 3 L. R. A. 733, 23 Am. St. Rep. 506 (1889).

Georgia.—Central R. R. & Banking Co. v. Strickland 90 Ga. 562, 16 S. E. 352 (1892).

Indiana.—Central Union Telegraph Co. v. Swoveland, 14 Ind. App. 341, 42 N. E. 1035 (1895).

Maryland.—Northern Central R. R. Co. v. O'Connor, 76 Md. 207, 24 Atl. 449, 16 L. R. A. 449, 35 Am. St. Rep. 422 (1892).

Ohio.—City of Newark v. Newark Waterworks Co., 4 Ohio N. P. 341 (1897).

West Virginia.—Boster v. Chesapeake & O. Ry. Co., 36 W. Va. 318, 15 S. E. (1892).

[3] Pennsylvania C. Co. v. Delaware & H. C. Co., 31 N. Y. 91 (1865).

See the language in Louisville, N. A. & C. Ry. Co. v. Wright, 18 Ind. App. 125, 47 N. E. 491 (1897).

as their directors deemed best calculated to promote their own interests and the interests of those engaged in navigating the canal." But one should not go so far in his concession of the right of regulation as did an early Michigan court,[1] in allowing a steamboat to make a rule that negroes should not go first cabin, although its general principle was sound: "The right to be carried, is a right superior to the rules and regulations of the boat, and can not be affected by them. If defendant had refused to carry the plaintiff generally, he would be liable, unless he could show some good excuse, releasing him from the obligation. While this is a right that can not be touched by rules and regulations, the accommodation of passengers while being transported, is subject to such rules and regulations as the carrier may think proper to make, provided they be reasonable."

§ 866. Proper enforcement of regulations.

It is properly held that the power to make regulations carries with it the power to enforce them. Thus the carrier of passengers may exclude those who attempt to get service in violation of its regulations,[2] and it may expel those who are found violating its regulations.[3] It should be said that such rejection or ejection must be done and accomplished at a proper time and place and in a proper method and manner without the use of excessive force or wanton indignity.[4] And it may be necessary to

[1] Day v. Owen, 5 Mich. 520, 72 Am. Dec. 62 (1858).

See the language in Platt v. Lecocq, 158 Fed. 723, 734 (1907).

[2] The cases to this effect are very numerous. See for example, Illinois Central R. R. Co. v. Loutham, 80 Ill. App. 579 (1898); and Dickerman v. St. Paul Union Depot Co., 44 Minn. 433, 46 N. W. 907 (1890).

[3] The cases to this effect are almost innumerable, see for example Gregory v. Chicago & N. W. Ry. Co., 100 Iowa, 345, 69 N. W. 532 (1896), and Decker v. Atchison, T. & S. F. R. R. Co., 3 Okla. 553, 41 Pac. 610 (1895).

[4] For this general doctrine the cases are very numerous. The principles are stated sufficiently in Hudson v. Lynn & B. Ry. Co., 178 Mass.

point out that when the expulsion is for failure to pay
the whole fare, what has been collected should be returned
less fare for the distance already covered, if the railroad
wishes to rescind the arrangement on which the carriage
is proceeding.   And there is considerable authority for the
proposition that if acceptance has once been made with
knowledge of the noncompliance with the regulation, it
is too late after such waiver to eject the passenger.[1] The
power to regulate does not include the power to fix a
pecuniary penalty without special legislation in aid of it.
But a higher charge may be made for service that is being
obtained in violation of regulations, as excess fare when
traveling without a ticket [2] or high demurrage for holding
cars beyond a fixed time.[3] The law for other public services seems to follow that for carriage.   A supplying company can refuse service to those who do not conform to its
regulations [4] and service may be shut off from those who
have failed to obey regulations.[5] Such cutting off is not
justifiable however, if the patron is acting in good faith; [6]
and a pecuniary penalty cannot be imposed for resuming
service, not even for the service of turning it on.[7]

64, 59 N. E. 647 (1901); and Cath-
ery v. St. Louis & S. F. R. R. Co.
(Mo. App.), 130 S. W. 130 (1910).

[1] See Braum v. Northern Pacific
Ry. Co., 79 Minn. 404, 82 N. W.
675, 49 L. R. A. 319, 79 Am. St.
Rep. 497 (1900).

See Lynch v. Metropolitan E. R.
Co., 90 N. Y. 77 (1882)—restraining
a passenger illegal.

[2] Elsworth v. Chicago, B. & Q.
Ry. Co., 95 Iowa, 98, 63 N. W.
584, 29 L. R. A. 173 (1895).

[3] Kentucky Wagon Mfg. Co. v.
Ohio & M. Ry. Co., 17 Ky. Law
Rep. 726, 32 S. W. 595 (1895).

[4] Harbinson v. Knoxville Water

Co. (Tenn.), 53 S. W. 993 (1899);
Robbins v. Railway Co., 100 Me.
496, 62 Atl. 136, 1 L. R. A. (N. S.)
963 (1905).

[5] Shiras v. Ewing, 48 Kan. 170,
29 Pac. 320 (1892); Huffman v.
Marcy Mutual Telephone Co., 143
Iowa, 590, 12 N. W. 1033, 23 L.
R. A. (N. S.) 1010 (1909).

[6] McEntee v. Kingston Water
Co., 165 N. Y. 27, 58 N. E. 785
(1900); Cumberland Telephone &
Telegraph Co. v. Baker, 85 Miss.
489, 37 So. 1012 (1905).

[7] State ex rel. v. Jones, 141 Mo.
App. 299, 125 S. W. 1169 (1910);
American Waterworks Co. v. State,

Topic B. Regulations Governing the Service

§ 867. Regulations limiting the service.

Speaking generally, a public service company may establish and promulgate rules and regulations governing the time and place and the manner and form in which it will render the service asked.[1] Such regulations, however, must not go so far in any of the points mentioned as to work prejudice to an applicant in any of his substantial rights, or operate so as to constitute a virtual refusal to perform the real duties imposed upon the company.[2] The difficulty in applying these general principles to particular facts has been seen already in at least two classes of cases, the result being in one class an irreconcilable conflict in the authorities and in the other a final agreement on the extent to which the regulation can go. It will be remembered that it is a common regulation for the supply companies to make that supply will not be continued for a patron who tenders payment for present service unless he will also pay the arrears he owes for past service. Many distinctions were to be seen in a preceding chapter in which this general problem was discussed at great length.[3] As to the extremes of possibility there is agreement. A regulation requiring a taker to pay the arrears of his predecessor in tenancy is held void as in the face of public duty to the present applicant, while a regulation that a patron must pay at any time within a given period is held valid unless the period is made unreasonably long. But there was irreconcilable conflict as to the validity of a regulation compelling a patron to pay for his own arrears, either at the same premises or at different premises. By

46 Neb. 194, 64 N. W. 711, 30 L. R. A. 447, 50 Am. St. Rep. 610 (1895).

[1] See the general language in United States v. Oregon Ry. & Nav. Co., 159 Fed. 975 (1908). And see generally, § 419.

[2] See the general language in the 318½ Tons of Coal, 14 Blatch. (U. S.) 453 (1878). And see generally, § 420.

[3] See §§ 450–460, *passim*, and cases cited.

many authorities this has been held a reasonable regulation to secure payment, but by many others such a regulation is held in the face of the public duty of the companies.
Another class of cases which has been discussed too elaborately already for repetition here, are the cases as to the
distribution of facilities. As to these there is now substantial agreement.[1] Rules establishing priorities are justifiable provided that adequate provision is made for all
business under normal conditions. And regulations as
to the prorating of the available facilities may supercede
the traditional rule requiring service in rotation in the
order of application, provided that these operate without
discrimination.

§ 868. Regulations relating to acceptance.

Regulations relating to the conditions under which
service will be undertaken are to be tested by the general
principles just discussed. Thus regulations may limit
the time within which acceptance will be made and define
the place at which acceptance will be made, provided the
time given is not unreasonably short and place designated
is not unreasonably inconvenient. Thus a railroad may
refuse to take goods or passengers unless they are tendered
or present themselves within a reasonable time before
the scheduled departure of its trains.[2] And so freight or
passengers may be refused if the tender is not made or
the demand is not made at its regular stations.[3] Moreover, the railroad may by reasonable regulations require
that certain freight shall be tendered to it at a particular
place or in a certain way.[4] And it may also require that

[1] See §§ 850–857, passim, and
cases cited.

[2] See Frazier & Co. v. Kansas
City, St. J. & B. Ry. Co., 48 Ia.
571 (1878).

[3] See Nashville Street Ry. Co. v.

Griffin, 104 Tenn. 81, 57 S. W. 153,
49 L. R. A. 451 (1900).

[4] See Robinson v. Baltimore & O.
R. R. Co., 64 C. C. A. 281, 129
Fed. 753 (1904).

certain freight shall be tendered to it before a certain hour, without any discrimination being involved therein.[1] But even if there is agreement as to the general principles, the application of them is not always beyond dispute. Thus the authorities are divided as to whether a rule of an express company that currency will not be received on any day after the departure of the last train is reasonable [2] or not.[3]

§ 869. Reasonable conditions of performing service.

Similarly the proprietors of the service may insist upon reasonable conditions upon which alone they will perform service, many of which have been discussed already. Thus an express company may reasonably ask that valuables shall be sealed in certain ways, although such precautions are not necessary for ordinary goods.[4] And a rule of a railroad that passengers upon freight trains must board them in the freight yards is reasonable.[5] All regulations may be waived in this respect as in others. Thus whether a shipper complied with a rule of the carrier requiring shippers desiring a car to be forwarded on a certain date to deliver the shipment before a certain hour is immaterial, if the conditions are waived and the shipment is in fact accepted by the carrier for transportation and delivery to the consignee.[6] An English case [7] is often

---

[1] See Central of Georgia Ry. Co. v. Butler Marble & G. Co. (Ga.), 68 S. E. 775 (1910).

[2] Platt v. Lecocq, 158 Fed. 723, 85 C. C. A. 621, 15 L. R. A. (N. S.) 558 (1907), the regulation held reasonable.

[3] Alsop v. Southern Exp. Co., 104 N. C. 278, 10 S. E. 297, 6 L. R. A. 271 (1889), the regulation held unreasonable.

[4] St. John v. The Express Co., 1 Woods (U. S.), 612 (1871).

[5] Connell v. Mobile & O. Ry. Co. (Miss.), 7 So. 344 (1890).

[7] Central of Georgia Ry. Co. v. Butler Marble & Granite Co., 68 S. E. 775 (1910).

[7] Palmer v. London L. R. I. C. P. 588.

cited to show that all the circumstances must be considered to see whether the regulation is reasonable.

§ 870. Establishment of stopping places.

It has been seen in dealing with stational facilities [1] that the true justification for the establishment of stopping places at which alone passengers will be taken up and set down, is that it is a reasonable regulation for the best interests of all concerned. It would of course seem to be best for each individual if a train would stop for him wherever he wanted to alight, but upon experiment it would be shown that this system would probably prejudice him; for his delays in reaching his own point might be so great with stops made at every point that anyone wished, that even for him the service might be worse. [2] Whether this be so in a particular case or not is immaterial, however, as the general defense for the regulation is sufficient. Indeed, this principle that established stopping places at reasonable intervals are better for all concerned than the individual right, has been appreciated recently even in the conduct of street railways, where formerly the custom was to stop wherever a passenger desired. Once a stopping place is established, however, the public have a right to be taken up and set down there upon reasonable conditions. [3] This does not mean that all trains must stop at every station; on the contrary they may adhere to a reasonable schedule, notwithstanding the desire of some particular passengers. [4] But a rule

[1] See Chapter XXIII, Topic C.

[2] Jackson v. Grand Ave. Ry. Co., 118 Mo. 199, 24 S. W. 192 (1893).

[3] Evansville & T. H. R. R. Co. v. Wilson, 20 Ind. App. 5, 50 N. E. 90 (1898).

[4] *Indiana.*—Pittsburg, C. & St. L. Ry. Co. v. Nuzum, 50 Ind. 141 (1875).

Kansas.—Atchison, T. & S. F. R. R. Co. v. Gants, 38 Kan. 608, 17 Pac. 54, 5 Am. St. Rep. 780 (1888).

Michigan.—Lake Shore & M. S. R. R. Co. v. Pierce, 47 Mich. 277, 11 N. W. 157 (1882).

Tennessee.—Trotlinger v. East Tenn. & Va. & Ga. R. R. Co., 11 Lea, 533 (1883).

that trains which have negligently passed an established stop will not be backed for the convenience of a passenger, has been held unreasonable.[1] Still a rule that passengers may only board trains at established stations is reasonable.[2] But if a train is actually stopping without being scheduled, it may be that passengers can board it.[3]

§ 871. Delivery districts.

Upon similar principles, really, the establishment of districts within which service will be rendered is justified; this is particularly true of telegraph messages[4] and express packages.[5] All the community should have the service unless reasonable limits are established; but once established these regulations govern even in particular cases of apparent hardship. Thus if one applicant is a few feet over the border he will not get delivery, although another near by may. And as limits may be established in reference to the distribution of population, it will not

[1] Jackson El. Ry. L. & P. Co. v. Lowry, 79 Miss. 431, 30 So. 634 (1901).

[2] Nashville St. Ry. v. Griffin, 104 Tenn. 812, 57 S. W. 153, 49 L. R. A. 451 (1900).

[3] Allen v. Lake Shore & M. S. Ry. Co., 57 Ohio St. 79, 47 N. E. 1037 (1897).

[4] See for examples:

Illinois.—Western Union Telegraph v. Trotter, 55 Ill. App. 659 (1894).

Kentucky.—Western Union Telegraph Co. v. Scott, 87 S. W. 289, 27 Ky. Law Rep. 975 (1905).

Missouri.—Reynolds v. Western Union Telegraph Co., 81 Mo. App. 223 (1899).

North Carolina.—Gainey v. Telegraph Co., 136 N. C. 261, 48 S. E. 653 (1904).

South Carolina.—Hellams v. Western Union Telegraph Co., 70 S. C. 83, 49 S. E. 12 (1904).

Tennessee.—Western Union Telegraph Co. v. McCaul, 115 Tenn. 99, 90 S. W. 856 (1906).

Texas.—Western Union Telegraph Co. v. Swearingen, 95 Tex. 420, 67 S. W. 767 (1902).

[5] See for examples:

Indiana.—United States Express Co. v. State ex rel., 164 Ind. 196, 73 N. E. 101 (1905). But see American Express Co. v. Southern Ind. Ex. Co., 167 Ind. 292, 78 N. E. 1021 (1906).

Michigan.—Bullard v. American Express Co., 107 Mich. 695, 65 N. W. 551 33 L. R. A. 66, 61 Am. St. Rep. 358 (1895).

be true that all within a certain distance of the office are on an equality. If, however, the company has undertaken either generally[1] or in the particular instance to deliver outside the delivery district upon the payment of an additional charge, it will be held according to its usual or actual undertaking.[2]

§ 872. Time-tables.

Upon similar principles time-tables are justified whereby transportation will only be given according to an established schedule. Without such regularity it might be the right of each passenger to have transportation given without any unreasonable delay to him. But a time-table which provides a service sufficiently frequent to handle the whole business offered, is a justification for not giving individual attention to particular cases. Time-tables should, of course, be established with due regard to the real needs of the community, more frequent service being demanded where there is much travel than where there is little. Moreover, train movements should be so arranged as to

[1] *Alabama.*—Western Union Telegraph Co. v. Burns, 51 So. 373 (1910).

North Carolina.—Bright v. Western Union Telegraph Co., 132 N. C. 317, 43 S. E. 841 (1903).

Texas.—Western Union Tel. Co. v. Cain (Tex. Civ. App.), 40 S. W. 624 (1897).

[2] *South Carolina.*—Campbell v. Western Union Telegraph Co., 74 S. C. 300, 54 S. C. 571 (1906).

Tennessee.—Western Union Telegraph Co. v. Robinson, 97 Tenn. 638, 37 S. W. 545, 34 L. R. A. 431 (1896).

When a telegraph company was unwilling to deliver a message beyond the free delivery limits, without its charges being paid or guaranteed, it was negligence for it not to wire to the sender, demanding payment or guaranty. Bryan v. Western Union Telegraph Co., 133 N. C. 603, 45 S. E. 738 (1903).

Where a telegraph company has contracted to transmit and deliver a message, it cannot excuse its liability for nondelivery on the ground that the business of the office was insufficient to justify the employment of an operator or a messenger boy to deliver messages. Western Union Tel. Co. v. Henderson, 89 Ala. 510, 18 Am. St. Rep. 148 (1889).

take care of the business properly.[1] The making and changing of schedules are problems of management, properly belonging to the company in the first instance; and the court should make every presumption in favor of these schedules.[2] Moreover, power to supervise schedules and order changes has recently been given to the regulating commissions; and their commands must be obeyed unless unreasonable. Two recent cases in the United States Supreme Court will serve to bring out the fundamental inquiry. In one case it was held that a commission could in revising time-tables have in mind the making of connections between intersecting roads for the convenience of the whole community, and that in the particular case it was sufficiently plain that it was not unreasonable to make the order revising the schedules.[3] In the other

[1] *United States.*—Atlantic C. L. R. R. Co. v. North Carolina Corp. Com., 206 U. S. 1 (1906).

Indiana.—Ohio & M. R. W. Co. v. Swarthout, 67 Ind. 567, 33 Am. Rep. 104 (1869).

Kansas.—Atchison, T. & S. F. R. R. Co. v. Gants, 38 Kan. 608, 5 Am. St. Rep. 780, 17 Pac. 54 (1888).

North Carolina.—Hutchinson v. Railroad Co., 140 N. C. 123, 52 S. E. 263 (1905).

Oklahoma.—Noble v. Atchison, T. & S. F. Ry. Co., 4 Okla. 534, 46 Pac. 483 (1896).

Texas.—St. Louis, S. W. Ry. Co. v. McCullough, 18 Tex. Civ. App. 534, 45 S. W. 324 (1898); Texas & P. Ry. Co. v. White (Tex. Civ. App.), 17 S. W. 419 (1891); Albin v. Gulf C. & S. F. Ry. Co. (Tex. Civ. App.), 95 S. W. 589 (1906).

[2] *Arkansas.*—St. Louis & S. F. R. R. Co. v. Vaughan, 84 Ark. 311, 105 S. W. 573 (1907).

Delaware.—Truax v. Philadelphia, W. & B. R. R. Co., 3 Houst. 233 (1864).

Georgia.—Riley v. Wrightsville & T. R. R. Co., 133 Ga. 413, 65 S. E. 890, 24 L. R. A. (N. S.) 379 (1909).

Indiana.—Ohio & Mississippi R. W. Co. v. Hatton, 60 Ind. 12 (1877).

Michigan.—Lake Shore & M. S. Ry. Co. v. Pierce, 47 Mich. 277, 11 N. W. 157 (1882); Van Camp v. Michigan Central Ry. Co., 137 Mich. 467, 100 N. W. 771 (1904).

New Hampshire.—Gordon v. Manchester & L. Ry. Co., 52 N. H. 596 (1873).

Ireland.—Tobin v. London & N. W. R. R. Co., 2 Ir. 22 (1895).

[3] Atlantic C. L. Ry. Co. v. North Carolina Corp. Comm., 206 U. S. 1, 51 L. ed. 933 (1906).

See also Southern Ry. Co. v. Commonwealth, 98 Va. 758, 37 S. E. 294 (1900).

case it was held that a State commission had jurisdiction to order the stopping of through trains although interstate, when such stoppage would be consistent with the proper rights of the through business, but that in the particular case the locality complaining was sufficiently served by the local trains, so that there would be no need for converting the high speed through trains into local trains.[1] Once the time-table is established the railroad is liable for damage caused by failure to make its trains run in accordance with the schedule.[2] But its liability in this regard is only for negligence in failing to perform its undertaking, and there are many cases where the railroad is held not blameworthy under the circumstances.[3]

[1] Atlantic C. L. Ry. Co. v. Wharton, 207 U. S. 328, 52 L. ed. 230 (1907).

See also Riley v. Wrightsville & T. Ry. Co., 133 Ga. 413, 65 S. E. 890, 24 L. R. A. (N. S.) 379 (1909).

[2] *Delaware.*—Reed v. Philadelphia, W. & B. R. R. Co., 3 Houst. 176 (1872).

Florida. — Florida So. R. R. Co. v. Katz, 23 Fla. 139, 1 So. 473 (1887).

Georgia.—Savannah, S. & S. R. R. Co. v. Bonand, 58 Ga. 180 (1877).

Indiana.—Pittsburg, C. & St. L. Ry. Co. v. Nuzum, 50 Ind. 141, 19 Am. Rep. 703 (1875).

Maryland.—Duling v. Philadelphia, W. & B. R. R. Co., 66 Md. 120 (1886).

Massachusetts.—Sears v. Eastern R. R. Co., 14 Allen, 433, 92 Am. Dec. 780 (1867).

Mississippi.—Wilson v. New Orleans & N. E. R. R. Co., 63 Miss. 352 (1885).

New York.—Weed v. Panama R. R. Co., 17 N. Y. 362, 72 Am. Dec. 474 (1858).

North Carolina.—H a n s l e y v. Jamesville & W. R. R. Co., 115 N. C. 602, 20 S. E. 528, 32 L. R. A. 544 (1894).

Texas.—Eddy v. Harris, 78 Tex. 661, 15 S. W. 107, 22 Am. St. Rep. 88 (1890).

[3] *Alabama.*—Louisville & N R. R. Co. v. Dancy, 97 Ala. 338, 11 So. 796 (1892).

Michigan.—Reed v. Duluth S. S. & A. Ry. Co., 100 Mich. 507, 59 N. W. 144 (1894).

New Hampshire.—G o r d o n v. Manchester & L. R. R. Co., 52 N. H. 596, 13 Am. Rep. 97 (1873).

South Carolina.—See Martin v. Columbia & G. R. R. Co., 32 S. C. 592, 10 S. E. 960 (1890).

As has been seen, a time-table cannot be changed without due and reasonable notice. Sears v. Eastern R. R. Co., 14 Allen (Mass.), 433, 92 Am. Dec. 780 (1867); Geer v. Michigan Central Ry. Co., 142 Mich. 511, 106 N. W. 72 (1905).

§ 873. Waiting rooms.

In many public businesses there are either premises maintained for the use of the public in the course of the service, or offices established for the convenience of the public dealing with the company. It is true as a general theory that the public have the right of access at all times; but as a matter of practice reasonable hours may be established. A railroad may certainly by proper regulations close its stations for certain periods. It is usually enough if they are opened a reasonable time before and after the departure of trains.[1] Thus it will be sufficient in the smaller stations, at least, to keep the waiting room open for a comparatively short time before and after the departure of trains. Similarly the ticket offices need only be open a reasonable time before the departure

In England it is apparently necessary to make a statement upon the time-table that the company will not hold itself liable for failure to meet the time-table liability except for negligence. Prevost v. Gt. Eastern Ry. Co., 13 L. T. (N. S.) 20 (1865); Thompson v. Midland Ry. Co., 34 L. T. (N. S.) 34 (1875). But the company cannot thus absolve itself from liability for negligence. Denton v. Gt. Northern Ry. Co., 5 El. & Bl. 860 (1856); Buckmaster v. Gt. Eastern Ry. Co., 23 L. T. (N. S.) 471 (1870).

A carrier of live stock need not run a special train with a car of stock of a shipper. Berry v. Chicago, M. & St. P. Ry. Co. (S. D.), 124 N. W. 859 (1910).

But if an express company has agreed to ship goods by a certain train and failed to do so the company is liable. Cantwell v. Pacific Express Co., 58 Ark. 487, 25 S. W. 503 (1894).

[1] *United States.*—Grimes v. Pennsylvania Ry. Co., 36 Fed. 72 (1888), need not be open six hours before train time at night.

Alabama.—Alabama Gt. So. Ry. Co. v. Arnold, 84 Ala. 159, 4 So. 359, 5 Am. St. Rep. 354 (1888), short time before and after train arrival at night.

Indiana.—Draper v. Evansville & T. H. R. R. Co., 165 Ind. 117, 74 N. E. 889 (1905), reasonable time before and after the departure of trains.

North Carolina.—Phillips v. Southern Ry. Co., 124 N. C. 123, 32 S. E. 388, 45 L. R. A. 163 (1899), regulation that thirty minutes before and after arrival of trains.

Oregon.—Abbot v. Oregon Ry. & Nav. Co., 46 Oreg. 549, 80 Pac. 1012, 1 L. R. A. (N. S.) 851 (1905), reasonable time before and after

of trains so as to give fair opportunity to purchase tickets.[1] And in the small places they may be closed for a short time before the departure of trains, in order to give the employé opportunity to attend to other duties. On the other hand in great cities the station and its office ought to be open from the time of the first arrival to the last departure.

§ 874. Office hours.

These principles as to established hours are of general

train time, a question of fact for the jury.

If train is delayed station should be kept open for waiting passenger. Texas & P. R. R. Co. v. Cornelius, 10 Tex. Civ. App. 125, 30 S. W. 720 (1895).

But if one is left at a station by a train failing to stop for him the agent is not bound to keep the station open for him all night. Brown v. Georgia C. & N. Ry. Co., 119 Ga. 88; 46 S. E. 71 (1903).

Intending passengers getting into a lighted car on a siding long before its departure are owed no protection. Archer v. Union Pacific Ry. Co., 110 Mo. App. 349, 85 S. W. 934 (1904).

Rule for closing a station does not justify putting a sick woman out into a storm. Texas Midland Ry. Co. v. Geraldon (Tex.), 128 S. W. 611 (1910).

[1] *Alabama.*—Evans v. Memphis & C. R. R. Co., 56 Ala. 246, 28 Am. Rep. 771 (1876).

Georgia.—Cent. Railroad & Banking Co. v. Strickland, 90 Ga. 562, 16 S. E. 352 (1892).

Illinois.—St. Louis, A. & T. H.

R. R. Co. v. South, 43 Ill. 176, 92 Am. Dec. 103 (1867).

Iowa.—Everett v. Chicago, R. I. & P. Ry. Co., 69 Iowa, 15, 28 N. W. 410 (1886).

Massachusetts.—Swan v. Manchester & L. R. R. Co., 132 Mass. 116, 42 Am. Rep. 432 (1882).

New York.—Nellis v. New York Central R. R. Co., 30 N. Y. 505 (1864).

In small communities the railroad may close its stations altogether at night.

Indiana.—Louisville, N. A. & C. Ry. Co. v. Wright, 18 Ind. App. 125, 47 N. E. 491 (1897).

Kentucky.—Louisville & N. R. R. Co. v. Commonwealth, 102 Ky. 300, 19 Ky. L. Rep. 1462, 43 S. W. 458, 53 L. R. A. 149 (1897).

At small stations where the station agent has many duties it is not to be expected that he will be in the ticket office every minute up to the time of the actual departure of the train.

Illinois.—St. Louis, A. & T. H. R. R. Co. v. South, 43 Ill. 176, 92 Am. Dec. 103 (1867).

New York.—Bordeaux v. Erie Ry. Co., 8 Hun, 579 (1876).

application. But there is so sizeable a body of law as to the office hours of telegraph companies as to require separate treatment. The telegraph companies also may establish reasonable hours.[1] If, however, the office is actually open at any time, messages should be received.[2] What is reasonable depends ultimately upon the demands of the community. Thus in most cities they should be opened from early in the morning until late at night; indeed, in the largest cities the central stations should be open all the time. In smaller places shorter hours are permissible; but still the telegraph business would require generally that the office should be open during most of the hours of the business day, even if there were a small amount of business.[3] On Sundays and holidays

[1] *United States.*—Winters v. Cowen, 90 Fed. 99 (1898).

Arkansas.—Western Union Telegraph Co. v. Love Banks Co., 73 Ark. 205, 83 S. W. 949 (1904).

Indiana.—Western Union Telegraph Co. v. Harding, 103 Ind. 505, 3 N. E. 172 (1885).

Kentucky.—Western Union Telegraph Co. v. Fisher, 21 Ky. Law Rep. 1293, 54 S. W. 830 (1900).

North Carolina.—Carter v. Western Union Telegraph Co., 141 N. C. 374, 54 S. E. 274 (1906).

South Carolina.—Bonner v. Western Union Telegraph Co., 71 S. C. 303, 51 S. E. 117 (1904).

Texas.—Western Union Telegraph Co. v. Wingate, 6 Tex. Civ. App. 394, 21 S. W. 439 (1894); Western Union Telegraph Co. v. Rawls (Tex. Civ. App.), 62 S. W. 136 (1901); Western Union Telegraph Co. v. Gibson (Tex. Civ. App.), 53 S. W. 712 (1899); Western Union Tel. Co. v. Hill (Tex. Civ. App.), 26 S. W. 252 (1894).

West Virginia.—Davis v. Western Union Telegraph Co., 46 W. Va. 48, 32 S. E. 1026 (1899).

[2] *Kentucky.*—Western Union Telegraph Co. v. Crider, 107 Ky. 600, 21 Ky. L. Rep. 1336, 54 S. W. 963 (1900).

North Carolina.—Bright v. Western Union Telegraph Co. 132 N. C. 317, 43 S. E. 841 (1903).

But even if a message is actually taken by an operator at the receiving office after hours, if no messengers are then available there is an excuse for not delivering it.

Tennessee.—McCaul v. Telegraph Co., 114 Tenn. 661, 88 S. W. 325 (1905).

Texas.—Western Union Telegraph Co. v. Neel, 86 Tex. 368, 25 S. W. 15, 40 Am. St. Rep. 847 (1894).

[3] Western Union Telegraph Co. v. Crider, 107 Ky. 600, 54 S. W. 963, 21 Ky. Law Rep. 1336 (190); Western Union Telegraph Co. v. Van Cleave, 107 Ky. 464, 54 S. W.

an early hour and a late hour will be enough.[1]   There is
conflict of authority as to whether if messages are accepted
at one point for delivery at another and arrive at the
destination after office hours, there is an obligation to
deliver them before the next office hours there.   But
in absence of any explicit undertaking, it would seem
that all parties must be governed by the reasonable regulation in force at the destination.   And where a company
has thousands of offices, the office hour at any particular
point cannot be known to a certainty at every point.[2]
There are, however, cases which hold in effect that everything which is received for transmission must be promptly
delivered without regard to office hours; but most of
these cases are those of exceptional messages obviously
requiring urgent haste, and under such circumstances it
is well recognized that all regulations must be set aside.[3]

§ 875. Proper baggage.

The carrier by its customary regulation takes his
personal baggage with the passenger without making an

827, 22 Ky. Law Rep. 53, 94 Am.
St. Rep. 366 (1900).

[1] See Western Union Telegraph
Co. v. Ford, 77 Ark. 531, 92 S. W.
528 (1906), and Western Union
Telegraph Co. v. Pierce, 170 S. W.
360 (1902).

[2] *United States.*—Given v. Western Union Telegraph Co., 24 Fed.
119 (1885).

Georgia.—Western Union Telegraph Co. v. Georgia Cotton Co.,
94 Ga. 444 (Ga.), 21 S. E. 835
(1894).

Indiana.—Western Union Telegraph Co. v. Harding, 103 Ind. 505,
3 N. E. 172 (1885).

Maryland.—Birney v. New York

& W. P. Telegraph Co., 18 Md. 341
(1862).

South Carolina.—Roberts v. Western Union Telegraph Co., 73 S. C.
520, 53 S. E. 985, 114 Am. St. Rep.
100 (1906).

Texas.—Western Union Telegraph Co. v. Neel (Tex. Civ. App.),
25 S. W. 15, 40 Am. St. Rep. 847
(1894); Western Union Telegraph
Co. v. Wingate, 6 Tex. Civ. App.
394, 25 S. W. 439 (1894).

[3] *Iowa.*—McPeek v. Western Union Telegraph Co., 107 Iowa, 356
78 N. W. 63, 43 L. R. A. 214, 70
Am. St. Rep. 205 (1899).

Utah.—Brown v. Western Union Telegraph Co., 6 Utah, 219, 21
P. 988 (1889).

additional charge. Nevertheless, it would not be proper to say that the service was gratuitous in such a case. The truth is that the compensation for the carriage of the baggage is included in the fare paid by the passenger, and the carrier is therefore liable for the baggage that he undertakes to accept as an insurer.[1] The baggage which the company so carries in consideration of the passenger's fare consists merely of the ordinary personal effects of the passenger which he will need on his journey.[2] It is almost impossible to summarize as briefly as is necessary at this point what constitutes baggage. In Woods v. Devin[3] to quote from one case, an excellent summary of the general law is given by Chief Justice Treat: "The principle of the authorities is, that the term 'baggage'

[1] See for example on this point:
Indiana.—Perkins v. Wright, 37 Ind. 27 (1871).
New Hampshire.—Smith v. Boston & M. R. R. Co., 44 N. H. 325 (1862).
New Jersey.—Runyan v. Cent. R. R. Co., 61 N. J. L. 537, 41 Atl. 367, 68 Am. St. Rep. 711, 43 L. R. A. 284, also 64 N. J. Law, 67, 44 Atl. 985, 48 L. R. A. 744 (1898).
Ohio.—First Nat. Bk. v. Marietta & C. R. R. Co., 20 Ohio St. 259, 5 Am. Rep. 655 (1870).
[2] See for examples of this:
United States.—New York C. & H. R. R. Co. v. Fraloff, 100 U. S. 24, 25 L. ed. 531 (1879).
Connecticut.—Hickox v. Naugatuck R. R. Co., 31 Conn. 281, 83 Am. Dec. 143 (1863).
Illinois.—Michigan C. R. R. Co. v. Carrow, 73 Ill. 348, 24 Am. Rep. 248 (1874).
Indiana.—Ohio & Miss. R. W. Co. v. Nickless, 71 Ind. 271 (1880);

Staub v. Kendrick, 121 Ind. 226, 23 N. E. 79 (1889).
Kansas.—Kansas City, F. S. & G. R. R. Co. v. Morrison, 34 Kan. 502, 9 Pac. 225, 55 Am. Rep. 252 (1886).
Massachusetts.—Connolly v. Warren, 106 Mass. 146, 8 Am. Rep. 300 (1870); Blumantle v. Fitchburg R. R. Co., 127 Mass. 322, 34 Am. Rep. 376 (1879).
Missouri.—McLean v. Rutherford, 8 Mo. 109 (1843).
North Carolina.—Bland et al. v. Womack, 2 Murphy, 373 (1818).
Oregon.—Oakes v. No. Pac. R. R. Co., 20 Ore. 392, 26 Pac. 230, 12 L. R. A. 318 (1891).
Wisconsin.—Gleason v. Transportation Co., 32 Wis. 85, 14 Am. Rep. 716 (1873).
England.—Hudston v. Midland Ry. Co., L. R. 4 Q. B. 366 (1869); Macrow v. Great Western Ry. Co., L. R. 6 Q. B. 612 (1871).
[3] 13 Ill. 746 (1852).

includes a reasonable amount of money in the trunk of a passenger intended for traveling expenses, and such articles of necessity and convenience as are usually carried by passengers for their personal use, comfort, instruction, amusement or protection; and that it does not extend to money, merchandise, or other valuables, although carried in the trunks of passengers, which are designed for different purposes. And regard may with propriety be had to the object and length of the journey, the expenses attending it, and the habits and condition in life of the passenger." A more definite rule cannot well be laid down. Upon this general principle that baggage is personal paraphernalia taken for use in connection with the journey, the carrier will not be liable for it unless the passenger is forwarding it at the time he is traveling; but of course if the carrier sends it at a different time for its own purposes it is liable.[1]

§ 876. Unusual baggage.

Since baggage is by the usual regulation limited to personal baggage, if the passenger takes ordinary merchan-

[1] The possibilities in this whole situation are seen in:

United States.—The Elvira Harbeck, 2 Blatchf. 336, Fed. Cas. No. 4,424 (1851).

Connecticut.—Beers v. Boston & A. R. R. Co., 67 Conn. 417, 34 Atl. 541, 52 Am. St. Rep. 293, 32 L. R. A. 535 (1896).

Indiana.—Perkins v. Wright, 37 Ind. 27 (1871).

Iowa.—Warner v. Burlington & Mo. R. R. R. Co., 22 Ia. 166, 92 Am. Dec. 389 (1867).

Maine.—Graffam v. Boston & M. R. R. Co., 67 Me. 234 (1877); Wilson v. Grand Trunk Ry. Co., 56 Me. 60, 96 Am. Dec. 435 (1868);

Wood v. Maine Central Ry. Co., 98 Me. 98, 56 Atl. 457 (1903).

Michigan.—Flint & Pere M. Ry. Co. v. Weir, 37 Mich. 111, 26 Am. Rep. 499 (1877); Marshall v. Pontiac, O. & N. R. R. Co., 126 Mich. 45, 85 N. W. 242, 55 L. R. A. 650 (1901).

New York.—Fairfax v. New York Cent. R. R. Co., 37 N. Y. Sup. Ct. 516 (1874); Burkett v. New York Cent. & H. R. R. R. Co., 24 Misc. (N. Y.) 76, 53 N. Y. Supp. 394 (1898).

Virginia.—Wilson v. Chesapeake & O. R. R. Co., 21 Gratt. (Va.) 654 (1872).

dise he cannot hold the carrier liable.[1] "There is no undertaking to carry merchandise and he had no right to impose his goods subtly upon the company, and then seek to make its obligation that of a common carrier."[2] But when the carrier, knowing the nature of the goods, charges and accepts extra compensation, he is responsible for them as a common carrier.[3] If, however, the carrier has notice that the articles are merchandise and accepts them for carriage, notwithstanding he is a gratuitous carrier, he is responsible for any negligent injury to the goods.[4]

[1] See for examples of this:
United States.—Humphreys v. Perry, 148 U. S. 627, 37 L. ed. 587, 13 Sup. Ct. 711 (1893).

Georgia.—Georgia R. R. Co. v. Johnson, 113 Ga. 589, 38 S. E. 954 (1901).

Indiana.—Doyle v. Kiser, 6 Ind. 242 (1855).

Maine.—Blumenthal v. Maine Cent. R. R. Co., 79 Me. 550, 11 Atl. 605 (1887).

Massachusetts.—Jordan v. Fall River R. R. Co., 5 Cush. 69, 51 Am. Dec. 44 (1849).

Minnesota.—McKibbin v. Great Northern Ry. Co., 78 Minn. 232, 80 N. W. 1052 (1899); Haines v. Chicago, St. P., M. & O. Ry. Co., 29 Minn. 160, 12 N. W. 447, 43 Am. Rep. 199 (1882).

Mississippi.—Miss. Cent. Ry. Co. v. Kennedy, 41 Miss. 671 (1868).

Missouri.—Rider v. Wabash, St. L. & P. Ry. Co., 14 Mo. App. 529 (1884).

New York.—Blanchard v. Isaacs, 3 Barb. 388 (1848); Bell v. Drew, 4 E. D. Smith 59 (1855).

Ohio.—Toledo & O. C. R. R. Co.

v. Bowler & B. Co., 63 Ohio St. 274, 58 N. E. 813 (1900).

Pennsylvania.—Verner v. Sweitzer, 32 Pa. St. 208 (1858).

Texas.—Jones v. Priester, 1 Tex. Civ. App. Cas. 613 (1877).

England.—Belfast & B. Ry. Co. v. Keys, 9 H. L. Cas. 556, 8 Jus. (N. S.) 367 (1861); Great North. Ry. Co. v. Shepherd, 8 Ex. 30 (1852).

[2] The quotation is from Michigan C. R. R. Co. v. Carrow, 73 Ill. 348, 24 Am. Rep. 248 (1874).

[3] *New York.*—Stoneman v. Erie Ry. Co., 52 N. Y. 429 (1873); Sloman v. Great Western Ry. Co., 67 N. Y. 208 (1876); Millard v. Missouri, K. & T. R. R. Co., 86 N. Y. 441 (1881).

Texas.—Texas & P. Railway Co. v. Capps, 2 Wills App., § 34 (1883).

[4] *United States.*—Hannibal R. R. Co. v. Swift, 12 Wall. (U. S.) 262, 20 L. ed. 423 (1870); Jacobs v. Tutt, 33 Fed. 412 (1888).

Arkansas.—Kansas City, F. S. & M. Ry. Co. v. McGahey, 63 Ark. 344, 38 S. W. 659, 58 Am. St. Rep. 111, 36 L. R. A. 781n (1897).

Topic C. Regulation of Patron's Conduct

§ 877. Regulations requiring prepayment.

The first regulations with which a patron is met are those which designate the conditions with which he must conform in order to obtain service. The most common of these are designed to secure prepayment, which, as has been seen, may always be made a condition precedent, although it may be waived. Thus a street car company may require by a reasonable regulation that a passenger shall deposit his fare in cash in a box upon entering the car.[1] But it would be unreasonable to enforce against a passenger a regulation unknown to him that fares should in rush hours be paid to a conductor instead.[2] One of the most illuminating illustrations of the operation of a regulation is that while a street car company must apparently accept a five dollar bill tendered for its small fare,[3] yet a

Illinois.—Hamburg Am. Packet Co. v. Gattman, 127 Ill. 598, 20 N. E. 662 (1889).

Kansas.—Chicago, R. I. & P. R. R. Co. v. Conklin, 32 Kan. 55, 3 Pac. 762 (1884).

Missouri.—Minter v. Pac. R. R. Co., 41 Mo. 503, 97 Am. Dec. 288 (1867).

New York.—Stoneman v. Erie Ry. Co., 52 N. Y. 429 (1873).

Ohio.—Toledo & O. C. Ry. Co. v. Dages, 57 Ohio St. 38, 47 N. E. 1039, and see 63 Am. St. Rep. 702 (1897).

Oregon.—Oakes v. No. Pac. R. R. Co., 20 Ore. 392, 26 Pac. 230, 23 Am. St. Rep. 126, 12 L. R. A. 318 (1891).

Texas.—Snaman v. Mo., K. & T. Ry. Co. (Tex. Civ. App.), 42 S. W. 1023 (1897).

England.—Great Northern Ry. Co. v. Shepherd, 8 Exch. 30, 21 L. J. Exch. 286, 7 R. & Can. Cas. 310 (1852).

But see Blumantle v. Fitchburg R. R. Co., 127 Mass. 322, 34 Am. Rep. 376n (1879); Scott, J., in Michigan Cent. R. R. Co. v. Carrow, *supra.*

[1] Nye v. Marysville & Y. C. St. Ry. Co., 97 Cal. 461, 32 P. 530 (1893). See also Elder v. International Ry. Co., 122 N. Y. Supp. 880 (1910).

[2] Perry v. Pittsburg Pass. Ry. Co., 153 Pa. St. 236, 125 Atl. 772 (1893).

[3] *California.*—Barrett v. Market Street Ry. Co., 81 Cal. 296, 22 Pac. 859, 6 L. R. A. 336, 15 Am. St. Rep. 61 (1889).

Tennessee.—Knoxville Traction Co. v. Wilkerson, 117 Tenn. 482, 99 S. W. 992, 9 L. R. A. (N. S.) 579 (1906).

regulation is not unreasonable which provides that change will not be given for a larger bill than two dollars.[1] There are many examples of these principles; and regulations tending to facilitate the making of payment or to secure the company its payment will be supported unless they are outrageous. Thus the common regulation in the supply services that the company may require a deposit as security for bills not yet incurred is held to be justifiable, provided that the amount of the deposit required is not far from what a current bill would be.[2] Such a requirement requiring deposit in advance of ascertainment of the amount due could only be made obligatory by a general regulation to this effect.[3] There can be no doubt

[1] *Georgia.*—W y n n v. Georgia Ry. & El. Co., 6 Ga. App. 77, 64 S. E. 278 (1909).

New York.—Barker v. Central Park N. & E. R. R. Co., 151 N. Y. 237, 45 N. E. 550, 35 L. R. A. 489, 56 Am. St. Rep. 626 (1896).

Pennsylvania. — Muldowney v. Pittsburg & B. Tr. Co., 8 Pa. Super. Ct. 335, 43 W. N. C. 52 (1898).

South Carolina.—Funderburg v. Augusta & A. Ry. Co., 81 S. C. 141, 61 S. E. 1075, 21 L. R. A. (N. S.) 868 (1908).

[2] In the following cases the propriety of securing a deposit was recognized:

United States.—Hewlett v. Western Union Telegraph Co., 28 Fed. 181 (1886).

Idaho.—Bardsly v. Boise Irr. & L. Co., 8 Idaho, 155, 67 Pac. 428 (1901).

Indiana.—Western Union Telegraph Co. v. McGuire, 104 Ind. 130, 2 N. E. 201 (1885).

Kentucky.—Owensboro Gaslight Co. v. Hildebrand, 19 Ky. L. Rep. 983, 42 S. W. 351 (1897).

Massachusetts.—Turner v. Revere Water Co., 171 Mass. 329, 50 N. E. 634, 40 L. R. A. 657, 68 Am. St. Rep. 432, 40 L. R. A. 657 (1898).

Michigan.—Williams v. Mutual Gas Co., 52 Mich. 499, 18 N. W. 236, 50 Am. Rep. 266 (1884).

Missouri.—Vanderberg v. Kansas City Mo. Gas Co., 126 Mo. App. 600, 105 S. W. 17 (1907).

New York.—Ford v. Brooklyn Gaslight Co., 3 Hun, 621 (1875).

Wisconsin.—S h e p a r d v. Milwaukee Gaslight Co., 6 Wis. 539, 70 Am. Dec. 479 (1858).

[3] But the requirement of such a deposit must be by a general regulation universally enforced or else the arrangement can be complained of for discrimination.

Kentucky.—Owensboro Gaslight Co. v. Hildebrand, 19 Ky. L. Rep. 983, 42 S. W. 351 (1897).

Pennsylvania.—Long v. Spring-

of the validity of a rule that telephone subscribers must pay before a certain day after bills have been rendered, on pain of having their service cut off.[1]   And further, a railroad may have a list of those whom it deems worthy of credit, from whom it does not require prepayment,[2] without its being considered discrimination against those not on the list.

§ 878. Regulations to prevent escape from payment.

Moreover, in order to make sure that none are obtaining service without payment, elaborate regulations may be devised.   Thus a railroad may require that passengers shall purchase a ticket before presenting themselves for transportation,[3] that they shall show their tickets before passing the gates leading to the trains,[4] that these tickets

field Water Co., 8 Del. Co. 151 (1901).

But in other cases it is left to the discretion of the company to demand a deposit from such customers as it fears are financially irresponsible.

Massachusetts.—Turner v. Revere Water Co., 171 Mass. 329, 50 N. E. 634, 68 Am. St. Rep. 432, 40 L. R. A. 657 (1898).

Iowa.—Phelan v. Boone Gas Co. 125 N. W. 208 (1910).

[1] Irvin v. Rushville Coöperative Telephone Co., 161 Ind. 521, 69 N. E. 258 (1903).

[2] Brown & B. C. Co. v. Grand Trunk Ry. Co. (Mich.), 124 N. W. Rep. 528 (1910).

[3] *Arkansas.*—McCook v. Northrup, 65 Ark. 225, 45 S. W. 547 (1898).

California.—Nye v. Marysville & Y. C. R. R. Co., 97 Cal. 461, 32 Pac. 530 (1893).

Illinois.—Chicago, B. & Q. R. R. Co. v. Boger, 1 Ill. App. 472 (1877).

Georgia.—Harp v. Southern Ry. Co., 119 Ga. 927, 47 S. E. 206 (1904).

Kansas.—South Kansas Ry. v. Hinsdale, 38 Kan. 507, 16 Pac. 937 (1888).

Michigan.—Van Dusan v. Grand Trunk Ry. Co., 97 Mich. 439, 56 N. W. 848, 37 Am. St. Rep. 354 (1893).

Mississippi.—Louisville & N. R. R. Co. v. Maybin, 66 Miss. 83, 5 So. 401 (1888).

New York.—Corwin v. Long Is. R. R. Co., 2 N. Y. City Ct. 106 (1885), *semble.*

Ohio.—Cleveland C. & C. Ry. Co. v. Bartram, 11 Ohio St. 457 (1860).

Vermont.—Hams v. Stevens, 31 Vt. 79, 73 Am. Dec. 337 (1858).

[4] *Indiana.*—Pittsburg, C. & St. L. R. W. Co. v. Vandyne, 57 Ind. 576, 26 Am. Rep. 68 (1877).

shall be produced upon request of the conductor taking up fares,[1] and that the ticket shall be exchanged for a train check which must be shown during the journey.[2] Similarly street car companies may require that a proper transfer be presented upon changing cars,[3] that transfers shall be asked for when paying fares,[4] that transfers shall only be good at intersecting points,[5] and that passengers shall not go from one car in charge of one conductor into another in charge of another conductor.[6] It is obvious

Maryland.—Northern C e n t r a l Ry. Co. v. O'Connor, 76 Md. 207, 24 Atl. 449, 35 Am. St. Rep. 422 (1892).

Minnesota.—Dickerman v. St. Paul Union Depot Co., 44 Minn. 433, 46 N. W. 907 (1890).

Missouri.—Cathey v. St. Louis & S. F. Ry. Co., 130 S. W. 130 (1910).

[1] *Illinois.*—Illinois Central R. R. Co. v. Loutham, 80 Ill. App. 579 (1898).

Nebraska.—Burlington & M. R. R. R. Co. v. Rose, 11 Neb. 177, 8 N. W. 433 (1881).

New York.—Hibbard v. N. Y. & Erie R. R. Co., 15 N. Y. 455 (1857).

North Carolina.—A m m o n s v. Railroad, 138 N. C. 555, 49 S. E. 1038 (1905).

[2] *New York.*—Veeder v. Fellows, 20 N. Y. 126 (1859).

West Virginia.—Price v. Chesapeake & O. Ry. Co., 46 W. Va. 538, 39 Am. St. Rep. 517, 33 S. E. 255 (1899).

So a passenger can refuse to give up his ticket unless he is given a train check where this regulation prevails. State v. Thompson, 20 N. H. 250 (1850).

[3] An ordinance prohibiting, under a penalty, the selling or giving away of any street car transfer issued to a passenger to enable him to make a continuous trip over a connecting line of the street railway company is not unconstitutional. City of Chicago v. Openheim, 229 Ill. 313, 82 N. E. 294 (1907).

Where a passenger takes a car having placards indicating that it ran only to a point two miles short of his destination with a ticket entitling him to ride over the line to his destination, he is not entitled to a transfer upon the car's reaching the end of its run, contrary to rules of the company. Mills v. Seattle, Renton & S. R. Co., 50 Wash. 20, 96 Pac. 520 (1908).

[4] Ketchum v. New York City Ry. Co., 118 N. Y. App. Div. 248, 103 N. Y. Supp. 486 (1907).

[5] Hanley v. Brooklyn Heights R. R. Co., 110 App. Div. 429 (1905); Percy v. Metropolitan Ry. Co., 58 Mo. App. 75 (1894).

[6] Birmingham R. L. & P. Co. v. McDonough, 153 Ala. 122, 44 So. 960, 13 L. R. A. (N. S.) 445 (1907).

Minnesota.—Faber v. Chicago

that as parts of a system designed to prevent escape from payment these particular regulations are all justified.

§ 879. Personal behavior of patron.

Various regulations may be made as to the personal conduct of the patron, whatever may seem to be necessary for the convenience of the company itself, as well as for the protection of other patrons. Most of this is properly discussed under the head of excuses for refusal in a former chapter, for most persons of this sort could almost always be refused without such regulations. Rules for the exclusion or expulsion of disorderly people,[1] or diseased persons [2] are, generally speaking, justifiable. And so are regulations for the rejecting or ejecting of intoxicated persons [3] or gamblers.[4] All this could doubtless be done without showing a regulation in justification; but in close cases the existence of a regulation will turn the scale. For example, smoking [5] and even spitting [6] apparently cannot be forbidden without a regulation. And although regulations forbidding interrupting conversations over the telephone by another party on the same line [7] or

Gt. Western Ry. Co., 62 Minn. 433, 64 N. W. 918, 36 L. R. A. 789 (1895).

A rule that coupons of such tickets, if detached, will not be accepted for a passage, is reasonable. Norfolk & W. R. R. Co. v. Wysor, 82 Va. 250 (1886).

A regulation of a railroad company that a monthly commutation ticket shall be surrendered by the passenger to the conductor on the last trip taken during the period for which it is issued is a reasonable regulation. Rogers v. Atlantic City R. R. Co., 57 N. J. L. 703, 34 Atl. 11 (1895).

[1] Nashville, C. & St. L. Ry. Co. v. Moore, 148 Ala. 63, 41 So. 984 (1906).

[2] Pullman Car Co. v. Krauss, 145 Ala. 395, 40 So. 398, 4 L. R. A. (N. S.) 103 (1906).

[3] O'Neill v. Lynn & B. R. Co., 155 Mass. 371, 29 N. E. Rep. 630 (1892).

[4] Tall v. Baltimore Steam Packet Co., 90 Md. 248, 44 Atl. 1007, 47 L. R. A. 120 (1899).

[5] McQuerry v. Metropolitan St. Ry. Co., 117 Mo. App. 255 (1906).

[6] People v. McKay, 46 Mich. 430, 9 N. W. 486 (1881).

[7] Huffman v. Marcy Mut. Telephone Co. (Iowa), 121 N. W. 1033, 23 L. R. A. (N. S.) 1010 (1909).

sleeping upon the benches of a waiting room [1] may be enforced, it is a question whether without such rules any action could be taken in the particular instance. The very nature of the service undertaken exacts control to this extent, for without this power there could be no assurance of its character or efficiency. This power to regulate is essential in order to enable the company involved to perform its service, and is clearly to be implied from the nature of the enterprise.

§ 880. Bringing dangerous things prohibited.

There are many reasonable rules to protect both the others carried and carrier itself. To protect all concerned the bringing of weapons [2] or animals [3] within public vehicles may be forbidden. These regulations could be enforced although the weapon was in fact not loaded or the animal in fact docile. Upon the same principles the bringing of cumbrous [4] or deleterious [5] parcels which might obstruct passageway or cause damage may be forbidden by regulations. But it does not follow that such regulations may be unreasonably enforced. A mechanic's tools cannot be thrown off the car,[6] but he may be told to go upon the platform with them.[7] The conductor cannot take his parcels away from a passenger,[8] but he may eject him with his undesirable property.[9]

[1] Central of Ga. Ry. Co. v. Motes, 117 Ga. 923, 43 S. W. 990, 62 L. R. A. 507, 97 Am. St. Rep. 223 (1903).

[2] Dowd v. Albany Ry. Co., 47 N. Y. App. Div. 202, 62 N. Y. Supp. 179 (1900).

[3] Daniel v. New Jersey St. Ry. Co., 64 N. J. L. 603, 46 Atl. 625 (1900).

[4] See also O'Gorman v. New York & Q. C. Ry. Co., 89 N. Y. Supp. 589 (1904).

[5] Mackintosh v. Augusta & A. Ry. Co., 69 S. E. 159 (1910).

[6] Smith v. Atchison, T. & S. F. Ry. Co., 122 Mo. App. 85 (1906).

[7] Nuttleman v. Philadelphia R. T. Co., 221 Pa. St. 485, 70 Atl. 828, 18 L. R. A. (N. S.) 503 (1908).

[8] Bullock v. Delaware, L. & W. R. R. Co., 60 N. J. L. 24, 36 Atl. 773 (1897).

[9] Gregory v. Chicago & N. W.

§ 881. Restriction of patron's position.

The usual right of a carrier of passengers to assign accommodations may be reinforced by the making of a regulation as to the position the passengers should take. And those who disobey it may be held to be affected thereby although they have had no personal warning. Thus a rule of a railway which requires that passengers shall remain in the cars set apart for them and shall not ride in a baggage or an express car, or other place of increased danger, is reasonable.[1]   And so is a rule that drovers on freight trains with their live stock must be in the caboose while the train is in motion.[2]   Likewise a regulation requiring passengers upon mixed trains to vacate their cars at stations while the train is being switched is proper.[3]   And a regulation forbidding employés of a street railway in uniform to ride upon the front seat of open cars where they are apt to talk with the motorman, has been held reasonable.[4]   To a certain extent such orders would be proper in individual cases.   But it is only by general regulations that the white and colored races could be confined to their respective accommodations.[5]   And so

Ry. Co., 100 Iowa, 345, 69 N. W. 532 (1906).

[1] Florida, etc., Ry. Co. v. Hirst, 30 Fla., 1, 11 So. 506, 16 L. R. A. 631, 32 Am. St. Rep. 17 (1892).

[2] Lake Shore & M. S. Ry. Co. v. Teeters, 166 Ind. 335, 77 N. E. 335, 5 L. R. A. (N. S.) 425 (1906). See further Ft. Scott, W. & W. Ry. Co. v. Sparks, 55 Kan. 288, 39 P. 1032 (1895), and Missouri, K. & T. Ry. Co. v. Cook, 8 Tex. Civ. App. 376, 27 S. W. 769 (1894).

[3] Hardin v. Fort Worth & D. C. R. R. Co. (Tex. Civ. App.), 100 S. W. 995 (1907).

[4] Rowe v. Brooklyn Heights Ry.

Co., 75 N. Y. Supp. 893 (1902). But see s. c., 81 N. Y. S. 106, 80 App. Div. 477 (1903).

[5] *United States.*—Chiles v. Chesapeake & O. Ry. Co., 218 U. S. 71, 30 Sup. Ct. 667 (1910).

Alabama.—Carleton v. Central of Ga. Ry. Co., 155 Ala. 326, 46 So. 495 (1908).

Arkansas.—Bradford v. St. Louis, I. M. & B. Ry. Co., 124 S. W. 516 (1910).

Kentucky.—Chiles v. Chesapeake & O. Ry. Co., 125 Ky. 299, 101 S. W. Rep. 386, 11 L. R. A. (N. S.) 268, 30 Ky. Law Rep. 1332 (1907).

Mississippi.—So. Light & T. Co.

regulations are necessary to set aside certain cars for women and their escorts, excluding men unaccompanied by women.[1] As regulations are indispensable to work this separation, it is necessary that their enforcement shall work no discrimination by consigning one race to inferior accommodations.[2] And if superior accommodations are provided for one race and not for the other, such accommodations cannot be refused anyone of whatever race he may be.[3]

§ 882. Passengers forbidden upon platforms.

Other common rules relate to the position which a patron may take while being served. The rule is usual that he must not ride upon the platforms of railroad cars,[4] or

v. Compton, 86 Miss. 269, 38 So. 629.

Michigan.—Day v. Owen, 5 Mich. 520, 72 Am. Dec. 62 (1858).

Pennsylvania.—Westchester & P. R. R. Co. v. Miles, 55 Pa. St. 209, 93 Am. Dec. 744 (1867).

North Carolina.—Britton v. Atlanta & C. A. L. Ry. Co., 88 N. C. 536, 43 Am. Rep. 749 (1883).

Tennessee.—Chesapeake, O. & S. W. R. R. Co. v. Wells, 85 Tenn. 613, 4 S. W. 5 (1887).

South Carolina.—Smith v. Chamberlain, 38 S. C. 529, 17 S. E. 371, 19 L. R. A. 710 (1892). *Contra*, Coger v. Northwestern Union Packet Co., 37 Iowa, 145 (1873). And see Gray v. Cincinnati So. Ry. Co., 11 Fed. 683 (1882).

[1] *United States.*—Brown v. Memphis & C. R. R. Co., 5 Fed. 499 (1880).

Iowa.—McKinley v. Chicago & N. W. Ry. Co., 44 Iowa, 314, 24 Am. Rep. 748 (1877).

Missouri.—Chilton v. St. Louis, I. M. & So. Ry. Co., 114 Mo. 88, 21 S. W. 457, 192 L. R. A. 269 (1892).

New York.—Peck v. New York, C. & H. R. R. R. Co., 70 N. Y. 587 (1877).

Tennessee.—Memphis & C. R. R. Co. v. Benson, 85 Tenn. 627, 4 S. W. 5, 4 Am. St. Rep. 776 (1887).

Wisconsin.—Bass v. Chicago & N. W. Ry. Co., 36 Wis. 450, 17 Am. Rep. 495 (1874).

[2] *United States.*—Houck v. Southern Pacific Ry. Co., 38 Fed. 226 (1888).

Texas.—Henderson v. Galveston, H. & S. A. Ry. Co. (Tex. Civ. App.), 38 S. W. 1136 (1896).

[3] *Illinois.*—Chicago & N. W. Ry. Co. v. Williams, 55 Ill. 185, 8 Am. Rep. 641 (1870).

Texas.—Pullman Palace Car Co. v. Cain, 15 Tex. Civ. App. 503, 40 S. W. 220 (1897).

[4] *Alabama.*—McCauley v. Ten-

even of street cars.[1] If a passenger who has notice of a
rule of a street railway company that persons riding on
the front platform of a car do so at their own risk, chooses
to ride on the front platform of a car of the company because the car is crowded and he prefers to stand outside, he
cannot recover from the company for injuries caused by
the negligence of the motorman in suddenly starting the
car.[2] But where notwithstanding a rule has been promulgated forbidding passengers to stand upon the platforms,
this has been habitually disregarded and passengers are
taken after the car is full and permitted to ride upon the
platform, many cases hold the carrier to the strictest
responsibility.[3]

§ 883. Regulations governing the supply.

Supplying companies may make regulations to prevent
abuse of the supply by waste,[4] or fraud upon them by
diverting the supply from the meter.[5] But those regulations must not be pressed so far as to be unreasonable.
Thus a regulation providing that the agents of the gas

nessee Coal, Iron & Railroad Co.,
93 Ala. 356, 9 So. 611 (1891).

Georgia.—Macon & W. R. R. Co.
v. Johnson, 38 Ga. 409 (1868).

New York.—Higgins v. New York
& H. R. R. Co., 2 Bosw. 132 (1857).

Tennessee.—Memphis & C. R. R.
Co. v. Benson, 85 Tenn. 627, 4 S. W.
5, 4 Am. St. Rep. 776 (1887).

[1] *Arkansas.*—Dobbins v. Little
Rock Ry. & El. Co., 79 Ark. 85, 95
S. W. 794 (1906).

New York.—Montgomery v. Buffalo Ry. Co., 165 N. Y. 139, 58 N. E.
770 (1900).

Pennsylvania.—McMillan v. Federal St. & P. V. Pass. Co., 172 Pa.
St. 523, 33 Atl. 560 (1896).

West Virginia.—Fisher v. West

Va. & P. R. Co., 42 W. Va. 183, 24
S. E. 570, 33 L. R. A. 69 (1896).

[2] See particularly McDonough v.
Boston Elevated Ry. Co., 191 Mass.
509, 78 N. E. 141 (1906).

[3] See particularly Central of Ga.
Ry. Co. v. Brown (Ala.), 51 So. 565
(1910).

[4] Watauga Water Co. v. Wolfe, 99
Tenn. 429, 41 S. W. 1060 (1897).
See also Robbins v. Bangor Ry. &
El. Co., 100 Me. 496, 62 Atl. 136
(1905).

[5] Krunemaker v. Dougherty, 77
N. Y. Supp. 467, 74 App. Div. 452
(1902).

See also Ferguson v. Metropolitan Gaslight Co., 37 How. Pr.
189 (1868).

company should have free access to the premises at all hours for examining appliances was held to be outrageous.[1] And in another case it was held that regulations which unconditionally forbade the attachment of governors near gas meters would be unreasonable.[2] Two recent cases in Tennessee involving the validity of the regulations of two water companies show very clearly the extent of this power to make regulations. In one 'of them it was held that the supply of a customer could be cut off for letting the water run, although he offered to prove that it was necessary to do this in order to get the water fresh.[3] In the other a regulation withholding of a supply from a customer was held justified which provided that during the sprinkling season hydrants, which were a part of his piping system, must have the threads filed from them, if he would not pay for sprinkling service.[4] Both of these cases are well worth reading on account of their excellent discussion of the general scope of the regulating power.

§ 884. Use made of equipment.

Upon similar principles regulations may be made as to the conduct of patrons when they are making use of the facilities. Thus a regulation of a railroad forbidding passengers from lying down on the benches in a station waiting room is held reasonable enough in an edifying opinion in the Georgia reports.[5] Plainly, too, a passenger can be ejected for using his berth improperly.[6] And a telephone company can by regulation forbid its patrons

[1] Shepard v. Milwaukee Gaslight Co., 6 Wis. 539, 70 Am. Dec. 479 (1857).

[2] Consolidated Gas Co. v. Blondell, 89 Md. 732, 43 Atl. 817, 46 L. R. A. 187 (1899).

[3] Watauga Water Co. v. Wolfe, 99 Tenn. 429, 41 S. W. 1060, 63 Am. St. Rep. 841 (1897).

[4] Harbison v. Knoxville Water Co. (Tenn.) 53 S. W. 993 (1899).

[5] Central of Georgia Ry. Co. v. Motes, 117 Ga. 923, 43 S. E. 990, 62 L. R. A. 507, 97 Am. St. Rep. 223 (1903).

[6] Nevin v. Pullman P. C. Co., 106 Ill. 222, 46 Am. Rep. 688 (1883).

from tampering with the instruments provided;[1] also it can forbid the use of profane language over its wires.[2] Upon somewhat similar principles a ticker company may put its reporting instruments in a subscriber's office on condition that quotations shall not be repeated, and may remove them if he violates the condition.[3] And a telephone company can compel a patron to pay more if non-subscribers use his station.[4]

Topic D. Regulations Relating to Tickets

§ 885. Ticket may be made indispensable.

The ticket system is so necessary for the protection of the carriers that they may make a regulation that no one shall be accepted for transportation without the proper ticket. Thus upon elevated railways the rule may be made that cash fare will not be accepted, but every passenger must procure a ticket before going upon a train platform.[5] And indeed the same regulation may be made at railway terminals, forbidding anyone to pass the gate without presentation of proper tickets.[6] It is a common regulation that nothing but a proper ticket will entitle one to transportation from any station upon freight trains, not even cash fare being acceptable.[7] The regulation

[1] Gardner v. Providence Telephone Co., 23 R. I. 312, 50 Atl. 1014, 55 L. R. A. 115 (1901).

[2] Huffman v. Marcy Mutual Telephone Co. (Iowa), 121 N. W. 1033, 23 L. R. A. (N. S.) 1010 (1909).

[3] Shepard v. Gold Stock & T. Co., 38 Hun, 338 (1885).

[4] Johnson v. State, 113 Ind. 143, 15 N. E. 215 (1887).

[5] Corwin v. Long Island R. R. Co., 2 N. Y. City Ct. 106 (1885).

[6] *Indiana.*—Pittsburg, C. & St. L. R. W. R. Co. v. Vandyne, 57 Ind. 576, 26 Am. Rep. 68 (1877).

Minnesota.—Dickerman v. St. Paul Union Depot Co., 44 Minn. 433, 46 N. W. 907 (1890).

[7] McCook v. Northup, 65 Ark. 225, 45 S. W. 547, 1057 (1898).

Michigan.—Van Dusan v. Grand Trunk R. Co., 97 Mich. 439, 56 N. W. 848, 37 Am. St. Rep. 354 (1893).

Ohio.—Cleveland, C. & St. L. R. W. Co. v. Bartram, 11 Ohio St. 457 (1860).

Texas.—International, etc., R. R. Co. v. Goldstein, 2 Tex. Civ. App. Cas. 274 (1884).

in such cases may go further, and require the traveler to get a permit to go upon a freight train as well as a ticket.[1] Unless such extreme regulations are generally made known it would not be fair to enforce them against a passenger who was ready to pay fare but had no ticket.[2] And it would be unreasonable to require a passenger taking a train from a station where no tickets are sold to have a ticket.[3] The company must at its peril permit every traveler to pass who actually conforms to the requirements by presenting a good ticket. Thus the company is liable if its gateman honestly believing that the ticket was not good refused to let a passenger take his train, if the ticket was in fact good.[4] And even a special regulation of the company printed upon a ticket that, in case of dispute between passenger and conductor as to the right to transportation under it the passenger must pay his fare and apply to the company for redress, is held to be unreasonable, and not binding on a passenger having a valid contract for transportation.[5]

§ 886. Failure to produce ticket.

If a person has bought a ticket and loses it, he has by reason of his purchase no right to ride unless he presents the ticket he has bought to the proper conductor.[6] The

[1] *Michigan.*—Thomas v. Chicago & G. T. Ry. Co., 72 Mich. 355, 40 N. W. 463 (1888).

Texas.—Ellis v. Houston, E. & W. Tex. Ry. Co., 30 Tex. Civ. App. 172, 70 S. W. 114 (1902).

[2] Lane v. East Tenn., Va. & Ga. R. R. Co., 5 Tenn. 124 (1880).

[3] Southern Kansas Ry. Co. v. Hinsdale, 38 Kan. 507, 16 Pac. 937 (1888).

[4] Northern Central Ry. Co. v. O'Conner, 76 Md. 207, 24 Atl. 449, 16 L. R. A. 449, 35 Am. St. Rep. 422 (1892); Young v. Central of Ga.

Ry. Co., 120 Ga. 25, 47 S. E. 556, 65 L. R. A. 436, 102 Am. St. Rep. 68 (1904).

[5] Cherry v. Chicago & A. R. Co., 191 Mo. 489, 90 S. W. 381, 2 L. R. A. (N. S.) 695, 109 Am. St. Rep. 830 (1905).

See also Georgia Ry. & El. Co. v. Baker, 125 Ga. 562, 54 S. E. 639, 7 L. R. A. (N. S.) 103, 14 Am. St. Rep. 246 (1906).

[6] *Connecticut.*—Downs v. New York & N. Haven R. R. Co., 36 Conn. 287 (1869).

Georgia.—Harp v. Southern Ry.

mere fact that the passenger has had a ticket does not necessarily establish his right to be transported on a given train; and it makes no difference if the fact that he has once had a ticket is known.[1] When the conductor makes his demand, he is entitled to have the ticket surrendered; he cannot be required to hear evidence or investigate the bona fides of a passenger's excuse for its nondelivery. Had the passenger's money blown out of his hand, it is evident that his misfortune would have fallen upon himself and not upon the company. The same result would follow where the ticket itself was lost; for it might have come into the hands of another, and the company might thereby have been compelled to carry two passengers for one fare. Besides, any rule allowing an excuse as a substitute for a ticket would give rise to so much uncertainty and so many possibilities of fraud that the courts have almost uniformly held that the failure to pay the fare or produce the tickets warrants an eviction. And so if the conductor gives him a train check in return for his ticket, and he loses his check, he must pay fare again.[2]

Co., 119 Ga. 927, 47 S. E. 206 (1904).

Massachusetts.—Standish v. Narragansett Steamship Co., 111 Mass. 512, 18 Am. Rep. 66 (1873).

Mississippi.—Louisville & N. R. R. Co. v. Maybin, 66 Miss. 83, 5 So. 401 (1888).

New Jersey.—Ripley v. New Jersey R. R. & Transp. Co., 31 N. J. L. 388 (1866).

Ohio.—Crawford v. Cincinnati, H. & D. R. R. Co., 26 Ohio St. 580 (1875).

Pennsylvania.—Ham v. Delaware & H. C. Co., 142 Pa. 617, 21 Atl. 1012 (1891). And see, s. c., 155 Pa. 548, 26 Atl. 757, 20 L. R. A. 682.

[1] *Connecticut.*—Downs v. New York, N. H. R. R. Co., 36 Conn. 278 (1869).

New Jersey.—New Jersey City & B. Ry. Co. v. Morgan, 52 N. J. L. 60, 18 Atl. 904 (1889).

New York.—Hibbard v. New York & E. Ry. Co., 15 N. Y. 455 (1857).

Pennsylvania.—Cresson v. Philadelphia & R. R. R. Co., 11 Phila. 597 (1875).

[2] *Illinois.*—Pullman Palace Car Co. v. Reed, 75 Ill. 125, 20 Am. Rep. 232 (1874).

Michigan.—Lucas v. Michigan Central Ry. Co., 98 Mich. 1, 56 N. W. 1039, 39 Am. St. Rep. 517 (1893).

The passenger is, however, entitled to a reasonable opportunity to search for his ticket.[1]

§ 887. Extra charge when fare paid on train.

As the railroad company may require tickets absolutely, if it permits cash to be paid on the train in the alternative by those who have not procured tickets in advance, an extra charge may be made those who have not procured tickets.[2] It follows that a system of requiring a larger payment to the conductor accompanied with a refund check for the excess is reasonable.[3] As the company may refuse to carry without a ticket, it may properly refuse

Vermont—Jerome v. Smith, 48 Vt. 230, 21 Am. Rep. 125 (1876).

West Virginia—Dewing v. Hutton, 46 W. Va. 538.

[1] Maples v. New York & New Haven R. R. Co., 38 Conn. 557, 9 Am. Rep. 434 (1871); Pittsburg, C., C. & St. L. Ry. Co. v. Daniels, 90 Ill. App. 154 (1899); Anderson v. Louisville & N. R. Co., 134 Ky. 343, 120 S. W. 298 (1909); Gates v. Quincy, O. & K. C. R. R. Co., 125 Mo. App. 334, 102 S. W. 50 (1907).

[2] *Indiana.*—Sage v. Evansville & T. H. R. R. Co., 134 Ind. 100, 33 N. E. 771 (1892).

Iowa.—Ellsworth v. Chicago, B. & Q. Ry. Co., 95 Iowa, 98, 63 N. W. 584, 29 L. R. A. 173 (1895).

Kentucky.—Wilsey v. Louisville & N. R. R. Co., 83 Ky. 511 (1886).

Minnesota.—State of Minn. v. Harvey Hungerford, 39 Minn. 6, 38 N. W. 628 (1888).

Ohio.—Railroad Co. v. Skillman, 39 Ohio St. 444 (1883).

[3] *Maine.*—State v. Goold, 53 Me. 279 (1865).

Georgia.—Coyle v. Southern Ry.

Co., 112 Ga. 121, 37 S. E. 163 (1900).

Louisiana.—McGowen v. Morgan's La. & Tex. R. R. & S. S. Co., 41 La. Ann. 732, 6 So. 606, 52 L. R. A. 817, 17 Am. St. Rep. 415 (1889).

Oregon.—Poole v. Northern Pacific R. R. Co., 16 Oreg. 261, 19 Pac. 107, 8 Am. St. Rep. 289 (1888).

A penalty for not purchasing a ticket before entering the cars cannot be exacted which, when added to the regular rate, will make the sum exacted exceed the maximum charge allowed by law. See Zagelmeyer v. Cincinnati, etc., R. R. Co., 102 Mich. 214, 47 Am. St. Rep. 514 (1894). See Coy v. Detroit, Y. & P. A. Ry. Co., 125 Mich. 616, 85 N. W. 6 (1901), which goes further still.

But where a refund is given it seems that this is not really charging more than the statutory rate ultimately. See Railroad Co. v. Skillman, 39 Ohio St. 444 (1883), and Reese v. Pennsylvania R. R. Co., 131 Pa. St. 422, 19 Atl. 72, 62 L. R. A. 529, 17 Am. St. Rep. 818 (1890).

under the far less inconvenient alternative to the traveler of putting him to the trouble of going to an office to get his excess refunded. If the company may charge those failing to get a ticket an additional price, and keep it, certainly they may charge such price and refund it. And, as the regulation is not in itself unreasonable or needlessly inconvenient to the traveler, its validity, upon general principles and on authority, would seem to be beyond question, since only by the ticket system can the company effectively protect itself from fraud of all sorts; and this regulation tends to put all fare-paying upon the ticket basis.

§ 888. No opportunity to obtain ticket.

One difficult situation of this sort which has often come before the courts is where the ticket office at the station where the passenger comes to take the train is wrongfully closed by neglect of the station agent. Under such circumstances the great majority of the cases have held that as the passenger has had no opportunity to obtain a ticket, he should not be ejected for refusal to pay the extra charge. Such a regulation is usually said to be invalid unless the corporation affords reasonable opportunity to its passengers to procure tickets at the lower rate and thereby avoid the disadvantage of such discrimination. It is of course true that the passenger has been wronged, and he should have a right to recover the excess. But the question remains whether he may consequently resist ejection and get damages for the personal injuries caused thereby, as most of the authorities concede.[1] There is, however, some authority to the contrary.[2]

[1] *Alabama.*—Kennedy v. Birmingham Ry. L. & P. R. R. Co., 138 Ala. 225, 35 So. 108 (1902).

Connecticut.—Crocker v. New London, W. & P. R. R. Co., 24 Conn. 249 (1855).

[2] Monnier v. New York C. & H. R. R. Co., 175 N. Y. 281, 67 N. E. 569, 62 L. R. A. 357, 96 Am. St. Rep. 619 (1903).

§ 889. Ticket agent's mistake.

Where the ticket agent gives a ticket not good for the transportation asked for, so that when this ticket is presented to the conductor the passenger cannot get the

Georgia.—Brown v. Central of Ga. Ry. Co., 128 Ga. 635, 58 S. E. 163 (1907).

Illinois.—St. Louis & A. & C. R. R. Co. v. Dalby, 19 Ill. 353 (1857).

Indiana.—Jeffersonville R. R. Co. v. Rogers, 28 Ind. 1, 92 Am. Dec. 276, 36 Ind. 116, 10 Am. Rep. 103 (1867).

Louisiana.—McGowen v. Morgan's La. & Tex. R. R. & S. S. Co., 41 La. Ann. 732, 6 So. 606, 5 L. R. A. 817, 17 Am. St. Rep. 415 (1889).

Maine.—State v. Goold, 53 Me. 279 (1865).

Massachusetts.—Swan v. Manchester & L. R. R. Co., 132 Mass. 116, 42 Am. Rep. 432 (1882).

Minnesota.—DuLaurans v. St. Paul & P. R. R. Co., 15 Minn. 49, 2 Am. Rep. 102 (1870).

Mississippi.—Forsee v. Alabama Gt. So. R. R. Co., 63 Miss. 66 (paraphrased above), 56 Am. Rep. 801 (1885).

Missouri.—Gardner v. St. Louis & S. F. Ry. Co., 117 Mo. App. 38, 93 S. W. 917 (1906).

New Hampshire.—Hillard v. Goold, 34 N. H. 230, 66 Am. Dec. 765 (1856).

New York.—Porter v. New York Central R. R. Co., 34 Barb. 353 (1861).

Ohio.—Smith v. Pittsburg, Ft. W. & C. R. R. Co., 23 Ohio St. 10 (1872).

Oregon.—Poole v. Northern Pacific R. R. Co., 16 Oreg. 261, 19 Pac. 107, 8 Am. St. Rep. 289 (1888).

South Carolina.—Talbert v. Charleston & W. C. Ry. Co., 72 S. C. 137, 51 S. E. 564 (1905).

Texas.—Fordyce & S. v. Manuel, 82 Tex. 527, 18 S. W. 657 (1891).

West Virginia.—White v. Chesapeake & O. R. R. Co., 26 W. Va. 800 (1885).

Wisconsin.—Phettiplace v. Northern Pacific R. R. Co., 84 Wis. 412, 54 N. W. 1092, 20 L. R. A. 483 (1893).

When a railroad company invites the public to take passage upon a special train at a certain station at excursion rates, passengers have a right to expect that reasonable accommodations will be furnished there, or on the train, to obtain tickets; and if the company has no ticket office or agent to sell tickets at that station, it cannot insist that all who board the train shall first purchase excursion tickets. Chicago, St. L. & P. R. R. Co. v. Graham, 3 Ind. App. 28, 29 N. E. 170, 50 Am. St. Rep. 256 (1891).

Plaintiff presented his mileage book to the agent at a station, according to the regulations of the company, requesting an exchange ticket, but the agent was not supplied with such tickets and promised to explain such fact to the conductor. The company was held liable for his subsequent expulsion. Pennsylvania Co. v. Lenhart, 120 Fed. 61 (1903).

transportation which he expected, the company is, of course, in the wrong. But where the intending passenger makes a mistake in asking for a ticket so that the wrong ticket is given him, of course he cannot complain if that ticket is not honored for passage.[1] Some cases go so far as to say that the passenger may rely upon the representation of the agent, although inconsistent with the ticket.[2] And there are obviously cases where the passenger's acceptance of a wrong ticket is so palpably negligent that he is foreclosed.[3] Nevertheless many cases hold that the

---

[1] *Michigan.*—Haggerty v. Flint & P. M. R. R. Co., 59 Mich. 366, 26 N. W. 639, 60 Am. Rep. 301 (1886).

Missouri.—Randolph v. Quincy, O. & K. C. R. R. Co., 129 Mo. App. 1 (1908).

Utah.—Rudy v. Rio Grande W. Ry. Co., 8 Utah, 165, 30 Pac. 366 (1892).

[2] *Alabama.*—Southern Ry. Co. v. Bunnell, 138 Ala. 247, 36 So. 380 (1902).

Arkansas.—Hot Springs R. R. Co. v. Deloney, 65 Ark. 177, 45 S. W. 351, 67 Am. St. Rep. 913 (1898).

Georgia.—Head v. Georgia Pacific Ry. Co., 79 Ga. 358, 7 S. E. 217, 11 Am. St. Rep. 434 (1887).

Kentucky.—Louisville & N. R. R. Co. v. Gaines, 99 Ky. 411, 18 Ky. L. Rep. 387, 36 S. W. 174, 59 Am. St. Rep. 465 (1896).

Louisiana.—Randall v. New Orleans & N. E. R. R. Co., 45 La. Ann. 778, 13 So. 166 (1893).

Minnesota.—Morrill v. Minneapolis St. Ry. Co., 103 Minn. 362, 115 N. W. 395 (1908).

Mississippi.—Illinois Central R. R. Co. v. Gortikov, 90 Miss. 787, 45 So. 363, 14 L. R. A. 464 (1907).

Missouri.—Ferguson v. Missouri Pacific Ry. Co., 144 Mo. App. 262, 128 S. W. 799 (1910).

North Carolina.—Hutchinson v. Railroad Co., 140 N. C. 123, 52 S. E. 263 (1905).

Texas.—Gulf, etc., R. R. Co. v. Rather, 3 Tex. Civ. App. 72, 21 S. W. 951 (1893); San Antonio & A. P. Ry. Co. v. Newman, 17 Tex. Civ. App. 606, 43 S. W. 915 (1897).

Washington.—Olson v. Northern Pacific R. R. Co., 49 Wash. 626, 96 Pac. 150, 18 L. R. A. (N. S.) 209 (1908).

West Virginia.—Trice v. Chesapeake & O. Ry. Co., 40 W. Va. 271, 21 E. S. 1022 (1895).

[3] *District of Columbia.*—Baggett v. Baltimore & O. R. R. Co., 3 D. C. App. Cas. 522 (1894), *semble.*

Massachusetts.—Bradshaw v. South Boston Ry. Co., 135 Mass. 407, 46 Am. Rep. 481 (1883).

New York.—Nolan v. New York, N. H. & H. R. R. Co., 41 N. Y. Super. Ct. 541 (1876).

Texas.—Houston & T. C. Ry. Co. v. Ford, 53 Tex. 364 (1880).

conductor must at his peril give credence to the passenger's story.[1] The abstract question whether the company or the passengers are in the wrong is usually decided properly without any noteworthy conflict of authority. But there is an irreconcilable division in the authorities as to the consequences of the company's being in the wrong. There are many jurisdictions [2] which hold that since the company is in the wrong, the passenger may resist expulsion and recover damages for personal injuries caused thereby. But in as many other jurisdictions [3]

[1] It should be said, however, that the cases hardly go further than to require the conductor to give credence to the passenger's story when it is reasonable under the circumstances. See for example the language in:

Kansas.—Jevons v. Union Pacific R. R. Co., 70 Kan. 491, 78 Pac. 817 (1904).

New York.—Parish v. Ulster & D. R. R. Co., 192 N. Y. 353, 85 N. E. 153 (1908).

[2] *United States.*—Erie Ry. Co. v. Littell, 63 C. C. A. 44, 128 Fed. 546 (1904).

Alabama.—See Louisville & N. R. R. Co. v. Hine, 121 Ala. 234, 25 So. 857 (1898).

Arkansas.—Hot Springs Ry. Co. v. Deloney, 65 Ark. 177, 45 S. W. 351, 67 Am. St. Rep. 913.

Georgia.—Head v. Georgia Pacific Ry. Co., 79 Ga. 358, 7 So. 217, 11 Am. St. Rep. 434 (1887).

Indiana.—Pittsburg, C., C. & St. L. Ry. Co. v. Street, 26 Ind. App. 224, 59 N. E. 404 (1901).

Iowa.—Ellsworth v. Chicago, B. & Q. Ry. Co., 95 Iowa, 98, 63 N. W. 584, 29 L. R. A. 173 (1895).

Kentucky.—Louisville, etc., R. R. Co. v. Gaines, 99 Ky. 411, 36 S. W. 174, 59 Am. St. Rep. 465 (1896).

Massachusetts.—Murdock v. Boston & Albany R. R. Co., 137 Mass. 293, 50 Am. Rep. 307 (1884), *semble.*

North Carolina.—Mace v. Southern Ry. Co., 151 N. C. 404, 66 S. E. 342, 24 L. R. A. 1178 (1909).

Texas.—Houston, etc., R. R. Co. v. White (Tex. Civ. App., 1901), 61 S. W. 436.

West Virginia.—See Sheets v. Ohio R. R. Co., 39 W. Va. 475, 20 S. E. 560 (1894).

[3] *United States.*—Poulin v. Canadian Pacific Ry. Co., 52 Fed. 197 (1892).

Alabama.—See McGhee v. Reynolds, 129 Ala. 540, 2 So. 961 (1900).

District of Columbia.—Baggett v. Baltimore & O. R. R. Co., 3 D. C. App. Cas. 522 (1894).

Illinois.—Pittsburg R. R. Co. v. Daniels, 90 Ill. App. 154 (1899).

Kentucky.—Illinois Central R. R. Co. v. Jackson, 117 Ky. L. Rep. 208, 79 S. W. 1187 (1904).

Maryland.—Western Md. R. R. Co. v. Stocksdale, 83 Md. 245, 37 Atl. 880 (1896).

it is held that although the ticket agent was in the wrong, so that the company can be sued for his default, the passenger has in fact gained no right to travel, and the conductor commits no tort by ejecting him.   The writer favors this latter view because he believes in the inherent necessity of the ticket system.   With this policy it is reasonable to enforce in this case as in all others the regulation that only those will be passed by the conductor who present a good ticket.

§ 890. Mistakes of the conductors.

Where the first of two conductors wrongfully punches the ticket or collects the ticket without giving a check, so that the conductor upon another train either refuses return passage or further transportation, the same case again arises, and the same conflict of authority.   Some cases [1] hold that the second conductor expels such a passenger at his peril.   Others hold, [2] however, that the second

Michigan.—Frederick v. Marquette, H. & O. R. R. Co., 37 Mich. 342, 26 Am. Rep. 531 (1877).

New Jersey.—Shelton v. Erie R. R. Co., 73 N. J. L. 558, 66 Atl. 403, 9 L. R. A. (N. S.) 727, 118 Am. St. Rep. 704 (1907).

New York.—Nolan v. New York, N. H. & H. R. R. Co., 41 N. Y. Super. Ct. 541 (1876).

Texas.—Houston & T. C. R. R. Co. v. Ford, 53 Tex. 364 (1880).

Virginia.—Virginia & S. W. Ry. Co. v. Hill, 105 Va. 729, 54 S. E. 872, 6 L. R. A. (N. S.) 899 (1906).

[1] *Maryland.*—Philadelphia W. & B. R. R. Co. v. Rice, 64 Md. 63, 21 Atl. 97 (1885).

Mississippi.—Kansas City, M. & B. R. R. Co. v. Riley, 68 Miss. 765, 9 So. 443, 13 L. R. A. 38, 95 Am. St. Rep. 309 (1891).

West Virginia.—McKay v. Ohio R. R. R. Co., 34 W. Va. 65, 11 S. E. 737, 9 L. R. A. 132, 26 Am. St. Rep. 913 (1980).

The company is liable in an appropriate way for the original default.   Little Rock Ry. & El. Co. v. Goerner, 80 Ark. 158, 95 S. W. 1007, 7 L. R. A. (N. S.) 97 (1906); Brown v. Rapid Ry. Co., 134 Mich. 591, 96 N. W. 925 (1903).

[2] *Massachusetts.*—Bradshaw v. South Boston R. R. Co., 135 Mass. 407, 46 Am. Rep. 481 (1883).

New York.—Townsend v. New York Central & H. R. R. R. Co., 56 N. Y. 295, 15 Am. Rep. 419 (1874).

Ohio.—Shelton v. Lake S. & M. S. Ry. Co., 29 Ohio St. 214 (1876).

Washington.—Braymer v. Seattle & So. Ry. Co., 35 Wash. 346, 77 Pac. 495 (1904).

conductor may eject the passenger as he has not got a proper ticket, and the passenger must seek his redress from the company for the wrong done him by the first conductor. On the other hand if the whole mistake is made by the conductor himself, the expulsion will be wrongful.[1] Thus where a conductor collects a ticket and afterwards wrongfully expels a passenger, the conductor is responsible for the injury caused thereby, and the same law is applied to the action of a conductor who has actual knowledge of the circumstances of the original mistake. But where it happens that the same conductor who made the original mistake in punching a ticket is the one who without remembrance of it, expels the passenger upon a subsequent trip the rule is properly enough otherwise.[2]

§ 891. Argument for the passenger.

It will have been noted that there is a conflict of authority as to whether the carrier is responsible for the damage caused by expulsion of a passenger who is led by the fault of another official of the company to present to the conductor expelling him a ticket which it would be contrary to the orders given to this conductor to accept. The argument for the passenger in such cases is obvious. It

[1] *Alabama.*—Morning Star v. Louisville & N. R. R. Co., 135 Ala. 251, 33 So. 156 (1902).

California.—Gorman v. Southern Pacific Ry. Co., 97 Cal. 1, 31 Pac. 1112, 33 Am. St. Rep. 157 (1892).

Georgia.—See Brown v. Central of Ga. Ry. Co., 128 Ga. 635, 58 S. E. 163 (1907).

Indiana.—See Chicago & E. G. R. R. Co. v. Conley, 6 Ind. App. 9, 32 N. E. 96 (1892).

Massachusetts.—See Moore v. Fitchburg R. R. Co., 4 Gray, 465, 64 Am. Dec. 83 (1855).

Rhode Island.—Arnold v. Rhode Island Co., 28 R. I. 118, 66 Atl. 60 (1907).

South Carolina.—McCarter v. Greenville Tr. Co., 72 S. C. 134, 51 S. E. 545 (1905).

Tennessee.—Louisville & N. R. R. Co. v. Blair, 104 Tenn. 212, 55 S. W. 154 (1900).

[2] Western Maryland R. R. Co. v. Schaun, 97 Md. 563, 50 Atl. 701 (1903).

is put in a late Alabama case [1] thus: "The carrier cannot shield itself from the consequences of misconduct or mistake on the part of one of its agents acting within the scope of his duties, which has naturally betrayed another of its agents into the final act of injury to the passenger." A short answer to this would be that by refusing to pay fare first and litigate afterwards, the passenger did not avoid the consequential damages flowing from the wrong of the original agent, but chose to aggravate them by incurring personal injury by the expulsion. But this perhaps would prove to much; for there certainly are many cases, as have been seen, where without dissent it is held that the passenger may resist expulsion rather than pay when he is entitled to transportation. [2]

§ 892. Argument for the carrier.

The argument for the carrier must therefore go deeper. The real explanation lies in the right to make and enforce proper regulations. If the ticket system is reasonable, the expelling conductor acting in accordance with it is justified for the thing that he does. This was thoroughly worked out in a Massachusetts case [3] thus: "The conductor of a street railway car cannot reasonably be required to take the mere word of a passenger that he is entitled to be carried by reason of having paid a fare to the conductor of another car; or even to receive and decide upon the

[1] Louisville & N. R. R. Co. v. Hine, 121 Ala. 234 (1898).

[2] One is under no obligation to purchase even for a trifle what is already his own. Therefore, a passenger on an excursion train running at reduced rates, who has through the fault of the company, been unable to secure an excursion ticket, is under no obligation to pay the full excessive rate of fare de-

manded by the conductor on the train, in order to prevent his being ejected from the train, and thus lessen his damages. Chicago, St. L. & P. R. R. Co. v. Graham, 3 Ind. App. 28, 29 N. E. 170, 50 Am. St. Rep. 256 (1891).

[3] Bradshaw v. South Boston Ry. Co., 135 Mass. 407, 46 Am. Rep. 481 (1883).

verbal statements of others as to the fact. The conductor has other duties to perform, and it would often be impossible for him to ascertain and decide upon the right of the passenger, except in the usual, simple and direct way." [1]

[1] In Riley v. Chicago City Ry. Co., 189 Ill. 384, 59 N. E. 794 (1901), it is pointed out that the passenger should have paid fare and avoided the damage.

PART VII.   LIABILITY FOR DEFAULT

CHAPTER XXVI

CONDUCT OF THE UNDERTAKING

§ 900. Proper conduct of the undertaking.

Topic A. Delay in Performing Service

§ 901. Duty to act promptly.
902. Reasonable time allowed for performance.
903. Special circumstances calling for haste.
904. Adherence to schedule time.

Topic B. Deviation from the Undertaking

§ 905. Usual course of performing service.
906. Performance in unauthorized manner.
907. Transportation over wrong route.
908. Essential change by deviation.

Topic C. Excuses for Default in Performing Service

§ 909. Natural forces.
910. Governmental authority.
911. Violent intervention.
912. Interruption by strike.
913. Interference of patron.
914. Press of business.

Topic D. Liability Consequent upon Default

§ 915. Delay must be negligent.
916. Loss directly caused by delay.
917. Loss merely concurrent with delay.
918. Extreme liability according to other authorities.
919. Negligence contributing to the catastrophe.
920. Negligence in not avoiding the catastrophe.
921. Absolute liability the result of deviation.
922. Absolute liability of special contract.

[786]

§ 900. Proper conduct of the undertaking.

Those who have undertaken a public service have always been strictly held to use due diligence to carry it through promptly. Of course there are many unexpected obstacles which will excuse delay in performing services. But even if the delay is excused, their duty remains to complete performance as best they may. Indeed, quite extraordinary steps are often required by the law for the protection of the interests of the patron in such an emergency. Moreover, by the general rule public servants are held strictly accountable for any deviation from their undertaking. What they have assumed to do for their patrons they must do in the very way that they have undertaken to do, and if they fail to perform in the way they have undertaken they are held absolutely liable for the time being. But here again extraordinary events may intervene; and in the unexpected emergency not only are they excused for making a deviation, but in many instances it is their duty to complete performances in some other way.

Topic A. Delay in Performing Service

§ 901. Duty to act promptly.

One who has undertaken public service is bound to exercise due diligence to perform the service undertaken within proper time. The cases upon this elementary proposition are almost countless, particularly in common carriage.[1] Although no certain time be promised for

[1] See in general these cases among many others:

Arkansas.—St. Louis, I. M. & So. Ry. Co. v. Heath, 41 Ark. 476 (1883).

California.—Palmer v. Atchison, T. & S. F. Ry. Co., 101 Cal. 187, 35 Pac. 630 (1894).

Illinois.—Mich. So. & N. I. R. R. Co. v. Day, 20 Ill. 375, 71 Am. Dec. 278 (1858).

Louisiana.—Berje v. Texas & P. Ry. Co., 37 La. Ann. 468 (1885).

Mississippi.—Vicksburg & M. R. R. Co. v. Ragsdale, 46 Miss. 458 (1872).

completion, a reasonable time will be implied.[1] Sometimes this default is so obvious as to speak for itself. Thus the consumption of seventeen days for the carriage of goods usually taking but three days is certainly apparently negligent.[2] And of course a delay of seventy days in completing the carriage of goods where usually but a few days are taken, could only be explained away in the most extraordinary case.[3] Where a cattle train was stopped for six hours upon a journey covering in all two hundred miles, it was held to be an unreasonable delay.[4] So where the usual course of transporting freight was one day the taking of two days was held unreasonable, when the market for perishable goods was lost thereby.[5]

Maine.—Grindle v. Eastern Exp. Co., 67 Me. 317 (1877).

Minnesota.—Bibb, Broom Corn Co. v. Atchison, T. & S. F. R. R. Co., 94 Minn. 269, 102 N. W. 709, 110 Am. St. Rep. 361, 69 L. R. A. 509 (1905).

North Carolina.—Boner & C. v. Merchants' So. Co., 1 Jones (N. C.) 211 (1853).

Pennsylvania.—Empire Transp. Co. v. Wallace, 68 Pa. St. 302 (1871).

Texas.—International & Gt. R. R. Co. v. Harder, 36 Tex. Civ. App. 151, 81 S. W. 356 (1904).

England.—Briddon v. Gt. No. Ry. Co., 28 L. J. Ex. 51 (1858).

[1] See particularly:

Indiana.—Cleveland, C., C. & St. L. Ry. Co. v. Heath, 22 Ind. App. 47, 53 N. E. 198 (1899).

West Virginia.—McGraw v. Baltimore & O. R. R. Co., 18 W. Va. 361, 41 Am. Rep. 696 (1881).

[2] Michigan & S. & N. Indiana R. R. Co. v. Day, 20 Ill. 375, 71 Am. Dec. 278 (1858).

A fortiori when thirty days were taken for a similar distance. Illinois Central Ry. Co. v. Cobb C. & Co., 64 Ill. 128 (1872).

[3] St. Louis, Iron Mountain & So. Ry. Co. v. Heath, 41 Ark. 476 (1883).

See also Jennings v. Grand Trunk Ry. Co., 52 Hun, 227, 5 N. Y. Supp. 140 (1889).

[4] Minter v. Chicago, R. I. & P. Ry. Co., 82 Mo. App. 130 (1899).

See also Ormsby Ry. Co. v. Union Pacific Ry. Co., 2 McCreary, 48, 4 Fed. 706 (1880).

[5] Frey v. New York C. & H. R. R. R. Co., 114 N. Y. App. Div. 747, 100 N. Y. Supp. 225 (1906).

But see Pennsylvania R. R. Co. v. Clark, 2 Ind. App. 146, 28 N. E. 208 (1891).

Furthermore, aside from the common law liability for unreasonable delay there are in many jurisdictions special statutes penalizing delays beyond a fixed time in certain services. Such is the North Carolina statute, making the carrier lia-

§ 902. Reasonable time allowed for performance.

A reasonable time for performance is, however, allowed in all cases. What is reasonable time for performing transportation depends upon the mode of conveyance, the distance to be traversed, the nature of the goods, the season of the year, and the facilities available for transportation.[1] The requirement of reasonable dispatch in forwarding goods does not necessarily require performance at the earliest possible moment, not by the next train certainly,[2] nor even on the same day.[3] Nor is it at all unreasonable to make the halts in transportation which are incident to the ordinary transaction of the business.[4] Similarly a telephone company is allowed a reasonable time after notice of the trouble for the repair of a sub-

ble for delay for more than four days in beginning transportation and for delay during transportation at any intermediate point for more than two days. See Parker v. Atlantic Coast Line R. R. Co., 133 N. C. 335, 45 S. E. 658, 63 L. R. A. 827 (1903), and Meredith v. Railroad Co., 137 N. C. 478, 50 S. E. 1 (1905).

As this statute and similar statutes are along the lines of the common law obligation they are held constitutional; but in order to be constitutional it would seem that such statutes should receive common law interpretation and the delays forbidden should be held subject to the excuses for delay at common law. See Grocery Co. v. Railroad Co., 136 N. C. 396, 48 S. E. 801 (1904), and Stone Co. v. Atlantic Coast Line R. R. Co., 144 N. C. 220, 56 S. E. 932 (1907).

[1] See the following cases among many others:

Illinois.—Adams Express Co. v. Bratton, 106 Ill. App. 563 (1902).

Indiana.—Cincinnati, I., St. L. & C. Ry. Co. v. Case, 122 Ind. 310, 23 N. E. 797 (1889).

Kentucky.—Louisville & C. Packet Co. v. Bottorff, 25 Ky. L. Rep. 1324, 77 S. W. 920 (1904).

Michigan.—McKenzie v. Michigan Central R. R. Co., 137 Mich. 112, 100 N. W. 260 (1904).

Nebraska.—Johnston v. Chicago B. & Q. R. R. Co., 70 Neb. 364, 97 N. W. 479 (1903).

Texas.—San Antonio & A. P Ry. Co. v. Turner, 42 Tex. Civ. App. 532, 94 S. W. 214 (1906).

West Virginia.—McGraw v. Baltimore & O. R. R. Co., 18 W. Va. 361, 41 Am. Rep. 690 (1881).

[2] Pennsylvania Co. v. Clark, 2 Ind. App. 146, 27 N. E. 586 (1891).

[3] Bank of W. V. v. Southern Exp. Co., 71 Miss. 741, 16 So. 300 (1894)

[4] Southern Pacific Co. v. Arnett, 61 C. C. A. 131, 126 Fed. 75 (1903).

scriber's line.[1] And the delivery of a telegram in its
regular order and within an hour from the time it was
received at the office in the city of delivery has been held
to be with reasonable dispatch.[2] But where several hours
were taken for the transmission of a message which would
ordinarily only take a few minutes the company was held
liable.[3] And a delay of eleven days before forwarding
property received for transportation made a railroad company liable.[4]

§ 903. Special circumstances calling for haste.

According to the general principle that what is due
diligence in performance depends upon the circumstances
of the case, special circumstances may call for unusual
haste. A sudden emergency may call for unusual haste to
extricate passengers from a perilous situation [5] or to rush
through to its designation perishable freight unexpectedly
exposed.[6] To cite an example from another business, telegraph messages announcing impending death should be
handled with extraordinary dispatch.[7] And the same is

[1] Buffalo County Tel. Co. v. Turner, 82 Neb. 841, 118 N. W. 1064,
19 L. R. A. (N. S.) 693 (1908).

[2] See Julian v. Western Union
Telegraph Co., 98 Ind. 327 (1884).

[3] See Western Union Telegraph
Co. v. Johnson, 9 Tex. Civ. App.
48, 28 S. W. 124 (1894).

[4] Alabama Gt. So. Ry. Co. v.
Quarles & C., 145 Ala. 436, 40 So.
120, 5 L. R. A. 867, 117 Am. St.
Rep. 54 (1906).

What is a reasonable time for
performance is a question of fact
to be submitted to the jury when
the evidence legally admits of more
than one conclusion. See Blod-
gett v. Abbott, 72 Wis. 516, 40 N.
W. 491, 7 Am. St. Rep. 873 (1888).

On proof of a delay in delivery
by the company at the destination, a *prima facie* case is made out
against it, and the burden of proof
then rests upon it to show that it
was not responsible for the delay.
See Bosley v. Baltimore & C. R. R.
Co., 54 W. Va. 563, 46 S. E. 613, 66
L. R. A. 871 (1904).

[5] See, for example, Pennsylvania
R. R. Co. v. Frees, 87 Pa. St. 234
(1878).

[6] See, for example, Frey v. New
York C. & H. R. R. R. Co., 114
N. Y. App. Div. 747, 100 N. Y.
Supp. 225 (1906).

[7] See, for example, Western Union Telegraph Co. v. Smith (Tex.
Civ. App.), 30 S. W. 937 (1894).

true of a telegram dealing with purchases in a fluctuating market.[1] Notwithstanding the special haste required in such circumstances the carrier cannot refuse to take perishable goods from a shipper who will not sign a release of his common law rights.[2] Nor can a telegraph company refuse to take a message from one who gives formal notice of the special importance of the prompt transmission of his message.[3] Contrasting different cases will bring out the general principle that what is due diligence depends upon the circumstances of the case. Thus as an express company from the nature of its business undertakes to transport goods with the utmost dispatch, it is liable for not forwarding promptly a box of souvenirs.[4] But as a railroad company practically only undertakes to handle ordinary freight without unreasonable delay, it may hold hay for a considerable time before forwarding it without being liable.[5]

§ 904. Adherence to schedule time.

A public service corporation which publishes a schedule undertaking to perform service at certain times and places is liable to anyone damaged by its default in failing to so perform in accordance with its professed undertaking.[6]

---

[1] See, for example, Western Union Telegraph Co. v. Scircle, 103 Ind. 227 (1885).

[2] See, for example, American Express Co. v. Smith, 33 Ohio St. 511, 31 Am. Rep. 561 (1878).

[3] See, for example, Vermilye v. Postal Telegraph Cable Co., 205 Mass. 598, 91 N. E. 904 (1910).

[4] Lambert-Murray Co. v. Southern Express Co., 146 N. C. 321, 59 S. E. 991 (1907).

[5] Strough v. New York Cent. & H. R. R. Co., 87 N. Y. S. 30 (1904).

[6] *Delaware.*—Reed & W. v. Philadelphia, W. & B. R. R. Co., 3 Houst. 176 (1873).

Georgia.—Savannah S. & S. R. R. Co. v. Bonaud, 58 Ga. 180 (1877).

Maryland.—Duling v. Philadelphia, W. & B. R. R. Co., 66 Md. 120, 6 Atl. 592 (1886).

Mississippi.—Wilson v. New Orleans & N. E. R. R. Co., 63 Miss. 352 (1885).

N e b r a s k a.—McClary v. Sioux City & P. R. R. Co., 3 Neb. 44, 19 Am. Rep. 631 (1873).

And indeed a corporation undertaking to do public service is usually bound to maintain a reasonably suitable schedule unless it is willing to perform any service requested whenever asked.[1] When such a schedule is established, generally speaking delays consequent upon awaiting the regular course of a reasonable schedule of service will not be ground of action against the company.[2] But when there have been unexpected stoppages, further delays cannot always be excused by relying upon the performance of the schedule as thus delayed; for it may well be necessary to provide an additional service if the delay is a considerable one and the new service can be arranged.[3] The duty of a railroad to transport passengers upon the advertised schedule time is held to impose upon it the highest degree of care and the utmost diligence under

New York.—Weed v. Panama R. R. Co., 17 N. Y. 362, 72 Am. Dec. 474 (1858).

South Carolina.—Miller v. Southern Ry. Co., 69 S. C. 116, 48 S. E. 99 (1903).

Texas.—Eddy v. Harris, 78 Tex. 661, 15 S. W. 107, 22 Am. St. Rep. 88 (1890).

England.—Denton v. R. R. Co., 6 El. & Bl. 860 (1856).

[1] *Georgia.*—Riley v. Wrightsville & T. R. R. Co., 133 Ga. 413, 65 S. E. 890, 24 L. R. A. (N. S.) 379 (1909).

Illinois.—Chicago, B. & Q. R. R. Co. v. George, 19 Ill. 510 (1858).

Indiana.—Pittsburg, C. & St. L. Ry. Co. v. Nuzum, 50 Ind. 141, 19 Am. Rep. 703 (1875).

Missouri.—Ratcliff v. Quincy, O. & K. C. R. R. Co., 118 Mo. App. 644, 94 S. W. 1005 (1906).

New Hampshire.—Gordon v. Manchester & L. R. R. Co., 52 N. H. 596 (1873).

New York.—Barker v. New York C. R. R. Co., 24 N. Y. 599 (1862).

Wisconsin.—Strohn v. Detroit & M. R. R. Co., 23 Wis. 126, 99 Am. Dec. 114 (1868).

England.—Hurst v. Gt. Western Ry. Co., 19 C. B. (N. S.) 310 (1865).

A change of schedules will not protect the company unless reasonable notice thereof is given to the public.

Massachusetts.—Sears v. Eastern R. R. Co., 14 Allen, 433, 92 Am. Dec. 780 (1867).

Michigan.—Van Camp v. Michigan Central Ry. Co., 137 Mich. 467, 100 N. W. 771 (1904).

[2] Galveston, H. & S. A. Ry. Co. v. Tuckett (Tex. Civ. App.), 25 S. W. 150 (1894).

[3] Gulf C. & S. F. Ry. Co. v. Porter, 25 Tex. Civ. App. 491, 61 S. W. 234 (1901).

the circumstances.[1] Nevertheless safety and promptness are not to be put on the same plane, for promptness must always yield to safety.[2]

Topic B. Deviation from the Undertaking

§ 905. Usual course of performing service.

In the absence of express agreement, the carrier is bound to transport the goods by the usual and ordinary route and by the usual means of conveyance.[3] The undertaking of a common carrier, in the absence of any special contract, is to transport the property to the place of destination by the most usual, safe, direct and expeditious route. Failing in any of these, unless prevented by inevitable accident, he is held liable for the loss. Thus, deviation may be defined in general terms as any substantial departure from the arrangement made between the company and the customer.[4] The salient example is a change in the route designated by the consignor.[5]

[1] Hansley v. Jamesville & W. R. R. Co., 115 N. C. 602, 20 S. E. 528, 44 Am. St. Rep. 474 (1894).

[2] Latour v. Southern Ry. Co., 71 S. C. 532, 51 S. E. 265 (1904).

[3] *United States.*—Express Company v. Kountze Bros., 8 Wall. 342 (1869).

Connecticut.—Crosby v. Fitch, 12 Conn. 410, 31 Am. Dec. 745 (1838).

Colorado.—Denver & R. G. R. R. Co. v. De Witt, 1 Colo. App. 419, 29 Pac. 824 (1892).

Georgia.—Phillips v. Brigham, 26 Ga. 617, 71 Am. Dec. 227 (1859).

New York.—Maghee v. Camden & A. R. R. Tr. Co., 45 N. Y. 514, 6 Am. Rep. 124 (1871).

South Dakota.—Church v. Chicago, M. & St. P. Ry. Co., 6 S. D.

235, 60 N. W. 854, 26 L. R. A. 616 (1894).

Texas.—Galveston, H. & H. R. R. v. Allison, 59 Tex. 193 (1883).

England.—Davis v. Garrett, 6 Bing. 716 (1830).

[4] *Illinois.*—Merchants' Dispatch Transportation Co. v. Kahn, 76 Ill. 520 (1875).

Indiana.—Powers v. Davenport, 7 Blackf. 497, 43 Am. Dec. 100 (1845).

Mississippi.—Bennet v. Byram, 38 Miss. 17, 75 Am. Dec. 90 (1859).

Tennessee.—Louisville & N. R. R. Co. v. Odill, 96 Tenn. 61, 33 S. W. 64, 54 Am. St. Rep. 820 (1896).

[5] *United States.*—The M a g g i e Hammond, 9 Wall. 435, 19 L. ed. 773 (1869).

Georgia.—Robinson v. Holst &

Mere delay, however, is not a deviation, unless it amounts to an abandonment of the contract or is so gross as to indicate departure from the undertaking.[1] Deviation is any dealing with the property taken in some way not authorized by the patron, but such intermeddling is not conversion although many of the consequences of a conversion flow therefrom for the time being.

§ 906. Performance in unauthorized manner.

In accordance with the general principles just discussed it has been held a deviation for a carrier, in violation of his undertaking, to ship goods before the time agreed upon;[2] or on a different vessel from that stipulated for.[3] So it is deviation to ship by rail instead of by water,[4] by water instead of by rail,[5] by sea instead of canal [6] and by an outside route rather than an inside route.[7] It may be a deviation to forward by steamship instead of sailing ves-

W., 96 Ga. 19, 23 S. E. 76 (1895).

Massachusetts.—Simkins v. Norwich & N. L. St. Co., 11 Cush. 102 (1853).

Missouri.—Glover v. Cape Girardeau & So. Ry. Co., 95 Mo. App. 369, 69 S. W. 599 (1902).

New York.—White v. Ashton, 51 N. Y. 280 (1873).

Pennsylvania.—Empire Co. v. Wallace, 68 Pa. St. 302, 8 Am. Rep. 178 (1871).

[1] *Arkansas.*—Chicago, R. I. & P. Ry. Co. v. Pfeifer, 90 Ark. 524, 119 S. W. 642, (1909).

K e n t u c k y.—Cassilay, etc., v. Young & Co., 39 Am. Dec. 505, 4 B. Mon. 265 (1843).

New York.—Wamsley v. Atlas S. S. Co., 168 N. Y. 533, 61 N. E. 896, 85 Am. St. Rep. 699 (1901).

Wisconsin.—Fahey v. Northern Transportation Co., 15 Wis. 129 (1862).

[2] Campion v. Canadian Pacific Ry. Co., 43 Fed. 775, 11 L. R. A. 128 (1890).

See also Louisville & C. Packet Co. v. Rogers, 20 Ind. App. 594, 49 N. E. 970 (1898).

[3] Green & B. R. Nav. Co. v. Marshall, 48 Ind. 596 (1874). And see Goddard v. Mallory, 52 Barb. 87 (1868).

[4] Merrick v. Webster, 3 Mich. 268 (1854).

[5] Philadelphia & R. R. Co. v. Beck, 125 Pa. St. 620, 17 Atl. 505, 11 Am. St. Rep. 924 (1889).

[6] White v. Ashton, 51 N. Y. 280 (1873).

[7] Empire Transportation Co. v. Wallace, 68 Pa. St. 302, 8 Am. Rep. 178 (1871).

sel;[1] and it is a deviation to transship goods.[2] But it would probably be going too far to call it a deviation to carry the goods in a position different from the directions given,[3] although the liability in such cases is very extreme. It is, however, clear that any material departure in the conduct of carriage from the special undertaking in regard to it constitutes a deviation, as in one case where there was a special contract for through transportation in the same cars.[4] In short any course which differs materially from the performance which was understood to have been undertaken is a deviation.

§ 907. Transportation over wrong route.

Carriers receiving property for transportation plainly make a deviation by forwarding the goods by a route inconsistent with their undertaking[5] or by forwarding property to a station other than that agreed upon.[6] And it is equally deviation to forward the goods to the specified destination by an indirect route,[7] the question whether the indirect route is outside the contemplation of the parties being a question for the jury.[8] Where there is a fair choice of routes it will be assumed that it is left to carrier to choose according to ordinary course of business;[9] but if the carrier chooses a more dangerous route he is liable.[10] Except in emergency the carrier has no right to

[1] Simkins v. Norwich & N. L. Stb. Co., 11 Cush. (Mass.) 102 (1853).

[2] The Maggie Hammond, 9 Wall. (U. S.) 435, 19 L. ed. 773 (1869).

[3] Colbath v. Bangor & A. R. R. Co., 105 Me. 379, 74 Atl. 918 (1909).

[4] Stewart v. Merchants' Dispatch Transp. Co., 47 Iowa, 229 (1877).

[5] Isaacson v. New York Central & H. R. R. R. Co., 94 N. Y. 278, 46 Am. Rep. 142 (1884).

[6] Gulf, C. & S. F. Ry. Co. v. Robinson (Tex. Civ. App.), 72 S. W. 71 (1903).

[7] White v. Ashton, 51 N. Y. 280 (1873).

[8] Wells, Fargo & Co.'s Exp. v. Fuller, 4 Tex. Civ. App. 213, 23 S. W. 412 (1893).

[9] Post v. Railroad Co., 103 Tenn. 184, 52 S. W. 301, 55 L. R. A. 481 (1899).

[10] Pierce v. Southern Pacific Co., 120 Cal. 156, 52 Pac. 302, 40 L. R. A. 350 (1898).

utilize another line,[1] or ship by another connection.[2]   A
carrier receiving the goods from the carrier who took them
from the consignor for transportation is directly liable
to the owner for injury to the goods, during such deviation
from the original contract for transportation,[3] unless the
first carrier under the circumstances had an apparent
authority in dealing with the second carrier to ship as it
did.[4]   If the connecting carrier designated has gone out
of business the goods should be forwarded by another
if one is running;[5] and if it appears later that transportation over the connecting line designated would be dangerous another should be chosen.[6]

§ 908. Essential change by deviation.

Deviation has from time immemorial been considered
a serious matter, fundamentally changing the character
of the service contemplated.   It seems, therefore, that
when there has been real deviation from the undertaking
assumed, the consequences of that deviation persist until
the service is completed.   Thus if a carrier has deviated
without justification, it would seem that he should be
absolutely liable for loss throughout the entire transit.
However, it is not altogether clear from the language of
the traditional authorities that the carrier after he is back
on his track would not be allowed to show that the loss
would have occurred if he had not deviated, if this is
conceivably possible.[7]   Certainly one should not go to the

[1] Seavey Co. v. Union Transit
Co., 106 Wis. 394, 82 N. W. 285
(1900).

[2] Brown & H. Co. v. Pennsylvania Co., 63 Minn. 546, 65 N. W.
961 (1896).

[3] See Fairfax v. New York Central & H. R. R. R. Co., 73
N. Y. 167, 29 Am. Rep. 119
(1878).

[4] See Patten v. Union Pacific Ry.
Co., 29 Fed. 590 (1886).

[5] Andrus v. Columbia & O. Stb.
Co., 47 Wash. 333, 92 Pac. 128
(1907).

[6] Empire State Cattle Co. v.
Atchison, T. & S. F. Ry. Co., 210
U. S. 1, 52 L. ed. 931, 28 Sup. Ct.
607 (1908).

[7] See Davis v. Garrett, 6 Bing.

other extreme of holding that deviation constitutes conversion with all the legal consequences that follow therefrom. It is in reality an intermeddling which should make the party failing to perform as he was authorized liable absolutely while he is performing in a way which by his deviation has become altogether wrong. But that this intermeddling does not amount to a conversion is shown by the cases which hold that the consignee must accept the goods upon their arrival after deviation and take appropriate action for his damages.[1]

Topic C. Excuses for Default in Performing Service

§ 909. Natural forces.

When delay is caused by the inevitable action of natural forces there is the established excuse of act of God. As this defense prevails against all liabilities whatever, even where the liability is otherwise practically that of an insurer, it will receive but summary treatment here, as it is more fully discussed later on in connection with these cases of more stringent liability.[2] It will be sufficient to

716 (1830); and Maghee v. Camden & A. R. R. Tr. Co., 45 N. Y. 514, 6 Am. Rep. 124 (1871).

[1] *Connecticut.*—Tucker v. Housatonic R. R. Co., 39 Conn. 447 (1872).

Georgia.—Phillips v. Brigham & Co., 26 Ga. 617, 71 Am. Dec. 227 (1859).

Kentucky.—Chesapeake & O. Ry. Co. v. Saulsberry, 126 Ky. 179, 31 Ky. L. Rep. 624, 103 S. W. 254, 12 L. R. A. (N. S.) 431 (1907).

Texas.—Southern Pacific Co. v. Booth (Tex. Civ. App.), 39 S. W. 585 (1897).

The collateral authorities are clear support for the doctrine advanced in the text. In case of deviation from the undertaking, all right to compensation is lost. De Colange v. The Chateau Margaux, 37 Fed. 157 (1888). All liens upon the property for the receiving of compensation are, of course, forfeited also. Marsh v. Union Pacific Ry. Co., 3 M'Crary, 236, 9 Fed. 873 (1882).

And the benefit of the contract under which the service is being rendered is also forfeited. Thorley, Ltd., v. Orchis S. S. Co., Ltd., 1 K. B. 660 (1907). See the full discussion of this matter in Waltham Mfg. Co. v. New York & T. S. S. Co., 204 Mass. 253, 90 N. E. 550 (1910).

[2] See §§ 655 *et seq., supra.*

cite here some illustrations of the general principle applied to the particular subjects in hand. Thus if a carrier is delayed by snowstorm,[1] or a shipmaster is obliged to deviate from his course by tempestuous weather,[2] the delay and the deviation are equally excused. So the freezing of a canal [3] or river,[4] low water [5] or a flood,[6]—to give an assortment of cases,—excuse both delay and deviation caused thereby, however serious may be the consequences. Even when caused by natural forces a delay is not necessarily excused. It is well established that the ordinary actions of the elements must be anticipated and guarded against so far as this is reasonably possible.[7] Where the delay might have been avoided by proper precautions there will be liability for any negligent action under the circumstances.[8]

§ 910. Governmental authority.

It has been seen in another connection that the inter-

[1] Ballentine v. North Missouri R. R. Co., 40 Mo. 491 (1867). See also Pruitt v. Hannibal & St. J. R. R. Co., 62 Mo. 527 (1786).

[2] Phelps, I. & Co. v. Hill, 1 Q. B. 605, 60 L. I. Q. B. 328 (1891).

[3] Beckwith v. Frisbie, 32 Vt. 559 (1860).

[4] Empire Transp. Co. v. Wallace, 68 Pa. St. 302, 8 Am. Rep. 178 (1871).

[5] Bennett v. Byram & Co., 38 Miss. 17, 75 Am. Dec. 90 (1859).

[6] American Express Co. v. Smith, 33 Ohio St. 511, 31 Am. Rep. 561 (1878). See further Norris v. Savannah, F. & W. Ry. Co., 23 Fla. 182, 1 So. 475, 11 Am. St. Rep. 355 (1887).

[7] Missouri, K. & T. Ry. Co. v. Truskett, 2 Ind. Terr. 633, 53 S. W. 444 (1899); s. c., 186 U. S. 480, 46 L. ed. 1259, 22 Sup. Ct. 943. See also Cleveland, C., C. & St. L. v. Heath, 22 Ind. App. 47, 53 N. E. 198 (1899).

[8] Wabash, St. L. & P. Ry. Co. v. McCasland, 11 Ill. App. 491 (1882). So if a telegraph company cannot forward its messages by reason of electric disturbances its delay is excused. See Beasley v. Western Union Telegraph Co., 39 Fed. 181 (1889).

Similarly atmospheric conditions making it impossible to telegraph train orders will excuse delay in train movements. International & G. N. R. R. Co. v. Hynes et al., 3 Tex. Civ. App. 20, 21 S. W. 622 (1893).

position of governmental authority will excuse a refusal to perform service so long as the prohibition is in force.[1] It is plain that such legal inhibitions equally excuse delay in completing performance to the extent that the delay is caused thereby. Where delay is caused by legal prohibition of any sort,[2] it is, of course, excusable. And orders proceeding from military authorities furnish an excuse to the extent that the delay is made necessary thereby.[3] But if the fault of the carrier is the cause of the interruption of the transit by the authorities he has of course no excuse.[4] And similarly if the delay is caused by process of the courts,[5] the carrier is excused for delay caused by obedience thereto. But he must show that the process is legally binding.[6]

§ 911. Violent intervention.

As the acts of public enemies will excuse a loss of goods, they will *a fortiori* excuse a delay [7] in performance. This is true where the situation is so serious as to justify the carrier in believing that there is real danger in continuing

[1] See §§ 590 *et seq.*, *supra.*

[2] Decker v. Atchison, T. & S. F. Ry. Co., 3 Okla. 553, 41 Pac. 610 (1895). See also Fort Worth & D. C. Ry. Co. v. Masterson, 95 Tex. 262, 60 S. W. 833 (1902).

[3] Illinois Central R. R. Co. v. McClellan, 54 Ill. 58, 5 Am. Rep. 83 (1870). Unless the condition was known at the time of acceptance. Illinois Central R. R. Co. v. Cobb, 64 Ill. 128 (1873).

[4] Dunn v. Becknall Bros., 2 K. B. 614, 71 L. J. K. B. 963 (1902). See also Railroad Co. v. O'Donnell, 49 Ohio St. 489, 32 N. E. 476, 34 Am. St. Rep. 579 (1892).

[5] Hynds v. Wynn, 71 Iowa, 593, 33 N. W. 73 (1887), for one example.

[6] Merz v. Chicago & N. W. Ry. Co., 86 Minn. 33, 90 N. W. 7 (1902), for another example.

[7] It is a general defense to any apparent liability that the default is caused by the act of public enemies. See:

United States.—Express Co. v. Kountz, 8 Wall. 342, 49 L. ed. 457 (1870).

Kentucky.—Bland v. Adams Express Co., 1 Duv. 232, 85 Am. Dec. 623 (1864).

New Mexico.—Seligman v. Armijo, 1 N. Mex. 459 (1870).

Tennessee.—Southern Express Co. v. Womack, 1 Heisk. 256 (1870).

See generally, § 666, *supra.*

the transportation. But the excuse for liability for delay
is not, as in the case of liability for loss, confined to public
enemies. If the delay is caused by mob violence which
cannot be overcome, or even by reasonable fear of such
violence, it is not negligent to cease operations. And the
delay is consequently excusable.[1]

§ 912. Interruption by strike.

The case of strikes presents a difficult situation, as has
been seen. In so far as the operations of the company
are prevented by the violent action of the strikers after
leaving the service,[2] or the violence of sympathizers,
with which the public authorities have not been able to
cope, delays are excusable until peaceful conditions are
restored.[3] Where, however, there is delay or damage
caused by the employés quitting work, the mere fact that
the company has not sufficient means to perform the
services at its disposal, is on general principles, no excuse,[4]

[1] *Arkansas.*—Railway Co. v. Ne-
ville, 60 Ark. 375, 30 S. W. 425,
28 L. R. A. 80, 46 Am. St. Rep.
208 (1895).

Georgia.—Haas v. Kansas City,
F. S. & G. R. R. Co., 81 Ga. 792,
7 S. E. 629 (1888).

New York.—Little v. Fargo, 43
Hun, 233 (1887).

Pennsylvania.—Lang v. Pennsylvania R. R. Co., 154 Pa. St.
342, 26 Atl. 370, 20 L. R. A. 360,
35 Am. St. Rep. 846 (1893).

See generally, § 667, *supra.*

[2] See these cases especially:

Georgia.—Haas v. Kansas City,
F. S. & G. R. R. Co., 81 Ga. 972,
7 S. E. 629 (1888).

Kentucky.—Louisville & N. R.
R. Co. v. Bell, 13 Ky. L. Rep. 393
(1891).

New York.—Grismer v. Lake
Shore & M. S. Ry. Co., 102 N. Y.
563, 7 N. E. 828, 55 Am. Rep. 837
(1886).

Texas.—Missouri Pacific Ry. Co.
v. Levi (Tex. Ct. of App.), 14 S.
W. 1062 (1889).

See generally, § 669, *supra.*

[3] See further:

Illinois.—Indianapolis & St. L.
R. R. Co. v. Juntgen, 10 Ill. App.
295 (1881).

Indiana.—Lake Shore, M. S. Ry.
Co. v. Bennett, 89 Ind. 457 (1883).

Mississippi.—Kansas City, M.
& B. R. R. Co. v. Spencer, 72 Miss.
491, 97 So. 168 (1894).

Montana.—State ex rel. v. Gt.
Northern Ry. Co., 14 Mont. 381,
36 Pac. 458 (1894).

[4] *Georgia.*—Central R. R. & B.

and delays from this cause are, therefore, not excused.[1] The existence of a strike upon a connecting railroad, however, may be an excuse for forwarding goods by another line than that originally contemplated; [2] but such deviation should not be resorted to without consulting the owner if this is practicable.[3]

§ 913. Interference of patron.

Where the default to which the patron objects is due to his own interference, he can hardly be heard to complain of it. A striking illustration of this principle was where the party was responsible for a fire set in the carrier's tunnel rendering the tracks impassable.[4] But the shipper is equally precluded from recovery if the loss was due to his delay in loading the car.[5] And he cannot complain if performance is not continued where he has failed to make prepayment.[6] So if his instructions in regard to icing cause the delay, he can have no complaint.[7] This

Co. v. Georgia Fruit, etc., Exch., 91 Ga. 389, 17 S. E. 904 (1893).

Missouri.—Read v. St. Louis, K. C. & N. R. R. Co., 60 Mo. 199 (1875).

Illinois.—Pittsburg, F. W. & C. R. R. Co. v. Hazen, 84 Ill. 36, 25 Am. Rep. 422 (1876).

New York.—Blackstock v. New York & E. R. R. Co., 20 N. Y. 48, 75 Am. Dec. 372 (1859).

See generally, § 668, *supra*.

[1] See further:

Georgia.—Southern Ry. Co. v. Atlanta Sand & S. Co., 68 S. E. 807 (1910).

Indiana.—Bartlett v. Pittsburg, C. & St. L. Ry. Co., 94 Ind. 281 (1883).

North Carolina.—Murphey Hardware Co. v. Southern Ry. Co., 150 N. C. 703, 64 S. E. 873, 22 L. R. A. (N. S.) 200 (1909).

Texas.—International & Gt. No. Ry. Co. v. Tisdale, 74 Tex. 8, 11 S. W. 900, 4 L. R. A. 545 (1889).

[2] Steiger v. Erie Ry. Co., 5 Hun, 345 (1875).

[3] Railroad v. Odil, 96 Tenn. 61, 33 S. W. 611 (1895).

[4] Railroad Co. v. O'Donnell, 49 Ohio St. 489, 32 N. E. 476, 34 Am. St. Ry. 579 (1892).

[5] Stoner v. Chicago Gt. W. Ry. Co., 109 Iowa, 551, 80 N. W. 569 (1899).

[6] Louisville & C. Packet Co. v. Bottorff, 25 Ky. Law Rep. 1324, 77 S. W. 920 (1904).

[7] Texas Central R. R. Co. v. Dorsey (Tex. Civ. App.), 70 S. W. 575 (1902).

was particularly plain in a recent case where the shipper
had the shipment stopped in transit to get time to nego-
tiate for special rates.[1] And probably the plainest case
of all is where the delay is due to the shipper's failure to
address the parcel properly.[2]

§ 914. Press of business.

It sometimes happens that there is a mass of business
which cannot be handled within reasonable time. This
matter has been already elaborately discussed.[3] A wholly
unexpected press of business is held an excuse for refusing
to undertake further service, provided that the company
has exercised due diligence in providing adequate facilities.[4]
Following these cases, the law for this situation will consequently be that where sufficient equipment has been provided to meet expected business, and by reason of unexpected demand prompt service cannot be given, there
is an excuse for such unavoidable delay.[5] This, however, is limited to cases where, when the business was accepted, it was not known that there was impending this
extraordinary pressure of business. For the management
is not excused for the delay in forwarding business which
it had accepted with knowledge of its inability to do so.[6]

[1] Herring v. Chesapeake & W.
R. R. Co., 101 Va. 778, 45 S. E.
322 (1903).

[2] McGowan v. Wilmington & W.
R. R. Co., 95 N. C. 417 (1886).

[3] See generally, §§ 663 et seq. and
§§ 798 et seq.

[4] See generally, §§ 800 et seq.

[5] See particularly:

Illinois.—Cobb C. & Co. v. Illinois Cent. R. R. Co., 88 Ill. 394
(1878).

Kentucky.—Newport News & M.
V. R. R. Co. v. Reed, 10 Ky. Law
Rep. 1020 (1889).

Missouri.—Dawson v. Chicago
& A. R. R. Co., 79 Mo. 296 (1883).

New York.—Wilbert v. New
York & E. Ry. Co., 12 N. Y. 245
(1855).

Texas.—Pecos & N. T. Ry. Co.
v. Evans-Snider-Buel Co., 42 Tex.
Civ. App. 60, 93 S. W. 1024 (1906).

Wisconsin.—Peet v. Chicago &
N. W. Ry. Co., 20 Wis. 594, 91
Am. Dec. 446 (1866).

See generally, §§ 665, 666.

[6] *United States.*—Helliwell v.
Grand Trunk Ry. Co., 10 Biss. 170,
7 Fed. 68 (1881).

Indeed, there are cases so extreme as to hold that a carrier is bound to know when he accepts property for shipment that he has, or can obtain, facilities for its transportation within a reasonable time.[1]   At all events, pressure of business resulting from lack of proper means of transportation cannot be an excuse for delay.[2]   Where this unexpected press of business will excuse the railroad for failure to move promptly all freight it has taken, it should usually normally move the freight on hand in the order of its receipt.[3]   But in extraordinary circumstances, it may postpone a later shipment for an earlier.[4]

Illinois.—Gt. Western Ry. Co. v. Burns, 60 Ill. 284 (1871).

Missouri.—Tucker v. Pacific R. R. Co., 50 Mo. 385 (1872).

North Carolina.—Branch v. Wilmington & W. R. R. Co., 77 N. C. 347 (1877).

Utah.—Nichols v. Oregon Short Line R. R. Co., 24 Utah, 83, 91 Am. St. Rep. 778, 66 Pac. 768 (1901).

Tennessee.—Southern Ry. Co. v. Deakins, 107 Tenn. 522, 64 S. W. 477 (1901).

Wisconsin.—Maclaren v. Detroit & M. R. R. Co., 23 Wis. 138 (1868).

[1] *United States.*—Thomas v. Wabash St. L. & P. Ry. Co., 63 Fed. 200 (1894).

Texas.—International & G. N. Ry. Co. v. Anderson (Tex. Civ. App.), 21 S. W. 691 (1893); Gulf, C. & S. F. Ry. Co. v. McAulay (Tex. Civ. App.), 26 S. W. 475 (1894); Gulf, C. & S. F. Ry. Co. v. Hodge (Tex. Civ. App.), 30 S. W. 829 (1895); Gulf, C. & S. F. Ry. Co. v. Hume, 6 Tex. Civ. App. 653, 24 S. W. 915.

But see:

Massachusetts.—Thayer v. Burchard, 99 Mass. 508 (1868).

Missouri.—Ballentine v. North Missouri Ry. Co., 40 Mo. 491, 93 Am. Dec. 315 (1867).

[2] See particularly:

United States.—Ormsby v. Union Pac. R. R. Co., 2 McCrary, 48, 4 Fed. 706.

Mississippi.—Yazoo & M. V. R. R. Co. v. Blum Co., 80 Miss. 180, 40 So. 748, 10 L. R. A. (N. S.) 432 (1906).

Wisconsin.—Ayres v. Chicago & N. W. R. R. Co., 71 Wis. 372, 37 N. W. 432 (1888).

Texas.—International & G. N. R. R. Co. v. Lecus (Tex. Civ. App.), 23 S. W. 323 (1893).

[3] See particularly, Marshall v. New York Central R. R. Co., 45 Barb. (N. Y.) 502 (1886), and Southern Ry. Co. v. Atlanta Sand & S. Co., 68 S. E. 807 (1910).

See generally, §§ 837–842, *supra*.

[4] See particularly, Michigan Central R. R. Co. v. Burrows, 33 Mich. 6 (1875), and Briddon v. Gt. Northern Ry. Co., 28 L. J. Ex. 51 (1858).

See generally, §§ 850–857, *supra*.

Topic D. Liability Consequent upon Default

§ 915. Delay must be negligent.

The rule is universal as to all public services that in order to make out a case of liability for delay in performing, some blameworthiness [1] must be shown, either the rare case of intention or the common case of negligence. What constitutes negligence is, of course, a question of due care under the circumstances. This may be tested generally by determining what is the time in which the service is usually completed. But the mere fact that there has been delay in performance beyond what would be the reasonable time under ordinary circumstances for completing performance, does not make out a conclusive case of liability, for there may be valid excuses for such delay as has just been seen. Unusual delay, to be sure, makes out a *prima facie* case; and where fault would be denied it must be shown that performance could not have been completed in less time by reason of unforeseen obstacles. [2] Sometimes the neglect of the carrier speaks for itself. If a train is delayed by one of its force being drunk, the railroad can obviously have no excuse. [3] And so if a locomotive is so negligently handled that certain

[1] *United States.*—Southern Pacific Co. v. Arnett, 126 Fed. 75 (1903).

Alabama.—Thompson v. Alabama Midland Ry. Co., 122 Ala. 378, 24 So. 931 (1898).

Georgia.—Smith v. Cleveland, C., C. & St. L. Ry. Co., 92 Ga. 539, 18 S. E. 977 (1893).

New Hampshire.—Favor v. Philbrick, 5 N. H. 358 (1831).

New York.—Parsons v. Hardy, 14 Wend. 215 (1835).

North Carolina.—Boner & C. v. Merchants' Steamboat Co., 1 Jones L. 211 (1853).

Texas.—International & G. N. Ry. Co. v. Hynes, 3 Tex. Civ. App. 20, 21 S. W. 622 (1893).

Virginia.—Southern Ry. Co. v. Wilcox, 99 Va. 394, 39 S. E. 144 (1901).

England.—Taylor v. Gt. No. Ry. Co., L. R. 1 C. P. 385 (1866).

[2] *Kentucky.*—Louisville, N. A. & C. Ry. Co. v. Brinley, 17 Ky. L. Rep. 9, 29 S. W. 305 (1895).

South Carolina.—Nettles v. South Carolina Ry. Co., 7 Rich. L. 190, 62 Am. Dec. 509 (1854).

[3] Weed v. Panama R. R. Co., 17 N. Y. 362, 72 Am. Dec. 474 (1858).

of its pipes freeze,[1] the carrier is to blame for the consequent delay.

§ 916. Loss directly caused by delay.

Where the delay is shown to be one for which the defendant company is to blame, it does not necessarily follow that there is liability for every loss connected with it. Of course, the liability is plain when the loss is obviously the result of the delay.[2] The result is still proximate if the actual loss of goods carried happened upon a connecting line by reason of the original delay.[3] Clearly when the carrier should have foreseen that such loss might result from his delay, there should be liability. And this may account for several cases which are sometimes held to decide more as, for instance, that case where a carter, delayed in his journey, left his wagon in mid-river at a ford where the goods were injured by a freshet.[4] In that case it would seem that the carrier should have foreseen that loss was much more likely to happen from the position in which he left the goods. And it may be admitted that liability may fairly be fastened upon the carrier for all the consequences of his delay resulting by ordinary natural

---

[1] Cleveland, C., C. & St. L. Ry. Co. v. Heath, 22 Ind. App. 47, 53 N. E. 198 (1899).

[2] *Alabama.*—Richmond & D. R. R. Co. v. Trousdale & Sons, 99 Ala. 389, 13 So. 23, 42 Am. St. Rep. 69 (1893).

Indiana.—Pittsburg, C., C. & St. L. Ry. Co. v. Mitchell, 91 N. E. 735 (1910).

Iowa.—Hewett v. Chicago, B. & Q. Ry. Co., 63 Iowa, 611 (1884).

Kansas.—Missouri Pacific R. R. Co. v. Peru-Van Zandt Imp. Co., 73 Kan. 295, 85 Pac. 408, 6 L. R. A. (N. S.) 1058, 117 Am. St. Rep. 468 (1906).

Missouri.—Wolf v. Express Co., 43 Mo. 421, 97 Am. Dec. 406 (1869).

Texas.—San Antonio & A. P. Ry. Co. v. Josey (Tex. Civ. App.), 71 S. W. 606 (1903).

[3] Fox v. Boston & M. R. R. Co., 148 Mass. 220, 19 N. E. 222, 1 L. R. A. 702 (1889). But see Michigan Central R. R. Co. v. Burrows, 33 Mich. 6 (1875).

[4] Campbell v. Morse, Harper (N. C.), 468 (1824).

See also Missouri, P. Ry. Co. v. Peru-Van Zandt Implement Co., 73 Kan. 295, 85 Pac. 408, 6 L. R. A. (N. S.) 1058 (1906).

sequence, whether foreseen by him or not. Such is the
case where the carrier transports unduly slowly in winter,
the exposure to the risk of freezing in some period of
severe cold being increased by the extension of the usual
period of transit.[1] Properly it would seem that these
are the sound distinctions to be taken. When the connection between the delay and the destruction is merely
accidental or fortuitous, the loss of the goods is a remote
consequence; but when the delay really increases the risk
of loss, the injury is not unnatural, and therefore proximate. Indeed delay, generally speaking, is quite as likely
to result in avoiding the catastrophe as it is to cause being
involved in it.[2] In accordance with this distinction it has
been said that when a passenger is negligently carried
by his station and compelled to walk back, the railroad
would not be liable if he was struck by lightning while
walking back, but it would be liable if he was struck by
a passing train.[3]

§ 917. Loss merely concurrent with delay.

There is a noteworthy conflict of authority upon the
question whether a carrier is liable who by a negligent
delay in transporting goods has involved them in the
course of transportation in a peril which has resulted in
their damage, it being admitted that the carrier would
not have been liable, had there been no negligent delay
intervening. According to what seems to the writer the
better authorities [4] it is held that the negligent delay of

[1] McGraw v. Baltimore & O. R.
R. Co., 18 W. Va. 361, 41 Am. Rep.
696 (1881). See also Michigan
Central R. R. Co. v. Curtis, 80 Ill.
324 (1875).

[2] Lewis v. Flint & P. M. Ry. Co.,
54 Mich. 55, 19 N. W. 744, 52 Am.
Rep. 790 (1884).

[3] Benson v. Central Pacific R. R.
Co., 98 Cal. 45, 32 Pac. 809 (1893).

[4] *United States.*—See Railroad
Co. v. Reeves, 10 Wall. 176, 19 L.
ed. 909 (1869); and Empire State
Cattle Co. v. Atchison, T. & S. F.
Ry. Co., 135 Fed. 135 (1905).

Kansas.—Rogers v. Missouri Pa-

the carrier in transportation should not be regarded as the proximate cause of the ultimate loss, even admitting that had the goods been transported with reasonable diligence they would not have been involved in the casualty. The leading authority to this effect is a Massachusetts case [1] in which delayed goods were while still *en route* overtaken by an unprecedented flood and destroyed thereby. And it was held that such a loss was in no sense caused by the delay, Mr. Justice Merrick saying: "The rise of waters in the Hudson, which did the mischief to the wool, occurred at a period subsequent to this, and consequently was the direct and proximate cause to which that mischief is to be attributed. The negligence of the defendants was remote; it had ceased to operate as an active, efficient and prevailing cause as soon as the wool had been carried on beyond Syracuse, and cannot therefore subject them to responsibility for an injury to the

cific Ry. Co., 75 Kan. 222, 88 Pac. 885, 10 L. R. A. (N. S.) 658 (1907).

Louisiana. — Dalzell v. Stb. Saxon, 10 La. Ann. 280 (1855).

Massachusetts. — Hoadley v. Northern Transp. Co., 115 Mass. 305 (1874).

Michigan.—Michigan Central R. R. Co. v. Burrows, 33 Mich. 6 (1875).

Mississippi.—Merchants' Wharfboat Assn. v. Wood & Co., 64 Miss. 661, 2 So. 76, 60 Am. Rep. 76 (1887).

Missouri.—Grier v. St. Louis Merchants' B. T. Ry. Co., 108 Mo. App. 565, 84 S. W. 158 (1904).

North Carolina. — Extinguisher Co. v. Railroad Co., 137 N. C. 278, 49 S. E. 208 (1904).

Ohio.—Daniels v. Ballantine, 23 Ohio St. 532, 13 Am. Rep. 264 (1872).

Pennsylvania. — Morrison v. Davis, 20 Pa. St. 171, 57 Am. Dec. 695 (1852).

Tennessee.—Lamont & Co. v. Nashville & C. R. R. Co., 9 Heisk. 58 (1871).

Texas.—International & G. N. R. R. Co. v. Bergman (Tex. Civ. App.), 64 S. W. 999 (1901).

Vermont.—Davis & G. v. Central Vt. R. R. Co., 66 Vt. 290, 29 Atl. 313, 44 Am. St. Rep. 852 (1893).

Virginia.—Herring v. Chesapeake & W. R. R. Co., 101 Va. 778, 45 S. E. 322 (1903).

West Virginia. — McGraw v. Baltimore & O. R. R. Co., 18 W. Va. 361, 41 Am. Rep. 696 (1881).

[1] Denny v. New York Central R. R. Co., 13 Gray (Mass.), 481, 74 Am. Dec. 645 (1859).

plaintiff's property, resulting from a subsequent inevitable accident which was the proximate cause by which it was produced. It is to the latter only to which the loss sustained by him is attributable."

§ 918. Extreme liability according to other authorities.

But the many cases must be reckoned with which hold that liability is made out from the mere fact that the loss would not have happened but for the negligent delay.[1] In a recent Iowa case[2] the carrier was held liable for the loss of goods destroyed by an extraordinary flood, Mr. Justice McClain concluding an elaborate opinion thus: "Now, while it is true that the defendant could not have anticipated this particular flood and could not have foreseen that its negligent delay in transportation would subject the goods to such a danger, yet it is now apparent that such delay did subject the goods to the danger, and that but for the delay they would not have been destroyed; and defendant should have foreseen, as any reasonable person could foresee, that the negligent delay would extend the time during which the goods would

---

[1] *Alabama.* — Alabama Gt. So. Ry. Co. v. Quarles & Co., 145 Ala. 436, 40 So. 120, 117 Am. St. Rep. 54, 5 L. R. A. (N. S.) 867 (1906).

Illinois.—Wald v. Pittsburg, C. C. & St. L. R. R. Co., 162 Ill. 545, 44 N. E. 888, 35 L. R. A. 356, 53 Am. St. Rep. 332 (1896).

Kentucky.—Hernshem Bros. v. Newport News & M. V. Co., 18 Ky. Law Rep. 227, 35 S. W. 1115 (1896).

Minnesota.—Bibb Broom Corn Co. v. Atchison, T. & S, F. Ry. Co., 94 Minn. 269, 102 N. W. 709, 69 L. R. A. 509, 110 Am. St. Rep. 361 (1905).

Missouri.—Davis v. Wabash, St. L. & P. Ry. Co., 89 Mo. 340, 1 S. W. 327 (1886), practically overruled.

Nebraska. — Wabash Ry. Co. v. Sharpe, 76 Neb. 424, 107 N. W. 758 (1906).

New York.—Michaels v. New York C. R. R. Co., 30 N. Y. 564, 86 Am. Dec. 415 (1864).

Texas.—Texas & P. Ry. Co. v. Smissen, 31 Tex. Civ. App. 549, 73 S. W. 42 (1903).

[2] Green-Wheeler Shoe Co. v. Chicago, R. I. & P. Co., 130 Iowa, 123, 106 N. W. 498 (1906).

be liable in the hands of the carrier to be overtaken by some such casualty, and would therefore increase the peril that the goods should be thus lost to the shipper."

§ 919. Negligence contributing to the catastrophe.

It may also be pointed out briefly that when the negligence of the carrier or the public servant is a contributing cause in the final loss, the carrier will be held liable therefor. Thus if a shipmaster sets forth in an unseaworthy vessel which is lost in a storm which a seaworthy vessel would probably have survived, the carrier was properly enough held liable.[1] In this case as in many others, the negligence may truly be said to be a cause contributing to the final catastrophe.[2] In another case, where in answer to an inquiry by a consignee for his goods the reply was negligently given that they had not arrived, the carrier was held liable for their subsequent destruction by inevitable accident.[3] The court felt that the carrier might well be held absolutely liable to the consignee for accidental loss during the period after such wrongful refusal. And indeed, this case of not giving over the goods upon demand is practically the same situation as that of deviation where the goods are carried in contravention of orders.[4]

§ 920. Negligence in not avoiding the catastrophe.

However, even if the damage is apparently caused exclusively by act of God, nevertheless if the public servant could have foreseen the catastrophe in time to have prevented it,[5] or could have avoided the results of it and

---

[1] Packard v. Taylor, C. & Co., 35 Ark. 402 (1880).

[2] See also Davis v. Wabash, St. L. & P. Ry. Co., 89 Mo. 340, 1 S. W. 327 (1886).

[3] Stevens v. Boston & M. R. R. Co., 1 Gray, 277 (1854).

[4] See also Railroad v. Kelly, 91 Tenn. 699 (1892).

[5] *United States.*—C a l d w e l l v.

negligently failed to do so, he will be liable.[1] This is brought out in two well known United States Supreme Court cases. In Express Company v. Kountz [2] it was pointed out that if the carrier chooses the route which would very probably expose the goods to capture by the enemy it will be liable for their capture. In Railroad Company v. Reeves [3] it was pointed out that unless the carrier failed to exercise whatever care was practicable to remove the goods from a rising flood it would not be held liable. These cases it will be seen are entirely consistent, being in effect complementary.

§ 921. Absolute liability the result of deviation.

It is generally agreed that proof of deviation and loss concurrent with it from whatever cause arising make out a case of liability without more.[4] By the general theory

Southern Express Co., 1 Flipp, 85, Fed. Cas. No. 2,303 (1866).

Alabama.—Smith v. Western Ry. of Ala., 91 Ala. 455, 8 So. 754, 11 L. R. A. 619 (1891).

Tennessee.—Express Co. v. Jackson, 92 Tenn. 326, 21 S. W. 666 (1893).

Texas.—St. Louis Ry. Co. v. Bland (Tex. Civ. App.), 34 S. W. 675 (1896).

[1] *Georgia.*—Savannah Ry. Co. v. Commercial Guana Co., 103 Ga. 590, 30 S. E. 555.

Nebraska.—Black v. Chicago, B. & O. R. R. Co., 30 Neb. 197 (1890).

New York.—Wing v. New York, etc., Ry. Co., 1 Hilton (N. Y. C. P.), 235.

South Carolina.—Ewart v. Street, 2 Bailey (S. C.), 157, 23 Am. Dec. 131 (1831).

[2] 8 Wall. 342, 19 L. ed. 457 (1869).

[3] 10 Wall. 176, 19 L. ed. 909 (1870).

[4] See:

United States.—The Maggie Hammond, 9 Wall. 435, 19 L. ed. 773 (1869).

Connecticut.—Crosby v. Fitch, 12 Conn. 410, 31 Am. Dec. 745 (1838).

Colorado.—Denver & R. G. R. R. Co. v. De Witt, 1 Colo. App. 419, 29 Pac. 824 (1892).

Georgia.—Phillips v. Brigham, 26 Ga. 617, 71 Am. Dec. 227 (1889).

Illinois.—Merchants' Dispatch Co. v. Kahn, 76 Ill. 520 (1875).

Indiana.—Powers v. Davenport, 7 Blackf. 497, 43 Am. Dec. 100 (1845).

Kansas.—Chicago & Gt. W. Ry. Co. v. Dunlap, 71 Kan. 67, 80 Pac. 34 (1905).

Iowa.—Stewart v. Merchants' Dispatch Transp. Co., 47 Iowa, 229 (1877).

taken in this chapter this liability is not based upon negligence in the conduct of the undertaking, nor do the cases require proof of negligence. The mere fact of deviation is essentially a wrong in itself, as it constitutes a repudiation of the arrangement under which the carrier was authorized to act. It has in fact never been an issue in any case of liability for deviation, whether the loss was directly or remotely caused by deviation. The carrier is unhesitatingly held liable, even when the act of God or the king's enemies is the plain cause of the loss. The explanation of this rule making the carrier who has deviated from his undertaking liable at all events thereafter, is the peculiar liability for improper intermeddling. Any bailee is regarded by the law as absolutely liable for any loss happening in the period after his intermeddling. As this intermeddling makes the whole performance thereafter fundamentally different, this absolute liability should persist until the goods are finally delivered. And very probably this is the law, although some doubts may be entertained after reading the opinions in the leading cases.[1]

Massachusetts.—Simkins v. Norwich & N. L. Stb. Co., 11 Cush. 102 (1853).

Mississippi.—Bennet v. Byram, 38 Miss. 17, 75 Am. Dec. 90 (1859).

New York.—White v. Ashton, 51 N. Y. 280 (1873).

Pennsylvania.—Empire Transp. Co. v. Wallace, 68 Pa. St. 302, 8 Am. Rep. 178 (1871).

South Dakota.—Church v. Chicago, M. & St. P. Ry. Co., 6 S. D. 235, 60 N. W. 854, 26 L. R. A. 616 (1894).

[1] See the *dicta* in Davis v. Garrett, 6 Bingham, 716 (1830), and in Maghee Camden & A. R. R. Tr.

Co., 45 N. Y. 514, 6 Am. Rep. 124 (1871).

Note the decisions in Thorley, Ltd., v. Orchis S. S. Co., Ltd. (1907), 1 K. B. 660, and in Galveston & H. Ry. Co. v. Allison, 59 Tex. 193 (1883).

See the analogy drawn in Wald v. Pittsburg, C., C. & St. L. R. R. Co., 162 Ill. 545, 44 N. E. 888, 35 L. R. A. 356, 53 Am. St. Rep. 332 (1896); and in Bibb Broom Corn Co. v. Atchison, T. & S. F. Ry. Co., 94 Minn. 269, 102 N. W. 709, 69 L. R. A. 509, 110 Am. St. Rep. 361 (1905).

But note the distinctions made

§ 922. Absolute liability when special contract.

In the last place, it should be stated that where the carrier has made an express contract to carry and deliver within a specified time, he is bound to fulfill his contract.[1] Nothing will excuse him, and he is liable for any delay, no matter from what cause it may have arisen.[2] There is nothing remarkable in holding that one who makes a contract must perform it at his peril, notwithstanding good explanations. A carrier need not make any special contract, but may insist upon taking the goods under his common-law liability, or not at all. Then his common-law excuses will be available; but if he actually contracts he has no more excuses than any other contractor.

in Rogers v. Missouri Pacific Ry. Co., 75 Kan. 222, 88 Pac. 885, 10 L. R. A. (N. S.) 658 (1907), and in Extinguisher Co. v. Railroad Co., 137 N. C. 278, 49 S. E. 208 (1904).

[1] See:

Arkansas.—Cantwell v. Pacific Express Co., 58 Ark. 487, 25 S. W. 503 (1894).

Illinois.—Chicago & A. R. R. Co. v. Thrapp, 5 Ill. App. 502 (1880).

Iowa.—See Stoner v. Chicago Gt. W. Ry. Co., 109 Iowa, 551 (1899).

Massachusetts.—Torrell v. Gage, 4 Allen, 245 (1862).

Missouri.—Collier v. Swinney, 16 Mo. 484 (1852).

Michigan.—Rudell v. Ogdensburg Transit Co., 117 Mich. 568 (1898).

New York.—Harmony v. Bingham, 1 Duer N. Y. 209, 62 Am. Dec. 142 (1852).

[2] *United States.*—The Harriman, 9 Wall. 161, 19 L. ed. 629 (1869).

Alabama.—Baxley v. Tallahassee & M. R. R. Co., 128 Ala. 183, 29 So. 451 (1900).

Indiana.—Pittsburg, C., C. & St. L. Ry. Co. v. Racer, 10 Ind. App. 503, 37 N. E. 280, 38 N. E. 186 (1894).

Iowa.—Wood v. Chicago, M. & St. P. Ry. Co., 68 Iowa, 491, 56 Am. Rep. 861 (1886).

Missouri.—Currell v. Hannibal & St. J. Ry. Co., 97 Mo. App. 93, 71 S. W. 113 (1902).

New Hampshire.—Deming v. Grand Trunk R. R. Co., 48 N. H. 455, 2 Am. Rep. 267 (1869).

North Carolina.—McAbsher v. Richmond & D. R. R. Co., 108 N. C. 344, 12 S. E. 892 (1891).

South Carolina.—M a t h i s v. Southern Ry. Co., 65 S. C. 271, 43 S. E. 684, 61 L. R. A. 824 (1902).

Tennessee.—Southern Ry. Co. v. Deakins, 107 Tenn. 522, 64 S. W. 477 (1901).

Texas.—International & B. N. R. R. Co. v. Young (Tex. Civ. App.), 28 S. W. 819 (1894); Texas & P. Ry. Co. v. Shawnee Cotton Oil Co. (Tex. Civ. App.), 118 S. W. 776 (1909).

CHAPTER XXVII

PROTECTION OWED DURING PERFORMANCE

§ 930. Extent of duty to protect.

All proprietors of public services who have persons or

[813]

property in their charge are bound to use their utmost efforts to protect them and safeguard them. As will be pointed out later, the carrier as to goods and the innkeeper as to baggage, are liable in many instances for injuries done to the property in their charge notwithstanding their utmost efforts; but as to their passengers and guests they owe no further duty than the rule just stated. The rule requiring protection is not necessarily limited to carriers and innkeepers, although almost all the cases upon the subject come from these departments. But the application of this law is necessarily confined to the services where the patrons and their belongings are taken in charge. Such is the case of passengers in sleeping cars and even of patrons in telegraph offices; and there are modern cases extending the rule requiring peculiar protection to such businesses.

Topic A. *Proper Protection of Patrons*

§ 931. Duty to care for patrons.

Of the general obligations to protect those with whom the proprietors are having business relations there can be no doubt. In a recent case [1] where a patron who had come to a telegraph office to send a message was insulted, the opinion was prefaced by these generalizations: "One of the great requirements which the government demands of every institution impressed with a public interest— and one which is thrown over every citizen as a great and protective shield—is the duty to act impartially with all. They are under obligations to extend their facilities to all persons, on equal terms, who are willing to comply with their reasonable regulations, and to make such compensation as is exacted from others in like circumstances.

---

[1] Dunn v. Western Union Telegraph Co., 2 Ga. App. 845, 59 S. E. 189 (1908).

From this principle, universally recognized, springs the corollary that all such persons, natural and artificial, shall afford to such members of the public, as have occasion to transact with them business of the nature they are holding themselves out as being accustomed to do, safe and decent access to the places opened up for the transaction of the business in question. This safety does not mean mere physical safety; nor this decency mere absence of obscenity, but by the employment of the expression safe and decent access it is intended to connote also the notion of freedom from abuse, humiliation, insult, and other unbecoming and disrespectful treatment. A member of the public is not to be deterred from transacting or offering to transact business which the law compels a telegraph company to accept impartially from every person, by reason of the fact that he cannot enter the public office without being subjected to insult or personal affront." [1]

§ 932. Extent of duty to care for patrons.

This duty of safeguarding and protecting passengers varies according to the passenger's apparent need of the same. The carrier is bound to warn all passengers of injuries likely to arise from the carrier's method of doing business which are known to the carrier and possibly unknown to the passenger. [2] But he is not bound to warn him of risks which should be apparent to any reasonable man. [3] For example, it is not the duty of the carrier to

---

[1] Likewise those coming to an express office are entitled to proper treatment. Richberger v. American Exp. Co., 73 Miss. 161, 18 So. 922, 55 Am. St. Rep. 522, 31 L. R. A. 390 (1895).

[2] See, for example:

Illinois.—Chicago & Alton R. R.

Co. v. Winters, 175 Ill. 293, 51 N. E. 901 (1898).

New Jersey.—Whalen v. Consolidated Traction Co., 61 N. J. L. 606, 40 Atl. 645, 41 L. R. A. 836, 68 Am. St. Rep. 723 (1898).

[3] See, for example:

Michigan.—Werbowlsky v. Ft.

awaken passengers upon their arrival at their stations,[1] except in the case of the proprietor of a sleeping car whose undertaking obviously includes this service.[2] As to whether the carrier need announce stations there is considerable conflict of authority.[3] It will depend doubtless upon the established custom in that regard; but at all events such a custom once established must not be departed from in a particular case. It should be added that even in the case where the passenger is receiving from the employés of the company assistance which could not have been demanded by the passenger as of right, the company will be held liable for any negligence while extending such assistance.[4]

§ 933. Special care in particular cases.

The amount of care required in giving proper protection depends obviously upon the particular circumstances. Thus special care must be given to women,[5] and still

Wayne & E. Ry. Co., 86 Mich. 236, 48 N. W. 1097, 24 Am. St. Rep. 120 (1891).

Missouri.—Miller v. St. Louis R. R. Co., 5 Mo. App. 471 (1878).

[1] See, for example:

Michigan.—Nichols v. Chicago & W. M. Ry. Co., 90 Mich. 203, 51 N. W. 364 (1892).

Texas.—Missouri, K. & T. Ry. Co. v. Kendrick (Tex. Civ. App.), 32 S. W. 42 (1895).

[2] See, for example:

Alabama.—Pullman Co. v. Lutz, 154 Ala. 517, 45 So. 675, 14 L. R. A. (N. S.) 907 (1908).

Kentucky.—Kentucky C e n t r a l Ry. Co. v. Biddle, 17 Ky. L. Rep. 1363, 34 S. W. 904 (1896).

Texas.—Pullman P. C. Co. v. Smith, 79 Tex. 468, 14 S. W. 993,

13 L. R. A. 215, 23 Am. St. Rep. 356 (1891).

Wisconsin.—McKeon v. Chicago, M. & St. P. Ry. Co., 94 Wis. 477, 69 N. W. 175, 35 L. R. A. 252, 59 Am. St. Rep. 910 (1896).

[3] See, for example:

New York.—Mearns v. Central R. R. of N. J. Co., 163 N. Y. 108, 57 N. E. 292 (1900).

Texas.—Houston & T. C. Ry. Co. v. Goodyear, 28 Tex. Civ. App. 206, 66 S. W. 862 (1902).

[4] See, for example:

Alabama.—Williams v. Louisville & N. Ry. Co., 150 Ala. 324, 43 So. 576, 10 L. R. A. (N. S.) 413 (1907).

Texas.—Missouri Pacific Ry. Co. v. Wortham, 73 Tex. 25, 10 S. W. 741, 3 L. R. A. 368 (1889).

[5] See, for example:

more perhaps to children unaccompanied.[1] If incapacitated persons are accepted without attendants they must be assisted,[2] and infirm persons should be given special attention.[3] Those who are taken ill upon a journey must be cared for until they can be disposed of safely.[4] And

Alabama.—Batton v. So. & No. Alabama R. R. Co., 77 Ala. 591, 54 Am. Rep. 80 (1884).

Colorado.—Pullman Palace Car Co. v. Barker, 4 Colo. 344, 34 Am. Rep. 89 (1878).

Missouri.—Craker v. Chicago & N. W. Ry. Co., 36 Wis. 657, 7 Am. Rep. 504 (1875).

But if a woman carrying a child is attended by friends, the carrier may be justified in relying upon them to furnish necessary assistance in entering car. St. Louis, I. M. & So. Ry. Co. v. Green, 85 Ark. 117, 107 S. W. 168, 14 L. R. A. (N. S.) 1148 (1908).

[1] See, for example:

Minnesota.—Jackson v. St. Paul City Ry. Co., 74 Minn. 48, 76 N. W. 956 (1898).

New York.—Sheridan v. Brooklyn City & N. R. R. Co., 36 N. Y. 39, 93 Am. Dec. 490 (1867).

Pennsylvania.—Pittsburg & M. Pass. Ry. Co. v. Caldwell, 74 Pa. St. 421 (1873).

[2] See, for example:

Minnesota.—Croom v. Chicago, M. & St. P. Ry. Co., 52 Minn. 296, 53 N. W. 1128, 18 L. R. A. 602, 38 Am. St. Rep. 557 (1893).

Mississippi.—New Orleans, J. & Gt. No. R. R. Co. v. Statham, 42 Miss. 607, 97 Am. Dec. 478 (1869).

And see Brady v. Springfield Traction Co. (Mo. App.), 124 S.

W. 1070 (1910). But see Louisville, N. & Gt. So. R. R. Co. v. Fleming, 14 Lea (Tenn.), 128 (1884).

[3] *Mississippi.*—Sevier v. Vicksburg & M. R. .R. Co., 61 Miss. 8, 48 Am. Rep. 74 (1883).

North Dakota.—Haug v. Gt. Northern Ry. Co., 8 N. D. 23, 77 N. W. 97, 42 L. R. A. 664, 73 Am. St. Rep. 727 (1898).

[4] *District of Columbia.*—Lemont v. Washington & G. Ry. Co., 1 Mackay, 180, 47 Am. Rep. 238 (1881).

Georgia.—Central of Ga. Ry. Co. v. Madden, 69 S. E. 165 (1910).

Kansas.—Atchison, T. & S. F. R. R. Co. v. Weber, 33 Kan. 543, 6 Pac. 877, 52 Am. Rep. 543 (1885).

Louisiana.—Conolly v. Crescent City R. R. Co., 41 La. Ann. 57, 5 So. 259, 17 Am. St. Rep. 389, 3 L. R. A. 133 (1889).

Massachusetts.—Connors v. Cunard S. S. Co., 204 Mass. 310, 90 N. E. 601, 26 L. R. A. (N. S.) 171 (1910), *semble.*

Ohio.—Railway Co. v. Salzman, 52 Ohio St. 558, 40 N. E. 891, 31 L. R. A. 261 (1895).

Pennsylvania.—McHugh v. Schlosser, 159 Pa. St. 480, 28 Atl. 291, 23 L. R. A. 574, 39 Am. St. Rep. 699 (1894), innkeeper.

Texas.—Gulf, T., S. F. Ry. Co. v. Coopwood (Tex. Civ. App.), 96 S. W. 102 (1906).

even drunken persons cannot be ejected where it would apparently not be safe to do so.[1] The difference between general undertaking and special undertaking may again be emphasized in these cases. A common carrier by his general profession must take women and cripples, although the care he must take of them will be greater than usual. Without special undertaking a carrier need not accept sick persons or intoxicated persons as passengers, but if he does so he must give them the special care which he is held to become bound to give them by voluntarily taking them in charge.

§ 934. Disposition of dangerous persons.

Insane passengers must be so restrained that they will not injure others,[2] if such injury is to be reasonably antici-

[1] *Alabama.*—Johnson v. Louisville & N. R. R. Co., 104 Ala. 241, 16 So. 75, 53 Am. St. Rep. 39 (1893).

Arkansas.—Price v. St. Louis, I. M. & So. Ry. Co., 75 Ark. 479, 88 S. W. 575, 112 Am. St. Rep. 79 (1905).

District of Columbia.—Converse v. Washington & G. R. R. Co., 2 MacAr. 504 (1876).

Georgia.—Peavy v. Georgia R. R. & Banking Co., 81 Ga. 485, 8 S. E. 70, 12 Am. St. Rep. 334 (1888).

Illinois.—Chicago City Ry. Co. v. Pelletier, 134 Ill. 120, 24 N. E. 770 (1890).

Indiana.—Cincinnati, I., St. L. & C. R. R. Co. v. Cooper, 120 Ind. 469, 22 N. E. 340, 16 Am. St. Rep. 334, 6 L. R. A. 241 (1889).

Kansas.—Atchison, T. & S. F. R. R. Co. v. Weber, 33 Kan. 543, 6 Pac. 877, 52 Am. Rep. 543 (1885).

Kentucky.—Chesapeake & O. Ry. Co. v. Saulsberry, 112 Ky. 915, 66 S. W. 1051, 23 Ky. L. Rep. 2341, 56 L. R. A. 580 (1902).

Maine.—Robinson v. Rockland, T. & C. St. Ry. Co., 87 Me. 387, 32 Atl. 994, 29 L. R. A. 530 (1895).

Massachusetts.—Hudson v. Lynn & Boston R. R. Co., 178 Mass. 64, 59 N. E. 647 (1901).

Michigan.—Strand v. Chicago & W. Ry. Co., 67 Mich. 380, 34 N. W. 712 (1887).

Missouri.—Eads v. Metropolitan Ry. Co., 43 Mo. App. 536 (1891).

New Hampshire.—Edgerly v. Union St. Ry. Co., 67 N. H. 312, 36 Atl. 558 (1892).

New York.—People v. Caryl, 3 Park Cr. 326 (1857).

Texas.—Paris & G. N. Ry. Co. v. Robinson (Tex. Civ. App.), 114 S. W. 658 (1908).

West Virginia.—Fisher v. West Virginia Co., 42 W. Va. 183, 24 S. E. 570, 33 L. R. A. 69 (1896).

[2] See particularly:

pated. And if a case of contagious disease is discovered, precautions for safe keeping of other passengers may be taken.[1] But the carrier is as before only bound to use due diligence. Moreover, it is the duty of the carrier to use the utmost care to protect passengers from the violence of other passengers who are [2] intoxicated or disorderly.[3] But even in ejecting such undesirable passengers, due care must be taken to avoid injuring them, and if they are unable to take care of themselves, they must be set down in a reasonably safe place, or else the company may be liable.

Topic B. Liability for Injuries Caused by Its Own Servants

§ 935. Duty to protect passenger.

The clearest examples of the duty to protect are the cases holding the railroads liable for assault upon passengers by its employés. The stringent general rule is well established that the company is responsible for such assaults [4] on passengers while the employés are on duty,

United States.—Meyer v. St. Louis, I. M. & So. Ry. Co., 54 Fed. 116, 4 C. C. A. 221 (1893).

Kentucky.—Louisville & N. R. R. Co. v. Logan, 88 Ky. 323, 10 S. W. 655, 21 Am. St. Rep. 332, 3 L. R. A. 80 (1889).

See generally, § 639, *supra.*

[1] *Alabama.*—Pullman P. C. Co. v. Krauss, 145 Ala. 395, 40 So. 398, 4 L. R. A. (N. S.) 103 (1906).

Wisconsin.—Walsh v. Chicago M. & St. P. Ry. Co., 42 Wis. 23, 24 Am. Rep. 376 (1877).

See generally, § 631, *supra.*

[2] See particularly:

Minnesota.—Lucy v. Chicago Gt. W. R. R. Co., 64 Minn. 7, 31 L. R. A. 551, 65 N. W. 944 (1896).

Tennessee.—West Memphis Pack-et Co. v. White, 99 Tenn. 256, 41 S. W. 583, 38 L. R. A. 427 (1897).

See generally, § 629, *supra.*

[3] See particularly:

Kansas.—Atchison, T. & S. F. Ry. Co. v. Weber, 33 Kan. 543, 6 Pac. 877, 52 Am. Rep. 543 (1885).

Massachusetts.—Hudson v. Lynn & B. R. R. Co., 178 Mass. 64, 59 N. E. 647 (1901).

See generally, § 632, *supra.*

[4] See, for example:

United States.—Lake Shore & M. S. Ry. Co. v. Prentice, 147 U. S. 101, 37 L. ed. 97, 13 Sup. Ct. 261 (1893).

Alabama.—Birmingham Ry. & E. Co. v. Baird, 130 Ala. 334, 30 So. 456, 54 L. R. A. 752, 89 Am. St. Rep. 43 (1900).

although the violence may have no apparent relation to
the conduct of the business. In the law of private relations when the assault is committed by a servant out of
personal spite or in a frolic of his own, many authorities
hold that the master is not liable. But practically all
the cases as to public employment hold the company liable for its failure to protect its patrons from all assaults
whatsoever by any employé whatever. And insults [1] directed against a passenger by a servant, also subject the
railroad to liability. Although for mere insults not published no liability would normally be recognized in private
relations, still a wrong is worked out in this case from the
failure of the company to perform its duty to protect the
passenger from insult.

Georgia.—Savannah, F. & W.
Ry. Co. v. Quo, 103 Ga. 125, 29 S.
E. 607, 40 L. R. A. 483, 68 Am.
St. Rep. 85 (1897).

Indiana.—Indianapolis P. & C.
Ry. Co. v. Anthony, 43 Ind. 183
(1873).

Kentucky.—Louisville & N. R.
R. Co. v. Ballard, 85 Ky. 307, 3 S.
W. 530, 7 Am. St. Rep. 600 (1887).

Maryland.—Baltimore & O. R.
R. Co. v. Barger, 80 Md. 23, 30
Atl. 560, 26 L. R. A. 220, 45 Am.
St. Rep. 319 (1894).

Massachusetts.—Coleman v. New
York & N. H. R. R. Co., 106 Mass.
160 (1870).

Maryland.—Baltimore & O. R.
R. Co. v. Blocher, 27 Md. 277
(1867).

New York.—Dwinelle v. New
York Central & H. R. R. R. Co.,
120 N. Y. 117, 24 N. E. 319, 8 L.
R. A. 224, 17 Am. St. Rep. 611
(1890).

North Carolina.—White v. Nor-

folk & S. R. R. Co., 115 N. C. 631,
20 S. E. 191, 44 Am. St. Rep. 489
(1894).

Ohio.—Passenger R. R. Co. v.
Young, 21 Ohio St. 518, 8 Am. Rep.
78 (1871).

Pennsylvania.—Pennsylvania R.
R. Co. v. Vandiver, 42 Pa. St. 365,
82 Am. Dec. 520 (1862).

Virginia.—Norfolk & W. R. R.
Co. v. Anderson, 90 Va. 1, 17 S. E.
757, 44 Am. St. Rep. 884 (1893).

Wisconsin.—Craker v. Chicago
& N. W. Ry. Co., 36 Wis. 657, 17
Am. St. Rep. 504 (1875).

[1] See, for example:

Illinois.—Chicago, B. & Q. R. R.
Co. v. Griffin, 68 Ill. 499 (1873).

Maine.—Goddard v. Grand
Trunk Ry. Co., 57 Me. 202, 2 Am.
St. Rep. 39 (1869).

M i s s o u r i.—McGinnis v. Missouri Pac. Ry. Co., 21 Mo. App.
399 (1886).

New York.—Gillespie v. Brooklyn Heights R. R. Co., 178 N. Y.

§ 936. Obligation to protect guest.

The situation is substantially the same in innkeeping as in passenger carriage and the same general principles should apply; but there is upon this matter a notable conflict of authority. It would seem that since his servants are provided, among other things, for the purpose of protecting guests, every injury inflicted upon the guest by a servant, either intentionally or negligently, is a breach of his duty of protection, and should render the innkeeper liable to the guest.[1] The innkeeper's duty, the breach of which by his servant causes the injury, is not the negative duty not to assault the guest, but the affirmative duty to protect him from assault. The servant, in assaulting the guest, is the one committing the battery; but he is at the same time causing a breach of the obligation of protection which rests on the innkeeper, and which the servant has himself been employed to carry out. To put an extreme case,[2] an innkeeper would certainly be liable who continued to receive guests without notifying them that there was a guest in the house stricken with smallpox. But these principles have not been accepted by all courts. In a California case,[3] for example, it was held that while the innkeeper must employ careful serv-

347, 70 N. E. 857, 66 L. R. A. 618, 102 Am. St. Rep. 503 (1904).

Tennessee.—Knoxville Traction Co. v. Lane, 103 Tenn. 376, 53 S. W. 557, 46 L. R. A. 549 (1899).

Texas.—Missouri, K. & T. Ry. Co. v. Kendrick (Tex. Civ. App.), 32 S. W. 42 (1895).

Wisconsin.—Craker v. Chicago & N. W. Ry. Co., 36 Wis. 657, 17 Am. Rep. 504 (1875).

[1] *Minnesota.*—Curran v. Olson, 88 Minn. 307, 92 N. W. 1124, 60 L. R. A. 733, 97 Am. St. Rep. 517 (1903).

Missouri.—Overstreet v. Moser, 88 Mo. App. 72 (1901).

Nebraska.—Clancy v. Barker, 71 Neb. 83, 98 N. W. 440, 69 L. R. A. 642, 115 Am. St. Rep. 559 (1904).

P e n n s y l v a n i a.—Rommel v. Schambacher, 120 Pa. St. 579, 11 Atl. 779, 6 Am. St. Rep. 732 (1887).

[2] Gilbert v. Hoffman, 66 Iowa, 205, 23 N. W. 632, 55 Am. Rep. 263 (1885).

[3] Rahmel v. Lehndorff, 142 Cal. 681, 76 Pac. 659, 65 L. R. A. 88, 100 Am. St. Rep. 154 (1904).

ants, and would be liable for negligence in employing his servants, and would furthermore be liable if he personally stood by and saw his servant injure a guest, yet he could not be held liable for an assault by his servant on a guest in the absence of personal negligence. The innkeeper's responsibility, the court said, is distinguishable from that of the carrier. There are other cases to the same effect,[1] based upon this idea that as the control of the innkeeper over his guests is not so intimate as that of a carrier he is not obliged to answer for their protection to the same extent. These must be regarded as ill-considered decisions. The obligation of the carrier and of the innkeeper in this respect should be placed on the same ground.

§ 937. Blameworthiness must be shown.

To hold a public servant for failure to protect his patrons as he has professed to do, is not to impose upon those who conduct these services the responsibility of an insurer of the safety of the patrons. Some one concerned in rendering the service must be found to be to blame for the injury complained of. The duty is to protect from such injurious acts as the proprietor may fairly be held responsible for. A rather recent case [2] well illustrates this. A passenger was injured by the accidental falling of a brakeman upon her; but the court found no ground for holding the railroad liable. "The declaration is founded on the careless and negligent manner in which the brakeman discharged his duty, and the only two questions in the case to be determined upon this motion are—*First*, whether the company failed to discharge the duty which it owed to the plaintiff as a passenger; and, *second*, whether

[1] Clancey v. Barker, 131 Fed. 161, 66 C. C. A. 469, 69 L. R. A. 653 (1904).

[2] Skinner v. Atchison, T. & S. F. Ry. Co., 39 Fed. 188 (1889). See also Goodloe v. Memphis & C. R. R. Co., 107 Ala. 233, 18 So. 166, 29 L. R. A. 729, 54 Am. St. Rep. 67 (1894).

the brakeman was negligent in the discharge of the duty committed to his care." The defendant owed, the court held, care and protection to the plaintiff,—such care and protection as, in the ordinary management and operation of trains, the highest degree of skill and care could exercise properly to protect her. But it appeared that the brakeman was in no way to blame for his slipping; and hence the railroad was held not liable. [1]

§ 938. Bases of liability for unauthorized injury.

Practically all the cases hold that those who have engaged themselves in a public service where people are in their charge are liable to a greater extent for injury to such persons than those engaged in a private business would be under similar circumstances. This is sometimes spoken of as exceptional; but as a matter of fact the apparently extreme liability of the public company in such cases is part of the general duty to protect those in its charge. This extends to outrageous action by the employé of a public servant against those whom it is the duty of the public company to protect, as well as to all other defaults in this respect.[2] Indeed, it may help in

[1] That the assault by the employé was provoked by the passengers is generally held no excuse. See, for example:

Illinois.—Chicago & Eastern R. R. Co. v. Flexman, 103 Ill. 546, 42 Am. Rep. 33 (1882).

Maryland.—Baltimore & O. R. R. Co. v. Barger, 80 Md. 23, 30 Atl. 560, 45 Am. St. Rep. 319, 26 L. R. A. 220 (1894).

New York.—Weber v. Brooklyn, Q. C. & S. R. R. Co., 47 App. Div. 306, 62 N. Y. Supp. 1 (1900).

North Carolina.—Strother v. Ab-

erdeen & A. R. R. Co., 123 N. C. 197, 31 S. E. 386 (1898).

But see:

Georgia.—City Electric Ry. Co. v. Shropshire, 101 Ga. 33, 28 S. E. 508 (1897).

New York.—Hibbard v. N. Y. & E. Ry. Co., 15 N. Y. 555 (1857).

[2] *United States.*—New Jersey Steamboat Co. v. Brockett, 121 U. S. 637, 7 S. Ct. 1039, 30 L. ed. 1049 (1886).

Alabama.—Birmingham Ry. & El. Co. v. Baird, 130 Ala. 334, 30 So. 456, 54 L. R. A. 752, 89 Am. St. Rep. 43 (1900).

understanding the law to say that every servant of the company has the duty to protect them from injury by himself as well as injury by third parties. This matter is well discussed in a leading case.[1] "We do not understand it to be denied that if such an assault on the respondent had been attempted by a stranger, and the conductor had neglected to protect her, the appellant would have been liable. But it is denied that the act of the conductor in maliciously doing himself what it was his duty, for the appellant to the respondent, to prevent others from doing, makes the appellant liable. It is contended that, though the principal would be liable for the

Georgia.—Savannah F. & W. Ry. Co. v. Quo, 103 Ga. 125, 29 S. E. 607, 40 L. R. A. 483, 68 Am. St. Rep. 85 (1897).

Indiana.—Louisville & N. R. R. Co. v. Kelley, 92 Ind. 371 (1883).

Maryland.—Baltimore & O. R. R. Co. v. Barger, 80 Md. 23, 30 Atl. 560, 26 L. R. A. 220, 45 Am. St. Rep. 319 (1894).

Massachusetts.—Hayne v. Union St. Ry. Co., 189 Mass. 551, 76 N. E. 219, 3 L. R. A. (N. S.) 605, 109 Am. St. Rep. 655 (1905).

New Jersey.—Haver v. Central of N. J. R. R. Co., 62 N. J. L. 282, 41 Atl. 916, 43 L. R. A. 84, 72 Am. St. Rep. 647 (1898).

New York.—Dwinelle v. New York Cent. & H. R. R. R. Co., 120 N. Y. 117, 24 N. E. 319, 8 L. R. A. 224, 17 Am. St. Rep. 611 (1890).

Nevada.—Quigley v. Central Pacific R. R. Co., 11 Nev. 350, 21 Am. Rep. 757 (1876).

Ohio.—Passenger R. R. Co. v. Young, 21 Ohio St. 518, 8 Am. Rep. 78 (1871).

Tennessee.—Pullman P. C. Co.

v. Gavin, 93 Tenn. 53, 23 S. W. 70, 21 L. R. A. 298, 42 Am. St. Rep. 902 (1893).

Texas.—St. Louis, S. W. Ry. Co. v. Johnson, 29 Tex. Civ. App. 184, 68 S. W. 58 (1902).

Virginia.—Norfolk & W. R. R. Co. v. Anderson, 90 Va. 1, 17 S. E. 757, 44 Am. St. Rep. 884 (1893).

Washington.—Cunningham v. Seattle El. R. & P. Co., 3 Wash. 471, 28 Pac. 745 (1892).

West Virginia.—Gillingham v. Ohio River Ry. Co., 35 W. Va. 588, 14 S. E. 243, 14 L. R. A. 798, 29 Am. St. Rep. 827 (1891).

[1] Craker v. Chicago & N. W. Ry. Co., 36 Wis. 657, 17 Am. Rep. 504 (1875).

In perhaps a majority of States the courts go so far as to permit the recovery of punitive damages against the company. Goddard v. Grand Trunk Ry. Co., 57 Me. 202, 2 Am. St. Rep. 39 (1869).

But this would seem to be going too far. Lake Shore & M. S. Ry. Co. v. Prentice, 147 U. S. 101, 37 L. ed. 97, 13 Sup. Ct. 261 (1893).

negligent failure of the agent to fulfill the principal's contract, the principal is not liable for the malicious breach by the agent, of the contract which he was appointed to perform for the principal; as we understand it, that if one hire out his dog to guard sheep against wolves, and the dog sleep while a wolf makes away with a sheep, the owner is liable; but if the dog play wolf and devour the sheep himself, the owner is not liable. The bare statement of the proposition seems a *reductio ad absurdum.*"

§ 939. Action outside of the employment.

For acts altogether outside of the employment there is in accordance with the general principle no liability, but it must be a very extreme case indeed in order to come within this saying. Only if the act is at some different time than the hours of duty, or at some different place than the premises of the company, may we have a case of private wrong by the employé disconnected from his general duty to protect the patron. Such cases of wholly independent private wrong may occur. Thus where the employé of a street railway assaulted a person who was outside the car barn waiting for a car the company was not held responsible.[1] And in a closer case [2] where the assault was committed by the driver after the passenger left the car for the purpose of making a complaint at the company's office and had reached the sidewalk, it was held that the company was not responsible. On general principles, however, wherever an altercation begun upon the cars is continued upon the street so that it may be said

---

[1] McGilvray v. West End St. Ry. Co., 164 Mass. 122, 41 N. E. 116 (1895).

See also Palmer v. Winston-Salem Ry. & Elec. Co., 131 N. C. 250, 42 S. E. 604 (1902).

[2] Central Ry. Co. v. Peacock, 69 Md. 257, 14 Atl. 709, 9 Am. St. Rep. 425 (1888).

But see Missouri Pacific Ry. Co. v. Divinney, 66 Kan. 776, 71 Pac. 855 (1903).

to be a continuous assault the company is liable.[1]   This was particularly true in a dramatic case where the conductor hurled a passenger off the car and assaulted him.[2] It may often be a close question of fact whether the assault was made upon one who was then having business relations with the company.[3]   And indeed it is sometimes doubtful for what company the agent is acting.[4]   There are certain cases which hold that the company is only liable for the assaults of those employés whose duty it is to protect passengers[5] during their hours of duty, but the weight of authority is overwhelmingly the other way.[6]

§ 940. Cumulative liability where two services involved.

Where the patron is receiving two services simultaneously, there may be a case of cumulative liability.   This is well brought out in the case of an assault upon a pas-

[1] McQuerry v. Metropolitan St. Ry. Co., 117 Mo. App. 255, 92 S. W. 912 (1906).

See also Blomsness v. Puget Sound El. Ry. Co., 47 Wash. 620, 92 Pac. 414, 17 L. R. A. (N. S.) 763 (1907).

[2] Peeples v. Brunswick & A. R. R. Co., 60 Ga. 281 (1878).

See also Wise v. Covington & C. St. Ry. Co., 91 Ky. 537, 16 S. W. 351 (1891).

[3] Bowen v. Illinois Central R. R. Co., 136 Fed. 306, 69 C. C. A. 444, 70 L. R. A. 915 (1905).

[4] Columbus Ry. Co. v. Christian, 97 Ga. 56, 25 S. E. 411 (1895).

[5] *United States.*—Bowen v. Illinois Central Ry. Co., 136 Fed. 306, 69 C. C. A. 444, 70 L. R. A. 915 (1905), express agent.

Illinois.—Henson v. Urbana &

C. St. Ry. Co., 75 Ill. App. 474 (1897), motorman.

[6] *Georgia.*—Georgia R. R. & Bk. Co. v. Richmond, 98 Ga. 495, 25 S. E. 565 (1896), baggage master.

Indiana.—Wabash Ry. Co. v. Savage, 110 Ind. 156, 9 N. E. 85 (1886), brakeman.

Kentucky.—Sherley v. Billings, 8 Bush (Ky.), 147, 8 Am. Rep. 451 (1871), clerk.

Massachusetts.—Bryant v. Rich, 106 Mass. 180, 8 Am. Rep. 311 (1870), waiter.

New York.—Steward v. Brooklyn & C. T. R. R. Co., 90 N. Y. 588 (1882), car driver assaulted passenger maliciously. Railroad held liable.

Wisconsin.—Fick v. Chicago & N. W. Ry. Co., 68 Wis. 469, 32 N. W. 527, 60 Am. Rep. 878 (1887), ticket agent.

senger riding in a sleeping car by an employé of the car company. It is plain that the car company is liable for failing in its duty to protect its patron when one of its employés employed for the very purpose of protecting him, commits an assault upon him.[1] Furthermore the railroad company is liable for the assault upon the passenger by the employé of the car company.[2] The railroad company remains liable to protect its passenger throughout the journey, and it cannot delegate its responsibility in that respect to the car company and escape liability thereon.

Topic C. Protection against Injury by Third Parties

§ 941. Limited extent of the duty.

Moreover, those engaged in the public services which involve the charge of persons and their belongings are under a stringent liability to use the utmost care in their protection from such injuries from third parties as they ought to have foreseen and could have prevented. The carrier or innkeeper ought not to admit to its conveyances or premises disorderly or dangerous persons who it might see are likely to cause harm to its patrons. This is because there is a special duty to protect passengers from insult by third parties whether intruders or fellow passengers.[3]

---

[1] Campbell v. Pullman P. C. Co., 42 Fed. 484 (1890).

See also Pullman P. C. Co. v. Lawrence, 74 Miss. 782, 22 So. 53 (1897).

[2] Dwinelle v. New York C. & H. R. R. R. Co., 120 N. Y. 117, 24 N. E. 319, 17 Am. St. Rep. 611 (1890).

Where a passenger from an ordinary coach enters a Pullman car without right the car company is not liable for the porter's assault. Williams v. Pullman P. C. Co., 40 La. Ann. 87, 3 So. 631 (1888).

[3] By the general principle the carrier is liable if he is negligent in not preventing the injury. See the language in:

United States.—Brown v. Chicago, R. I. & P. Ry. Co., 139 Fed. 972, 72 C. C. A. 20 (1905).

Alabama.—Birmingham Ry. & E. Co. v. Baird, 130 Ala. 334, 30 So. 456, 54 L. R. A. 752, 89 Am. St. Rep. 43 (1900).

Arkansas.—St. Louis, I. M. & So. Ry. Co. v. Wilson, 70 Ark. 136, 66 S. W. 661, 91 Am. St. 74 (1902).

Connecticut.—Flint v. Norwich

Indeed the law is very exacting as to all this, holding the carrier or innkeeper liable for injuries by third parties which ought to have been anticipated. Of the same nature is the duty to protect its patrons from exposure to indecent approach or scenes of violence. If these duties are neglected without good cause and a passenger receives injury, which might have been reasonably anticipated or naturally expected, from one who is improperly received or permitted to continue as a passenger, the carrier is responsible.[1]

§ 942. Protection against fellow passengers.

In particular there are many cases describing the liability which carriers are under to protect their patrons while in their charge from injuries to them by their fellow passengers which they had reason to anticipate, either from general circumstances or from particular facts.[2]

& N. Y. Transp. Co., 34 Conn. 554 (1868).

Georgia.—Savannah, F. & W. Ry. Co. v. Boyle, 115 Ga. 836, 42 S. E. 242, 59 L. R. A. 104 (1902).

Maryland.—United Rys. & E. Co. v. Deane, 93 Md. 619, 49 Atl. 923, 54 L. R. A. 942, 86 Am. St. Rep. 453 (1901).

Missouri.—Woas v. St. Louis Transit Co., 198 Mo. 664, 96 S. W. 1011, 7 L. R. A. (N. S.) 231 (1906).

Nebraska.—Bevard v. Lincoln Traction Co., 74 Neb. 802, 105 N. W. 635, 3 L. R. A. (N. S.) 318 (1905).

New Jersey.—Haver v. Central R. R. of New Jersey, 62 N. J. L. 282, 41 Atl. 916, 72 Am. St. Rep. 647, 43 L. R. A. 85 (1898).

Pennsylvania.—Graeff v. Philadelphia & R. R. R. Co., 161 Pa. St.

230, 28 Atl. 1107, 23 L. R. A. 606, 41 Am. St. Rep. 885 (1894).

Virginia.—Connell v. Chesapeake & O. Ry. Co., 93 Va. 44, 24 S. E. 467, 57 Am. St. Rep. 786 (1896).

[1] By this general principle the carrier is not liable if the negligence cannot be imputed to him in the premises. See particularly:

Alabama.—Batton v. So. & No. Ala. R. R. Co., 77 Ala. 591, 54 Am. Rep. 80 (1884).

New York.—Putnam v. Broadway & Seventh Ave. R. R. Co., 55 N. Y. 108, 14 Am. Rep. 190 (1873).

[2] *United States.*—St. Louis, I. M. & So. Ry. Co. v. Greenthal, 77 Fed. 150, 23 C. C. A. 100 (1896).

Connecticut.—Flint v. Norwich & N. Y. Transp. Co., 34 Conn. 554 (1868).

The argument was once made that the carrier should always be held liable for an assault by one passenger upon another, because he should be as answerable for the acts of one he had accepted as a passenger as he would be for one he had taken as a servant. But it is now universally recognized that there is no such privity in the conduct of the enterprise between the carrier and his passenger as to make him liable for the acts of his passenger as such. The most that can be required of the carrier, therefore, is the full performance of his duty to protect the passenger. And it is well established that there is no liability if the assault by the fellow passengers

District of Columbia.—Flannery v. Baltimore & O. R. R. Co., 4 Mackey, 111 (1885).

Georgia.—Richmond & D. R. Co. v. Jefferson, 89 Ga. 554, 16 S. E. 69, 17 L. R. A. 571, 32 Am. St. Rep. 87 (1892).

Illinois.—Chicago & A. R. R. Co. v. Pillsbury, 123 Ill. 9, 14 N. E. 23, 5 Am. St. Rep. 483 (1887).

Iowa.—Felton v. Chicago, R. I. & P. Ry. Co., 69 Ia. 577, 29 N. W. 618 (1886).

Kansas.—Spangler v. St. Joseph & G. I. Ry. Co., 68 Kan. 46, 74 Pac. 607, 63 L. R. A. 634, 104 Am. St. Rep. 391 (1903).

Kentucky.—Kinney v. Louisville & N. Ry. Co., 99 Ky. 59, 17 Ky. Law Rep. 1405, 34 S. W. 1066 (1896).

Maryland.—Tall v. Baltimore Steam Packet Co., 90 Md. 248, 44 Atl. 1007, 47 L. R. A. 120 (1899).

Massachusetts.—Kuhlen v. Boston & N. St. Ry. Co., 193 Mass. 341, 79 N. E. 815, 7 L. R. A. (N. S.) 729, 118 Am. St. Rep. 516 (1907).

Michigan.—MacWilliams v. Lake Shore & M. S. Ry. Co., 146 Mich. 216, 109 N. W. 272 (1906).

Minnesota.—Mullan v. Wisconsin C. Ry. Co., 46 Minn. 474, 49 N. W. 249 (1891).

Mississippi.—Illinois Central Ry. Co. v. Minor, 69 Miss. 710, 11 So. 101, 16 L. R. A. 627 (1892).

Missouri.—Jackson v. Missouri P. Ry. Co., 104 Mo. 448, 16 S. W. 413 (1891).

New Jersey.—Exton v. Central Ry. Co., 63 N. J. L. 356, 46 Atl. 1099, 56 L. R. A. 508 (1899).

North Carolina.—Penny v. Atlantic Coast Line Co., 133 N. C. 221, 45 S. E. 563, 63 L. R. A. 497 (1903).

Pennsylvania.—Pittsburg, F. W. & C. Ry. Co. v. Hinds, 53 Pa. St. 512, 91 Am. Dec. 224 (1866).

Tennessee.—Ferry Companies v. White, 99 Tenn. 256, 41 S. W. 583, 38 L. R. A. 427 (1897).

Washington.—Wescott v. Seattle R. & S. Ry. Co., 41 Wash. 618, 84 Pac. 588, 4 L. R. A. (N. S.) 947, 111 Am. St. Rep. 1038 (1906).

should not naturally be expected, or if there was no special notice of the particular danger.[1]

§ 943. Injuries from negligent conduct.

Not only must there be precautions to prevent injury by intentional acts, but also by negligent acts of other passengers or any other persons, so far as they can be reasonably anticipated.[2] And the carrier is bound to use

[1] *United States.*—Murphy v. Western & A. R. R. Co., 23 Fed. 637 (1885).

Alabama.—Batton v. So. & No. Ala. R. R. Co., 77 Ala. 591, 54 Am. Rep. 80 (1884).

Colorado.—Synder v. Colorado Springs & C. C. Dist. Ry. Co., 36 Colo. 288, 85 Pac. 686, 8 L. R. A. (N. S.) 781, 118 Am. St. Rep. 110 (1906).

Georgia.—Savannah, F. & W. Ry. Co. v. Boyle, 115 Ga. 836, 42 S. E. 242, 59 L. R. A. 104 (1902).

Illinois.—Springfield Consolidated Ry. Co. v. Flynn, 55 Ill. App. 600 (1894).

Iowa.—See Felton v. Chicago, R. I. & P. R. R. Co., 69 Iowa, 577, 29 N. W. 618 (1886).

Kentucky.—Kinney v. Louisville & N. R. R. Co., 99 Ky. 59, 17 Ky. L. Rep. 1405, 34 S. W. 1066 (1896).

Minnesota.—Mullan v. Wisconsin C. R. R. Co., 46 Minn. 474, 49 N. W. 249 (1891).

Mississippi.—Royston v. Illinois Central R. R. Co., 67 Miss. 376, 7 So. 320 (1889).

Missouri.—Sullivan v. Jefferson Ave. R. R. Co., 133 Mo. 1, 34 S. W. 556 (1895).

North Carolina.—Britton v. Atlanta & C. A. L. Ry. Co., 88 N. C. 536, 43 Am. Rep. 749 (1883).

New York.—Putman v. Broadway & 7th Ave. R. R. Co., 55 N. Y. 108 (1873).

Texas.—Thweatt v. Houston, E. & W. T. Ry. Co., 31 Tex. Civ. App. 227, 71 S. W. 976 (1903).

England.—P o u n d e r v. North Eastern Ry. Co., 1 Q. B. 385 (1892).

The owner of a steamboat is required to exercise the utmost vigilance and diligence in protecting its passengers from injuries from another passenger by the negligent and careless use of a loaded gun exhibited by him, where, under all the circumstances, might reasonably have expected or anticipated the injury. Ferry Companies v. White, 99 Tenn. 256, 41 S. W. 583, 38 L. R. A. 427 (1897).

Allowing passengers to play cards in the smoking room of a steamboat in violation of the rule of the carrier does not make the carrier liable for an injury to another passenger who was shot during a quarrel which occurred during the game as it could not reasonably have been foreseen that such shooting would occur. Tall v. Baltimore Steam Packet Co., 90 Md. 248, 44 Atl. 1007, 47 L. R. A. 120 (1899).

[2] Ayres v. Delaware, L. & W. R. R. Co., 28 N. Y. Supp. 789, 77 Hun, 414 (1894).

due diligence to prevent damage from such negligent acts if he sees that they are likely to cause harm, as for instance to stop a car negligently started by an unauthorized person [1] or to remove valises negligently left in an aisle,[2] or to protect passengers against other passengers who are fighting and causing danger of injury to other passengers.[3] If, however, the negligence of the fellow passenger or third party was not reasonably to be anticipated, as where it consisted of throwing open violently a car door,[4] carrying bombs in a parcel of the usual appearance[5] or setting fire to a fellow passenger, there is no liability.[6] If the carrier had no right to control the negligent persons, it is, of course, not responsible for their conduct.[7] The act of an intoxicated person in tripping a passenger while being removed has been held one for which the carrier was not responsible, there being no evidence of negligence in permitting the intoxicated person to board the car,[8] and mere contact with a person who is being removed because of intoxication has been held to afford no cause of action.[9]

§ 944. Liability for injuries by outsiders.

In defining the liability of a carrier of passengers for injuries to them by third parties the modern law makes

[1] North Chicago St. R. R. Co. v. Cook, 145 Ill. 551, 33 N. E. 958 (1893).

[2] Chicago & A. Ry. Co. v. Buckmaster, 74 Ill. App. 575 (1897).

[3] Holly v. Atlanta Street R. R. Co., 61 Ga. 215, 34 Am. Rep. 97 (1878).

[4] Graeff v. Philadelphia & R. R. R. Co., 161 Pa. St. 230, 28 Atl. 1107, 23 L. R. A. 606, 41 Am. St. Rep. 885 (1894).

[5] East Indian Ry. Co. v. Kalidas Mukerjee, App. Cas. 396, 70 Law J. P. C. 63, 84 Law T. 210 (1901).

[6] Sullivan v. Jefferson Ave. Ry. Co., 135 Mo. 1, 34 S. W. 566, 32 L. R. A. 167 (1895).

[6] Murphy v. Great Northern Ry. Co., 2 L. R. Irish, 301 (1897).

[8] Cobb v. Boston El. Ry. Co., 179 Mass. 212, 60 N. E. 476 (1901).

[9] Spade v. L. & Boston Ry. Co., 172 Mass. 488, 52 N. E. 747, 43 L. R. A. 832, 70 Am. St. Rep. 298 (1899).

this same distinction. The common carrier, it is granted, must use the utmost care in protecting passengers and their attendants, not only from the violence and rudeness of its own officers and agents but also of intruders and outside parties.[1] There are many well considered cases which support this view, but none of them fail to impose the qualification that the wrong or injury done the passenger by such strangers must have been of such a character, and perpetrated under such circumstances, as that it might reasonably have been anticipated, or naturally expected to occur.[2]

[1] *Colorado.*—Wright v. Chicago, B. & Q. R. R. Co., 4 Colo. App. 102, 35 Pac. 196 (1893).

Georgia.—Savannah, F. & W. Ry. Co. v. Boyle, 115 Ga. 836, 42 S. E. 242, 59 L. R. A. 104 (1902).

Illinois.—Chicago & A. R. R. Co. v. Pillsbury, 123 Ill. 9, 14 N. E. 23, 5 Am. St. Rep. 483 (1887).

Kentucky.—Tate v. Illinois Central R. R. Co., 26 Ky. L. Rep. 309, 81 S. W. 256 (1904).

Louisiana.—Clerc v. Morgan's La. & Tex. R. R. & S. S. Co., 107 La. 370, 31 So. 886, 90 Am. St. Rep. 319 (1902).

Massachusetts.—Ormandroyd v. Fitchburg & L. St. R. R. Co., 193 Mass. 130, 78 N. E. 739, 118 Am. St. Rep. 457 (1906).

Missouri.—O'Gara v. St. Louis Transit Co., 204 Mo. 724, 103 S. W. 54, 12 L. R. A. (N. S.) 840 (1907).

Nebraska.—Bevard v. Lincoln Traction Co., 74 Neb. 802, 105 N. W. 635, 3 L. R. A. (N. S.) 318 (1905).

North Carolina.—Seawell v. Carolina Central R. R. Co., 133 N. C. 515, 45 S. E. 850 (1903).

Rhode Island.—Bosworth v. Union R. R. Co., 26 R. I. 309, 55 Atl. 490 (1904).

Vermont.—Dufur v. Boston & M. R. R. Co., 75 Vt. 165, 53 Atl. 1068 (1902).

V i r g i n i a.—Connell v. Chesapeake & O. Ry. Co., 93 Va. 44, 24 S. E. 467, 57 Am. Rep. 786 (1896).

England.—Cobb v. Gt. Western R. R. Co., A. C. 419 (1894).

[2] *Alabama.*—Batton v. So. & No. Ala. R. R. Co., 77 Ala. 591, 54 Am. Rep. 80 (1884).

Georgia.—Savannah, F. & W. Ry. Co. v. Boyle, 115 Ga. 836, 42 S. E. 242, 59 L. R. A. 104 (1902).

Illinois.—Illinois Central R. R. Co. v. Laloge, 113 Ky. 896, 69 S. W. 795, 62 L. R. A. 405 (1902).

Minnesota.—Fewings v. Mendenhall, 88 Minn. 336, 93 N. W. 127, 60 L. R. A. 601, 97 Am. St. Rep. 519 (1903).

Missouri.—Woas v. St. Louis Transit Co., 198 Mo. 664, 96 S. W. 1017, 7 L. R. A. (N. S.) 231 (1906).

New York.—Weeks v. New York, N. H. & H. R. R. Co., 72 N. Y. 50, 28 Am. Rep. 104 (1878).

§ 945. Injuries resulting from overcrowding.

Injury to passengers resulting from overcrowding at stations is another danger from which the carrier is bound to protect its patrons.[1] Such liability may arise even when the carrier does nothing more than permit the crowd to gather and neglect to control it.[2] Particularly where the carrier controls the admission of passengers to the conveyances he is bound to exercise reasonable care so to regulate the movements of those whom they are undertaking to transport as to preserve the safety of all.[3] But when the facilities used by the traction company are not wholly within its control, the utmost that can be required of the company is to provide against the expected crush by having sufficient guards.[4] In the management of

Pennsylvania.—Pittsburg, F. W. & C. R. R. Co. v. Hinds, 53 Pa. St. 512, 91 Am. Dec. 224 (1866).

Texas.—Segal v. St. Louis S. W. Ry. Co., 35 Tex. Civ. App. 517, 80 S. W. 233 (1904).

England.—P o u n d e r v. North Eastern Railway Co., 1 Q. B. 385 (1892).

A carrier owes to passengers, and others lawfully using its station platform the duty to protect them from dangerous habits of the servants of an express company in negligently moving trucks about the platform without warning. St. Louis, I. M. & S. Ry. Co. v. Shaw (Ark.), 125 S. W. 654 (1910).

But see McGrath v. Eastern Ry. Co., 74 Minn. 363, 77 N. W. 136 (1898), where it was held that the railroad was not responsible for the hitting of a passenger upon a platform by a package of papers thrown from a train by a news agent.

[1] *Kansas.*—Topeka C. Ry. Co. v. Higgs, 38 Kan. 375, 16 Pac. 667, 5 Am. St. Rep. 754 (1888).

Nebraska.—Pray v. Omaha St. Ry. Co., 44 Neb. 167, 62 N. W. 447, 48 Am. St. Rep. 717 (1895).

New Jersey.—Hansen v. North Jersey St. Ry. Co., 64 N. J. L. 686, 46 Atl. 718 (1900).

New York.—McGearty v. Manhattan Ry. Co., 15 App. Div. 2, 43 N. Y. Supp. 1086 (1897).

[2] Viemeister v. Brooklyn Heights R. R. Co., 87 N. Y. S. 162, 91 App. Div. 510 (1904); Grogan v. Brooklyn Heights R. R. Co., 97 App. Div. 413, 89 N. Y. S. 1027 (1904).

[3] Dawson v. New York & Brooklyn Bridge, 31 App. Div. 537, 52 N. Y. Supp. 133 (1898).

And see Dittmar v. Brooklyn Heights R. R. Co., 91 App. Div. 378, 86 N. Y. Supp. 878 (1904).

[4] Kuhlen v. Boston & N. Street Ry. Co., 193 Mass. 341, 79 N. E. 815, 7 L. R. A. (N. S.) 729 (1907).

crowded vehicles due care must be used.[1] But it cannot be said to be negligence merely to take passengers on board when all the seats are taken.[2] But if so many are taken on board that one of the passengers is subsequently crowded off, the carrier is liable.[3] And the carrier is likewise liable if the jostling of the crowd causes injury to passengers.[4]

§ 946. Proper extent of the duty.

The proprietors of the service are, however, only liable to those who are in a position to claim its special protection. Thus a railroad owes a duty to protect travelers who come to its premises a reasonable time before the departure of its trains [5] or to passengers who remain upon its premises a reasonable time after their arrival.[6] The same duty is owed to persons coming to make an inquiry [7]

See also Wagner v. Brooklyn Heights R. R. Co., 95 App. Div. 219, 88 N. Y. Supp. 791 (1904).

[1] Merrill v. Eastern R. R. Co., 139 Mass. 238, 1 N. E. 548, 139 Mass. 252, 29 N. E. 666 (1885).

[2] Jacobs v. West End St. Ry. Co., 178 Mass. 116, 59 N. E. 639 (1901).

[3] Reem v. St. Paul City Ry. Co., 77 Minn. 503, 80 N. W. 638, 778 (1899).

[4] Buck v. Manhattan Ry. Co., 15 Daly, 48, 2 N. Y. Supp. 718 (1888). The carrier is not liable, however, for anything not the natural and probable result of the overcrowding, such as one passenger, because of vexation at being crowded, throwing another passenger off of the car. Synder v. Colorado Springs & C. C. Dist. Ry. Co., 36 Colo. 288, 85 Pac. 686, 8 L. R. A. (N. S.) 781, 118 Am. St. Rep. 110 (1906).

If a passenger appears well able to take care of himself and in no danger, it is not negligence in the conductor not to go to the passenger's assistance. Jarmy v. Duluth St. Ry. Co., 55 Minn. 271, 56 N. W. 813 (1893).

[5] See St. Louis S. W. Ry. Co. v. Griffith, 12 Tex. Civ. App. 631, 35 S. W. 741 (1896), and Texas & P. Ry. Co. v. Bowlin (Tex. Civ. App.), 32 S. W. 918 (1895).

[6] *Georgia.*—Brunswick & W. Ry. Co. v. Moore, 101 Ga. 684, 28 S. E. 1000 (1897).

Illinois.—Chicago & A. R. Co. v. Tracey, 109 Ill. App. 563 (1903).

Indiana.—Glenn v. Lake Erie & W. R. R. Co., 165 Ind. 659, 75 N. E. 282, 112 Am. St. Rep. 255, 2 L. R. A. (N. S.) 872 (1905).

Texas.—Houston & T. C. Ry. Co. v. Batchler, 37 Tex. Civ. App. 116, 73 S. W. 981 (1904).

[7] See particularly, D a n i e l v.

or a complaint.[1] But it owes no duty to protect one coming upon its premises out of curiosity merely;[2] and it does not even owe the extraordinary duty to protect to one who is waiting at a station in order to meet a passenger.[3]

§ 947. Duty of innkeepers to protect from third parties.

The innkeeper, while not an insurer of a guest against personal injury, should protect him against injury from third persons so far as it is within his power to do so. Thus, where in the presence of an innkeeper, and without being prevented by him, one guest pinned a piece of paper on the coat of another guest and set it on fire, the innkeeper was held responsible to the injured guest for the injury thus caused.[4] And so an innkeeper who, without warning, allows a guest to come to an inn in which he knows there is a contagious disease is responsible to the guest if he contracts the disease.[5] But an innkeeper would not be responsible for an assault committed on one of his guests within the hotel by a stranger, provided he has taken all reasonable precautions to prevent such occurrences by excluding disorderly persons from his premises.[6] There is one interesting case, which is probably

Petersburg Ry. Co., 117 N. C. 592, 23 S. E. 327, 4 L. R. A. (N. S.) 485 (1895), and cases cited.

[1] See particularly, S a v a n n a h Street Ry. Co. v. Bryan, 86 Ga. 312, 12 S. E. 307, 22 Am. St. Rep. 464 (1890), and cases cited.

[2] Gillis v. Pennsylvania R. R. Co., 59 Pa. St. 129, 98 Am. Dec. 317 (1868).

See generally, § 371.

[3] Houston & T. C. R. R. Co. v. Phillio, 98 Tex. 18, 69 S. W. 994, 97 Am. St. Rep. 868, 59 L. R. A. 392 (1902).

See generally, § 372.

[4] Rommel v. Schambacher, 120 Pa. St. 579, 11 Atl. 779, 6 Am. St. Rep. 732 (1887). And see to the same effect, Curran v. Olson, 88 Minn. 307, 92 N. W. 1124, 60 L. R. A. 733, 97 Am. St. Rep. 517 (1903).

[5] Gilbert v. Hoffman, 66 Ia. 205, 23 N. W. 632, 55 Am. Rep. 263 (1885); Levy v. Corey, 1 City Ct. Rep. Supp. 57 (1884), accord.

[6] Clancy v. Barker, 131 Fed. 161, 66 C. C. A. 469 (1904), semble.

correct, which holds that where a woman was the innkeeper, she was not responsible for an assault upon a guest by her husband, as she could not exclude him from the premises.[1]

§ 948. Special protection in sleeping cars.

It is the duty of the sleeping car company to guard its passengers from harm so far as it may reasonably do so. Thus it must guard passengers from the attacks of wrongdoers, if such attacks can be foreseen; but where the attack cannot be foreseen, as in a case where a passenger is killed by an assassin, the company is not liable. "While not directly responsible to a passenger for a wrong inflicted by an intruder, or a stranger, or a fellow passenger, they are responsible for such injury if it appears that the companies knew, or ought to have known, that danger existed or was reasonably to be apprehended, and that they could, by the use of the agencies at their disposal, have prevented the mischief."[2] So it the duty of the car company to protect its passenger, so far as it may, against annoyance and insult. Where the company allowed drunken persons to enter a sleeping car and use vulgar, profane and indecent language, it was liable in damages to a female passenger for the injury thereby sustained.[3]

Topic D. Duty to Act in Emergencies

§ 949. Duty to meet emergencies.

As is discussed more fully elsewhere, almost all public servants are excused for unavoidable accidents in respect to which they are not negligent; and even with their exceptional liability, neither the carrier nor the innkeeper is liable for loss from overruling causes. Yet in all these

[1] Curtis v. Dinneen, 4 Dak. 245, 30 N. W. 148 (1886).

[2] Levien v. Webb, 30 N. Y. Misc. 196, 61 N. Y. Supp. 1113 (1899).

[3] Connell v. Chesapeake & O. Ry. Co., 93 Va. 44, 24 S. E. 467, 57 Am. St. Rep. 786 (1896).

cases of excusable accident a duty of care at once arises to make proper arrangements under the circumstances.[1] This means that every effort must be taken to give adequate protection from further consequences of the accident.[2] For instance, if a conductor on a railroad finds further progress barred by a washout, it is evidence of negligence if he fails to back the train in order to discharge his passengers at a suitable spot.[3] But when a train stopped at a distance from burning oil cars, it was held that there was no necessity to warn passengers not to go nearer.[4]

§ 950. Duty to repair damage.

Where the injury may be repaired wholly or partially at the place of accident, and where such a course is peculiarly necessary to prevent further deterioration, the elements of this new duty are obvious. The carrier must do what is reasonable to prevent deterioration of the goods or damage to them as a result of an accident. Thus although there is an inherent tendency in perishable goods to rapid deterioration, still if they could be preserved by unusual precautions, these should be taken. Thus if a cargo has been wet it should be dried [5] if that is practicable.[6] So perishable provisions should be iced if the departure of the carrier has been delayed.[7] And wrecked cars

---

[1] Penn v. Buffalo & El. R. R. Co., 49 N. Y. 204, 10 Am. Rep. 355 (1872).

See also Black v. Chicago, B. & Q. Ry. Co., 30 Neb. 197, 46 N. W. 428 (1890).

[2] International & G. N. Ry. Co. v. Hynes, 3 Tex. Civ. App. 20, 21 S. W. 622 (1893).

But see Empire Transportation Co. v. Wallace, 68 Pa. St. 302, 8 Am. Rep. 178 (1871).

[3] Houston, E. & W. T. Ry. Co. v. Rogers, 16 Tex. Civ. App. 19, 40 S. W. 201 (1897).

[4] Conroy v. Chicago, St. P., M. & O. R. R. Co., 96 Wis. 243, 70 N. W. 486, 38 L. R. A. 419 (1897).

[5] Notara v. Henderson, L. R. 7 Q. B. 225 (1872).

[6] Steamboat Lynx v. King & F., 12 Mo. 272, 49 Am. Dec. 135 (1848).

[7] Peck v. Weeks, 34 Conn. 145 (1867).

should be guarded if that is possible.[1] Of course in these
as in other cases, if the law throws this rather extraordinary liability of care in emergencies on the companies,
they may recoup themselves by a proper charge.   And
clearly special instructions by the shipper not to take precautions will excuse the carrier from so doing in the absence of any unexpected delay.

§ 951. Liability to stop performance.

Unusual circumstances may call for the stopping of
performance.   Thus when a horse has been made sick by
being frightened by the motion of the train, the car containing it should be sidetracked upon request where this
is practicable.[2] In a more extreme case it was held lately
that where a woman traveling was taken with childbirth
pains it was the duty of the conductor to accede to her
request to stop the train at a town where there was a
hospital although the train was not scheduled to stop
there.[3] To put less obvious cases, it has been held that
where the transportation of peaches was stopped at a
bridge which had been swept away and the delay promised to be so long that in the weather conditions then
prevailing the fruit was sure to rot before it could be got
to market even if another route were next attempted, the
carrier had the extraordinary right, if indeed not the
duty, to sell the fruit on the spot.[4] The extraordinary
law of this section is for extreme cases.   A conductor is
not obliged to stop a train to enable a passenger to recover
a hand bag lost out a window.[5]

---

[1] Lang v. Pennsylvania R. R.
Co., 154 Pa. St. 342, 26 Atl. 370,
35 Am. St. Rep. 846 (1893).

[2] Coupland v. Housatonic R. R.
Co., 61 Conn. 531, 23 Atl. 870, 15
L. R. A. 534 (1892).

[3] Central of Ga. Ry. Co. v. Madden (Ga.), 69 S. E. 165 (1910).

[4] American Express Co. v. Smith,
33 Ohio St. 511, 31 Am. Rep. 561
(1878).

[5] Henderson v. Cent. Pass. Ry.

§ 952. Duty to take appropriate action.

It is now well established that in most cases of this sort, the first thing that should be attempted by the carrier is to communicate with the owner of the goods for his further directions.[1] Similarly a telegraph company should notify the sender, if there, of the cause preventing the delivery of the message.[2] It may be that there is a duty to forward by some other connection if one is available.[3] But there is no duty to go to extraordinary expense to complete one's own performance in a way never professed.[4] Generally speaking the duty is to take appropriate action. And the courts will properly hesitate to declare the course which the proprietors of the service took in the haste of an emergency unreasonable, if it was in good faith.

Co., 140 U. S. 683, L. ed. 11 Sup. Ct. 1021 (1891).

[1] *Mississippi.*—Alabama & V. Ry. Co. v. Brichett, 72 Miss. 891, 18 So. 421 (1895).

New York.—Johnson v. New York C. R. R., 33 N. Y. 610, 88 Am. Dec. 416 (1865).

[2] *United States.*—Swan v. Western Union Telegraph Co., 63 C. C. A. 550, 129 Fed. 318 (1904).

North Carolina. — Cogdell v. Western Union Telegraph Co., 135 N. C. 431, 47 S. E. 490 (1904).

[3] *Ohio.*—American Exp. Co. v. Smith, 33 Ohio St. 511, 31 Am. Rep. 561 (1878).

Washington.—Andrus v. Columbia & O. Stb. Co., 47 Wash. 333, 92 Pac. 128 (1907).

[4] *Missouri.*—Silver v. Hall, 2 Mo. App. 557 (1876).

Pennsylvania.—Empire Transportation Co. v. Wallace, 68 Pa. St. 302, 8 Am. Rep. 178 (1871).

CHAPTER XXVIII

FAILURE IN THE UNDERTAKING

§ 960. General theory of the liability.

§ 960. General theory of liability.

In this chapter no more will be attempted than to show the basis of liability for failure in the undertaking. There will be no attempt to collect the innumerable cases that there are in the books. Most of these cases involve the general principles of liability, not the peculiar principles of public service. All that is attempted in this chapter is to bring together material enough for generalization as to the real basis for liability in public service for plain failure in the undertaking professed. What complicates the matter is that the standard of liability for some services is notably different than for other services. In the two chief examples of public calling, which have always been recognized as such, common carriage and innkeeping, our law has for a long time held the proprietors practically liable absolutely as insurers for loss of the goods intrusted to them. It should be emphasized from the outset that this liability as an insurer is as abnormal in public service as it is in private business. It is imposed only upon carriers of goods, not upon carriers of passengers; it applies to the protection of the guest's belongings, not of his person. And it is not applied to any other public callings, however similar they may be to carriage and innkeeping, although they are equally public. The most that the law normally requires of those who profess a public employment is the utmost foresight, such as the peculiar importance of public service requires.

Topic A. Abnormal Liability as an Insurer

§ 961. Early liability in common calling.

There is much in the early books concerning the liability assumed by those who professed a common calling. All

who were engaged in common employment were subjected to what was in those days an extraordinary liability
in respect to the performance of their special assumption
in the particular business. Thus the common smith was
held to warrant against pricking the horse, but not for
its protection.[1] A common veterinarian was liable upon
this implied undertaking for doing injury to a horse intrusted to his care although he made no express promise,
but he could show that the horse died from other causes.[2]
The carrier was absolutely liable for theft while on the
road with his goods, but not while putting up at an inn
with them.[3] The innkeeper must answer for theft from
the guest, but apparently for no other kind of injury in
the same degree.[4] Each of these persons having assumed
performance of the undertaking was bound to his public
so to carry on his calling as to avoid losses by his unskill-
fulness in it. By undertaking this special calling he was
held to warrant his special preparation for it; but there
is no evidence in the case of these persons of anything approaching liability for loss of all kinds. The action was almost invariably in case on a *super se assumpsit*, the profession in the undertaking being the measure of the liability.
By the current reasoning he was held absolutely liable
for default in what he had undertaken to do, much as a
special contractor would be to-day. An innkeeper was
thus held liable for failure to guard if a mob broke in; and
so a carrier must answer for loss by robbers.

§ 962. Subsequent development of the carrier's liability.

In view of this consistent theory in the earlier law hold-

[1] F. N. B. 948.

[2] Y. B. 43 Ed. III, 33, pl. 38.

[3] Anon., Dall. 8; Y. B. 42 *Lib.
Assis.* 260, pl. 17.

[4] Y. B. 42 Ed. III, 3, pl. 11, Doc-
tor and Student, c. 38.

The citations in this section are
owed to Professor Ames, being
taken from his articles on the *History of Assumpsit*, 2 *Harvard Law
Review*, 1.

ing all in common calling to the standard of the profession that they had assumed, the subsequent development in the law making common carriers absolutely liable for all losses, which did not fall within arbitrary exceptions later developed, can hardly be explained on any other ground than spontaneous variation. True it is that in some early cases bailees are apparently held to a strict accountability[1] but this was applied to all bailees indifferently. The *dicta* in Coggs v. Barnard,[2] particularly the elaborate disquisition of Lord Holt are sometimes referred to as the starting point of the modern law. But taking these *dicta* together there is not enough to show that the carrier was thought to be liable for wholly unvoidable catastrophes. It was not until Forward v. Pittard,[3] as late as 1785, that there was squarely presented a loss of goods without fault by the carrier, caused in that case by an accidental fire for which the carrier was not in any way responsible. It remained for Lord Mansfield in that case to utter the portentous words "A carrier is in the nature of an insurer."

§ 963. Absolute liability of the common carrier.

As the law has stood for some time, therefore, the carrier of goods is absolutely liable for their loss or for injury to them. And he is thus liable as an insurer, whether the loss or injury is his fault or he contributes in any way to the loss or not.[4] The most striking cases of this are those holding him liable for the damage done to his goods

---

[1] See Southcote's Case, 4 Coke, 836.

[2] 2 Ld. Raym. 909.

[3] 1 T. R. 27 (1785).

The citations in this section are owed to Professor Beale, being taken from his article on *The Carrier's Liability: Its History*, in 11 *Harvard Law Review*, 158.

[4] The insurance liability with its peculiar excuses is discussed in the following cases among others:

United States.—Pendall v. Rench, 4 McLean, 259 (1847).

Alabama.—Southern Ry. Co. v. Levy, 39 So. 95, 144 Ala. 614 (1905).

California.—Jackson v. Sacramento & V. R. R. Co., 23 Cal. 268 (1863).

Georgia.—Van Winkle v. South

by a fire which originated outside his control, where not the slightest negligence can be imputed to him in any respect. And so a shipmaster is held liable, for an accidental loss of his vessel for which he could not be said to be in any way to blame.[1] It should be said that there are certain exceptions to this absolute liability in the modern law, most of which can be traced back to an early time when they had a logical place in the general scheme. These are discussed with some detail later on in this chapter. It will be sufficient at this point to give the list of these established excuses from absolute liability—(1) act of God, (2) public enemies, (3) vice of the goods and (4) interference of the party.

§ 964. Subsequent development of innkeeper's liability.

The protection of the weary wayfarer from nocturnal

Carolina R. R. Co., 38 Ga. 32 (1868).

Illinois.—Illinois Central R. R. Co. v. Frankenberg, 54 Ill. 88, 5 Am. Rep. 92 (1870).

Iowa.—Cownie Glove Co. v. Merchants' Dispatch Transp. Co., 106 N. W. 749, 130 Iowa, 327 (1906).

Kentucky.—Farley v. Lavary, 21 Ky. L. Rep. 1252, 54 S. W. 840, 47 L. R. A. 383 (1900).

Maine.—Parker v. Flagg, 26 Me. 181, 45 Am. Dec. 101 (1846).

Massachusetts.—Gage v. Tirrell, 9 Allen (Mass.), 299 (1864).

M i n n e s o t a.—Christenson v. American Express Co., 15 Minn. 270, 2 Am. Rep. 122 (1870).

Mississippi.—Powell v. Mills, 30 Miss. 231, 64 Am. Dec. 158 (1855).

Missouri.—McFadden v. Missouri, P. R. R. Co., 92 Mo. 343, 4 S. W. 689, 1 Am. St. Rep. 721 (1887).

Nebraska.—St. Joseph & G. I. Ry. Co. v. Palmer, 38 Neb. 463, 22 L. R. A. 335, 56 N. W. 957 (1893).

New York.—Sherman v. Wells, 28 Barb. 403 (1858).

South Carolina.—Campbell v. Morse, Harper, 468 (1824).

Tennessee.—Craig v. Childress, Peck, 270, 14 Am. Dec. 751 (1823).

Wisconsin.—Klauber v. American Express Co., 21 Wis. 21, 91 Am. Dec. 452 (1866).

England.—Trent Nav. Co. v. Wood, 1 T. R. 28, 3 Esp. 127; Nugent v. Smith, 1 C. P. D. 423 (1876).

[1] As may be seen in the cases just cited that the utmost care has been exercised is no excuse. See particularly:

California.—Agnew v. Steamer Contra Costa, 27 Cal. 425, 87 Am. Dec. 87 (1865).

New Jersey.—Mershon v. Hobensack, 22 N. J. L. 372 (1850).

robbers has always been included in the undertaking of the innkeeper; and at all times the innkeeper has been held absolutely liable for loss from theft.[1] In the leading case on the subject, Cayle's Case,[2] it was resolved that "the innholder shall not be charged, unless there be a default in him or his servants, in the well and safe keeping and custody of their guest's goods and chattels within his common inn; for the innkeeper is bound in law to keep them safe without any stealing or purloining." No trace can be found in the reports or abridgements of any different doctrine until the case of Richmond v. Smith.[3] In that case, however, for the first time in a judicial decision, the court likened the innkeeper to the common carrier; and Mr. Justice Bayley used language which seemed to carry his responsibility for loss as far as that of the common carrier. "It appears to me that an innkeeper's liability very closely resembles that of a carrier. He is prima facie liable for any loss not occasioned by the act of God or the king's enemies; although he may be exonerated where the guest chooses to have his goods under his own care." Although this case was questioned afterward [4] it has been affirmed since.[5] It is probable, therefore, that in England to-day the innkeeper is liable for all loss,

---

[1] *Alabama.*—Lanier v. Young-blood, 73 Ala. 587 (1883).

Illinois.—Johnson v. Richardson, 17 Ill. 302, 63 Am. Dec. 369 (1855).

Minnesota.—Lusk v. Belote, 22 Minn. 468 (1876).

New York.—Wise v. Hoffman House, 28 N. Y. Misc. 225, 59 N. Y. Supp. 38 (1899).

Ohio.—Gast v. Gooding, 1 Ohio Dec. 315 (1849).

Pennsylvania.—Shultz v. Wall, 134 Pa. St. 262, 19 Atl. 742, 19 Am. St. Rep. 686, 8 L. R. A. 97 (1890).

South Carolina.—N e w t o n v. Axon, 1 McCord, 509, 10 Am. Dec. 685 (1821).

Vermont.—McDaniels v. Robinson, 26 Vt. 316, 62 Am. Dec. 574 (1854).

England.—Cayle's Case, 8 Coke, 63 (1574). *Contra,* Baker v. Dessauer, 49 Ind. 28 (1874).

[2] 8 Coke, 63 (1574).

[3] 8 B. & C. 9 (1828).

[4] Dawson v. Channey, 5 Q. B. 164 (1843).

[5] Morgan v. Ravey, 6 H. & N. 265 (1861).

except what is caused by act of God, or the king's enemies.[1]

§ 965. Conflict in the American authorities.

In perhaps a majority of the American jurisdictions
the court has clearly imposed upon the innkeeper a liability analogous to that of the common carrier.[2] The
rule as commonly stated in these jurisdictions is that the
innkeeper is liable for the goods of the guest lost in the
inn, unless the loss has been by act of God or of a public
enemy or by fault of the owner or its own qualities. The
extent and reason of this doctrine are well expressed by
Mr. Justice Wilde in Mason v. Thompson:[3] "Nothing is
better settled than the general principle that innkeepers
are chargeable for the goods of their guests lost from their
inns. This liability is imposed upon them for considerations of public policy." However, in several jurisdictions
a much less stringent rule is laid down, the innkeeper
being held liable for loss of goods in the inn only if he is
negligent personally, or by his servants.[4] "It is a harsh

[1] Day v. Bather, 2 H. & C. 14
(1863).

[2] *California.*—Matere v. Brown,
1 Cal. 221, 52 Am. Dec. 303 (1850).

Delaware.—Russell v. Fagan, 7
Houst. 389, 8 Atl. 258 (1886).

Maine.—Shaw v. Berry, 31 Me.
478, 52 Am. Dec. 628 (1850); Norcross v. Norcross, 53 Me. 163
(1865).

Nebraska.—Dunbier v. Day, 12
Neb. 596, 12 N. W. 109, 41 Am.
Rep. 772 (1882).

New Hampshire.—Sibley v. Aldrich, 33 N. H. 553, 66 Am. Dec.
745 (1856).

New York.—Hulett v. Swift, 33
N. Y. 371, 88 Am. Dec. 405 (1865);

Lucia v. Omel, 53 N. Y. App. Div.
641, 66 N. Y. Supp. 1136 (1900).

Ohio.—Gast v. Gooding, 1 Ohio
Dec. 315 (1849).

West Virginia.—Cunningham v.
Bucky, 42 W. Va. 671, 26 S. E.
442, 35 L. R. A. 850, 57 Am. St.
Rep. 876 (1896).

[3] 9 Pick. (Mass.) 280, 20 Am.
Dec. 471 (1830).

[4] *Illinois.*—Johnson v. Richardson, 17 Ill. 302, 63 Am. Dec. 369
(1855).

Indiana.—Baker v. Dessaner, 49
Ind. 28 (1874).

L o u i s i a n a.—Woodworth   v.
Morse, 18 La. Ann. 156 (1866).

Maryland.—Towson v. Havre de

rule," said Judge Trumbull in Metcalf v. Hess,[1] "which makes a person in any case responsible for a loss which has occurred without any fault of his." Thus in jurisdictions which hold the innkeeper liable only for negligence or breach of undertaking, he is not responsible where the goods were lost by accidental fire.

§ 966. Insurance liability not extended to persons.

Strange as it may seem this law that holds the common carrier of goods as an insurer of them does not extend to the public carrier of passengers, who is liable only for negligence.[2] This distinction is the one that has been recognized and acted upon for nearly a century. The courts have always insisted that there was a difference, founded upon substantial reasons, between the liability of the common carrier of goods and the common carrier of passengers. The former was held to warrant the safe carriage of the goods, except against loss or damage from the act of God or the public enemy; but the latter was held to contract only for due and proper care in the carriage of passengers. The same applies to innkeeping; the innkeeper is at most responsible for proper care in the protection of his guest[3] whereas he is liable as an insurer of the belongings of the guest within his inn.

Grace Bank, 6 Har. & J. 47, 14 Am. Dec. 254 (1823).

Michigan.—Cutler v. Bonney, 30 Mich. 259, 18 Am. Rep. 127 (1874).

Texas.—Houth v. Franklin, 20 Tex. 798, 73 Am. Dec. 218 (1858).

Vermont.—Howe Machine Co. v. Pease, 49 Vt. 477 (1877).

[1] 14 Ill. 129 (1852).

[2] *Minnesota.*—Smith v. St. Paul City Ry. Co., 32 Minn. 1, 18 N. W. 827, 50 Am. Rep. 550 (1884).

Missouri.—Feary v. Metropoli-

tan St. Ry. Co., 162 Mo. 75, 62 S. W. 452 (1901).

New York.—McPadden v. New York Cent. Ry. Co., 44 N. Y. 478, 4 Am. Rep. 705 (1871).

T e n n e s s e e.—Railroad Co. v. Kuhn, 107 Tenn. 106, 64 S. W. 202 (1901).

Virginia.—Norfolk & W. Ry. Co. v. Marshall, 90 Va. 836, 20 S. E. 823 (1894).

[3] *Alabama.*—West v. Thomas, 97 Ala. 622, 11 So. 768 (1892).

New York.—Stott v. Churchill,

§ 967. Responsibility for animate chattels.

Upon similar principles animate property has often been distinguished from other chattels. This was brought out in one of the early American cases,[1] where the carrier of slaves was held not to be liable as an insurer of them. As Chief Justice Marshall said of such carriage: "The carrier has not, and cannot have, the same absolute control over him, that he has over inanimate matter. In the nature of things, and in his character, he resembles a passenger, not a package of goods." There has been some tendency to apply this law to the carriage of animals, but it has not gone so far except in one jurisdiction as to deny that the carrier of animals is a carrier of goods. The property is peculiar however because it is animate and the carrier has therefore in the most extreme degree the recognized excuse that a common carrier has whensoever the inherent vice of the goods itself contributes to the loss. As Judge Denio said in one leading case[2] dealing with the transportation of animals: "They may die of fright, or by refusing to eat, or they may, notwithstanding every precaution, destroy themselves in attempting to break away from the fastenings, by which they are secured in the vehicle used to transport them, or they may kill each other."

15 N. Y. Misc. 80, 36 N. Y. Supp. 476 (1895).

Tennessee.—Weeks v. McNulty, 101 Tenn. 495, 48 S. W. 809, 43 L. R. A. 185, 70 Am. St. Rep. 693 (1898).

England.—Sandys v. Florence, 47 L. I. C. P. 598 (1878).

[1] Boyce v. Anderson, 2 Pet. (U. S.) 150, 7 L. ed. 379 (1829).

[2] Penn v. Buffalo & E. R. R. Co., 49 N. Y. 204, 10 Am. Rep. 355 (1872).

In Michigan the taking of animals is not considered common carriage at all, see Michigan So. R. R. Co. v. McDonough, 21 Mich. 165, 4 Am. Rep. 466 (1870).

But elsewhere in the United States it is held common carriage, see Kansas Pacific Ry. Co. v. Nichols, 9 Kan. 235, 12 Am. Rep. 494 (1872).

See citations in § 256, *supra.*

Topic B. Abnormal Liability Rigidly Confined

§ 968. The service must be public.

The extraordinary liability as an insurer now under discussion is confined to the case where the service that is being rendered, whether by the carrier or the innkeeper, is public in character. Thus one who is merely a private carrier [1] or simply a boarding-house keeper [2] is never held liable as an insurer. It is usually said that unless the business is affected with a public interest there is no public policy calling for the insurance liability, and only those who have undertaken to serve the public can be held to this extraordinary liability. But what is nearer the truth is that the insurance liability is so extreme that the courts

---

[1] See particularly:

United States.—Lamb v. Parkman, 1 Sprague, 343 (1857).

Arkansas.—Shinn v. Cotton, 52 Ark. 90, 12 S. W. 157 (1889).

Georgia.—Self v. Dunn, 42 Ga. 528, 5 Am. Rep. 544 (1871).

Louisiana.—Flautt v. Lashley, 36 La. Ann. 106 (1884).

Michigan.—Allis v. Voight, 90 Mich. 125, 51 N. W. 190 (1892).

Mississippi.—Harrison v. Roy, 39 Miss. 396 (1860).

New Hampshire.—F a u c h e r v. Wilson, 68 N. H. 338, 28 Atl. 1002, 39 L. R. A. 431 (1895).

South Carolina.—Littlejohn v. Jones, 2 McMull, 366, 39 Am. Dec. 132 (1842).

Texas.—Chevallier v. Straham, 2 Tex. 115, 47 Am. Dec. 639 (1847).

Vermont.—Beckwith v. Frisbie, 32 Vt. 559 (1860).

England.—Tadhunter v. Buckley, 7 L. T. (N. S.) 273 (1862).

C a n a d a.—Roussel v. Aumais, Rap. Jud. Quebec, 18 C.S. 474 (1900).

But see the following cases in which there was a tendency shown to extend the absolute liabilities:

Pennsylvania.—Gordon v. Hutchison, 1 W. & S. 285, 37 Am. Dec. 464 (1841).

Tennessee.—Moss v. Bettis, 4 Heisk. 661, 13 Am. Rep. 1 (1871). See generally, Chapter VII.

[2] See particularly:

United States.—Ball v. Beck, Fed. Cas. No. 1,161.

Georgia.—Bonner v. Welborn, 7 Ga. 296 (1849).

Iowa.—Lyon v. Smith, Morris 184 (1843).

Kentucky.—Southward v. Myers, 3 Bush. 681 (1868).

North Carolina. — Holstein v. Phillips, 146 N. C. 366, 59 S. E. 1037, 14 L. R. A. (N. S.) 975 (1907).

Texas.—Howth v. Franklin, 20 Tex. 798, 73 Am. Dec. 218 (1858).

Vermont.—Clary v. Willey, 49 Vt. 55 (1875). See generally, Chapter VII.

rigidly confine it to the exact situation for which the law was originally laid down.

§ 969. The service must be upon a public basis.

By the same law a common carrier, who has in the particular case undertaken the service upon a private basis, is not liable as an insurer.[1] Nor is the innkeeper, who has accepted in some other capacity than as a guest one lodging with him, liable for more than due care.[2] As all of these distinctions have been elaborately made in previous chapters it will not be necessary to repeat here what has been said as to the difference between a public employment and a private enterprise, nor need the distinction which exists between acceptance upon the public basis and acceptance upon a private basis be emphasized further.

§ 970. Service undertaken gratuitously.

It has already been seen that the prepayment of a rea-

[1] See particularly:

United States.—Chicago, M. & St. P. Ry. Co. v. Wallace, 66 Fed. 506, 30 L. R. A. 161 (1895).

Arkansas.—Harvey v. Rose, 26 Ark. 3, 7 Am. Rep. 595 (1870).

Indiana.—Cleveland, C., C. & St. L. Ry. Co. v. Henry, 170 Ind. 94, 83 N. E. 710 (1908).

Massachusetts.—Robertson v. Old Colony R. R. Co., 156 Mass. 525, 31 N. E. 650, 32 Am. St. Rep. 482 (1892).

Michigan.—Goup v. Wabash St. L. & P. Ry. Co., 56 Mich. 111, 22 N. W. 215, 56 Am. Rep. 374 (1885).

New Jersey.—Dudley v. Camden & P. Ferry Co., 42 N. J. L. 25, 36 Am. Rep. 501 (1880).

Pennsylvania. — F o r e paugh v. Delaware L. & W. R. R. Co., 128 Pa. St. 217, 18 Atl. 503, 15 Am. St. Rep. 672, 5 L. R. A. 508 (1889).

See generally, Chapter XXII.

[2] *Arizona.*—Haff v. Adams, 6 Ariz. 395, 59 Pac. 111 (1899).

Connecticut.—Walling v. Potter, 35 Conn. 183 (1868).

Iowa.—Shoecraft v. Bailey, 25 Iowa, 553 (1868).

Maine.—Norcross v. Norcross, 53 Me. 163 (1865).

Massachusetts.—Hall v. Pike, 100 Mass. 495 (1868).

Tennessee.—Meacham v. Galloway, 102 Tenn. 445, 52 S. W. 859, 73 Am. St. Rep. 886 (1899).

Vermont.—Read v. Amidon, 41 Vt. 15, 98 Am. Dec. 560 (1868).

England.—Shaw v. Ray, 1 Cr. & Dix. C. C. (Ire.) 84 (1839).

See generally, Chapter XXII.

sonable compensation may be required in all public services, and that waiving that right in particular cases does not disable one from insisting on such prepayment in other cases.[1] And it has also been pointed out that it is possible for a person in a public service to go still further and waive all payment, and assume gratuitously the full obligations attached to the particular service. But naturally, persons engaged in public service, when acting gratuitously are disposed to cut down their liability so far as that is possible. This is peculiarly true of the carrier and the host who are held liable as insurers of goods intrusted to them when they are acting in their public capacity. But as a free service is not common service, they are not liable absolutely for goods which they have taken upon a private basis. Indeed it is said that in gratuitous service one is only liable for wanton action or gross negligence. And it is usually enough that the carrier or the innkeeper takes as much care of the goods so deposited as he would of his own.[2] The distinction between gratuitous service and compensated service must, therefore, be made with some nicety in these two services, as it has fundamental importance in determining liability. Numerous decisions illustrate the application of these principles to common carriers [3] and innkeepers.[4]

---

[1] See Chapter XIII, Topic A.

[2] See Chapter XXII, Topic D.

[3] See generally:

Alabama.—Louisville & W. R. R. Co. v. Gerson & Sons, 102 Ala. 409, 14 So. 873 (1893).

California.—Fay v. Steamer New World, 1 Cal. 348 (1850).

Connecticut.—Beers v. Boston & A. R. R. Co., 67 Conn. 417, 34 Atl. 541, 52 Am. St. Rep. 293, 32 L. R. A. 535 (1896).

Indiana.—Perkins v. Wright, 37 Ind. 27 (1871).

Illinois.—Rice v. Illinois Central Ry. Co., 22 Ill. App. 643 (1887).

Iowa.—Warner v. Burlington & M. R. R. R. Co., 22 Iowa, 166, 92 Am. Dec. 389 (1867).

---

[4] See generally:

Arkansas.—Wear v. Gleason, 53 Ark. 364, 12 S. W. 756, 20 Am. St. Rep. 186 (1889).

§ 971. Compensation included in the whole transaction.

In many cases, service is held to be for compensation although a charge was not expressly stipulated for. In the absence of an agreement to the contrary, when a common carrier takes goods to be carried the presumption is that he is a carrier for hire; [1] and even the intent upon the part of a carrier not to charge for his service, if not disclosed before the carriage is undertaken, will not make the service gratuitous. [2] Many services called "free" are properly held not gratuitous upon an examination of all the facts. Thus when grain bags are by a recognized custom returned to the shipper of grain without further payment in addition to the established freight rate, the transportation of the bags back was held not gratuitous; [3] and in a similar case the carrier was held liable as an insurer for oil tanks being returned to the shipper. [4] An important application of this principle is seen in the case of ship-

Kentucky.—Adams Express Co. v. Cressap, 6 Bush. 572 (1869).

Maine.—Knowles v. Atlantic & St. L. R. R. Co., 38 Me. 55, 61 Am. Dec. 234 (1854).

Michigan.—Flint & P. M. R. R. Co. v. Weir, 37 Mich. 111, 26 Am. Rep. 499 (1877).

New Hampshire.—Graves v. Ticknor, 6 N. H. 537 (1834).

New York.—Beardslee v. Richardson, 11 Wend. 25, 25 Am. Dec. 596 (1833).

Virginia.—Chesapeake & O. R. R. Co. v. Wilson, 21 Gratt. 654 (1872).

Georgia.—Stewart & P. v. Head, 70 Ga. 449 (1883).

Missouri.—Wiser v. Chesley, 53 Mo. 547 (1873).

New York.—Coykendall v. Eaton, 55 Barb. 188, 37 How. Pr. 438 (1869).

Ohio.—Arcade Hotel Co. v. Wiatt, 44 Ohio St. 32, 4 N. E. 398, 58 Am. Rep. 785 (1886).

Tennessee.—Tulane Hotel Co. v. Holohan, 112 Tenn. 214, 79 S. W. 113 (1903).

England.—Doorman v. Jenkins,

2 Ad. & El. 256, 4 Nev. & M. 170, 4 L. J. K. B. 29 (1834).

Canada.—Holmes v. Moore, 17 L. C. R. 143 (1867).

[1] Knox v. Rives, Battle & Co., 14 Ala. 249, 48 Am. Dec. 97 (1848).

[2] Gray v. Missouri River Packet Co., 64 Mo. 47 (1876).

[3] Pierce v. Milwaukee R. R. Co., 23 Wis. 38 (1868).

[4] Spears & G. v. Lake Shore & M. S. R. R. Co., 67 Barb. 513 (1876).

ments made C. O. D.; [1] it is properly held in these cases that the carrier is strictly liable as such in bringing back the funds. [2] One important instance of this general situation has already been discussed in another connection; the carriage of proper baggage is included in the price paid for the passenger's transportation; and hence the carrier is liable as an insurer for the loss of such baggage. [3] But the payment of fare only covers the transportation of proper baggage, and if the transportation of goods which are not within the limitations as to what is baggage, is imposed on the carrier, he will not be liable as a common carrier is. [4]

§ 972. The business must be carriage.

It is significant also that the courts have stood stiffly by their definition of carriage and refused to extend to anything else the extraordinary liability in common carriage. Services of almost exactly the same nature are not held to be subject to this law, even when these services are public in character. The courts insist upon two requisites to meet their conception of carriage; first, that the carrier shall have possession, second, that the carrier shall transport. It will be remembered that these tests came out in the earliest chapters where the public callings were discussed separately. That bridge proprietors [5] and ferrymen [6] were not held liable as insurers as carriers

---

[1] Zollinger v. The Emma, Fed. Cas. No. 18,218 (1876).

[2] Kemp v. Coughtry, 11 Johns. (N. Y.) 107 (1814).

[3] See Woods v. Devin, 13 Ill. 746 (1852).

What is properly baggage is discussed in § 875, *supra*.

[4] See Michigan Central R. R. Co. v. Carrow, 73 Ill. 348 (1874).

What is not properly baggage is discussed in § 876, *supra*.

[5] See particularly:

United States.—Kentucky & I. Bridge Co. v. Louisville & N. Ry. Co., 37 Fed. 567 (1889).

South Carolina.—Griegsby v. Chappelle, 5 Rich. 443 (1852).

See generally, § 53.

[6] See particularly:

were, although their service was recognized as public, was because they did not take possession; and the same thing was held later of towage [1] and switching. [2] On the other hand although wharfingers [3] and warehousemen [4] took possession they did not transport, and hence were not held liable as carriers; and the cases as to log drivers [5] and flume proprietors [6] are thus explained.

§ 973. Carrier's liability not extended to other employments.

It is to be noted further that this liability of the carrier as an insurer has not been extended by the courts to employments which might possibly be considered similar enough. Even when confronted with former *dicta* to the effect that a certain employment was like common carriage the courts promptly said that it was not enough like it to apply the insurance liability to it. It has been said at various times as to many a calling that it was

Massachusetts.—White v. Winnisimet Ferry Co., 7 Cush. 155 (1851).

New Jersey.—Dudley v. Camden & P. Ferry Co., 42 N. J. L. 25, 36 Am. Rep. 501 (1880).

See generally, § 771.

[1] See particularly:

United States.—S t e a m e r New Philadelphia, 1 Black, 62, 17 L. ed. 84 (1861).

Illinois.—Knapp v. McCaffrey, 178 Ill. 107, 52 N. E. 898, 29 Am. St. Rep. 290, aff'd 177 U. S. 638 (1899).

Maryland.—Pennsylvania D. & M. Steam Nav. Co. v. Dandridge, 8 Gill & J. 248, 29 Am. Dec. 543 (1833).

New York.—Alexander v. Greene, 3 Hill, 9 (1842).

See generally, § 774.

[2] See particularly, Swift & Co. v. Ronan, 103 Ill. App. 475 (1902). See generally, § 773.

[3] See particularly, Chattock & Co. v. Bellamy & Co., 64 L. J. Q. B. 250 (1895).

See generally, § 15.

[4] See particularly, Canterbury Meat Co. v. Shaw & Co., 7 L. R. New Zealand, 708 (1889).

See generally, § 143, *supra.*

[5] See particularly, Mann v. White River Log & B. Co., 46 Mich. 38, 8 N. W. 550, 41 Am. Rep. 141 (1881).

See generally, § 55, *supra.*

[6] See particularly, Queen v. McFarlane, 7 Can. Sup. 216 (1882).

See generally, § 74 *supra.*

For all the matters discussed in this section see generally, Chapter V.

virtually common carriage, for the reason that when new businesses became affected with a public interest, the desire of the courts to hold them to public duties could at first only find expression by saying that they were like one of the businesses where public duties were then imposed. That there was a general class of public callings in which public duties were owed was not at first appreciated. Thus the first telegraph companies were spoken of as common carriers[1] and so were the first water companies.[2] But when it came to imposing upon such companies absolute liability the courts rebelled. And in practically all cases the telegraph companies are held only to the exercise of that peculiar care which is due under the circumstances.[3] And water companies are only held liable where their negligence is shown.[4]

§ 974. The business must be innkeeping.

In a similar way the courts have stood stiffly by their definition of innkeeping and have continually refused to apply the extraordinary liability of the innkeeper except to those public houses which come clearly within that definition. The innkeeper must strictly supply all the entertainment which the weary traveler actually needs on his road, which in lowest terms is food and shelter. If the keeper of a house of entertainment does not undertake to furnish either of these necessities he is not a common innkeeper; and this requirement distinguishes inns from many similar houses of public entertainment. Thus a

[1] See for example, Parks v. Alta Cal. Telegraph, 13 Cal. 422, 73 Am. Dec. 589 (1859).

See generally, § 21, *supra*.

[2] See for example, Wheeler v. No. Colo. Irr. Co., 10 Colo. 582, 17 Pac. 487, 3 Am. St. Rep. 603 (1887).

See generally, § 93, *supra*.

[3] See for example, Leonard v. New York A. & B. Telegraph Co., 41 N. Y. 544 (1820).

See generally, § 980, *infra*.

[4] See for example, Green v. Ashland Water Co., 101 Wis. 258, 77 N. W. 722, 43 L. R. A. 117, 70 Am. St. Rep. 911 (1892).

See generally, § 981, *infra*.

house which does not supply lodging is not an inn; and
this rule excludes from among inns a restaurant or eating
house.[1] On the same principle a coffeehouse or a drink-
ing saloon is not an inn.[2] And for the same reason a house
that furnishes only lodging without food, like a lodging
house,[3] or an apartment hotel,[4] is not an inn.

§ 975. The innkeeper's liability not extended to other employments.

The extraordinary liability of the innkeeper is not extended by the courts to other employments somewhat
similar, as it might well have been, had this degree of liability really commended itself to the courts. Two examples of this will suffice—the case of the sleeping car
and the case of the steamboat. Although a sleeping car
is a place for the reception and entertainment of travelers,
it is plainly not an inn. For clearly it differs from an inn
in many particulars. The inn affords necessary protection
and accommodation to travelers while they rest from their
journey; the sleeping car offers a single accommodation,
a bed to passengers while they continue their journey.
The sleeping car does not afford needed personal protection—the carrier is obliged to protect the passenger even
if he rides in the ordinary coach. Nor does the sleeping
car afford entertainment; its proprietors do not supply
food and lodging both. Thus such car owners have never

[1] *Illinois.*—Sheffer v. Willoughby,
163 Ill. 518, 45 N. E. 253, 34 L. R.
A. 464, 54 Am. St. Rep. 483 (1896).

New York.—Block v. Sherry, 43
N. Y. Misc. 342, 87 N. Y. Supp.
160 (1904).

England.—Regina v. Rymer, 2
Q. B. Div. 136, 46 L. J. M. C. 108
(1877).

Canada.—Dunn v. Bean, Quebec
Rep., 11 Super. Ct. 538 (1897).

[2] *New York.* People v. Jones, 54
Barb. 311 (1863).

England.—Regina v. Rymer, 2
Q. B. D. 136, 46 L. J. M. C. 108
(1877).

[3] *New York.*—Kelley v. New
York Excise Comrs., 54 How. Pr.
327 (1877).

[4] Davis v. Gay, 141 Mass. 531,
6 N. E. 549 (1886).

See further, § 263, *supra.*

save in one case been held liable as insurers for the losses of their passengers.[1] Practically the same arguments can be made to show that even when a steamboat owner both provides staterooms and furnishes meals, he is liable as a carrier of passengers merely, not as an innkeeper. And it is now almost universally agreed that this situation is not to be governed by the liabilities attaching to innkeepers.[2]

Topic C. Extent of Normal Liability

§ 976. Absolute and relative liability.

As was insisted at the beginning of this chapter, the special liability imposed by the law upon the carrier of goods and the innkeeper of goods, is altogether exceptional. Probably it is due to a rather modern extension of the rather stringent ancient rule, and doubtless in those times

[1] *United States.*—Blum v. Southern P. P. C. Co., 1 Flip. 500, Fed. Cas. No. 1,574 (1876).

Alabama.—Pullman P. C. Co. v. Adams, 120 Ala. 581, 24 So. 921, 74 Am. St. Rep. 53, 45 L. R. A. 787 (1898).

Colorado.—Pullman P. C. Co. v. Freudenstein, 3 Colo. App. 540, 34 Pac. 578 (1893).

Georgia.—Pullman P. C. Co. v. Hall, 106 Ga. 765, 32 S. E. 923, 71 Am. St. Rep. 293, 44 L. R. A. 790 (1899).

Illinois.—Pullman P. C. Co. v. Smith, 73 Ill. 360, 24 Am. Rep. 258 (1874).

Indiana.—Woodruff S. & P. C. Co. v. Diehl, 84 Ind. 474, 43 Am. Rep. 102 (1882).

Massachusetts.—Whicher v. Boston & A. R. R. Co., 176 Mass. 275, 57 N. E. 601, 79 Am. St. Rep. 314 (1900).

Mississippi.—Illinois Central R.

R. Co. v. Handy, 63 Miss. 609, 56 Am. Rep. 846 (1886).

New York.—Tracy v. Pullman P. C. Co., 67 How. Pr. 154 (1884).

Tennessee.—Pullman P. C. Co. v. Gavin, 93 Tenn. 53, 23 S. W. 70, 42 Am. St. Rep. 902, 21 L. R. A. 289 (1893).

But see Pullman P. C. Co. v. Lawrence, 74 Miss. 782, 22 So. 53 (1897).

See generally, § 153, *supra.*

[2] *United States.*—Walsh v. The Wright, Newb. Adm., 494 Fed. Cas. No. 17, 115 (1854).

Kentucky. — Steamboat Crystal Palace v. Vanderpool, 16 B. Mon. 302 (1855).

Massachusetts. — Clark v. Burns, 118 Mass. 275 (1875).

Contra, New York. — Crozier v. Boston, N. Y. & M. Stb. Co., 43 How. Pr. 466 (1871).

See generally, § 769.

a practically absolute liability for breach of the undertaking was felt to be necessary in order to prevent connivance with robbers, with which the country was infested.
Then, too, there was nothing shocking to the mediæval
mind in absolute liability as such, where it was felt that
a desirable end could be reached by that process. Fortunately, these notions did not persist in respect to public
employment in general, for the prevalence of this law
would be altogether out of touch with modern conditions
and present views of liability. What the modern law
demands of one engaged in public service is his utmost;
but one is not held liable for not doing more than his best.
And this is the general rule throughout public employment to-day.

§ 977. Development of the rule requiring blameworthi-
ness.

This development of this policy for liability only when
fault can be imputed may best be seen in the law relating
to the liability of the carrier of passengers. The public
carriage of passengers is, indeed, comparatively recent,
so that the suits against such carriers for personal injuries date only from the beginning of the nineteenth
century. In one of the first of the English cases in 1824 [1]
the doctrine apparently held was that the stage proprietor
should be liable to the passengers he carried for the land-
worthiness of his coach, much as the shipowner was liable
for a loss of goods due to the unseaworthiness of his vessel.
And in some American cases the same disposition was
shown, a case in New York as late as 1862 [2] apparently
going to the extent of holding a railroad liable for injury
to a passenger on a railroad train due to a hidden defect.
But this not unnatural tendency to follow the near anal-

[1] Bremner v. Williams, 1 C. &
P. (Eng.) 414 (1824).

[2] Alden v. New York C. R. R.

Co., 26 N. Y. 102, 82 Am. Dec. 401
(1862).

ogy of the law of the carriage of goods in dealing with the carriage of persons was soon arrested. The honor of being the first court to bring out clearly the modern notion that the liability is relative and blameworthiness must be shown belongs to the Massachusetts Supreme Court,[1] which held in 1845 that notwithstanding the way in which some of the current English cases could be read, they were convinced that the most that the law could fairly require of a stage owner was the utmost human care and foresight. As it turned out, this was not long afterwards in 1869 decided by an English court in a leading case,[2] which held that a railroad was not responsible for injury to a passenger caused by the breaking of a car wheel due to a latent defect in it. And this has been the law both in America and England ever since.

§ 978. Liability of carrier of passengers.

This modern law has never better been summarized than in that early leading Massachusetts case just mentioned [3] which concludes by holding: "that carriers of passengers for hire are bound to use the utmost care and diligence in the providing of safe, sufficient and suitable coaches, harnesses, horses and coachmen, in order to prevent those injuries which human care and foresight can guard against; and that if an accident happens from a defect in the coach, which might have been discovered and remedied upon the most careful and thorough examination of the coach, such accident must be ascribed to negligence, for which the owner is liable in case of injury to a passenger happening by reason of such accident. On the other hand, where the accident arises from a hidden and internal defect, which a careful and thorough

---

[1] Ingalls v. Bills, 9 Met. (Mass.) 1, 43 Am. Dec. 346 (1845).

[2] Readhead v. Midland Ry. Co., L. R. 4 Q. B. 379 (1869).

[3] Ingalls v. Bills, 9 Met. 1, 43 Am. Dec. 346, per Hubbard, J. (1845).

examination would not disclose, and which could not be guarded against by the exercise of a sound judgment and the most vigilant oversight, then the proprietor is not liable for the injury, but the misfortune must be borne by the sufferer, as one of that class of injuries for which the law can afford no redress in the form of a pecuniary recompense.[1]

§ 979. Liability of innkeepers for guests personally.

The duties of the innkeeper to his guests personally

[1] And see among the almost innumerable cases in which these principles have been applied to all the modern forms of passenger carriage:

Arkansas.—Little Rock, F. & S. Ry. Co. v. Miles, 40 Ark. 298, 48 Am. Rep. 10 (1883).

California.—Fisher v. Southern Pacific Co., 89 Cal. 399, 26 Pac. 894 (1891).

Connecticut.—Hall v. Connecticut River Stb. Co., 13 Conn. 319 (1839).

Florida.—Florida Southern R. R. Co. v. Hirst, 30 Pa. St. 1, 32 Am. St. Rep. 17 (1892).

Kentucky.—Davis v. Paducah Ry. & L. Co., 113 Ky. 267, 24 Ky. L. Rep. 135, 68 S. W. 140 (1902).

Illinois.—North Chicago St. Ry. Co. v. Cook, 145 Ill. 551, 33 N. E. 958 (1893).

Iowa.—Sales v. Western Stage Co., 4 Iowa, 547 (1857).

Maine.—Libby v. Maine Central R. R. Co., 85 Me. 34, 26 Atl. 943, 20 L. R. A. 812 (1892).

Maryland.—Philadelphia, W. & B. R. R. Co. v. Anderson, 72 Md. 519, 20 Atl. 2, 20 Am. St. Rep. 483, 8 L. R. A. 673 (1890).

Massachusetts.—Pitcher v. Old Colony St. Ry. Co., 196 Mass. 69, 81 N. E. 876, 13 L. R. A. 481 (1907).

Missouri.—Gilson v. Jackson Co. Horse Ry. Co., 76 Mo. 282 (1882).

Nebraska.—Spellman v. Lincoln Rapid Tr. Co., 36 Neb. 890, 55 N. W. 270, 38 Am. St. 753, 20 L. R. A. 316 (1893).

New York.—Graham v. Manhattan Ry. Co., 149 N. Y. 336, 43 N. E. 917 (1896).

North Carolina.—Porter v. Raleigh & G. R. R. Co., 132 N. C. 71, 43 S. E. 547 (1903).

Pennsyl v a n i a.—Fredericks v. Northern Cent. R. R. Co., 157 Pa. St. 103, 27 Atl. 689, 22 L. R. A. 306 (1893).

South Carolina.—Renneker v. South Carolina R. R. Co., 20 S. C. 219 (1883).

Tennessee.—Weeks v. McNulty, 101 Tenn. 495, 48 S. W. 809, 70 Am. St. Rep. 693 (1898).

Texas.—McCarty v. Houston & T. C. Ry. Co. (Tex. Civ. App.), 54 S. W. 421 (1899).

West Virginia.—Gillingham v. Ohio River R. R. Co., 35 W. Va. 588, 14 S. E. 243, 14 L. R. A. 798 29 Am. St. Rep. 827 (1891).

may be divided into three classes: he must furnish shelter, protection and food. He is therefore called upon to provide safe premises, to protect the guests against personal harm, and to furnish a sufficient quantity of wholesome food. The innkeeper is bound to provide reasonably safe premises.[1] This duty the innkeeper cannot escape by delegating it to another, even though the latter is a proper and generally careful person.[2] The innkeeper is responsible if his delegate is negligent. Thus, where an innkeeper had his elevator inspected in the usual way by a proper inspector and the latter negligently failed to find a defect, the innkeeper was held liable to a guest who was injured by reason of the defect.

§ 980 Liability of telegraph companies.

Another illustration of the true extent of liability in public employment according to modern notions may be found in the established law as to the liability of telegraph companies.[3] That the liabilities of a common carrier do not attach to business of this kind may now be considered as well settled. That messages of the highest importance are often sent requiring a proportionate de-

[1] *Kentucky.*—Woodward v. Birch, 4 Bush. 510 (1869).

Maine.—Hilton v. Adams, 71 Me. 19 (1879).

New York.—Washburn v. Jones, 14 Barb. 193 (1851).

Tennessee.—Dickerson v. Rogers, 4 Humph. 179, 40 Am. Dec. 642 (1843).

[2] *Alabama.*—West v. Thomas, 97 Ala. 622, 11 So. 768 (1892).

New York.—Stott v. Churchill, N. Y. Misc. 80, 36 N. Y. Supp. 476 (1895).

Nebraska.—Hotel Assn. v. Walters, 23 Neb. 280, 36 N. W. 561 (1888).

England.—Sandys v. Florence, 48 L. J. C. B. 597 (1878).

[3] What follows is virtually a quotation from Bartlett v. Western Union Telegraph Co., 62 Me. 209 (1873).

The liability of telephone companies is analogous to that of telegraph companies. See the elaborate discussion of the liabilities of telephone companies in McLeod v. Pacific Telephone Co., 52 Oreg. 22, 94 Pac. 468, 95 Pac. 1009, 15 L. R. A. (N. S.) 810, 18 L. R. A. (N. S.) 954 (1908).

gree of care, may be considered equally certain. To require a degree of care and skill commensurate with the importance of the trust reposed, is in accordance with the principles of law applicable to all undertakings of whatever kind, whether professional, mechanical, or that of the common laborer. There is no reason why the business of sending messages by telegraph should be made an exception to the general rule. This requires skill as well as care. If the work is difficult, greater skill is required.[1]

§ 981. Liability of water companies.

There have been several cases of late in which the lia-

---

[1] To the same effect, see:

United States.—Abraham v. Western Union Telegraph Co., 23 Fed. 315 (1885).

Arkansas.—Western Union Tel. Co. v. Short, 53 Ark. 434, 14 S. W. 649, 9 L. R. A. 744 (1890).

Florida.—Western Union Telegraph Co. v. Hyer Bros., 22 Fla. 637, 1 Am. St. Rep. 222 (1886).

Georgia.—Stamey v. Western Union Telegraph Co., 92 Ga. 613, 18 S. E. 100, 44 Am. St. Rep. 95 (1893).

Illinois.—Tyler V. & Co. v. Western Union Telegraph Co., 60 Ill. 421, 14 Am. Rep. 38 (1871).

Indiana.—Western Union Telegraph Co. v. Meredith, 95 Ind. 93 (1888).

Maine.—Fowler v. Western Union Telegraph Co., 80 Me. 381, 6 Am. St. Rep. 211 (1888).

Maryland.—Birney v. New York & W. Pr. Telegraph Co., 18 Md. 341, 81 Am. Dec. 607 (1862).

Massachusetts.—Grinnell v. Western Union Telegraph Co., 113 Mass. 299, 18 Am. Rep. 485 (1873).

Michigan.—Birkett v. Western Union Telegraph Co., 103 Mich. 361, 61 N. W. 645, 33 L. R. A. 404, 50 Am. St. Rep. 374 (1894).

Ohio.—Telegraph Co. v. Griswold, 37 Ohio St. 301, 41 Am. Rep. 500 (1881).

New York.—Kiley v. Western Union Telegraph Co., 109 N. Y. 231 (1888).

Pennsylvania.—New York & W. Pr. Telegraph Co. v. Dryburg, 35 Pa. St. 298, 78 Am. Dec. 338 (1860).

South Carolina.—Pinckney v. Western Union Telegraph Co., 19 S. C. 71, 45 Am. Rep. 499 (1883).

Tennessee.—Telegraph Co. v. Frith, 105 Tenn. 167, 58 S. W. 118 (1900).

Texas.—Western Union Telegraph Co. v. Boots (Tex. Civ. App.), 31 S. W. 825 (1895).

But see:

California.—Parks v. Alta Cal. Tel. Co., 13 Cal. 422, 73 Am. Dec. 589 (1859).

Oklahoma.—Blackwell M. & E. Co. v. Western Union Telegraph Co., 17 Okla. 376, 89 Pac. 235 (1906).

bility of water companies to their patrons as purveyors of water has been discussed. It is clear on all these authorities that the water companies are not held to anything like an absolute liability for the purity of the water supplied. It is recognized that the most that they can be held to is what it is reasonable to require of them. Indeed, in relation to other public services the standard to which the law holds up the water companies does not seem perhaps high enough. Thus when the supply must be taken from the turbid streams of the locality, it is held that it cannot be expected that clear water should be supplied.[1] And generally the most that can be expected is that the water supplied shall be reasonably potable, it cannot be required that it shall be really pure.[2] It is not impossible that these standards may be raised in the course of time to conform to the general standard in public service, which requires extraordinary efforts to do the best that is really possible. The cases do go far enough now to hold a water company liable for negligence if the water supplied to its patrons is really dangerous.[3] But in such cases the duty is at most to use due care, the companies not being liable for the pollution of the water supplied, even when it is carrying disease germs, unless their negligence is plainly shown in not safeguarding their watershed and in not inspecting their supply.[4]

[1] *Alabama.*—Stein v. State, 37 Ala. 123 (1861).

Colorado.—Grand Junction v. Grand Junction Water Co., 14 Colo. App. 424, 60 Pac. 196 (1900).

K e n t u c k y.—Georgetown v. Georgetown Water, G. & E. P. Co., 121 S. W. 428, 24 L. R. A. (N. S.) 303 (1909).

Missouri.—Aurora Water Co. v. Aurora, 129 Mo. 540, 31 S. W. 946 (1895).

[2] *New York.*—People v. New York Suburban Water Co., 56 N. Y. Supp. 364 (1899).

Pennsylvania.—DuBois Borough v. DuBois City Waterworks Co., 176 Pa. St. 430, 35 Atl. 248, 53 Am. St. Rep. 678, 34 L. R. A. 92 (1896).

[3] *England.*—Green v. Chelsea W. W. Co., 70 L. T. 547 (1894).

[4] *New York.*—Danaher v. Brooklyn, 119 N. Y. 1, 23 N. E. 745 (1890).

§ 982. Liability of gas companies.

In regard to the liability of gas companies to their patrons in course of supplying them, the cases from the outset have held the companies to that high degree of care [1] which the circumstances of this public service demand.[2] In a recent Indiana case [3] this law was thus applied to the special facts of the case. "Appellant was engaged in dealing in and furnishing to its patrons a dangerous, deadly, explosive, and inflammable element. The character of the product it furnished required of it the highest degree of care and caution, and imposed upon it a continuing duty of oversight and inspection." [4]

§ 983. Liability of electric companies.

The cases as to the liability of an electric company in

Wisconsin.—Green v. Ashland Water Co., 101 Wis. 258, 77 N. W. 722, 43 L. R. A. 117, 70 Am. St. Rep. 911 (1892).

[1] *Illinois.*—Belvidere Gaslight & F. Co. v. Jackson, 81 Ill. App. 244 (1898).

Indiana.—Coy v. Indianapolis Gas Co., 146 Ind. 655, 46 N. E. 17, 20, 36 L. R. A. 535 (1896).

New Jersey.—Benedict v. Columbus Construction Co., 49 N. J. Eq. 23, 23 Atl. 485 (1891).

New York.—Lannen v. Albany Gaslight Co., 46 Barb. 264 (1865).

Pennsylvania.—Hoehle v. Allegheny Heating Co., 5 Pa. Super. Ct. 21 (1897).

West Virginia.—Barrickman v. Marion Oil Co., 45 W. Va. 634, 32 S. E. 327, 44 L. R. A. 92 (1898).

[2] Negligence therefore must be shown in the course taken by the gas company. Lodge v. United Gas & Imp. Co., 209 Pa. St. 553, 58 Atl. 925 (1904). And it must be shown as to a matter which the gas company had control. Tremaine v. Halifax Gas Co., 3 Nova Scotia, 360.

[3] Indiana Natural & Illuminating Gas Co. v. Long, 27 Ind. App. 219, 59 N. E. 410 (1901).

[4] Quoting with approval the leading case of Holly v. Boston Gaslight Co., 8 Gray (Mass.), 123, 69 Am. Dec. 233 (1857), where the chief justice said that gas companies owed it to their patrons "to institute and maintain an efficient system of oversight and superintendence, and to be prepared with a sufficient force ready to be put in action, and fully competent to supply and furnish a prompt remedy for all such accidents, defects, and interruptions in their affairs, as from experience and character of their works there was reasonable ground to anticipate might occur."

the course of supplying its patrons have followed the analogy of the gas cases. There are peculiar dangers to all concerned in the supplying of electric current, which call for due care. This was brought out in one case where a patron was killed by an electric shock in turning out a lamp. It was shown that by the crossing of a primary and a secondary wire a death dealing current of a high voltage was conducted into the house. The company attempted to defend itself by showing that the direct connection with this deadly current was made through a lamp socket installed by the customer himself, but the court held that the company was liable as the customer need not install such appliances as would handle such currents safely.[1] In another recent case it was pointed out that the responsibility of the electric company in such cases all depended upon showing its diligence in the matter. The company it was said was not liable for injuries caused patrons by a defect or break in the transformer unless they knew of it or could have known of it by the exercise of such reasonable inspection and care as the circumstances call for in this dangerous business.[2]

---

[1] Gilbert v. Duluth General Electric Co., 93 Minn. 99, 100 N. W. 653 (1904).

A fortiori the company is liable if it did the interior wiring itself. Herzog v. Municipal Electric Light Co., 89 N. Y. App. Div. 569, 85 N. Y. Supp. 712 (1904).

[2] Denver Consolidated Electric Co. v. Lawrence, 31 Colo. 301, 73 Pac. 39 (1903).

See also Memphis Consol. Gas & E. Co. v. Letson, 135 Fed. 969, 68 C. C. A. 453 (1905).

In Alexander v. Nanticoke Light Co., 209 Pa. St. 571, 58 Atl. 1068 (1904), it was said that to a patron turning on light the company is held to a high standard of duty to protect its patrons from the perilous current it is furnishing by doing all that human care, skill and vigilance can suggest.

In McCabe v. Narragansett Electric Co., 26 R. I. 427, 59 Atl. 112 (1904), it was held that expert testimony could be adduced in such a case to show that better safeguards and inspection were possible.

Topic D. Established Excuses from All Liability

§ 984. What constitutes act of God.

From time immemorial a loss caused solely by the act of God has been excused,[1] but what constitutes an act of God has never been defined with exactness. Indeed, it is evident that the extent of this excuse has varied in the history of the law, having been formerly, very probably, more extensive than it is at present. The awful convulsions of nature are plainly acts of God. Losses caused altogether by earthquakes, eruptions, landslides and tidal waves, to select four instances, are plainly excused. Violent storms are also plainly acts of God, such as tornadoes, whirlwinds or cloud-bursts, and extraordinary floods or the bursting of dams. And snowstorms or blizzards furnish other examples, with snow blockades and snow slides as their result. A sudden change in temperature such as an unexpected frost, or an unforseen period of extreme cold constitutes an act of God, as well as warm weather and extreme heat. An electrical disturbance also may excuse as an act of God. This is not only true of the extreme case of lightning, but it may be true of a less apparent electrical disturbance which makes the

[1] This general paragraph is written with the following cases particularly in mind:

United States.—Gleeson v. Virginia Midland R. R. Co., 140 U. S. 435, 35 L. ed. 458, 11 Sup. Ct. 859 (1889).

Colorado.—Blythe v. Denver & R. G. Ry. Co., 15 Colo. 333, 25 Pac. 702, 11 L. R. A. 615, 22 Am. St. Rep. 403 (1891).

Iowa.—Green Wheeler Shoe Co. v. Chicago, R. I. & P. Ry. Co., 130 Iowa, 123, 106 N. W. 498 (1906).

Minnesota.—Bibb Broom Corn Co. v. Atchison, T. & S. F. Ry. Co.,

94 Minn. 269, 102 N. W. 709, 69 L. R. A. 509 (1905).

Nebraska.—Wabash Ry. Co. v. Sharpe, 76 Neb. 424, 107 N. W. 758, 124 Am. St. Rep. 823 (1906).

New York.—Colt v. M'Mechen, 6 Johns. (N. Y.) 160 (1810).

Pennsylvania.—Long v. Pennsylvania R. R. Co., 147 Pa. St. 343, 23 Atl. 459, 14 L. R. A. 741, 30 Am. St. Rep. 732 (1892).

South Carolina.—Slater v. South Carolina R. R. Co., 29 S. C. 96, 6 S. E. 936 (1888).

England.—Trent Navigation Co. v. Wood, 3 Esp. 127 (1785).

working of telegraph wires unmanageable for the time being. It should be added that the ceasing of the natural forces which are unusually manifesting themselves constitutes an act of God. Thus a sudden dying of the wind is as much an act of God as an unexpected squall; and an unusual drought is as much an act of God as a torrential rain.[1]

§ 985. Act of God merely contributory.

The plain rule to be deduced from the cases is that the act of God does not furnish an excuse unless the loss be solely caused by it.[2] If, therefore, human action concurs with act of God to such degree that it may be said to be active in the final catastrophe, the excuse of act of God is unavailable.[3] Thus the Chicago fire originating by

[1] Act of God as an excuse in innkeeping, see Mason v. Thompson, 9 Pick. 283, 20 Am. Dec. 471 (1830).

Act of God as an excuse in water supply, see: Pawnee Land & C. Co. v. Jenkins, 1 Colo. App. 425 (1892).

Act of God as an excuse in electric supply, see Phœnix L. & F. Co. v. Bennett, 8 Ariz. 314, 74 Pac. 48 (1903).

Act of God as an excuse in telephone service, see Southern Bell Telephone & Telegraph Co. v. McTyer, 137 Ala. 601, 34 So. 1020 (1903).

Act of God as an excuse in telegraphing, see White, W. & K. v. Western Union Telegraph Co., 14 Fed. 710 (1882).

[2] *Arkansas.*—Packard v. Taylor, 35 Ark. 402 (1880).

Maryland.—Ferguson v. Brent, 12 Md. 9, 71 Am. Dec. 582 (1857).

New York.—McArthur & H. v. Sears, 21 Wend. 190 (1839).

New Jersey.—New Brunswick S. B. & C. Co. v. Tiers, 24 N. J. L. (4 Zab.) 697, 64 Am. Dec. 394 (1853).

North Carolina.—Briggs v. Durham Traction Co., 147 N. C. 389, 61 S. E. 373 (1908).

South Carolina.—Slater v. South Carolina Ry. Co., 29 S. C. 96, 6 S. E. 936 (1888).

[3] *Alabama.*—Smith v. Western Ry. of Ala., 91 Ala. 455, 8 So. 754, 24 Am. St. Rep. 929, 11 L. R. A. 619 (1890).

Connecticut.—See Williams v. Grant, 1 Conn. 487, 7 Am. Dec. 235 (1816).

Mississippi.—Gilmore v. Carman, 1 Sm. & M. 279, 40 Am. Dec. 96 (1843).

New York.—Gould v. Hill, 2 Hill, 623 (1842).

Tennessee.—Nashville, C. & St. L. Ry. Co. v. Stone & H., 112 Tenn. 348, 79 S. W. 1031, 105 Am. St. Rep. 955 (1904).

human negligence in a remote part of the city was not
an act of God, and so the railroads were held liable
for freight ultimately destroyed thereby, although its destruction could not have been avoided by the exercise of
the utmost efforts on their part.[1] But the Johnstown flood
caused by the bursting of a storage reservoir was held an
act of God, excusing the railroads from liability for the
goods in their possession thus destroyed.[2] Another comparison of two other cases may make this plainer. If by
failure of the wind a vessel is driven upon the shore notwithstanding the efforts of its navigators, the loss is by
act of God.[3] But if a ship while being steered in its usual
course runs upon the wreck of another ship which had
sunk below the surface of the water in mid channel by
a sudden squall, the loss is by act of man.[4]

§ 986. Damage by public enemies.

From time immemorial seizure by the king's enemies
has been an excuse in public service. As a foundation for
the excuse, a state of war must exist between the community to which the carrier belongs and the country whose
forces have made the seizure. It makes no difference
whether the foreign government waging the war is *de jure*
or *de facto;* but it must be sufficiently organized to be
regarded as a belligerent party in a war actually begun.
The case of domestic forces arrayed against each other
sometimes is thought to be difficult. But it makes no
difference which is the government *de jure*. If one part of
a country is under one *de facto* government and the other
under another, the forces of each are enemy forces in the

Texas.—Chevalier v. Strahan, 2
Tex. 115, 47 Am. Dec. 639 (1847).

[1] Merchants' Dispatch Co. v.
Smith, 76 Ill. 542 (1875).

[2] Wald v. Pittsburg, C., C. & St.
L. R. R. Co., 162 Ill. 545, 44

N. E. 88, 53 Am. St. Rep. 322, 35
L. R. A. 356 (1896).

[3] Merritt v. Earle, 29 N. Y. 115,
86 Am. Dec. 292 (1864).

[4] Trent Navigation v. Wood
(Eng.), 3 Esp. 127 (1785).

other's territory.   The American cases chiefly relate to the situation at the time of our civil war.   It was finally generally agreed that the Confederate government was so far *de facto* as not only to make its forces public enemies to Federal carriers [1] but also to make the Federal forces enemies to Confederate carriers. [2]

§ 987. How far the defense extends.

On the other hand, damage caused by mere marauders does not come within the excuse. [3]   And if a carrier be robbed by a hundred men, he is never the more excused. [4] Perhaps one justification for this distinction from a technical point of law is that while there is no remedy over against the public enemy, such a remedy does exist theoretically against the domestic marauder.   Thus where

[1] Thus a Federal carrier would be excused for injuries done goods in his hands by Confederate forces, but not by the Federal forces.

Illinois.—Illinois Central R. R. Co. v. McClellan, 54 Ill. 58, 5 Am. Rep. 83 (1870).

Kentucky.—Bland v. Adams Express Co., 1 Duval, 232, 85 Am. Dec. 623 (1864).

New Mexico.—Seligman Bros. v. Armijo, 1 New Mex. 459 (1870).

Rhode Island.—Hubbard v. Harnden Express Co., 10 R. I. 244 (1872).

[2] So a Confederate carrier could not excuse himself for losses attributed to the Confederate forces, but could do so for losses caused by the Federal forces.

Georgia.—Wallace v. Sanders, 50 Ga. 134, 42 Ga. 486 (1871).

Tennessee.—Southern Ex. Co. v. Womack, 1 Heisk. 256 (1870).

[3] See the discussion in Morse v. Slue, 1 Mod. 85 (1671).   See also Rusell v. Nervian, 17 C. B. (N. S.) 163 (1864).

The term "public enemy" under the rule that a carrier is liable for the loss of goods except by act of God or the public enemy, means enemy of the country, and does not include mobs.   Pittsburg, C., C. & St. L. Ry. Co. v. City of Chicago, 89 N. E. 1022, 242 Ill. 178 (1909).

[4] *United States.*—S h e r m a n v. Pennsylvania R. R. Co., Fed. Cas. No. 12,769, 8 Wkly. Notes Cas. (Pa.) 269 (1880).

Arkansas.—Missouri Pacific Ry. Co. v. Nevill, 60 Ark. 375, 30 S. W. 425, 28 L. R. A. 360, 35 Am. St. Rep. 846 (1893).

Pennsylvania.—Lancy v. Pennsylvania R. R. Co., 154 Pa. St. 342, 26 Atl. 370, 26 L. R. A. 360, 35 Am. St. Rep. 846 (1893).

Texas.—Gulf, C. & S. F. Ry. Co. v. Levi, 76 Tex. 337, 13 S. W. 191, 8 L. R. A. 323 (1889).

the absolute liability as an insurer exists, the fact that the goods are injured or seized by a mob of rioters, which the carrier is absolutely unable to resist, furnishes no excuse, however unexpected the attack may have been. It should be added in this connection that pirates are enemies of all mankind, although outlaws are not.

§ 988. Vice of the property.

Moreover, there is an established excuse if the loss happens by deterioration or disintegration of the goods in transit, whether it is due to inherent characteristics or precipitated by external factors. If for example the loss happens by a freezing in winter [1] or if by melting in summer [2] there is an apparent excuse. Likewise a loss caused by the fermentation of the molasses [3] being carried, or by the decay of the fruit in transit, will be excused. [4] In any case, the deterioration of the goods must be the result of natural causes. [5] But it is not necessary to show that the loss would have occurred if the goods had not been moved. [6]

§ 989. Natural propensities of animals.

This excuse finds its chief scope in the law relating to the carriage of animals. [7] It is almost universally agreed that this is common carriage with all the law thereto

[1] McGraw v. Baltimore & O. R. R. Co., 18 W. Va. 361 (1881).

It is otherwise if the carrier was negligent in the matter. Fox v. Boston & M. R. R. Co., 148 Mass. 220, 19 N. E. 222 (1889).

[2] Nelson v. Woodruff, 1 Black (U. S.), 156 (1861).

It is otherwise if the carrier was negligent in not providing against this. Beard v. Illinois Central R. R. Co., 79 Iowa, 518, 44 N. W. 800, 18 Am. St. Rep. 381, 7 L. R. A. 280 (1890).

[3] Faucher v. Wilson, 68 N. H.

338, 38 Atl. 1002, 39 L. R. A. 431 (1895).

[4] The Collenberg, 1 Black (U. S.), 170, 17 L. ed. 89 (1861).

[5] Southern Express Co. v. Bailey, 7 Ga. App. 331, 66 S. E. 960 (1910).

[6] Lester v. Lancashire & Y. Ry. Co. (1903), 1 K. B. 878, 72 L. I. K. B. 385.

[7] The better way of stating the law is to say that the carrier of animals has in an extreme degree for a common carrier the recognized excuse that the inherent vice of the goods was a contributing cause.

applying, but since animals are being dealt with losses which can be traced primarily to their proper vice are held excused.[1] Of course special care must be taken of animals because they are alive. And in emergencies unusual steps must be taken to save them.[2] But if, notwithstanding due care for them, they injure themselves or die by accident the carrier cannot be held liable. [3]

§ 990. Interference by patron.

The patron should not recover when the loss can be

Kansas.—Kansas Pacific Ry. Co. v. Nichols, K. & Co., 9 Kan. 235, 12 Am. Rep. 494 (1872).

Nebraska.—Chicago, B. & Q. R. R. Co. v. Williams, 61 Neb. 608, 85 N. W. 832 (1901).

Pennsylvania. — R i t z & P. v. Pennsylvania R. R. Co., 3 Phil. 82 (1858).

Vermont.—Kimball v. Rutland & B. R. R. Co., 26 Vt. 247, 62 Am. Dec. 567 (1854).

But see, going to a greater length in favor of the carrier:

Michigan.—Heller v. Chicago Gt. T. Ry. Co., 109 Mich. 53, 66 N. W. 667, 63 Am. St. Rep. 541 (1896).

New York.—Penn, Jr., v. Buffalo & E. R. R. Co., 49 N. Y. 204, 10 Am. Rep. 355 (1872).

[1] *Alabama.*—So. & No. Alabama R. R. Co. v. Henlein & B., 52 Ala. 606, 23 Am. Rep. 578 (1875).

Illinois.—Illinois Central R. R. Co. v. Brelsford, 13 Ill. App. 251 (1883).

Kentucky.—Hall v. Renfro, 3 Met. 51 (1860).

Massachusetts.—Evans v. Fitchburg R. R. Co., 111 Mass. 142, 15 Am. Rep. 19 (1872).

Minnesota. —Lindsley v. Chicago, M. & St. P. Ry. Co., 36 Minn. 539, 1 Am. St. Rep. 692 (1887).

Mississippi.—Illinois Cent. Ry. Co. v. Scruggs, 69 Miss. 418, 13 So. 698 (1891).

Missouri.—Cash v. Wabash R. R. Co., 81 Mo. App. 109 (1899).

New Hampshire.—R i x f o r d v. Smith, 52 N. H. 355, 13 Am. Rep. 42 (1872).

New Jersey.—Feinberg v. Delaware, L. & W. R. R. Co., 52 N. J. 451, 20 Atl. 33 (1890).

North Carolina.—Selby v. Wilmington & W. R. Co., 113 N. C. 588, 18 S. E. 88, 37 Am. St. Rep. 635 (1893).

South Carolina.—Ramberg v. South Carolina R. R. Co., 9 S. C. 61 (1877).

Texas.—Ft. Worth & D. C. Ry. Co. v. Greathouse, 17 S. W. 834 (1891).

England.—Blower v. Great Western Ry. Co., L. R., 7 C. P. 655 (1872).

[2] See Coupland v. Housatonic R. R. Co., 61 Conn. 531, 23 Atl. 870 (1892).

[3] See Ames v. Fargo, 114 N. Y. App. Div. 666, 99 N. Y. Supp. 994 (1906).

attributed to his own action. Thus if wrong directions for the performance of service are given the patron cannot complain of the failure caused thereby.[1] And if the patron conceals the true character of the service asked he cannot complain of the loss caused thereby.[2] Furthermore, if the patron interferes with the performance of the service he cannot complain of any loss to which his action contributes. Thus where the shipper put hay into a stock car in violation of regulations of the company forbidding the putting of combustibles into the car, it was said that the carrier should not be held liable for a subsequent loss by fire.[3] Similarly where a servant of the shipper accompanying stock took a lantern into the car which set the car on fire, it was held that the railroad was not liable whether the lantern was handled negligently or not.[4]

§ 991. Assumption by patron.

To the extent that the patron takes control, from that

[1] *United States.*—See The Huntress, 2 Ware, 89 Fed. Cas. No. 6,914 (1840).

Illinois.—Erie Ry. Co. v. Wilcox, 84 Ill. 239, 25 Am. Rep. 251 (1870).

North Carolina.—See Grocery Co. v. Railroad Co., 136 N. C. 396, 48 S. E. 861 (1904).

Pennsylvania.—The Lake Shore & M. S. Ry. Co. v. Hodapp, 83 Pa. St. 22 (1876).

Tennessee.—Southern Exp. Co. v. Kaufmann, 12 Heisk. 161 (1873).

Wisconsin.—Wells v. American Express Co., 44 Wis. 342 (1878).

[2] *Georgia.*—Southern Express Co. v. Everett, 37 Ga. 688 (1868).

Illinois.—Oppenheimer v. United States Exp. Co., 69 Ill. 62, 18 Am. Rep. 596 (1873).

Massachusetts.—See Phillips v. Earle, 8 Pick. 182 (1829), pointing out that unless deceit is practiced on him the carrier cannot complain if value is not declared, as he should ask for value if he wishes to know it.

New York.—Richards v. Westcott, 2 Bosw. (N. Y.) 589 (1858).

Pennsylvania.—Relf v. Rapp, 3 Watts & S. 21, 37 Am. Dec. 528 (1841).

England.—Gibbon v. Paynton, 4 Burr. 2298 (1769).

See generally, § 737, *supra*.

[3] Pratt et al. v. Ogdensburg & L. C. R. R. Co., 102 Mass. 557 (1869).

[4] Hart v. Chicago & N. W. Ry. Co., 69 Iowa, 485, 29 N. W. 597 (1886).

time forth he assumes responsibility. To refer to a considerable list of cases, if the loss is due to the improper packing of the goods the carrier is not liable.[1] But if the improper condition of the goods for the purpose of shipment is fairly apparent when they are shipped, then the carrier should refuse to receive the goods, or else, having received them, he will be liable for the loss.[2] Likewise if the shipper assumes the responsibility for loading the goods upon the vehicle, the carrier is thereby relieved from liability for loss caused thereby.[3] But if the improper loading should have been apparent to the carrier from the ordinary inspection which he or his servants would naturally give it, the carrier will be liable.[4]

[1] *Illinois.*—American Express Co. v. Perkins, 42 Ill. 458 (1867).

New York.—Cohen v. Platt, 48 N. Y. Misc. 378, 95 N. Y. Supp. 535 (1906).

[2] The David & C., 5 Blatchf. 266 (1865).

New York.—Ames v. Fargo, 114 N. Y. App. Div. 666, 99 N. Y. Supp. 994 (1906).

Ohio.—Union Express Co. v. Graham, 26 Ohio St. 595 (1875).

Oregon.—Goodman v. Oregon Ry. & Nav. Co., 22 Oreg. 14, 28 Pac. 894 (1892).

[3] *Alabama.*—McCarthy v. Louisville & N. R. R. Co., 102 Ala. 193, 14 So. 370, 48 Am. St. Rep. 29 (1893).

Illinois.—Pennsylvania Co. v. Kenwood Bridge Co., 170 Ill. 645, 49 N. E. 215 (1897).

Massachusetts.— L o v e l a n d v. Burke, 120 Mass. 139, 21 Am. Rep. 507 (1876).

New York.—J a c k s o n Architectural Works v. Hurlbut, 158 N. Y. 34, 52 N. E. 665, 70 Am. St. Rep. 432 (1899).

Texas.—Gulf, W. T. & P. Ry. Co. v. Wittnebert, 101 Tex. 368, 108 S. S. 150, 130 Am. St. Rep. 858 (1908).

Vermont.—Ross v. Troy & B. R. R. Co., 49 Vt. 364, 24 Am. Rep. 144 (1877).

Wisconsin.—Miltimore v. Chicago & N. W. R. R. Co., 37 Wis. 190 (1875).

England.—Richardson v. North Eastern Ry. Co., L. R. 7 C. P. 75 (1872).

[4] *Alabama.*—Atlantic C. L. Ry. Co. v. Rice, 52 So. 918 (1910).

Illinois.—Elgin, J. & E. Ry. Co. v. Bates Machine Co., 200 Ill. 636, 66 N. E. 326, 93 Am. St. Rep. 218 (1903).

Minnesota.—Calender v. Vanderhoof Co., 99 Minn. 295, 109 N. W. 402 (1906).

North Dakota.—Duncan v. Gt. Northern R. R. Co. (N. D.), 118 N. W. 826 (1908).

T e x a s.—International & Gt. Northern Ry. Co. v. Dwight & Co. (Tex. Civ. App.), 100 S. W. 1011 (1907).

CHAPTER XXIX

LIMITATION OF LIABILITY

§ 1000. Limitation upon liability possible.

[874]

§ 1000. Limitation upon liability possible.

The liability of those engaged in a public employment has, as has been seen, two principal aspects—liability for damage neither intentionally caused nor due to negligence (which is limited to the carrier of goods and the innkeeper as to goods) and liability for willful or negligent default (which prevails in all public service). It may well be that the abnormal liability of an insurer which the law imposes upon the carrier and the innkeeper may be cut down by special arrangement. But it would seem to be against public policy for a public servant to stipulate that he shall not be liable for his negligence in the performance of his undertaking. At all events this is the working hypothesis with which this chapter is begun. And as a matter of fact this distinction will be found to be supported by an almost overwhelming weight of authority.

Topic A. Methods of Making Limitations

§ 1001. Mere notice not sufficient.

In England towards the end of the eighteenth century, and for a considerable time thereafter, cases became common where by mere notice the common carrier sought to limit, in various ways, his liability as an insurer at common law, and to a considerable extent he was successful in the courts in this attempt. A general public notice brought to the attention of the patron was held to limit liability by cutting down the scope of the employment professed by the person giving the notice.[1] The delivery of a handbill containing the notice [2] the publication of a notice for three

---

[1] Hide v. Proprietors of T. & M. Navigation Co., 1 Esp. 36 (1793); Riley v. Horne, 5 Bing. 217 (1828); Mayhew v. Eames, 3 B. & C. 601 (1825); Gibbon v. Paynton, 4 Burr. 2298 (1769).

Contra, as to liability for negligence, Newborn v. Just, 2 C. & P. 76 (1825); Slim v. Great Northern R. R. Co., 14 C. B. 647 (1854).

[2] Phillips v. Edwards, 3 H. & N. 813 (1858).

months in a newspaper to which the plaintiff subscribed [1] and an advertisement which in all probability would attract the attention of the plaintiff [2] were held, as matter of law, to affect the shipper. Posting the notice in the carrier's office,[3] however, was held insufficient when the circumstances were not such that the shipper should have known of the notice, or as against a shipper who could not read.[4] This practice was finally put an end to by statute. A few decisions in the United States, following to a certain extent the English doctrine, have said that a limitation of liability by implied assent may be proved by evidence of a general public notice brought to the knowledge of the shipper before he makes his shipment and his apparent acquiescence therein.[5] But generally in the United States, a common carrier cannot restrict his liability by a mere notice in any form, though brought home to the shipper.[6] There are certain statutes on the subject in America also.

[1] Rowley v. Horne, 3 Bingham, 2 (1825).

[2] Lesson v. Holt, 1 Starkie, 186 (1816).

[3] Kerr v. Willan, 6 M. & S. 150 (1817).

[4] Davis v. Willian, 2 Starkie, 279 (1817).

[5] *Georgia.*—See Cooper v. Berry, 21 Ga. 526, 68 Am. Dec. 468 (1857).

Kentucky.—Orndorff v. Adams Express Co., 3 Bush. 194, 96 Am. Dec. 207 (1867).

Maine.—Sager v. The Portsmouth, S. & B. & E. R. R. Co., 31 Me. 228, 50 Am. Dec. 659 (1850).

Pennsylvania.—See Beckman v. Shouse, 5 Rawle, 179, 28 Am. Dec. 653 (1835).

[6] *Connecticut.*—Hale v. New Jersey Steam Nav. Co., 15 Conn. 539, 39 Am. Dec. 398 (1843).

Dakota.—Hartwell v. Northern Pac. Exp. Co., 5 Dak. 463, 41 N. W. 732, 3 L. R. A. 342 (1889).

Delaware.—Flinn v. Philadelphia, W. & B. R. R. Co., 1 Houst. 469 (1858).

Georgia.—Fish v. Chapman, 2 Ga. 349, 46 Am. Dec. 393 (1847).

Illinois.—Oppenheimer v. United States Exp. Co., 69 Ill. 62, 18 Am. Rep. 596 (1873).

Kentucky.—Louisville & N. R. R. Co. v. Brownlee, 14 Bush. 590 (1879).

New Hampshire.—Moses v. Boston & Maine R. R. Co., 32 N. H. 523, 64 Am. Dec. 381 (1856).

Oregon.—Seller v. Steamship Pacific, 1 Oreg. 409 (1861).

South Carolina.—Piedmont Mfg. Co. v. Columbia & G. R. R. Co., 19 S. C. 353 (1882).

§ 1002. Special contract necessary.

In the present law, therefore, it is impossible by a mere notice to relieve one's self from legal obligations. And such notice is held insufficient in itself to make out a special contract, unless it may fairly be said to have been expressly incorporated in an actual contract by one of the modes hereinafter mentioned in the contract for service.[1] But a special contract, if it has all the requisite ele-

South Dakota.—Mener v. Chicago, M. & St. P. Ry. Co., 5 S. Dak. 568, 49 Am. St. Rep. 898 (1894).

Vermont.—Kimball v. Rutland & B. R. R. Co., 26 Vt. 247, 62 Am. Dec. 567 (1854).

The English Carriers' Act of 1830 contained a provision that common carriers by land could not affect their liability for goods committed to them to carry by a mere public notice or declaration, but expressly sanctioned any special contract which might be entered into by the shipper and the carrier. Under this act it was held (see Walker v. York & N. M. Ry. Co., 2 E. & B. 750 [1853]) that the shipping of goods with knowledge of a general notice limiting liability and without dissent therefrom, made a special contract by notice,—notwithstanding the provision of the act. In 1854 the Railway and Canal Traffic Legislation was passed. This statute contained a provision that no contract made by a railroad or canal company respecting the receiving, forwarding, or delivering property should bind any other goods for carriage.

Note the American statutes permitting innkeepers to limit their liability, discussed in Lanier v.

Youngblood, 73 Ala. 587 (1883); Murchison v. Sergent, 69 Ga. 206, 47 Am. Rep. 754 (1882); Olson v. Crossman, 31 Minn. 222, 17 N. W. 375 (1883); Porter v. Gilkey, 57 Mo. 235 (1874). See Purvis v. Coleman, 1 Bosw. 321, affirmed in 21 N. Y. 111 (1860).

[1] *United States.*—N e w J e r s e y Steam Nav. Co. v. Merchants' Bank, 6 How. 344, 12 L. ed. 465 (1848).

Alabama.—Southern Express Co. v. Caperton, 44 Ala. 101, 4 Am. Rep. 118 (1870).

Connecticut.—Coupland v. Housatonic R. R. Co., 61 Conn. 531, 23 Atl. 870, 15 L. R. A. 534 (1892).

Georgia.—Central of Georgia Ry. Co. v. Lippman, 110 Ga. 665, 36 S. E. 202, 50 L. R. A. 673 (1900).

Illinois.—Illinois Central R. R. Co. v. Frankenberg, 54 Ill. 88, 5 Am. Rep. 92 (1870).

Indiana.—Indianapolis & C. R. R. Co. v. Cox, 29 Ind. 360, 95 Am. Dec. 640 (1868).

Louisiana.—Logan v. Pontchartrain R. R. Co., 11 Rob. 24, 43 Am. Dec. 199 (1845).

Maine.—Fillebrown v. Grand Trunk Ry. Co., 55 Me. 462, 92 Am. Dec. 606 (1867).

Maryland.—Baltimore & O. R.

ments for a contractual obligation, may in almost all jurisdictions be made, by the operation of which the common law liability may be limited [1] to an extent that will be much discussed presently.   There is no reason in the nature of things why special contracts as to the limitation of liability should not be made between a public service company and its patrons.   The company cannot force its patrons to make such special contracts, but they may enter into them voluntarily.   Generally speaking, one who has common law rights may bargain them away, but not if the contract is against public policy.   But since the common law basis is the regular course, proof of the receipt of goods for transportation by the carrier and the agreement to carry the goods raises the presumption that the goods are taken under the common law liability, sub-

R. Co. v. Brady, 32 Md. 333 (1869).

Massachusetts.—Buckland v. Adams Express Co., 97 Mass. 124, 93 Am. Dec. 68 (1867).

Michigan.—McMillan v. Michigan S. & N. I. R. R. Co., 16 Mich. 79, 93 Am. Dec. 208 (1867).

Nebraska.—Atchison & Neb. R. R. Co. v. Miller, 16 Neb. 661, 21 N. W. 451 (1884).

New York.—Hollister v. Nowlen, 19 Wend. 234, 32 Am. Dec. 455 (1888).

New Hampshire. — Moses v. Boston & Maine R. R. Co., 24 N. H. 71, 55 Am. Dec. 222 (1851).

North Carolina.—Gardner v. Southern R. R. Co., 127 N. C. 293, 37 S. E. 328 (1900).

Ohio.—Gaines v. Union Transp. & Ins. Co., 28 Ohio St. 418.

Tennessee.—Walker v. Skipwith, Meigs, 502, 33 Am. Dec. 161 (1838).

Vermont.—Farmers' & M. Bank v. Champlain Trans. Co., 23 Vt. 186, 56 Am. Dec. 68 (1851).

West Virginia.—Brown v. Adams Express Co., 15 W. Va. 812 (1879).

Canada.—Fitzgerald v. Grand Trunk Ry. Co., 4 Ont. App. 601 (1880).

[1] *United States.*—Railroad Co. v. Lockwood, 17 Wall. 357, 21 L. ed. 627 (1873).

Connecticut.—Lawrence v. New York P. & B. R. R. Co., 36 Conn. 63 (1869).

Indiana.—Thayer v. St. Louis, A. & T. H. R. R. Co., 22 Ind. 26, 85 Am. Dec. 409 (1864).

Michigan.—Feige v. Michigan Central R. R. Co., 62 Mich. 1 (1886).

Virginia.—Richmond & Danville R. R. Co. v. Payne, 86 Va. 481, 10 S. E. 749 (1890).

West Virginia.—Zouch v. Chesapeake & O. Ry. Co., 36 W. Va. 524, 15 S. E. 185, 17 L. R. A. 116 (1892)

ject only to such modifications in the common law liability as may have been made by statute.[1] This presumption of common law liability cannot be rebutted by mere proof of a local custom.[2]

§ 1003. Acceptance of an instrument.

The acceptance of an instrument commonly used to embody the contract, such as a bill of lading, will usually be conclusive proof of the contract it evidences. This doctrine is most commonly applied to bills of lading,[3] but it has also been applied to other shipping receipts.[4]

[1] Dorr v. New Jersey Steam Nav. Co., 11 N. Y. 485, 62 Am. Dec. 125 (1854).

[2] Coxe v. Heisley, 19 Pa. St. 243 (1852).

[3] *United States.*—Railroad Co. v. Manufacturing Co., 16 Wall. 318, 21 L. ed. 297 (1872).

Alabama.—Logan v. Mobile Trade Co., 46 Ala. 513 (1871).

Arkansas.—St. Louis, I. M. & S. Ry. Co. v. Weakly, 50 Ark. 397, 8 S. W. 134, 7 Am. St. Rep. 104 (1887).

Indiana.—Adams Express Co. v. Carnahan, 29 Ind. App. 606, 64 N. E. 647, 94 Am. St. Rep. 279 (1902).

Iowa.—Mulligan v. Illinois Central Ry. Co., 36 Iowa, 181, 14 Am. Rep. 514 (1873).

Kansas.—Atchison, T. & S. F. R. R. Co. v. Dill, 48 Kan. 210, 29 Pac. 148 (1892).

Kentucky.—Adams Express Co. v. Nock, 2 Duv. 562, 87 Am. Dec. 510 (1866).

Maryland.—Brehme v. Adams Express Co., 25 Md. 328 (1866).

Mississippi.—Southern Express Co. v. Moon, 39 Miss. 822 (1863).

Missouri.—Snider v. Adams Express Co., 63 Mo. 376 (1876).

New Hampshire.—Merrill v. American Express Co., 62 N. H. 514 (1883).

New York.—Kirkland v. Dinsmore, 62 N. Y. 171, 20 Am. Rep. 475 (1875).

Pennsylvania.—American Express Co. v. Second Nat. Bank, 69 Pa. St. 394, 8 Am. Rep. 268 (1871).

Rhode Island.—Ballou v. Earle, 17 R. I. 441, 22 Atl. 1113, 33 Am. St. Rep. 881 (1891).

Tennessee.—East Tennessee, Va. & Ga. R. R. Co. v. Brumley, 5 Lea, 401 (1880).

Vermont.—Davis & G. v. Central Vermont R. R. Co., 66 Vt. 290, 29 Atl. 313, 44 Am. St. Rep. 852 (1893).

[4] *Connecticut.*—Mears v. New York, N. H. & H. Ry. Co., 75 Conn. 171, 52 Atl. 610, 56 L. R. A. 884, 96 Am. St. Rep. 192 (1902).

Indiana.—Adams Express Co. v. Carnahan, 29 Ind. App. 606, 64 N. E. 647 (1902).

Massachusetts.—Graves v. Adams Express Co., 176 Mass. 280, 57 N. E. 462 (1900).

The opinion in Grace v. Adams,[1] contains this clear statement of the justification for this doctrine: "The acceptance of it (a bill of lading) by the plaintiff, at the time of the delivery of his package,[2] without notice of his dissent from its terms, authorized the defendants to infer assent by the plaintiff. It was his only voucher and evidence against the defendants. It is not claimed that he did not know, when he took it, that it was a shipping contract or bill of lading. It was his duty to read it. The law presumes, in the absence of fraud or imposition, that he did read it, or was otherwise informed of its contents and was willing to assent to its terms without reading it. Any other rule would fail to conform to the experience of all men."

§ 1004. Such acceptance not conclusive.

Although the acceptance of the instrument is generally held to be at least *prima facie* evidence of an agreement to its stipulations,[3] there are many jurisdictions where the stipulations contained in a bill of lading,[4] for example

New York.—Wilson v. Platt, 84 N. Y. Supp. 143 (1903).

South Carolina.—Dunbar v. Charleston & W. C. Ry. Co., 62 S. C. 414, 40 S. E. 884 (1902).

[1] 100 Mass. 505, 97 Am. Dec. 117 (1868).

[2] Note, however, that where the instrument is issued after the shipment is made without any previous understanding it cannot affect the common law relationship already established.

Illinois.—Merchant's Dispatch Transp. Co. v. Furthmann, 149 Ill. 66, 36 N. E. 624, 41 Am. St. Rep. 265 (1893).

Indiana.—Louisville, N., A. & C. Ry. Co. v. Craycraft, 12 Ind. App. 203, 39 N. E. 523 (1894).

Massachusetts.—Gott v. Dinsmore, 111 Mass. 45 (1872).

Wisconsin.—Strohn v. Detroit & M. Ry. Co., 21 Wis. 554, 94 Am. Dec. 554 (1867).

[3] *Indiana.*—Louisville, N., A. & C. Ry. Co. v. Craycraft, 12 Ind. App. 203, 39 N. E. 523 (1894).

Tennessee.—Dillard Bros. v. Louisville & N. R. R. Co., 2 Lea, 288 (1879).

Texas.—Missouri, K. & T. Ry. Co. v. Carter, 9 Tex. Civ. App. 677 (1895).

Wisconsin.—Boorman v. American Express Co., 21 Wis. 152 (1866).

[4] *United States.*—Railroad Co. v. Manufacturing Co., 16 Wall. 318, 21 L. ed. 297 (1872).

are held not to be made part of the contract by the mere acceptance of the instrument. These jurisdictions require that something more shall be shown in evidence of mutual assent than the mere fact of the issue of the instrument in question. And, indeed, the real question in every case is whether the document received is of such a character that under the circumstances, by the general understanding of the community, the receipt of the document is an assent to its terms. It is often insisted that provisos on tickets and passes do not necessarily govern,[1] but there is more law to the contrary.[2] The conservative view indicated in the footnotes to this section does not generally prevail as to such significant instruments as bills of lading and passenger tickets, as reference to the citations in this and the preceding paragraph will show.

Alabama.—Southern Express Co. v. Armstead, 50 Ala. 350 (1873).

Dakota.—Hartwell v. Northern Pacific Exp. Co., 5 Dak. 463, 41 N. W. 732, 3 L. R. A. 342 (1889).

Georgia.—Central R. R. Co. v. Dwight Mfg. Co., 75 Ga. 609 (1885).

Illinois.—Anchor Line v. Dater, 68 Ill. 369 (1873).

Mississippi.—Mobile & O. R. R. Co. v. Weiner, 49 Miss. 725 (1874).

New York.—Blossom v. Dodd, 43 N. Y. 264 (1870).

Ohio.—Gaines v. Union Transp. & Ins. Co., 28 Ohio St. 418 (1876).

Oregon.—Seller v. Steamship Pacific, 1 Oreg. 409 (1861).

[1] *United States.*—The Majestic, 166 U. S. 375, 17 Sup. Ct. 597, 41 L. ed. 1039 (1897).

Delaware.—Flinn v. Philadelphia, W. & B. R. R. Co., 1 Houston, 469 (1858).

Kansas.—Kansas City, St. J. & C. B. R. R. Co. v. Rodebaugh, 38 Kan. 45, 15 Pac. 899 (1887).

New York.—Lechowitzer v. Hamburg-American Packet Co., 27 N. Y. Supp. 140, 57 N. Y. St. Rep. 862 (1894).

South Carolina.—Norman v. Southern Ry. Co., 65 S. C. 517, 44 S. E. 83, 95 Am. St. Rep. 809 (1903).

[2] *United States.*—Boering v. Chesapeake Beach Ry. Co., 193 U. S. 442, 48 L. ed. 742, 24 Sup. Ct. 515 (1904).

Maryland.—Johnson v. Philadelphia, W. & B. R. R. Co., 63 Md. 106 (1884).

Massachusetts.—Quimby v. Boston & Maine R. R. Co., 150 Mass. 365, 23 N. E. 205, 5 L. R. A. 846 (1890).

Utah.—Drummond v. Southern Pacific Co., 7 Utah, 118, 25 Pac. Rep. 733 (1891).

§ 1005. Where consideration is found.

Inasmuch as by law the person engaged in a public service is bound, upon the tender of a reasonable charge, or rather of the established rate, to serve anyone to the extent of the service professed, the mere undertaking of the performance of what it is one's duty to perform would not seem to be a consideration sufficient to support the contract for limitation of liability. Where there is a reduced rate, that is, a rate lower than what would be reasonable or what has been fixed for the performance of the service under full common law liability, a proper consideration for the contract for limitation of liability may be found.[1] And to render this reduced rate really a consideration, it would seem that a fair option of shipping the goods at the higher rate upon common law liability must have been afforded the shipper.[2] However, where the agree-

---

[1] *Alabama.*—Mouton v. Louisville & N. R. R. Co., 128 Ala. 537, 29 So. 602 (1900).

Connecticut.—M e a r s v. N e w York, N. H. & H. R. R. Co., 75 Conn. 171, 52 Atl. 610, 56 L. R. A. 884, 96 Am. St. Rep. 192 (1902).

Indiana.—Adams Express Co. v. Harris, 120 Ind. 73, 21 N. E. 340, 7 L. R. A. 214 (1889).

Kentucky.—Baughman v. Louisville, E. & St. L. Ry. Co., 94 Ky. 150, 21 S. W. 757 (1893).

Minnesota.—Wehmann v. Minneapolis, St. P. &. S. S. M. Ry. Co., 58 Minn. 22, 59 N. W. 546 (1894).

Missouri.—Richardson v. Chicago & A. Ry. Co., 149 Mo. 311, 50 S. W. 782 (1899).

Tennessee.—Railroad Co. v. Gilbert, Parkes & Co., 88 Tenn. 430, 12 S. W. 1018 (1889).

Texas.—Texas & P. Ry. Co. v. Klepper (Tex. Civ. App.), 24 S. W. 567 (1893).

Wisconsin.—Ulman v. Chicago & N. W. Ry. Co., 112 Wis. 150, 88 N. W. 41, 56 L. R. A. 246, 88 Am. St. Rep. 949 (1901).

Ireland.—Gallagher v. Gt. Western Ry. Co., I. R. 8 C. L. 326 (1874).

[2] *Arkansas.*—Pacific Express Co. v. Wallace, 60 Ark. 100, 29 S. W. 32 (1895).

Indiana.—Pittsburg, C., C. & St. L. Ry. Co. v. Mitchell, 000 Ind. 000, 91 N. E. 735 (1910).

Kansas.—Atchison, T. & S. F. R. Co. v. Dill, 48 Kan. 210, 29 Pac. 148 (1892).

Missouri.—Phœnix Powder Mfg. Co. v. Wabash Ry. Co., 101 Mo. App. 442, 74 S. W. 492 (1903); Bowrin v. Wabash Ry. Co., 90 Mo. App. 324 (1901).

North Carolina.—Gardner v.

ment relates to the performance of services which the carrier as a public servant was not bound to render,[1] or has some other legal consideration in it,[2] this objection cannot be raised.

§ 1006. Certain authorities more easily satisfied.

However, the view has been advanced that the limitation of liability agreed upon will be valid, even if the alternative is not presented of shipping under the common law at a higher rate. This view was recently adopted apparently by the Supreme Court of the United States in a recent decision [3] where Mr. Justice McKenna said: "If it means that the alternative must be actually presented to the shipper by the carrier, we cannot agree. From the standpoint of the law the relation between carrier and shipper is simple. Primarily the carrier's responsibility is that expressed in the common law, and the shipper may insist upon the responsibility. But he may consent to a limitation of it, and this is the 'option and opportunity' which is offered to him. What other can be necessary?" It is believed that this case is distinguishable; [1] if not, it is submitted that it is not likely to make

Southern Ry. Co., 127 N. C. 293, 37 S. E. 328 (1900).

Tennessee.—Nashville, C. & St. L. Ry. Co. v. Stone & H., 112 Tenn. 348, 79 S. W. 1031 (1904).

Texas.—Texas & P. Ry. Co. v. Avery, 19 Tex. Civ. App. 235, 46 S. W. 897 (1898).

[1] See Gardner v. Southern Ry. Co., 127 S. C. 293, 37 S. E. 329 (1900).

[2] See Wehmann v. Minneapolis, St. P. & S. S. M. Ry. Co., 58 Minn. 22, 59 N. W. 546 (1894).

[3] Cau v. Texas & P. R. R. Co.,

194 U. S. 427, 24 S. Ct. 663, 48 L. ed. 1053 (1904).

If the shipper asks for the "lowest rate" and a limited liability contract is tendered to him, which he accepts, he cannot avoid the limitation of liability upon the ground that he requested a rate for service under common law liability and that such rate was refused. Jennings v. Grand Trunk Ry. Co., 52 Hun, 227 (1889).

[4] The circumstances showing want of consideration must be specially pleaded. Gulf, C. & S. F. Ry. Co.

law, in view of the fact that it stands alone in its opposition to the whole theory of the common law on this subject.

Topic B. Limitation of Exceptional Liability as Insurer

§ 1007. Such limitation not inconsistent with public duty.
The most important point in relation to the limitation of liability is that the exceptional liability, such as that making the common carrier of goods liable as an insurer, may be done away with by a special contract properly made.[1]   By the overwhelming weight of authority, it

v. Wright, 1 Tex. Civ. App. 402, 21 S. W. 80 (1892).

[1] *United States.*—York Co. v. Central R. R. Co., 3 Wall. 107, 18 L. ed. 170 (1865).

Alabama.—Louisville & N. R. R. Co. v. Landers, 135 Ala. 504, 33 So. 482 (1903).

Arkansas.—St. Louis, I. M. & S. Ry. Co. v. Bone, 52 Ark. 26, 11 S. W. 958 (1889).

Georgia.—Nicoll v. East Tennessee, Va. & Ga. Ry. Co., 89 Ga. 260, 15 S. E. 309 (1892).

Indiana.—Thayer v. St. Louis, A. & T. H. R. R. Co., 22 Ind. 26, 85 Am. Dec. 409 (1864).

Iowa.—Hazel v. Chicago, M. & St. P. Ry. Co., 82 Iowa, 477, 48 N. W. 926 (1891).

Maine.—Morse v. Canadian Pacific Ry. Co., 97 Me. 77, 53 Atl. 874 (1902).

Maryland.—McCoy & P. v. Erie & West. Transp. Co., 42 Md. 498 (1875).

Massachusetts. — Hoadley v. Northern Transp. Co., 115 Mass. 304, 15 Am. St. Rep. 106 (1874).

Minnesota.—Hull v. Chicago, St. P., M. & O. Ry. Co., 41 Minn. 510,

43 N. W. 391, 16 Am. St. Rep. 722 (1889).

Mississippi.—Illinois Central R. R. Co. v. Scruggs, 69 Miss. 418, 13 So. 698 (1891).

Missouri.—Rice v. Kansas Pacific Ry. Co., 63 Mo. 314 (1876).

New Jersey.—Russell v. Erie R. R. Co., 70 N. J. 808, 59 Atl. 150, 67 L. R. A. 433 (1904).

New Hampshire.—Rand v. Merchant's Dispatch Transp. Co., 59 N. H. 363 (1879).

New York.—Boswell v. Hudson River R. R. Co., 5 Bosw. 699 (1860).

North Carolina.—Smith & Melton v. North Carolina R. R. Co., 64 N. C. 235 (1870).

Ohio.—Gaines v. Union Transp. & Ins. Co., 28 Ohio St. 418 (1876).

Pennsylvania.—Allam v. Pennsylvania R. R. Co., 183 Pa. 174, 38 Atl. 709, 39 L. R. A. 535 (1897).

Tennessee.—Dillard v. Louisville & N. R. R. Co., 2 Lea, 288 (1879).

Vermont.—Davis v. Central Vt. R. R. Co., 66 Vt. 290, 29 Atl. 313 (1893).

Wisconsin.—Boorman v. American Express Co., 21 Wis. 152 (1866).

is conceded that a contract which goes no further than this is not against public policy. As the carrier is still held liable for any negligence that may be found in him, it is enough. A contract which only relieves from liability a carrier who has exercised the utmost human foresight certainly cannot be said really to tend in any way to impair that efficiency which is so requisite in a public service. If there ever was any reason for the earlier law, making the carrier liable when he was not blameworthy, the necessities for any such law ceased before it had really become law. According to modern notions of responsibility, there is almost never reason enough to make a party to whom no fault can be attributed liable for a loss. Certainly there is no policy in favor of such responsibility strong enough to declare against public policy a contract limiting liability to blameworthy conduct.[1]

§ 1008. Statutory regulation of such contracts.

In several jurisdictions there are statutes forbidding common carriers to reduce their common law liability by contract in certain respects.[2] Such statutes are constitutional so far as their being due process of law is concerned.[3] They are not generally construed beyond their normal meaning to apply to limitation of liability to a stated valuation.[4] Very properly they are held not ap-

[1] See particularly the general language in Railroad Co. v. Lockwood, 17 Wall. 357, 21 L. ed. 627 (1873).

[2] *Texas.*—Houston & T. C. R. R. Co. v. Burke, 55 Tex. 323, 40 Am. Rep. 808 (1881).

Virginia.—Chesapeake & O. Ry. Co. v. Beasley, 104 Va. 788, 52 S. E. 566, 3 L. R. A. 183 (N. S.) (1906).

[3] *United States.*—Atlantic C. L. R. R. Co. v. Riverside Mills, 31 Sup.

Ct. 164 (1911). (The provision of § 20 of the Interstate Commerce Act of February 4, 1887, as amended by the Hepburn Act of June 29, 1906, c. 3591, § 7, held constitutional.)

Kentucky.—Western Union Tel. Co. v. Eubank, 100 Ky. 591, 66 Am. St. Rep. 361 (1897).

[4] *California.*—Donlon v. Southern Pacific Co., 151 Cal. 763, 91 Pac. 603, 11 L. R. A. (N. S.) 911 (1907).

plicable to limitation of liability in matters beyond the true extent of the public profession, such as limitation of liability as carrier to the time during which goods are upon its own line,[1] and limitation of liability in operating private side tracks[2] erected by permission upon its right of way. But the reasonableness of the particular contract will not take it out of the application of the statute.[3] And such statutes have been held to render invalid an agreement that the shipper shall feed, water and attend to stock shipped.[4]

§ 1009. Construction of the contract.

The limitation of the carrier's exceptional liability is, however, as will be seen presently, the sole limitation which, by general agreement among the authorities, the carrier may make without danger to the public interests. That limitation of the carrier's liability for negligence is always attended by some danger to the public interests, is apparently recognized by all the authorities in the general rule of strict construction for the exempting clauses.[5] At all events, it is generally agreed that a clause exempting a carrier generally from all liability will never be construed as covering exemption from liability for negligence. Even in such a jurisdiction as New York where an explicit contract exempting from liability for negligence has repeatedly been held not to be against public policy, this rule of construction has thus been stated: "A common carrier is subject to two distinct classes of liabilities—one

Texas.—Missouri Pacific Ry. Co. v. Sherwood, 84 Tex. 125, 19 S. W. 455, 17 L. R. A. 643 (1892).

[1] Barnes v. Long Island Ry. Co., 100 N. Y. Supp. 593, 115 App. Div. 44 (1906).

[2] Griswold v. Illinois Central Ry. Co., 90 Iowa, 265, 57 N. W. 843, 24 L. R. A. 647 (1894).

[3] Pacific Express Co. v. Hertzberg, 17 Tex. Civ. App. 100, 42 S. W. 795 (1897).

[4] Cincinnati, N. O. & T. P. Ry. Co. v. Sanders & Russell, 118 Ky. 115, 80 S. W. 488 (1904).

[5] See generally Erie Ry. Co. v. Lockwood, 28 Ohio St. 358 (1876).

where he is liable as an insurer without fault on his part; the other, as an ordinary bailee for hire, when he is liable for default in not exercising proper care and diligence; or, in other words, for negligence. General words from whatever cause arising may well be satisfied by limiting them to such extraordinary liabilities as carriers are under without fault or negligence on their part. When general words may operate without including the negligence of the carrier or his servants, it will not be presumed that it was intended to include it." [1]

§ 1010. Conflict of laws.

It is said in most jurisdictions that the validity of a contract limiting liability should be governed by the law of the place where the contract for the shipment was made.[2] But in many other jurisdictions it is insisted that the law of the place where performance is going on when the damage is caused should govern.[3] In these latter juris-

---

[1] Quoted from Mynard v. Syracuse, B. & N. Y. R. R. Co., 71 N. Y. 180, 27 Am. Rep. 28 (1877).

[2] *United States.*—Liverpool & G. W. Steam Co. v. Phœnix Ins. Co., 129 U. S. 397, 32 L. ed. 788, 9 S. Ct. 469 (1889).

California.—Palmer v. Atchison, T. & S. F. R. R. Co., 101 Cal. 187, 35 Pac. 630 (1894).

Connecticut.—Camp v. Hartford & N. Y. Steamboat Co., 43 Conn. 333 (1876).

Illinois.—Illinois Central R. R. Co. v. Beebe, 174 Ill. 13, 50 N. E. 1019, 43 L. R. A. 210, 66 Am. St. Rep. 253 (1898).

Massachusetts.—Brockway v. American Express Co., 168 Mass. 257, 47 N. E. 87 (1897).

Minnesota.—Powers Mercantile Co. v. Wells-Fargo & Co., 93 Minn. 143, 100 N. W. 735 (1904).

Mississippi.—Shaw v. Postal Telegraph & C. Co., 79 Miss. 670, 31 So. 222, 56 L. R. A. 486, 89 Am. St. Rep. 666 (1901).

Missouri.—Otis Co. v. Missouri Pacific Ry. Co., 112 Mo. 622, 20 S. W. 676 (1892).

New York.—Valk v. Erie R. R. Co., 130 N. Y. App. Div. 446, 114 N. Y. Supp. 964 (1909).

Oklahoma.—Western Union Telegraph Co. v. Pratt, 18 Okla. 274, 89 Pac. 237 (1907).

Texas.—Western Union Telegraph Co. v. Cooper, 29 Tex. Civ. App. 591, 69 S. W. 427 (1902).

[3] *Georgia.*—Carter v. Southern Ry. Co., 3 Ga. App. 34 (1907).

New Hampshire.—Gray v. Jack-

dictions theoretically the law of the place where the cause
of action arose will govern the rights of the parties, including the effect in the tort action of the contract limiting
liability.   But there is the practical difficulty in very
many cases of interstate carriage that the transit involves
crossing several States; and in despair in this situation
some of these latter jurisdictions revert to the law of the
place of contract where the initial carriage was begun.[1]
But a contract limiting the liability of the carrier, though
valid where made, is sometimes refused enforcement in
other States as against their public policy.[2]   And an
agreement contained in the contract of carriage to the effect that the contract is to be governed by the law of some
other State will not avail to make valid a limitation of
liability against the public policy of the state in which the
contract is made.[3]   It is generally held that, in the absence
of evidence, the law of any other State will be presumed
to be the same as the law of the forum.[4]

Topic C. Stipulations Against Liability for Negligence

§ 1011. Such stipulation inconsistent with public duty.

By the great weight of authority a contract in any
public service that the patron will not hold the company

son, 51 N. H. 9, 12 Am. Rep. 1
(1871).

Ohio.—Pittsburg, C., C. & St. L.
Ry. Co. v. Sheppard, 56 Ohio St.
68, 46 N. E. 61, 60 Am. St. Rep.
732 (1897).

Pennsylvania.—Hughes v. Penn-
sylvania R. R. Co., 202 Pa. 222, 51
Atl. 990, 63 L. R. A. 513, 97 Am. St.
Rep. 713, aff'd in 191 U. S. 477, 48
L. ed. 268 (1902).

[1] *Iowa.*—Hudson & Co. v. Northern Pacific R. R. Co., 92 Iowa, 231,

60 N. W. 608, 54 Am. St. Rep. 550
(1894).

South Dakota.—Mener v. Chicago, M. & St. P. Ry. Co., 5 S. D.
568, 59 N. W. 945, 25 L. R. A. 81,
49 Am. St. Rep. 898 (1894).

[2] Chicago, B. & Q. Ry. Co. v.
Gardiner, 51 Neb. 70, 70 N. W. 508
(1897).

[3] The New England, 110 Fed. 415
(1901).

[4] Pierce v. Southern Pacific Co.,
120 Cal. 156, 52 Pac. 302, 40 L. R.
A. 350 (1898).

liable for loss or damage caused by its negligence or that
of its servants is held against public policy.[1]   The real

[1] *United States.*—Bank of Kentucky v. Adams Express Co., 93 U. S. 174, 23 L. ed. 872 (1876).

Alabama.—South & North Alabama R. R. Co. v. Henlein, 52 Ala. 606, 23 Am. Rep. 578 (1875).

Arkansas.—St. Louis, I. M. & So. Ry. Co. v. Jones, 93 Ark. 537, 125 S. W. 1025 (1910).

Connecticut.—Welch v. Boston & A. R. R. Co., 41 Conn. 333 (1874).

Colorado.—Merchants' Dispatch & Tr. Co. v. Cornforth, 3 Colo. 280, 25 Am. Rep. 757 (1877).

Dakota.—Hartwell v. Northern Pacific Exp. Co., 5 Dak. 463, 41 N. W. 732 (1889).

Delaware.—Flinn v. Philadelphia, W. & B. R. R. Co., 1 Houst. 469 (1857).

Georgia.—Central of Ga. Ry. Co. v. Hall, 124 Ga. 322, 52 S. E. 679, 4 L. R. A. (N. S.) 898, 110 Am. St. Rep. 170 (1905).

Illinois.—Illinois Central R. R. Co. v. Beebe, 174 Ill. 13, 50 N. E. 1019, 43 L. R. A. 210, 66 Am. St. Rep. 253 (1898).

Indiana.—Pittsburg, C., C. & St. L. Ry. Co. v. Higgs, 165 Ind. 694, 76 N. E. 299, 4 L. R. A. (N. S.) 1081 (1905).

Iowa.—Rose v. Des Moines Valley Ry. Co., 39 Iowa, 246 (1874).

Louisiana.—Randall v. New Orleans & N. E. R. R. Co., 45 La. Ann. 778, 13 So. 166 (1893).

Maine.—Sager v. Portsmouth, S. & B. E. R. R. Co., 31 Me. 228, 50 Am. Dec. 659 (1850).

Maryland.—Baltimore & O. R. R. Co. v. Brady, 32 Md. 333 (1869).

Massachusetts.—Graves v. Lake Shore & M. S. R. R. Co., 137 Mass. 33, 50 Am. Rep. 282 (1884).

Minnesota.—Starr v. Gt. Northern Ry. Co., 67 Minn. 18, 69 N. W. 632 (1896).

Michigan.—Hawkins v. Great Western R. R. Co., 17 Mich. 57, 97 Am. Dec. 179 (1868).

Mississippi.—Southern Exp. Co. v. Moon, 39 Miss. 822 (1863).

Missouri.—Jones v. St. Louis S. W. Ry. Co., 125 Mo. 666, 28 S. W. 883, 26 L. R. A. 718, 46 Am. St. Rep. 514 (1894).

Nebraska. — Pacific Telegraph Co. v. Underwood, 37 Neb. 315, 55 N. W. 1057, 40 Am. St. Rep. 490 (1893).

New Jersey.—Ashmore v. Pennsylvania S. T. & Tr. Co., 4 Dutch (N. J.), 180 (1860).

New Hampshire.—Durgin v. American Express Co., 66 N.' H. 277, 20 Atl. 328, 9 L.R.A. 453 (1890).

North Carolina.—Parker v. Atlantic Coast Line Ry. Co., 133 N. C. 335, 45 S. E. 658, 63 L. R. A. 827 (1903). McBee v. Carolina Central Ry. Co., 89 N. C. 311 (1883).

Ohio.—Pittsburg, C., C. & St. L. Ry. Co. v. Sheppard, 56 Ohio St. 68, 46 N. E. 61, 60 Am. Rep. 732 (1897).

Oklahoma.—Missouri, K. & T. Ry. Co. v. Davis, 24 Okla. 677, 104 Pac. 34, 24 L. R. A. (N. S.) 866 (1909).

Oregon.—Richmond v. Southern Pacific Co., 41 Oreg. 54, 67 Pac. 947, 57 L. R. A. 616, 93 Am. St. Rep. 694 (1902).

reason for this seems to be that if such contracts were permitted there would be an inevitable deterioration in the public service.   Indeed, that the invalidity of such exemptions is due to the character of the service is shown by the fact that when the matter under contract does not directly pertain to the public service as such, the contract is held valid.   As the United States Supreme Court said on the general issue in Railroad v. Lockwood [1]—"The proposition to allow a public carrier to abandon altogether his obligations to the public, and to stipulate for exemptions that are unreasonable and improper, amounting to an abdication of the essential duties of his employment, would never have been entertained by the sages of the law."

§ 1012. Authorities permitting such limitation.

However, there are a few jurisdictions where such limitation is permitted.[2]   Other jurisdictions permit such a limitation of liability for ordinary but not for gross negligence.[3]   Other cases permit limitation of liability for any

Pennsylvania.—Willock v. Pennsylvania R. R. Co., 166 Pa. St. 184, 45 Am. St. Rep. 674 (1895).

South Carolina.—Gilliland & G. v. Southern Ry. Co., 85 S. C. 26, 67 S. E. 20, 27 L. R. A. 1106 (1910).

Texas.—Harris v. Howe, 74 Tex. 534, 12 S. W. 224, 5 L. R. A. 777, 15 Am. St. Rep. 862 (1889).

Utah.—McIntosh v. Oregon Ry. & Nav. Co., 17 Idaho, 100, 105 Pac. 66 (1909).

Vermont.—Mann & W. v. Birchard & P., 40 Vt. 326 (1867).

Virginia.—Virginia & T. R. R. Co. v. Sayers, 26 Gratt. 328 (1875).

West Virginia.—Maslin v. Baltimore & O. R. R. Co., 14 W. Va. 180, 35 Am. Rep. 748, (1878).

Washington.—Muldoon v. Seattle City Ry. Co., 7 Wash. 528, 35 Pac. 422, 38 Am. St. Rep. 901 (1893).

Wisconsin.—Davis v. Chicago, M. & St. P. Ry. Co., 93 Wis. 470, 67 N. W. 16, 1132, 33 L. R. A. 654, 57 Am. St. Rep. 935 (1896).

[1] 17 Wall. 357, 21 L. ed. 627 (1873).

[2] *New York.*—Cragin v. New York Central R. R. Co., 51 N. Y. 61, 10 Am. Rep. 559 (1872).

West Virginia.—Baltimore & O. R. R. Co. v. Rathbone, 1 W. Va. 87, 88 Am. Dec. 664 (1865), overruled by Maslin v. Baltimore & O. R. R. Co., 14 W. Va. 180, 35 Am. Rep. 748 (1878).

[3] *District of Columbia.*—Galt v.

negligence of servants but not that directly attributable to the carrier himself.[1] It should be pointed out once more that even in these jurisdiction a general clause exempting liability will not cover losses due to negligence, unless *ipsissimis verbis* included in the limitation.[2] The argument in favor of permitting such limitations is that parties should be free to contract as they please. But the overwhelming weight of authority against permitting such limitation is proof positive of the public policy against it.

§ 1013. Such stipulations invalid in other services.

From the authorities already discussed the generalization is now justifiable in regard to all public services, that a contract got from a patron by one engaged in public service, exempting the proprietor from liability for injuries caused by negligence in the performance of the service, will be of no avail. Upon this general principle a Texas [3] court declared void a provision in a special contract with a water taker that he would not hold the city liable for its negligence in supplying water. Likewise a Colorado [4] court held recently that a contract between an electric lighting company and its patron, stipulating that it should not in any event be liable for damage to person or property

Adams Express Co., MacA. & M. 124, 48 Am. Rep. 742 (1879).

Georgia.—Cooper v. Raleigh & G. R. R. Co., 110 Ga. 659, 36 S. E. 240 (1900).

Illinois.—Wabash Ry. Co. v. Brown, 152 Ill. 484, 39 N. E. 273 (1894).

Kansas.—Kallman v. United States Express Co., 3 Kan. 205 (1865).

[1] *Michigan.*—McMillan v. Michigan S. & N. I. R. R. Co., 16 Mich. 79, 93 Am. Dec. 208 (1867).

England.—Shaw v. Gt. Western Ry. Co. (1894), 1 Q. B. 373 (1893).

[2] *New York.*—Mynard v. Syracuse & B. & N. Y. R. R. Co., 71 N. Y. 180, 27 Am. Rep. 28 (1877).

Ohio.—Erie R. R. Co. v. Lockwood, 28 Ohio St. 358 (1876).

[3] Dittmar v. New Braunfels, 20 Tex. Civ. App. 293, 48 S. W. 114 (1899).

[4] Denver Consolidated Electric Co. v. Lawrence, 31 Colo. 301, 73 Pac. 39 (1903).

arising or resulting from the use of light, was an attempt to relieve the company of its obligation to perform properly its public duty and was consequently void as against public policy.   Similarly an Indiana court [1] has held that a stipulation by a telephone company that it would not be liable for messages delivered would not protect it against a suit for default in this regard, if this service were shown to be part of its regular course of business.   And further, a New York court [2] has held a gas company liable for an explosion caused by its imperfectly closing a supply pipe leading into its customer's premises, notwithstanding a stipulation in the original application to the company exempting the company from all damages caused by explosion.

§ 1014. Difficulties in the telegraph cases.

The telegraph cases generally profess the same principles.   Thus by the overwhelming weight of authority a telegraph company cannot by a stipulation exempt itself from liability for negligence in handling a message,[3] al-

[1] Central Union Telephone Co. v. Swoveland, 14 Ind. App. 341, 42 N. E. 1035 (1895).

[2] Bastian v. Keystone Gas Co., 27 App. Div. 584, 50 N. Y. Supp. 537 (1898).

[3] *United States.* — Abraham v. Western Union Tel. Co., 23 Fed. 315 (1885).

Alabama.—Western Union Telegraph Co. v. Henderson, 89 Ala. 510, 7 So. 419, 18 Am. St. Rep. 148 (1889).

Arkansas.—Western Union Telegraph Co. v. Cobbs, 47 Ark. 344, 1 S. W. 558, 58 Am. Rep. 756 (1880).

Colorado.—Western Union Telegraph Co. v. Graham, 1 Colo. 230, 9 Am. Rep. 136 (1871).

Georgia.—Western Union Telegraph Co. v. Blanchard, 68 Ga. 299, 45 Am. Rep. 480 (1882).

Illinois.—Western Union Telegraph Co. v. Tyler, 74 Ill. 168, 24 Am. Rep. 279 (1874).

Indiana.—Western Union Telegraph Co. v. Jones, 95 Ind. 228, 48 Am. Rep. 713 (1883).

Iowa.—Garrett v. Western Union Tel. Co., 83 Iowa, 257, 49 N. W. 88 (1891).

Kansas.—Russell v. Western Union Telegraph Co., 57 Kan. 230, 45 Pac. 598 (1906).

Kentucky.—Western Union Telegraph Co. v. Eubanks & R., 100 Ky. 591, 38 S. W. 1068, 36 L. R. A. 711, 66 Am. St. Rep. 361 (1897).

though there are cases to the contrary.¹ But as to errors in the transmission of unrepeated messages, although many cases hold that they cannot stipulate against liability for negligence,² there are probably more which held that they may.³ These cases may perhaps be explained

Maine.—Ayer v. Western Union Telegraph Co., 79 Me. 493, 10 Atl. 495, 1 Am. St. Rep. 353 (1887).

Massachusetts.—Ellis v. American Telegraph Co., 13 Allen, 226 (1866).

Nebraska.—Pacific Telegraph Co. v. Underwood, 37 Neb. 315, 55 N. W. 1057, 40 Am. St. Rep. 490 (1893).

North Carolina.—Thompson v. Western Union Telegraph Co., 107 N. C. 449, 12 S. E. 427 (1890).

Ohio.—Telegraph Co. v. Griswold, 37 Ohio St. 301, 41 Am. Rep. 500 (1881).

Pennsylvania.—Western Union Telegraph Co. v. Stevenson, 128 Pa. St. 442, 18 Atl. 441, 5 L. R. A. 515, 15 Am. St. Rep. 687 (1889).

Tennessee.—Pepper v. Telegraph Co., 87 Tenn. 554, 11 S. W. 783, 4 L. R. A. 660, 10 Am. St. Rep. 699 (1889).

Texas.—Mitchell v. Western Union Tel. Co., 12 Tex. Civ. App. 262 (1896).

Vermont.—Gillis v. Western Union Tel. Co., 61 Vt. 461, 15 Am. St. Rep. 917 (1889).

West Virginia.—Beatty Lumber Co. v. Western Union Telegraph Co., 52 W. Va. 410, 44 S. E. 309 (1903).

¹ *Michigan.*—Birkett v. Western Union Tel. Co., 103 Mich. 361, 61 N. W. 645, 33 L. R. A. 404, 50 Am. St. Rep. 374 (1894).

New York.—Dixon v. Western

Union Tel. Co., 3 App. Div. 60. 38 N. Y. Supp. 1056 (1896).

² *Alabama.*—Western Union Telegraph Co. v. Chamblee, 122 Ala. 428, 25 So. 232, 82 Am. St. Rep. 89 (1898).

Illinois.—Tyler v. Western Union Telegraph Co., 60 Ill. 421, 14 Am. Rep. 38, 74 Ill. 168 (1871).

Kansas.—Western Union Telegraph Co. v. Crall, 38 Kan. 679, 17 Pac. 309, 5 Am. St. Rep. 795 (1888).

Maine.—Ayer v. Western Union Telegraph Co., 79 Me. 493, 10 Atl. 495, 1 Am. St. Rep. 353 (1887).

Missouri.—Reed v. Western Union Telegraph Co., 135 Mo. 661, 37 S. W. 904 (1896).

North Carolina.—Brown v. Postal Telegraph Co., 111 N. C. 187, 16 S. E. 179, 17 L. R. A. 648, 32 Am. St. Rep. 793 (1892).

Ohio.—Telegraph Co. v. Griswold, 37 Ohio St. 301, 41 Am. Rep. 500 (1881).

³ *United States.*—Primrose v. Western Union Tel. Co., 154 U. S. 1, 38 L. ed. 883, 14 Sup. Ct. 1098 (1894).

California.—Coit v. Western Union Tel. Co., 130 Cal. 657, 63 Pac. 83, 53 L. R. A. 678, 80 Am. St. Rep. 153 (1900).

Florida.—Western Union Telegraph Co. v. Milton, 53 Fla. 484, 43 So. 495, 11 L. R. A. (N. S.) 560, 125 Am. St. Rep. 1077 (1907).

Kentucky.—Camp v. Western

by saying (what is not the fact in the business) that the repeated message is the regular service in which liability cannot be limited and the unrepeated message is special service in the performance of which the company may make its own terms. It is only upon some such assumption as this that certain classes of telegraph cases can be explained. Only by conceiving that the service which is being rendered is beyond obligation can cases be supported which hold that a telegraph company can stipulate against liability for negligence of boys, sent for messages from the office[1]. And only in this way can the cases be explained which permit a telegraph company to limit to a nominal sum the damages recoverable for negligence in transmitting night messages.[2]

§ 1015. Services outside of the profession.

But these restrictions upon the limitation of liability do not apply to the case where the service which is being rendered cannot be demanded as a common law right. Such service being without the public obligation is outside the public policy. Accordingly, common carriers of passengers may contract against liability for the negligence of themselves or their servants as regards mail

Union Telegraph Co., 1 Met. (Ky.) 164, 71 Am. Dec. 461 (1858).

Maryland.—United States Tel. Co. v. Gildersleeve, 29 Md. 232, 96 Am. Dec. 519 (1868).

Michigan.—Western Union Telegraph Co. v. Carew, 15 Mich. 525 (1867).

New York.—Halsted v. Postal Telegraph-Cable Co., 193 N. Y. 295, 85 N. E. 1078, 19 L. R. A. (N. S.) 1021, 127 Am. St. Rep. 952 (1908).

Nevada.—Barnes v. Western Union Telegraph Co., 24 Nev. 125, 50 Pac. 438, 77 Am. St. Rep. 791 (1897).

Pennsylvania.—Western Union Telegraph Co. v. Stevenson, 128 Pa. 442, 18 Atl. 441, 5 L. R. A. 515, 15 Am. St. Rep. 687 (1889).

England.—McAndrew v. Electric Telegraph Co., 17 C. B. 3 (1855).

Canada.—Baxter v. Dominion Telegraph Co., 37 U. C. Q. B. 470 (1875).

[1] See Stamey v. Western Union Telegraph Co., 92 Ga. 613, 18 S. E. 1008, 44 Am. St. Rep. 95 (1893).

[2] See Aiken v. Western Union Telegraph Co., 5 S. C. 358 (1874).

clerks,[1] express messengers,[2] car employés,[3] or train boys.[4] Carriers of goods may make similar stipulations. A railroad may stipulate against liability for negligence in carrying express matter for express companies,[5] against liability while hauling circus trains,[6] against liability for cotton while in a compress,[7] or for goods on private sidings.[8]

§ 1016. Services in course of business.

On the other hand where any public duty may really be said to be involved, such clauses exempting the public servant from liability for negligence cannot stand. The citation of some recent cases will serve to bring out this

[1] See:
United States.—Baltimore & O. S. W. R. R. Co. v. Voigt, 176 U. S. 498, 44 L. ed. 560, 20 Sup. Ct. 385 (1899).
Indiana.—Louisville, N. A. & C. Ry. Co. v. Keefer, 146 Ind. 21, 44 N. E. 796, 38 L. R. A. 93, 58 Am. St. Rep. 348 (1896).
See generally § 777, *supra*.
[2] See:
Illinois.—Blank v. Illinois Central R. R. Co., 182 Ill. 332, 55 N. E. 332 (1899).
New Jersey.—Dodd v. Central R. R. of N. J. (N. J. L.), 76 Atl. 544 (1910).
See generally § 778, *supra*.
[3] *Illinois.*—Chicago, R. I. & P. Ry. Co. v. Hamler, 215 Ill. 525, 74 N. E. 705, 1 L. R. A. (N. S.) 674, 106 Am. St. Rep. 187 (1905).
Indiana.—Russell v. Pittsburg, C., C. & St. L. Ry. Co., 157 Ind. 305, 61 N. E. 678, 87 Am. St. Rep. 214 (1901).
See generally § 779, *supra*.
[4] See:
Connecticut. — Griswold, Admr., v. New York & N. E. R. R. Co., 53

Conn. 371, 4 Atl. 261, 55 Am. Rep. 115 (1885).
Louisiana.—Higgins v. New Orleans, M. & C. R. R. Co., 28 La. Ann. 133 (1876).
See generally § 782, *supra*.
[5] *Indiana.*—Pittsburg, C., C. & St. L. Ry. Co. v. Mahoney, 148 Ind. 196, 46 N. E. 917, 40 L. R. A. 101 62 Am. St. Rep. 503 (1897).
Texas.—Trinity Val. Ry. Co. v. Stewart (Tex. Civ. App.), 62 S. W. 1085 (1901).
[6] See:
Michigan.—Coup v. Wabash, St. L. & P. Ry. Co., 56 Mich. 111, 22 N. W. 215, 56 Am. Rep. 374 (1885).
Pennsylvania.—Forepaugh v. Delaware, L. & W. R. R. Co., 128 Pa. St. 217, 18 Atl. 503, 15 Am. St. Rep. 762, 5 L. R. A. 508 (1889).
Discussed in § 755, *supra*.
[7] See Deming v. Merchants' Cotton-Press & Storage Co., 90 Tenn. 306, 17 S. W. 89, 13 L. R. A. 518 (1891).
[8] Mann v. Pere Marquette Ry. Co., 135 Mich. 210, 97 N. W. 721 (1903).
See generally § 404, *supra*.

distinction.   In one it was held that shippers of cattle must not be asked to contract away the protection which the law gives them.[1]   In the other the same thing was held in regard to employés of a milk contractor.[2]   Even the employés of the carrier itself are to be regarded as passengers when riding as passengers travel.[3]   And wherever a passenger is being carried under such circumstances that there can be seen to be compensation in the transaction he cannot, even in view of the lower rate he accepts, be allowed to sign away his rights.[4]

§ 1017. Arrangements with connecting services.

As has been seen the further transportation of goods beyond its own route is service outside of the profession of a common carrier.   And it is generally agreed that the carrier may, if it participates in connecting carriage, make its terms with the shipper with regard to its liability beyond its own route.   Stipulations against liability for damage to goods, however caused, while in the custody of an independent connecting carrier are, therefore, generally upheld.[5]   In this case of connecting carriage [6] a limitation

[1] See Illinois Central R. R. Co. v. Anderson, 184 Ill. 294, 56 N. E. 331 (1900).
  Discussed in § 780, *supra*.

[2] See Baker v. Boston & Maine R. R. Co., 74 N. H. 100, 65 Atl. 386 (1906).
  Discussed in § 781, *supra*.

[3] See:
  Massachusetts.—Doyle v. Fitchburg R. R. Co., 162 Mass. 66, 37 N. E. 770, 25 L. R. A. 157, 44 Am. St. Rep. 335 (1894).
  Pennsylvania.—McNulty v. Pennsylvania R. R. Co., 182 Pa. St. 479,

38 Atl. 524, 38 L. R. A. 576, 61 Am. St. Rep. 721 (1897).
  See generally §§ 783, 784, *supra*.

[4] See:
  United States.—Grand Trunk Ry. Co. v. Stevens, 95 U. S. 655, 24 L. ed. 535 (1877).
  Indiana.—Pittsburg, C., C. & St. L. Ry. Co. v. Higgs, 165 Ind. 694, 76 N. E. 299, 4 L. R. A. (N. S.) 1081 (1905).
  See generally § 785, *supra*, § 970, *infra*.

[5] *United States.*—St. John v. Southern Express Co., 1 Woods, 612 (1871).

[6] *Georgia.*—Mosher v. Southern Express Co., 38 Ga. 37 (1868).
  Missouri.—Marshall & A. v.

Kansas City, Ft. S. & M. Ry. Co., 74 Mo. App. 81 (1898).
  Tennessee.—Merchants' Dispatch

against liability as an insurer and the like, agreed upon between the shipper and the first of a series of carriers, will inure to the benefit of a succeeding carrier, as the first carrier may be held to have negotiated the contract in behalf of the succeeding carrier.[1] But where the original carrier undertakes the whole carriage, although such limitation of liability will protect the original carrier from suit by the shipper for damage to the goods without negligence,[2] it is difficult to see how the subordinate carrier will be covered by it.

Connecticut.—Mears v. New York, N. H. & H. Ry. Co., 75 Conn. 171, 52 Atl. 610, 56 L. R. A. 884, 96 Am. St. Rep. 192 (1902).

Georgia.—East Tennessee & Georgia R. R. Co. v. Montgomery, 44 Ga. 278 (1871).

Indiana.—United States Exp. Co. v. Rush, 24 Ind. 403 (1865).

Iowa.—Peterson v. Chicago, R. I. & P. Ry. Co. (Iowa), 45 N. W. 573 (1890).

Kansas.—Berg v. The Atchison, T. & S. F. R. R. Co., 30 Kan. 561 (1883).

Maine.—Bacon v. Casco Bay Steamboat Co., 90 Me. 46, 37 Atl. 328 (1897).

Massachusetts. — Pendergast v. Adams Express Co., 101 Mass. 120 (1869).

Transp. Co. v. Block Bros., 86 Tenn. 392, 6 S. W. 881, 6 Am. St. Rep. 847 (1888).

Texas.—Gulf, C. & S. F. Ry. Co. v. Vaughn (Tex. Civ. App.), 16 S. W. 775 (1890).

[1] *United States.*—Merchants' Bk. v. New Jersey Steam Nav. Co., 6 How. (U. S.) 344, 12 L. ed. 465 (1848).

Michigan.—McEacheran v. Michigan Central R. R. Co., 101 Mich. 264, 59 N. W. 612 (1894).

Minnesota.—Wehmann v. Minneapolis, St. P. & S. S. M. Ry. Co., 58 Minn. 22, 59 N. W. 546 (1894).

New York.—Hunt v. New York, etc., R. R. Co., 1 Hilton, 228 (1856).

Ohio.—Cincinnati R. R. Co. v. Pontius, 19 Ohio St. 221, 2 Am. Rep. 391 (1869).

Pennsylvania. — Pennsylvania Central R. R. Co. v. Schwarzenberger, 45 Pa. St. 208 (1863).

South Carolina.—Hill v. Georgia, C. & N. Ry. Co., 43 S. C. 461, 21 S. E. 337 (1895).

The same principles apply to telegraph companies. Western Union Telegraph Co. v. Sorsby, 29 Tex. Civ. App. 345, 69 S. W. 122 (1902).

New York.—Maghee v. Camden & A. R. R. T. Co., 45 N. Y. 514, 6 Am. Rep. 124 (1871).

[2] *Missouri.*—Halliday v. St. Louis, K. C. & N. Ry. Co., 74 Mo. 159, 41 Am. Rep. 309 (1881).

Ohio.—Cincinnati R. R. Co. v. Pontius, 19 Ohio St. 221, 2 Am. Rep. 391 (1869).

If the contract in terms applies

§ 1018. Stipulations in gratuitous arrangements.

It is particularly plain in the case of gratuitous arrangements that a definite arrangement limiting liability will
be held valid.   If it is made plain to the recipient that the
service which he is receiving is being rendered him upon
a private basis, this is all that is really requisite; [1] but if
the proprietors choose to undertake a gratuitous service
upon the same basis as their obligatory service, they are
held liable as in their public service. [2] Gratuitous service
is not public service; and there is no general policy to
set aside whatever arrangements the parties may choose
to make, nor can it be said that in limiting their gift
the proprietors are overreaching their patrons.   The most
striking cases which come under this heading are those
where a railroad in issuing a free pass makes it plainly a
condition of its acceptance that the recipient shall agree
not to hold it liable as a public carrier for personal injuries
as it would be liable to a real passenger.   By what is
now the plain weight of authority such agreements are
respected; [3] but there is still a considerable amount of
law to the contrary. [4]

only to the initial carrier the result
may be different,—a subsequent
carrier may be held to its common
law liabilities. Bancroft & Co. v.
Merchants' Dispatch Transp. Co.,
47 Iowa, 262, 29 Am. Rep. 482
(1877).

It would seem to be improper in
theory for the shippers in a case
where the initial carrier undertakes
through carriage to be suing the
subordinate carrier, since the bail-
ment is solely to the through carrier; but when the through carrier
has a full common right against the
subordinate carrier, although the
shipper has only a limited right
against the through carrier, it would
seem that the through carrier should
enforce this right for the shipper.

[1] See generally Chapter XXII,
Topic A.

[2] See generally Chapter XXII,
Topic D.

[3] *United States.*—Northern Pacific Ry. Co. v. Adams, 192 U. S.
440, 48 L. ed. 513, 24 Sup. Ct. 408
(1904); Boering v. Chesapeake

[4] *Alabama.*—Mobile & Ohio R.
R. Co. v. Hopkins, 41 Ala. 486, 94
Am. Dec. 607 (1868).

Indiana.—Indiana C. Ry. Co. v.
Mundy, 21 Ind. 48, 83 Am. Dec.
339 (1863).

Topic D. Validity of Special Stipulations

§ 1019. Limitation of valuation generally permitted.

Stipulations limiting the recovery to an agreed amount in case of loss by negligence do not necessarily tend to defeat public service, and therefore are not held against public policy by the great majority of cases.[1] As the Mas-

Beach Ry. Co., 193 U. S. 442, 48 L. ed. 742, 24 Sup. Ct. 515 (1903).

Connecticut.—Griswold v. New York & N. E. R. R. Co., 53 Conn. 371, 4 Atl. 261, 55 Am. Rep. 115 (1885).

Illinois.—Toledo, W. & W. Ry. Co. v. Beggs, 85 Ill. 80, 28 Am. Rep. 613 (1877).

Indiana.—Payne v. Terre Haute & I. Ry. Co., 157 Ind. 616, 62 N. E. 472, 56 L. R. A. 472 (1902).

Maine.—Rogers v. Kennebec Stb. Co., 86 Me. 261, 29 Atl. 1069, 25 L. R. A. 491 (1894).

Massachusetts.—Quimby v. Boston & Maine R. R. Co., 150 Mass. 365, 23 N. E. 205, 5 L. R. A. 846 (1890).

Minnesota.—Jacobus v. St. Paul & C. Ry. Co., 20 Minn. 125, 18 Am. Rep. 360 (1873).

Missouri.—Bryan v. Missouri Pacific Ry. Co., 32 Mo. App. 228 (1888).

Pennsylvania.—Camden & A. R. R. Co. v. Bausch 7 Atl. 731 (1887).

[1] *United States.*—See Hart v. Pennsylvania R. R. Co., 112 U. S. 331, 28 L. ed. 717, 5 S. Ct. 151 (1884).

Alabama.—Southern Express Co. v. Owens, 146 Ala. 412, 41 So. 752, 8 L. R. A. (N. S.) 369, 119 Am. St. Rep. 41 (1906).

New Jersey.—Kinney v. Central R. R. Co., 34 N. J. L. 513, 3 Am. Rep. 265, 32 N. J. L. 407, 90 Am. Dec. 675 (1869).

New York.—Wells v. New York Central R. R. Co., 24 N. Y. 181 (1862).

Tennessee.—Marshall v. Nashville Ry. & Light Co., 118 Tenn. 254, 101 S. W. 419, 9 L. R. A. (N. S.) 1246 (1906).

Texas.—Gulf, C. & S. F. Ry. Co. v. McGown, 65 Tex. 640 (1886).

Washington.—Muldoon v. Seattle City Ry. Co., 7 Wash. 528, 35 Pac. 422, 22 L. R. A. 794 (1893).

Wisconsin.—Annas v. Milwaukee & N. R. R. Co., 67 Wis. 46, 30 N. W. 282, 58 Am. Rep. 848 (1886).

California.—Donlon v. Southern Pacific Co., 151 Cal. 763, 91 Pac. 603, 11 L. R. A. (N. S.) 811 (1907).

Indiana.—Rosenfield v. Peoria, D. & E. Ry. Co., 103 Ind. 121, 2 N. E. 344, 53 Am. Rep. 500 (1885).

Massachusetts.—Hill v. Boston H. T. & W. R. R. Co., 144 Mass. 284, 10 N. E. 836 (1887).

Minnesota.—Douglas Co. v. Minnesota Transfer Ry. Co., 62 Minn. 288, 64 N. W. 899, 30 L. R. A. 860 (1895).

Missouri.—H a r v e y v. Terre Haute & I. R. R. Co., 74 Mo. 538 (1881).

sachusetts court said in the leading case:[1] "The plaintiffs
cannot recover a larger sum without violating their own
agreement. Although one of the indirect effects of such a
contract is to limit the extent of the responsibility of the
carrier for the negligence of his servants, this was not the
purpose of the contract. We cannot see that any considerations of a sound public policy require that such contracts
should be held invalid, or that a person, who in such contract fixes a value upon his goods which he intrusts to the
carrier, should not be bound by his valuation."

§ 1020. Qualification of this statement.

In some jurisdictions,[2] however, the doctrine of the
preceding section is altogether denied, the thoroughgoing
doctrine being that it is always contrary to the policy of
the law that a public servant should ever be permitted
to stipulate for any exemption from liability for defaults

New Hampshire.—D u r g i n v.
American Express Co., 66 N. H.
277, 20 Atl. 328, 9 L. R. A. 453
(1890).

New York.—Zimmer v. New
York Central & H. R. R. R. Co.,
137 N. Y. 460, 33 N. E. 642 (1893).

South Carolina. — Johnstone v.
Richmond & D. Ry. Co., 39 S. C.
55, 17 S. E. 512 (1893).

Tennessee.—Louisville & N. Ry.
Co. v. Sowell, 90 Tenn. 17, 15 S.
W. 837 (1891).

West Virginia.—Zouch v. Chesapeake & O. Ry. Co., 36 W. Va. 524,
15 S. E. 185, 17 L. R. A. 116 (1892).

[1] Graves v. Lake Shore & M. S.
R. R. Co., 137 Mass. 33, 50 Am.
Rep. 282 (1884).

[2] *Colorado.*—Overland Mail &
Express Co. v. Carroll, 7 Colo. 43,
1 Pac. 682 (1883).

Illinois.—Adams Express Co. v.
Stettaners, 61 Ill. 184, 14 Am. Rep.
57 (1871).

Kentucky.—Baughman v. Louisville, E. & St. L. Ry. Co., 94 Ky.
150, 21 S. W. 757 (1893).

Mississippi.—Chicago, St. L. &
N. O. R. R. Co. v. Abels, 60 Miss.
1017 (1883).

North Carolina.—Everett v. Norfolk & S. R. R. Co., 138 N. C. 68,
50 S. E. 557, 1 L. R. A. (N. S.) 985
(1905).

Pennsylvania.—Hughes v. Pennsylvania R. R. Co., 202 Pa. St. 22,
51 Atl. 990, 63 L. R. A. 513, 97 Am.
St. Rep. 713, aff'd in 191 U. S. 477,
48 L. ed. 268, 24 Sup. Ct. Rep. 132
(1902).

Texas.—Galveston, H. & S. A.
Ry. Co. v. Ball, 80 Tex. 602, 16 S.
W. 441 (1891).

for which he is to blame. And indeed it would probably be generally agreed that where the value set is so small as to virtually relieve the company from liability, such a stipulation should be set aside as practically the same thing as a limitation of liability for negligence.[1] Where a valuation is given and there is a partial loss the authorities are divided. According to some cases the carrier must pay the actual loss with the limitation as an up limit.[2] But according to the many authorities the shipper can recover only such proportion of the agreed valuation as the partial loss bears to the actual value.[3] The decision of this issue depends ultimately upon whether the contract theory or the estoppel theory is held.

[1] See for this general doctrine the language in:

Alabama.—Southern Express Co. v. Owens, 146 Ala. 412, 41 So. 752, 8 L. R. A. (N. S.) 369, 119 Am. St. Rep. 41 (1906).

Kentucky.—Baughman v. Louisville, E. & St. L. R. R. Co., 94 Ky. 150, 21 S. W. 757 (1893).

Massachusetts.—Phillips v. Earle, 8 Pick. 182 (1829).

Minnesota.—Douglas Co. v. Minnesota Transfer Ry. Co., 62 Minn. 288, 64 N. W. 899, 30 L. R. A. 860 (1895).

North Carolina.—Everett v. Norfolk & S. R. R. Co., 138 N. C. 68, 50 S. E. 557, 1 L. R. A. (N. S.) 985 (1905).

T e n n e s s e e.—Railway Co. v. Wynn, 88 Tenn. 320, 14 S. W. 311 (1890).

[2] *C a l i f o r n i a.*—Michalitschke Bros. & Co. v. Wells, F. & Co., 118 Cal. 683, 50 Pac. 847 (1897).

Massachusetts.—Brown v. Cunard S. S. Co , 147 Mass. 58, 16 N. E. 717 (1888).

M o n t a n a.—Nelson v. Great Northern Ry. Co., 72 Pac. 642, 28 Mont. 297 (1903).

[3] *United States.*—Hart v. Pennsylvania R. R. Co., 112 U. S. 331, 28 L. ed. 717, 5 S. Ct. Rep. 151 (1884).

Indiana.—United States Express Co. v. Joyce, 36 Ind. App. 1, 69 N. E. 1015 (1905).

Minnesota.—O'Malley v. Great Northern Ry. Co., 86 Minn. 380, 90 N. W. 974 (1902).

Missouri.—Goodman v. Missouri, K. & T. Ry. Co., 71 Mo. App. 460 (1897).

Tennessee.—Starnes v. Railroad Co., 91 Tenn. 516 (1892).

Where there is a statute prohibiting the carrier from limiting his liability there is apparently a tendency to hold the restriction of liability to a certain amount in violation of the statute, with the result that the shipper may hold the carrier liable for the full amount of the loss. See Greenwald v. Weir, 111 N. Y. Supp. 235, 59 Misc. Rep. 431 (1908).

§ 1021. Liability limited to set amount.

Furthermore, where a limitation is made to a set amount fixed by the company in the special contract for shipments at a certain rate, the patron (having the alternative to ask service upon a common law basis) is bound by the stipulation, even in case of the carrier's negligence.[1]

But if the shipper in order to get the lower rate which is fixed for parcels below a certain value, fraudulently fails to declare the value of his extraordinarily costly parcel the contract is so tainted with illegality that he cannot sue the company at all. Ellison v. Adams Express Co., 245 Ill. 410, 92 N. E. 277 (1910).

[1] *United States.*—Jennings v. Smith, 106 Fed. 139, 45 C. C. A. 249 (1901).

Alabama.—Louisville & N. R. R. Co. v. Sherrod, 84 Ala. 178, 4 So. 29 (1887).

Arkansas.—St. Louis, I. M. & S. Ry. Co. v. Weakly, 50 Ark. 397, 8 S. W. 134, 7 Am. St. Rep. 104 (1887).

California.—Pierce v. Southern Pacific Co., 120 Cal. 156, 47 Pac. 874, 52 Pac. 302, 40 L. R. A. 350 (1898).

Connecticut.—Coupland v. Housatonic R. R. Co., 61 Conn. 531, 23 Atl. 870, 15 L. R. A. 534 (1892).

Georgia.—Georgia Southern & F. Ry. Co. v. Johnson, 121 Ga. 231, 48 S. E. 807 (1904).

Indiana.—Adams Express Co. v. Carnahan, 29 Ind. App. 606, 63 N. E. 245, 94 Am. St. Rep. 279 (1902).

Illinois.—Oppenheimer v. United States Express Co., 69 Ill. 62 (1873).

Kansas.—Pacific Express Co. v. Foley, 46 Kan. 457, 26 Pac. 665, 12

L. R. A. 799, 26 Am. St. Rep. 107 (1891).

Maine.—Little v. Boston & M. R. R. Co., 66 Me. 239 (1876).

Massachusetts.—Squire v. New York Central R. R. Co., 98 Mass. 239, 93 Am. Dec. 162 (1867).

Minnesota.—Alair v. Northern Pacific Ry. Co., 53 Minn. 160, 45 N. W. 1072, 19 L. R. A. 764 (1893).

Missouri.—Harvey v. Terre Haute R. R. Co., 74 Mo. 538 (1881).

New Hampshire.—Duntley v. Boston & Maine R. R. Co., 66 N. H. 263, 20 Atl. 327, 9 L. R. A. 449, 49 Am. St. Rep. 610 (1890).

Rhode Island.—Ballou v. Earle, 17 R. I. 441, 22 Atl. 1113, 14 L. R. A. 433, 33 Am. St. Rep. 881 (1891).

Tennessee.—Railway Co. v. Sowell, 90 Tenn. 17, 15 S. W. 837 (1890).

South Carolina.—Johnstone v. Richmond R. R. Co., 39 S. C. 55, 17 S. E. 512 (1892).

Virginia.—Richmond & D. Ry. Co. v. Payne, 86 Va. 481, 10 S. E. 749, 6 L. R. A. 849 (1890).

West Virginia.—Zouch v. Chesapeake & Ohio Ry. Co., 36 W. Va. 524, 15 S. E. 185, 17 L. R. A. 116 (1892).

Wisconsin.—Ullman v. Chicago & N. W. Ry. Co., 112 Wis. 150, 88 N. W. 41, 56 L. R. A. 246, 88 Am. St. Rep. 949 (1901).

In the leading case [1] the United States Supreme court put the matter upon this ground. "The subject-matter of a contract may be valued, or the damages in case of a breach may be liquidated in advance. In the present case the plaintiff accepted the valuation as 'just and reasonable.' The bill of lading did not contain a valuation of all animals at a fixed sum for each, but a graduated valuation according to the nature of the animal. It does not appear that an unreasonable price would have been charged for a higher valuation."

§ 1022. Authorities opposed to such limitation.

This doctrine, however, is not followed in many jurisdictions, [2] the general doctrine of the dissenting cases

[1] Hart v. Pennsylvania R. R. Co., 112 U. S. 331, 28 L. ed. 717, 5 S. Ct. 151 (1884).

In many of these cases the point is made that the amount set must not be outrageously disproportionate to the actual amount at risk as the carrier sees it. See particularly:

Alabama.—Southern Express Co. v. Owens, 146 Ala. 412, 41 So. 752, 8 L. R. A. (N. S.) 369, 119 Am. St. Rep. 41 (1906).

Minnesota.—Douglas Co. v. Minnesota Transfer Ry. Co., 62 Minn. 288, 64 N. W. 899, 30 L. R. A. 860 (1895).

And see the stronger language in:

Massachusetts.—Phillips v. Earle, 8 Pick. 182 (1829).

England.—Great Western Ry. Co. v. McCarthy, 12 App. Cas. 182 (1887).

[2] *United States.*—Calderon v. Atlas S. S. Co., 170 U. S. 272, 42 L. ed. 1033, 18 Sup. Ct. 588 (1898); Eells v. St. Louis, K. & N. W. Ry. Co., 52 Fed. 903 (1892).

Colorado.—Overland Mail & Express Co. v. Carroll, 7 Colo. 43, 1 Pac. 682 (1883).

District of Columbia.—Galt v. Adams Express Co., MacA. & M. 124, 48 Am. Rep. 742 (1879).

Georgia.—Georgia R. R. Co. v. Gann, 68 Ga. 350 (1882).

Illinois.—Chicago & N. W. Ry. Co. v. Chapman, 133 Ill. 96, 24 N. E. 417, 8 L. R. A. 508 (1890).

Indiana.—Adams Express Co. v. Harris, 120 Ind. 73, 21 N. E. 340, 7 L. R. A. 214, 16 Am. St. Rep. 315 (1889).

Iowa.—Solan v. Chicago, M. & St. P. Ry. Co., 95 Iowa, 260, 63 N. W. 692, 28 L. R. A. 718, 58 Am. St. Rep. 430, aff'd in 169 U. S. 133, 42 L. ed. 688, 18 Sup. Ct. Rep. 289 (1895).

Kansas.—St. Louis & S. F. Ry. Co. v. Sherlock, 59 Kan. 23, 51 Pac. 899 (1898).

Kentucky.—Orndorff v. Adams Express Co., 3 Bush (Ky.), 194, 96 Am. Dec. 207 (1867).

being that a restriction to a given amount of liability for negligence is in effect a limitation of liability in case of negligence. It is quite true that no real exception to the general liability to use due care can be permitted. But provided that the carrier is always chargeable in a substantial amount for negligence, that may well be enough to keep him sufficiently careful in the conduct of the service. The point is granted in many of the jurisdictions,[1] that they will permit the limitation to stand as an estoppel when the shipper makes a statement or agreement as to the value of the property, and thereby obtains a lower rate or causes the carrier to omit precautions which would have been taken if the true value of the property had been disclosed.

§ 1023. Stipulation for notification of loss.

In view of the general principles now established, the usual stipulation in the còntract of carriage, that notice of loss must be given to the carrier within a reasonable time, must obviously be held valid.[2] As Mr. Justice Strong

Louisiana.—Kember v. Southern Express Co., 22 La. Ann. 158, 2 Am. Rep. 719 (1870).

Minnesota.—Moulton v. St. Paul, M. & M. Ry. Co., 31 Minn. 85, 16 N. W. 497, 47 Am. Rep. 781 (1883).

[1] *Arkansas.*—Southern Express Co. v. Hill, (Ark.) 98 S. W. 371 (1906).

Mississippi.—Southern Express Co. v. Seide, 67 Miss. 609 (1890).

North Carolina.—Everett v. Railroad Co., 138 N. C. 68, 50 S. E. 557, 1 L. R. A. (N. S.) 985 (1905).

Ohio.—United States Express Co. v. Backman, 28 Ohio St. 144 (1875).

Pennsylvania.—Grogan & Merz v. Adams Express Co., 114 Pa. St. 523, 7 Atl. 134 (1886); Ruppel v.

Allegheny Ry. Co., 167 Pa. St. 166, 31 Atl. 478 (1895).

T e n n e s s e e.—Railway Co. v. Wynn, 88 Tenn. 320, 14 S. W. 311 (1890).

Texas.—St. Louis S. W. Ry. Co. of Texas v. McIntyre, 36 Tex. Civ. App. 399, 82 S. W. 346 (1904).

Virginia.—Virginia & T. R. R. Co. v. Sayers, 26 Gratt. 328 (1875).

West Virginia.—Maslin v. Baltimore & O. R. R. Co., 14 W. Va. 180, 35 Am. Rep. 748 (1878).

Wisconsin.—Ullman v. Chicago & N. W. Ry. Co., 112 Wis. 150, 88 N. W. 41, 56 L. R. A. 246, 88 Am. St. Rep. 949 (1901).

[2] *U n i t e d States.*—Metropolitan Trust Co. of New York v. Toledo,

clearly said in concluding his opinion in the leading case [1] in the United States Supreme court: "Our conclusion, then, founded upon the analogous decisions of courts, as well as upon sound reason, is that the express agreement between the parties averred in the plea was a reasonable one, and hence that it was not against the policy of the law. It purported to relieve the defendants from no part of the obligations of a common carrier. They were bound to the same diligence, fidelity, and care as they would have been required to exercise if no such agreement had been made. All that the stipulation required was that the shipper, in case the package was lost or dam-

St. L. & K. C. Ry. Co., 107 Fed. 628 (1901).

Arkansas.—St. Louis & S. F. Ry. Co. v. Hurst, 67 Ark. 407, 55 S. W. 215 (1900).

Georgia.—Southern Ry. Co. v. Adams, 115 Ga. 705, 42 S. E. 35 (1902).

Indiana.—United States Express Co. v. Harris, 51 Ind. 127 (1875).

Illinois.—Baxter v. Louisville, N., A. & C. Ry. Co., 165 Ill. 78, 45 N. E. 1003 (1897).

Kansas.—Atchison, T. & S. F. Ry. Co. v. Morris, 65 Kan. 532, 70 Pac. 651 (1902); Sprague v. Missouri Pacific Ry. Co., 34 Kan. 347, 8 Pac. 465 (1885).

Massachusetts.—S a n d f o r d v. Housatonic R. R. Co., 11 Cush. 155 (1853).

Mississippi.—Southern Express Co. v. Hunnicutt, 54 Miss. 566, 28 Am. Rep. 385 (1877).

Minnesota.—Armstrong v. Chicago, M. & St. P. Ry. Co., 53 Minn. 183, 54 N. W. 1059 (1893).

Missouri.—W a r d v. Missouri

Pacific Ry. Co., 158 Mo. 226, 58 S. W. 28 (1900).

New York.—American Grocery Co. v. Staten Island R. T. Ry. Co., 51 N. Y. Supp. 307, 23 Misc. Rep. 356 (1898).

North Dakota.—Hatch v. Minneapolis, St. P. & S. S. M. Ry. Co., 15 N. D. 490, 107 N. W. 1087 (1906).

Ohio.—P e n n s y l v a n i a Co. v. Shearer, 75 Ohio St. 249, 79 N. E. 431, 116 Am. St. Rep. 730 (1906).

Oklahoma.—St. Louis & S. F. Ry. Co. v. Phillips, 17 Okla. 264, 87 Pac. 470 (1906).

Pennsylvania.—Pavitt v. Lehigh Valley Ry. Co., 153 Pa. St. 302, 25 Atl. 1107 (1893).

Texas.—McCarty v. Gulf, C. & S. F. Ry. Co., 79 Tex. 33, 15 S. W. 164 (1890).

Utah.—Houtz v. Union Pacific R. R. Co., 33 Utah, 175, 93 Pac. 439, 17 L. R. A. (N. S.) 628 (1908).

England.—Simons v. Gt. Western Ry. Co., 18 C. B. 805 (1856), three days.

[1] Express Co. v. Caldwell, 21 Wall. 264, 22 L. ed. 556 (1874).

aged, should assert his claim in season to enable the defendants to ascertain the facts, in other words, that he should assert it within ninety days."

§ 1024. Little qualification of this doctrine.

There are but few cases directly to the contrary; and that any exist can only be explained by the inveterate prejudice against any stipulations affecting the common law liability of public carriers.[1] Where there are general statutes against limitation of liability there is conflict of authority, as will be seen in the cases subjoined, as to whether this sort of stipulation can be said to be a real limitation.[2] All the safeguards that the law throws about any modification of his common law liabilities by a common carrier apply to this stipulation as to any other qualification. A special contract must be shown;[3] but the acceptance of a shipping paper containing this clause will usually be enough.[4] The stipulation will govern in

[1] *Alabama.*—Southern Express Co. v. Caperton, 44 Ala. 101, 4 Am. Rep. 118 (1870), perhaps against all limitations thirty days held too short. But see Western Ry. of Alabama v. Little, 86 Ala. 159, 5 So. 563 (1888).

North Carolina.—Capehart v. Seaboard & Roanoke R. R. Co., 81 N. C. 438, 31 Am. Rep. 505 (1879). But see Hinkle v. Southern Ry. Co., 126 N. C. 932, 36 S. E. 348, 78 Am. St. Rep. 685 (1900).

[2] Some cases even go so far as to hold that the stipulation is valid although there is a statute in the jurisdiction generally prohibiting a common carrier to exempt itself from its liability as such.

Texas.—Gulf, C. & S. F. Ry. Co. v. Trawick, 68 Tex. 314, 4 S. W. 567, 2 Am. St. Rep. 494 (1887).

Virginia.—Liquid Carbonic Co. v. Norfolk & W. Ry. Co., 107 Va. 323, 58 S. E. 569, 13 L. R. A. (N. S.) 753 (1907).

But this is apparently against the weight of authority.

Iowa.—Grieve v. Illinois Central R. R. Co., 104 Iowa, 659, 74 N. W. 192 (1898).

Kentucky.—Brown v. Illinois Central R. R. Co., 100 Ky. 525, 38 S. W. 862 (1897).

Nebraska.—Cook v. Chicago, R. I. & P. Ry. Co., 78 Neb. 64, 110 N. W. 718 (1907).

Texas.—Missouri, K. & T. Ry. Co. v. Allen, 39 Tex. Civ. App. 236, 87 S. W. 168 (1905).

[3] Southern Express Co. v. Barnes, 36 Ga. 532 (1867).

[4] Express Co. v. Caldwell, 21 Wall. 264, 22 L. ed. 556 (1874).

cases of damage done by negligence as well as in those where the carrier is charged as an insurer; [1] but in order to cover cases of negligence the stipulation must so provide either in the very clause or by fair construction of the whole instrument. [2]

§ 1025. Similar stipulations in telegraph blanks.

There has been much litigation concerning the validity of the usual stipulation in telegraph blanks requiring the party aggrieved by the fault of the company to file his claim within a relatively short time. According to the great weight of authority such a stipulation is held valid. [3] But the qualification is sometimes made that the stipulation will not be enforced where it would be unreasonable to do so. [4] This qualification is particularly plain where

[1] Houtz v. Union Pacific R. R. Co., 33 Utah, 175, 93 Pac. 439, 17 L. R. A. (N. S.) 628 (1908).

[2] Isham v. Erie Ry. Co., 112 App. Div. 612, 98 N. Y. Supp. 609 (1906), aff'd in 191 N. Y. 547, 85 N. E. 1111 (1908).

[3] *Arkansas.*—W e s t e r n Union Telegraph Co. v. Cobbs, 47 Ark. 344, 1 S. W. 558, 58 Am. Rep. 756 (1886).

Colorado.—Western Union Telegraph Co. v. Dunfield, 11 Colo. 335, 18 Pac. 34 (1888).

Illinois.—Western Union Telegraph Co. v. Beck, 58 Ill. App. 564 (1895).

Indiana.—Western Union Telegraph Co. v. Jones, 95 Ind. 228, 48 Am. Rep. 713 (1883).

Iowa.—Albers v. Western Union Tel. Co., 98 Iowa, 51, 66 N. W. 1040 (1896).

Kansas.—Russell v. Western Union Telegraph Co., 57 Kan. 230, 45 Pac. 598 (1896).

Missouri.—Massengale v. Western Union Telegraph Co., 17 Mo. App. 257 (1885).

Nebraska.—Pacific Tel. Co. v. Underwood, 37 Neb. 315, 55 N. W. 1057, 40 Am. St. Rep. 490 (1893).

New York.—Young v. Western Union Telegraph Co., 34 N. Y. Super Ct. 390 (1872).

Pennsylvania.—Wolf v. Western Union Telegraph Co., 62 Pa. St. 83, 1 Am. Rep. 387 (1869).

Tennessee.—Western Union Telegraph Co. v. Courtney, 113 Tenn. 482, 82 S. W. 484 (1904).

Texas.—Western Union Telegraph Co. v. Rains, 63 Tex. 27 (1885).

Wisconsin.—Heimann v. Western Union Telegraph Co., 57 Wis. 562, 16 N. W. 32 (1883).

[4] *North Carolina.*—Sherrell v. Western Union Telegraph Co., 109 N. C. 527, 14 S. E. 94 (1891).

Virginia.—Western Union Telegraph Co. v. Reynolds, 77 Va. 173, 46 Am. Rep. 715 (1883).

the message never was sent, as it will then often take a considerable time for this fact to transpire.[1]   And there may be other cases where it will be so impracticable for the party aggrieved to comply with the stipulation that it would be outrageous to enforce it.[2]   There are some jurisdictions which consider this stipulation so against public policy as to be absolutely void.[3]   Moreover there are statutory provisions in some States which are held to make it impossible for a telegraph company to stipulate in any way against full common law liability for negligence.[4]   In certain jurisdictions this stipulation is held valid in the case of night messages, the idea being that such service is offered as an alternative to the regular service.[5]   It might be added that where this stipulation is respected, beginning a suit within the time limited is generally held to be a sufficient compliance with it.[6]

---

[1] *Alabama.*—Western Union Telegraph Co. v. Way, 83 Ala. 542, 118 Ind. 248, 20 N. E. 222 (1887).

Indiana.—Western Union Telegraph Co. v. Yopst, 118 Ind. 248, 20 N. E. 222, 3 L. R. A. 224 (1889).

[2] *Georgia.*—Western Union Telegraph Co. v. Hines, 96 Ga. 688, 51 Am. St. Rep. 159 (1895).

Iowa.—Wells v. Western Union Telegraph Co. (Iowa), 123 N. W. 371, 24 L. R. A. (N. S.) 1045 (1909).

[3] *United States.*—Johnston v. Western Union Telegraph Co., 33 Fed. Rep. 362 (1887).

Kentucky.—Smith v. Western Union Telegraph Co., 83 Ky. 104, 4 Am. St. Rep. 126 (1885).

Maine.—Ayer v. Western Union Telegraph Co., 79 Me. 493, 10 Atl. 495, 1 Am. St. Rep. 353 (1887).

New Mexico.—Western Union Telegraph Co. v. Longwill, 5 New Mex. 308, 21 Pac. 339 (1889).

[4] *Arkansas.*—Western Union Telegraph Co. v. Cobbs, 47 Ark. 344, 1 S. W. 558, 58 Am. Rep. 756 (1886).

Indiana.—Western Union Telegraph Co. v. McKibben, 114 Ind. 511, 14 N. E. 894 (1887).

[5] *United States.*—Jones v. Western Union Telegraph Co., 18 Fed. 717 (1883).

Minnesota.—Cole v. Western Union Telegraph Co., 33 Minn. 227, 22 N. W. 385 (1885).

[6] *Alabama.*—Western Union Telegraph Co. v. Henderson, 89 Ala. 510, 7 So. 419, 18 Am. St. Rep. 148 (1889).

North Carolina.—Sherrell v. Western Union Telegraph Co., 109 N. C. 527, 14 S. E. 94 (1891).

§ 1026. What time is reasonable.

By the accepted doctrine, reasonable time for such notice must be given. Thus sixty days [1] or thirty days [2] is usually held reasonable. On the other hand if an unreasonably short time is fixed, as that immediate complaint shall be made, the stipulation will generally be considered unreasonable. In some cases it has been decided that thirty days,[3] or even sixty days,[4] may not be enough to provide; but unless abnormal circumstances appear these

[1] *Alabama.*—Harris v. Western Union Telegraph Co., 121 Ala. 519, 25 So. 910, 77 Am. St. Rep. 70 (1898).

Arkansas.—Western Union Telegraph Co. v. Dougherty, 54 Ark. 221, 15 S. W. 468, 11 L. R. A. 102, 26 Am. St. Rep. 33 (1891).

Georgia.—Hill v. Western Union Telegraph Co., 85 Ga. 425, 11 S. E. 874, 21 Am. St. Rep. 166 (1890).

Indiana.—Western Union Telegraph Co. v. Meredith, 95 Ind. 93 (1883).

Iowa.—Albers v. Western Union Telegraph Co., 98 Iowa, 51, 66 N. W. 1040 (1896).

North Carolina.—Sherrill v. Western Union Telegraph Co., 109 N. C. 527, 14 S. E. 94 (1891).

Pennsylvania.—Wolf v. Western Union Telegraph Co., 62 Pa. St. 83, 1 Am. Rep. 387 (1869).

South Dakota.—Kirby v. Western Union Telegraph Co., 7 S. D. 623, 65 N. W. 37, 30 L. R. A. 612 (1895).

Texas.—Western Union Telegraph Co. v. Phillips (Tex. Civ. App.), 30 S. W. 494 (1893).

[2] *Colorado.*—Western Union Telegraph Co. v. Dunfield, 11 Colo. 335, 18 Pac. 34 (1888).

Minnesota.—Armstrong v. Chicago, M. & St. P. Ry. Co., 53 Minn. 183, 54 N. W. 1059 (1893).

Texas.—Western Union Telegraph Co. v. Culberson, 79 Tex. 65, 15 S. W. 219 (1890).

Virginia.—Liquid Carbonic Co. v. Norfolk & W. Ry. Co., 107 Va. 323, 58 S. E. 569, 13 L. R. A. (N. S.) 753 (1907).

[3] See:

United States.—Pacific Coast S. S. Co. v. Bancroft-Whitney Co., 94 Fed. 180, 36 C. C. A. 135 (1899).

Alabama.—Southern Express Co. v. Caperton, 44 Ala. 101, 4 Am. Rep. 118 (1870).

Arkansas.—Western Union Telegraph Co. v. Cobbs, 47 Ark. 344, 1 S. W. 558, 58 Am. Rep. 756 (1886).

North Carolina. — Capehart v. Seaboard & R. R. R. Co., 81 N. C. 438, 31 Am. Rep. 505 (1879).

[4] See further:

Kentucky.—Davis v. Western Union Telegraph Co., 107 Ky. 527, 54 S. W. 849, 92 Am. St. Rep. 371 (1900).

Nebraska.—Pacific Tel. Co. v. Underwood, 37 Neb. 315, 55 N. W. 1057, 40 Am. St. Rep. 490 (1893).

cases cannot be supported. The conflict of authority in
one class of cases deserves notice. It is a usual stipulation
for a railroad to make in the bill of lading under which
live stock is shipped, that the consignee shall make his
complaint before taking the stock away. In some cases
this is held unreasonable; and so it may seem, particularly
in the case where the effects of the injury cannot be known
for some time.[1] But other cases consider even this extreme
stipulation justified, as necessary for the protection of
the railroad; and the further clause which is usually found
that the claim must be made before the consignment is
mixed with other stock is apparently reasonable.[2] In
all the cases under this topic the reasonableness of the
stipulation is the problem.[3] The reasonableness of the
time stipulated for is determined by the usual circumstances of the case. As will be seen in the cases cited,
weight will be attached to various circumstances, such
as—the distance of the transportation contracted for,
whether the shipper is to accompany the shipment, what
time must naturally elapse before the owner will learn

[1] *United States.*—Ormsby v. Union Pacific Ry. Co., 2 MacCrary, 48
(1880).

Illinois.—Wabash R. R. Co. v.
Thomas, 222 Ill. 337, 78 N. E. 777,
7 L. R. A. (N. S.) 1041 (1906).

Ohio.—Baltimore & O. R. R. Co.
v. Hubbard, 72 Ohio St. 302, 74 N.
E. 214 (1905), five days too short to
determine injury to live stock.

Tennessee.—Smitha v. Louisville
& N. Ry. Co., 86 Tenn. 198, 6 S. W.
209 (1887).

[2] *Arkansas.*—Kansas & A. V. Ry.
Co. v. Ayres, 63 Ark. 331, 38 S. W.
515 (1897).

Illinois.—Baxter v. Louisville, N.
A. & C. Ry. Co., 165 Ill. 78, 45 N. E.
1003 (1897).

Iowa.—Hudson & Co. v. Northern Pacific Ry. Co., 92 Iowa, 231,
60 N. W. 608, 54 Am. St. Rep. 550
(1894).

Missouri.—Smith v. Chicago, R.
I. & P. Ry. Co., 112 Mo. App. 610,
87 S. W. 9 (1905).

[3] *United States.*—Express Co. v.
Caldwell, 21 Wall. 264, 22 L. ed.
556 (1874).

Illinois.—Chicago, C., C. & St.
L. Ry. Co. v. Bozarth, 91 Ill. App.
68 (1900).

Missouri.—Thompson v. Chicago
& Alton R. R. Co., 22 Mo. App. 321
(1886).

North Carolina.—Wood v. Southern Ry. Co., 118 N. C. 1056, 24 S. E.
704 (1896).

of his loss, whether the damage would make itself apparent at once, whether sufficient directions are given as to the making of the complaint, and whether a claim agent is accessible.[1]

[1] *Alabama.*—Western Ry. Co. v. Harwell, 91 Ala. 340, 8 So. 649 (1890).

Indiana.—Adams Exp. Co. v. Reagan, 29 Ind. 21, 92 Am. Dec. 332 (1867).

New York.—Ghormley v. Dinsmore, 19 Jones & S. 196 (1885).

Tennessee.—Glenn & Sons v. Southern Express Co., 86 Tenn. 594, 8 S. W. 152 (1888).

Texas.—St. Louis, A. & T. Ry. Co. v. Turner, 1 Tex. Civ. App. 625, 20 S. W. 1008 (1892).

PART VIII. TERMINATION OF SERVICE

CHAPTER XXX

END OF THE UNDERTAKING

§ 1030. When the undertaking is completed.

§ 1030. When the undertaking is completed.

As has been sufficiently shown in a former chapter, the

carrier and the innkeeper are subject to an extraordinary liability in respect to the goods intrusted to them, although strangely enough not as to the persons in their care. This extraordinary liability, which makes them practically insurers, continues, however, only so long as the public service that they have undertaken is being performed; and as will be seen presently, the obligation they are thereafter under is simply the obligation to exercise due care. As there is this great difference in the liability, the cases upon it are so numerous that even to deal with them briefly requires some space. The subject has its general interest because here is a case where the extent of the undertaking assumed in the provision of a public service is minutely measured, for the special liability attaches only so long as this public service is being performed. Aside from this particular problem there is the general problem of the proper termination of all liability by completed performance. This is to a large extent a question of the full scope of the particular undertaking, which would involve detailed description of the usual course of each particular business if it were to be treated in detail.

Topic A. How Long Service Continues

§ 1031. Interruption in transit.

The undertaking of the carrier is to transport. His special liability, therefore, should be confined to the time of transportation. It has already been sufficiently discussed when this transportation may have been said to have begun. It will be seen very soon when this transportation may be said to have been ended. And by the usual rule all that goes on between these two extremes is held to be during transit.[1] If the carrier stops the trans-

---

[1] The transit continues while the passenger is upon a transfer car. Citizens' St. R. R. Co. of Ind. v. Merl, 134 Ind. 609, 33 N. E. 1014 (1893).

By temporarily alighting from a

portation for his own convenience, from time to time, transit is still considered as continued. Even if there is an interruption in the transit which is unvoidable, the carrier is still held strictly accountable as such for loss of the goods.[1]

§ 1032. Temporary absence from an inn.

The time from which an innkeeper comes under exceptional liability for the goods of his guest has already been defined; and the time when he ceases to be under that liability will soon be fixed. Between these two times one may certainly hold the host liable for goods left in the inn, while he is absent about his business in the neighborhood. There are a variety of cases holding that a temporary absence of the guest of a considerable length does not terminate the relationship.[2] But the law is rather

crowded car to permit another passenger to conveniently get off one does not cease to be a passenger. Tompkins v. Boston Elevated Ry. Co., 201 Mass. 114, 87 N. E. 488, 20 L. R. A. (N. S.) 1063, 131 Am. St. Rep. 392 (1909).

A temporary departure by a passenger from the train for any good or reasonable cause, without intent to abandon transportation does not end the relation of carrier and passenger. Austin v. St. Louis & S. F. Ry. Co. (Mo. App.), 130 S. W. 385 (1910).

For example, if a passenger steps off at a station before reaching his destination intending to return to the train, he does not lose his rights as a passenger. Parsons v. New York Central & H. R. R. R. Co., 113 N. Y. 355, 21 N. E. 145, 10 Am. St. Rep. 450 (1889).

[1] The same law prevails if the goods are stopped in transit for any reason whether excusable or not. Fenner v. Buffalo & S. L. R. R. Co., 44 N. Y. 505, 4 Am. Rep. 709 (1871).

And so it is even if the goods are warehoused in transit. Mason v. Grand Trunk Ry. Co., 37 Upp. Can. Q. B. 163 (1875).

[2] *Colorado.*—Brown Hotel Co. v. Burckhardt, 13 Col. App. 59, 56 Pac. 188 (1899).

Iowa.—Hayes v. Turner, 23 Ia. 214 (1867).

New York.—McDonald v. Edgerton, 5 Barb. (N. Y.) 560 (1849).

Tennessee.—Whitemore v. Haroldson, 2 Lea (Tenn.), 312 (1879).

Vermont.—McDaniels v. Robinson, 26 Vt. 316, 62 Am. Dec. 574 (1854).

England.—Allen v. Smith, 12 C. B. (N. S.) 638, 31 L. J. C. P. 306, 9 Jur. (N. S.) 230, 6 L. T. 459, 10 W.

strict upon this matter, requiring that the absence must be really temporary with an intent to return known to the innkeeper within a definite and reasonable time.[1] And, of course, since the relationship continues, the liability to compensate the innkeeper must be understood to continue during the absence.

§ 1033. Transfer to connecting service.

Where the carriage involves the services of several carriers, the transit is considered to proceed without interruption. Of course, if the arrangement is found to be that the original carrier undertakes a through transit, there will be one transit, and the initial carrier will be responsible for the goods during the entire journey.[2] The

R. 646, affirmed, 9 Jur. (N. S.) 1284, 11 W. R. 440 (Eng., 1862).

[1] *Alabama.*—Glenn v. Jackson, 93 Ala. 342, 9 So. 259, 12 L. R. A. 382 (1890).

Florida.—O'Brien v. Vaill, 22 Fla. 627, 1 So. 137, 1 Am. St. Rep. 219 (1886).

Mississippi.—Miller v. Peebles, 60 Miss. 819, 45 Am. Rep. 423 (1883).

New York.—W i n t e r m u t e v. Clarke, 5 Sandf. (N. Y.) 242 (1851).

Tennessee.—Whitemore v. Haroldson, 2 Lea (Tenn.), 312 (1879).

Vermont.—McDaniels v. Robinson, 28 Vt. 387, 67 Am. Dec. 720 (1856).

[2] *United States.*—Central Trust Co. of N. Y. v. Wabash, St. L. & P. Ry. Co., 31 Fed. 247 (1887).

Alabama.—Mobile & Girard R. R. Co. v. Copeland, 63 Ala. 219 (1879).

Connecticut.—Hood v. New York & H. R. R. R. Co., 22 Conn. 1 (1852).

Georgia.—Falvey v. Georgia R. R. Co., 76 Ga. 597, 2 Am. St. Rep. 58 (1886).

Illinois.—Illinois Cent. R. R. Co. v. Frankenberg, 54 Ill. 88, 5 Am. Rep. 92 (1870).

Maine.—Skinner v. Hall, 60 Maine, 477 (1872).

Minnesota.—Leo v. St. Paul, M. & M. Ry. Co., 30 Minn. 438, 15 N. W. 872 (1883).

Mississippi.—Mobile & Ohio R. R. Co. v. Tupelo Furniture Mfg. Co., 67 Miss. 35, 7 So. 279, 19 Am. St. Rep. 262 (1889).

Nebraska.—Richardson v. Halstead, 44 Neb. 606, 62 N. W. 1077 (1895).

North Carolina.—Knott v. Raleigh & Gaston R. R. Co., 98 N. C. 73, 3 S. E. 735, 2 Am. St. Rep. 321 (1887).

Tennessee.—Louisville & Nash-

policy of the law is that some one should be liable as a common carrier from the beginning of the connecting service to its end. And in the more usual case of connecting carriage a prior carrier is not relieved of responsibility until the subsequent carrier has received the goods.[1] By the accepted law this liability of a first carrier continues until the first carrier has deposited the goods where the second carrier receives them, and given notice, as would generally be requisite, to the succeeding carrier that the goods were there awaiting his transportation,[2] together with the necessary instructions for forwarding the goods.[3] If, however, the second carrier finally refuses the goods,

ville R. R. Co. v. Campbell et al., 7 Heisk. 253 (1872).

Wisconsin.—Laughlin v. Chicago & N. Ry. Co., 28 Wis. 204, 9 Am. Rep. 493 (1871).

[1] *Alabama.*—Mount Vernon Co. v. Alabama Gt. S. R. R. Co., 92 Ala. 296, 8 So. 687 (1890).

Connecticut.—Palmer v. Chicago, B. & Q. R. R. Co., 56 Conn. 137, 13 Atl. 818 (1888).

Georgia.—Wallace v. Rosenthal, 40 Ga. 419 (1869).

Illinois.—Illinois Central R. R. Co. v. Mitchell, 68 Ill. 471, 18 Am. Rep. 564 (1873).

Michigan.—Moore v. Michigan Central R. R. Co., 3 Mich. 23 (1853).

South Carolina.—M i l l e r Bros. v. Railway Co., 33 S. C. 359 (1890).

Tennessee.—I n s u r a n c e Co. v. Railroad Co., 8 Baxt. 268 (1874).

West Virginia.—Lewis v. Chesapeake & Ohio Ry. Co., 47 W. Va. 656, 35 S. E. 908, 81 Am. St. Rep. 816 (1900).

Wisconsin.—Hooper v. Chicago & N. Ry. Co., 27 Wis. 81, 9 Am. Rep. 439 (1870).

[2] *United States.*—Myrick v. Michigan Cent. R. R. Co., 9 Biss. 44 (1879).

California.—C o l f a x Mountain Fruit Co. v. Southern Pac. Ry. Co., 118 Cal. 648, 46 Pac. 668 (1896), 50 Pac. 775, 40 L. R. A. 78 (1897).

Connecticut.—Palmer v. Chicago, B. & Q. R. R. Co., 56 Conn. 137, 13 Atl. 818 (1888).

Kentucky.—Louisville, St. L. & T. Ry. Co. v. Bourne & Embry, 16 Ky. L. Rep. 825, 29 S. W. 975 (1895).

Michigan.—Rickerson R o l l e r Mill Co. v. Grand Rapids & I. R. R. Co., 67 Mich. 110, 34 N. W. 269 (1887).

Missouri.—Dunn v. Hannibal & St. J. R. R. Co., 68 Mo. 268 (1878).

New York.—Sprague v. New York Cent. R. R. Co., 52 N. Y. 637 (1873).

[3] *Illinois.*—Michigan S. & N. I. R. R. Co. v. Day, 20 Ill. 375, 71 Am. Dec. 278 (1858).

Michigan.—Hutchings v. Ladd, 16 Mich. 493 (1868).

the first carrier has performed its duty as such. But there rests upon it in this case, as in many other cases of unexpected interruption, the duty to store [1] the goods refused and notify the consignor of the situation.[2]

§ 1034. End of innkeeper's liability as such.

After a guest pays his bill and departs, the innkeeper continues liable as such during a reasonable time for bag-

New York.—Sherman v. Hudson River R. R. Co. 64 N. Y. 254 (1876).

Ohio.—Little Miami R. R. Co. v. Washburn, 22 Ohio St. 324 (1872).

Pennsylvania. — F o r s y t h e v. Walker, 9 Pa. St. 148 (1848).

Tennessee.—R a i l r o a d Co. v. Southern Seating & Cabinet Co., 104 Tenn. 568, 58 S. W. 303, 50 L. R. A. 729 (1900).

Texas.—Fort Worth & D. C. Ry. Co. v. Masterson, 95 Tex. 262, 66 S. W. 833 (1902).

[1] *United States.*—Buston v. Pennsylvania Ry. Co., 119 Fed. 808, 56 C. C. A. 320 (1903).

Alabama.—Louisville & N. R. R. Co. v. Duncan & Orr, 137 Ala. 446, 34 So. 988 (1902).

Louisiana.—Dalzell v. Steamboat Saxon, 10 La. Ann. 280 (1855).

Maryland.—Baltimore & Ohio R. R. Co. v. Schumacher, 29 Md. 168, 96 Am. Dec. 510 (1868).

Minnesota.—Wehmann v. Minneapolis, St. P. & S. Ste. M. Ry. Co., 58 Minn. 22, 59 N. W. 546 (1894).

New York.—Rawson v. Holland, 59 N. Y. 611, 17 Am. Rep. 394 (1875).

Tennessee.—Bird v. Railroad Co., 99 Tenn. 719, 42 S. W. 451, 63 Am. St. Rep. 856 (1897).

Wisconsin.—Wood v. Milwaukee & St. P. Ry. Co., 27 Wis. 541, 9 Am. Rep. 465 (1871).

[2] *United States.*—In re Peterson, 21 Fed. 885 (1884).

Kentucky.—Louisville & N. R. R. Co. v. F. & D. Live Stock Commission Firm, 21 Ky. L. Rep. 708, 52 S. W. 972 (1899).

Maine.—Fisher v. B o s t o n & Maine R. R. Co., 99 Me. 338, 59 Atl. 532, 68 L. R. A. 390, 105 Am. St. Rep. 283 (1904).

Missouri.—Cramer v. American M. U. Express Co. & Merchants' Dispatch Co., 56 Mo. 524 (1874).

New York.—Johnson v. New York Central R. R. Co., 33 N. Y. 610, 88 Am. Dec. 416 (1865).

A stipulation in the contract that the carrier is not to be liable after the property is ready for delivery to the next carrier or to the consignee does not relieve the carrier from liability for goods withheld in transit and injured by its negligence as aforesaid. Isham v. Erie R. R. Co., 112 N. Y. App. Div. 612, 98 N. Y. Supp. 609 (1906).

A car is delivered to the connecting carrier when it is placed on its transfer track, and it is notified of that fact. McMillan v. Chicago, R. I. & O. Ry. Co. (Iowa), 124 N. W. 1069 (1910).

gage left in his charge.[1] So, after the bill had been paid
and while the guest's horse was being harnessed in order
that he might drive away, the innkeeper continued liable
as such for the safety of the horse.[2] Where a traveler
was told he could have a room only until an expected
guest who had engaged it should arrive, and on these
terms he took the room and put his goods in it, and when
the expected guest arrived the innkeeper's servants put
the goods in the corridor, where they were lost, it was held
that the innkeeper's liability continued after the goods
had been placed in the corridor.[3] And where the innkeeper undertook to deliver the baggage at a steamboat
or at a railroad station, the innkeeper's liability was held
to continue until it was so delivered.[4]

§ 1035. Termination of the carrier's liability as such.

There is irreconcilable conflict among the authorities
upon the question as to when the special liability of the
common carrier comes to its end. Upon abstract principles it should end when the transportation undertaken
may properly be said to have been completed; but there
are no less than four principal theories as to the termination of the special liability, viz.: (1) In some jurisdictions
the end of the movement of the goods is the end of their
carriage. (2) In other jurisdictions the liability of a
common carrier continues until a reasonable time for the
consignee to get the goods has expired. (3) In still other

[1] *Colorado.*—Murray v. Marshall,
9 Colo. 482, 13 Pac. 589, 59 Am.
Rep. 152 (1886).

Georgia.—Adams v. Clem, 41 Ga.
65, 5 Am. Rep. 524 (1870).

Michigan.—Baehr v. Downey,
133 Mich. 163, 94 N. W. 750 (1903).

New York.—Maxwell v. Gerard,
84 Hun, 537, 32 N. Y. Supp. 849
(1895).

[2] Seymour v. Cook, 53 Barb. 451,
35 How. Pr. (N. Y.) 180 (1868).

[3] Medewar v. Grand Hotel Co.,
2 Q. B. 11, 60 L. J. Q. B. 209, 64 L.
T. 851, 55 J. P. 614 (1891).

[4] *Georgia.*—Sasseen et al. v. Clark,
37 Ga. 242 (1867).

Maryland.—Giles v. Fauntleroy,
13 Md. 126 (1858).

jurisdictions the common carrier remains liable as such until he has given reasonable notice. (4) Some carriers must offer personal delivery before they are exonerated. These matters will be considered briefly in substantially this order in the following sections. In all jurisdictions, however, the extraordinary liability as a common carrier may at length come to an end with the carrier still in possession of the goods. And during this period of custody awaiting delivery the carrier's liability becomes that of a warehouseman, viz.: a liability for failure to use due care to protect and guard the goods according to their nature. But the carrier may in special cases by a new agreement with the owners hold the goods for them as a warehouseman. No citations are given for the matters described in this paragraph as the various aspects of the problem are sufficiently discussed with appropriate citations in the paragraphs immediately following.

§ 1036. End of transportation.

According to what would seem to be the proper test, common carriage should come to its end when the undertaking assumed has been performed. A common carrier, as such, undertakes only transportation to a certain place. When he has deposited the goods at that point on the route he has done all that he has professed, and it seems therefore that his exceptional liability as a common carrier should then terminate. The cases to this effect are sufficiently numerous to justify its acceptance; and it has, moreover, the practical advantage of a fixed rule always capable of exact application.[1] In the Massachusetts case [2]

[1] *Georgia.* — Knight v. Wrightsville & T. Ry. Co., 127 Ga. 204, 56 S. E. 363 (1906).

Illinois.—Chicago & A. R. R. Co. v. Scott, 42 Ill. 132 (1866).

Iowa.—Mohr & Smith v. Chicago

[2] Norway Plains Co. v. Boston & Maine R. R. Co., 1 Gray (Mass.), 263, 21 Am. Dec. 423 (1854).

in which this doctrine was first clearly announced Chief Justice Shaw said: "From this necessary condition of the business, and from the practice of these transportation companies to have platforms on which to place goods from the cars, in the first instance, and warehouse accommodation by which they may be securely stored, the goods of each consignment by themselves, in accessible places, ready to be delivered, the court are of opinion that the duty assumed by the railroad corporation is—and this, being known to owners of goods forwarded must, in the absence of proof to the contrary, be presumed to be assented to by them so as to constitute the implied contract between them—that they will carry the goods safely to the place of destination, and there discharge them on the platform and there and then deliver them to the consignee or party entitled to receive them, if he is there ready to take them forthwith or if the consignee is not there ready to take them, then to place them securely and keep them safely a reasonable time, ready to be delivered when called for."

& N. W. R. R. Co., 40 Ia. 579 (1875).

Massachusetts.—Norway Plains Company v. Boston & Maine R. R. Co., 1 Gray, 263, 61 Am. Dec. 423 (1854).

Michigan.—Michigan Central R. Co. v. Lentz, 32 Mich. 502 (1875).

Missouri. — Gashweiler v. Wabash St. L. & P. R. R. Co., 83 Mo. 112 (1884).

North Carolina.—Hilliard v. Wilmington & W. R. R. Co., 6 Jones' Law, 343 (1859).

Pennsylvania.—McCarthy v. New York & Erie R. R. Co., 30 Pa. St. 247 (1858).

South Carolina.—Speers & C. v. Spartanburg, U. & C. R. R. Co., 11 S. C. 158 (1878).

In some of these jurisdictions there must be some definite act of warehousing. See, for example:

Delaware.—McHenry v. Philadelphia W. & B. R. R. Co., 4 Harr. 448 (1846).

Illinois.—Chicago & R. I. R. R. Co. v. Warren, 16 Ill. 502, 63 Am. Dec. 317 (1855).

Minnesota.—Arthur et al. v. St. Paul & D. Ry. Co., 38 Minn. 94, 35 N. W. 718 (1887).

New Mexico.—MacVeagh v. Atchison, T. & S. F. Ry. Co., 3 N. Mex. 205, 5 Pac. 457 (1885).

§ 1037. Reasonable time for removal.

There are, however, a great number of cases in which the rule is stated to be that the common carrier is an insurer of the goods until the expiration of a reasonable time for the consignee to get them after the transit is completed.[1] In one of the leading cases [2] on this point in New York this law is thus succinctly summarized by Commissioner Earle: "I think we may fairly infer the following rules as to the delivery of goods at their place of destination by a railroad carrier. If the consignee is present upon the arrival of the goods, he must take them without unreasonable delay. If he is not present, but lives at or in

[1] *Alabama.*—Bowdon v. Atlantic C. L. Ry. Co., 148 Ala. 29, 41 So. 294 (1906).

Arkansas.—Kansas City, F. S. & M. Ry. Co. v. McGahey, 63 Ark. 344, 38 S. W. 659, 36 L. R. A. 781, 58 Am. St. Rep. 111 (1897).

California.—Wilson v. California Cent. Ry. Co., 94 Cal. 166, 29 Pac. 861, 17 L. R. A. 685 (1892).

Indiana.—Pennsylvania Co. v. Liveright, 14 Ind. App. 518, 41 N. E. 350 (1895).

Kansas.—Leavenworth, L. & G. R. R. Co. v. Maris, 16 Kan. 333 (1876).

Kentucky.—Jeffersonville R. R. Co. v. Cleveland, 2 Bush, 468 (1867).

Minnesota.—Derosia v. Winona & St. P. R. R. Co., 18 Minn. 133 (1872).

Mississippi.—Gulf & C. R. R. Co. v. Fuqua, 84 Miss. 490, 36 So. 349 (1904).

New Jersey.—Morris & E. R. R. Co. v. Ayres, 29 N. J. L. 393, 80 Am. Dec. 215 (1862).

New York.—Huntley v. Dows, 55 Barb. (N. Y.) 310 (1864).

Ohio.—Lake Erie & W. Ry. Co. v. Hatch, 52 Ohio St. 408, 39 N. E. 1042 (1895).

Vermont.—Blumenthal v. Brainerd et al., 38 Vt. 402, 91 Am. Dec. 349 (1866).

Washington.—Normile v. Northern Pacific Ry. Co., 36 Wash. 21, 77 Pac. 1087, 67 L. R. A. 271 (1904).

Wisconsin.—Wood v. Crocker, 18 Wis. 345, 86 Am. Dec. 773 (1864).

England.—Chapman v. Gt. Western Ry. Co., 5 Q. B. D. 278 (1880).

In some of these jurisdictions all that is required is that the consignee should have access to the goods.

Connecticut.—Graves v. Hartford & N. Y. Stb. Co., 38 Conn. 143, 9 Am. Rep. 369 (1871).

West Virginia.—Berry v. West Va. & P. R. R. Co., 44 W. Va. 538, 30 S. E. 143, 67 Am. St. Rep. 781 (1898).

[2] Fenner v. Buffalo & St. L. R. R. Co., 44 N. Y. 505, 4 Am. Rep. 709 (1871).

the immediate vicinity of the place of delivery, the carrier must notify him of the arrival of the goods, and then he has a reasonable time to take and remove them. If he is absent, unknown, or cannot be found, then the carrier can place the goods in its freight-house; and, after keeping them a reasonable time, if the consignee does not call for them, its liability as a common carrier ceases. If, after the arrival of the goods, the consignee has a reasonable opportunity to remove them, and does not, he cannot hold the carrier as an insurer. The carrier's liability thus applied and limited, I believe, will be found consonant with public policy, and sufficiently convenient and practicable."

§ 1038. Whether notification is necessary.

The third view, that reasonable notice must be given to the consignee before liability is terminated, is generally law as to carriage by sea; and, indeed, this has a real justification in the case of carriage by sea, inasmuch as the arrival of ships can never be known with any exactness, and it cannot always be told at which wharf the ship will discharge.[1] In the case of the railroad, the usual carrier

---

[1] As to notice by a shipmaster see:

United States.—The Eddy, 5 Wall. 481, 18 L. ed. 486 (1866).

Maryland.—United Fruit Co. v. New York & B. Tr. Line, 104 Md. 567, 65 Atl. 415, 8 L. R. A. (N. S.) 240 (1906).

Missouri.—Steamboat Keystone v. Moies, 28 Mo. 243, 75 Am. Dec. 123 (1859).

New York.—Zinn v. New Jersey Stb. Co., 49 N. Y. 442, 10 Am. Rep. 402 (1872).

There is a duty on the consignee to make arrangements to get notice. St. Louis, I. M. & S. Ry. Co.

v. Townes, 93 Ark. 430, 26 L. R. A. (N. S.) 572, 124 S. W. 1036 (1910).

But the carrier must make diligent inquiry to discover consignee's whereabouts in order to give notice. Butler v. East Tenn. & Virginia R. R. Co., 8 Lea (Tenn.), 32 (1881).

See:

Michigan.—Michigan Ry. Co. v. Ward, 2 Mich. 538 (1853)—charter proviso.

Missouri.—Herf & Frerichs Chemical Co. v. Lackawanna Line, 100 Mo. App. 164, 73 S. W. 346 (1903)—local usage.

by land, this is different, as the arrival of freight trains may be reasonably anticipated, and the carrier provides proper sheds for warehousing goods after transit. But even as to railroad carriage there are many cases requiring the carrier to give notice in addition to holding it liable as a common carrier for a reasonable time.[1]

Topic B. How the Service Is Terminated

§ 1039. Extent of obligation to deliver.

The service assumed in common carriage does not necessarily go so far as to impose upon the common carrier the obligation of seeking out the consignee and offering to make delivery to him personally, any more than it imposes the duty to go to the consignor and get the goods from him. But personal delivery is professed in certain

[1] *Arkansas.*—Railway Company v. Nevill, 60 Ark. 375, 30 S. W. 425, 46 Am. St. Rep. 208, 28 L. R. A. 80 (1895).

California.—Cavallaro v. Texas & P. Ry. Co., 110 Cal. 348, 42 Pac. 918, 52 Am. St. Rep. 94 (1895).

Colorado.—Denver & R. G. R. R. Co. v. DeWitt, 1 Colo. App. 419, 29 Pac. 524 (1892).

Mississippi.—New Orleans, J. & Gt. No. R. R. Co. v. Tyson, 46 Miss. 729 (1872).

New Hampshire.—Moses v. Boston & M. R. R. Co., 32 N. H. 523, 64 Am. Dec. 381 (1856).

New York.—Fenner v. Buffalo & St. Louis R. R. Co., 44 N. Y. 505, 4 Am. Rep. 709 (1871).

Ohio.—Lake Erie & W. Ry. Co. v. Hatch, 52 Ohio St. 408, 39 N. E. 1042 (1895).

Tennessee.—Pennsylvania R. R. Co. v. Naive, 112 Tenn. 239, 79 S. W. 124, 64 L. R. A. 443 (1903).

Washington.—Normill v. Northern Pacific Ry. Co., 36 Wash. 21, 77 Pac. 1087, 67 L. R. A. 271 (1904).

Wisconsin.—Hermann et al. v. Goodrich, 21 Wis. 536, 94 Am. Dec. 562 (1867).

No notice is required in many of the jurisdictions which hold the carrier liable as such for a reasonable time after the arrival of the goods.

Kentucky.—Lewis v. Louisville & N. Ry. Co., 135 Ky. 361, 122 S. W. 184 (1909).

New Jersey.—Morris & E. R. R. Co. v. Ayres, 29 N. J. L. 393, 80 Am. Dec. 215 (1862).

North Carolina.—Hilliard v. Wilmington & W. R. R. Co., 51 N. C. 343 (1859).

West Virginia.—Berry v. West Virginia & P. R. R. Co., 44 W. Va. 538, 30 S. E. 143, 67 Am. St. Rep. 781 (1898).

kinds of carriage, and in such businesses it is therefore owed. This distinction was marked in the early law by the difference between carriage by sea, where the most that the shipmaster could fairly be said to undertake was to deliver the goods at the wharf,[1] and carriage by land, where the carrier was usually held to undertake personal delivery to the consignee.[2] This distinction is marked in modern times by the difference between the railroad business as it is usually conducted, where delivery to the consignee is not undertaken beyond its own rails,[3] and the express business, where facilities are usually provided for delivery to the addressee personally.[4]

§ 1040. Delivery by express companies.

Express companies generally undertake personal delivery to the consignee. They are therefore liable as common carriers until delivery, or rather until they have made reasonable efforts to deliver.[5] In order to discharge

[1] *United States.*—The Eddy, 5 Wall. 481, 18 L. ed. 486 (1866).

Arkansas.—Turner v. Huff, 46 Ark. 222, 55 Am. Rep. 580 (1885).

Illinois.—Scholes v. Ackerland, 15 Ill. 474 (1854).

Pennsylvania.—Cope v. Cordova, 1 Rawle (Pa.), 203 (1829).

But see the qualifications of this doctrine in:

Alabama.—Stone et al. v. Rice, 58 Ala. 95 (1877).

South Carolina.—G a l l o w a y v. Hughes, 1 Bailey, 553 (1830).

[2] *New York.*—Gibson v. Culver, 17 Wend. 305, 31 Am. Dec. 297 (1837).

England.—Hyde v. Trent & M. Nav. Co., 5 T. R. 389, 1 Esp. 36 (1793).

[3] See:

California.—Dresbach v. California R. R. Co., 57 Cal. 462 (1881).

Massachusetts.—Norway P l a i n Co. v. Boston & M. R. R. Co., 1 Gray, 263, 61 Am. Dec. 423 (1854).

Michigan.—Michigan Central R. R. Co. v. Ward, 2 Mich. 538 (1853).

Mississippi.—New Orleans, J. & Gt. No. R. R. Co. v. Tyson, 46 Miss. 729 (1872).

[4] See:

Michigan.—Bullard v. American Express Co., 107 Mich. 695, 65 N. W. 551, 33 L. R. A. 66, 61 Am. St. Rep. 358 (1895).

West Virginia.—Hutchinson v. United States Express Co., 63 W. Va. 128, 59 S. E. 949, 14 L. R. A. (N. S.) 393 (1907).

[5] *Alabama.*—Southern Exp. Co. v. Armstead, 50 Ala. 350 (1873).

the express company from its liability as a common carrier it must tender the goods at the consignee's address during business hours; and its liability as a carrier is terminated if it finds him absent, or he refuses to take the goods.[1] However, an express company may, at least in small communities where the business does not justify the provision of an equipment for delivering parcels, make the rule that it will not undertake personal delivery at all.[2] In such a case, or when the consignee assents to the goods being held instead of being delivered, the company remains liable as a carrier at most only for a reasonable time after notifying the addressee.[3]

Illinois.—American Express Co. v. Haggard, 37 Ill. 465, 87 Am. Dec. 257 (1865); Baldwin v. American Express Co., 23 Ill. 197, 74 Am. Dec. 190 (1859).

Indiana.—American Express Co. v. Hockett, 30 Ind. 250, 95 Am. Dec. 691 (1868); Adams Express Co. v. Darnell, 31 Ind. 20, 99 Am. Dec. 582 (1869).

New York.—Haslam v. Adams Express Co., 6 Bosw. 235 (1860); Pelton v. Rensselaer & S. R. R. Co., 54 N. Y. 214, 13 Am. Rep. 568 (1873).

Oregon.—Bennett v. Northern Pacific Express Co., 12 Oreg. 49 (1885).

Pennsylvania.—Union Express Co. v. Ohleman, 92 Pa. St. 323 (1879).

[1] *New York.*—Cappel v. Weir, 45 Misc. 419, 90 N. Y. Supp. 394 (1904).

Tennessee.—Kremer v. Southern Express Co., 6 Cold. 356 (1869).

Wisconsin.—Marshall v. American Express Co., 7 Wis. 1, 73 Am. Dec. 381 (1858).

[2] *Indiana.*—State ex rel. R. R. Comm. v. Adams Express Co., 171 Ind. 138, 85 N. E. 337, 19 L. R. A. (N. S.) 93 (1908).

Michigan.—Bullard v. American Express Co., 107 Mich. 695, 65 N. W. 551, 33 L. R. A. 66, 61 Am. St. Rep. 358 (1895).

Missouri.—Downs v. Pacific Express Co., 135 Mo. App. 330, 116 S. W. 9 (1909).

West Virginia.—Hutchinson v. United States Express Co., 63 W. Va. 128, 59 S. E. 949, 14 L. R. A. (N. S.) 393 (1907).

[3] *New Jersey.*—Burr v. Adams Express Co., 71 N. J. L. 263, 58 Atl. 609 (1904).

New York.—Laporte v. Wells F. Express Co., 23 App. Div. 267, 48 N. Y. Supp. 292 (1897).

It is otherwise if the custom is not brought home to the customer. Packard v. Earle, 113 Mass. 280 (1873).

Where the consignee instead of accepting delivery which is offered him requests the agent to hold it for him until another day the com-

§ 1041. Delivery by telegraph companies.

It is the duty of a telegraph company to use due diligence to find the addressee of the telegram and make delivery with reasonable promptness.[1] The telegraph company may establish reasonable free delivery limits in connection with its offices;[2] and, in the absence of such limits it is not bound, unless there is special contract, to deliver a message outside of the town to which it is addressed.[3] The telegraph company may also establish

pany ceases to be liable as a carrier. Southern Express Co. v. Holland, 109 Ala. 362, 19 So. 66 (1895).

[1] *Alabama.*—Tidwell v. Western Union Tel. Co. (Ala.), 51 So. 934 (1910).

Arkansas.—Louisiana & N. W. Ry. Co. v. Reeves (Ark.), 128 S. W. 1051 (1910).

Illinois.—Pope v. Western Union Tel. Co., 9 Ill. App. (9 Bradw.) 283 (1881).

Indiana.—State v. Western Union Tel. Co. (Ind.), 87 N. E. 641 (1909).

Iowa.—Herron v. Western Union Tel. Co., 90 Ia. 129, 57 N. W. 696 (1894).

Kentucky.—Western Union Tel. Co. v. Price (Ky.), 126 S. W. 1100 (1910).

Missouri.—Fitch v. Western Union Tel. Co. (Mo. App.), 130 S. W. 44 (1910).

North Carolina.—Lyne v. Western Union Tel. Co., 123 N. C. 129, 31 S. E. 350 (1898).

South Carolina.—Martin v. Western Union Telegraph Co., 81 S. C. 432, 62 S. E. 833 (1908).

Texas.—Western Union Tel. Co. v. Moran (Tex. Civ. App.), 113 S. W. 625 (1908).

[2] *Alabama.*—Western Union Tel. Co. v. Henderson, 89 Ala. 510, 7 So. 419, 18 Am. St. Rep. 148 (1889).

Illinois.—Western Union Tel. Co. v. Trotter, 55 Ill. App. 659 (1894).

Kentucky.—Western Union Tel. Co. v. Scott, 27 Ky. L. Rep. 975, 87 S. W. 289 (1905).

Missouri.—Reynolds v. Western Union Tel. Co., 81 Mo. App. 223 (1899).

Texas.—Western Union Tel. Co. v. Shockley (Tex. Civ. App.), 122 S. W. 945 (1909).

But payment in advance is not a necessary condition of the obligation to deliver beyond free delivery limits. Western Union Tel. Co. v. Moore, 12 Ind. App. 136, 39 N. E. 874, 54 Am. St. Rep. 515 (1894).

[3] *Kansas.*—Western Union Tel. Co. v. Harvey, 67 Kan. 729, 74 Pac. 250 (1903).

Kentucky.—Western Union Tel. Co. v. Mathews, 107 Ky. 663, 21 Ky. Law Rep. 1405, 55 S. W. 427 (1900).

Tennessee.—Western Union Tel. Co. v. McCaul, 115 Tenn. 99, 90 S. W. 856 (1905).

Texas.—Western Union Tel. Co. v. Swearingen, 95 Tex. 420, 67 S. W. 767 (1902).

reasonable office hours; [1] and such regulation will limit the obligation assumed, unless controlled by a special contract with the sender. [2] Delivery may be made to anyone authorized to receive telegrams for the addressee, such as to the person "care of" whom the telegram is addressed [3] or to the clerk of the hotel at which the addressee is stopping; [4] but a delivery to the addressee's

[1] *Alabama.*—Western Union Tel. Co. v. Jackson, 163 Ala. 9, 50 So. 316 (1909).

Georgia.—Western Union Tel. Co. v. Georgia Cotton Co., 94 Ga. 444, 21 S. E. 835 (1893).

Illinois.—Western Union Tel. Co. v. Trotter, 55 Ill. App. 659 (1894).

Indiana.—Western Union Tel. Co. v. Harding, 103 Ind. 505, 3 N. E. 172 (1885).

Kentucky.—Western Union Tel. Co. v. Bibb (Ky.), 125 S. W. 257 (1910).

New York.—Ayres v. Western Union Tel. Co., 72 N. Y. Supp. 634, 65 App. Div. 149 (1901).

North Carolina.—Cates v. Western Union Tel. Co., 151 N. C. 497, 66 S. E. 592, 24 L. R. A. (N. S.) 1286 (1909).

Rhode Island.—Sweet v. Postal Tel. & Cable Co., 22 R. I. 344, 47 Atl. 881, 53 L. R. A. 732 (1901).

South Carolina.—Bonner v. Western Union Tel. Co., 71 S. C. 303, 51 S. E. 117 (1905).

Tennessee.—McCaul v. Western Union Tel. Co., 114 Tenn. 661, 88 S. W. 325 (1905).

Texas.—Western Union Tel. Co. v. Neel, 86 Tex. 368, 25 S. W. 15, 40 Am. St. Rep. 847 (1894).

West Virginia.—Davis v. Western Union Tel. Co., 46 W. Va. 48, 32 S. E. 1026 (1899).

[2] *Alabama.*—Western Union Tel. Co. v. Hill, 163 Ala. 18, 50 So. 248, 23 L. R. A. (N. S.) 648 (1909).

Iowa.—McPeek v. Western Union Tel. Co., 107 Ia. 356, 78 N. W. 63, 43 L. R. A. 214, 70 Am. St. Rep. 205 (1899).

North Carolina.—Suttle v. Western Union Tel. Co., 148 N. C. 480, 62 S. E. 593 (1908).

Texas.—Western Union Tel. Co. v. Wingate, 6 Tex. Civ. App. 394, 25 S. W. 439 (1894).

[3] *Alabama.*—Western Union Tel. Co. v. Wright (Ala.), 53 So. 95 (1910).

Michigan.—Sweet v. Western Union Tel. Co., 139 Mich. 322, 102 N. W. 850 (1905).

North Carolina.—Hinson v. Postal Tel. Cable Co., 132 N. C. 460, 43 S. E. 945 (1903).

Tennessee.—Western Union Tel. Co. v. McCaul, 115 Tenn. 99, 90 S. W. 856 (1905).

Texas.—Western Union Tel. Co. v. Shaw, 40 Tex. Civ. App. 277, 90 S. W. 58 (1905).

[4] Western Union Tel. Co. v. Trissal, 98 Ind. 566 (1884); Western Union Tel. Co. v. Cullers, 3 Willson Cir. Cas. Ct. App. (Tex.), § 289 (1887).

minor son,[1] or to his partner,[2] or by telephone to his residence[3] or even to his wife,[4] has been held not a good delivery. When, however, personal delivery proves impossible, or delivery otherwise is directed, leaving at the residence[5] or mailing[6] has been held permissible.

§ 1042. Delivery of goods by railroad companies.

The obligations of railroad companies in respect to delivery are now well settled. Generally speaking the modern railroad company does not deliver goods except at its established stations.[7] But where there is no freight

Contra, Western Union Tel. Co. v. Cobb, 95 Tex. 333, 67 S. W. 87, 58 L. R. A. 698, 93 Am. St. Rep. 862 (1902); and compare Western Union Tel. Co. v. Barefoot, 97 Tex. 159, 76 S. W. 914, 64 L. R. A. 491 (1903).

[1] Western Union Tel. Co. v. Whitson, 145 Ala. 426, 41 So. 405 (1906).

[2] Western Union Tel. Co. v. Hendricks, 29 Tex. Civ. App. 413, 68 S. W. 720 (1902).

[3] Brashears v. Western Union Tel. Co., 45 Mo. App. 433 (1891).

Delivery by telephone may, however, be provided for by special contract. Lyles v. Western Union Tel. Co., 77 S. C. 174, 57 S. E. 725, 12 L. R. A. (N. S.) 534 (1907); and it has been held that a telegraph company receiving a message at its office of delivery, after the hours for delivery by messenger, is bound to use a telephone connected with the addressee to deliver the message or give notice of the same. Western Union Tel. Co. v. Price, 13 Ky. 7 758, 126 S. W. 1100 (1910).

[4] Western Union Tel. Co. v. Mitchell, 91 Tex. 454, 44 S. W. 274,

40 L. R. A. 209, 66 Am. St. Rep. 906 (1898); Western Union Tel. Co. v. Moseley, 28 Tex. Civ. App. 562, 67 S. W. 1059 (1902).

But see Western Union Tel. Co. v. McCaul, 115 Tenn. 99, 90 S. W. 856 (1905); and see Western Union Tel. Co. v. Rowell (Ala.), 51 So. 880 (1910).

[5] *United States.*—Given v. Western Union Tel. Co., 24 Fed. 119 (1885).

Alabama.—Tidwell v. Western Union Tel. Co. (Ala.), 51 So. 934 (1910).

Kansas.—Western Union Tel. Co. v. Woods, 56 Kan. 737, 44 Pac. 989 (1896).

[6] *Arkansas.*—King v. Western Union Tel. Co., 89 Ark. 402, 117 S. W. 521 (1909).

Kentucky.—Taylor v. Western Union Tel. Co., 136 Ky. 1, 123 S. W. 311 (1909).

[7] *Alabama.*—South. & No. Alabama Ry. Co. v. Wood, 66 Ala. 167, 41 Am. Rep. 740 (1880).

Massachusetts.—Norway Plains Co. v. Boston & M. R. R. Co., 1 Gray, 263, 61 Am. Dec. 423 (1854).

Michigan.—Michigan C e n t r a l

depot, giving the consignee access to a car upon a siding containing his freight may be equivalent.[1] Where the company has agreed to deliver goods elsewhere or differently, it will become responsible to the extent of its special undertaking.[2] Thus, where a carrier is transporting goods in bond, knowing that under the regulations of the Treasury Department they can only be properly delivered into a bonded warehouse, the railroad is held to have undertaken to make such delivery.[3] Moreover, the railroad company is generally bound to unload the goods from the cars before delivery can usually be said to have taken place.[4] And this is especially plain where the consignee could not have the opportunity of inspecting the goods before accepting without such unloading.[5] The consignee

R. R. Co. v. Ward, 2 Mich. 538 (1853).

Mississippi.—New Orleans, J. & Gt. No. R. R. Co. v. Tyson, 46 Miss. 729 (1872).

[1] Chicago, R. I. & P. Ry. Co. v. Kendall, 72 Ill. 423 (1897). But see Bachant v. Boston & M. R. R. Co., 187 Mass. 392, 73 N. E. 642, 105 Am. St. Rep. 408 (1905).

[2] *Arkansas.* — Railway Co. v. Bruce, 55 Ark. 65, 17 S. W. 363 (1891).

New York.—New York C. & H. R. R. R. Co. v. Standard Oil Co., 87 N. Y. 486 (1882).

Pennsylvania.—Allam v. Pennsylvania R. R. Co., 183 Pa. St. 174, 38 Atl. 709, 39 L. R. A. 535 (1897).

Vermont.—Cutts v. Brainerd, 42 Vt. 566, 1 Am. Rep. 353 (1870).

[3] Chicago & N. W. R. R. Co. v. Lawyer, 69 Ill. 285, 18 Am. Rep. 613 (1873). Compare Galloway v. Hughes, 1 Bailey (S. C.), 553 (1830).

[4] *United States.*—Hudson River

L. Co. v. Wheeler, C. & E. Co., 93 Fed. 374 (1899).

Kentucky.—Louisville & N. Ry. Co. v. Owen, 12 Ky. L. Rep. 716 (1890).

Massachusetts.—Benson v. Gray, 154 Mass. 391, 28 N. E. 275, 13 L. R. A. 262 (1891).

North Carolina. — Benbow v. North Carolina R. R. Co., Phillips' L. 421, 98 Am. Dec. 76 (1868).

Texas.—Galveston, H. & S. A. Ry. Co. v. Jones (Tex. Civ. App.), 123 S. W. 737 (1910).

Washington.—Normile v. Northern Pac. Ry. Co., 36 Wash. 21, 77 Pac. 1087, 67 L. R. A. 271 (1904).

[5] *Alabama.*—Louisville & N. R. R. Co. v. Gilmer, 89 Ala. 534, 7 So. 654 (1889).

Georgia.—See Kenny Co. v. Atlanta & W. P. R. R. Co., 122 Ga. 365, 50 S. E. 132 (1905).

New Hampshire.—Jewell v. Grand Trunk Ry. Co., 55 N. H. 84 (1874).

West Virginia.—Dudley v. Chi-

may, however, accept delivery in a different place at an earlier time from what is usual; and by such acceptance a delivery may be made good when tender merely would have been bad.[1] And the existence of a customary mode of delivery may be sufficient to justify the carrier in delivering in a certain manner which would otherwise be unusual.[2]

§ 1043. Delivery of bulky freight.

It has been noted already that the railroads owe unusual duties with respect to the delivery of bulky freight. When coal, ore, grain or oil are shipped in bulk in car-load lots as they generally are, the consignee may properly insist, if he has a private siding connected with his premises or if there is a public siding adjoining his premises, that the cars shall be shunted to his premises; for only in this way can such bulk freight be conveniently unloaded.[3] Moreover, if the shipment is of great bulk, such as quarried stone or heavy castings, the request is equally proper, since it is extremely disadvantageous to cart such freight through the streets.[4] There is apparently no such obliga-

cago, M. & St. P. Ry. Co., 58 W. Va. 604, 52 S. E. 718, 3 L. R. A. (N. S.) 1135, 112 Am. St. Rep. 1027 (1906).

[1] *Massachusetts.*—Lewis v. Western R. R. Corporation, 11 Met. 509 (1846).

New Hampshire.—Jewell v. Grand Trunk Ry. Co., 55 N. H. 84 (1874).

[2] *Illinois.*—Chicago, R. I. & P. Ry. Co. v. Kendall, 72 Ill. App. 105 (1897).

Indiana.—Pittsburg, C. & St. L. Ry. Co. v. Nash, 43 Ind. 423 (1873).

Pennsylvania.—McMasters v. Pennsylvania R. R. Co., 69 Pa. St. 374, 8 Am. Rep. 264 (1871).

Utah.—Sharp & M. v. Clark et al., 13 Utah, 510, 45 Pac. 566 (1896).

[3] *United States.*—Olanta Coal M. Co. v. Beech Creek R. R. Co., 144 Fed. 150 (1906).

Illinois.—Chicago & N. W. Ry. Co. v. People, 56 Ill. 365, 8 Am. Rep. 690 (1870).

[4] *United States.*—Coe v. Louisville & N. Ry. Co., 3 Fed. 775 (1880).

Kentucky. — Bedford-Bowling Green Stone Co. v. Oman, 115 Ky. 369, 73 S. W. 1038, 24 Ky. L. Rep. 2274 (1903).

tion to the consignee of ordinary freight, however large
his business with the railroad may be; even if he habitually
receives freight in car-load lots, it is not outrageous to
make him go to the public sidings or the regular freight
houses for his goods.[1] It should be said, however, that the
terminal railways of various sorts usually undertake the
delivery of all cars whatever they contain to the premises
of the consignees, if they have a special switch or they
have a siding adjacent.[2] There are certain special instances
which deserve special mention. It seems to be settled
now in the "stockyard cases," although the controversy
has been a long one, that the railroad may refuse to deliver car-loads of cattle to the particular stockyards to
which they are consigned, and instead force all consignees
of cattle to come to a particular stockyards, which it thus
virtually designated as its cattle station.[3] But in the
"telegraph pole cases" the courts have held that, when a
railroad has delivered telegraph poles one by one at short
intervals along its route for one customer, it would be
discrimination not to do so for another desiring like service.[4] In practically all cases where delivery at private
sidings is conceded, it is held that when the car is placed

[1] *Georgia.*—Durden v. Southern
Ry. Co., 2 Ga. App. 66, 58 S. E. 299
(1907).

Michigan.—Mann v. Pere Marquette R. R. Co., 135 Mich. 210, 97
N. W. 721 (1903).

[2] *United States.*—Interstate S. Y.
Co. v. Indianapolis U. Ry. Co., 99
Fed. 477 (1900); United States v.
Sioux City S. Y. Co., 162 Fed. 556
(1908).

Illinois.—Wiggins Ferry Co. v.
East St. L. Union Ry. Co., 107 Ill.
450 (1883); Peoria & P. U. Ry. Co.
v. United States R. S. Co., 136 Ill.

643, 27 N. E. 59, 29 Am. St. Rep.
348 (1891).

[3] For the earlier view, see Covington S. Y. Co. v. Keith, 139 U. S.
128, 35 L. ed. 73, 11 Sup. Ct. 461
(1891).

For the latest law, see Louisville
& N. R. R. Co. v. Central S. Y. Co.,
212 U. S. 132, 53 L. ed. 441, 29 Sup.
Ct. 246 (1909).

[4] *Florida.*—State v. Atlantic C.
L. R. R. Co., 51 Fla. 543, 41 So. 529
(1906).

Louisiana.—Cumberland T. & T.
Co. v. Morgan's L. & T. Ry. Co.,

upon the siding the liability of the carrier ceases.[1]   And
this may also be true where at request of the consignee
the car is put upon a special siding and he is given access
thereto.[2]

§ 1044. Setting down passengers.

The obligation to the passenger upon a railroad is fully
performed when the passenger has been allowed to alight
at the station of his destination and has safely left, or had
a reasonable opportunity safely to leave, the station.[3]

51 La. Ann. 29, 24 So. 803, 72 Am.
St. Rep. 442 (1899).

[1] *Alabama.*—South & North Alabama R. R. Co. v. Wood, 66 Ala.
167, 41 Am. Rep. 749 (1880).

Illinois.—East St. L. Connecting
Ry. Co. v. Wabash, St. L. & P. Ry.
Co., 123 Ill. 594, 15 N. E. 45 (1888).

Indiana.—Pittsburg, C. & St. L.
Ry. Co. v. Nash, 43 Ind. 423 (1873).

New York.—McAndrew v. Whit-
lock, 52 N. Y. 40, 11 Am. Rep. 657
(1873).

[2] *Illinois.*—Chicago, R. I. & P.
Ry. Co. v. Kendall, 72 Ill. App. 105
(1897).

Iowa.—Independence Mills Co.
v. Burlington, Cedar R. & N. Ry.
Co., 72 Ia. 535, 34 N. W. 320, 2 Am.
St. Rep. 258 (1887).

Massachusetts.—Rice v. Boston
& W. R. R. Corp., 98 Mass. 212
(1867).

North Carolina.—Brooks Mfg.
Co. v. Southern Ry. Co. (N. C.), 68
S. E. 243 (1910).

[3] *United States.*—Chicago, R. I. &
P. Ry. Co. v. Wood, 104 Fed. 663,
44 C. C. A. 118 (1900).

Delaware.—Wallace v. Wilmington & N. Ry. Co., 8 Houst. 529, 18
Atl. 818 (1889).

Georgia.—Caldwell v. Richmond
& D. Ry. Co., 89 Ga. 550, 15 S. E.
678 (1892).

Illinois. — Chicago T e r m i n a l
Transfer R. R. Co. v. Helbreg, 99
Ill. App. 563 (1902).

Indiana.—Glenn v. Lake Erie &
W. Ry. Co., 165 Ind. 659, 75 N. E.
282, 2 L. R. A. (N. S.) 872, 112 Am.
St. Rep. 255 (1905).

Iowa.—Patterson v. Omaha & C.
B. Ry. & Bridge Co., 90 Iowa, 247,
57 N. W. 880 (1894).

Kansas.—A delay of one-half
hour before leaving train after
reaching destination terminates the
relation of carrier and passenger.
Chicago, K. & W. Ry. Co. v. Frazer,
55 Kan. 582, 40 Pac. 923 (1895).

Kentucky.—Louisville & ·N. Ry.
Co. v. Keller, 104 Ky. 768, 47 S. W.
1072 (1898), passenger entitled to a
reasonable time.

Louisiana.—Dave v. Morgan's
Louisiana & T. R. R. & Steamship
Co., 47 La. Ann. 576, 17 So. 128
(1895).

Maryland.—Johnson v. Philadelphia, W. & B. R. R. Co., 63 Md. 106
(1884).

Massachusetts.—Legge v. New
York, N. H. & H. R. R. Co., 197

In the case of a street railway company, it is fulfilled by leaving the passenger when he has arrived at his destination, safely in the street.[1] The street railway company,

Mass. 88, 83 N. E. 367, 23 L. R. A. (N. S.) 633 (1908).

Minnesota.—Wyman v. Northern Pac. R. R. Co., 34 Minn. 210, 25 N. W. 349 (1885).

Michigan.—Burnham v. Wabash Ry. Co., 91 Mich. 523, 52 N. W. 14 (1892).

Nebraska.—Omaha & R. V. Ry. Co. v. Chollette, 33 Neb. 143, 49 N. W. 1114 (1891).

North Carolina.—Hansley v. Jamesville & W. R. C. Co., 115 N. C. 602, 20 S. E. 528, 32 L. R. A. 543, 44 Am. St. Rep. 474 (1894).

North Dakota.—Haug v. Great Northern Ry. Co., 77 N. W. 97 (1898).

New Jersey.—Falk v. New York, S. & W. R. R. Co., 56 N. J. L. 380, 29 Atl. 157 (1894).

New York.—Van Ostran v. New York Central & H. R. R. R. Co., 35 Hun (N. Y.), 590 (1885).

North Carolina.—Hinshaw v. Raleigh & A. A. L. R. R. Co., 118 N. C. 1047, 24 S. E. 426 (1896).

Ohio.—Pittsburg, C. & St. L. R. R. Co. v. Krouse, 30 Ohio St. 222 (1876).

Pennsylvania.—Hartzig v. Lehigh Val. R. R. Co., 154 Pa. St. 364, 26 Atl. 310 (1893).

South Carolina.—Samuels v. Richmond & D. R. R. Co., 35 S. C. 493, 14 S. E. 943, 28 Am. St. Rep. 883 (1891).

Texas.—Texas & P. Ry. Co. v. Dick, 26 Tex. Civ. App. 256, 63 S. W. 895 (1901); Houston & T. C. Ry.

Co. v. Batchler, 37 Tex. Civ. App. 116, 83 S. W. 902 (1904).

Wisconsin.—Ellis v. Chicago, M. & St. P. Ry. Co., 120 Wis. 645, 98 N. W. 942 (1904). But the relation of carrier and passenger ceases after a reasonable time for the passenger to get off the car at his destination elapses. Imhoff v. Chicago & M. Ry. Co., 20 Wis. 344 (1866).

West Virginia.—The relation of carrier and passenger does not terminate by the act of the passenger in alighting from the car at his destination, but continues until a reasonable time for the passenger to leave the railroad premises has elapsed. McDade v. Norfolk & W. Ry. Co. (W. Va.), 68 S. E. 378 (1910).

[1] *Alabama.*—Calderwood v. North Birmingham St. Ry. Co., 96 Ala. 318, 11 So. 66 (1892).

Illinois.—West Chicago St. R. R. Co. v. Walsh, 78 Ill. App. 595 (1898).

Indiana.—Anderson v. Citizens' St. R. R. Co., 12 Ind. App. 194, 38 N. E. 1109 (1894).

Maryland.—United Railways & Electric Co. v. Hertel, 97 Md. 382, 55 Atl. 428 (1903).

Missouri.—Jackson v. Grand Ave. Ry. Co., 118 Mo. 199, 24 S. W. 192 (1893).

New York.—Timpson v. Manhattan Ry. Co., 52 Hun (N. Y.), 489, 5 N. Y. Supp. 684 (1889).

Oregon.—Smith v. City & Suburban Ry. Co., 29 Oreg. 539, 46 Pac. 136 (1896).

however, is bound to warn any passenger who is about to alight in a dangerous place that is known to the carrier itself.[1] But if the passenger's injury is due solely to his jumping from the conveyance while it is in motion, he cannot recover damages.[2] It has been held that if passengers are given permission to remain upon the conveyance for a time after their destination is reached, they will remain passengers until they have had a reasonable time to leave in addition to the extension of time granted.[3] But the act of a passenger in remaining upon the premises of the carrier after arriving at his destination for an unlawful purpose, or for objects not contemplated by the contract of transportation, has been held to deprive him of his rights as a passenger.[4]

Topic C. Whether Delivery Is Properly Made

§ 1045. Performance according to instructions.

It would seem that completion of performance according to the instructions given by the person entitled to give directions would always be justifiable in the absence of complicating circumstances. Thus delivery to the consignee would normally be a discharge from all further liability;[5] and so would delivery to the consignor be, if

Pennsylvania.—Fairmount & A. St. Pass. Ry. Co. v. Stutler, 54 Pa. St. 375 (1867).

[1] *Alabama.*—Montgomery St. Ry. Co. v. Mason, 133 Ala. 508, 32 So. 261 (1902).

Arkansas.—Little Rock & Ft. S. Ry. Co. v. Tankersley, 54 Ark. 25, 14 S. W. 1099 (1890).

Kentucky.—Sweet v. Louisville Ry. Co., 113 Ky. 15, 67 S. W. 4 (1902).

Massachusetts.—Bigelow v. West End St. Ry. Co., 161 Mass. 393, 37 N. E. 367 (1894).

[2] *Minnesota.*—Butler v. St. Paul & D. R. R. Co., 59 Minn. 135, 60 N. W. 1090 (1894).

North Carolina.—Burgin v. Richmond & D. Ry. Co., 115 N. C. 673, 20 S. E. 473 (1894).

[3] Prickett v. New Orleans Anchor Line, 13 Mo. App. 436 (1883).

[4] Hendrick v. Chicago & A. Ry. Co., 136 Mo. 548, 38 S. W. 297 (1896); Chicago, R. I. & P. Ry. Co. v. Barrett, 16 Ill. App. 17 (1884).

[5] See:

Massachusetts.—Forbes v. Bos-

title has not passed to the consignee.[1] Where a bill of lading is issued, delivery according to its tenor will usually be considered the performance of the undertaking;[2] and therefore it is often said that the carrier may require the production of the bill of lading before he can be asked to deliver the goods.[3] A distinction should be taken, however, which is not invariably observed. A carrier who has issued an "order" bill of lading delivers the goods to anyone else than the holder of the bill of lading at his peril, as the commercial community deals with such bills as representing the goods themselves.[4] But it is usually held

ton & Lowell R. R. Co., 133 Mass. 154 (1882).

New York.—Marshall et al. v. New York Central R. R. Co., 45 Barb. 502 (1866).

[1] See:

United States.—Southern Express Co. v. Dixon, 94 U. S. 549, 24 L. ed. 285 (1876).

New York.—Thompson v. Fargo, 49 N. Y. 188, 10 Am. Rep. 342 (1872).

[2] See:

Alabama.—Louisville & N. R. R. Co. v. Britton, 149 Ala. 552, 43 So. 108 (1907).

New Hampshire.—First Nat. Bank v. Northern R. R. Co., 58 N. H. 203 (1877).

[3] See:

Kansas.—Atchison, T. & S. F. Ry. Co. v. Schriver, 72 Kan. 550, 84 Pac. 119, 4 L. R. A. (N. S.) 1056 (1906).

Maryland.—Chesapeake Steamship Co. v. Merchants' Bank, 102 Md. 589, 63 Atl. 113 (1906).

New York.—Lyons v. New York Cent. & H. R. R. R. Co., 120 N. Y. Supp. 1132, 136 App. Div. 903 (1909).

Texas.—Dwyer v. Gulf, C. & S. F. Ry. Co., 69 Tex. 707, 7 S. W. 504 (1888).

One case has said that the carrier must ask for production of bill of lading if he has any reason to suspect consignee. Nashville, C. & St. L. Ry. Co. v. Grayson County Nat. Bank, 100 Tex. 17, 93 S. W. 431 (1906).

Another case has said that the carrier is liable for damages for delay caused by refusing to deliver goods without production of the bill of lading. George & Co. v. Louisville & N. Ry. Co., 88 Miss. 306, 40 So. 486 (1906).

[4] *Arkansas.*—Arkansas Southern Ry. Co. v. German Nat. Bank, 77 Ark. 482, 92 S. W. 522 (1906).

Kentucky.—Douglas v. People's Bank, 86 Ky. 176, 5 S. W. 420, 9 Am. St. Rep. 276 (1887).

Massachusetts.—Wright & C. Co. v. Warren, 177 Mass. 283, 58 N. E. 1082 (1901).

Minnesota.—Ratzer v. Burlington, C. R. & N. Ry. Co., 64 Minn. 245, 66 N. W. 988, 58 Am. St. Rep. 530 (1896).

otherwise as to the "straight" bill of lading, for it would be hampering business too much to hold the carrier liable for delivering to the addressee without his producing the bill.[1]

§ 1046. Legal excuse for withholding delivery.

If goods are claimed from the carrier in proceedings affecting the goods shipped by the consignor,[2] or by process after the arrival of the goods in a suit involving the consignee,[3] or if the goods themselves are seized,[4] or if they are stopped in transit [5]—these proceedings will excuse

Missouri.—Midland Nat. Bank v. Missouri Pacific Ry. Co., 132 Mo. 492, 33 S. W. 521, 53 Am. St. Rep. 505 (1896).

Nebraska.—Union Pacific Ry. Co. v. Johnson, 45 Neb. 57, 63 N. W. 144, 50 Am. St. Rep. 540 (1895).

[1] *Arkansas.* — Nebraska M e a l Mills v. St. Louis S. W. Ry. Co., 64 Ark. 169, 38 L. R. A. 358, 62 Am. St. Rep. 183 (1897).

Massachusetts.—Forbes v. Boston & L. R. R. Co., 133 Mass. 154 (1892).

[2] *United States.*—Stiles v. Davis, 1 Black, 101, 17 L. ed. 33 (1861).

Michigan.—Pingree v. Detroit, L. & N. R. R. Co., 66 Mich. 143, 33 N. W. 298, 11 Am. St. Rep. 479 (1887).

New Hampshire.—Hett v. Boston & M. R. R. Co., 69 N. H. 139, 44 Atl. 910 (1897).

New York.—Bliven & M. v. Hudson River R. R. Co., 36 N. Y. 403 (1867).

[3] *Illinois.*—Illinois Central R. R. Co. v. Cobb, 48 Ill. 402 (1868).

Iowa.—Montrose Pickle Co. v. Dodson & H. Mfg. Co., 76 Iowa, 172, 40 N. W. 705, 2 L. R. A. 417, 14 Am. St. Rep. 213 (1888).

Minnesota.—Cooley v. Minnesota Transfer Ry. Co., 53 Minn. 327, 55 N. W. 141, 39 Am. St. Rep. 609 (1893).

Missouri.—Landa v. Holck & Co. et al., 129 Mo. 663, 31 S. W. 900 (1895).

[4] See:

Indiana.—Ohio & Mississippi Ry. Co. v. Yohe, 51 Ind. 181, 19 Am. St. Rep. 727 (1875).

New York.—Bliven & M. v. Hudson River R. R. Co., 36 N. Y. 403 (1867).

[5] See:

California.—Jones v. Earl, 37 Cal. 630, 99 Am. Dec. 338 (1869).

Maine.—Allen v. Maine Central R. R. Co., 79 Me. 327, 9 Atl. 895, 1 Am. St. Rep. 310 (1887).

Where process was served upon a general solicitor of the railroad and goods were let go by a freight agent at the point of delivery a few hours later before the solicitor could investigate or get in touch with the situation the railroad was held not liable. Bates v. Chicago, M. & St.

the carrier for withholding delivery.[1] The carrier will at least have the right to hold the goods for a reasonable time to investigate the merits of the claim.[2] And the carrier is bound to give his patron notice of any interference with the goods by legal process.[3] It should be noted that if the goods are not held up by the process served, the carrier will have no excuse for abandoning their transportation.[4] And it is still more noteworthy that unless the seizure to which he submits is really valid, the carrier is not excused.[5]

P. Ry. Co., 60 Wis. 296, 19 N. W. 72, 50 Am. Rep. 369 (1884).

A carrier is not held liable for failing to take extraordinary steps to protect the interests of the consignor, such as stopping the goods in transit for him. French v. Star Union Transp. Co., 134 Mass. 288 (1883).

[1] *Iowa.*—Skinner v. Chicago & R. I. R. R. Co., 12 Iowa, 191 (1861).

Maryland.—Baltimore & O. R. R. Co. v. Pumphrey, 59 Md. 390 (1882).

New Mexico.—MacVeagh v. Atchison, T. & S. F. R. R. Co., 3 N. M. 205, 5 Pac. 457 (1885).

New York.—McEntee v. New Jersey Steamboat Co., 45 N. Y. 34, 6 Am. Rep. 28 (1871).

[2] *Maine.*—Bennett v. American Express Co., 83 Me. 236, 22 Atl. 159, 13 L. R. A. 33, 23 Am. St. Rep. 774 (1891).

Massachusetts.—E d w a r d s v. White Line Tr. Co., 104 Mass. 159, 6 Am. Rep. 213 (1870).

New York.—V a n W i n k l e v. United States Mail S. S. Co., 37 Barb. 122 (1862).

Vermont.—Burton v. Wilkinson, 18 Vt. 186, 46 Am. Dec. 145 (1846).

[3] *United States.*—The M. M. Chase, 37 Fed. 708 (1889).

Georgia.—Savannah, G. & N. A. R. R. Co. v. Wilcox, Gibbs & Co., 48 Ga. 432 (1873).

Indiana.—Ohio & Mississippi Ry. Co. v. Yohe, 51 Ind. 181, 19 Am. Rep. 727 (1875).

Oregon.—Jewett v. Olsen, 18 Oreg. 419, 23 Pac. 262, 17 Am. St. Rep. 745 (1890).

[4] See:

United States.—The Mary Ann Guest, Olcott, 498, Fed. Cas. No. 9197 (1847).

South Carolina.—Faust v. South Carolina R. R. Co., 8 S. C. 118 (1877).

[5] See:

Maine.—Bennett v. American Express Co., 83 Me. 236, 22 Atl. 159, 13 L. R. A. 33, 23 Am. St. Rep. 774 (1891).

Michigan.—Gibbons v. Farwell, 63 Mich. 344, 29 N. W. 855, 6 Am. St. Rep. 301 (1886).

Where the liquor in the custody of the carrier was seized and destroyed in conformity with a state statute, and the carrier gave notice to the owner, it was held that he was relieved from all liability.

§ 1047. Delivery to true owner.

It is a good defense to an action upon the contract for transportation against a common carrier by a party to the consignment, if the carrier shows that it delivered the goods to the true owner.[1] Indeed, it is liable for conversion if it refuses to surrender the goods to the true owner upon demand.[2] But it should be noted that if the transportation undertaken is for one who in reality has no right to the goods, the carrier after delivery cannot be held liable for conversion by reason of such dealing with the goods.[3] It may be noted that if the owner demands his goods at any place, he is entitled to have them; but he must pay the freight for the whole carriage originally arranged.[4]

§ 1048. Delivery to wrong person.

Such is the responsibility of bailees, that delivery by the carrier to a person other than the person designated is a

Wells v. Maine Steamship Co., 4 Cliff. (U. S.) 228, 29 Fed. Cas. No. 17,401 (1879).

And so where delivery of bananas was withheld in accordance with orders of the local sanitary commission which had declared a quarantine the carrier was excused. Alabama & V. Ry. Co. v. Tirelli Bros., 93 Miss. 797, 48 So. 962 (1909).

[1] *United States.*—The Idaho, 93 U. S. 575, 23 L. ed. 978 (1876).

Illinois.—American Express Co. v. Greenhalgh, 80 Ill. 68 (1875).

Indiana.—Cleveland, C., C. & St. L. Ry. Co. v. Moline Plow Co., 13 Ind. App. 225, 41 N. E. 480 (1895).

Minnesota.—National Bank of Commerce v. Chicago, B. & N. R. R. Co., 44 Minn. 224, 46 N. W. 342, 560, 20 Am. St. Rep. 566, 9 L. R. A. 263 (1890).

New York.—Bates v. Stanton, 1 Duer, 79 (1852).

[2] *Colorado.*—Florence & C. C. Ry. Co. v. Jensen (Colo.), 108 Pac. 974 (1910).

Georgia.—Southern Express Co. v. Palmer et al., 48 Ga. 85 (1873).

Nebraska.—Shellenberg v. Fremont, E. & M. V. R. R. Co., 45 Neb. 487, 63 N. W. 859, 50 Am. St. Rep. 561 (1895).

Wisconsin.—Wells v. American Express Co., 55 Wis. 23, 11 N. W. 537, 12 N. W. 441, 42 Am. Rep. 695 (1882).

[3] *United States.*—Rosenfield v. Express Co., 1 Woods (U. S.), 131 (1871).

Missouri.—White Live Stock Commission Co. v. Chicago, M. & St. P. R. R. Co., 87 Mo. App. 330 (1900).

[4] *United States.*—The Mohawk,

misdelivery for which the carrier is absolutely liable as for a conversion, even if there is no negligence that can be imputed to him.[1] But if the negligence of the shipper is a factor in the mistake, then the carrier is excused, as where the address of the consignee is so wrong as naturally to mislead the carrier.[2] Furthermore, delivery to an unauthorized person is misdelivery,[3] while delivery to an agent with apparent authority to receive is good.[4] It is, for example, not good delivery to hand the goods over to a spouse [5] or a guarantor.[6] But it is good delivery to hand a package addressed to the Secretary of the Treasury to a clerk in his office,[7] or in care of the conductor of a train to whomsoever may be the conductor at the time.[8]

8 Wall. 153, 19 L. ed. 406 (1868).

North Dakota.—Braithwaite v. Power, 1 N. Dak. 455, 48 N. W. 354 (1891).

[1] Alabama.—Mobile, J. & K. C. Ry. Co. v. Bay Shore L. Co. (Ala.), 51 So. 956 (1910).

Arkansas.—Little Rock, M. R. & T. R. R. Co. v. Glidwell, 39 Ark. 487 (1882).

Illinois.—Illinois Cent. R. Co. v. Parks, 54 Ill. 294 (1870).

Indiana.—Cleveland, C., C. & St. L. R. R. Co. v. Wright, 25 Ind. App. 525, 58 N. E. 559 (1900).

New York.—Packard v. Getman, 4 Wend. 613, 21 Am. Dec. 166 (1830).

West Virginia.—Clarke-Lawrence Co. v. Chesapeake & O. Ry. Co., 63 W. Va. 423, 61 S. E. 364 (1908).

[2] New York.—Mott v. Long I. Ry. Co., 123 N. Y. Supp. 49 (1910).

Pennsylvania.—Lake Shore & M. S. Ry. Co. v. Hodapp, 83 Pa. St. 22 (1876).

[3] California.—Adams & Co. v. Blankenstein, 2 Cal. 413, 56 Am. Dec. 350 (1852).

Missouri.—Wilson Sewing Machine Co. v. Louisville & N. R. R. Co., 71 Mo. 203 (1879).

New York.—Schlesinger & Sons v. New York, N. H. & H. R. R. R. Co., 85 N. Y. Supp. 372 (1903).

Wisconsin. — Ela v. American Merch. Union Exp. Co., 29 Wis. 611, 9 Am. Rep. 619 (1872).

[4] Georgia.—Brunswick & W. Ry. Co. v. Rotchild & Co., 119 Ga. 604, 46 S. E. 830 (1904).

Illinois.—American Merch. Un. Exp. Co. v. Milk, 73 Ill. 224 (1874).

[5] Missouri Pacific Ry. Co. v. Weil, 8 Kans. App. 839, 57 Pac. 853 (1899).

[6] Mahon v. Blake, 125 Mass. 477 (1878).

[7] Aldrich C. S. Mfg. Co. v. American Exp. Co., 117 Mich. 32, 75 N. W. 94 (1898).

[8] Southern Express · Co. v. Wil-

§ 1049. Delivery to the designated person.

There is a noteworthy conflict of authority in that class of cases where a swindler, taking a name and address practically the same as that of an established concern in good credit, orders goods shipped to him. When the carrier subsequently delivers the goods to the swindler, he is by many cases held liable for a misdelivery, and responsible therefore for the loss of the goods thereby.[1] But there are strong opinions to the effect that in such cases this is delivery by the carrier to the party designated by the consignor, and it is therefore a proper performance of the obligation.[2] In the cases first cited, it is insisted that a carrier is always liable for misdelivery although he is absolutely without blameworthiness, and that in this instance the consignor intended that the goods should be delivered to the person whom he supposed wrote the letter ordering the goods. But in the cases cited on the other side, it is insisted

liams, 99 Ga. 482, 27 S. E. 743 (1896).

[1] *Florida.*—Southern Express Co. v. Van Meter, 17 Fla. 783, 35 Am. Rep. 107 (1880).

Illinois.—Pacific Express Co. v. Shearer, 160 Ill. 215, 43 N. E. 816, 52 Am. St. Rep. 324, 37 L. R. A. 177 (1896).

Iowa.—Brunswick v. United States Express Co., 46 Iowa, 77 (1877).

Kentucky.—Louisville & N. R. R. Co. v. Ft. Wayne Electric Co., 108 Ky. 113, 21 Ky. L. R. 1544, 55 S. W. 918 (1900).

New York.—Price v. Oswego & S. R. R. Co., 50 N. Y. 213, 10 Am. Rep. 475 (1872).

Ohio.—Oskamp et al. v. Southern Express Co., 61 Ohio St. 341, 56 N. E. 13 (1899).

Tennessee.—Sword v. Young, 89 Tenn. 126, 14 S. W. 481, 604 (1890).

Vermont.—Winslow v. Vermont & M. R. R. Co., 42 Vt. 700, 1 Am. Rep. 365 (1870).

[2] *United States.*—The Drew, 15 Fed. 826 (1883).

Massachusetts. — Samuel v. Cheney, 135 Mass. 278, 46 Am. Rep. 467 (1883).

Missouri.—Wilson v. Adams Express Co., 27 Mo. App. 360 (1887).

Pennsylvania.—Seibert v. Railway Co., 15 Pa. Super. Ct. 435 (1900).

Texas.—Pacific Express Co. v. Hertzberg, 17 Tex. Civ. App. 100, 42 S. W. 795 (1897).

England.—M'Kean v. M'Ivor, L. R. 6 Ex. 36 (1870).

that if a carrier simply performs his undertaking according to the instructions given he is always protected, and that if the seller is shipping goods in response to an order his intention is to send the goods to the writer of that letter. The inherent difficulty in the problem is that there is truth in both arguments; and probably the issue is what is predominant in the shipper's mind. There are those who will say that it is to sell to the reputable concern, but the writer believes that as business goes it is to fill the actual order.

§ 1050. Demurrage charges.

It would seem that corresponding to the carrier's duty to deliver within a reasonable time or else be liable for the delay, there should be a duty upon the consignee to take away the goods within a reasonable time or else be liable for the extra service of the carrier in holding the goods for him after the carriage has ceased. However, there is a noteworthy conflict of opinion as to the basis of such a charge against the consignee for a delay in taking the goods from the carrier or detention of his vehicles. Even in admiralty this conflict appears, the English view being that the charge can only be made if stipulated for in the bill of lading,[1] while the American view has been that there may be a charge for unnecessary detention imposed regardless of contract.[2] As to the right of a railroad to make a charge in the nature of demurrage, there are two opinions in the American authorities. In the earlier cases it was usually decided that unless there was a stipulation for demurrage in the contract of shipment, such a charge could not be imposed.[3] In other jurisdictions

[1] Brouncker v. Scott, 4 Taunt. 1 (1811).

See, however, Ford v. Cottesworth, L. R. 4 Q. B. 127 (1868).

[2] The Apollon, 9 Wheat. 362 (1824).

See also Hawgood v. 1,310 Tons of Coal, 21 Fed. 681 (1884).

[3] *United States.*—Sutton v. Housa-

it is held when the railroad posts regulations imposing demurrage these charges may be collected.[1] At all events the demurrage charge must be reasonable;[2] but it is not necessarily based upon the mere cost of the storage to the railroad.[3] As a consequence of this difference of opinion as to the basis of this demurrage there is conflict of authority as to whether there is a lien for the charge. According to the earlier view, as this was a separate matter outside of common-law obligation, there was no common-law lien;[4] but according to the modern view the carrier is at least given a warehouseman's lien for such storage.[5]

tonic R. R. Co., 45 Fed. 507 (1891).

Illinois.—Chicago & N. W. Ry. Co. v. Jenkins, 103 Ill. 588 (1882).

Nebraska.—Burlington & M. R. R. Co. v. Chicago Lumber Co., 15 Neb. 390, 19 N. W. 451 (1884).

Tennessee.—Swan v. Railroad Co., 106 Tenn. 229, 61 S. W. 57 (1901).

[1] *Georgia.*—M i l l e r & C o. v. Georgia R. R. & Banking Co., 88 Ga. 563, 15 S. E. 316, 18 L. R. A. 323, 30 Am. St. Rep. 170 (1891).

Massachusetts.—Miller v. Mansfield, 112 Mass. 260 (1873).

Mississippi.—Yazoo & M. V. R. R. Co. v. Searles, 85 Miss. 520, 37 So. 939, 68 L. R. A. 715 (1904).

Pennsylvania.—Pennsylvania R. R. Co. v. Midvale Steel Co., 201 Pa. St. 624, 51 Atl. 313, 88 Am. St. Rep. 836 (1902).

[2] *Illinois.*—Schumaker v. Chicago & N. W. Ry. Co., 207 Ill. 199, 69 N. E. 825 (1904).

Pennsylvania.—Baltimore & O. R. R. Co. v. Gray's Ferry Abattoir Co., 27 Pa. Super. Ct. 511 (1905).

[3] *Kentucky.*—Kentucky W a g o n

Mfg. Co. v. Ohio & M. Ry. Co., 98 Ky. 152, 17 Ky. L. Rep. 726, 32 S. W. 595, 36 L. R. A. 850, 56 Am. St. Rep. 326 (1895).

Missouri.—Darlington v. Missouri Pac. R. R. Co., 99 Mo. App. 1, 72 S. W. 122 (1903).

[4] *New York.*—Crommelin v. New York & H. R. R. R. Co., 10 Bosw. (N. Y.) 77 (1862).

Pennsylvania.—Nicolette Lumber Co. v. People's Coal Co., 213 Pa. St. 379, 62 Atl. 1060, 3 L. R. A. (N. S.) 327, 110 Am. St. Rep. 550 (1906).

Tennessee.—East Tenn.,' Va. & Ga. R. R. Co. v. Hunt, 15 Lea (Tenn.), 261 (1885).

Wyoming.—Kansas Pac. Ry. Co. v. McCann, 2 Wyo. 3 (1877).

[5] *Alabama.*—Southern Ry. Co. v. Lockwood Mfg. Co., 142 Ala. 322, 37 So. 667, 68 L. R. A. 227 (1904).

Massachusetts.—Miller v. Mansfield, 112 Mass. 260 (1873).

Mississippi.—New Orleans & N. E. R. R. Co. v. George, 82 Miss. 710, 35 So. 193 (1903).

Ohio.—Pittsburg, C., C. & St. L.

§ 1051. Full completion of performance.

Although the problem of the completion of performance of the undertaking is of vital moment only in the case of carriers and innkeepers, it would seem that whenever it is of importance in other services the same general principles should govern. The principles which have been discussed in this chapter justify the large generalization that the special obligation due imposed upon one engaged in a public service terminates when there has been full performance of the service which has been undertaken, but not until then. It is difficult to find cases in the other public services where the issue is whether the public service is ended. Perhaps the explanation of those cases which hold that when water supply is cut off for nonpayment, a price cannot be charged for turning on the water again [1] is that the service is regarded as simply interrupted by the nonpayment. Another interesting set of cases holds that even when the service of the telephone company has been permanently discontinued, the company has not altogether terminated its liability for possible damages until it has removed its wires from the structure. [2]

Ry. Co. v. Mooar Lumber Co., 27 Oh. Cir. Ct. 588 (1905).

Under the Interstate Commerce Act a demurrage charge scheduled by the railroad must be paid in the absence of action by the Commission setting it aside. Texas & P. Ry. Co. v. Abilene Oil Co., 204 U. S. 426, 51 L. ed. 553, 27 S. Ct. Rep. 350 (1907).

Note should be made of the very modern statutes providing for reciprocal demurrage charges for unwarranted delay by the carrier or the shipper. St. Louis, I. M. & So. Ry. Co. v. Edwards (Ark.), 127 S. W. 713 (1910).

[1] See State ex rel. Jones, 141 Mo. App. 299, 125 S. W. 1169 (1910).

[2] See Southern Bell Telephone & T. Co. v. McTyer, 137 Ala. 601, 34 So. 1020 (1902).

BOOK IV. REGULATION OF PUBLIC SERVICE

PART IX. RESTRICTION OF CHARGES

CHAPTER XXXI

GENERAL THEORY OF RATE REGULATION

§ 1060. General principles governing reasonableness.

§ 1060. General principles governing reasonableness.

The question of the reasonableness of rates is a complex one. As there are two parties having an interest in the rates, the company serving and the customer served, and their interests are diverse and, to a considerable extent, opposed, a rate which is reasonable from the point of view of one may be quite unreasonable from the point of view of the other. The interest of the company is entirely directed toward framing a schedule of rates which as a whole shall produce a certain return, and so long as the return is realized it is immaterial to it what the proportion of contribution of each individual customer is to the whole amount. On the other hand, the customer is interested in the individual rate charged to him, and in that alone. So long as his rate is a fair one it is immaterial to him that the whole schedule is so arranged as to yield a great profit to the company. As the case stands thus, it is necessary in framing a schedule to require a proper amount of concession from all parties concerned. The principles on which the fairness of the whole schedule would be determined will be limited by the requirement of fairness to the individual customer; and on the other hand the principles on which the reasonableness of a particular rate would be determined may need modification because of the just claim of the company to a fair compensation. The examination of the reasonableness of the charges must therefore involve a study both of the reasonableness of the schedule as a whole and also of the reasonableness of the separate rates.

Topic A. The Schedule as a Whole

§ 1061. Reasonableness of the schedule as a whole.

The reasonableness of the schedule as a whole depends upon whether it yields a fair return to the proprietors of the service. This is largely a mathematical question governed by principles which may now be said to be well recognized.[1] The public service company is entitled first of all to pay all its expenses of operation. These include not only the actual disbursements for operation in each

---

[1] The latest of the long line of Federal cases in which these elements are fully considered is Missouri, K. & T. Ry. Co. v. Love, 177 Fed. 493 (1910).

year, but also certain annual charges which must be paid before any real profit is realized. Moreover the company is entitled by the modern decisions to gain a fair profit upon its reasonable capitalization. The determination of what constitutes a reasonable capitalization and what a fair return, is a matter which is not altogether clear in its details upon the authorities as yet. But generally speaking it may be said that by the present policy a total return will be allowed in normal cases sufficient to yield the company a net profit above proper charges equal to that which would be realized from any other business where the capital and the risk were the same.[1]

§ 1062. Many elements to be taken into account.

That these various elements are all taken into consideration by a modern court in passing upon the reasonableness of a schedule of rates is shown in many leading cases. For example in the case of Brymer v. Butler Water Company,[2] the court being called upon under a statute to pass upon the complaint that the schedule of rates of the water company was too high, Mr. Justice Williams said: "By what rule is the court to determine what is reasonable, and what is oppressive? Ordinarily that is a reasonable charge or system of charges which yields a fair return upon the investment. Fixed charges and the costs of maintenance and operation must first be provided for, then the interests of the owners of the property are to be considered. They are entitled to a rate of return, if their property will earn it, not less than the legal rate of interest; and a system of charges that yields no more income than is fairly required to maintain the plant, pay fixed charges and operating expenses, provide a suitable sink-

[1] The latest of the many State cases in which these elements are all taken into account is Coal & Coke Ry. Co. v. Conley (W. Va.), 67 S. E. 613 (1910).

[2] 179 Pa. St. 231, 36 Atl. 249, 36 L. R. A. 260 (1897).

ing fund for the payment of debts, and pay a fair profit to the owners of the property, cannot be said to be unreasonable." [1]

§ 1063. Reduction of particular rates leaving sufficient total earnings.

It should be admitted at the outset that there are several decisions which rely too much upon this conception,— holding that the legislature may reduce the rates for a particular service below its cost provided that the total earnings from all business will still constitute a fair return upon the capital invested. The leading case to this effect is Minneapolis & St. Louis Railroad v. Minnesota [2] in which the plaintiff railroad attacked as unconstitutional a rate fixed by the railroad commission for the carriage of coal. The railroad did not claim that the reduction of this rate alone would deprive it of a fair return, but only that if the reduced rate were applied to all freights the income of the road would be insufficient. The United States Supreme Court held the rate legal, notwithstanding this fact, Mr. Justice Brown saying: "Notwithstanding the evidence of the defendant that if the rates upon all merchandise were fixed at the amount imposed by the commission upon coal in carload lots, the road would not pay its operating expenses, it may well be that the existing rates upon other merchandise, which are not disturbed by the commission, may be sufficient to earn a large profit to the company, though it may earn little or nothing upon coal in carload lots." [3]

[1] See particularly Smyth v. Ames 169, U. S. 466, 42 L. ed. 819, 18 Sup. Ct. 418 (1898), among the many cases containing similar generalizations.

[2] 186 U. S. 257, 46 L. ed. 1151, 22 Sup. Ct. 901 (1902). The court had already committed itself to this doctrine in St. Louis & S. F. R. R. Co. v. Gill, 156 U. S. 649, 39 L. ed. 567, 15 Sup. Ct. 484 (1895).

[3] See further, much to the same effect:

United States.—Interstate Consolidated St. Ry. Co. v. Massachusetts, 207 U. S. 79, 28 Sup. Ct. 26

§ 1064. Rule of proportionality in sharing costs.

There is however dissent from this doctrine, as may be seen in those cases which go so far as to hold the imposition of disproportionate rates improper. As an abstract matter the fairest way to determine the cost of any particular service would be to apportion ratably the total disbursements of every sort to the various items of traffic and so to arrive at proportionate rates. Theoretically, perhaps, any other method is less just to all concerned. In determining what is a reasonable rate for services rendered, it is hardly proper to take the road as existing and as maintained, with its track and terminal equipments, salaries and all other expenses, and to regard as the total cost of any particular service merely the increased expense necessary to add to its business the service in question; truly the cost of that service ought to include its fair share of the interest on investments and of the general expenses.[1] Theoretically therefore a proportionate rate should be established for each article of traffic. This rate will be fixed according to the share of the entire burden of charge which ought reasonably to be borne by that particular article.[2] In determining the reasonable share of the burden to be borne by an article, various considerations

(1908); Willcox v. Consolidated Gas Co., 212 U. S. 19, 53 L. ed. 382, 29 Sup. Ct. 192 (1909); Southern R. R. Co. v. McNeill, 155 Fed. 756 (1907); Central of Ga. Ry. Co. v. McLendon, 157 Fed. 961 (1907).

Arkansas.—Missouri Pacific R. R. Co. v. Smith, 60 Ark. 221, 29 S. W. 752 (1895).

Florida.—Pensacola & A. R. R. Co. v. Florida, 25 Fla. 310, 5 So. 833 (1889).

Georgia.—Southern Ry. Co. v. Atlanta Stove Wks., 128 Ga. 207, 57 S. E. 429 (1907).

Minnesota.—State v. Minneapolis & St. L. Ry. Co., 80 Minn. 191, 83 N. W. 60 (1900).

North Dakota.—State ex. rel. v. Northern Pacific Ry. Co., N. D. 120 N. W. 869, 25 L. R. A. (N. S.) 1001 (1909).

[1] See particularly Pennsylvania Ry. Co. v. Philadelphia County, 220 Pa. St. 100, 68 Atl. 676, 15 L. R. A. (N. S.) 108 (1908).

[2] See particularly Gulf C. & S. F. R. R. Co. v. Railroad Commission (Tex.), 116 S. W. 795 (1909).

must be weighed, and the rate when finally established will be determined as a result of all such considerations.

§ 1065. Rates must be fair to all concerned.

The fundamental principle as to the reasonableness of a particular rate is that it should be fair compensation for the service rendered. There are, therefore, limits within which the railroad company must act in fixing its rates. The company must have reasonable compensation; but the customer must not be charged more than a reasonable price. The compensation, in order to be reasonable, must be fair to both parties.[1] It is not enough that the whole schedule shall bring in a fair return to the company; the particular rate fixed for carriage must be in itself no more than a reasonable amount for the customer to pay under the circumstances for the service rendered him. The question of reasonableness involves the element of reasonableness both as regards the company and as regards the public.[2] Stated in more accurate terms, the law requiring fair compensation has two distinct sides. It is desirable that the carrier should receive the full cost to it of performing the service. It is desirable, also, that the shipper should not pay more than the value of the service to him. These two limitations are diverse, but their reconciliation upon the basis of compromise is not altogether impossible.

§ 1066. Interests of the companies to be considered.

As a general rule therefore it will be unjustifiable for the government to reduce the total net returns from the

[1] See the language of Harlan, J., in San Diego L. & T. Co. v. National City, 174 U. S. 739, 43 L. ed. 1154, 19 Sup. Ct. 804 (1899); and of Brewer, J., in Cotting v. Kansas City S. Y. Co., 183 U. S. 79, 46 L. ed. 92, 22 Sup. Ct. 30 (1901).

[2] See the language of Savage, J., in Kennebec Water Dist. v. Waterville, 97 Me. 185, 54 Atl. 6, 60 L. R. A. 856 (1902); and Canty, J., in Steenerson v. Gt. Northern Ry. Co., 69 Minn. 353, 72 N. W. 713 (1897).

schedule as a whole below what will produce a fair return upon a proper capitalization. However desirable it may be to provide lower rates for the public which is receiving the service, it is equally necessary to leave a reasonable return to the company that is performing the service. According to modern views upon the constitutional guaranties an adequate return upon the true value of the property devoted to the public use by those who conduct a public service ought in all normal cases to be left; otherwise it is said that they are in effect deprived of their property without due process of law, if their rates are so reduced by public authority as to leave no such adequate return. And this is based upon sound public policy. It ought always to be plain that those who invest their funds in some public employment are going to get a fair per cent upon their investment.[1] For unless they are well assured of this they will employ their money elsewhere, and many enterprises necessary for the public convenience will not be undertaken, nor will existing plants be extended.[2] "As popularly expressed, the rights of the people —the rights of shippers who use it as a carrier—have to be regarded; but, as judicially expressed, these last have to be so regarded as not to disregard the inherent and reasonable rights of the projectors, proprietors, and operators of these carriers."

§ 1067. Interests of the public to be considered.

But that there are in reality two tests, not one, is pointed out by the most discriminating judges in the more recent cases, and it is the avowed policy of the United States Supreme Court that both parties to the service,

---

[1] Paraphrased from the language of Mitchell, C. J., in Pennsylvania R. R. Co. v. Philadelphia County, 220 Pa. St. 100, 68 Atl. 676, 15 L. R. A. (N. S.) 108 (1908).

[2] Quoted from McCormick, J., in Metropolitan T. Co. v. Houston & T. C. R. R. Co., 90 Fed. 683 (1898).

the carrier and the shipper, should be considered in deciding all cases. Thus, in the leading case of Smyth v. Ames,[1] the court, in declaring the Nebraska maximum freight law unconstitutional, guarded itself against being understood as taking an extreme position in favor of the carrier by saying: "It cannot therefore be admitted that a railroad corporation maintaining a highway under authority of the state may fix its rates with a view solely to its own interests and ignore the rights of the public. But the rights of the public would be ignored if rates for transportation of persons or property on a railroad are exacted without reference to the fair value of the property used for the public and the fair value of the services rendered, but in order simply that the corporation may meet operating expenses, pay the interest on its obligations, and declare a dividend to its stockholders." And in Covington & Lexington Turnpike Road Company v. Sandford,[2] that court, in considering legislation, reducing rates said: "A corporation is not entitled as of right and without reference to the interests of the public, to realize a given per cent upon its capital stock. Stockholders are not the only persons whose rights or interests are to be considered. The rights of the public are not to be ignored. The public cannot properly be subjected to unreasonable rates in order simply that stockholders may earn dividends.

§ 1068. Accommodation of both sought.

So many considerations must be taken into account in passing upon rates that the problem is always a complex one. The difficulties, many of them, arise from the desire to give scope to a variety of principles which must inevitably come into a more or less irreconcilable conflict.

---

[1] 169 U. S. 466, 42 L. ed. 819, 18 Sup. Ct. 418 (1898).

[2] 164 U. S. 596, 41 L. ed. 566, 17 Sup. Ct. 198 (1896).

But this accommodation of conflicting desires is the usual end of legal effort. And it is to be hoped that by the general discussion of this great problem of rate regulation some lasting compromise may be brought about. That the rights of all concerned are to receive recognition in the final settlement may be seen in this summary of the present situation by one of the masters [1] of the subject. "The elemental principles thus far noted may be summarized as, on the one hand, the right of the company to derive a fair income, based upon the fair value of the property at the time it is being used for the public, taking into account the cost of maintenance or depreciation, and current operating expenses; and, on the other hand, the right of the public to have no more exacted than the services in themselves are worth. While the company is entitled, so far as this case shows, to a fair return upon the value of the property used for the public at the time it is being used, the public (that is, the customers) may demand that the rates shall be no higher than the services are worth to them, not in the aggregate, but as individuals. The value of the services in themselves is to be considered, and not exceeded. These views seem to be consonant with reason. They are also established by the highest judicial authority in our country." [2]

§ 1069. Enlightened policy in rate regulation.

That the courts are approaching this great issue with the enlightened policy of fair compromise of conflicting interest is plain. " The courts in clear cases ought not to hesitate to arrest the operation of a confiscatory law, but they ought to refrain from interfering in cases of any other kind. Regulation of public service corporations,

[1] Savage, J., in Kennebec Water District v. Waterville, 97 Me. 185, 54 Atl. 6, 60 L. R. A. 856 (1902).

[2] See also the language of Poffenbarger, J., in Coal & Coke Ry. v. Conley (W. Va.) 67 S. E. 613 (1910).

which perform their duties under conditions of necessary monopoly, will occur with greater and greater frequency as time goes on. It is a delicate and dangerous function, and ought to be exercised with a keen sense of justice on the part of the regulating body, met by a frank disclosure on the part of the company to be regulated. The courts ought not to bear the whole burden of saving property from confiscation, though they will not be found wanting where the proof is clear. The Legislatures and subordinate bodies to whom the legislative power has been delegated, ought to do their part. Our social system rests largely upon the sanctity of private property, and that state or community which seeks to invade it will soon discover the error in the disaster which follows. The slight gain to the consumer, which he would obtain from a reduction in the rates charged by public service corporations is as nothing compared with his share in the ruin of which would be brought about by denying to private property its just reward, thus unsettling values and destroying confidence. On the other hand, the companies to be regulated will find it to their lasting interest to furnish freely the information upon which a just regulation can be based." With these the views of the United States Supreme Court [1] it would seem that the present crisis may be faced with confidence. [2]

Topic B. The Particular Rate

§ 1070. Reasonableness of the separate rates.

The question of the reasonableness of any separate rate is more complex. Even if it be assumed that the individual patron ought not to pay more than his fair

---

[1] Per Moody, J., in Knoxville v. Knoxville Water Co., 212 U. S. 1, 53 L. ed. 371, 29 Sup. Ct. 148 (1909).

[2] See also the language of Speer, J., in Tift v. Southern Ry. Co., 138 Fed. 753 (1905).

share of the whole amount received by the company, what his fair share may be depends upon too many considerations to make the solution of the problem easy. Moreover fairness to the customer requires that under no circumstances should he be forced to pay a rate greater than the value of the service rendered to him, and this involves a determination of the value to him of the service, which will not always be the cost to the company of the particular service.[1] It is obvious that all these considerations, which taken together enter into a determination of the reasonableness of the separate rate are rather vague,[2] and that it will in the ordinary case be a matter of great difficulty to determine the question.

§ 1071. Relation of the particular rate to the whole schedule.

The proper method in passing upon the reasonableness of rates is to discover whether the particular rate is fair, judging the schedule as a whole. As has been seen, this involves the consideration of many factors, some of them conflicting, but it may be said that rates fixed are fair to the company if from the schedule as a whole it gets a reasonable return, and fair to the people served if they pay in each particular case no more than the service is worth. In order to meet, as far as may be, both requisites, a particular rate should seldom be passed upon without considering the relations to the schedule as a whole, especially as the reasonableness of one rate may be judged

[1] The principle that the separate rate charged to particular persons must not be unfair to the person served may be said to be well established. See the general language of Savage, J., in Brunswick & T. Water Dist. v. Maine Water Co., 99 Me. 371, 59 Atl. 537 (1904).

[2] But the courts have not yet been able to apply this general principle in a satisfactory manner. See the exposition of the inconsistent theories as to the determination of railroad rates in the opinion of Bethea, J., in Interstate Comm. Comm. v. Chicago G. W. R. R. Co., 141 Fed. 1003 (1905).

with reference to other rates in the same schedule.[1] Examples of the way in which such problems are worked out, considering all factors and then giving most weight to one held to be controlling in the particular case, may be seen in various cases.[2]

§ 1072. Rates unreasonable in themselves.

Occasionally a case will come up when the problem of the character of the rate charged will be easy to decide. Sometimes the rate demanded is plainly extortionate when judged by the standard of what is usual for such service. Thus in a recent case where railroads charged a contractor $700 for the transportation of a monument a comparatively short distance, this was held so outrageous that recovery could be had.[3] The court pointed out that like transportation for similar articles cost but a few dollars, and for the railway to stipulate for such a sum constituted in effect a breach of their public duty. In the still famous "Naval stores" case [4] the court found the rates complained

[1] The leading case thus far in the supreme court for the consideration of the results of the total schedule in determining the reasonableness of the particular rates composing it is Smyth v. Ames, 169 U. S. 466, 42 L. ed. 819, 18 Sup. Ct. 418 (1898).

[2] The proper relation of a particular rate to the whole schedule is elaborately worked out hereafter. The way of approaching the subject that is supported throughout this treatise is well set forth in the brief opinion of Brewer, J., in Atlantic C. L. R. R. Co. v. Florida, 203 U. S. 256, 51 L. ed. 174, 27 Sup. Ct. 108 (1906).

[3] Harrison Granite Co. v. Pennsylvania R. R. Co., 145 Mich. 712, 108 N. W. 1081 (1906).

A petition against a carrier to re-cover excessive freight rates, alleging the distance from the starting point to destination, that a certain sum was a reasonable compensation for carrying the commodity over defendant's line for such distance, that defendant charged plaintiff a larger sum, which charge was paid under protest—states a cause of action. Ft. Smith & W. R. Co. v. Chandler Cotton Oil Co. (Okla.), 106 Pac. 10 (1909).

[4] Interstate Comm. Comm. v. Louisville & N. Ry. Co., 118 Fed. 613 (1902).

A complaint states a good cause of action in an action to recover for a freight overcharge which alleges that defendant was a common carrier who instead of charging plaintiff the stipulated freight rate, ex-

of unreasonable, largely upon the evidence adduced as to the charges made for similar transportation by the railroads concerned and other railroads operating in the same territory. The usual charge for similar service constitutes therefore an external test by which to check all internal computations, if one may use these phrases.

§ 1073. Value of the service.

It is highly desirable, if indeed not indispensable, that no more should be charged the individual patron than the service is worth to him. This principle is succinctly stated in a leading case [1] thus: "The public—that is the customers—may demand that the rates shall be no higher than the services are worth to them not in the aggregate, but as individuals. The value of the services in themselves is to be considered and not exceeded." This as the judge further insisted was true irrespective of whether the gross returns received from such rates gave a fair return upon reasonable investment or not, for the public duty which the company fundamentally owes its customers makes obligatory upon it the rendering of individual service at fair rates for the service required, regardless of any other considerations.[2]

§ 1074. What the traffic will bear.

It is often urged particularly in the discussion of the

torted an excessive freight rate, and refused to haul or deliver the logs unless plaintiff would pay such sum, that plaintiff offered to pay the reasonable charge, and demanded that the logs should be hauled for such freight charges, which defendant refused to do, and the plaintiff was compelled to pay such extortionate and illegal rate to an amount stated, in order to have the freight moved, and that plaintiff paid such charge under protest. Fairford Lumber Co. v. Tombigbee Valley R. Co. (Ala.), 51 So. 770 (1910).

[1] Quoted from Savage, J., in Kennebec Water Dist. v. Waterville, 97 Me. 185, 54 Atl. 6, 60 L. R. A. 856 (1902).

[2] See the language of Carter, J., in State ex rel. R. R. Comm. v. Seaboard Air Line Ry. Co., 48 Fla. 129, 37 So. 314 (1904).

railway rate problem that it is justifiable to make rates according to what the traffic will bear. This is a factor in the situation undoubtedly; for the management in order to get business enough to carry on its service with economy and profit must to some extent make some concessions to the low grade commodities which it will inevitably recoup from the high grade freight. And yet this is clearly a principle which can only be justified under strict limitations; and, indeed, any considerable concession to the principle of charging what the traffic will bear is dangerous. The public service company is acting primarily for the benefit, not for the exploitation of the public. To allow a carrier, for instance, to charge what the traffic will bear is to foster an unjust increase of railroad rates in particular cases.[1] To assert that the self-interest of carriers may be safely relied upon to prevent unjust exaction is to deny the necessity of any public service law.[2]

§ 1075. Making rates compared with levying taxes.

It is a common statement in the discussion of rate making that the situation is the same as in the levying of taxes. This may be used as a figure of speech but it is loose talk at best. There is a certain truth in the principle of charging more against valuable goods than against cheap goods as has been conceded; but that the carrier can, in analogy to taxation, throw the burden upon the more valuable goods and relieve the cheaper goods in direct proportion to their respective values cannot be admitted. The duty of the carrier is to move all goods at a reasonable price for the service rendered, a matter not to be determined upon any *ad valorem* basis. It is clear, at any rate, that the charge is not necessarily limited to the advantage

[1] Tift v. Southern Ry., 138 Fed. 753 (1905). Comm. v. Chicago G. W. Ry. Co., 141 Fed. 1003 (1905).

[2] But see Interstate Com.

which the customer derives from the service; and the fact that the rule does not work both ways makes one suspicious of it. When the price of a commodity goes up the railroads certainly have no right to raise their charges in proportion to the prosperity of their shippers.[1] Nor could a water company justify a greater charge for water against a man who lives in a costly house than against a house of less value in the market.[2] It is needless to add that such taxation without representation is opposed to the genius of the American people; and indeed, the government has not authorized any such private corporations to be tax-gatherers for their own benefit.

§ 1076. Service of unusual value.

That the service in question will be of unusual value to the particular patron is no reason why he should be called upon to pay more than any other member of the public should pay. If it were attempted to extend this theory of charging what the traffic will bear to other public services its oppressive character would be obvious. Suppose a water company should charge particular householders individually what they would pay rather than have their service cut off.[3] It is obvious as a Maine judge has pointed out that in many instances householders would pay several hundred per cent more than some others would pay who have their own sources of supply. And as a Federal judge recently said, if lumber will bear the advance, that is no reason why it should.[4] That business will still be done at the rate charged is no evidence that it is not unreasonable when a public service is in question, although doubtless it would be in the case of a private

[1] Tift v. Southern R. R. Co., 138 Fed. 753 (1905).

[2] Preston v. Water Commissioners, 117 Mich. 589, 76 N. W. 92 (1898).

[3] See Brunswick & T. Water Dist. v. Maine Water Co., 99 Me. 371, 59 Atl. 537 (1904).

[4] Tift v. Southern Ry. Co., 138 Fed. 753 (1905).

business. The monopolistic conditions which characterize public employment would result in extortionate prices being possible, while in a private business the asking of an unreasonable price would simply result in a refusal to do business, since the party quoted the outrageous price could resort to a competitor. The ordinary postulates of political ecomony are applicable only to private businesses where the law of competition prevails. In the case of public business the law of the land must be invoked to keep charges down to a reasonable level.

§ 1077. Service not worth usual amount.

Conversely the managers of public service, who are on the outlook for all the business they can get at whatever price the business will bear, claim the right to make extraordinary reductions to those of their patrons who find the service of less value to them than it would be to the average customer. Thus railroads make extraordinarily low rates for certain commodities of such an inferior grade that at the average freight rate it would not move at all, so disproportionate would the freight charge be to its actual value. Sometimes the railroads go further, and make a lower charge to these who are going to utilize the commodity in further manufactures and those to whom it is of sufficient value in its present shape.[1] This same problem of getting additional business by quoting a price to certain customers which will make it worth while to them, is coming up in the other public services as well. Thus the proprietors of gas works claim the right to make lower rates to those who utilize the supply for fuel.[2] It

---

[1] According to Hoover v. Pennsylvania R. R. Co., 156 Pa. St. 220, 27 Atl. 282, 36 Am. St. Rep. 43, 22 L. R. A. 263 (1893), such reductions may be made. But according to Lumber Co. v. Railroad, 136 N. C. 479, 48 S. E. 813 (1904), such reductions constitute illegal discrimination.

[2] A gas company may make a lower rate for fuel gas. State v. New Orleans Gas Light Co., 108

may often be that there are such substitutes for fuel gas that unless a much lower rate than the average is charged the business cannot be got. This argument in itself is no justification for making disproportionate rates against other members of the public who have no cheaper substitute. It may be said for allowing these practices, that provided it is understood that no business shall be done unless there is some margin above the bare cost of operation such additional business will benefit those who must pay the fixed charges to some extent by reducing the average cost of their service. It should be noted, however, that no court has ever suggested that a company which neglected its opportunities to make more money by such discriminating rates was doing wrong.

§ 1078. Average cost always modified.

In the determination of rates upon the basis of proportionality the average cost of service must play an important part. The ton-mile cost of moving freight on the railroad in question must be considered always.[1] But the average cost of service is at best only a standard with which to make comparisons.[2] As a practical matter some factors are present in every particular case which will either raise or lower the actual cost in its relation to the average cost. Thus the establishment of a ton-mile rate as a standard merely brings rates down to the narrowest point of scrutiny, and for that purpose is valuable; but it excludes consideration of other circumstances and conditions which enter into the making of rates, no matter how compulsory or imperious they may be, and it cannot,

La. 67, 32 So. 179 (1902). But it need not do so. People's Gaslight Co. v. Hale, 94 Ill. App. 406 (1900).

[1] See particularly, Atlantic C. L. Ry. Co. v. Florida, 203 U. S. 256,

51 L. ed. 174, 27 Sup. Ct. 108 (1906).

[2] See further Seaboard Air Line Ry. Co. v. Florida, 203 U. S. 261, 51 L. ed. 175, 27 Sup. Ct. 109 (1906).

therefore, be accepted as altogether controlling in determining the reasonableness of rates. A particular rate is thus the resultant of many factors. While there are certain economic forces which must be recognized as playing a legitimate part in the establishment of a particular rate, it is the office of the law to interfere to prevent the working out of these forces in an oppressive way.

CHAPTER XXXII

PROPER BASIS OF CAPITALIZATION

§ 1080. Various theories as to proper capitalization.

Topic A. The Original Cost as the Common-law Basis

§ 1081. Actual investment entitled to return.
1082. Argument for the rule of total investment.
1083. What is the actual cost.
1084. Cost enhanced by fraudulent contract.
1085. Plant built unnecessarily large.
1086. Plant adapted for a larger population.
1087. Construction now thought unwise.
1088. Proportion of plant not now utilized.
1089. Equipment long since superseded.
1090. Capital sunk in past operations.

Topic B. Outstanding Capitalization

§ 1091. Normal capitalization outstanding unconclusive.
1092. The problem of watered stock.
1093. Abandonment of par values.
1094. Bonded indebtedness beyond actual value.
1095. Stock issues based upon surplus earnings.
1096. Securities issued upon reorganization.
1097. State scrutiny of the issue of securities.
1098. Existing capitalization hardly excessive.

Topic C. Present Value as the Constitutional Basis

§ 1099. Protection of present values.
1100. Original cost as affecting present value.
1101. Value as a going concern.
1102. Whether return allowed on such value.
1103. Franchise value upon purchase.
1104. Franchise values not considered in rate regulation.
1105. Values returned for taxation inconclusive.
1106. Tax valuation does not estop the State.

§ 1080. Various theories as to proper capitalization.

In order to decide upon what principles the amount of capital devoted to a public service and therefore entitled to a return is to be estimated it is important to examine the various theories which have been brought forward for determining what amount is proper. There is as yet no real agreement among the authorities which have dealt with this problem; but it is desirable that some theory should be found with a sufficient preponderance to be taken as a working basis in a given situation. For without a basal theory as to proper capitalization, rate regulation is virtually impossible; since unless this is determined it cannot be told whether the receipts from any given business are excessive or not. Many theories as to proper capitalization have been advanced at different times, and, indeed, each of them still has some advocates at the present time. But, various as these are, they may be reduced to four. Thus (1) the outstanding capitalization is by a few still regarded as sacred; while at the other extreme are those who refer everything to what might be shown to be (2) the bare cost of substantial reproduction at the present moment. But to most persons both of these standards seem essentially unfair, either to the company concerned or to the public served. And the real controversy it is submitted is between the two remaining theories, (3) the original cost. of the property in question to its owners, or (4) the fair value of the property at the present time. It will be seen that, although these amounts may sometimes nearly approximate each other, there is such an inherent difference between these cases that one or the other must ultimately be adopted in a particular case.

Topic A. The Original Cost as the Common-Law Basis

§ 1081. Actual investment entitled to return.

The doctrine that the company would be entitled to a fair return on the money actually invested, whether originally or during the operation of the company, is expressed in some cases. This view is substantially held by the Supreme Court of Pennsylvania in Brymer v. Butler Water Company [1] where Mr. Justice Williams summed up the law relating to this matter thus: "The cost of the water to the company includes a fair return to the persons who furnished the capital for the construction of the plant, in addition to an allowance annually of a sum sufficient to keep the plant in good repair and to pay any fixed charges and operating expenses. A rate of water rents that enables the company to realize no more than this is reasonable and just." [2]

§ 1082. Argument for the rule of total investment.

It is submitted that this rule that a return may be

[1] 179 Pa. St. 231, 36 Atl. 249, 36 L. R. A. 260 (1897).

[2] In several jurisdictions the amount actually invested in good faith is given almost controlling weight.

United States.—Milwaukee El. Ry. Co. v. Milwaukee, 87 Fed. 577 (1898).

California.—San Diego Water Co. v. San Diego, 118 Cal. 556, 50 Pac. 633, 62 Am. St. Rep. 261 (1897).

Pennsylvania.—Pennsylvania R. R. Co. v. Philadelphia County, 220 Pa. St. 100, 68 Atl. 676, 15 L. R. A. N. S. 108 (1908).

West Virginia.—Coal & Coke Ry. Co. v. Conley (W. Va.) 67 S. E. 613 (1910).

But as in most cases the rule of present value is now favored, it is pointed out that original cost can only be important data in estimating what is the present value. This point is made most strongly in:

United States.—Seaboard Air L. Ry. Co. v. Florida, 203 U. S. 261, 51 L. ed. 175, 27 Sup. Ct. 109 (1906).

Minnesota.—State ex rel. v. Minneapolis & St. L. Ry. Co., 80 Minn. 191, 83 N. W. 60, 89 Am. St. Rep. 514 (1900).

based upon the total investment sunk in the construction of the plant from first to last, with certain limitations, may be adopted not improperly by a public service company in making up its own schedule of rates. The advantages of this rule, and the disadvantages of any other, are well dealt with in the Pennsylvania cases [1] brought under the peculiar statute which gives the court power to say whether the rates fixed by the water company in its schedule are unreasonable or not. In one of the fullest of these cases, the court found that allowing only one per cent for depreciation, the net income available for dividends was five per cent upon the total cost of construction of the water works. The Justice before whom the case was brought, held the schedule reasonable; he said, in part: "The primary basis of any calculator as to the value of a water plant must be the money actually invested by the owners. If the earnings of the company have been used to improve the property, it is counted as so much more cash invested. In a case in another State, the market value of the plant was suggested as the proper basis of calculation. This is open to two objections. The plant, for many reasons, may have depreciated in value and the consumers of water may have decreased in their number, thus working an injustice to the owners, or the plant, owing to favorable natural conditions and the rapid growth of the territory supplied, may have greatly enhanced in value, thus increasing the rates beyond reason and equity." [2]

[1] Wilkes-Barre v. Spring Brook Water Co., 4 Lack. (Pa.) Leg. News, 367 (1899). This is based upon Brymer v. Butler Water Co., 179 Pa. St. 231, 36 Atl. 249, 36 L. R. A. 260 (1897), cited in the last paragraph.

[2] See further the still more ex- treme case of Metropolitan Trust Co. v. Houston & T. C. R. R. Co., 90 Fed. 683 (1898); and the almost equally extreme case of Pennsylvania R. R. Co. v. Philadelphia County, 220 Pa. St. 100, 68 Atl. 676, 15 L. R. A. (N. S.) 108 (1908).

§ 1083. What is the actual cost.

The question of what constitutes the actual cost of the plant was raised and much discussed in the case of the Town of Falmouth v. Falmouth Water Company.[1] A statute gave the plaintiff town a right to take the corporate property of the defendant company on payment of the actual cost with interest. The town exercised the right, and this suit was brought to determine the actual cost. The court held in the litigation which followed that the actual cost mentioned in the statute was the actual cost of the plant to the water company; and this cost they held to be the amount actually paid to the contractor by the water company, although the contractor had done the work under a rather peculiar contract which yielded him a somewhat unusual profit. Mr. Justice Loring said in part: "It is argued by the town that this result amounts to substituting market value for actual cost, and actual cost excludes everything in the nature of a profit. It is true that actual cost excludes everything in the nature of a profit; but what is actual cost to the company includes a profit to the contractor, just as what is actual cost to the contractor includes a profit to the merchants of whom he buys his material." [2]

§ 1084. Cost enhanced by fraudulent contract.

It should be clear, however, that if the contract under which the works are constructed is collusively made, the company cannot later rely upon the contract price as the true measure of actual cost. For instance, it has not been uncommon, in the past at least, for the promoters of a public service company to organize a construction group, which was thereafter paid extravagant prices. If such were shown to be the facts, a court to-day would have no

[1] 180 Mass. 325, 62 N. E. 255 (1902).

[2] See to the same effect: Glouces-ter Water Co. v. Gloucester, 179 Mass. 365, 60 N. E. 977 (1901).

hesitation in going behind the returns to discover what would have been a proper cost. In a recent case in the United States Supreme Court [1] Mr. Justice Moody said: "The cause for the large variation between the real value of the property and the capitalization in bonds and preferred and common stock is apparent from the testimony. All, or substantially all, the preferred and common stock was issued to contractors for the construction of the plant, and the nominal amount of the stock issued was greatly in excess of the true value of the property furnished by the contracts. A single instance taken from the testimony will illustrate this. At the very start of the enterprise a contract was entered into for the construction of a part of the plant, which was of a value slightly, if at all, exceeding $124,000. The price paid the contractor was $125,000 in bonds and $200,000 in common stock. Other contracts for construction showed a like disproportion between value furnished and nominal capitalization received for that value. It perhaps is unnecessary to say that such contracts were made by the company with persons who, at the time, by stock ownership controlled its action. Bonds and preferred and common stock issued under such conditions afford neither measure of nor guide to the value of the property." [2]

§ 1085. Plant built unnecessarily large.

If the plant as originally constructed is unnecessarily large the company should not expect a return upon its

[1] Knoxville v. Knoxville Water Co., 212 U. S. 1, 53 L. ed. 371, 29 Sup. Ct. 148 (1909).

[2] The following cases, among others, make this point plain:

United States.—Dow v. Biedelman, 125 U. S. 680, 31 L. ed. 841, 8 Sup. Ct. 1028 (1888).

Maine.—Kennebec Water Dist. v. Waterville, 97 Me. 185, 54 Atl. 6, 60 L. R. A. 856 (1902).

Minnesota.—Steenerson v. Gt. Northern Ry. Co., 69 Minn. 353, 72 N. W. 713 (1897).

West Virginia.—Coal & Coke Ry. Co. v. Conley (W. Va.), 67 S. E. 613 (1910).

total investment. This is put in a striking manner in a recent case, thus: [1] "For a simple illustration, suppose that a five hundred horse power engine was used for pumping when a one hundred horse power engine would do as well. As property to be fairly valued the larger engine might be more valuable than the smaller one, yet it could not be said that it would be reasonable to compel the public to pay rates based upon the value of the unnecessarily expensive engine." The reason for this is best expressed in another recent case [2] thus: "If a plant is built, as probably this was, for a larger area than it finds itself able to supply, or, apart from that, if it does not, as yet, have the customers contemplated, neither justice nor the Constitution requires that, say, two-thirds of the contemplated number should pay a full return."

§ 1086. Plant adapted for a larger population.

But where the plant is built larger at the outset than is required immediately with the idea of supplying an increased population a more complex problem arises; for it has recently been appreciated that in many cases the public interests may often be served best by such expenditures. In the late case of the Tintern Manor Water Company [3] the court in determining what rates it would be reasonable to charge, made an elaborate investigation into the capital expenditures of the company, the results

---

[1] Per Savage, J., in Brunswick & T. W. D. v. Maine Water Co., 99 Me. 371, 59 Atl. 537 (1904). See, also, Capital Gas Light Co. v. Des Moines, 72 Fed. 829 (1896).

[2] San Diego L. & T. Co. v. Jasper, 189 U. S. 439, 47 L. ed. 892, 23 Sup. Ct. 571 (1903).

See also Boise City I. & L. Co. v. Clark, 131 Fed. 415, 65 C. C. A. 399 (1904).

[3] Long Branch Commission v. Tinturn Manor Water Co., 70 N. J. Eq. 71, 62 Atl. 474 (1905).

But see, Capital City Gaslight Co. v. Des Moines, 72 Fed. 829 (1896), doubting whether the expense of carrying an option on land for possible extensions of a gas plant is to be allowed for.

of which are detailed by the court in one of the most practical discussions as yet to be found among all the opinions dealing with rate problems. The Vice Chancellor found in almost all items large excess in cost if the standard was a plant which would barely meet present needs; but this he said was not a conclusive test, as it was the right of the company, if indeed not its duty to its public, to provide against the future growth of the community to a reasonable extent. In applying these principles the Vice Chancellor makes plain the compromise he has in mind. For example, the main supply pipes are thirty-six inch; he estimates that this is providing in advance for more population than can reasonably be expected for fifty years, while a thirty inch main would provide for perhaps twenty years in advance. He deducts therefore, the difference, $75,000, the guiding principle being what will prove in the long run to be an enlightened policy for the best interests of all concerned. With much the same consideration in mind a Federal judge recently held [1] that if a railroad is built in a new, sparsely settled territory with a view to serving a large future population and developing business, the Constitution does not require the few people and the small business of the present time to pay rates which will yield an income equal to the full return to be gathered when the country is populated and business developed in the full capacity of the road.

§ 1087. Construction now thought unwise.

It may turn out in some cases that some parts of the plant will prove of little value in the working of the system at a later time. In fairness it would seem that in such cases the question should be whether the expenditure seemed wise at the time it was made; if so that expenditure

[1] Southern Pacific R. R. Co. v. Bartine, 170 Fed. 725 (1909). See further, In Re Arkansas R. R. Rates, 168 Fed. 720 (1908).

should be considered like any other. This was put in extreme form in a Pennsylvania case,[1] where upon the reorganization of a system of water supply, one source formerly needing an expensive filtration plant was exclusively assigned to manufacturing purposes where filtering was unnecessary. Nevertheless the court held that the cost of the filtration plant remained capital entitled to full return. "It was a proper purchase under the circumstances," said the court, "and unquestionably represents a part of the investment of the Wilkes-Barre Water Company. Whether under the present system its function is as important as under the old system is immaterial. The money it represents was judiciously expended." [2]

§ 1088. Portion of plant not now utilized.

As to such portion of the plant as is not utilized at all in the present operation, the problem is more difficult still. If this is being held in condition to operate in emergencies, which are not altogether improbable, it would seem plain in analogy to the decisions just discussed that it may be included. On the other hand, if it is not devoted to any present use, then it should be plain that allowance should not be made for it in estimating the cost. In this case property no longer of any use should be carried in a separate account, as property should be which is being held for use in the remote future. In accordance with these distinctions, a Federal court [3] has allowed for

[1] Wilkes-Barre v. Spring Brook Water Co., 4 Lack. (Pa.) Leg. News 367 (1899).

[2] See Capital City Gaslight Co. v. Des Moines, 72 Fed. 829 (1896), where the court more cautiously suggests that as it is not shown that two gas plants, one for water gas, and the other for coal gas is even now altogether bad practice it will allow for both, although by the preponderance of expert opinion in new construction such an arrangement would not be made.

[3] Willcox et al. v. Consolidated Gas. Co., 212 U. S. 19, 53 L. ed. 381, 29 Sup. Ct. 192 (1909).

old gas works superseded but held in reserve, while the Minnesota court [1] refused to consider large tracts of land held for possible future freight terminals.   These decisions are not necessarily inconsistent.   The plant in the first case would be by most business men regarded as sufficiently devoted to the immediate business, while the land in the second case is plainly being carried more as a speculation.   Business men would demand a business profit on the whole plant in the first case, but they might well be content to carry without profit unimproved lands, relying upon the appreciation of the property for their ultimate profit.

§ 1089. Equipment long since superseded.

The extreme form of this problem relates to superseded equipment.   Take the case of a street railway which is constructed as a horse railway, then at great expense is changed to a cable road, then later at still greater expense is converted to an electric road, and then is obliged by statute to build a subway and place its tracks underground. It may have happened that all these expenditures were provided for by the raising of new capital for which securities are still outstanding.   Would it be outrageous to ask that some return on this capital should still constitute a charge upon the present concern?   In several cases some respect has been paid to this capitalization long after its tangible results have disappeared, notably in Milwaukee Electric Railway & Light Co. v. Milwaukee,[2] where District Judge Seaman allowed $2,000,000 in addition to the actual value of the present properties, making an allowance for the necessary and reasonable investment in the purchase of the old lines and equipments, which

[1] Steenerson v. Gt. Northern Ry. Co., 69 Minn. 353, 72 N. W. 713 (1897).

[2] 87 Fed. 577 (1898).

were indispensable to the contemplated improvement, and for the large investment arising out of the then comparatively new state of the art of electric railways for a large system.[1]

§ 1090. Capital sunk in past operations.

On the other hand, where the constitutional question is raised whether the Legislature may without confiscation so reduce rates as to leave a return only on the value of the present property, it would seem that it cannot be said to be taking that which no longer exists—capital sunk in the enterprise. Thus in disallowing the cost of unsuccessful experiments a Federal court [2] said: "Nor should there be included any amounts expended or investments made by plaintiff in its attempt or experiment, however laudable these attempts may have been, to supply fuel gas to the citizens of Des Moines, and which were expended or invested in directions not now required, or not properly · serviceable for the company's present uses. These must be laid aside, among any other unprofitable investments in the history of the company. These may evidence the creditable desire of the company to keep its works fully abreast with progressive ideas of gas making. But they are now of no market value. In other words, the court may not now regard the rates as properly to be increased above what would otherwise be reasonable for the purpose of allowing plaintiff to recoup losses heretofore incurred in any unfortunate or unprofitable investments it has made, or to charge and receive interest on losses thus incurred." [3]

---

[1] See also Metropolitan Trust Co. v. Houston & T. C. R. R. Co., 90 Fed. 683 (1898).

[2] Capital City Gaslight Co. v. Des Moines, 72 Fed. 829 (1896).

[3] But see Metropolitan Trust Co. v. Houston & T. C. R. R. Co., 90 Fed. 683 (1898).

Topic B. Outstanding Capitalization

§ 1091. Nominal capitalization outstanding unconclusive.

If stock is issued for no real consideration, or for more than the actual consideration received, it clearly cannot be taken as any indication of the capital. This was vigorously said by Mr. Justice Harlan in a leading case:[1] "It cannot, therefore, be admitted that a railroad corporation maintaining a highway under the authority of the State may fix its rates with a view solely to its own interests, and ignore the rights of the public. The rights of the public would be ignored if rates for the transportation of persons or property on a railroad are exacted without reference to the fair value of the property used for the public or the fair value of the services rendered, but in order simply that the corporation may meet operating expenses, pay the interest on its obligations, and declare a dividend to stockholders. If a railroad corporation has bonded its property for an amount that exceeds its fair value, or if its capitalization is largely fictitious, it may not impose upon the public the burden of such increased rates as may be required for the purpose of realizing profits upon such excessive valuation or fictitious capitalization; and the apparent value of the property and franchises used by the corporation, as represented by its stocks, bonds, and obligations, is not alone to be considered when determining the rates that may be reasonably charged." [2]

---

[1] Smyth v. Ames, 169 U. S. 466, 42 L. ed. 819, 18 Sup. Ct. 418 (1898).

And see particularly the language of Mr. Justice Moody in Knoxville v. Knoxville Water Co., 212 U. S. 1, 53 L. ed. 371, 29 Sup. Ct. 148 (1909).

[2] Outstanding capitalization was

said to be inconclusive in the following cases, among others:

United States.—Reagan v. Farmer's Loan & Trust Co., 154 U. S. 362, 38 L. ed. 1014, 14 Sup. Ct. 1047 (1894); San Diego Land & T. Co. v. National City, 174 U. S. 739, 43 L. ed. 1154, 19 Sup. Ct. 804 (1899); Spring Valley Water Works

§ 1092. The problem of watered stock.

Those who examine into these questions even in the most superficial manner are soon convinced of one thing, and that is that the par value of the outstanding stock issues does not necessarily constitute a proper basis for the capital charge. To make the capital account of a public service company the measure of its legitimate earnings would place, as a rule, the corporation which has been honestly managed from the outset under enormous disadvantages. Little if any weight, therefore, is to be attached to the nominal capitalization of the company, even although these shares may now be in the hands of innocent holders.[1] For, however distressing this circumstance may be, the law must take the attitude that these holders purchased with imputed knowledge of the public service law by which the state may always reduce the rates without unconstitutionality to a point where they will yield no more than a fair return upon actual values. So notorious is it that outstanding securities may have no relation to actual values, that their par value is hardly regarded by anyone to-day.[2]

v. San Francisco, 124 Fed. 574 (1903); Perkins v. Northern Pac. Ry. Co., 155 Fed. 445 (1908).

California.—Spring Valley Water Works v. San Francisco, 82 Cal. 286, 22 Pac. 910 (1890).

Maine.—Kennebec Water Dist. v. Waterville, 97 Me. 185, 54 Atl. 6, 60 L. R. A. 856 (1902).

Minnesota.—Steenerson v. Gt. Northern Ry., 69 Minn. 353, 72 N. W. 713 (1897).

North Carolina.—Griffin v. Goldsboro Water Co., 122 N. C. 206, 30 S. E. 319, 41 L. R. A. 240 (1898).

West Virginia.—Coal & Coke Ry.

Co. v. Conley (W. Va.), 67 S. E. 613 (1910).

[1] The plight of such holders appealed to Judge Hough in Consolidated Gas Co. v. Willcox, 157 Fed. 849 (1907). But Judge Ross had no sympathy for such holders in San Diego L. & T. Co. v. National City, 74 Fed. 79 (1896).

[2] Allegations as to outstanding securities are pertinent. Houston & T. C. Ry. Co. v. Storey, 149 Fed. 499 (1906).

But they are inconclusive. Perkins v. Northern Pacific Ry. Co., 155 Fed. 445 (1908).

For an excellent recent case in

§ 1093. Abandonment of par values.

So disproportionate is capitalization that to some students of the problem who have considered this matter of watered stock attentively it has seemed that the business-like solution would be to have the shares in the corporation without any designated par value, representing simply fractions of the ownership. This theory has been taken up by practical promoters who frankly admit that the real reason for issuing more in par value than the actual expenditures is so that a return commensurate with the risk may be obtained, should the corporation succeed. The general public however unjustly would almost always object in a particular case to seeing a shareholder getting a fourteen per cent dividend on a $100 share, but not perhaps to his getting a $14 dividend on an undenominated share which he bought for $200. Those who propose thus to elimate par values altogether must of course concede the power of the state to reduce rates so that there shall be no more than a fair return proportionate to the risk upon the actual value of the physical properties at any given time.

§ 1094. Bonded indebtness beyond actual value.

It was at one time supposed that bonded indebtedness was to be held sacred; [1] but from the modern point of view property held in mortgage is subject to revaluation as much as any other. As Mr. Justice Canty said in the leading case of Steenerson v. Great Northern Railway

which it is pointed out that fictitious valuations indicated by over issues of securities are to be rejected in dealing with this problem. See Coal & Coke Ry. Co. v. Conley (W. Va.), 67 S. E. 613 (1910).

In Southern Pacific R. R. Co. v. Bartine, 170 Fed. 751 (1910), it was said that the fair value of the outstanding securities was one of the elements to be considered.

[1] Of the cases to this effect see especially, Chicago & N. W. R. R. v. Dey, 35 Fed. 866, 1 L. R. A. 744 (1888).

Company:[1] "In determining what are reasonable rates, it is perfectly immaterial whether the railroad is mortgaged for two or three times what it would cost to reproduce it, or whether it is free from incumbrance. To hold otherwise would be to hold that the State or the public have indirectly guaranteed the payment of the mortgage bonds of every railroad. The State may as well guaranty the bonds directly as indirectly. But neither the state nor the public have done either the one or the other. It is immaterial how the property has been split up into different rights, interests, and claims. For the purpose of fixing rates, the holders of all these stand in the shoes of the sole owner of the property, unincumbered. The rights of the bondholders are no more and no less sacred than the rights of such an owner."

§ 1095. Stock issues based upon surplus earnings.

Doubts have sometimes been expressed as to the standing of securities issued to stockholders when surpluses have been accumulated. That this process may be stopped for the future by the reduction of rates to a point where no such surplus will be earned is true. But if at some past time a surplus has been earned and either held as cash or utilized in new construction, an issue of new securities against this would seem to represent capital belonging to the stockholders devoted to the business of the company as much as any other securities paid for by their holders.[2] As Mr. Justice Williams clearly explained in the Brymer case:[3] "In determining the amount of the

---

[1] 69 Minn. 353, 72 N. W. 713 (1897).

Perhaps the two best cases to read in support of the principal case are:

United States.—Knoxville v. Knoxville Water Co., 212 U. S. 1, 53 L. ed. 371, 29 Sup. Ct. 148 (1909).

North Carolina.—Griffin v. Goldsboro Water Co., 122 N. C. 206, 30 S. E. 319, 41 L. R. A. 240 (1898).

[2] See Logansport Gas Co. v. Peru, 89 Fed. 185 (1898).

[3] 179 Pa. St. 231, 36 Atl. 249, 36 L. R. A. 260 (1897).

investment by the stockholders it can make no difference that money earned by the corporation, and in a position to be distributed by a dividend among its stockholders, was used to pay for improvements and stock issued in lieu of cash to the stockholders. It is not necessary that the money should first be paid to the stockholder and then returned by him in payment for new stock issued to him. The net earnings, in equity, belonged to him, and stock issued to him in lieu of the money so used that belonged to him was issued for value, and represents an actual investment by the holder."

§ 1096. Securities issued upon reorganization.

A complication frequently met is that the operating company is the result of the consolidation of several previous companies or the reorganization of a previous corporation. In many actual cases both reorganization and consolidation are to be found so many times at various stages of the corporate history of the given concern that the outstanding issues tell little or nothing of real investment now devoted to the public service.[1] A reorganization may mean an increase in the nominal capitalization to placate certain interests or it may mean drastic elision of securities that represented actual investment. A consolidation similarly may mean increase or decrease in nominal capitalization. Obviously when a holding company is utilized there is a duplication of stock issues, at the very least. And when the consolidation is effected by buying the former properties outright an inflated price is usually paid. When in any of these ways the actual property is buried beneath corporate finance, little respect is to be paid to the outstanding issues as such, but the question should be as to the real values underlying

[1] See Chicago Union Traction Co. v. Chicago, 199 Ill. 579, 65 N. E. 470 (1902).

all these. It has been held, however, that whenever the capitalization of the present company is the result of some arrangement with the State by which the securities then issued may be said to have been approved, the State may not later be heard to question the values thus practically validated.[1]

§ 1097. State scrutiny of the issue of securities.

Of late years there has been an increasing tendency for the State to control this matter from the outset, by giving to the regulating commission the power to pass upon the issue of securities by public service corporations, and to scrutinize the arrangements under which these are paid for. Massachusetts which led the way in this direction went so far as to require not only authorization from the commission for new issues, but required further that all such issues should be paid for upon a cash basis at the market price. But very recently it has been seen that this legislation is too exacting, and the commission now has power to fix a somewhat lower price at which the new securities may be distributed if it believes that the conditions require it. Under the New York legislation, to take another type, the State is principally concerned in seeing to the application of the funds derived from new issues, whether in refunding obligations already incurred or in constructing new works.[2] To judge from the decisions thus far rendered, the question of what expenditures are a proper basis for permanent capitalization is the principal problem. This general sort of stock regulation is however not confined to these two States, but has spread

---

[1] See Willcox v. Consolidated Gas Co., 212 U. S. 19, 53 L. ed. 382, 29 Sup. Ct. 192 (1909).

[2] Power to pass upon the issue of securities may constitutionally be given to the commissions.

Minnesota.—State ex rel. v. Gt. Northern R. R. Co., 100 Minn. 445, 111 N. W. 289 (1907).

Wisconsin.—State ex rel. v. Railroad Commission, 137 Wis. 80, 117 N. W. 846 (1908).

rapidly over the country.[1] The results to be expected from it are in the end a great simplification of the problem of regulation, as under it the outstanding securities will gradually come to be at least the *prima facie* measure of the real investment devoted to public service upon which it may ultimately be conceded a proper return is due. What would be needed to bring this condition about immediately would be physical valuation of the present properties and an entire revision of the present holdings upon that basis.

§ 1098. Existing capitalization hardly excessive.

The only way in which investments in public service corporations could be jeopardized by any solution of the present problem which has been proposed, would be by proof that the outstanding capitalization is excessive; but although this has been loudly claimed, the claim can probably not be supported. Various theories for determining capitalization have been suggested which as has been seen, may be analyzed into four—the actual investment, the nominal outstanding capitalization, the actual present value, and the cost of reproduction. The law has not as yet made any invidious choice among these, but has considered them all with respect. The Constitution, as its interpretation has been settled by the Supreme Court, secures to the companies the opportunity for a fair return on the actual present value of the property; if hampered improperly in getting this it is said that their property is taken without due process of law. In respect to this test the commission has pointed out that the pres-

---

[1] As to the attitude of the courts in revision of the action of the commissions under such legislation, see:

New York.—People ex rel. Delaware & H. R. R. Co. v. Stevens, 197 N. Y. 1, 90 N. E. 60 (1909).

Texas.—United States & M. T. Co. v. Delaware W. Const. Co. (Tex. Civ. App.), 112 S. W. 447 (1908).

ent value is certainly as great as the reproduction value, and that the outstanding capitalization is little if at all greater than this is at the present time. It is true that there are outstanding many billions of securities which did not represent any original cash investment, in other words, "watered stock." But the probabilities are that when the enormous increase in the value of the rights of way and terminal facilities, together with the immense expenditures in improving trackage, roadbeds, grades and structures out of current earnings are all considered, the real value of railroad securities even may be as great as the face value of the securities.

Topic C. Present Value as the Constitutional Basis

§ 1099. Protection of present values.

The leading case on this point on the constitutional side of this problem is Smyth v. Ames.[1] This was a suit to test the constitutionality of certain statutes regulating railroad rates. In the course of this opinion Mr. Justice Harlan said: "We hold that the basis of all calculations as to the reasonableness of rates to be charged by a corporation maintaining a highway under legislative sanction must be the fair value of the property being used by it for the convenience of the public. And in order to ascertain that value, the original cost of construction, the amount expended in permanent improvements, the amount and market value of its bonds and stock, the present as compared with the original cost of construction, the probable earning capacity of the property under particular rates prescribed by statute, and the sum required to meet operating expenses, are all matters for consideration, and were to be given such weight as may be just and right in each case. We do not say that there

---

[1] 169 U. S. 466, 42 L. ed. 819, 18 Sup. Ct. 419 (1898).

may not be other matters to be regarded in estimating the
value of the property. What the company is entitled to
ask is a fair return upon the value of that which it employs
for the public convenience." [1]

§ 1100. Original cost as affecting present value.

It follows from the rule just recited that present value
may be shown to be less than actual cost. The true inquiry in constitutional cases is the present value of the
plant, and the evidence should be directed to that issue.
Without some proof as to that the case must fail.[2] But
this does not mean that evidence as to original cost is to

[1] By the prevalent law the present value may be the basis of rate
regulation by legislative process,
etc.

United States.—Reagan v. Farmers' Loan & Trust Co., 154 U. S.
362, 38 L. ed. 1014, 14 Sup. Ct. 1047
(1894); San Diego Land & T. Co. v.
National City, 174 U. S. 739, 43
L. ed. 1154, 19 Sup. Ct. 804 (1899);
San Diego, L. & T. Co. v. Jasper,
189 U. S. 439, 47 L. ed. 892, 23
Sup. Ct. 571 (1903); Stanislaus Co.
v. San Joaquin & K. R. C. & I. Co.,
192 U. S. 201, 48 L. ed. 406, 24 Sup.
Ct. 241 (1903); Cleveland Gaslight
Co. v. Cleveland, 71 Fed. 610
(1891); Atlantic & P. Ry. v. U. S.,
76 Fed. 186 (1896); Northern Pac.
Ry. v. Keyes, 91 Fed. 47 (1898);
Spring Valley Waterworks v. San
Francisco, 124 Fed. 574 (1903).
See Southern Pac. Ry. v. Railroad
Commissioners, 78 Fed. 236 (1896);
Cumberland Tel. & Tel. Co. v.
Railroad Comm., 156 Fed. 823
(1907); Southern Pacific R. R. Co.
v. Bartine, 170 Fed. 725 (1909); St.
Louis & S. F. Ry. Co. v. Hadley,
168 Fed. 317 (1909); Missouri, K.

& T. Ry. Co. v. Love, 177 Fed. 493
(1910).

California.—Spring Valley Waterworks v. San Francisco, 82 Cal.
286, 23 Pac. 910 (1890); Redlands,
L. & C. D. Water Co. v. Redlands,
121 Cal. 365, 53 Pac. 843 (1898).

Indiana.—Chicago, I. & L. Ry.
Co. v. Railroad Commission, 39
Ind. App. 358, 79 N. E. 520 (1907).

Iowa.—Cedar Rapids Co. v. Cedar Rapids, 118 Ia. 234, 91 N. W.
1081 (1902);

Maine.—Kennebec Water Dist.
v. Waterville, 97 Me. 185, 54 Atl.
6, 60 L. R. A. 856 (1902); Brunswick & T. W. Dist. v. Maine Water
Co., 99 Me. 371, 59 Atl. 537 (1904).

Minnesota.—Steenerson v. Gt.
Northern Ry., 69 Minn. 353, 72
N. W. 713 (1897); State ex rel. v.
Minneapolis & St. L. Ry., 80 Minn.
191, 83 N. W. 60 (1900).

West Virginia.—Coal & Coke Ry.
Co. v. Conley (W. Va.), 67 S. E.
613 (1910).

[2] See particularly State v. Minneapolis & St. L. Ry. 80 Minn. 191,
83 N. W. 60 (1900).

be excluded. As Mr. Justice Savage said in a water works case [1] already quoted: "The rates which it would be reasonable for the company to ask depend upon what would be a fair return, under the circumstances, upon the value of the property used—a question which we shall discuss later on. In determining what would be a fair return, undoubtedly the amount of money actually and wisely expended is a primary consideration. Actual cost bears upon reasonableness of rates, as well as upon the present value of the structure as such. It thus bears upon what is a fair return upon the investment, and so upon the value of the property. In estimating structure value prior cost is not the only criterion of present value, and present value is not what is to be ascertained. The present value may be affected by the rise and fall of prices of materials. If in such way the present value of the structure is greater than the cost, the company is entitled to the benefit of it. If less than the cost, the company must lose it. And the same factors should be considered in estimating the reasonableness of returns."

§ 1101. Value as a going concern.

There is more to present value than a mere inventory will show. Certain it is that, when the question is as to the present value of a public service property that is being taken over by the State or a municipality either by eminent domain or by virtue of some clause in the original franchise, the value of the property as a going concern is to be taken. In Gloucester Water Supply Company v. Gloucester, before cited, [2] Mr. Justice Loring said: "It is

---

[1] Kennebec Water Dist. v. Waterville, 97 Me. 185, 54 Atl. 6, 60 L. R. A. 856 (1902).

See State ex rel. v. Seaboard Air Line Ry. Co., 48 Fla. 129, 37 So. 314 (1904).

Compare Seaboard Air Line Ry.

Co. v. Florida, 203 U. S. 261, 51 L. ed. 175, 27 Sup. Ct. 109 (1906).

[2] 179 Mass. 365, 60 N. E. 977, (1901). See also Spring Valley Waterworks v. San Francisco, 124 Fed. 574 (1903).

plain that the real, commercial, market value of the property of the water company is, or may be, in fact greater than 'the cost of duplication, less depreciation, of the different features of the physical plant.' Take, for example a manufacturing plant: Suppose a manufacturing plant has been established for some ten years and is doing a good business and is sold as a going concern; it will sell for more on the market than a similar plant reproduced physically would sell for immediately on its completion, before it had acquired any business." On this point also Mr. Justice Savage in Kennebec Water District v. Waterville [1] gave this instruction: "In consideration of the fact that the system is a going concern, the appraisers should consider, among other things, the present efficiency of the system, the length of time necessary to construct the same *de novo*, the time and cost needed after construction to develop such new system to the level of the present one in respect to business and income, and the added net incomes and profits, if any, which by its acquirement as such going concern, would accrue to a purchaser during the time required for such new construction, and for such development of business and income."

§ 1102. Whether return allowed on such value.

So far as the value of a "going business" is increased by the mere element of good will, it cannot demand a return from the rates charged. "The fact that the business is established is, of course, a material fact in ascertaining the value of the plant, and especially is this true where the property is being estimated for the purposes of sale or condemnation; but as a basis for estimating profits

[1] 97 Me. 185, 54 Atl. 6, 60 L. R. A. 856 (1902). See also Brunswick & T. Water Dist. v. Maine Water Co., 99 Me. 371, 59 Atl. 537 (1904). In case of sale to a municipality the value of the plant as a going concern is to be considered. Norwich Gas & E. Co. v. City of Norwich, 76 Conn. 565, 57 Atl. 746 (1904).

its significance is less apparent. The merchant who sells an established business may properly place a high value on the good will which he relinquishes to the buyer; but so long as he continues in the enjoyment of the business he has created he does not add the value of the good will to his capital stock in estimating the percentage of his annual profits."[1] To a certain extent however, a going business is actually more valuable than the mere physical elements of which the plant is composed. The physical connections of its plant, the cost of fitting it for its purpose, the loss of interest on the investment during construction and until the plant is in complete and lucrative operation, all add an actual value to the plant and are properly included in the construction account and form part of the actual capital employed in the enterprise. " The fact that it is a system in operation, not only with a capacity to supply the city, but actually supplying many buildings in the city,—not only with a capacity to earn, but actually earning,—makes it true that the 'fair and equitable value' is something in excess of the cost of reproduction." [2]

§ 1103. Franchise value upon purchase.

Whether when the plant of a public service company is taken by a city, by eminent domain or by contract, compensation is to be made for the franchises of the company is not entirely clear on the authorities. The question should of course be determined according to whether, in view of the purchase or taking, any value remains in the franchise. Although the company may be compelled to submit to statutory rates which make no account of the existence of a franchise, the franchise may nevertheless be of some value. Even when the rates are so limited,

[1] Quoted from Cedar Rapids Water Co. v. Cedar Rapids, 118 Iowa, 234, 91 N. W. 1081 (1902).

[2] Quoted from Kennebec Water Dist. v. Waterville, 97 Me. 185, 54 Atl. 6, 60 L. R. A. 856 (1902).

the company is still permitted to receive a return on its capital which is greater than that on a government bond; the ownership of the plant may, therefore, have a certain value which the franchise gives. And if the franchise actually has a value, compensation for it should be made. If, then, a public service company has obtained from the public authorities an exclusive franchise for a term of years, which has been granted in such a way as to form a contract which the State cannot impair, the franchise has obviously a certain value, for the opportunity to make a fair rate of return in a business so safe as this is by reason of its monopoly in a public necessity is worth a certain sum in itself.[1] But no more than this need really be paid even for such an exclusive franchise, no matter what its present profits may be, since the State may at any time reduce its rates to a fair return upon its actual investment. Even if there is no monopoly, if the franchise is practically exclusive, it presumably has a value, for which the company must be paid if the plant is taken by eminent domain or is bought under a clause in the charter. The value of this franchise is greater or less according to the practical possibility of competition; it is greatest if the franchise is legally exclusive, and grows less as the likelihood of actual competition increases.[2]

§ 1104. Franchise values not considered in rate regulation.

It should be clear that in estimating the capital upon

[1] Bristol v. Bristol & Warren Waterworks, 23 R. I. 274, 49 Atl. 974 (1901). Compare Gloucester Water Co. v. Gloucester, 179 Mass. 365, 60 N. E. 977 (1901).

[2] Quoted from Kennebec Water Dist. v. Waterville, 97 Me. 185, 54 Atl. 6, 60 L. R. A. 856 (1902), citing, among other cases, Long Island Water Supply Co. v. Brooklyn, 166 U. S. 685, 41 L. ed. 1165, 17 Sup. Ct. 718 (1897).

In case of sale to a city the value of company's contract with the city is to be considered. Covington Gaslight Co. v. City of Covington, 22 Ky. L. Rep. 796, 58 S. W. 805 (1900).

which a public service company is entitled to a fair return the value of a franchise enjoyed by the company cannot be considered. The value of the franchise is itself based on the capacity of the company to earn profits; and it becomes greater when the earnings of the company are increased. If, therefore, a high rate of income could be justified on account of the great value of the franchise, this fact would in turn enhance the value of the franchise itself and so justify a still higher charge; and there would be no limit to the legal charge of the company which could be enforced should such franchise value be permitted to increase in this way the capital charges. As Mr. Justice Savage said in a late Maine case [1] involving this point: "In connection it should be noticed that to say that the reasonableness of rates depends upon the fair value of the property used, and that the fair value of the property used depends upon the rates which may be reasonably charged, seems to be arguing in a circle. If we should say that reasonableness of rates depended solely upon the value of the property, and that value of the property depended solely upon the rates which may be reasonably charged, such would be the case. But neither proposition is true." It unquestionably follows that such franchise values cannot stand in the way of rate regulation. As Mr. Justice Peckham recently said in the Supreme Court of the United States as to a valuation of the property of the Consolidated Gas Company [2] which included some mil-

---

[1] In Brunswick & T. Water Dist. v. Maine Water Co., 99 Me. 371, 59 Atl. 537 (1904). But see Spring Valley Works v. San Francisco, 124 Fed. 574 (1903).

It may well be that if a price is paid for the franchise to the governmental authorities granting the franchise this sum must be ac-

counted a part of the cost of the plant; and if this must be periodically renewed a provision for its amortization would also seem proper.

[2] Willcox v. Consolidated Gas Co., 212 U. S. 19, 53 L. ed. 382, 29 Sup. Ct. 192 (1909).

It seems that if the State in the

lions for its franchises: "Its past value was founded upon the opportunity of obtaining these enormous and excessive returns upon the property of the company, without legislative interference with the price for the supply of gas, but that immunity for the future was, of course, uncertain, and the moment it ceased and the legislature reduced the earnings to a reasonable sum the great value of the franchises would be at once and unfavorably affected."

§ 1105. Values returned for taxation inconclusive.

It is sometimes urged that the valuation placed upon the property of the company for taxation should establish the present value. While it is true that this furnishes some criterion, it certainly is open to show the common fact that assessments on the district in question are usually no more than a certain percentage of actual values.[1] Even its sworn return of tangible property has been held not to estop the company from showing higher value in disputing the reasonableness of legislative rates.[2] But such returns are evidence against the company which seeks to establish higher value. Returns made to local bodies for parts of the physical property do not however prevent the company from showing that the value of the property as a whole is greater than the aggregate of these parts.

§ 1106. Tax valuation does not estop the State.

On the other hand the State by assessing a value for taxation does not estop itself from reducing that value by

past has authorized a capitalization which includes some franchise value it cannot later refuse to let the corporation get a fair return on the capitalization thus validated. And so it would be probably where the State has insisted that a certain price should be got for the shares of the corporation which were issued against all the assets of the corporation franchises included.

[1] Southern Pacific Ry. Co. v. Railroad Commrs., 78 Fed. 236 (1896).

[2] Louisville, & N. Ry. Co. v. Brown, 123 Fed. 946 (1903).

later regulation of rates. As the United States Supreme Court recently pointed out in the Consolidated Gas case [1] even a franchise tax is a tax on the actual value of the franchise as it exists at any particular time; and the imposition of it is quite consistent with the value of the franchise being subject to diminution by a diminished income as a result of legislation reducing rates.[2] The company may be taxed upon its franchise when by reason of the failure of the State to keep its rates down it is earning an extraordinary amount upon its physical value. But when the State choses to so reduce the rates that the company can earn nothing beyond the fair value of its tangible property, it will find that it has little or no franchise value left to tax.

Topic D. Cost of Reproduction as the Basis

§ 1107. The Minnesota rule.

According to the rule adopted in Minnesota the value on which a railroad is entitled to a fair return is the cost of reproducing the road in its present condition at present prices. If extraordinary expenses were necessary in establishing the road, or if higher prices prevailed at the time it was built, these would not enter into consideration at all. The leading case on this point is Steenerson v. Great Northern Railway.[3] The railway commission having fixed grain rates, the railway company appealed, and the question was finally determined in the Supreme Court of Minnesota. In delivering the principal opinion in the case Mr. Justice Canty said: "The railroad may have been

---

[1] Willcox v. Consolidated Gas Co., 212 U. S. 19, 53 L. ed. 382, 29 Sup. Ct. 192 (1909).

[2] Overruling s. c., 157 Fed. Rep. 849 (1908).

[3] 69 Minn. 353, 72 N. W. 713 (1897).

See also State ex rel. Ry. Comm. v. Minneapolis & St. L. R. R. Co., 80 Minn. 191, 83 N. W. 60, 89 Am. St. Rep. 514 (1900).

constructed years ago, when iron rails cost $85 per ton, and everything else in proportion, or it may have been constructed yesterday, when steel rails cost but $16 per ton, and everything else nearly in proportion. Counsel for the railway company dwell much upon the original cost of the older portions of these lines of road. If a railroad was built 30 years ago at a cost of $40,000 per mile, and another one equally as good was built within a year through the same territory at a cost of $12,000 per mile, on what principle should it be held that the old road is entitled to three and one third times as much income as the new road? No guaranty was ever given by the State to the old road that the price of materials and the cost of construction would not decline, or that capital invested in railroads should not be subject to like vicissitudes as capital invested in other enterprises. Modern improvements and other causes have continued to reduce the cost of construction of all kinds of new plants, and to reduce the value of old plants, or render them wholly worthless, and the State did not guaranty that those causes should not in like manner affect the capital invested in railroads. Then the material question is not what the railroad cost originally, but what it would now cost to reproduce it."

§ 1108. The Federal courts opposed.

The Minnesota rule having been applied by the Texas Railway Commission in fixing railroad rates in that State, the railroads filed in the Federal court a bill for an injunction against the rates. The rule was held to be an improper and unreasonable one, and the exaction of the rates as fixed by the commission was restrained.[1] Circuit Judge McCormick said: "It is therefore not only impracticable,

---

[1] Metropolitan Trust Co. v. Houston & T. C. R. R., 90 Fed. 683 (1898).

but impossible to reproduce this road, in any just sense, or according to any fair definition of those terms. And a system of rates and charges that looks to a valuation fixed on so narrow a basis as that shown to have been adopted by the commission, and so fixed as to return only a fair profit upon that valuation, and which permits no account for betterments made necessary by the growth of trade, seems to me to come clearly within the provision of the Fourteenth Amendment to the Constitution of the United States, which forbids that a State shall deprive any person of property without due process of law, or deny any person within its jurisdiction the equal protection of the laws." [1]

§ 1109. Explanation of the California decisions.

Two California decisions [2] appear to hold that nothing but the cost of reproduction is to be considered. The cases did not, however, go quite so far. They are well considered and explained by Circuit Judge Morrow in the Federal court in the Ninth Circuit: [3] "Neither of these cases goes to the extent of holding that in determining the value of the property of a corporation neither the capital stock nor bonded indebtedness can be considered. It is doubtless true that in many cases these elements may be excessive or fictitious, and represent speculative, rather than real and substantial, values. But there may be cases where both stock and bonds represent in the market a present actual value in the property of the corporation, and a value that could not be otherwise very well established. In such a case, what objection can there be to

[1] Milwaukee Electric Ry. & L. Co. v. Milwaukee, 87 Fed. 577 (1898), goes almost to the same extent.

[2] San Diego Water Co. v. San Diego, 118 Cal. 556, 50 Pac. 633 (1897); Redlands L. & C. D. Water Co. v. Redlands, 121 Cal. 365, 53 Pac. 843 (1898).

[3] Spring Valley Waterworks v. San Francisco, 124 Fed. 574 (1903).

giving the evidence such consideration as, under all the circumstances, it deserves?   It seems to me there can be none."

§ 1110. Factors disregarded by the reproduction rule.

The essential inadequacy of the reproduction rule has often been remarked.   The different factors that should be considered are well set forth in the case of the National Waterworks Company v. Kansas City,[1] a suit brought by a water company to enforce the statutory obligation resting upon the city to pay to the company the "fair and equitable value" of the whole works.   In answer to the theory that this would be satisfied by finding what the works could be reproduced for, Mr. Justice Brewer said that reproducing the waterworks plant would not be a fair test, because that did not take into account the value which flows from the established connections between the pipes and the buildings of the city.   It is obvious that the mere cost of purchasing the land, constructing the buildings, putting in the machinery, and laying the pipes in the streets—in other words, the cost of reproduction— does not give the present value of the property.   A completed system of waterworks, such as the company has, without a single connection between the pipes in the streets and the buildings of the city, would be a property of much less value than that system connected, as it is, with so many buildings, and earning, in consequence thereof, the money which it does earn.   On the other hand in the case of Knoxville v. Knoxville Water Company,[2] Mr. Justice Moody pointed out that in estimating for regulating purposes the value of a plant the cost of reproduction is not a fair measure of value unless a substantial allowance is made for the actual depreciation which makes

---

[1] 62 Fed. 853, 10 C. C. A. 653 (1894).

[2] 212 U. S. 1, 53 L. ed. 371, 29 Sup. Ct. 148 (1909).

an old plant of less value than a new one. And this he said in the particular case resulted in putting too high a valuation upon the waterworks. Its present physical value he thought was not more than the cost of reproduction less the actual depreciation.

§ 1111. Abandonment of the investment test impolitic.

Emphasis has thus far been laid upon the essential injustice of any reproduction rule to the proprietors of the enterprise in ignoring large elements of value which exist in a going concern. And unless the promoters of an enterprise can rest assured of the fruits of their labor there may not be sufficient inducement to bring about a proper development of public works. It is an unfair rule which would subject investors to great chances of loss without any corresponding chances of gain.[1] But there is, moreover, the grave danger that in the course of time this rule devised by advocates for the public for the dismay of the companies may be turned upon the public to its own distress. So rapidly does advantageous realty of all sorts increase in value in a growing community that it will soon be seen that to reproduce many public works would cost much more now than the original cost.[2] The few miles of trackage by which the New York Central Railroad enters the city of New York, a strip of land which cost originally comparatively nothing, could not be paralleled to-day for several hundred millions. The land grants stretching on each side of several of the Pacific railroads for thousands of miles could not in many tracts be replaced for many times their original valuation. One may prophesy with confidence that before the century is much older, regret will be felt that a short-sighted

---

[1] See the language in Wilkes-Barre v. Spring Brook Water Co., 4 Lack. L. News (Pa.) 367 (1899).

[2] See the language in San Diego Water Co. v. San Diego, 118 Cal. 556, 50 Pac. 633 (1897).

public opinion in the last century refused to protect the honest investor in his original investment, as the common law was inclined to do, and made the constitutional test for the regulation of rates that of the value of the property at any particular time.

§ 1112. Two principles still persist.

Finally it must be borne in mind that the problem presented to a court which is asked to set aside an established rate as unconstitutional because it amounts to a confiscation of property, is not precisely the same problem as that presented to a court which is asked to pass upon the fairness of a rate established by a public service company. If a statutory rate takes property, the property affected by it is not the original investment, but the property actually existent and owned by the company. If it is a taking of property to deprive the owner of a fair return upon it, the return must be unfair as income derived from that actual property. In determining whether the return allowed to the railroad is a fair return on their property the property is that actually in use, at its present value. Where, however, the question is whether the company is exacting too great a return on its investment by means of an unfair schedule the question is as to the amount actually and bona fide invested. Justifying legislative rates under the constitution therefore is one thing, and holding that unreasonable charges are not being made as a matter of common law is quite another matter.

CHAPTER XXXIII

RATE OF RETURN

§ 1120. Elements in determining a fair return.

§ 1120. Elements in determining a fair return.

What constitutes a fair rate of return is difficult to determine by general rule as it is dependent upon the

[997]

particular case.   It depends to a certain extent upon the
character of the enterprise; in established businesses a
lower rate should be expected than in new ventures.   It
depends moreover upon the nature of the security; upon
bonds a lower rate of interest is to be expected than the
usual percentage paid in dividends upon stocks.   These
are the principal considerations, but as the discussion
advances it will be seen that there are other minor matters
to be taken into account.   It will make some difference,
also, in what manner the matter comes before the court
for decision.   If the question is whether a rate fixed by
one engaged in a public service is producing an unreasonably high rate of return, that is one thing.   If the question
is whether a rate fixed by public authority, either by the
Legislature directly or by a commission acting in pur-
suance of legislative authority, is unreasonably low, that
is another matter.   It is obvious that there is all the
difference of reasonable alternatives between these two
aspects of the problem.   Eight per cent might not be too
much return by a schedule fixed by the company in one
case, while a reduction of a schedule by legislation so as
not to produce more than six per cent, might not be
outrageous in the other.

Topic A. Establishment of the Doctrine

§ 1121. Establishment of the power to restrict charges.

The earlier cases under the Fourteenth Amendment
simply established that the State might regulate the rates
of those engaged in public employment.   The attention
of the court was directed to showing that the power to
regulate existed, and practically nothing was said about
the limitations upon that power.[1]   And indeed the com-

[1] Where a company has accepted
a franchise providing that it shall
not charge more than certain rates,
it cannot of course later make the
complaint that these rates are inadequate.

plainants did not adduce evidence that the rates fixed by the State were inadequate; they denied altogether that the rates could be regulated at all. The idea of these earlier cases, so far as one can judge from the language used, was that regulation of rates might go to any extent, so long as a deficit was not brought about.[1]

§ 1122. Rates fixed must not produce a deficit.

As soon as the power to regulate was once established the point was urged that the power had its limitations, and this the court conceded in very guarded language. For example, in the Railroad Commission cases [2] Chief Justice Waite said: "From what has thus been said it is not to be inferred that this power of limitation or regulation is itself without limit. This power to regulate is not a power to destroy, and limitation is not the equivalent of confiscation." As late as the case of Reagan v. Farmers' Loan & Trust Company [3] this requisite was not stated unequivocally. In that case Mr. Justice Brewer said:

United States.—Chesapeake & P. Tel. Co. v. Manning, 186 U. S. 238, 46 L. ed. 1144, 22 S. Ct. 881 (1902).

New York.—Condon v. New Rochelle Water Co., 136 App. Div. 897, 120 N. Y. Supp. 1119 (1909).

[1] The Federal cases of this period, which held that if there was any net profit left, apparently no matter how small, the legislation was not confiscatory, were: Munn v. Illinois, 94 U. S. 113, 24 L. ed. 72 (1876); Peik v. Chicago & N. W. Ry. Co., 94 U. S. 164, 24 L. ed. 97 (1876); Chicago, B. & Q. Ry. Co. v. Iowa, 94 U. S. 155, 24 L. ed. 94 (1876); Chicago M. & St. P. R. R. Co. v. Ackley, 94 U. S. 179, 24 L. ed. 99 (1876); Tilley v. Savannah, F. & W. R. R. Co., 5 Fed. 641 (1881); Wells v. Oregon Ry. & Nav. Co., 15 Fed. 561 (1883.)

[2] 116 U. S. 307, 29 L. ed. 636 (1886).

[3] 154 U. S. 362, 38 L. ed. 1014, 14 Sup. Ct. 180 (1894).

The Federal cases of this transition period when it was hoped that a profit would normally be left the public service company whose rates had been reduced by legislation were: Dow v. Beidelman, 125 U. S. 680, 31 L. ed. 841, 8 Sup. Ct. 1028 (1888); Chicago & G. T. Ry. v. Wellman, 143 U. S. 339, 36 L. ed. 176, 12 Sup. Ct. 400 (1892); Chicago N. W. R. R. v. Dey, 35 Fed. 866, 1 L. R. A. 744 (1888); Chicago & P. M. & O. R. R. Co. v. Becker, 35 Fed. 883 (1888).

"It is unnecessary to decide, and we do not wish to be understood as laying down an absolute rule that in every case a failure to produce some profit to those who have invested their money in the building of a road is conclusive that the tariff is unjust and unreasonable. And yet justice demands that every one should receive some compensation for the use of his money and property, if it be possible without prejudice to the rights of others."

§ 1123. Adequate return must be left.

But in 1898, in the important case of Smyth v. Ames,[1] a disposition was shown to give more protection to the owners of the railroads. It was proved in that case that the regulation complained of might very probably leave some return above all proper charges. But this did not satisfy the court, Mr. Justice Harlan saying: "What the company is entitled to ask is a fair return upon the value of that which it employs for the public convenience. On the other hand, what the public is entitled to demand is that no more be exacted from it for the use of a public highway than the services rendered by it are reasonably worth." Ever since this case the doctrine has been well established that except in abnormal cases legislation reducing rates which does not leave a fair profit upon the capital involved is virtually confiscatory.[2]

[1] 169 U. S. 466, 42 L. ed. 819, 18 Sup. Ct. 418 (1898).

[2] In the following cases, among others, the new rates imposed by governmental authority were held confiscatory by the above principles on the showing made by the evidence adduced.

United States.—St. Louis & San Francisco Ry. Co. v. Gill, 156 U. S. 649, 39 L. ed. 567, 15 Sup. Ct. 484 (1895); Cotting v. Kansas City S. Y. Co., 183 U. S. 79, 46 L. ed. 92, 22 Sup. Ct. 30 (1901); Cleveland Gas Light Co. v. Cleveland, 71 Fed. 610 (1891); New Memphis Gas Light Co. v. Memphis, 72 Fed. 952 (1896); Southern Pac. Ry. Co. v. Railroad Commission, 78 Fed. 236 (1896); Northern Pac. Ry. Co. v. Keyes, 91 Fed. 47 (1898); Milwaukee Electric Ry. Co. v. Milwaukee, 87 Fed. 577 (1898); Spring Valley Waterworks v. San Francisco, 124 Fed. 574 (1903); Palatka Waterworks v. Palatka, 127 Fed. 161 (1903); Ozark

§ 1124. Reduction leaving reasonable return.

The present doctrine of the United States Supreme Court, as seen in Stanislaus County v. San Joaquin Canal and Irrigation Company [1] is that the rates of public service companies may be reduced to any extent, provided reasonable return is left to the owners upon the value of the property devoted to the public use. In that case an ordinance adopted by a board of supervisors fixing water rates was objected to because the result would work a reduction of its rates from eighteen to six per cent. The reply to this contention by Mr. Justice Peckham, in the Supreme Court of the United States was: "It is not confiscation, nor a taking of property without due process of law, nor a denial of the equal protection of the laws, to fix water rates so as to give an income of six per cent upon the then value of the property actually used for the purpose of supplying water as provided by law, even though the company had prior thereto been allowed to fix rates that would secure to it one and one-half per cent a month income upon the capital actually invested in the undertaking. If not hampered by an unalterable contract,

Bell Telephone Co. v. Springfield, 140 Fed. 666 (1905); Southern R. R. Co. v. M'Neill, 155 Fed. 756 (1907); Seaboard Air Line Ry. Co. v. Railroad Comm. 155 Fed. 792 (1907).

California.—Spring Valley Waterworks v. San Francisco, 82 Cal. 286, 22 Pac. 910 (1890).

Illinois.—Chicago v. Rogers Pk. Co., 214 Ill. 212, 73 N. E. 375 (1905).

Maryland.—Maryland Tel. Co. v. Simons Sons Co., 103 Md. 137, 63 Atl. 314 (1906).

Michigan.—Alpena Electric Co. v. Alpena, 130 Mich. 413, 90 N. W. 36 (1902).

Nebraska.—Wabaska Electric Co. v. City of Wymore, 60 Neb. 199, 82 N. W. 626 (1900).

New York.—Brooklyn Union Gas Co. v. City of New York, 115 App. Div. 69, 100 N. Y. Supp. 571 (1906).

Pennsylvania.—Pennsylvania R. R. Co. v. Philadelphia County, 220 Pa. St. 100, 68 Atl. 676, 15 L. R. A. (N. S.) 108 (1908).

Texas.—Texas & N. O. R. R. Co. v. Sabine Tram. Co. (Tex. Civ. App.), 121 S. W. 256 (1909).

Vermont.—State v. Central Vt. Ry. Co., 81 Vt. 463, 71 Atl. 194, 130 Am. St. Rep. 1065 (1908).

[1] 192 U. S. 201, 48 L. ed. 406, 24 Sup. Ct. 241 (1903).

providing that a certain compensation should always be received, we think that a law which reduces the compensation theretofore allowed to six per cent upon the present value of the property used for the public is not unconstitutional. There is nothing in the nature of confiscation about it." [1]

Topic B. Extent to Which Return is Protected

§ 1125. Reasonableness of return now judicial question.

The result of this is that reasonableness of return has become a judicial question; and therefore the rules by which this shall be determined have become matters of law. The present situation is perhaps best summed up in

[1] In the following cases among others, the new rates imposed by governmental authority were held not to be confiscatory by the above principles on the showing made by the evidence adduced;

United States.—San Diego Land & Town Co. v. National City, 174 U. S. 739, 43 L. ed. 1154, 19 Sup. Ct. 804 (1899); Minneapolis & St. Louis R. R. Co. v. Minnesota, 186 U. S. 257, 46 L. ed. 1151, 22 Sup. Ct. 900 (1902); San Diego Land & Town Co. v. Jasper, 189 U. S. 439, 47 L. ed. 892, 23 Sup. Ct. 571 (1903); Prentice v. Atlantic C. L. Ry. Co., 211 U. S. 210, 53 L. ed. 150, 29 Sup. Ct. 67 (1908); Willcox v. Consolidated Gas Co., 212 U. S. 19, 53 L. ed. 382, 29 Sup. Ct. 192 (1909); Old Colony Trust Co. v. City of Atlanta, 83 Fed. 39 (1897); Ball v. Rutland R. Co., 93 Fed. 513 (1899); Kimball v. City of Cedar Rapids, 99 Fed. 130 (1900); Perkins v. Northern Pac. Ry. Co., 155 Fed. 445 (1907); Home Tel. & Tel. Co. v. Los Angeles, 155

Fed. 554 (1907); Central of Ga. Ry. Co. v. M'Lendon, 157 Fed. 961 (1907); Oregon Ry. & W. v. Campbell, 173 Fed. 957 (1909).

Florida.—State v. Seaboard Air Line, 48 Fla. 129, 37 So. 314 (1904).

Illinois.—Chicago v. Rogers Pk. Co., 214 Ill. 212, 73 N. E. 375 (1905).

Indiana.—Chicago I. & L. Ry. Co. v. Railroad Commission, 39 Ind. App. 358, 79 N. E. 520 (1907).

Iowa.—Cedar Rapids W. Co. v. Cedar Rapids, 118 Ia. 234, 91 N. W. 1081 (1902).

Kansas.—T u c k e r v. Missouri Pacific Ry. Co. (Kans.), 108 Pac. 89 (1910).

Maine.—Kennebec Water Dist. v. Waterville, 97 Me. 185, 54 Atl. 6, 60 L. R. A. 856 (1902).

Minnesota.—State ex rel. v. Minneapolis & St. Louis R. R. Co., 80 Minn. 191, 83 N. W. 60, 89 Am. St. Rep. 514 (1900).

New York.—Richman v. Consolidated Gas Co., 114 App. Div. 216, 100 N. Y. S. 81 (1906).

one [1] of the recent cases, dealing with the reduction of water rates, in which Judge Shelby said: "Conceding the legislative right to regulate the charges to be made by the complainant for water, such regulation must be within reasonable limits. It could not lawfully go to the extent of depriving the complainant of all income from its investment, and in effect confiscate its property. The power to regulate could not legally be used as the power to destroy. The question of the reasonableness of such regulations is one for judicial examination and determination. But the judiciary ought not to interfere with the rates established under legislative sanction, where the legislature has the right to act, unless they are plainly and palpably so unreasonable as to make their enforcement equivalent to depriving the complainant of reasonable returns on its investment; but judicial interference is proper when the case shows an attack upon the rights of property, under the guise of regulating, which will make the plaintiff's property valueless in his hands, by annulling or making inoperative existing contracts." [2]

§ 1126. Fair return generally conceded.

It is now generally conceded that an adequate return upon the true value of the property devoted to the public use by those who conduct a public service ought in all normal cases to be left. Otherwise it is now conceded that they are in effect deprived of their property without due

Wisconsin.—State ex rel. v. Railroad Commission, 137 Wis. 80, 116 N. W. 905 (1908).

[1] Palatka Waterworks v. Palatka, 127 Fed. 161 (1903).

[2] Whether a railroad rate is confiscatory so as to deprive the company of its property without due process of law within the meaning of the Fourteenth Amendment depends upon the valuation of the property, the income derivable from the rates and the proportion between the two, which are matters of fact which the company cannot be prevented from trying before a competent tribunal of its own choosing. Where a state railroad commission, which is granted power by the state constitution to make

process of law, if their rates are so reduced by public authority as to leave no such adequate return. It is not only a due consideration for the rights of others who have already invested their money in public services, but also an enlightened selfishness with a view to the future which dictates the present policy that a reasonable return upon the value of the property devoted to the public service shall be protected by the Constitution. That a fair return in this sense is generally conceded is apparent in all the recent cases, as a quotation from the latest decision [1] will show: "It therefore does not seem that rates producing no more than a reasonable return on their fair value could be unjust to any one. In fixing the measure of return upon property devoted to public use, regard should be had to the character of the business, the locality and the risk, whether the return will be uniform and secure; whether the patronage is steady or fluctuating and quickly responsive to financial and commercial changes, interest rates legal and contractual and the rates customarily sought and required in like investments in the locality; if a railroad, the character of the traffic, whether largely of a kind dependent upon uncertain conditions or so diversified that causes affecting part will not greatly affect the whole. The return should be a fair, just, and reasonable one, and not so meager as to repel investment in the property or to embarrass the owner in operating it." [2]

§ 1127. Reasonable rates not necessarily profitable.

It should not be inferred that the rule that regulation

and enforce rates, enacts and attempts to enforce rates which are so low as to be confiscatory, then enforcement may be enjoined. Prentice v. Atlantic Coast Line Ry. Co., 211 U. S. 210, 53 L. ed. 150, 29 Sup. Ct. 192 (1909).

[1] Missouri K. & T. Ry. Co. v. Love, 177 Fed. 493 (1910).

[2] See also late case in the State courts: Coal & Coke Ry. Co. v. Conley (W. Va.) 67 S. E. 613 (1910).

of rates shall leave a fair return by way of profit is without exception. There are decisions which show that this is not an inviolable right. A recent Florida case [1] will bring this out, where Mr. Justice Carter said of a plea that at the rates imposed by the commission the company would not make a fair return above operating expenses: "The vice in this method of pleading lies in the fact that the question of reasonableness is made to depend upon the capacity of the rates to yield a net income over and above the cost of constructing and maintaining the road and the payment of fixed charges, whereas circumstances may exist under which rates are reasonable which do not afford a net income above the cost of operation and taxes, or the cost of operation, taxes and fixed charges. The returns set forth a few elements entering into the question as to what constitutes a reasonable rate, and attempt to make these elements controlling; whereas the conditions surrounding the operation of the road may deprive them of controlling force." [2]

§ 1128. Reduction ruinous only to certain companies.

A difficult question arises where although there has been a drastic reduction of rates, certain companies are in so strong a position that their earnings are not cut below the minimum of fair profit, while with other companies the reductions will not only wipe out all profits whatsoever, but compel them to conduct their business at a loss.

[1] State v. Seaboard Air Line, 48 Fla. 129, 37 So. 314 (1904).

[2] See to the same effect:

United States.—In re Arkansas R. R. Rates, 168 Fed. 720 (1909).

Arkansas.—St. Louis & S. F. Ry. v. Gill, 54 Ark. 101, 15 S. W. 18, 11 L. R. A. 452 (1891).

Florida.—Pensacola & A. R. R.

v. Florida, 25 Fla. 310, 5 So. 833 (1889).

Indiana.—Southern Indiana R. R. Co. v. Railroad Commission, 172 Ind. 113, 87 N. E. 966 (1909) Adams Exp. Co., 85 Neb. 25, 122 N. W. 691 (1909)

West Virginia.—Coal & Coke R. Co. v. Conley (W. Va.), 67 S. E. 613 (1910).

Whenever this is brought to the attention of the court their attitude must be that they are dealing only with the case in hand, their sole function being to determine in the particular case before them whether this legislation will virtually confiscate the business property of this complainant.[1] The consequence follows inevitably that while the rates imposed may be found unreasonable, and therefore not enforceable as to some of the roads in the State, this does not necessarily render them unreasonable and unenforceable as to other roads doing business in the State.[2]

§ 1129. Possibility of increase of business at the lowered rates.

The point is urged from time to time that the reduction ordered in existing rates should not be questioned at the outset, but the company should be compelled to give the new rates a fair trial. It may turn out that there will be no reduction in earnings after all, since the increased business consequent upon the lower rate might more than make good that loss. Although this has much force from a theoretical point of view, it must obviously be acted upon in an actual case with the greatest caution. This was one of the many matters discussed in the important case of Chicago & Northwestern Railway v. Dey,[3] when

[1] Pennsylvania R. R. Co. v. Philadelphia County, 220 Pa. St. 100, 68 Atl. 676, 15 L. R. A. (N. S.) 108 (1908). See also Nebraska Tel. Co. v. Cornell, 59 Neb. 737, 82 N. W. 1 (1900).

[2] St. Louis & S. F. R. R. v. Hadley, 168 Fed. 317 (1909). Legislation applying only to railroads of a certain class should therefore be held constitutional. Coal & Coke Ry. Co. v. Conley (W. Va.), 67 S. E. 613 (1910).

But in a leading case the United States Supreme Court held legislation applying only to stock yards of a certain size outrageous. Cotting v. Kansas City S. Y. Co., 183 U. S. 79, 46 L. ed. 92, 22 Sup. Ct. 30 (1901).

[3] 35 Fed. 883, 1. L. R. A. 744, and note (1888).

Southern Ry. Co. v. Tift, 206 U. S. 428, 51 L. ed. 1124, 27 Sup. Ct. 1124 (1906), the court will enjoin threatened rates without allowing

Mr. Justice Brewer disposed of it in this wise: "The only fair judicial test is to apply the rates to the business that has been done in the past, and see whether, upon that basis such rates will be remunerative, or compel the transaction of business at a loss." However within a few years some of the Federal judges have shown a disposition to refuse to grant a preliminary injunction against the present enforcement of the new rates imposed by the governmental authorities until the outcome may be seen.[1] Of course the issuance of a preliminary injunction lies within the discretion of the judge; and it may be that it should not be granted, unless the court feels that there is high probability of irreparable injury.[2] And indeed the United States Supreme Court in Willcox v. Consolidated Gas Co.[3] seems to have committed itself to the doctrine that it should be considered in the final disposition of the case whether increased consumption at the lower rate might not result in increased earnings—"as the cost of furnishing the gas would not increase in proportion to the increased amount of gas furnished." It was conceded, however, that a company should not be put to this practical test unless it

trial of them if it feels that the probabilities are that the parties concerned will be injured.

Macon Grocery Co. v. Atlantic Coast Line, 163 Fed. 738 (1908), the court will enjoin outrageous rates put in force by the carriers pending passing upon by commission.

[1] See In re Arkansas Railroad Rates, 168 Fed. 720 (1909); Central of Ga. Ry. R. Co. v. McLendon, 157 Fed. 961 (1907).

[2] See Seaboard A. L. Ry. Co. v. Railroad Commission, 155 Fed. 793 (1907). And see St. Louis & S. F. R. R. Co. v. Hadley, 168 Fed. 317 (1909).

[3] 212 U. S. 19, 53 L. ed. 382, 29 Sup. Ct. 192 (1909).

In the extraordinary case of the telephone, as increased business means increased cost, this doctrine has no application. Louisiana R. R. Commission v. Cumberland Telephone Co., 212 U. S. 414, 53 L. ed. 577, 29 Sup. Ct. 357 (1909).

But in a business such as common carriage where increasing business means increasing returns the court will not grant an injunction where it feels confident that this result will follow. State v. Adams Exp. Co., 85 Neb. 25, 122 N. W. 691 (1909).

was plain in a particular case that such a result was distinctly probable. And of course in the event of loss actually resulting from the new rates the complainant originally dismissed may file a new bill without prejudice.

§ 1130. Reasonable profit upon each transaction.

It will be assumed throughout this discussion that all that the law secures to those who devote their capital to public business is the enjoyment of total receipts from that business, be it large or small, sufficient to show a fair per cent of profit upon that capital each year. This undoubtedly is the general rule with which the courts have been working. However, there are some decisions as to certain businesses which must be reckoned with that suggest a different basis. According to these dicta in certain businesses at least, the proprietors are entitled to a fair percentage of profit upon each service it renders, regardless of the total return this in the aggregate may show upon the capital that is employed. There are dicta which seem to go to this extent in the highest courts of both the United States and the British Empire. In deciding against legislation reducing the charges of a stock yard the Supreme Court [1] said: "The question is not how much he makes out of his volume of business, but whether in each particular transaction the charge is an unreasonable transaction for the service rendered." What the Privy Council had previously said in regard to bridge tolls was approved. "The principle must be, when reasonableness comes in question, not what profit it may be reasonable for a company to make, but what it is reasonable to charge to the person who is charged." These dicta as will be seen when the cases are discussed more fully later on, are by the con-

[1] Cotting v. Kansas City Stock Yards Co., 183 U. S. 79, 46 L. ed. 92, 22 Sup. Ct. 30 (1901).

[2] Canada So. R. R. Co. v. International Bridge Co., L. R. 8 App. Cas. 723 (1883).

text confined to that small class of public services which receive no public aid either by way of grant or of privilege; thus confined it should not affect the general law. But certainly were it to be held a proper principle for all cases it would subvert the whole basis of the established law. Those businesses in which there are naturally but few transactions comparatively, would be ruined, while those in which a great number of transactions are carried on would profit enormously.

Topic C. Fair Rate of Return

§ 1131. Interest upon bonds protected.

It was generally agreed from the very first that whatever might be the right to earn a dividend upon stock, the interest upon the outstanding bonds must be protected. Thus in Chicago and Northwestern Railway v. Dey,[1] Mr. Justice Brewer would protect the interest upon outstanding bonds in all contingencies, although he left the question of whether any surplus should be left for dividends to the discretion of the legislature. But certainly, as the United States Supreme Court said some years later, bond issues which have no actual values behind them have no protection.[2] And if the interest in the bonds is fixed unduly high at the outset, it will not be protected against legislation reducing rates, as the California courts hold.[3] Indeed it has been questioned whether more than the current rate of interest upon borrowings in an enterprise of similar character can be secured to bondholders. In the case of Steenerson v. Great

---

[1] 35 Fed. 866 (1888). See also Brymer v. Butler Water Co., 179 Pa. St. 231, 36 Atl. 249, 36 L. R. A. 260 (1897).

[2] Smyth v. Ames, 169 U. S. 466, 42 L. ed. 819, 18 Sup. Ct. 418 (1897). See also: Spring Valley Waterworks v. San Francisco, 124 Fed. 574 (1903).

[3] Spring Valley Waterworks v. San Francisco, 124 Fed. 574 (1903). And compare Redlands L. & C. D. Water Co. v. Redlands, 121 Cal. 365, 53 Pac. 843 (1898).

Northern Railway Company [1] the court answered the question in the negative, Mr. Justice Canty saying: "If a railway company has made what turns out to be a bad bargain by issuing its bonds for six per cent or seven per cent interest per annum that should be its misfortune and not the misfortune of the public." [2]

§ 1132. Dividends upon stock protected.

Within the last ten years, as has been seen, the general principle has become established that there must be left to those who conduct a public enterprise some adequate return on their investment as a whole. This newer view was well put in one sentence in New Memphis Gas Light Company v. New Memphis,[3] thus: "The company has a right to such gross revenue from the sale of gas as will enable it to pay all legitimate operating expenses, pay interest on valid fixed charges, so far as bonds or securities represent an expenditure actually made in good faith, and also to pay a reasonable dividend on stock, so far as this represents an actual investment in the enterprise." What then is reasonable dividend? Dividends upon stock at least where there are outstanding bonds ought to be permitted to be somewhat larger than the interest upon the bonds. Since the bonds have a prior lien upon the assets, the risk to the holders of them is much less than to the holders of stock, and the stockholders should therefore have a higher rate of return because of the risk of passing of dividends in bad times or of foreclosure in case of complete failure. This question of reasonable dividend depends chiefly upon the current rate of return.[4]

[1] 69 Minn. 353, 72 N. W. 713 (1897). But see Pennsylvania R. R. Co. v. Philadelphia County, 220 Pa. St. 100, 68 Atl. 676, 15 L. R. A. (N. S.) 108 (1908).

[2] See contra, Norwich Gas & E. Co. v. City of Norwich, 76 Conn. 565, 57 Atl. 746 (1904).

[3] 72 Fed. 952 (1896).

[4] Among the many cases to this effect, see:

United States.—Cotting v. Kan-

§ 1133. Current rate of return.

The current rate of return to capital it is submitted is the true basis of fixing the percentage. This is said in the more discriminating cases which discuss the problem carefully. Some illustrations of the way the court treats the matter now will illustrate this further. In Brymer v. Butler Water Company [1] the court said in reviewing the schedule of a water company, that it is entitled to a rate of return, if the property will earn it, not less than the legal rate of interest; a return of something over six per cent was held not unreasonable therefore. Furthermore this court in the still later case of the Pennsylvania Railroad Company v. Philadelphia County [2] frankly said that it regarded its previous suggestion of six per cent as simply fixing a minimum return, not the maximum one at all. Men do not put their money into business enterprises for small interest, as the court well says. In a recent Federal case [3] the court thought that the owners of a railroad should have a profit above the necessary expense of conducting

sas City S. Y. Co., 183 U. S. 79, 46 L. ed. 92, 22 Sup. Ct. 30 (1901); Stanislaus Co. v. San Joaquin & K. R. C. & I. Co., 192 U. S. 201, 48 L. ed. 406, 24 Sup. Ct. 241 (1903); Cleveland Gas Co. v. Cleveland, 71 Fed. 610 (1891); Milwaukee Electric Ry. Co. v. Milwaukee, 87 Fed. 577 (1898); Central Ry. Co. v. Railroad Commission, 161 Fed. 996 (1908); St. Louis & S. F. R. R. Co. v. Hadley, 168 Fed. 317 (1909).

Florida.—State v. Seaboard Air Line, 48 Fla. 152, 37 So. 658 (1904).

Iowa.—Cedar Rapids Co. v. Cedar Rapids, 118 Ia. 234, 91 N. W. 1081 (1902).

Maine.—Brunswick & T. W. Dist. v. Maine Water Co., 99 Me. 371, 59 Atl. 537 (1904).

Minnesota.—State v. Minneapolis & St. L. R. R. Co., 80 Minn. 191, 83 N. W. 60, 89 Am. St. Rep. 514 (1900).

Mississippi.—Alabama & V. Ry. v. Railroad Commission, 86 Miss. 667, 38 So. 356 (1905).

Pennsylvania.—Pennsylvania R. R. Co. v. Philadelphia County, 220 Pa. St. 100, 68 Atl. 676, 15 L. R. A. (N. S.) 108 (1908).

West Virginia.—Coal & Coke Co. v. Conley (W. Va.), 67 S. E. 613 (1910).

[1] 179 Pa. St. 231, 36 Atl. 249 (1897).

[2] 220 Pa. St. 100, 68 Atl. 676, 15 L. R. A. (N. S.) 108 (1908).

[3] Central R. Co. v. Railroad Commission, 161 Fed. 925 (1908).

such business equal to eight per cent per annum upon the value of the property so employed, that being the legal rate of interest in Alabama on loans of money, and the current rate of profit upon property used in business enterprises similar to railroads. And upon the same general principle another Federal judge held recently that a local Louisiana telephone company which was making seven per cent ought not to be disturbed.[1] With these cases in mind one is justified in saying that the current rate of return to capital invested [2] in the community served may confidently be expected.[3]

§ 1134. Reasonable profits sufficiently safe.

In any normal case the proprietor of a public service may therefore expect a dividend equal to the current rate of return in enterprises of similar character. It should be borne in mind, however, that public services have in general more assured permanence and less danger of ruinous competition than most private businesses. However opinions must necessarily differ as to what would be a reasonable profit in a given case, most courts when asked to declare the action of some legislative body in reducing certain rates to be virtual confiscation will take the attitude that unless the reduction worked is really indefensible the legislative rate will not be disturbed. Thus in a recent Iowa case [4] the court did not consider an ordinance confiscatory which so reduced rates as to leave the company about five per cent on the value of the property which resulted in this case in over six per cent on its outstanding securities. A recent Florida case,[5]

[1] Cumberland Tel. & Tel. Co. v. R. R. Commission, 156 Fed. 823 (1907).

[2] Missouri R. & T. R. Co. v. Love, 177 Fed. 493 (1910).

[3] Louisville & N. Ry. Co. v. Brown, 123 Fed. 946 (1903).

[4] Cedar Rapids Water Co. v. Cedar Rapids, 118 Iowa 234, 91 N. W. 1081 (1902).

[5] State ex rel. v. Seaboard A. L. R. R. Co., 48 Fla. 129, 37 So. 314 (1904).

where it was held that the court could not say that even three and one-half per cent upon the cost of a system was confiscatory, is to be explained by the fact that the present value might be one-half of the actual cost.

§ 1135. Unreasonable profits not protected.

Generally speaking proof that the net earnings which will be left by the proposed reduction will leave an absurdly low percentage as in one recent case [1] two and one-third per cent is enough to condemn the legislative rate. In one of the latest Federal cases [2] it is said succinctly that the authorities practically establish a six per cent minimum. But in Stanislaus County v. The San Joaquin Company,[3] the United States Supreme Court permitted the dividend of an irrigation company not yet developed to be cut to six per cent. On the other hand, in the case of Cotting v. Kansas City Stock Yards Company [4] the court held that legislation cutting the return of the company below six per cent was unconstitutional. Administered in this spirit rate regulation should have no terror to the general investor. Bonds and stocks thus protected will not be brought below par by governmental action; indeed they will sell at a handsome premium.

§ 1136. Business profit now recognized.

It should be said in fairness that much more than this six per cent may be earned in many instances, without the profit being unreasonable. Except in the most highly developed communities public service has certain risks even as compared with private business, besides its obvious advantages. They must run whatever the times, and their fate is linked with that of the community.

[1] Coal & Coke Ry. Co. v. Conley (W. Va.), 67 S. E. 613 (1910).

[2] St. Louis & S. F. R. Co. v. Hadley, 168 Fed. 317, 354 (1909).

[3] 192 U. S. 201, 48 L. ed. 406, 24 Sup. Ct. 245 (1903).

[4] 183 U. S. 79, 46 L. ed. 92, 22 Sup. Ct. 30 (1901).

They are engaged in a business with the ordinary incidents of a business, with some of the hopes and hazards of a business.[1] It is plain, for example, that the rates at which investors will lend their money to governmental bodies furnishes little criterion of the return that will be required to induce them to invest in the various securities of the public service companies.[2] The whole problem of rate regulation has been seen more steadily of late. It has been appreciated that in dealing with a public service company the State is really dealing with a private business concern, however many the obligations may be which it owes to the public.[3] The risks they run are such that their financial management should be left to them unless they be shown to be taking profit with outrageous disregard of their public obligation. With these broader views it would not be surprising if some consideration should be given to the *entrepreneur*.[4] And to some extent the ability to conceive and execute new projects or a comprehensive consolidation deserve a return.

§ 1137. Greater profit for better service.

Reference might here be made to some recent theories, already resulting in some legislation dealing with the rate of return. The best of these proposals at present is for a sliding scale, the rate of dividend being permitted to increase as the price of the product to the public decreases. The advantages to the public of such a deal are obvious; but it has hidden disadvantages. There will be a spur to intensive improvement, to cheapen the product, certainly; but a deterent to extensive work, to extend the

[1] Brunswick & T. Water Dist. v. Maine Water Co., 99 Me. 371, 59 Atl. 537 (1904).

[2] Spring Valley Waterworks v. San Francisco, 124 Fed. 574 (1903).

[3] Pennsylvania R. R. Co. v. Philadelphia County, 220 Pa. St. 100, 68 Atl. 676, 15 L. R. A. (N. S.) 108 (1908).

[4] Metropolitan Trust Co. v. Houston & T. C. R. R. Co., 90 Fed. 683 (1898).

service, accompanies this. There is danger to the public that the product will be cheapened to its detriment, and to the stockholders that proper depreciation accounting will be abandoned. It seems therefore a policy to be reserved for adoption in particular cases of special bargaining. And this is a matter to be thought out carefully before action is taken in a particular case. Some better method of profit sharing with increased returns for the corporations and better service for the communities may be thought out which will spur the company not only to greater output, but to wider extensions, not only to larger dividends, but to better maintenance.

Topic D.   Character of the Enterprise
§ 1138. Larger returns in risky enterprises.

It follows from what has just been said that in a risky enterprise a large return may be demanded. The principle that as large a return is permissible as is obtained in businesses of similar character covers the case. And the policy to induce people to undertake such services for the benefit of the public requires a larger return for a more risky enterprise. In Brunswick Water District v. Maine Water Company [1] Mr. Justice Savage made the point very clearly indeed: " 'Reasonable' is a relative term, and what is reasonable depends upon many varying circumstances. An equivalent to the prevailing rate of interest might be a reasonable return, and it might not. It might be too high or it might be too low. It might be reasonable, owing to peculiar hazards or difficulties in one place to receive greater returns there than it would in another upon the same investment." [2]

[1] Brunswick & T. W. Dist. v. Maine Water Co., 99 Me. 371, 59 Atl. 537 (1904).

[2] The following cases mention the character of the enterprise as a factor in determining the rate of return:

United States.—Cotting v. Kansas City S. Y. Co., 183 U. S. 79, 46 L. ed. 92, 22 Sup. Ct. 30 (1901);

§ 1139. Public service has its peculiar risks.

Just what rate of interest a public service company should be allowed to pay upon its securities is difficult to determine by rule, since the circumstances will be different in different cases. Whatever it is obliged to pay to sell its bonds at par if the negotiations for the issue are conducted with good faith would be the test. And that would depend upon the stability of the business to the mind of the lenders. Public service bonds are sold on the exchanges from as low as a three per cent basis to as high as a sixteen per cent basis, and doubtless will always continue to do so. Enterprise and industrial progress would be at a standstill if the rate was kept down to that on government bonds.[1] It must be remembered that those who embark in public services place their property to a great extent in the hands of the public. They must be always ready to supply the public demand, and must take the risk of any falling off in that demand. They cannot convert their property to any other use, however unprofitable the public use may have become.[2] They must

Stanislaus Co. v. San Joaquin & K. R. C. & I. Co., 192 U. S. 201, 48 L. ed. 406, 24 Sup. Ct. 241 (1903); Cleveland Gas Light Co. v. Cleveland, 71 Fed. 610 (1891); Milwaukee Elec. Ry. Co. v. Milwaukee, 87 Fed. 577, B. & W. 336 (1898); Metropolitan Trust Co. v. Houston & Texas Cent. R. R. Co., 90 Fed. 683 (1898); Louisville & N. Ry. v. Brown, 123 Fed. 946 (1903); Palatka Waterworks v. Palatka, 127 Fed. 161 (1903); Missouri K. & T. Ry. Co. v. Love, 177 Fed. 493 (1910).

Kentucky.—Troutman v. Smith, 105 Ky. 231, 48 S. W. 1084 (1899).

Maine.—Kennebec Water Dist. v. Waterville, 97 Me. 185, 54 Atl. 6, 60 L. R. A. 856 (1902).

Minnesota.—Steenerson v. Great No. Ry. 69 Minn. 353, 72 N. W. 713 (1897).

Pennsylvania.—Wilkes-Barre v. Spring Brook Water Co., 4 Lack. Leg. News, 367 (1898).

West Virginia.—Coal & Coke Ry. Co. v. Conley (W. Va.), 67 S. E. 613 (1910).

[1] This is in part paraphrased from Wilkes-Barre v. Spring Brook Water Co., 4 Lack. Leg. News, 367 (1898).

See also Brunswick & T. Water Dist. v. Maine Water Co., 99 Me. 371, 59 Atl. 537 (1904).

[2] Long Branch Comm. v. Tintern Manor Water Co., 70 N. J. Eq. 71, 62 Atl. 474 (1905).

run in good times and bad with substantially the same expense. If they lose in bad times they cannot recoup themselves by extraordinary profits in good times. These risks exist to some extent in all communities but they are greater in some than in others.

§ 1140. Special hazards of the business considered.

The hazards of the business are therefore to be considered in determining what is a reasonable rate of return in the particular enterprise in question. An excellent example of this problem is to be found in the case of Canada Southern Railway v. International Bridge Company.[1] It was shown in that case that the bridge company at its established charges was earning something like fifteen per cent upon its investment. The opinion of Lord Chancellor Selbourne alluded to the peculiar risks of the enterprise rather by way of dictum than as the basis of his decision. He said, on this point: " You cannot ask a court to say that the persons who have projected such an undertaking as this, who have encountered all the original risks of executing it, who are still subject to the risks which from natural and other causes every such undertaking is subject to, and who may possibly, as in the case alluded to by the learned judge in the court below, the case of the Tay Bridge, have the whole thing swept away in a moment, are to be regarded as making unreasonable charges, not because it is otherwise than fair for the railway company using the bridge to pay those charges, but because the bridge company gets a dividend which is alleged to amount, at the utmost, to fifteen per cent. Their Lordships can hardly characterize that argument as anything less than preposterous." [2]

See also Kennebec Water Dist. v. Waterville, 97 Me. 185, 54 Atl. 6, 60 L. R. A. 856 (1902).

[1] L. R. 8 App. Cas. 723 (1883).
[2] To the same effect is Troutman v. Smith, 105 Ky, 231, 48 S. W.

§ 1141. Commercial conditions affecting dividends.

To a certain extent the dividends which a railroad company can earn are dependent upon commercial conditions generally. When crops fail or when commercial crises come the general business of the common carrier inevitably falls off. Even if it should raise its rates very considerably it would be difficult for it to maintain its regular dividends and it is doubtful whether it ought to do so and increase thereby the general distress. This may be pressed too far, and perhaps the point is overstated in Steenerson v. Great Northern Railway,[1] where Mr. Justice Canty insists that a railroad cannot say—When times are prosperous and dividends large, we win, when times are hard and business dull, the public must lose. The business of the carrier cannot but be affected by the State of commerce in the country at large. It is perhaps true that with good times and rising prices the value of the property of a public service company increases with other values and consequently it may justify higher earnings. And if the carrier must suffer to a certain extent with others in bad times he ought be allowed to recoup himself to some extent in prosperous times. This is hinted in Metropolitan Trust Company v. Houston and Texas Central Railroad Company,[2] where Mr. Justice McCormick, in holding that the commission ought not to have reduced the rates of the railroad in the way that they did, said: "Promoters and proprietors of roads have looked to the future, as they had a right to do, and as they were induced to do by the solicitation of the various communities through which they run, and by various encourage-

1084, (1899) allowing a ferryman a large profit on the capital invested because of the notorious hazards of the business.

[1] 69 Minn. 353, 72 N. W. 713 (1897).

The same idea is expressed in Matthews v. Board of Corp. Commrs., 106 Fed. 7 (1901).

[2] 90 Fed. 683 (1898).

See also Missouri, K. & T. R. R. Co. v. Love, 177 Fed. 493 (1910).

ments offered by the State." It may be that in good times small amounts may be set aside to maintain uniform dividends. For it is certainly desirable that there should be as few fluctuations as possible in the conduct of the finances of a public service company. And if commercial conditions are such that a four per cent bond may be sold at eighty-five, to better advantage than a five per cent bond at par, the writer sees little objection to accommodating the financing of the company to the times.

CHAPTER XXXIV

OPERATING EXPENSES

§ 1150. Real cost of operation.

Topic A. Cost of Performing Service

§ 1151. Cost of rendering service.
  1152. Salaries paid to officials.
  1153. Expenditures to get business.
  1154. Current taxes.
  1155. Outstanding loans.
  1156. Interest payable.
  1157. Dividends declared.

Topic B. Expenditures on the Plant

§ 1158. Expense of maintaining equipment.
  1159. Losses due to accident.
  1160. Betterments considered as maintenance.
  1161. Replacement considered as repair.
  1162. Renewal of equipment to offset depreciation.
  1163. Permanent improvements should not be annual charge.
  1164. New construction should be charged to capital account.
  1165. A liberal policy desirable.

Topic C. Amortization Requirements

§ 1166. Depreciation now generally allowed.
  1167. Full allowance still begrudged.
  1168. Refusal to allow depreciation.
  1169. Fund to repair depreciation.
  1170. Capitalization of past depreciation.
  1171. Payments into sinking fund.
  1172. Sinking fund for municipal bonds.
  1173. Amortization of franchise rights.

Topic D. Operations of Consolidated Properties

§ 1174. Complications in case of systems.
  1175. System generally taken as a whole.
  1176. Unprofitable portions of the line not considered.

§ 1150. Real cost of operation.

The real cost of operation is not so easy a figure to determine as one might first suppose. Certain items of annual expenditure should obviously be included as annual charges, such as wages and supplies, provided that such expenditures have not been unreasonable. But as to other expenditures there is difficulty in deciding whether they should be included as current expenses or provided for out of new capital, such as replacements and betterments. Involved in this problem is the accounting permissible in allowing for depreciation and reparation. And in this connection the propriety of setting aside a sinking fund or providing against amortization should be considered. Altogether it will be seen that this is not a matter to be dismissed with the accepted rule that only proper annual charges should be deducted from gross income, while all expenditures for lasting improvements should be provided for from new capital.[1]

Topic A. Cost of Performing Service

§ 1151. Cost of rendering service.

Before there can be any question of income on the capital employed, the necessary annual charges must be met by the rates; and first of all the actual cost of service furnished. This involves most obviously the payment of wages, and the purchase of current supplies. The general principle was concisely stated by Mr. Justice Brewer

[1] A waterworks company must make full disclosure of its earnings and expenses when it assails as confiscatory rates fixed by ordinance. McCook Waterworks Co. v. City of McCook, 85 Neb. 677, 124 N. W. 100 (1909).

in Chicago and Northwestern Railway v. Dey:[1] "Cost of service implies skilled labor, the best appliances, keeping the road-bed and the cars and machinery and other appliances in perfect order and repair. The obligation of the carrier to the passenger and the shipper requires all these." And in the Long Branch [2] waterworks case the Vice Chancellor recently allowed without discussion the estimate made for "the costs of maintainance and administration, including ordinary repairs and taxes." It should, of course, be said that it does not follow that in every case the company will be entitled to credit for all of its current expenditures. Reckless and unnecessary expenditures, not legitimately incurred in the actual operations of the company cannot be allowed.

§ 1152. Salaries paid to officials.

The salaries of officials must, of course, be paid, as part of the annual charges; but these salaries must not be fixed at an extravagant amount. If a group of stockholders who controlled a majority of the stock could vote themselves enormous salaries and deduct the amount from the receipts of the company before making a return to capital, the highest possible rates might be justified, and the rights of the public be ignored. This question was considered, and well discussed, by Mr. Justice Brewer in Chicago and Grand Trunk Railway v. Wellman:[3] "It is agreed that the defendant's operating expenses for 1888 were $2,404,516.54. Of what do these operating expenses consist? Are they made up partially of extravagant sal-

[1] 35 Fed. 866, I. L. R. A. 744 (1888).

See also Brewer, J., in Chicago, M. & S. P. Ry. Co. v. Tompkins, 176 U. S. 167, 44 L. ed. 418, 20 Sup. Ct. 336 (1900).

[2] Long Branch Commission v. Tintern Manor Water Co., 70 N. J. Eq. 71, 62 Atl. 474 (1905).

See also the opinion of Savage in Brunswick & T. Water Dist. v. Maine Water Co., 99 Me. 371, 59 Atl. 537 (1904).

[3] 143 U. S. 339, 36 L. ed. 76, 12 Sup. Ct. 400 (1892).

aries,—fifty to one hundred thousand dollars to the president, and in like proportions to subordinate officers? Surely, before the courts are called upon to adjudge an act of the legislature fixing the maximum passenger rates for railroad companies to be unconstitutional, on the ground that its enforcement would prevent the stockholders from receiving any dividends on their investments, or the bondholders any interest on their loans, they should be fully advised as to what is done with the receipts and earnings of the company; for, if so advised, it might clearly appear that a prudent and honest management would, within the rates prescribed, secure to the bondholders their interest, and to the stockholders reasonable dividends." [1]

§ 1153. Expenditures to get business.

A public service company can no doubt expend a reasonable amount in advertising. Perhaps it may be said that reasonable advertising is for the benefit of the customer. But it seems to be agreed that large commissions cannot be given by a public service company to those who get it business. For money spent in efforts by one company to secure certain business in preference to another company benefits the company only, not the customer, and it is not just that the customer should be forced to pay it. In the case of Pannell v. Louisville Tobacco Warehouse Company, [2] a case involving the reg-

---

[1] This quotation is included with approval in the opinion of the court in Tucker v. Missouri Pacific Ry. Co. (Kans.), 108 Pac. 89 (1910).

According to a recent decision, a court will take into account the increased cost of labor by reason of the reduction of hours. In re Arkansas R. R. Rates, 168 Fed. 720 (1909).

In St. Louis & S. F. Ry. Co. v. Hadley, 168 Fed. 317 (1909), the court refused to take it into consideration as against a legislative reduction of rates that the companies would be compelled to reduce the wages of their employés.

[2] 113 Ky. 630, 68 S. W. 662, 23 Ky. L. Rep. 2423 (1902).

ulation of rates of tobacco warehouses, Mr. Justice Hobson said: "We know that the larger the fee, the more the warehouseman can afford to pay out to get the trade; and it is not the policy of the law that the warehousemen should be allowed to charge a large fee against the shipper, in order that he may be able to spend a portion of it in securing the trade. To illustrate: If the fees were so large that the warehousemen could give half of them to get the business, it is manifest that this would lead to practices that ought not to be encouraged, and would be a hardship on the tobacco raiser, which the statute was designed to prevent." [1]

§ 1154. Current taxes.

Taxes for the year are obviously a proper annual charge. Overdue taxes for past years paid during the year are just as obviously not to be regarded as an annual charge. [2] Upon the policy for the State to pursue in taxing public service companies in general and railroads in particular, there is and may be much difference of opinion. Such companies should, of course, be taxed upon their tangible property at its locus, and this is generally done. But upon the question of whether there should be a high franchise tax opinion differs, although it is now recognized that such taxes are constitutional enough. It may be pointed out, however, that if too heavy a franchise tax is levied upon a railroad company, it is bound in the end to react upon the rates which the railroad will charge the public, as the payments made for taxation requirements are obviously annual charges. [3]

[1] Compare United States v. Delaware L. & W. Ry. Co., 152 Fed. 269 (1907).

[2] See Southern Pacific R. R. Co. v. Railroad Commrs. 78 Fed. 236 (1896).

[3] See Long Branch Commission v. Tintern Manor Water Co., 70 N. J. Eq. 71, 62 Atl. 474 (1905).

§ 1155. Outstanding loans.

It is obvious that a loan made by a company during the year cannot be charged as an annual expense. In Southern Pacific Co. v. Railroad Commissioners,[1] that question actually came up for decision. It appeared that the Southern Pacific Company, as lessee, had entered into an elaborate lease with the Oregon & California Company as lessor, by the terms of which the net earnings received by the lessee should be applied to pay the interest on the bonded indebtedness of the lessor with a proviso that if there should not be a sufficiency of net earnings upon the line to pay this interest the Southern Pacific Company might pay the same on account of the Oregon & California Company and charge the payment to it, being entitled to reimburse itself from future net earnings with six per cent interest until paid. The Southern Pacific Company claimed that a payment which it had made on this account should be put in as a current expenditure in determining whether the rates fixed by the California Commission left it a reasonable return above proper expenses. But the court held otherwise; on this point Judge McKenna said: "Was the payment of the interest a loss to the Southern Pacific Company? Clearly not. It is secured to it, and is to be reimbursed to it, and is charged in the report as a 'balance deficit payable by Oregon & California Railroad Company.' Clearly, again, if it had not been paid, it could not be claimed as a loss. If paid, and to be reimbursed and secured, it cannot be claimed as a loss, if the debtor or the security be good. I cannot assume now that the debtor or the security will not be good."

§ 1156. Interest payable.

It is very common and not unnatural to speak of in-

[1] 78 Fed. 236 (1896).

terest payable upon bonded indebtedness as fixed charge
and therefore one of the items in making up the total of
annual expenditures. Thus Mr. Justice Brewer speaks of
it in the well-known case of Chicago and Northwestern
Railway Company v. Dey: [1] "The fixed charges are the
interest on the bonds. This must be paid, for otherwise
foreclosure would follow, and the interest of the mortgagor
swept out of existence. The property of the stockholders
cannot be destroyed any more than the property of the
bondholders. Each has a fixed and vested interest, which
cannot be taken away. I know that often the stockholder and the bondholder are regarded and spoken of as
having but a single interest; but the law recognizes a clear
distinction. A mortgage on a railroad creates the same
rights in mortgagor and mortgagee as a mortgage on my
homestead. The legislature cannot destroy my property
in my homestead simply because it is mortgaged, neither
can it destroy the stockholders' property because the
railroad is mortgaged. It cannot interfere with a contract between the company mortgagor and the mortgagee,
or reduce the stipulated rate of interest; and so, unless
that stipulated interest is paid, foreclosure of course follows, and the mortgagors' rights, the property of the
stockholders, are swept away." [2]

§ 1157. Dividends declared.

Nor in determining the net income is it permissible
to include dividends on the stock. Dividends must be
paid, if at all, out of net income, and are in no sense annual
charges or operating expenses. "It seems to us very
clear that in estimating the operating expenses of a rail-

[1] 35 Fed. 866, 1 L. R. A. 744
(1888). Cited with approval in
Southern Pacific Co. v. Railroad
Commrs., 78 Fed. 236 (1896).

[2] Smyth v. Ames, 169 U. S. 466,

42 L. ed. 819, 18 Sup. Ct. 418, B. &
W. 347 (1898), affirming s. c. 64
Fed. 165. See Steenerson v. Gt.
Northern Ry. 69 Minn. 353, 72
N. W. 713 (1897).

way stock dividends cannot be included. They are no part of the cost of operation. Nor should they be included, under any of the authorities, when ascertaining the reasonableness of a rate tariff. This is in no manner denying the defendant's right to earn sufficient to pay its operating expenses, interest upon its bona fide bonded indebtedness, and a proper dividend upon its lawfully issued stock shares or value of the investment." [1] Upon appeal to the Supreme Court of the United States this language of the Minnesota court was affirmed: [2] "In proving that the cost of transporting *all* merchandise exceeded the rate fixed by the commission on this coal, the interest upon bonds and dividends upon stock were included in operating expenses. The propriety of the first is at least doubtful, the impropriety of the second is plain. We do not intend, however, to intimate that the road is not entitled to something more than operating expenses."

Topic B. Expenditures on the Plant

§ 1158. Expense of maintaining equipment.

As the public service company is obliged to provide a sufficient equipment for the proper accommodation of the public, and to keep all its appliances and premises in good condition, the cost of maintaining the equipment is of course to be repaid from the rates. Thus, in the case of a ferry, the court [3] in passing on the reasonableness of a rate took it into account that the owner of the ferry "is compelled, in the operation of the ferry, to keep for the accommodation of the public two large boats for the transportation of vehicles, a waiting boat, a large flat outside waiting boat for convenience in getting in and out of skiffs,

---

[1] State ex. rel. v. Minneapolis & St. L. R. R. Co., 80 Minn. 191, 83 N. W. 60 (1900).

[2] Minneapolis & S. L. R. R. Co.

v. Minnesota, 186 U. S. 257, 46 L. ed. 1151, 22 Sup. Ct. 900 (1902).

[3] Troutman v. Smith, 105 Ky. 231, 48 S. W. 1084 (1899).

four skiffs, a large reflecting lamp, that throws light across the river; and that she owns, and is compelled to keep in repair and free from mud, the approaches to the ferry on both sides, and employ regularly two men, and frequently three or four additional hands to perform the necessary work." And in a recent gas works case in determining what constitutes "net profits," the court [1] said that: "The cost of operation in furnishing gas within the city upon which profits are to be divided, including necessary repairs must be charged as expenses to be deducted from the amount received therefrom in order to determine the profit thereon."

§ 1159. Losses due to accident.

A certain amount of loss by accident is inseparable from the conduct of any business, and this is particularly true of a business having so many unavoidable dangers as that of a railroad operation. In so far as these losses are without fault of anyone concerned the sums paid to make reparation for them may obviously be charged as an expense of operation. But more than this, it seems, must be conceded; a certain amount of negligence by employés cannot be avoided, and these losses also seem inseparable from the conduct of the business. The only losses which the railroad company may not properly charge against the public, therefore, are those which result from its own reckless management, or its willful failure to provide adequate facilities.[2] Similarly a supply company can claim allowance for that amount of wastage which experience proves is not inconsistent with proper management.[3] Reference should be made here to the employés' compensation acts which are being urged to-day. In the case of

[1] Erie v. Erie Gas & M. Co., 78 Kans. 348, 97 Pac. 468 (1908).

[2] See In re Arkansas R. R. Rates, 168 Fed. 720 (1909).

[3] See Rieker v. Lancaster, 14 Lanc. L. Rev. (Pa.) 393 (1897).

a public service company particularly the personal accident seems to be a part of the cost of performing the service which the community should bear.

§ 1160. Betterments considered as maintenance.

It is not always easy to determine whether replacement construction of the plant of a public service company constitutes annual or capital charges. Current repairs obviously constitute annual charges. Outright extensions just as obviously should be put into the capital account. But as to replacement, and more particularly as to improvements, problems arise which may be handled in different ways. Since they may be handled in different ways not unreasonably, it cannot be said that a corporation is acting unreasonably in adopting one policy or the other. This was pointed out by Mr. Justice Bradley when in Union Pacific Railroad Company v. United States,[1] the Supreme Court was called upon to decide whether that company had acted unreasonably in so arranging its finances that it did not appear to be making such net earnings as by the terms thereof were to be applied to the reduction of certain of its bonds. "As a general proposition, net earnings are the excess of the gross earnings over the expeditures defrayed in producing them, aside from and exclusive of the expenditure of capital laid out in constructing and equipping the works themselves. It may often be difficult to draw a precise line between expenditures for construction and the ordinary expenses incident to operating and maintaining the road and works of a railroad company. Theoretically, the expenses chargeable to earnings include the general expenses of keeping up the organization of the company, and all expenses incurred in operating the works and keeping them in good condition and repair; while expenses

---

[1] 99 U. S. 402, 25 L. ed. 274 (1878).

chargeable to capital include those which are incurred in the original construction of the works, and in the subsequent enlargement and improvement thereof." [1]

§ 1161. Replacement considered as repair.

In the leading case of Reagan v. Farmers' Loan & Trust Company,[2] where it was contended that the cost of new rails should be charged to construction, and not to expenses of operation, Mr. Justice Brewer said: "Now, it goes without saying that, in the operation of every road, there is a constant wearing out of the rails, and a constant necessity for replacing old with new. The purchase of these rails may be called "permanent improvements," or by any other name; but they are what is necessary for keeping the road in serviceable condition. Indeed, in another part of the report, under the head of 'Renewals of rails and ties,' is stated the number of tons of 'New rails laid' on the main line. Other items therein are for fencing, grading, bridging, and culvert masonry, bridges and trestles, buildings, furniture, fixtures, etc. It being shown affirmatively that there were no extensions, it is obvious that these expenditures were those necessary for a proper carrying on of the business required of the company."[3]

§ 1162. Renewal of equipment to offset depreciation.

The equipment of the road must be renewed from time to time; and an expenditure of the proper proportionate amount in each year for new equipment is a proper annual charge. So in Milwaukee Electric Railway and Light Company v. Milwaukee,[4] it was held proper to buy yearly and charge to annual expenses a sufficient number of cars, with motors and complete electrical equipment,

[1] See also Metropolis Trust Co. v. Houston & T. C. R. R. Co., 90 Fed. 683 (1898).

[2] 154 U. S. 362, 38 L. ed. 1014, 14 Sup. Ct. 1047 (1894).

[3] See also Long Branch Commission v. Tintern Manor Water Co., 70 N. J. Eq. 71, 62 Atl. 474 (1905).

[4] 87 Fed. 577 (1898).

to keep up the necessary standard of equipment. It may aid one to appreciate the nature of the problem and the method of its solution to cite from the expert testimony adduced in that case and adopted by the court. "In reference to the element of depreciation, the witness Beggs thought that experience had demonstrated that the most life that could be expected from the best roadbed was twelve years, when it would have to be almost entirely renewéd. The street railway company must now of necessity lay about twelve miles of track annually, being about one-twelfth of its total mileage; and would be required, whether they wish to or not, to lay that amount annually hereafter, to keep their tracks fairly up to the standard. The same applied to the equipment. The company should put on not less than twenty of the most modern equipments, thereby keeping its standard up to the minimum as it had, 240 equipments; because he thought it fair to assume that the average life of the equipment, taken as a whole, will not exceed twelve years, the life of the motor being somewhat less than that, and that of the car we hope may exceed it possibly several years." [1]

§ 1163. Permanent improvements should not be annual charge.

However it may be in doubtful cases, where continual replacements going on from year to year may not unreasonably be considered as equivalent to annual charges to repair account, it is obvious that permanent improvements should not be charged as annual expenditures in the year in which they are constructed, but should be carried to capital account. The United States Supreme Court [2]

[1] See however Nashua & L. R. R. Co. v. Boston & L. R. R. Co., 136 U. S. 356, 34 L. ed. 363, 10 Sup. Ct. 1004 (1893).

[2] Illinois C. R. R. Co. v. Interstate Com. Comm. 206 U. S. 441, 51 L. ed. 1128, 27 Sup. Ct. 700 (1907).

was perhaps speaking within limits when it held that the Interstate Commerce Commission was not acting unreasonably in disallowing as operating expenses of the Illinois Central Railroad expenditures for real estate, right of way, tunnels, bridges, and other strictly permanent improvements; and also for equipment such as locomotives and cars. The Commission expressed the opinion that such expenditures should not be charged to a single year, but should be so far as practicable projected proportionally over the future. And this view Mr. Justice McKenna, speaking for the court, adopted. "It would seem," he said, "as if expenditures for additions to construction and equipment, as expenditures for original construction and equipment, should be reimbursed by all of the traffic they accommodate during the period of their duration, and that improvements that will last many years should not be charged wholly against the revenue of a single year." [1]

§ 1164. New construction should be charged to capital account.

The rule will be generally conceded that outright new construction should be charged to capital and should not therefore be admitted as an annual expense of operation. As Mr. Justice Carter of the Florida court recently put it in a case [2] where the railroad in complaining of the rates put in force by a commission alleged that its total receipts would not now be sufficient to recoup it for its "costs of operation" and its "cost of construction:"

---

[1] In the latest case on this point it is held that the earnings of a railroad company applied to the purchase of additional equipment, extension of its lines, and other improvements, must be regarded as a part of the net earnings, and are not properly chargeable to operating expenses. Coal & Coke Ry. Co. v. Conley (W. Va.) 67 S. E. 613 (1910).

[2] State ex rel. v. Seaboard A. L. Ry. Co., 48 Fla. 129, 37 So. 314, (1904).

"The use of the words 'reasonable cost of constructing' renders the pleading very ambiguous. The reasonable cost of construction is to be considered in determining the fair value of the company's property, which is an element entering into the question of reasonableness of the rate; but the cost of construction is not to be deducted from the earnings under the proposed rates in ascertaining if those rates are reasonable; for under such a rule the public would be compelled to pay for constructing the road without being entitled to its ownership." So in estimating the net profits of a gas company it was held that operating expenses would not include "expenditures for new wells, mains, or other permanent improvements or betterments." [1]

§ 1165. A liberal policy desirable.

This problem under discussion is peculiarly one where the desirable principle should be adhered to, that the State should as far as possible confine itself to regulation leaving the companies to work out their own problems of management. Public service companies should not be prevented from making substantial betterments out of current earnings as private companies advisedly do, if they can manage it. There are extremes here as to which all must agree; but there remains a middle ground where discretion may well be left to the railways themselves. No one would deny that current repairs should come out of current earnings; and every one would concede that new construction should be provided for by additional capital. There remains the debatable ground of improvements and betterments to which the American railways have been used to devote such part of their annual earnings as they could afford. When the results of this progressive American policy are compared with

---

[1] Erie v. Erie Gas & C. Co., 78 Kans. 348, 97 Pac. 468 (1908).

the physical condition to which the English railways have been brought by the opposite policy of distributing all earnings and issuing new capital, it will be seen how necessary to the community it is that a railroad should increase its standard from year to year out of current earnings. At all events, if the American railways are to be restricted henceforth in this manner, they are likely to be much hampered in keeping their facilities up to the modern requirements of their business. It seems fair enough for each generation to pay its share of continual betterment.

Topic C. Amortization Requirements

§ 1166. Depreciation now generally allowed.

In general an annual charge for depreciation in value of the plant by use is proper.[1] This is again a matter which cannot be decided by general rules as to a standard percentage, but is a matter of careful investigation into the

[1] The general proposition is supported by the following cases, among others:

United States.—Union Pac. Ry. v. U. S., 99 U. S. 402, 25 L. ed. 274 (1878), reversing 13 Court Cl. 401; Reagan v. Farmers' L. & T. Co., 154 U. S. 362, 38 L. ed. 1014, 14 Sup. Ct. 1047 (1893); San Diego L. & T. Co. v. National City, 174 U. S. 739, 43 L. ed. 1154, 19 Sup. Ct. 804 (1899), affirming 74 Fed. 79; San Diego L. & T. Co. v. Jasper, 189 U. S. 439, 47 L. ed. 892, 23 Sup. Ct. 571 (1901); Knoxville v. Knoxville Water Co., 212 U. S. 1, 53 L. ed. 371, 29 Sup. Ct. 148 (1909); So. Pac. Ry. v. Railroad Comm., 78 Fed. 236 (1896); Milwaukee Electric Ry. & L. Co. v. Milwaukee, 87 Fed. 577 (1898); Perkins

v. Missouri Pac. Ry. Co., 155 Fed. 445 (1897); San Joaquin & Kings R. C. & I. Co. v. Stanislaus County, 163 Fed. 567 (1898).

Michigan.—G r a n d Haven v. Grand Haven W. W., 119 Mich. 652, 78 N. W. 890 (1899).

Minnesota.—Steenerson v. Gt. N. Ry., 69 Minn. 353, 72 N. W. 713 (1897).

Ohio.—Hamilton v. Hamilton Gas Light & C. Co., 11 Ohio Dec. 513 (1901).

Pennsylvania.—Pennsylvania R. R. Co. v. Philadelphia County, 220 Pa. St. 100, 68 Atl. 676, 15 L. R. A. (N. S.) 108 (1908).

Washington.—Twitchell v. Spokane, 55 Wash. 86, 104 Pac. 150, 24 L. R. A. (N. S.) 290 (1909).

character of the particular plant. It is now seen that the question of depreciation is too difficult for offhand estimation. The courts have as yet usually contented themselves with saying that some fair per cent should be allowed. Undoubtedly in the future, such expert evidence of the amount of the probable depreciation in the particular plant will be relied upon. Waterworks, for example, apparently suffer a very slight depreciation,[1] while a street railway depreciates very fast.[2] The probabilities are that sufficient allowance is not being made for the physical depreciation that the usual equipment used in most public services undergoes, to say nothing of the intangible fall in the value of the present machinery of any sort due to the fact of the usually lower cost of replacement at present. A well conducted company may indeed see to it that provision is made for the renewal of equipment which is obviously deteriorating, but few indeed are making under present conditions provision against the slow but sure depreciation of the plant as a whole. Now that it is becoming recognized in the decisions that such allowance is a proper operating cost, more attention will doubtless be paid to this vital matter.[3]

§ 1167. Full allowance still begrudged.

Even now courts are apparently proceeding too cautiously in conceding allowance for depreciation. As an illustration of this attitude the treatment accorded this

[1] See for example: Wilkes-Barre v. Spring Brook W. Co., 4 Lack. Leg. News (Pa.), 367 (1898).

[2] See for example: Milwaukee Electric Ry. Co. v. Milwaukee, 87 Fed. 577 (1898).

[3] Modern cases for justifying the courts in going searchingly into the amount of actual depreciation are:

Maine.—Kennebec Water Dist. v. Waterville, 97 Me. 185, 54 Atl. 6, 60 L. R. A. 856 (1902).

New Jersey.—Long Branch Comm. v. Tintern Manor Water Co., 70 N. J. Eq. 71, 62 Atl. 474 (1905).

item in the cases of the Tintern Manor Water Company [1] may be cited: "I think they ought to get at the start a moderate rate of interest, say 5%, on their investment, after paying all expenses of operation and maintenance and a moderate allowance for depreciation in value. This latter item, as applied to the water mains, is slight. If originally laid of iron of proper quality and properly coated on the interior, they are practically immortal. They are, however, liable to diminution in carrying capacity due to the growth on the interior of tubercles of rust. This is an unascertainable quantity, which varies materially with the quality of the iron, the character of the coating and the characteristics of the eater. The five hydrants, steam pumps, boilers and filters, and buildings certainly do depreciate in value each year to an appreciable extent over and above the amount which may be expended upon them for reasonable and ordinary repairs. Mr. LaMonte put this depreciation at 5% on all mains and hydrants. I think that too great and fix it at 1% on so much of the $847,000, as is represented by the material so subject to depreciation. Just what proportion of the whole that represents must be a mere estimate, with insufficient data. I put it at $600,000." [2]

§ 1168. Refusal to allow depreciation.

There are, however, at least two jurisdictions—California and Iowa—refusing any allowance for depreciation among the annual charges. The argument in the Iowa case [3] was this: "We see no reason why plaintiff, in addition to operating expenses, repairs, and other ordinary charges, should be allowed to reduce the apparent profits

[1] Long Branch Comm. v. Tintern Manor Water Co., 70 N. J. Eq. 71, 62 Atl. 474 (1905).

[2] See also Wilkes-Barre v. Spring Brook Water Co., 4 Lack. L. News (Pa.) 367 (1899), fixing one per cent arbitrarily.

[3] Cedar Rapids Co. v. Cedar Rapids, 118 Iowa, 234, 91 N. W. 1081 (1902).

by deductions for a restoration or rebuilding fund. The setting aside of such a fund may be good business policy, and, if the company sees fit to devote a portion of its profits to that purpose (though as we understand the record, no such fund has yet been created), no one can complain; but it is in no just sense a charge affecting the net earnings of the works. To hold otherwise is to say that the public must not only pay the reasonable and fair value of the services rendered, but must, in addition, pay the company the full value of its works every 40 years—the average period estimated by plaintiff—for all time to come." [1]

§ 1169. Fund to repair depreciation.

This line of argument is well met by that advanced by Sir George Jessel, Master of the Rolls, in the case of Davison v. Gillies. [2] The by-laws of a tramway company required a "contingencies fund" to be set aside before the payment of dividends; and the court held this proper: "A tramway company lay down a new tramway. Of course the ordinary wear and tear of the rails and sleepers, and so on, causes a sum of money to be required from year to year in repairs. It may or may not be desirable to do the repairs all at once, but if at the end of the first year the line of tramway is still in so good a state of repair that it requires nothing to be laid out on it for repairs in that year, still, before you can ascertain the net profits, a sum of money ought to be set aside as representing the amount in which the wear and tear of the line has, I may say, so far depreciated it in value as that sum will be required for the next year or next two years. It appears to me that you can have no net profits unless this sum

[1] San Diego Water Co. v. San Diego, 118 Cal. 556, 50 Pac. 633 (1897), accord. See also Redlands L. & C. D. Water Co. v. Redlands, 121 Cal. 365, 53 Pac. 843 (1898).
[2] 16 Ch. D. 347n (1879).

has been set aside. When you come to the next year, or the third or fourth year, what happens is this: As the line gets older the amount required for repairs increases. If you had done what you ought to have done, that is, set aside every year the sum necessary to make good the wear and tear in that year, then in the following years you would have fund sufficient to meet the extra cost." Where, however, the line had worn out without a proper fund having been provided for repairs, it was held that the whole amount necessary could not be charged to a single year, but only the proportionate amount.[1]

§ 1170. Capitalization of past depreciation.

That depreciation is an actual cost to be included in the annual charges of a corporation is shown in a striking manner in a late decision of the United States Supreme Court [2] to the effect that it must be provided for from year to year out of annual earnings, and cannot be ignored for a long period and then capitalized. The problem as presented to the court, and the solution of it, is so well stated in the opinion of Mr. Justice Moody that to paraphrase it would be inexcusable. "A clear appreciation of this error can be best obtained by a comprehensive review of the hearing. The company's original case was based upon an elaborate analysis of the cost of construction. To arrive at the present value of the plant large deductions were made on account of the depreciation. This depreciation was divided into complete depreciation and incomplete depreciation. The complete depreciation represented that part of the original plant which through destruction or obsolescence had actually perished as useful property. The incomplete

---

[1] Dent v. London Tramway Co., 16 Ch. Div. 344 (1880).

[2] Knoxville v. Knoxville Water Co., 212 U. S. 1, 53 L. ed. 371, 29 Sup. Ct. 148 (1909).

depreciation represented the impairment in value of the parts of the plant which remained in existence and were continued in use. It was urgently contended that in fixing upon the value of the plant upon which the company was entitled to earn a reasonable return the amounts of complete and incomplete depreciation should be added to the present value of the surviving parts. The court refused to approve this method, and we think properly refused. A water plant, with all its additions, begins to depreciate in value from the moment of its use. Before coming to the question of profit at all the company is entitled to earn a sufficient sum annually to provide not only for current repairs but for making good the depreciation and replacing the parts of the property when they come to the end of their life. The company is not bound to see its property gradually waste, without making provision out of earnings for its replacement. It is entitled to see that from its earnings the value of the property invested is kept unimpaired, so that at the end of any given term of years the original investment remains as it was at the beginning. It is not only the right of the company to make such a provision, but it is its duty to its bond and stockholders, and, in the case of a public service corporation at least, its plain duty to the public. If a different course were pursued the only method of providing for replacement of property which has ceased to be useful would be the investment of new capital and the issue of new bonds or stocks. This course would lead to a constantly increasing variance between present value and bond and stock capitalization—a tendency which would inevitably lead to disaster either to the stockholders or to the public, or both. If, however, a company fails to perform this plain duty and to exact sufficient returns to keep the investment unimpaired, whether this is the result of unwarranted dividends upon over-issues of securities, or of omission to exact proper prices for the output, the fault is its own. When, therefore, a public regulation of its prices comes under question the true value of the property then employed for the purpose of earning a return cannot be enhanced by a consideration of the errors in management which have been committed in the past." [1]

§ 1171. Payments into sinking fund.

The suggestion is made in one case that a provision out of current earnings for a sinking fund is proper. In Brymer v. Butler Water Company [2] already quoted, it was said that out of income might be set aside a "suitable sinking fund for the payment of debts." On the other hand, in the recent case of Houston & Texas Central Railway Company v. Storey,[3] it was held that a railroad company would not be allowed to earn an amount sufficient to provide a sinking fund for the discharge of its indebtedness in addition to paying the interest thereon. It is indeed very questionable how far it is true that a public service company should be allowed to include in its annual charges a percentage sufficient to provide for the redemption of its bonds in so far as these bonds represent cost of construction.[4] To adopt such a policy would make the generation during which these bonds are being paid off pay for the railroad to that extent, and yet after that it would be hard to say that the next generation could demand carriage free of fixed charges. The

---

[1] Where a public service corporation raises more money in a particular year than is required for actual depreciation it cannot carry the excess to capital for the purpose of estimating the amount on which it is entitled to pay dividends. Louisiana Railroad Comm. v. Cumberland Telephone Co., 212 U. S.

414, 53 L. ed. 577, 29 Sup. Ct. 357 (1909).

[2] 179 Pa. St. 231, 36 Atl. 249 (1897).

[3] 149 Fed. 499 (1906).

[4] See San Diego Water Co. v. San Diego, 118 Cal. 556, 50 Pac. 633 (1897).

startling truth seems to be, therefore, that a public service company should not any more expect to pay off its bonded indebtedness than to return the subscribers the subscriptions on their stock. The bonds should be refunded as they fall due, the interest remaining a fixed charge; and the stock should remain outstanding, only reasonable dividends being distributed to it. What the law secures is a return on the capital invested, not a return of it. But if the bond issue represents some expenditure not resulting in everlasting addition to the plant utilized, this may properly be provided for by an installment purchase. Such financial arrangements as equipment bonds are justifiable whereby the amount which the bond issue represents is sunk by periodical payments [1] with the same result as an installment purchase.

§ 1172. Sinking fund for municipal bonds.

Whatever may be the case where the company is owned by private stockholders, so that a payment of the bonded debt would inure to the benefit of private owners, it seems clear that a city which has issued bonds for works and supplies its citizens with water, gas, or other commodity of public concern may establish a sinking fund and sink its bonds out of annual income from the works.[2] Two differences, at least, exist between this case and the ordinary case of bonds of a public service company. First, the credit of the city is ordinarily higher than that of the company and the rate of interest on its bonds is so much lower that the combined interest and sinking fund requirements are not much greater than the interest which

[1] Compare Milwaukee Electric Ry. Co. v. Milwaukee, 87 Fed. 577 (1898).

[2] It is clear enough on the authorities that a municipality may conduct these public services on a business basis making the rates high enough to produce to good profit above proper expenditures including depreciation. Twitchell v. Spokane, 55 Wash. 86, 104 Pac. 150, 24 L. R. A. (N. S.) 290 (1909).

the company would pay; second, that the benefit of the payment is realized, not by individuals, but by the very body of citizens which is paying the rates. The right of a city to sink its construction bonds from annual income was recognized in Preston v. Detroit Water Commissioners.[1]

§ 1173. Amortization of franchise rights.

Where a franchise for a limited period is granted to a public service company, it may perhaps be proper to deduct from gross income a sufficient amount to sink the value of a secured franchise which will disappear at the end of the period, since the value of the plant is annually depreciated by that amount. In Milwaukee Electric Railway v. Milwaukee,[2] recently cited, the court said: "There is much force in the argument of counsel that consideration should also be given to the factor of depreciation by amortization of franchises, as all the franchises in question terminate in the year 1924." In certain of the schemes now much in favor in bargaining between a municipality and a public service company, it is provided that the works shall be constructed at the expense of the public service company and operated by it as its own for a fixed period, at the end of which time the subway, or whatever it may be, thus becomes the property of the municipality free of payment. It is obvious that in such a case the public service company must be allowed to sink the cost of such works from sums set aside from annual earnings by some process.

Topic D. Operations of Consolidated Properties

§ 1174. Complications in case of systems.

If the business carried on by the public service com-

---

[1] 117 Mich. 589, 76 N. W. 92 (1898). [2] 87 Fed. 577 (1898).

pany covers a large territory, the difficult question arises whether the system is to be taken as a whole or whether each locality is to be taken by itself. Additional complications are added to the problem when it is shown that the present system is the result of a consolidation, more or less integrated, of several properties; then the question becomes whether each of these original constituents is to be taken by itself in rate regulation, or whether all are to be taken together as before. These are practical problems of great importance; and therefore this separate topic is devoted to the consideration of the propriety of such apportionment, for it is sometimes attempted. Like most questions of rate regulation, this question may arise in one of two ways: one aspect of it will be whether a railroad company operating leased lines or held lines is justified in treating its system as a whole; the other side of the question will be whether such an operating company can be required at all to consider its system as a whole in making rates. In regard to both questions it may be pointed out that the law of corporations, and particularly the law of public service companies, forbids absolutely one such company leasing itself to another, and also the holding of the controlling interest in the stock of one such corporation by another. The only way in which combination along these lines may be perfected, therefore, with safety is by express permission of the Legislature of the State, obtained in one form or another at one time or another. It may fairly be argued, therefore, that since this railway system is organized with the consent of the State, it is not unjustifiable for the management of that company to deal with the public upon the basis that the system is a unit; and furthermore, it cannot be complained by the owners of this system, who have applied for the power to combine, if the State in regulating charges in the future treats the system as a whole.

§ 1175. System generally taken as a whole.

It must, however, be insisted upon as the usual solution of this problem, that the railway system, for example, shall be treated as an entirety.[1] By this conception every division is as much an integral part of the whole system as the different portions of the main line are. And the contention is that it is not proper to segregate a division and fix rates for it upon the basis of its own finances taken by themselves, although some slight scope may be given to such considerations. The typical railroad system has trunk lines with ramifying branches. To a certain extent it is plain that the main lines with their denser traffic can be operated at less cost per ton mile than the lateral branches. At the same time if in a total haulage the distance upon the branch is short relatively to the distance upon the main line, it may not be unjustifiable to make the same proportionate rate for the whole distance. And on the whole it would seem in most cases justifiable for the company conducting a consolidated system to take the attitude that the system should be treated as an entirety. This is also true of a supplying system serving only one locality wherein the conditions are substantially the same. All the revenue received from the whole operations of the system should be accounted for in order to decide whether a company is receiving a fair return on the total cost of the plant. [2]

---

[1] The general rule is that railway systems shall be treated as units.

United States.—Chicago, Milwaukee & St. P. Ry. v. Tompkins, 176 U. S. 167, 44 L. ed. 417, 20 Sup. Ct. 336 (1900); Minneapolis & St. L. Ry. v. Minnesota, 186 U. S. 257, 46 L. ed. 1151, 22 Sup. Ct. 900 (1902); Atlantic & P. Ry. v. U. S., 76 Fed. 186 (1896); Interstate Comm.

Comm. v. Louisville & N. R. R., 118 Fed. 613 (1902).

Arkansas.—St. Louis & S. F. Ry. v. Gill, 54 Ark. 101, 15 S. W. 18, 11 L. R. A. 452 (1891).

Florida.—Pensacola & A. R. R. v. Fla., 27 Fla. 310, 5 So. 833 (1889).

West Virginia.—Coal & Coke Ry. Co. v. Conley (W. Va.), 67 S. E. 613 (1910).

[2] The problem is treated in the

§ 1176. Unprofitable portions of the line not considered.

In Steenerson v. Great Northern Railway [1] the court considered at length the subject of unprofitable lines; and held that the profitable portions of the system could not be compelled to pay the loss on lines built through a newly and sparsely settled country. The reasoning of Mr. Justice Canty is as follows: "If," he said, "the road was profitable a certain reasonable rate would be fixed. If then a new and unprofitable extension were made, and the accounts covered the whole system, the rates on the older portion of the road would necessarily be raised, and that portion would bear the burden of the new extension. But why should the older portion of the line bear a loss due to the mistaken management of the company? A portion of a line that is not self-supporting is not a feeder, but an incumbrance; and in determining what are reasonable rates on the rest of the line or system, any State has a right to reject such portion from the line or system. Of course, in rejecting the same all benefit to the rest of the line or system from traffic passing over such portion must also be rejected, and nothing can be allowed to the rest of the line or system on such traffic, except the operating expenses on the same, including the additional wear and tear on the rest of the road caused by such traffic. Whether this rule would apply where such a portion of a line or system ceased to be self-supporting by reason of some temporary cause, such as an unusual drought or a pestilence, we need not consider." [2] It is perhaps fair to point out that in a later portion of the same opinion the

same way in other public services. See:

Maine.—Kennebec Water Dist. v. Waterville, 97 Me. 185, 54 Atl. 6, 60 L. R. A. 856 (1902).

New Jersey.—Long Branch Comm. v. Tintern Manor Water Co., 70 N. J. Eq. 71, 62 Atl. 474 (1905).

[1] 79 Minn. 353, 72 N. W. 713 (1897).

[2] See also Chicago & G. T. Ry. v. Wellman, 143 U. S. 339, 36 L. ed. 176, 12 Sup. Ct. 400 (1892).

court expressed the opinion that the whole system should be entitled to share the prosperity of each constituent part of it.

§ 1177. Expenditures for different parts apportioned.

But in other cases it has been held that the receipts and charges of each part of a system should be considered separately. In San Diego Land and Town Company v. National City,[1] where it appeared that a water company was supplying a town and also a large agricultural territory outside the town, the court held that in determining what were reasonable rates for supplying water to the inhabitants of the town the charges should be fixed with a view to yielding a fair rate of interest on the value of that part of the plant referable to the territory embraced in the town, without attempting to make compensation for losses sustained in the distribution of water to the territory outside the town. On appeal to the Supreme Court of the United States this was upheld, and Mr. Justice Harlan said:[2] "One of the points in dispute involves the question whether the losses to the appellant arising from the distribution of water to consumers *outside of the city* are to be considered in fixing the rate for consumers within the city. In our judgment the Circuit Court properly held that the defendant city was not required to adjust rates for water furnished to it and to its inhabitants so as to compensate the plaintiff for any such losses. This is so clear that we deem it unnecessary to do more than to state the conclusion reached by us on this point."

§ 1178. Constituent companies operated under separate charters.

It is held in some cases that the fact that the constituent roads still preserve their original charters and are theo-

[1] 74 Fed. 29 (1896).

[2] San Diego L. & T. Co. v. National City, 174 U. S. 739, 43 L. ed. 1154, 19 Sup. Ct. 804 (1899).

retically operated under them is sufficient to justify the requirement that each shall be treated by itself in rate regulation. Thus in one recent case,[1] where the propriety of a reduction in rates ordered by the railroad commission of Florida was in question, it was shown that the Pensacola & Atlantic division of the Louisville & Nashville Railroad system was in reality a separate corporation. It was shown that the rates enforced would not give an adequate return upon the Pensacola & Atlantic Railroad itself, although the Louisville & Nashville system was shown to be profitable. Upon these facts Judge Pardee granted an injunction to prevent the enforcement of these rates, saying in substance: "The fact that a line of railroad is operated in connection with other lines owned by the same company, but under separate charters, whereby the earnings of such line are increased and its operating expenses reduced, does not prevent its being considered as a separate and independent line for the purpose of determining the reasonableness of rates thereon, fixed by the State; full consideration of the joint operation being given when the road is credited for the increased business and reduced expenses."[2]

§ 1179. Rent of leased portions.

Where a *bona fide* lease of one road to another is made, the operating road is entitled to include the rent of the leased road in its operating expenses.[3] It is the annual expense of providing its appliances for carrying on its public business, and as such is a proper annual charge against gross income. The rent must be agreed upon in good faith; otherwise it would be in the power of the owners of a railroad to increase the annual charges, by successive

[1] Louisville & N. R. R. Co. v. Brown, 123 Fed. 946 (1903).

[2] Compare State ex rel. v. Sea-board A. L. Ry. Co., 48 Fla. 129, 37 So. 314 (1904).

[3] 78 Fed. 236 (1896).

leases, to such an extent that any rate would be reasonable. But granting the good faith of the lease and the reasonableness of the rent, it is a proper element of charge.

§ 1180. If rental becomes unjustifiable.

According to the Minnesota doctrine [1] by which the reproduction value of the road is the only proper basis of charge, the operating line cannot charge to annul operating expenses the agreed rental of a leased line, even though it was reasonable at the time the lease was made, if it is now higher than is justified by the present rate of income and reproduction value of the leased road. "If the amount of such fixed charges exceed the amount of what is a reasonable income on the cost of reproducing the road, the patrons of the road should not be required to pay the excess."

[1] Canty, J., in Steenerson v. Gt.   Northern Ry. Co., 69 Minn. 353, 72 N. W. 713 (1897).

CHAPTER XXXV

DETERMINATION OF PARTICULAR RATES

§ 1190. Various theories as to rate making.

§ 1190. Various theories as to rate making.

Various theories as to the making of particular rates
are still in vogue. Indeed, the first impression, which
lasts after much reading on the topic, is that where
there is not confusion upon the subject, there is disagree-
ment. But apparently the more lawyerlike persons would
base all particular rates upon the cost of the service to the
company, while the more businesslike persons would
make the universal test the value of the service to the
patron. Opportunists would leave the making of rates to
competition; paternalists would attempt to equalize the
advantage of customers in making rates. But, however
various they may seem, these theories as to the proper
basis of rate making align themselves into two opposed
groups, the legal, which gives chief place to the cost of
service, and the economic, which makes the value of the
service the basis. There used to be these two schools as to
the whole schedule, one maintaining that the total receipts which a public service company might take was
limited by law, the other one asserting that the corporations were entitled to what they could get out of the public.
This matter of the whole schedule has so long been settled against economic freedom and in favor of legal restriction that no one would reopen the controversy with
any hope of success. But still at the present time with all
conceding that the gross earnings which a company may

take are limited by law in any given case to a determinate amount, the economic school still persists in saying that the company can get these gross receipts by any distribution of the burden that it finds most advantageous.

Topic A. Cost of Service as the Basis

§ 1191. Proper proportion of total costs.

In the preceding chapters the total amount of gross receipts which a public service company is justified in taking from its whole business has been discussed. These were in brief all annual expenditures, including an allowance for upkeep, and in addition the fair capital charges for the year, arrived at by determining what would be in the particular case a reasonable return upon proper capitalization. As an abstract matter the fairest way to all concerned to determine the price for any particular service would seem to be to apportion ratably the total disbursements of every sort to the various items of business, and so to arrive at proportionate rates.[1] Theoretically certainly any other method is less just to all concerned. In determining thus what is a reasonable rate for a service to be rendered, it is not proper to take the plant as existing and as maintained, and to regard as the whole cost of any subsequent service merely the increased expense necessary to add to its business the service in question. Truly, the cost of each service ought to include its fair share of the interest on investment and of the general expense; and it is necessary, therefore, to consider what rules there may be devised for proper apportionment.[2] To look at the problem from another

[1] In Pennsylvania R. R. Co. v. Philadelphia County, 220 Pa. St. 100, 68 Atl. 676, 15 L. R. A. (N. S.) 108 (1908), it was held that passenger rates could not be so reduced as to prevent the railroad company from earning a fair profit upon that branch of its business.

[2] In Gulf C. & S. F. R. R. Co. v. Railroad Commission (Tex.), 116 S. W. 795 (1909), the court held a railroad could charge for trans-

point of view, the entire schedule of rates having been established, and the amount to be raised by the entire schedule of rates having been determined, the sum of all the particular rates must equal that amount; and this sum is tested by adding together the rates received.

§ 1192. Apportionment of separable costs to different services.

Even in a complicated business it ought to be possible to determine the peculiar cost of a particular service with some degree of accuracy. Take the most difficult of all, railway transportation. The first difficulty that presents itself is that the ordinary railroad is engaged in at least two different businesses, the transportation of freight and the transportation of passengers, with their costs intermingled. Now, many of the particular costs of moving traffic can be separated, the wages paid the train crews of freight trains from those paid to the train crews of passenger trains, and the fuel burned by freight locomotives from that burned by passenger locomotives, to take two important items. Moreover, to a certain extent the entire expense of transportation may thus be judged from the sums expended in operation.[1] When the average amount expended in moving quantities of a given commodity is known, a standard is established by which it may be seen whether there is not a full return to the railroad of the entire cost attributable to the transportation of these goods. And an expert railway management ought to be able to estimate with a sufficient degree of accuracy the

porting lumber not merely the separable costs of such transportation, but also its proper proportion of the fixed charges of the railroad.

[1] In Chicago, St. P. Mo. & O. Ry. Co. v. Becker, 35 Fed. 883 (1888), a rate for switching cars fixed by a commission was enjoined, the complainant's testimony showing that the actual cost of the service, viz., wages of employés, rent of engines, keeping the track in repair, etc., exceeded per car by fourteen cents the one dollar allowed in the schedule as compensation.

particular expenditures involved in moving a carload from one point to another—wages, coal, oil and the like. It would be wrong upon any theory to ignore the cost of service in so far as it may thus be estimated; for to serve some shippers for less than the special costs of serving them would be plainly unfair to other shippers, who would almost inevitably be called upon to make up the deficiency. [1]

§ 1193. Allocation of joint costs.

When the separable costs of operation have thus been distributed to the different kinds of services rendered, it will be found that from forty to sixty per cent of the total expenditures for which the company should be recouped have been thus accounted for, the percentage depending upon the kind of business in general and the accounting of the company in particular. This determination of half of the average cost for particular services with sufficient accuracy gives to the further computation greater reliability, as it greatly diminishes the percentage of error in the total due to the comparative inaccuracy of the other half. This other half consists of the part allocated to the particular business in question of the joint costs of operation, which consist principally of the general expenses and capital charges. Even here some distribution can be made. Thus to consider still railroad operation, in so far as the freight management and passenger management are divided between different officials the salaries may be apportioned; and as to a large extent freight equipment and to a smaller extent freight terminals are divided their capital charges may be divided. There remains, how-

[1] Conversely no complaint can be made of a charge for a particular service which not only covers the full cost of the particular service asked but also yields a fair profit above that cost: Southern Ry. Co. v. St. Louis H. & G. Co., 214 U. S. 297, 53 L. ed. 1004, 29 Sup. Ct. 678 (1909).

ever, a very considerable total of joint costs inextricably combined, the salaries of the executive officers and the capital charges upon roadbed, as example. At this point we are for the first time really driven to computation upon an artificial basis to arrive at some distribution. Obviously this is to be arrived at by striking some proportion. Some students of this subject are content to rest this upon respective utilization, dividing these joint costs in the proportion (say) of freight ton-mileage to passenger mileage. But this proportion seems to throw too great a burden upon the passenger service, the receipts from the passenger train being so much less than those from the freight train. Other persons maintain that the volume of business done should determine the proportion, dividing these joint costs (say) in the proportion of freight receipts to passenger receipts. But this proportion in turn seems to throw too great a burden upon the freight traffic, the passenger business obviously receiving more service than its proportion of the total receipts. Confronted suddenly with this problem in the late litigation resulting from the recent two cent passenger legislation, the State courts have hardly got further at first, than to say that they would not permit a reduction in rates in one branch of railroad service whether passenger [1] or freight,[2] which did not leave a fair profit upon each branch above its proper proportion of the expense of operation.

§ 1194. Apportionment between interstate and intrastate business.

Where a road runs through several States the Constitu-

---

[1] Pennsylvania R. R. Co. v. Philadelphia Co., 220 Pa. St. 100, 68 Atl. 676, 15 L. R. A. (N. S.) 108 (1908).

[2] Coal & Coke Ry. Co. v. Conley (W. Va.), 67 S. E. 613 (1910).

See also State v. Atlantic C. L. Ry. Co., 48 Fla. 114, 37 So. 657 (1904).

See further Tucker v. Missouri Pacific R. R. Co. (Kans.), 108 Pac. 89 (1910).

tion as interpreted by the Supreme Court of the United States requires that the value of the plant utilized in the intrastate business and the net earnings from such business must both be ascertained in order to determine whether the rates fixed by the State or its Commission are reasonable or confiscatory. In the leading case in the United States Supreme Court on this point Smyth v. Ames,[1] Mr. Justice Harlan said: "In our judgment, it must be held that the reasonableness or unreasonableness of rates prescribed by a State for the transportation of persons and property wholly within its limits must be determined without reference to the interstate business done by the carrier, or to the profits derived from it. The State cannot justify unreasonably low rates for domestic transportation, considered alone, upon the ground that the carrier is earning large profits on its interstate business, over which, so far as rates are concerned, the State has no control. Nor can the carrier justify unreasonably high rates on domestic business upon the ground that it will be able only in that way to meet losses on its interstate business. So far as rates of transportation are concerned, domestic business should not be made to bear the losses on interstate business, nor the latter the losses on domestic business. It is only rates for the transportation of persons and property between points within the State that the State can prescribe; and when it undertakes to prescribe rates not to be exceeded by the carrier, it must do so with reference exclusively to what is just and reasonable, as between the carrier and the public, in respect of domestic business. The argument that a railroad is an entirety; that its income goes into, and its expenses are provided for, out of a common fund; and that its capitalization is on its entire line, within and without the State, can have no application where the State is without authority over

[1] 169 U. S. 466, 42 L. ed. 89, 18 Sup. Ct. 418 (1898).

rates on the entire line, and can only deal with local rates
and make such regulations as are necessary to give just
compensation on local business." [1]

§ 1195. Apportionment of total expense.

The Federal courts with a much more complicated problem to deal with have been driven to stating the theory
upon which they will proceed. The State legislation reducing passenger fares could only apply to intrastate
business. To determine whether this reduction was unjustifiable the Federal courts saw that they were required
not only to allocate the respective costs of passenger and
freight business but also to apportion these to the intrastate and interstate business. In one of the latest cases [2] on
this subject Judge McPherson narrowed the discussion to
two theories—the mileage proportion and the revenue
proportion. He admitted that neither of these would
result in mathematical accuracy; but he insisted that as a
practical matter the one which promised to be most
satisfactory should be taken as the basis of action. "The
theory to now recognize must be either the proportion of
earnings state or interstate, or ton and passenger mile."
After reviewing what few cases there are bearing upon the
point, all of which agree upon the greater proportionate
cost of local business as compared with through business,
he said that, although other standards are suggested, the

---

[1] In Minnesota the state court
had taken the other alternative possible by assuming that a similar rate
would be adopted throughout the
whole system, the court feeling that
there was not any good reason why
a railway system should be divided
on state lines at all. Steenerson v.
Gt. Northern Ry. Co., 69 Minn.
353, 72 N. W. 713 (1897).

[2] In St. Louis & S. F. R. R. Co. v.
Hadley, 168 Fed. 317 (1909).

Citing Northern Pacific R. R. Co.
v. Keyes, 91 Fed. 47 (1899); Chicago M. & St. P. Ry. Co. v. Smith,
110 Fed. 473 (1901); In re Arkansas
R. R. Rates, 163 Fed. 141 (1908);
Chicago M. & St. P. Ry. Co. v.
Tompkins, 176 U. S. 167, 44 L. ed.
417, 20 Sup. Ct. 336 (1900).

more satisfactory and accurate was "the difference in cost in relation to the revenue."

§ 1196. Basis of the distribution.

Furthermore in the very latest case [1] at the present time this view is elaborately defended by Judge Hook. "From the very nature of the case, therefore, some rule must be adopted for charging to each of them their fair and equitable proportion of the common expense. Of necessity it must proceed upon average conditions commonly known or shown to exist, and it argues nothing to say that it does not fully apply to this or that exceptional instance. A general rule based on experienced observation is fair, and what is lost by its application in one place is doubtless gained in another, and an equitable equilibrium maintained. Of those suggested the revenue basis appears to be much more uniform in its adaptibility and much less subject to substantial objection. It has been frequently employed. It is the one to which the mind naturally turns in every problem involving the charging of common expense to different departments of a business. When a general or common expense cannot be located what is more obviously reasonable than to say in the first place the different branches or departments shall bear it according to the value of their products of their gross earnings, and then make due allowance for exceptional conditions if any are perceived? That seems at the start to satisfy the mind intent on equity. It is a working basis for the distribution of all expense incident to railroad business among its revenue yielding operations of every character."

[1] Missouri K. & T. Ry. Co. v. Love, 177 Fed. 493 (1900). Citing Smyth v. Ames, 169 U. S. 466, 18 Sup. Ct. 418, 42 L. ed. 819 (1898); Chicago M. & St. P. R. Co. v. Tompkins, 176 U. S. 167, 20 Sup. Ct. 336, 44 L. ed. 417 (1900); Northern Pacific v. Keyes, 91 Fed. 47 (1899); In re Arkansas R. R. Rates, 163 Fed. 141 (1908); St. Louis & S. F. R. Co. v. Hadley, 168 Fed. 317 (1909).

With due deference to those who have been worried in choosing between these two proportions, each of which it is admitted has its error, the writer would suggest that by a compound proportion, utilizing both proportions, the respective errors in the single proportions would be largely offset, and an entirely defensible result would be reached.

§ 1197. Proportionate share of different classes.

This proposal to fix rates by the computation of the costs is not mere theory but is followed in present practice, as may be seen by an examination of the elaborate opinion of the Vice Chancellor in the recent case of Tintern Manor Water Company and Long Branch,[1] where the principal issue was as to the amount which Long Branch should pay for the water supplied for its municipal requirements. His computation well fortified by careful reasoning from point to point was somewhat as follows. First, he decided by exhaustive examination what would constitute in the particular case a fair return to the proprietors of the waterworks upon their reasonable capitalization. To this figure, he added what the expert testimony showed, would be the fair annual cost of operation and maintenance—all this he pointed out must be recouped to the company from its total receipts. Then, after consideration, he decided how much of this amount should be contributed by the private consumers and how much by the various municipal consumers. And finally he decided what proportion of this amount should be paid by Long Branch itself. It is believed that in intricate cases of real importance all these steps are necessary to determine the reasonableness of a particular charge. In another recent case[2] dealing with the franchise obligations of a gas com-

[1] Long Branch Commission v. Tintern Manor Water Co., 70 N. J. Eq. 71, 62 Atl. 474 (1905).

[2] Erie v. Erie Gas Light & C. Co., 78 Kan. 348, 97 Pac. 408 (1909).

pany which was supplying gas both for domestic and commercial purposes within and without the city the question came up as to the respective costs of each branch of the business, and the consequent profit in each. Confronted by this problem the court while recognizing its difficulty did not despair. It may be difficult to distinguish the items, the court admitted, especially as expenditures of the company had not been classified but were entered in one common account, including the cost of the establishment and the operation of the service, and this confusion included the sales within and without the city. But this difficulty the court said could not affect the rights involved and probably would not be found to be as great as anticipated. For example, in making the estimates for the computation of profits within the cities, simply deduct from the amount of sale within the city the amount received from sales to manufacturers.

§ 1198. Average rate per unit of service.

In dealing with a multiplicity of rates for particular services, the computations described in this topic may be carried with advantage one step further, to the determination of the average cost per unit of service, which may be used thereafter as a standard for testing the charge for any particular service. Thus of any given gas company it may be said that it is entitled to take as gross receipts from its whole business a certain sum determined by adding together its operating expenses, including therewith all proper maintenance charges, and its fixed charges, rather a fair return upon a reasonable capitalization. Then if the probable sales, judged by its actual sales, amount to approximately certain thousands of cubic feet, its proper average price per cubic foot may be found. In testing freight rates, the most difficult problem of all, this standard is the ton-mile cost. If the sum of the whole amount of freight carried be one hundred thousand ton miles, and the gross revenue required from freight be two thousand dollars, the average rate of freight will be two cents per ton mile. If there were no other factors in the problem, therefore, a fair proportionate rate would be the ton-mile average charge.[1] Because, however, of other factors, which cause a difference between commodities with respect to the fair charge for carrying them, a uniform ton-mile rate applied to all cases would not result in reasonable rates.[2]

§ 1199. Recognition of the ton-mile cost basis.

Although generally abhorrent to economists, the ton-mile cost basis is well recognized by judges to-day as the first test to be employed in determining the reasonableness of particular rates. In a recent case [3] in the United States Supreme Court, where the issue was whether a certain rate upon phosphates fixed by a commission was fair to the railroad affected, Mr. Justice Brewer, speaking for the court said: "And here we face this situation: The order of the commission was not operative upon all local rates but only fixed the rates on a single article, to wit, phosphate. There is no evidence of the amount of phosphates carried locally; neither is it shown how much a change in the rate of carrying them will affect the income, nor how much the rate fixed by railroads for carrying phosphate has been changed by the order of the commission. There is testimony tending to show the gross income from all local freights and the value of the railroad property, and also certain

[1] As will be seen in Atlantic C. L. Ry. Co. v. Florida, 203 U. S. 256, 51 L. ed. 174, 27 Sup. Ct. 108 (1906), discussed in the next paragraph, resort is often had to the ton-mile cost as a basis for regulation.

[2] As the Supreme Court of the United States held at the same term, if the State uses such a basis in regulation it is not oppressive. Seaboard Air L. Ry. Co. v. Florida, 203 U. S. 261, 51 L. ed. 175, 27 Sup. Ct. 109 (1908).

[3] Atlantic C. L. Ry. Co. v. Florida, 203 U. S. 256, 51 L. ed. 174, 27 Sup. Ct. 108 (1906).

difficulties in the way of transporting phosphates owing to the lack of facilities at the terminals. But there is nothing from which we can determine the cost of such transportation. We are aware of the difficulty which attends proof of the cost of transporting a single article, and in order to determine the reasonableness of a rate prescribed it may be sometimes necessary to accept as a basis the average rate of all transportation per ton per mile. We shall not attempt to indicate to what extent or in what cases the inquiry must be special and limited. It is enough for the present to hold that there is in the record nothing from which a reasonable deduction can be made as to the cost of transportation, the amount of phosphates transported, or the effect which the rate established by the commission will have upon the income. Under these circumstances it is impossible to hold that there was error in the conclusions reached by the Supreme Court of the State of Florida, and its judgment is affirmed." [1]

§ 1200. Ton-mile cost basis not oppressive.

At all events it may be said that governmental regulation based upon the ton-mile basis is not oppressive. This is shown sufficiently in another case [2] involving a similar issue decided by the same Justice on the same day. "With reference to the second of these cases the order made by the railroad commission is said by the plaintiff in error to be an 'irregular, unjust and unreliable method of rate fixing,' and this upon the theory that the order makes the rate per mile the same for any distance, whether one mile or a hundred miles. It appears the 16.43 per cent of all the local freight business of the company in Florida comes from the carrying of phosphates, and ref-

---

[1] See also Gulf & S. F. R. R. Co. v. Railroad Commission (Tex.), 116 S. W. 795 (1909).

[2] Seaboard Air Line Ry. Co. v. Florida, 203 U. S. 261, 51 L. ed. 175, 27 Sup. Ct. 109 (1908).

erence is made to several cases in which the courts have
noticed the fact that the cost of moving local freight is
greater than that of moving through freight, and the
reasons for the difference. But evidently counsel mis-
interprets the order of the railroad commission. It does
not fix the rate at one cent per ton per mile. It simply
provided that it shall not exceed one cent per ton per mile,
prescribes a maximum which may be reduced by the railroad company, and if distance demands a reduction the
company may and doubtless will make it. In addition it
must be borne in mind that it is to be presumed that the
railroad commission acted with full knowledge of the
situation; that phosphates were in Florida possibly carried
a long distance, the place of mining being far from the
place of actual use or preparation for use. Further, when
we turn to the report of the railroad company (which of
course is evidence against it) we find that the company's
average freight receipt per ton per mile in the State of
Florida was $8\frac{15}{100}$ mills; so that the rate authorized for
phosphates was nearly two mills per ton larger than such
average. Under these circumstances it is impossible to
say that there was error in the conclusions of the Supreme
Court of the State, and its judgments are affirmed." [1]

§ 1201. Authorities permitting disproportionate rates.

So far as there is as yet actual law upon this problem of
the revision of particular rates the outcome hangs in the
balance where it is not unlikely it will long remain. It
must be conceded that at first sight the weight of authority
would seem to be against one who is claiming that the
particular rates in a schedule should not be unreasonably
disproportionate. But upon examination this weight of
authority will be found only for a limited proposition.

[1] But see Tucker v. Missouri   Pacific R. R. Co. (Kan.), 108 Pac.
89 (1910).

It is true that by what is still the weight of authority the imposition of a rate by legislation, which fixes so disproportionately low a rate for a particular service as to make that service admittedly unprofitable will nevertheless not be held to be unconstitutional, if from its total receipts the company in question will get a fair return on its proper capital above operating expenses and reasonable charges. The Supreme Court of the United States still holds to the doctrine first clearly announced in Minneapolis & St. Louis Railroad Company v. Minnesota [1] where Mr. Justice Brown in justifying an order of the State commission so reducing the rate on coal that its transportation would be at a loss said: "Notwithstanding the evidence of the defendant that if the rates upon all merchandise were fixed at the amount imposed by the commission upon coal in carload lots, the road would not pay its operating expenses, it may well be that the existing rates upon other merchandise, which are not disturbed by the commission, may be sufficient to earn a large profit to the company, though it may earn little or nothing upon coal in carload lots." [2]

---

[1] 186 U. S. 257, 46 L. ed. 1151, 22 Sup. Ct. 901 (1902). The court had already committed itself to this doctrine in St. Louis & S. F. R. R. Co. v. Gill, 156 U. S. 649, 39 L. ed. 567, 15 Sup. Ct. 484 (1895).

[2] See further to the same effect:

United States.—Interstate Consolidated St. Ry. Co. v. Massachusetts, 207 U. S. 79, 52 L. ed. 111, 28 Sup. Ct. 26 (1908); Willcox v. Consolidated Gas Co., 212 U. S. 19, 53 L. ed. 382, 29 Sup. Ct. 192 (1909); Southern R. R. Co. v. McNeill, 155 Fed. 756 (1907); Central of Ga. Ry. Co. v. McLendon, 157 Fed. 974 (1907); In re Arkansas R. R. Rates,

168 Fed. 720 (1908). But see Lake Shore & M. S. Ry. Co. v. Smith, 173 U. S. 684, 43 L. ed. 858, 19 Sup. Ct. 565 (1899).

Arkansas.—Missouri Pacific R. R. Co. v. Smith, 60 Ark. 221, 29 S. W. 752 (1895).

Minnesota.—State v. Minneapolis & St. L. Ry. Co., 80 Minn. 191, 83 N. W. 60 (1900).

Florida.—Pensacola & A. R. R. Co. v. Florida, 25 Fla. 310, 5 So. 833 (1889).

Georgia.—Southern Ry. Co. v. Atlanta Stove Works, 128 Ga. 207, 57 S. E. 429 (1907).

North Dakota.—State ex rel. v.

§ 1202. Authorities opposed to disproportion.

It should be noted, however, that there has been vigorous protest of late years against this proposition, even as it has been limited.   In this connection the recent case of the Pennsylvania Railroad Company v. Philadelphia County [1] deserves full consideration as the latest expression of the modern tendency to look into the different departments of the business in their relation to one another.   In that case there was bill in equity to restrain the enforcement of the Pennsylvania statute imposing a two cent passenger rate.   It was urged in defense of the legislation that, although it might leave no profit to the railroad in question upon its passenger traffic, the gross receipts of that railroad would, notwithstanding this, be sufficient to pay a fair profit upon its whole capital.   But the Pennsylvania Supreme Court held the legislation unconstitutional upon this showing, Chief Justice Mitchell saying: "True business principles require that the passenger and freight traffic not only may, but should be separately considered. The intelligent business of the world is done in that way. Every merchant and manufacturer examines and ascertains the unprofitable branches of his business with a view to reducing or cutting them off entirely, and there is no reason why a railroad or other corporation should not be permitted to do the same thing as long as its substantial corporate duties under its franchise are performed.   While the public has certain rights which in the case of conflict must prevail, yet it must not be forgotten that even so-called public service corporations are private property organized and conducted for private corporate profit. And unless necessary for the fulfillment of their corporate duties they should not be required to do any part of their

Northern Pacific Ry. Co. (N. D.),   [1] 220 Pa. St. 100, 68 Atl. 676, 15
120 N. W. 869, 25 L. R. A. (N. S.)   L. R. A. (N. S.) 108 (1908).
1001 (1909).

business in an unbusinesslike way with a resulting loss. If part is unprofitable it is neither good business nor justice to make it more so because the loss can be offset by profit on the rest. To concede that principle would, as the court below indicated, permit the legislature to compel the carriage of passengers practically for nothing though the inexorable result would be that freight must pay inequitable rates that passenger travel may be cheap." [1]

Topic B. Factors Modifying Average Cost

§ 1203. Cost of service insufficient in itself.

To be entirely fair the cost of service is not always the decisive factor in determining a railroad rate, even if it could in all cases be fairly approximated. The ton-mile average cost in railroad transportation will always be found to be much modified by other factors in actual application. For, in the first place, it must always be impossible to arrive at the exact cost of a particular carriage. No goods, as a practical matter, are carried by themselves under such circumstances that an exact computation can be made of the cost of carriage. In the second place, even if such a computation were possible it would not necessarily be fair to make a shipper pay the exact cost of carriage of each shipment. To do so would make the freight vary according to the circumstances of each journey; no man could know what he must pay for any particular shipment, and for similar carriages of the same article two shippers would pay very different charges. Practical convenience requires that the charge shall be uniform for a certain article carried over a certain route, although the exact cost of carriage

---

[1] See further to the same effect:

Texas.—Gulf C. & S. F. R. R. Co. v. Railroad Commission (Tex.), 116 S. W. 795 (1909).

West Virginia.—Coal & Coke Ry. Co. v. Conley (W. Va.), 67 S. E. 613 (1910).

may at one time be very much greater than at another. The exact cost of carriage, therefore, or such approximation to it as may be possible, can never be used as the sole factor in a particular rate. But while the cost of carriage cannot be used by itself to determine a particular rate, neither should it ever be neglected. Considered along with other factors, it must have a strong influence in raising or lowering the particular rate.

§ 1204. Current theories as to relative rates.

All the principles governing the fixing of rates which have ever been suggested may be seen in brief compass in a still recent opinion of Judge Bethea: [1] "There are a great many factors and circumstances to be considered in fixing a rate.[2] Among other things: (1) The value of the service to the shipper, including the value of the goods and the profit he could make out of them by shipment. This is considered an ideal method, when not interfered with by competition or other factors. It includes the theory so strenuously contended for by petitioners, the commission, and its attorneys, of making the finished product carry a higher rate than the raw material. This method is considered practical, and is based on an idea similar to taxation.[3] (2) The cost of service to the carrier would be an ideal theory, but is not practical. Such cost can be reached approximately, but not accurately enough to make this factor controlling. It is worthy of consideration, however.[4] (3) Weight, bulk, and conven-

---

[1] Interstate Commerce Commission v. Chicago Gt. Western R. R. Co., 141 Fed. 1003 (1905).

[2] Citing Noyes, Am. R. R. Rates, 61, 85–109.

[3] Citing Interstate Commerce Commission v. B. & O. Ry. Co. (C. C.), 43 Fed. 37.

[4] Citing Western Union Tel. Co. v. Call Publishing Co., 181 U. S. 92, 21 Sup. Ct. 561, 45 L. ed. 765; Interstate Commerce Commission v. Detroit, Grand Haven & Milwaukee R. R. Co., 167 U. S. 633, 17 Sup. Ct. 986, 42 L. ed. 306, etc.

ience of transportation. (4) The amount of the product or the commodity in the hands of a few persons to ship or compete for, recognizing the principle of selling cheaper at wholesale than at retail.[1] (5) General public good, including good to the shipper, the railroad company and the different localities.[2] (6) Competition, which the authorities, as well as the experts, in their testimony in these cases, recognize as a very important factor.[3] None of the above factors alone are considered necessarily controlling by the authorities. Neither are they all controlling as a matter of law. It is a question of fact to be decided by the proper tribunal in each case as to what is controlling."[4]

§ 1205. Amount of service asked as a factor.

As the amount of service asked at a particular time increases, the cost thereof tends in normal cases to fall below the average. This is a familiar rule in the transportation of freight by railroads; and it has become axiomatic that while the aggregate charge is continually increasing the further the freight is carried, yet the rate per ton per mile is constantly growing less all the time. In consequence of the existence of this rule the increase of the aggregate charge continues to be less in proportion every hundred miles after the first, arising out of the character and nature of the service performed and the cost

[1] Citing Interstate Commerce Commission v. B. & O. Ry. Co., 145 U. S. 263, 12 Sup. Ct. 844, 36 L. ed. 699.

[2] Citing Interstate Commerce Commission v. B. & O. Ry. Co., 145 U. S. 263, 12 Sup. Ct. 844, 36 L. ed. 699.

[3] Citing Phipps v. London & Northwestern Ry. Co., 2 Q. B. D. 229 (1892).

[4] Citing Interstate Commerce Commission v. Alabama Midland Ry. Co., 168 U. S. 144, 18 Sup. Ct. 45, 42 L. ed. 414; East Tennessee, Virginia & Georgia Railway Co. v. Interstate Commerce Commission, 181 U. S. 1, 21 Sup. Ct. 516, 45 L. ed. 719; Texas & Pac. Ry. Co. v. Interstate Commerce Commission, 162 U. S. 197, 16 Sup. Ct. 666, 40 L. ed. 940; Interstate Commerce Commission v. Louisville & Nashville R. R. Co., 190 U. S. 273, 23 Sup. Ct. 687, 47 L. ed. 1047, etc.

of service; and thus it is that staple commodities and merchandise are enabled to bear the charges of transportation from and to the most distant portions of the country. The reason for this rule is that the cost of railway transportation is made up of the expense of the two terminals and the intermediate haul, and the terminal expenses are the same whether the haul be long or short. A few miles, or even a considerable number of miles, of additional haul may in some instances of long distance transportation be practically of very little importance, and the aggregate rate therefore may be very little affected by the additional mileage.

§ 1206. Local business peculiarly expensive.

Sometimes the cost of a particular service is peculiarly expensive. Thus local shipments are more expensive to handle in proportion to the mileage than long distance shipments, and a greater proportionate charge is therefore justified. "The operating expenses of a railroad consist of two principal items: (1) cost of maintenance of plant; (2) cost of conducting transportation. The former item is constant, and can justly be divided between the different kinds of traffic in proportion to their volume. As to the second item, however, such a division cannot properly be made; for it is agreed, by all who have had occasion to consider the subject, railroad commissioners as well as railroad officials, that the cost of conducting transportation is, relative to income, much higher for local business than for the general business of a road. The causes of this added cost are chiefly three: (1) the shortness of the haul; (2) the lightness of the train loads; (3) expense of billing and handling the traffic." [1] But be-

[1] Northern Pacific Ry. Co. v. Keyes, 91 Fed. 47 (1898). See also Chicago, M. & St. P. Ry. Co. v. Tompkins, 176 U. S. 167, 44 L. ed. 417, 20 Sup. Ct. 336 (1900).

cause a greater charge may be made on local than on through business, it by no means follows that all the charge of maintaining a station can be laid upon the business done at that station. If, for instance, a small amount of business is done at a station the rates cannot be made much greater at that station than at a neighboring way station, where three or four times as much business is done. Some particular losses are inseparable from the conduct of a general public service.[1]

§ 1207. Special conditions affecting cost.

There may be special circumstances connected with a particular transaction which increase or decrease the cost of service; and the effect of such circumstances on the rate must be considered. For instance, the expense of constructing a mountain branch may be very much greater than that of building the main line; or the population served by the company may in places be so sparse as to make the cost of operation very great in proportion to the service demanded. All these circumstances may properly affect the rate charged in those portions of the territory served by the company; yet it appears unjust to place the whole burden upon such territory, thus accentuate its poverty, and place another handicap upon it in the effort to become prosperous. Not all the extra cost of service should be placed upon the particular customers. Thus many things besides the mere mileage run must be considered in fixing the rates. A uniform mileage rate imposed upon all railroads would be in reality unequal and unjust. As Mr. Justice Morse said in Wellman v. Chicago & Grand Trunk Railway:[2] "If no clas-

[1] In Missouri, K. & T. Ry. Co. v. Love, 177 Fed. 493 (1910), the court considered elaborately the greater cost of local business in comparison with through business. See also St. Louis & S. F. Ry. Co. v. Hadley, 168 Fed. 317 (1908).

[2] 83 Mich. 592, 47 N. W. 489 (1890).

sification can be made, and the maximum rate must be fixed the same for all, then the law is admitted to operate unequally and unjustly, because some companies are to less expense than others in the same length of road by reason of the nature of the country through which they run; some have costly terminal facilities, and some have not; some owe large amounts, and some do not; and some do a large amount of business, and some do not."

§ 1208. Circumstances of particular service.

The point that the cost of service may be different for different parts of the same system was insisted upon in Interstate Commerce Commission v. Lehigh Valley Railroad Company.[1] It appeared in that case that the Interstate Commerce Commission, upon complaint of a shipper, had adjudged a certain rate upon coal unreasonable. The Commission based its finding upon its deductions from the annual report of the defendant company that the average cost of carrying a ton of coal from the Lehigh anthracite regions to Perth Amboy was 85 cents. Judge Acheson held that this was an inadequate basis to justify the finding that the particular rate in question was unreasonable; he said: "Having adopted an estimated average rate of revenue, namely, $1.495 from each ton of coal carried over the 149 miles from the Lehigh and Mahanoy regions to Perth Amboy, the Commission assumed that the expenses of the transportation of coal over this particular branch of the defendant's railroad system was necessarily only the average cost of the carriage of all coal upon the defendant's entire system. The assumption which thus underlies the Commission's estimate is unwarrantable. Merely because the cost of carriage of all coal upon the defendant's entire railroad system from all points of shipment to all destinations was

[1] 74 Fed. 784 (1897).

56 per cent of the gross receipts from all coal is no reason for concluding that upon a particular line or part of the system the cost of carriage bears the same ratio to the coal receipts from that particular line or part."

§ 1209. Proportionate rates always legal.

Upon the other proposition there is no conflict of authority whatever. The rate maker may always with the approbation of the law work out a schedule of rates in which the respective rates are based upon their proportional cost of the whole service rendered. Not only would all courts undoubtedly agree that legislation forbidding disportionality in rates is constitutional,[1] but also it is doubtless law that a public service company may so arrange its schedule as to make each rate yield a reasonable profit for each service above the fair cost, without any question as to the legality of such a course.[2] It is, therefore, well within limits to say in summarizing what has gone before, that although the rate making party is as yet by the weight of authority not held to act illegally in imposing a schedule where the particular rates are out of proportion,[3] it is unanimously agreed that if the policy of proportional distribution of the real costs is adopted by the rate making body, no objection can be made on any grounds whatsoever.[4]

§ 1210. Full extent of the doctrine.

The suggestion is sometimes made that a distinction is to be drawn between keeping the different classes of

[1] Seaboard Air Line Ry. Co. v. Florida, 203 U. S. 261, 51 L. ed. 175, 27 Sup. Ct. 109 (1906), and cases cited.

[2] Pennsylvania R. R. Co. v. Philadelphia County, 220 Pa. St. 100, 68 Atl. 676, 15 L. R. A. (N. S.) 108 (1908), and cases cited.

[3] Willcox et al. v. Consolidated Gas Co., 212 U. S. 19, 53 L. ed. 382, 29 Sup. Ct. 192 (1909), and cases cited.

[4] Interstate Comm. Comm. v. Western A. R. R. Co., 88 Fed. 186 (1898), and cases cited.

charges proportionate and making the different items proportionate. Except for the inherent difficulties of pursuing the inquiry further the writer perceives no difference in principle between the two; and he has no reason to believe that the distinction has foundation in law. It is true that by the weight of authority a rate on coal [1] or oil,[2] may be made disproportionately small; provided the total receipts of the railroad are sufficient. But it is also true that if the rate on phosphates [3] or lumber [4] is kept in proportion to other rates no one can complain that the rates are illegally made. This policy is altogether in accordance with the tendency of the modern law of public service against all discriminatory practices. Indeed any method of fixing rates which results in disproportionate treatment to different customers asking somewhat different services would seem to be against that fundamental principle of equality which of late years has been held to be violated by discriminatory treatment of different patrons asking substantially similar services.

Topic C. Value of Service as the Basis

§ 1211. What the traffic will bear.

It is sometimes suggested that the value of the service to the customer is "what the traffic will bear," that is, what he will be willing to pay rather than go without service. This Mr. Judge Bethea ventured to call the "ideal method." [5] In one sense the service is worth what one will pay for it; and this is the rule which usually ap-

[1] See Minneapolis & St. Louis Ry. Co. v. Minnesota, 186 U. S. 257, 46 L. ed. 1151, 22 Sup. Ct. 901 (1902).

[2] See Tucker v. Missouri Pacific Ry. Co. (Kan.), 108 Pac. 89 (1910).

[3] Seaboard Air Line Ry. Co. v. Florida, 203 U. S. 261, 51 L. ed. 175, 27 Sup. Ct. 109 (1908).

[4] Gulf C. & S. F. R. R. Co. v. Railroad Commission (Tex.), 116 S. W. 795 (1909).

[5] In Interstate Com. Comm. v. Chicago G. W. R. R. Co., 141 Fed. 1003 (1905).

peals to the company as fair. This consideration, it may be, has some place in the philosophy of rate making; although it is submitted that it is a dangerous principle which may often operate to the disadvantage of the public, unless it is much limited. But so necessary is some such principle felt to be by the managers of a company that it will always be employed in rate making. And this is one of the prime causes for the necessity of governmental revision for the protection of the public, of the rates established by the corporation. "This domination" by the corporations Judge Speer says prophetically the American people will "never tolerate."[1] The real truth of this matter seems to be that charging what will produce the largest profits is fundamental in private business, but often wholly opposed to public duty.

§ 1212. Necessity of legal limitation.

It is urged sometimes that this principle of charging what the traffic will bear contains it own safeguards; for if more is charged than the value of the service to the customer business will cease, and the managers, realizing this, as they are in close touch with the situation will never intentionally or permanently charge more than the service is worth. The answer to this seems to be that many customers will pay for service more than its true value if that is necessary in order to get service.[2] They will shift this undue burden upon the ultimate consumer if they can, and if not, they will be obliged to shoulder it themselves. From a legal point of view it is a conclusive answer to the economic argument that people will continue to pay for service at unfair rates. Indeed, any considerable concession to the principle of charging what the

---

[1] In Tift v. Southern R. R. Co., 138 Fed. 753 (1905).

[2] See Brunswick & T. W. D. v. Maine Water Co., 99 Me. 371, 59 Atl. 537 (1904).

traffic will bear is dangerous.   The public service company is acting primarily for the benefit, not for the exploitation of the public.   To allow a carrier, for instance, to charge what the traffic will bear is to foster a continual increase of railroad rates, at least when prices are rising.[1]

§ 1213. Worth of the service to the individuals taken as a whole.

An excellent distinction is made in a recent case [2] as to the methods of arriving at the value of the service to the person served by a public service company.   It is pointed out that what is sought is the worth to the individuals served, taken as a whole, of such service as they are receiving from a company, such as that which is serving them.   This shows the true test of the value of the service to the person served to be far from what the person in question will pay rather than to go without service.   As this is a matter not often discussed with discrimination a considerable quotation is necessary.   Mr. Justice Savage said: "When the worth of the water to a consumer is estimated, we are not limited to the value of water itself, for it is an absolute necessity.   Its value has no limit. Water, speaking abstractly, is priceless; it is inestimable. To sustain life it must be had at any price.   And in this respect a public water service differs from all other kinds of public service.   In estimating what it is reasonable to charge for a water service—that is, not exceeding its worth to the consumers—water is to be regarded as a product, and the cost at which it can be produced or distributed is an important element of its worth.   It is not the only element, however.   The individuals of a com-

[1] See Tift v. Southern Ry., 138 Fed. 753 (1905).

[2] Brunswick & T. W. Dist. v.

Maine Water Co., 99 Me. 371, 59 Atl. 537 (1904).

munity may with reason prefer to pay rates which yield a return to the money of other people higher than the event shows they could serve themselves for, rather than make the venture themselves and risk their own money to lose in an uncertain enterprise. It was said by us in the Waterville case [1] that the investor is entitled to something for the risk he takes, and it is not unreasonable for the customer to be charged with something on that account. That is one of the things which make up the worth of the water to the customer. The same element enters always into the relations between producer and consumer. But such a consideration as this last one must always be treated with caution. The company is only entitled to fair returns, in any event, and "fair" to the customer as to itself. In the aspect now being considered, the worth of a water service to its customers does not mean what it would cost some one individual or some few individuals to supply themselves, for one may be blessed with a spring, and another may have a good well. It means the worth to the individuals in a community taken as a whole. It is the worth to the customers as individuals, but as individuals making up a community of watertakers."

§ 1214. Cost of obtaining a substitute for the service.

In at least one case the suggestion was made that the cost to the consumer of obtaining the service for himself was the true criterion. In Grand Haven v. Grand Haven Waterworks, [2] the court was obliged to determine the proper amount to be allowed by the city for water furnished by the defendant company. The court held that in the absence of definite evidence of the value of the

[1] Kennebec Water Dist. v. Waterville, 97 Me. 185, 54 Atl. 6, 60 L. R. A. 856 (1902).

[2] 119 Mich. 652, 78 N. W. 890 (1899).

services, the company should be allowed what the city had been saved by the water furnished, which was found to be eight per cent upon the amount necessary to build a plant which would furnish the water. The course of the court in this case is certainly open to criticism. The rule adopted gives to the company all the profit on the transaction, leaving the consumer no better off than if he had supplied the water for himself. Yet there was presumably a considerable profit in the transaction; at least, such would ordinarily be the case. A fair share of this profit ought to be extended to the consumer. In the ordinary case, such a rule would be prohibitive. A farmer, a thousand miles from market, could not afford to pay as freight on his grain what it would cost him to build a railroad or to cart his crops to market; nor could a person who desires to cross a river pay a bridge company by way of toll what it would cost him to get across on his own account. Such a basis of compensation is certainly unreasonable to the customer.[1]

§ 1215. External standards of value.

While not the legal measure of proper charge, the current rates for other transportation within the same territory by the company in question or by other companies performing similar services, is evidence which will furnish a test for the value of the particular services in question. This was one of the strongest arguments brought forward in the "Naval Stores Case," [2] to show that the Savannah rates were themselves unreasonable. This comparison cannot be made as the cases hold without considering dissimilar conditions; and conditions may be so dis-

---

[1] Canada Southern Ry. Co. v. International Bridge Co., L. R. 8 App. Cas. 723 (1883).

[2] Interstate Commerce Commission v. Louisville & N. Ry. Co., 118 Fed. 613 (1902). Compare Southern Pacific Co. v. Interstate Commerce Commission, 177 Fed. 963 (1910).

similar that no comparison would be proper. Thus in a recent Illinois case,[1] involving the reasonableness of switching rates, the court, in holding that it was error to deny the company the right to prove the usual and customary charges during the time in question for like services in other cities and places in the State, said that while charges which are usual and customary are not necessarily fair and reasonable, and a charge which is fair and reasonable in one place is not necessarily fair and reasonable in another, yet proof of what is usual and customary under substantially like conditions in many places in the State tends more or less to prove what is fair and reasonable in any particular place in the State.

§ 1216. Rates reasonable per se.

In arriving at the real value of anything its current price is good evidence. To a certain extent there are external standards as to what constitutes a fair rate in that community for a given service, so that it might often be possible to say of a particular rate demanded by a particular public service company that it was reasonable or unreasonable in itself.[2] Where there are such standards the rate which the company has established to meet its own policies or necessities must yield something.[3] But

---

[1] Chicago, P. & St. L. R. R. Co. v. People, 136 Ill. App. 2 (1909). But proof as to charges in different communities is not admissible. Hooper v. Chicago, M. & St. P. Ry. Co., 91 Iowa, 639, 60 N. W. 487 (1894).

[2] Thus it has often been remarked in the water cases that the particular rate charged is obviously reasonable in itself. City of Madison v. Madison Gas & El. Co., 129 Wis. 249, 108 N. W. 65, 116 Am. St. Rep. 944, 8 L. R. A. (N. S.) 529 (1906).

[3] A telephone company has been held not entitled to charge a telegraph company a greater rate for service than it charged other business houses for similar service, because the telegraph company derived a greater profit from the use of its telephone in its telegraph business. Postal Cable-Telegraph Co. v. Cumberland Telephone & Telegraph Co., 177 Fed. 726 (1910).

does it follow that if the rates of a certain company are no higher than these standard rates that it may justify any profits however large which may result from its business? It would seem that this is a situation where one or the other of the fundamental limitations upon a public service company must be applied, since the public is entitled to protection in either case. Thus no public service company, whatever its necessities, can charge the public more than reasonable rates; while if it is making exorbitant dividends it is not open to it to urge that its rates are not above the ordinary.

§ 1217. The Kansas City stock yards case.

A certain opposition to the views put forward in this treatise is shown in the dicta in the opinion of Justice Brewer when he delivered the judgment of the court in Cotting v. Kansas City Stock Yards Company.[1] This was a bill in equity to enjoin the enforcement of a statutory rate for the use of the defendant's stock yards. The court said of one engaged in such a public service: "He has a right to charge for each separate service that which is reasonable compensation therefor, and the legislature may not deny him such reasonable compensation, and may not interfere simply because out of the multitude of his transactions the amount of his profits is large. Such was the rule of the common law, even in respect to those engaged in a quasi-public service, independent of legislative action. In any action to recover for an excessive charge, prior to all legislative action, who ever knew of an inquiry as to the amount of the total profits of the party making the charge? Was not the inquiry always limited to the particular charge, and whether that charge was an unreasonable exaction for the service rendered?" What there is in this case may be judged only after a

[1] 183 U. S. 79, 46 L. ed. 92, 22 Sup. Ct. 30 (1901).

consideration of the case which follows upon which it is founded.

§ 1218. The Niagara bridge case.

The same rule appears to have been the basis of decision of the judicial committee of the Privy Council in the case of Canada Southern Railway v. International Bridge Company.[1] This was a suit in which the railroad claimed that the bridge company was charging it too high a toll for the transportation of passengers across the bridge, the toll charged being ten cents for each passenger. Lord Selborne said: "It certainly appears to their Lordships that the principle must be, when reasonableness comes in question, not what profit it may be reasonable for a company to make, but what it is reasonable to charge to the person who is charged. That is the only thing he is concerned with. They do not say that the case may not be imagined of the results to a company being so enormously disproportionate to the money laid out upon the undertaking as to make that of itself possibly some evidence that the charge is unreasonable, with reference to the person against whom it is charged. But that is merely imaginary. Here we have got a perfectly reasonable scale of charges in everything which is to be regarded as material to the person against whom the charge is made. One of their Lordships asked counsel at the bar to point out which of these charges were reasonable. It was not found possible to do so. In point of fact, every one of them seems to be, when examined with reference to the service rendered and the benefit to the person receiving that service, perfectly unexceptionable, according to any standard of reasonableness which can be suggested."

§ 1219. These cases apparently distinguishable.

In these cases the court apparently concedes the neces-

[1] 8 App. Cas. 723 (1883).

sary limitation of the rule. If the income of the company from the rates is so great as to give an unreasonably great profit to the company upon all its operations, it will be inferred that the rates, though *prima facie* reasonable, must be too high. Thus in the Niagara Gorge case fifteen per cent was not an unduly high rate of profit for so hazardous an investment but one hundred per cent would doubtless have proved that the individual rate was too high, even though it was reduced neither by competition nor by the limit of desire of the traveler. So in the Kansas City stock yards case, while eighteen and one-half cents seemed in itself reasonably cheap for the care and feeding of an animal, and was so where the net profit was less than five per cent, the finding might have been different if the seemingly reasonable individual rates had in the aggregate brought in a net profit of fifty per cent.

Topic D. Economic Principles Affecting Rate Making

§ 1220. Law of decreasing costs.

Economists in dealing with the problem of rate making in public service have been prone to consider chiefly what policies it should behoove the managers of a business to follow in order to get their due return from it most advantageously. It has been pointed out, for example, in all discussions of the railroad problem by economists that the fixed expenses, which constitute so considerable a proportion of the disbursements by a railroad, are to a very large extent independent of the amount of its traffic carried. It follows that additional business will always be done at a decreasing relative cost. The net income rises as the business expands, and the law of increasing returns is again demonstrated. This may be shown in a simple formula if it be assumed only one-half of the expenditures of a railroad varies with the traffic. "If it costs x to deal with 1,000,000 units of traffic, 5,000,000 units will cost not $5\,x$, but $1\text{-}2\,x+(1\text{-}2\,x\times5)=3\,x$." [1] How far it is possible to justify by this economic law the making of differences in freight rates in consistency with existing legal restrictions is another matter. [2]

§ 1221. Exceptions to law of decreasing cost.

While it is fortunately true in most public business that an increase in custom means a decrease in the average cost, it is by no means universally true. In the telephone service, for example, we have the phenomenon of increasing cost with increasing business. This the United States Supreme Court pointed out in a recent opinion [3] in which the whole situation was examined. To the argument that with the lower rates which had been ordered by the State commission there might be an increased business, the court sagely answered that this would make the plight of the complaining telephone company all the worse. "We say this because the evidence shows that in the case of telephone companies the general result of a reduction of rates in some other kinds of business does not always follow, namely that there would be an increased demand, which could be supplied at a proportionately less

[1] Noyes: A m e r i c a n Railroad Rates, p. 19, citing Acworth: Elements cf Railway Economics, 50.

[2] This law, greater returns usually resulting from an increased business as the result of decreasing cost on the additional transactions, is at the bottom of the present doctrine of the Federal courts that they will not stay the enforcement of the new scale of rates imposed by governmental bodies if they feel that there is high probability that there will be increased business at the lowered rates which will make them profitable. See: In re Arkansas R. R.

Rates, 163 Fed. 141 (1908); Central of Ga. Ry. v. McLendon, 157 Fed. 961 (1907); Seaboard A. L. Ry. Co. v. Railroad Comm., 155 Fed. 793 (1907); Willcox v. Consolidated Gas Co., 212 U. S. 19, 53 L. ed. 382, 29 Sup. Ct. 192 (1909). But see Chicago & N. W. Ry. Co. v. Dey, 35 Fed. 883 (1888); St. Louis & S. F. Ry. Co. v. Hadley, 168 Fed. 317 (1909).

[3] Louisiana R. R. Comm. v. Cumberland Tel. Co., 212 U. S. 414, 53 L. ed. 577, 29 Sup. Ct. 357 (1909).

cost than the original business. Such, it is admitted, would be the case generally in regard to water companies, gas companies, railroad companies, and perhaps some others, where the rate is a reasonable one. For example, it is said that it would cost no more, or certainly scarcely an appreciable amount more, to haul a train of two cars both filled than it would to haul the same train with both cars half filled, and if the reduction in rates should result in filling the cars where previously they had not been half filled, there might be an increased carriage at a cost very little more than before, and probably an increased profit. So, in the case of a water company, the reduced rate might result in furnishing more water to consumers already existing, and the increased cost of furnishing the same would be infinitesimal, where there was a supply sufficiently large to fill the demand. So, also, in furnishing gas at reduced rates, the reduction in the rate would very probably result in increased consumption, not only in increased demands from more consumers, but also an increased consumption by consumers already existing, and the increased cost of furnishing the gas would be nothing like in proportion to the increase in consumption. In these cases increased profits might be the result of decreased rates. But with telephone companies, as shown by the testimony of the president of the complainant, the reduction in toll rates does not bring an increased demand, ecxept upon the condition of corresponding increase in expenses."

§ 1222. Competition as a factor.

Much of the disproportion between individual rates existing is explained by the presence or absence of competition.[1] Indeed this competition is put forward as a

[1] That competition may justify grossly disproportionate rates between localities is well established by the Federal decisions. See

justification for making disproportionate rates, upon the ground that the increased business obtained by cutting rates to meet competition reacts favorably upon the whole business by decreasing costs. And it must be admitted that this law of increasing returns may be considered in making rates. If traffic may be acquired by a specially low rate which would otherwise be lost, to acquire the traffic would benefit rather than burden other traffic of a different kind, since if under the law of increasing returns it is remunerative, the profit thus earned will tend to diminish the rates charged on the remaining traffic. On this ground competition may be considered as a factor in fixing rates. If a carrier is carrying goods from two stations, at one of which there is competition, the rate at the station where the competition exists may fairly be reduced, so far as is absolutely necessary to secure the traffic, provided the reduced rate remains a remunerative one under the law of increasing returns. If the rate were not reduced, *ex hypothesi*, the traffic would be lost, and the profit realized upon it must be exacted from the non-competitive traffic; if on the other hand the rates were reduced equally all over the road, the carrier could not earn a fair return from his whole schedule, since we are assuming that the necessary competitive rate is so low as

Cincinnati, N. O. & T. P. Ry. Co. v. Interstate Comm. Comm., 162 U. S. 184, 40 L. ed. 935, 16 Sup. Ct. 700 (1896); Texas & P. Ry. Co. v. Interstate Comm. Comm., 162 U. S. 197, 40 L. ed. 940, 16 Sup. Ct. 666 (1896); Interstate Comm. Comm. v. Alabama Mid. Ry., 168 U. S. 144, 42 L. ed. 414, 18 Sup. Ct. 45 (1897); Louisville & N. Ry. Co. v. Behlmer, 175 U. S. 648, 44 L. ed. 309, 20 Sup. Ct. 209 (1898); East Tenn., V. & G. Ry. v. Interstate Comm. Comm., 181 U. S. 1, 45 L. ed. 719, 21 Sup. Ct. 516 (1901); Interstate Comm. Comm. v. Clyde S. S. Co., 181 U. S. 29, 45 L. ed. 729, 21 Sup. Ct. 512 (1901). In addition to the above cases, while in various stages below, see: Missouri Pac. Ry. v. Texas & P. Ry. Co., 31 Fed. 862 (1887); Ex parte Koehler, 31 Fed. 315 (1887); Interstate Comm. Comm. v. Atchison, T. & S. F. Ry., 50 Fed. 295 (1892); Interstate Comm. Comm. v. Southern Ry. Co., 105 Fed. 703 (1900).

to be profitable only as a result of the law of increasing
return. The same result will follow if the competition
affects a particular kind of business as electric power, but
not another class as electric illumination. It is urged
strongly to-day that such reductions are fair, even to the
patron who does not get the benefit of the competition, as
a factor in reducing his rate.[1]

§ 1223. Policy for permitting competitive rates.

The policy of this matter seems to be to permit the
making of rates to meet competition, even if proportionately they seem preferential, in order that competition
may be possible, which it could not be without this permission. This is very acutely said by Lord Herschell in
Phipps v. London & North Western Railway Company: [2]
"Suppose that to insist on absolutely equal rates would
practically exclude one of the two railways from the
traffic, it is obvious that those members of the public who
are in the neighborhood where they can have the benefit
of this competition would be prejudiced by any such proceedings. And further, inasmuch as competition undoubtedly tends to diminution of charge, and the charge
of carriage is one which ultimately falls upon the consumer, it is obvious that the public have an interest in the
proceedings under this act of Parliament not being so
used as to destroy a traffic which can never be secured,
but by some such reduction of charge, and the destruction of which would be prejudicial to the public by tending to increase prices." It must be admitted that this
line of argument has to a considerable extent prevailed.
And without going into the many problems as to local
discrimination, the result largely of statutory provisions

---

[1] But see Louisville & N. Ry.   L. Rep. 232, 51 S. W. 164, 1012
Co. v. Commonwealth, 21 Ky.   (1899).
     [2] 2 Q. B. 229 (1892).

and their construction, which are discussed later, it must be conceded that it is a general principle recognized in all of those cases that it is permissible to make the competitive rate low enough to get business and to hold it. But this principle permitting the carrier to make in particular instances low rates to meet competition has its limitations; it will not justify the making of rates which will not be remunerative, as that must result in throwing undue burdens upon others. [1]

§ 1224. Necessary limitation upon these principles.

That the law of increasing returns cannot be permitted to go too far in rate making has been pointed out many times by those who deal with this question from the legal standpoint. While few economists would go to the logical extreme of justifying any whimsical distribution of the total burden upon particular kinds of business any more than they would defend personal discrimination, many would still defend charging against particular classes of business that can bear the burden of the larger proportion of the cost, and still more they would justify the making of lower rates for classes of business which could not stand the higher rates in order to gain the advantages of increased volume of business resulting in decreasing costs. To a lawyer, however, who believes that discrimination in public service is the abhorrent thing such relative discrimination can no more be defended by business motives than personal discrimination can be. All that can be said of the advantages of getting the higher price for all the business you can, and then making concessions to get more business still, can be said in defense of personal discrimination as well as relative discrimination. But it will not do to come to a conclusion here without full examina-

[1] See also the language in Interstate Commerce Commission v. Alabama Midland Ry. Co., 69 Fed. 227 (1895).

tion of the merits of the controversy, for policy may materially modify logical rules. And if there be real policy in permitting charging what the traffic will bear against particular traffic or in permitting reductions to increase business and thereby reduce cost, it will have its influence in making the law.

§ 1225. Equalization of commercial advantage.

A theory of fixing rates which appeals to many economists, which is in fact a modification or special application of the policy for charging what the traffic will bear, is the theory that rates should be so fixed as to equalize the advantage of shippers and thus establish conditions of business for the good of the whole country.[1] It is in substance a sort of legal protection to beneficiaries thought to be meritorious. Thus if wheat cannot be raised in Wyoming as cheaply as in Iowa, the rates from Wyoming to the seaboard should be correspondingly reduced; unless indeed it does not seem to the rate fixers to be for the country's good that wheat should be raised in Wyoming. A practical objection to this doctrine will at once appear. It calls on the private individuals who happen to have power over rates to act in such a way as to subserve the public good, rather than their own advantage; and thus without election as legislators and without the responsibility of office, to perform one of the most difficult of legislative functions. It must be admitted that certain judges in certain opinions have given some countenance to this doctrine, but only to the extent of saying that if a rate making body has acted upon these theories its course will not be held to be irrational. While the equalization of advantage cannot be a chief factor in

[1] See for example:

Georgia.—Southern Ry. Co. v. Atlanta Stove Works, 128 Ga. 207, 57 S. E. 429 (1907).

Minnesota.—State v. Minneapolis & St. L. Ry. Co., 80 Minn. 191, 83 N. W. 60 (1900).

rate fixing, it may legitimately be considered as one of the subordinate factors tending to lower the particular rate, and may be taken into account with the other factors enumerated in this chapter. It is notable, however, that the courts have never required the making of rates to proceed upon this basis; they have at most, and only to a very slight degree, given some justification to companies which have had such policies in mind.[1]

§ 1226. Argument against preferential rates.

It is often urged that a carrier should so arrange its rates as to bring about some desirable commercial result, either by equalizing commercial advantages between two localities or between two commodities. This theory is dangerous. The carrier's rates may seldom be fixed with such an object in view. There should be no attempt to deprive a community of its natural advantage or supply the lack of these advantages to another community. A carrier has no right to concern itself with the advantages of one point on its line as against another, or to adjust its tariff so as to equalize the natural advantages between the two places.[2] Localities should not be deprived, through a carrier's adjustment of relative rates, of advantages supplied from a common market for the finished product nor of the other advantages which the enterprise of its citizens has secured, and upon the strength of which business conditions have grown up. Certainly such consideration cannot prevail in place of a statute prohibiting

[1] *United States.*—Interstate Commerce Commission v. Chicago Gt. Western Ry. Co., 209 U. S. 108, 52 L. ed. 705, 28 Sup. Ct. 493 (1908).

Illinois.—Peoples Gaslight Co. v. Hale, 94 Ill. App. 406 (1900).

[2] See for example: Chicago, R. I. & P. Ry. Co. v. Interstate Commerce Commission, 171 Fed. 680 (1909). This opinion is much modified in favor of allowing the public welfare to be considered by a regulating commission in Interstate Commerce Commission v. Chicago, R. I. & P. Ry. Co., 218 U. S. 88, 54 L. ed. 000, 30 Sup. Ct. 651 (1910).

the charging of more for a short haul than for a long haul which includes it.[1]

§ 1227. Conclusion as to proportionate rate.

As a result of these considerations, the hypothesis may be drawn that a rate should be established for each article of traffic. This rate will be fixed according to the share of the entire burden of charge which ought reasonably to be borne by that particular article. In determining the reasonable share of the burden to be borne by an article, various considerations must be weighed, and the rate when finally established will be determined as a result of all such considerations. It must be clear, therefore, that the establishment of the particular rate is not, like the establishment of the general schedule of charges, a matter which can be settled altogether by a mathematical formula. There are too many economic factors operating in bringing about a particular rate for that to be possible really. The division of rates among the particular commodities involves judgment and experience; it is not an exact division, but only the closest possible approximation to fairness.

§ 1228. Conflicting theories still persist.

Charging what the traffic will bear will always prove the easiest way to get the proper amount of money, if no legal limitations are put upon this distribution of the burden. To leave the distribution of the burden without law, when the total charge is restricted by law, seems almost stultification. For a disproportionate rate to a particular customer may be more oppressive than a system which, although somewhat too large in its total returns, was one

[1] See for example: Behlmer v. Louisville & N. Ry. Co., 83 Fed. 398 (1900), holding that economic equalization cannot justify charging more for short hauls than for long hauls in the face of an explicit statute.

in which he contributed only a proportionate share. Of course, on actual application neither of these theories would to-day be pushed to its logical extreme, the economists would profess to deplore actual extortion in an individual charge; the lawyer would not demand exact distribution of the burden. Legal restriction to some degree is admitted by the economist; economic modification is recognized to some extent by the lawyer. For practical purposes the various theories may be thus reduced to modifications in various degrees of these two persisting theories.

CHAPTER XXXVI

CHARACTERISTICS OF THE RATE

§ 1230. Fixing the particular rate.

§ 1230. Fixing the particular rate.

There are certain details relating to the fixing of a rate which must be considered. Rate making has become enough of a science to have its own technique. The separate rate is the definite charge fixed by the person conducting a public employment as the price regularly demanded for performing the service asked. So many kinds of service are asked by so many people of most public service corporations, that it would be inconvenient to conduct the business without some established schedule of rates. It would indeed usually be a practical impossibility to fix a separate rate for each service by itself. Thus a classified schedule of regular rates is the usual characteristic of a public business. Indeed by modern legislation such rate schedules are made obligatory to make sure that all may know the rate in advance, and to make certain that all shall be charged the same rate. Various methods of charging, it will be seen, may be adopted in framing such schedules, so long as the rate imposed may be known with certainty. And this end is furthered by basing rates upon some unit of service. This is indeed the most salient characteristic of a rate, considered abstractly, that it is an entirety—the single charge for the whole service which is performed.

Topic A. Classification in Rate Schedules

§ 1231. Prevalence of classification.

It is obvious that classification is in many businesses necessary for convenience in rate fixing if for no other reason. And indeed some form of classification has been used from time immemorial. The first formal classification appears to have been made for toll roads, a system which was taken up naturally enough for canal tolls. For as soon as public service became a diversified business of large proportions fairness to the patrons as well as the convenience of the proprietors required a classification as the basis of fixing rates. In modern times classification has become the very foundation of railroad rates, and the question of charge is primarily a question of into which class the goods shipped fall. In other businesses than railroad operation elaborate classification of the services offered prevails,—the various kinds of service which a telephone company offers its subscribers is one example. It may be admitted that as a classification gains in convenience, it loses in accuracy. No classification can be so minute as to conform to the differing varieties and conditions of traffic; and to separate differing grades or varieties of the same service into different classes with varying rates, even if it could be accomplished, would go far to defeat the real purpose of classification.

§ 1232. History of railroad classification.

From the very nature of the case classification goes far back into the law of public service. Carriers and shipmasters were driven to it when their business became of general scope, and canal proprietors and highway owners published rough schedules from the outset. As the situation has developed in recent years the methods of classification of freight in the United States furnish the best illustration of the system. All goods that may by any possibility be offered for shipment are classified in such a way as to bring together into a few large classes such articles as can fairly be subjected to the same charge for carriage. A rate is then fixed for each class; not a difficult matter, since it has been found quite practicable to make the number of classes small. Unfortunately this classification is not uniform throughout the United States, the country being divided into three parts where different classifications prevail—the Official, the Southern and the Western, the boundaries being respectively the Potomac, the Ohio, and the Mississippi. As the existing classification goes far back and it has changed very slowly in details so that business has adjusted itself to the established classification, it requires considerable evidence of injustice to induce the commission to displace the existing classification.

§ 1233. Usual division into classes.

The standard classification, which in each system contains five or six classes, while sufficient for ordinary commodities, does not and in the nature of things cannot cover exceptional cases, and especially cases of especially difficult carriage. In order to cover such exceptional cases, it is the custom to give certain commodities a rating above the first class, such as "double first class rates," or even higher. Furthermore, there is a continual tendency to differentiate commodities, and to seek a means of giving to some article a rate which falls outside, (usually below) these class rates. But sometimes there are intraclass ratings; such as a rate "forty per cent less than third class." This tendency is of course, opposed in its fundamental principle to the whole theory of classification, and if given play enough would soon put an end to the system on which present rates are based; and it is therefore not to be commended as a general expedient. If it seems necessary in any particular case, it is probably because the difference in rates of the two classes concerned is unduly great.

§ 1234. Distribution of the burden by classification.

Not only would it be altogether inexpedient to fix the same rate for all service but it would be highly unjust. This is especially obvious in railroad transportation. Different articles require such different care in carriage that it would be unjust to fix a single rate that should apply to all articles carried.[1] If a uniform rate were fixed for each pound carried, lead would be more expensive to ship than live stock; and if the rate were proportioned to bulk, a diamond would be carried more cheaply than fence posts. It is necessary in order to distribute fairly among the shippers the burden of the entire schedule of rates to graduate the charge according to the nature of the article carried. Classification is recognized as a necessary method of adjusting the burdens of transportation equitably upon the various articles of traffic, in view of differing circumstances and conditions, and but for the necessity of such adjustment, considerations based alone on weight and distance of haul would probably determine rates, except as modified by competition. This method, while securing practical uniformity, would probably deprive many articles which are now important factors in commerce of the benefit of transportation to distant points.[2]

§ 1235. Reasonableness of classification requisite.

As a practical matter, therefore, the reasonableness of a particular rate depends upon the reasonableness of classification. Manifestly in determining respective classi-

[1] Rules for the intervention of classification sheets. See Smith v. Gt. Northern Ry. Co., 15 N. D. 195, 107 N. W. 56 (1906).

[2] Results of making false classification. See Illinois Central R. R. Co. v. Seitz, 214 Ill. 350, 73 N. E. 585 (1905).

fication an attempt should be made to obtain a fair relation between the services rendered, and a classification which fails to do this is unreasonable. When the rate for a particular service is in question the decision primarily involves a comparison with other services as now classified. Classification by its very nature involves the relation of one service to all others, and such comparison is therefore essential in testing any scheme of classification. Classification furnishes the best index of reasonable rate for particular service. If the schedule of rates as a whole is producing too much or too little this as has been seen can be determined with reasonable certainty upon well established principles; but whether the particular rates are proper ones it was conceded could not be determined by mere computation with any such degree of accuracy. If the returns on the whole schedule are too high there should be a general reduction of rates or if too low there should be a general advance; in neither case should a particular class be selected for benefit of reduction or the burden of advance. But granting that the whole returns from the schedule are reasonable, then the question as to the reasonableness of a particular rate is whether it is properly placed in a reasonable classification. A classification to be reasonable must not only put similar services in the same classes, but must make proportionate differences between the rates charged against the respective classes. Thus the law as to particular rating reverts to its original test of proportionate share of the proper burden. But granting that the existing classification constitutes a reasonable system, the question remains as to a particular service whether it is properly placed in that system.

§ 1236. Influences determining proper classification.

It has been said that similarity between services is the determining factor in making classification. Thus freight classification is based upon the relations which commodities bear to each other in such respects as character, use, bulk, weight, value, tonnage, risk, cost of carriage, ease of handling and other controlling conditions. It will be noticed that all these considerations are concerned with the nature of the commodity itself; either its material qualities or its use. They affect either the cost of carriage to the carrier, or the value of carriage to the shipper. It is plain then that classification is a method of rate making based upon all the principles governing the establishment of particular rates which have been discussed in the preceding chapter.

§ 1237. Like classification for similar goods.

The comparison commonly instituted is that between similar things, for the purpose of placing them in the same class. Thus the following articles have upon comparison been ordered by the Interstate Commerce Commission in the same class: envelopes for correspondence and merchandise envelopes,[1] celery with egg plant,[2] eggs with berries,[3] soap with groceries,[4] box shooks with laths,[5] bitters with ink [6] and cowpeas with grain,[7] to select a few examples from the great mass of rulings on these points.

§ 1238. Different classification for dissimilar goods.

On the other hand the impropriety of putting things utterly unlike into the same class has often been pointed

[1] Wolf Brothers v. Allegheny Valley R. R. Co., 7 I. C. C. Rep. 40 (1897).

[2] Tecumseh Celery Co. v. Cincinnati, J. & M. Ry. Co., 4 Int. Com. Rep. 318, 5 I. C. C. Rep. 663.

[3] Brownell v. Columbus & C. M. R. R. Co., 5 I. C. C. (O. S.) 638 (1893).

[4] Pyle v. East Tenn. Va. & Ga. Ry. Co., 1 I. C. C. (1888).

[5] Michigan Box Co. v. Flint & P. M. R. R., 6 I. C. C. Rep. 335 (1897).

[6] Myers v. Pennsylvania Co., 2 Int. Com. Rep. 403, 2 I. C. C. Rep. 573 (1889).

[7] Swaffield v. Atlantic Coast Line, 10 I. C. C. Rep. 281 (1904).

out even in cases before the judicial courts. Thus hay is of a lower class than soap,[1] ice than bricks [2] and steam coal than domestic grades.[3] Upon the whole these examples of similarity and dissimilarity are rather obvious. Raw material is usually of lower class than the finished product, as holland cloth is in comparison with window shades.[4] But when a prepared fertilizer is simply the acid phosphate mixed with cinders no higher rate is justifiable.[5] And in a striking case [6] lately decided it was held that the rate of packing house products could be made less than that on live stock by reason of the difference in cost and risk being in favor of dead freight over live freight.

§ 1239. Business expensive to handle.

Where the service is usually expensive to handle a relatively larger rate is plainly justifiable. Thus passengers who travel in chair cars must expect to pay higher rates for the much more expensive accommodations than those who go in the regular coaches.[7] So when perishable meats are forwarded a special equipment is required resulting in a higher rate. Where, however, no special equipment is necessary, as for lumber which may go by any kind of car without special equipment, the rate must be much lower.[8] And although not perishable a much higher rate could be charged upon valuable ores than upon

[1] Cincinnati, H. & D. R. R. Co. v. Interstate Comm. Comm., 206 U. S. 142, 51 L. ed. 995, 27 Sup. Ct. 648 (1907).

[2] Fitchburg R. R. Co. v. Gage, 12 Gray (Mass.), 393 (1859).

[3] Com. v. Louisville & N. R. R. Co., 24 Ky. L. Rep. 509, 68 S. W. 1103 (1902).

[4] Interstate Comm. Comm. v. Delaware L. & W. R. R. Co., 64 Fed. 723 (1894).

[5] Southern R. R. Co. v. Railroad Commission, 42 Ind. App. 90, 83 N. E. 727 (1907).

[6] Interstate Commerce Commission v. Chicago, Gt. Western Ry. Co., 209 U. S. 108, 52 L. ed. 705, 28 Sup. Ct. 493 (1908).

[7] St. Louis, A. & T. R. R. Co. v. Hardy, 55 Ark. 134, 17 S. W. 711 (1891).

[8] Tift v. Southern R. R. Co., 138 Fed. 753 (1905).

coal by reason of the additional risk of loss in transit. So if an article is bulky, out of usual proportion to its weight, as straw hats, a much higher rate per hundred pounds can be charged than for pig lead. So if goods are packed in convenient packages for handling, as hardware in casks, a lower rate can be made than for uncrated furniture. And to reserve the most important illustration of this principle to the last, a much lower rate can be made for goods shipped in car load lots than for package freight by reason of the obvious economy of carrying through unbroken car loads. These matters would receive further discussion at present were it not that these differences are fully treated under the head of discrimination later on.

§ 1240. Service performed at lower cost.

It is not inconsistent with the principles of rate making here defended that lower rates can be made for a service which is less expensive to handle. Thus an electric company can make lower rates for current supplied for power during the daytime, when its dynamos are not being operated to full capacity, than for illumination at night, as no addition need be made to its plant to take on this business.[1] So a gas company may make a lower rate for fuel gas supplied upon the basis that the service may be cut off when extraordinary conditions make it necessary to devote the supply to illumination. So a telegraph company may make lower rates for the slower transmission of messages over night, the same force not being maintained to handle them. And so a telephone company can make a lower rate for an ordinary installation than for a metallic circuit and long distance equipments in which they must tie up more capital.[2] It will be noted as

[1] Metropolitan Electric Co. v. Ginder, 2 Ch. D. 799 (1901).

[2] Gardner v. Providence Telephone Co., 23 R. I. 312, 50 Atl. 1014, 55 L. R. A. 113 (1901).

to these examples that not only is the rate lower by reason of the lessened cost to the company, but also by reason of the lower value of the service to the customer. And it is well that these two desirable ends can both be met in most cases.

Topic B. Method of Fixing Rates

§ 1241. Basis upon which charges may be made.

It is proper for a public service company in establishing its rates to adopt various methods of charging for measuring the price which the public shall pay for the service. Thus a gas company may charge by the cubic foot, a water company by the gallon, an electric company by the watt, a cabman by the hour, a grain elevator man by the bushel, a telegraph company by the word, a telephone company by the minute, a railroad by the mile. Whatever the method of measuring adopted by the company it will be supported by the court provided that it is a reasonable one. And its reasonableness is to be tested by its propriety; whether this scheme of computing the rate is or is not unnatural in dealing with the subject matter will be the test.

§ 1242. Establishment of the unit of charge.

It is proper for a public service company, moreover, in fixing its rates to determine upon certain units of charge which shall be the minimum of charge for its services. Thus a gas company may fix a monthly minimum charge; and so an electric company may demand a certain amount per month whether that amount of electricity is used or not. A water company may charge by the quarter; and so may a telephone company by the quarter. A telegraph company may charge for ten words even if less are sent; and an innkeeper may charge for a night though the guest remain in his room but an hour. Upon similar principles a railroad may decline to take any package for less than twenty-five cents. The question as to all of these charges is again whether their imposition is reasonable.

§ 1243. Methods of computing freights.

In the case of freight rates it will commonly be not unreasonable to employ different methods in arriving at the proper rate in different cases; and if these differing methods are respectively used in appropriate treatment of varying subject-matter, it is plain that this is not only consistent with public duty, but cases can even be imagined where not to do so would be inconsistent with public duty. But what has been said is of course subject to the limitation that there must be no illegal discrimination of any sort by charging some by one measure and others by another. It is, for example, plainly justifiable for a railroad in making its freight rates to charge for coal by the ton, but for paper boxes by the cubic yard. The space required is rightly taken into account in the adjustment of freight charges, when the bulk is so considerable in comparison with weight as to occupy space which if taken up by heavier freight would yield larger receipts.

§ 1244. Different basis in supply services.

In the supply services there are two methods of charging which might be adopted, neither of which can be said to be improper. Thus those who manage a waterworks may charge by measure, installing meters, or they may charge a flat rate, estimated largely by the number and character of the taps. The water company may, of course, be restrained either by statute or charter to charge for water according to a particular method.[1] In the absence of any such limitation it seems unquestionable that the

[1] *Alabama.*—Birmingham W. W. Co. v. Truss, 135 Ala. 530, 33 So. 657 (1903).

California.—Shaw v. San Diego Water Co., 50 Pac. 693 (1897).

water company may either employ the flat method altogether in dealing with its customers; or it may impose the meter system upon all its customers.[1] It is more usual in the supply services for the company to offer different bases to its patrons; and it is entirely proper. Thus water companies usually offer their customers the choice between a flat rate and a meter rate.[2] Certainly the customer can have no complaint in such a case if he is given his choice between the two methods.[3]

§ 1245. Requiring metering not discrimination.

It might seem that when a company is giving service upon two bases it would be discrimination to impose one system upon particular customers against their desire, while others are given their choice. But it seems to be universally held that in the absence of any special statute or franchise provision forbidding it, a water company may at its pleasure insist upon a particular customer paying for water at the meter rate.[4] This will not always result in any particular consumer paying substantially the

[1] *Maine.*—Robbins v. Bangor Ry. & El. Co., 100 Me. 496, 62 Atl. 136, 1 L. R. A. (N. S.) 963 (1906), uniform meter basis valid.

Michigan.—Goebel v. Grosse Point Waterworks, 126 Mich. 307, 85 N. E. 744 (1901), uniform flat rate valid.

[2] *Massachusetts.*—Shaw Stocking Co. v. Lowell, 199 Mass. 118, 85 N. E. 90, 18 L. R. A. (N. S.) 765 (1909).

Virginia.—Exchange & Building Co. v. Roanoke & Water Co., 90 Va. 83, 17 S. E. 789 (1893).

[3] *California.*—Sheward v. Citizen's Water Co., 90 Cal. 635, 27 Pac. 439 (1891).

New York.—Brass v. Rathbone, 8 App. Div. 78, 40 N. Y. Supp. 666 (1892).

[4] *California.*—Shaw v. San Diego Water Co., 50 Pac. 693 (1907).

Maine.—Robbins v. Bangor R. & Electric Co., 100 Me. 496, 62 Atl. 136, 1 L. R. A. (N. S.) 963 (1906).

Massachusetts. — Shaw Stocking Co. v. Lowell, 199 Mass. 118, 85 N. E. 90, 18 L. R. A. (N. S.) 765 (1909).

Minnesota.—Powell v. Duluth, 91 Minn. 53, 97 N. W. 450 (1903).

Virginia.—Exchange & B. Co. v. Roanoke G. & W. Co., 90 Va. 83, 17 S. E. 789 (1893).

Wisconsin.—State v. Gosnell, 116 Wis. 606, 93 N. W. 542, 61 L. R. A. 33 (1907).

same amount under either system. The prices must be so fixed as to bring in substantially the same return whatever system is adopted; and the flat rate must accordingly be fixed according to the average consumption. Persons who consume less than the average amount will be benefited by the adoption of a meter system; persons who consume more than an average amount will be required to pay more. In either case, the meter rate, as it results in a payment proportioned to the amount supplied, is essentially fair. It may therefore be conceded that the company may always impose the meter basis upon a particular consumer. In one of the leading cases [1] this is positively said: "There is nothing unjust or inequitable to either party, since in each the company receives and the consumer pays for the exact amount of water supplied."

§ 1246. Query as to the flat rate.

When however, it is the flat rate which is imposed upon a particular customer the result may not be reasonable. In Ladd v. Boston [2] for example a householder who was paying the minimum meter rate of fifteen dollars per year was threatened by the city with a change from meter basis to the fixture basis which would cost him about one hundred dollars a year. He filed a bill to enjoin the city from doing so, but in vain. It must be clear in this case that if the plaintiff paid the fixture rate he would be using far less than the average amount of water used by consumers paying that rate. This fact the court said was not material. "Under any general and uniform system other than measuring the water, some will pay more per

[1] In Sheward v. Citizen's Water Co., 90 Cal. 635, 27 Pac. 439 (1891).

[2] 170 Mass. 332, 49 N. E. 627, 40 L. R. A. 171 (1898).

The point is that this treatment of the complainant was the result of a general policy. If it were not true that all consumers in exactly the same class of the complainant were to be similarly treated the case would certainly be wrong. See Powell v. Duluth, 91 Minn. 53, 97 N. W. 456 (1903).

gallon than others." This is doubtless true, so far as the question is whether the fixture rate was a reasonable one; but it may perhaps be doubted whether under the circumstances it was reasonable to force upon the plaintiff a rate which compelled him to pay more than his fair share for the water he used, when the alternative was fair both to him and to the city.[1]

§ 1247. Justification of the minimum charge.

A minimum rate is an excellent illustration of the characteristics of the rate. Such a rate may be supported, although it operates in some cases somewhat differently than it does in others; for this is the normal operation of a regulation. It may therefore be true that some applicants are paying for a little more than others upon a pro rata basis, and the objection of discrimination cannot be taken. Thus the general minimum charge upon any single shipment of freight for one hundred pounds at the rate applying to the article. It is reasonable for carriers to fix a minimum weight and charge for the transportation of less than car load shipments. This is justified by the necessary expense and clerical work attending the carriage of such shipments, large or small, which, aside from the actual manual labor involved, are practically the same irrespective of the weight and bulk of the package. Noth-

---

[1] Where a telephone company charged a flat rate for similar service against other business patrons, it was held that it could not require telegraph companies in order to obtain full telephone service, to share with the telephone company an arbitrary percentage of receipts from business received by the telegraph company from the telephone. Postal Cable Telegraph Co. v. Cumberland Telephone & T. Co., 177 Fed. 726 (1910).

Business service as used in the franchise of a telephone company in fixing the maximum rate for such service means the ordinary service between business men and other citizens within the radius specified, and does not include service rendered to a telegraph company under a joint traffic arrangement. East Tenn. Telephone Co. v. City of Harrodsburg (Ky.), 122 S. W. 126 (1909).

ing can be more scientific in this regard than the graduate scale of the express companies whereby a very much higher charge than its proportion of the hundred pound rate is made against a five pound package, a lesser disproportion against ten pounds, and less still as the weight increases.

§ 1248. Principle applicable in all public service.

Indeed in every service there is a certain constant expense in each individual service which justifies a relatively high minimum charge for any service at all, but becomes relatively inconsiderable as the service rendered increases in amount. This is peculiarly true of such separated services as the domestic services. Every householder that the service company equips itself to supply with water, gas, electricity, or telephonic connection involves not only a very considerable additional capital charge but a very considerable regular expense. It is therefore altogether justifiable for the company to protect itself against this cost by the establishment of a minimum charge. This principle is carried to its logical extreme by some electric lighting companies which base the consumer's rate upon his maximum takings on the theory that the installation required is the proper basis.

§ 1249. Unit must be reasonable.

It may be difficult to determine with exactness by any satisfactory tests what the unit of service should be, but there will be cases occasionally where it is obvious that so large a unit has been fixed by the public service company that it would be outrageous to compel the applicant to pay for so much. The most striking case of this came up by a petition for the mandamus against an irrigation company [1] which had required the applicant to enter into

---

[1] Wheeler v. Northern Colorado Irrigation Co., 10 Colo. 582, 17 Pac. 487 (1887).

See also Rockland Water Co. v. Adams, 84 Me. 472, 24 Atl. 840, 30 Am. St. Rep. 368 (1892).

what was in effect a ten year arrangement, refusing to supply him with water for his land at the proper rate of $2.50 per acre per annum, unless he would sign this contract not only paying $1.50 for each acre, the annual charge, but $10 down for each acre as an advance. In agreeing in the overruling of the demurrer Mr. Justice Helm said in part: "If the carrier may collect a part of its annual transportation charge in advance for the remaining years of its corporate life, it may collect all. Suppose the company just organized; under counsel's view, the consumer may, there being no legislation on the subject, be compelled to pay the cost of delivering water to him for the entire twenty years of its existence, before he can exercise his constitutional right during a single season." [1]

§ 1250. Reasonableness of the period fixed.

It is only in certain kinds of public businesses that the unit of service is so plainly indicated by the nature of the service that any other would be unreasonable. In most public businesses there are no natural units. And the only question therefore will be whether the unit fixed by the company conducting the service will appear to the court to be outrageously long. Perhaps the quarterly period is roughly the limit within which the ordinary supply company should keep itself. Certainly the cases generally would sanction a company supplying a householder with water, gas, electricity, or telephone service in demanding that it should be paid quarterly in advance.[2] But to de-

---

[1] So a water company can require those who wish sprinkler service to engage for the whole season.

Alabama.—Ward v. Birmingham Water Works Co., 152 Ala. 285, 44 So. 570 (1907).

Tennessee.—Wautauga Water Co. v. Wolfe, 99 Tenn. 429, 41 S. W.

1060, 63 Am. St. Rep. 1841 (1897).

[2] Wautauga Water Co. v. Wolfe, 99 Tenn. 429, 41 S. W. 1060, 63 Am. St. Rep. 1841 (1897).

It has been held, indeed, that a telephone company may compel its subscribers to pay for six months

mand pay for a year in advance in such services would doubtless be unreasonable. As the Maine court said in a recent case [1] of this sort: "We do not think that a regulation providing that every taker of water should be liable to pay rent for the whole year, whether he actually uses it for that length of time or not, and to make the payment in advance on the first day of July without a special undertaking therefor, is reasonable. It casts upon the public who have occasion to use water for a short time only, an unjust and unreasonable burden."

§ 1251. Minimum rate distinguished from equipment charge.

Objection has previously been taken to the making of a charge for equipment employed, such as meter rent.[2] It

in advance. Buffalo County Telephone Co. v. Turner, 82 Neb. 841, 118 N. W. 1064, 19 L. R. A. (N. S.) 693 (1909).

[1] Rockland Water Co. v. Adams, 84 Me. 472, 24 Atl. 840, 30 Am. St. Rep. 368 (1892).

However it may not be unjustifiable to demand pay in advance for the year in water supply provided a rebate is given if the water is not used for the whole year. See Turner v. Revere Water Co., 171 Mass. 329, 50 N. E. 634, 68 Am. St. Rep. 432, 40 L. R. A. 657 (1898).

In a recent case it was held that a contract providing that telephone service would be furnished for one year, and that at the expiration of the year the lease should be considered renewed from month to month on the payment of the stipulated sum in advance, was reasonable. Southwestern Telegraph & Tele-

phone Co. v. Luckett (Tex. Civ. App.), 127 S. W. 856 (1910).

[2] Cases forbidding meter rent as such are:

Alabama.—Montgomery Light & P. Co. v. Watts (Ala.), 51 So. 726 (1909).

New York.—Buffalo v. Buffalo Gas Co., 81 App. Div. 505, 80 N. Y. Supp. 1093 (1903).

Kentucky.—Louisville Gas Co. v. Dulaney, 100 Ky. 405, 38 S. W. 703, 36 L. R. A. 125 (1897).

Ohio.—Newark v. Newark Water Works Co., 4 O. N. P. 341 (1897).

Some cases permit meter rent principally upon the ground that it is price of privilege to have service on meter.

California.—Sheward v. Citizen's Water Co., 90 Cal. 635, 27 Pac. 439 (1891).

Minnesota.—Powell v. Duluth, 91 Minn. 53, 97 N. W. 450 (1903).

Others justify the supplying mu-

is believed that a public service company ought to provide all the facilities necessary for rendering the service it undertakes, and upon its total investment therein base its general rates. In accordance with this theory, meter rent as a charge for facilities furnished should never be charged. But many supply companies term the price which they require their customers to pay at all events "meter rent" when upon the whole facts it is really a minimum charge; and many courts in permitting the charging of such meter rent are really on the facts only justifying a minimum charge.[1] It is therefore necessary to make the distinction between what is truly a meter rent and what is really a minimum charge very carefully. A dollar meter charge would be added to each bill regardless of consumption; the dollar minimum charge would not only be made if actual consumption was below that amount, while if it was above, the actual measurement would alone be charged. Therefore while an equipment charge is essentially wrong (and is indeed so regarded by most authorities which have had this distinction called to their attention) a minimum charge is essentially right. The one makes a charge for the provision of facilities as such, which is wrong; the other is designed to compensate for the essential costs of small service, which is right.

nicipality in passing an ordinance compelling the customer to pay for the meter.

Arkansas.—Wilson Water & E. Co. v. Arkadelphia (Ark.), 129 S. W. 1091 (1910).

Kansas.—Cooper v. Goodland, 80 Kan. 121, 102 Pac. 244 (1909).

[1] Cases permitting a minimum charge however denominated are:

Missouri.—State ex rel. v. Sedalia Gas Light Co., 34 Mo. App. 501 (1889).

New York.—Gould v. Edison Electric Co., 29 N. Y. Misc. 241, 60 N. Y. Supp. 559 (1899).

It is generally agreed that the minimum imposed in advance cannot be justified if it is not the same for all customers.

Pennsylvania.—Long v. Springfield Water Co., 8 Del. Co., 151 (1901).

Kentucky.—Owensboro Gas Co. v. Hillebrand, 19 Ky. L. Rep. 983, 42 S. W. 351 (1897).

§ 1252. Initial unit distinguished from repeat unit.

It will be noticed from time to time in the discussion of the proper unit in particular services that at the original installation of service the applicant may be required to commit himself to a longer period than he could be required to oblige himself for later. When an applicant requires the company to supply him with electricity he can be required to sign for a year, but later it may be that a quarter would be the longest period.[1] When a telephone is originally installed the applicant must take for a year, [2] later he may perhaps withdraw on a quarter's notice. The reasonableness of this is obvious enough. Where an expensive installation of a special character must be made the company should at least have the small security of the obligation to pay for a year. And the noticeable operation of this principle will therefore be limited to where such special installation is necessary. Simple illustrations of this will appear in all services. Thus in shipping a package by a railroad the original basis is a hundred pounds, a flat rate beyond that the charge is graduated often as low as by the pound. So in telegraphing the original limit is the ten word message beyond which the unit is the single word.

Topic C. The Journey the Unit

§ 1253. The journey is a single entire unit.

The journey for which a passenger has a right to be received and upon which he enters when he is received, is the whole transit from his point of departure to his destination; the entire journey which he means at that particular time to take. This journey is a single unit of service; for it the carrier is entitled to make a single

[1] Gould v. Edison Electric Co., 60 N. Y. Supp. 559, 29 N. Y. Misc. 241 (1899).

[2] Williams v. Maysville Telephone Co., 26 Ky. L. Rep. 945, 82 S. W. 995 (1904).

charge, and the passenger is entitled only to an unbroken carriage. Neither party has a right to break this single unit of service into two.

§ 1254. Ticket good only for through transportation.

For the reason that the journey is an entirety, the ticket with which a passenger pays his fare is good only for the single journey on which the passenger is then engaged. It is good for any journey which is included within its terms, thus it is good from its starting point to any station short of its destination or from any station between its *termini* and the point of destination.[1] If presented for use and accepted in payment of fare it is at once used, and cannot be used again. So where a ticket from Buffalo to New York expired on the 26th of September, and the bearer took the train for New York on the evening of that day and his ticket was called for and punched, he had paid his fare for the whole journey, although the train did not reach his destination until the next day.[2]

§ 1255. Passenger cannot take two journeys for a single fare.

A passenger cannot for a single fare travel part of the distance for which he has paid his fare upon one train and part on another; for that would be paying for a single journey and really taking two. A stop-over without the payment of an additional fare can be taken only by the express permission of the carrier.[3] This law is sum-

[1] Auerbach v. New York C. & H. R. R. R. Co., 89 N. Y. 281, 42 Am. Rep. 290 (1882).

[2] Auerbach v. New York C. & H. R. R. R. Co., *supra.*

[3] *Massachusetts.*—Cheney v. B. & M. R. R., 11 Met. 121, 45 Am. Dec. 190 note (1846).

New Jersey.—State v. Overton, 24 N. J. Law, 435, 61 Am. Dec. 671 (1854).

Ohio.—Cleveland, Col. & Cinn. R. R. v. Bartram, 11 Ohio St. 457 (1860).

Pennsylvania.—Vankirk v. Pennsylvania R. R., 76 Pa. St. 66, 18 Am. Rep. 404 (1874).

marized thus by Mr. Justice Deady in Roberts v. Koehler: [1] "A ticket for transportation on a railway between certain *termini*, which is silent as to the time when or within which it may be used, does not authorize the holder to stop over at any point between such *termini*, and resume his journey thereon on the next or any following train. The contract involved in the sale and purchase of such a ticket is an entire one, and not divisible. It is a contract to carry the passenger through to the point of his destination as one continuous service, and not by piecemeal, to suit his convenience or pleasure.

§ 1256. Two partial fares for a single journey.

For this reason a passenger has no right to split up a single journey into two by tendering fare from the point of departure to an intermediate station, and then, continuing on the train, tender fare from the intermediate station to his destination, even though he might thus secure a cheaper passage by taking advantage of cheaper rates between two of the stations. This point was fully considered in the case of the London & Northwestern Railway v. Hinchcliffe. [2] On this principle it was held in an Australian case that a rule providing that no passenger should take a ticket at any intermediate station for the purpose of continuing his journey in the same train as that in which he arrived, except from some stopping place where booking clerks are not provided, was reasonable and valid. [3]

§ 1257. Part of journey completed before fare collection.

It not infrequently happens that a passenger has completed part of his journey before the fare is demanded and

---

[1] *United States.*—Roberts v. Koehler, 30 Fed. 94 (1887).

California.—Drew v. Central Pac. R. R. Co., 51 Cal. 425 (1875).

[2] 2 K. B. 32 (1903).

[3] Davies v. Williamson, 21 N. S. W. L. R. 124 (1899).

collected; and a passenger is sometimes found dishonest enough to attempt to ride to his destination upon payment of fare for the remaining distance. That this attempt is illegal has been made plain. The journey in which he is engaged is the whole journey from his place of departure to his destination; and the fare which is due, and which alone is due, is the fare for the whole distance.[1] The same thing is true if for some reason he would have a legal right to leave the train at an intermediate station without paying fare, but instead of doing so chooses to remain on the train and complete his journey. This was the ground of the decision in a case decided by the Supreme Court of Missouri. In that case the plaintiff, bound on a journey from A to B, could not get a seat until he reached X, an intermediate station; and he then refused to pay fare from A to B, but instead of doing so tendered fare from X to B only. He was ejected for nonpayment of fare, and the court held that the ejection was justified, though he might lawfully have left the train at X, the first station, without paying fare, since he could get no seat.[2]

§ 1258. Resumption of journey by ejected passenger.

Although the penalty of ejection which is visited upon a rejected passenger is much discussed later on, there is one phase of it that comes up in this connection. Suppose the passenger has been properly ejected may he be refused further transportation? Certainly by the principles first discussed he cannot take the train again without paying full fare from the original point of departure to his destination, since what he desires is the completion of the original journey.[3] In Pennington v. Philadelphia,

[1] Manning v. Louisville & N. R. R., 95 Ala. 392, 11 So. 8, 36 Am. St. Rep. 225, 16 L. R. A. 55 (1891).

[2] Davis v. Kansas City, S. J. & C. B. R. R., 53 Mo. 317, 14 Am. Rep. 457 (1873).

[3] *Alabama.*—Manning v. Louisville & N. R. R., 95 Ala. 392, 11 So.

Wilmington and Baltimore Railroad Company, Mr. Justice Bryan said in the course of an excellent discussion: "The plaintiff was required to leave the cars at Back River Station, on his journey back to Baltimore from Perryman's. After he had left the cars and while on the platform he offered to pay the conductor his fare from that station to Baltimore, but the conductor refused to give him admission to the cars. The plaintiff had already accomplished a portion of the return journey to Baltimore without paying his fare. He clearly was not entitled to be conveyed from Perryman's to Baltimore without paying fare for the whole distance. If he had been carried from Back River Station to Baltimore, on payment of the fare only from that place, he would have escaped payment of a portion of the fare: and so, in fact, he would have accomplished the return trip at a reduced rate. The company was under no obligation to carry him for less than the full rate for the whole distance and so he was properly excluded from the cars." [1]

§ 1259. Passenger expelled at a regular station.

If the passenger is expelled at a regular station, where passengers have a right to demand reception, he certainly cannot take the train again without paying full fare from the original point of departure to his destination, since what he also desires to do is to continue on his journey. [2]

8, 16 L. R. A. 55, 36 Am. St. Rep. 225 (1891).

Iowa.—Stone v. Chicago & N. W. R. R. Co., 47 Iowa, 82, 29 Am. Rep. 458 (1877).

Maryland.—Pennington v. Phila., W. & B. R. R., 62 Md. 95 (1883).

Massachusetts.—Swan v. Manchester & L. R. R., 132 Mass. 116, 42 Am. Rep. 432 (1882).

[1] *Supra.*

[2] *United States.*—Missouri, K. & T. Ry. Co. v. Smith, 152 Fed. 608 (1902).

Georgia.—Georgia So. & Fla. Ry. Co. v. Asmore, 88 Ga. 529, 15 S. E. 13, 16 L. R. A. 53 (1891).

Iowa.—Hoffbauer v. O. & N. W. Ry. Co., 52 Iowa, 342 (1879).

Maryland.—Garrison v. United Ry. & E. Co., 97 Md. 347, 55 Atl. 371, 99 Am. St. Rep. 452 (1903).

Where, however, the passenger had a ticket for the station at which he was ejected, but wrongfully claimed that his ticket entitled him to be carried further, he was held entitled to take the train and ride on to his destination upon paying the additional fare.[1] Mr. Justice Guffy said: "Lebanon Junction is admitted to be a point where the train stopped, and it did not stop there for the purpose of ejecting the plaintiff, and after he had quietly and submissively yielded to expulsion he was entitled to the same rights and privileges that any other citizen or passenger had, who wanted to go to Louisville, as he manifestly did, for he took the next train for that point."

§ 1260. Change of destination during the journey.

If a passenger takes a train intending to go to an intermediate station, but during his journey changes his mind and determines to go further, he is still proposing to take a single journey, and must pay the difference between the fare he has already paid and the entire fare for the whole journey he decides to take; but upon doing so he would, it seems, have a right to stay in the train and complete his journey. Such a case was supposed in the argument of an Australian case, and it was urged that the passenger might be obliged to wait at the intermediate station for the next train. The court, however, said: "He need do nothing of the kind. All that he would have to do would be to remain in his seat, and tell the guard that he wanted

New Jersey.—State v. Campbell, 32 N. J. L. 309 (1867).

New York.—Pease v. Delaware, L. & W. R. R. Co., 101 N. Y. 367, 5 N. E. 37, 54 Am. St. Rep. 699 (1886).

North Carolina.—Clark v. Wilmington & W. R. R. Co., 91 N. C. 506, 49 Am. Rep. 647 (1884).

Ohio.—Railroad Co. v. Skillman, 39 Ohio St. 444 (1883).

Tennessee.—Louisville & N. R. R. Co. v. Garrett, 8 Lea (Tenn.), 438, 41 Am. Rep. 640 (1881).

[1] Louisville & N. R. R. Co. v. Breckinridge, 99 Ky. 1, 34 S. W. 702 (1896).

See Choctaw, O. & G. R. R. Co.

to go on to Dubbo, and pay the difference in the fare." [1]
Even if he originally bought a ticket to the intermediate
station he would not have a right to buy a ticket for the
remaining portion of his journey; the railroad could insist
that he pay the excess fare. On the other hand, the railroad could doubtless require that he buy a ticket for the
remainder of his journey or else pay the fare for the entire
journey, receiving back his ticket for the first part of it.
In London & Northwestern Railway v. Hinchcliffe [2] it is
so held.

§ 1261. Second journey on same train.

Although a single journey is treated as an entirety, it
does not necessarily follow because a person goes beyond
his first destination on the same train that there may not
really be two separate journeys. [3] If the train waits long
enough at the intermediate station, the passenger may
complete the object of his first journey and undertake
another quite independent journey on the same train. [4]
Thus where the defendant bought a ticket from M to F,
intending to remain at F long enough to transact some
business there and then go on to X; and the train waited
at F forty minutes, which proved to be long enough for
the defendant to transact his business, and he therefore
took the same train for X, he was held not to be guilty of
rebooking at an intermediate station while upon the same
journey.

§ 1262. No separate charge for a part of the transit.

By the general principle governing this matter, the
carrier, it seems, cannot divide up his route so as to make

v. Hill, 110 Tenn. 396, 75 S. W. 963
(1903).

[1] Davies v. Williamson, 21 New
So. Wales L. R. (Law), 124 (1899).

[2] 2 K. B. 32 (1903).

[3] Louisville & N. R. R. Co. v.
Breckinridge, 99 Ky. 1, 34 S. W.
702 (1896).

[4] Flannery v. Hastings, 15 Aus-
tral. L. T. 1 (1893).

a separate charge for crossing a bridge. In the case of Southern Pacific Company v. Patterson,[1] the railroad company had conveyed its right of way across a river to an independent bridge company, which exacted a toll of fifty cents for crossing the river. This was held to be an illegal exaction. The court seems to have thought that no separate charge could properly be made, and this, it is submitted, is the correct view. In the actual case the decision was that, whether or not a separate charge could be made, it could not at any rate exceed the maximum mileage rate imposed by law upon railroad companies.

Topic D. The Shipment the Unit

§ 1263. Maritime freight.

Freight is a single thing, and cannot be broken up into two or more separate claims. The carrier may be entitled to it, or he may not yet have entitled himself to it; but he is entitled to the whole or nothing. It becomes important, therefore, to examine more closely into the nature of freight, and determine just when the right to it accrues. In the maritime law, the freight is a separate maritime interest, distinct from vessel and cargo, and like them dependent upon the safety of the voyage. It comes into being as an existent interest as soon as the voyage begins, that is, at the moment when the vessel "breaks ground;"[2] but it is not earned until the voyage is completed, and it is for that reason at risk until it is earned. It may be insured, libelled, or transferred as a separate interest. Wherever there is an agreement, on the one side to carry and on the other to pay freight, it is a necessarily implied term of the contract that the carrier shall be allowed to

[1] 7 Tex. Civ. App. 451, 27 S. W. 194 (1894).

[2] Curling v. Long, 1 Bos. & P. (Eng.) 634 (1797). See also Burgess v. Gun, 3 Har. & J. (Md.) 225 (1811); Bailey v. Damon, 3 Gray (Mass.), 92 (1854).

fulfil the contract on his side and thus earn the freight; and if the shipper takes away his goods before the voyage begins, and thus prevents the carrier from earning freight, the carrier is entitled to compensation. Under such circumstances the orthodox cases give the carrier his entire freight, but this is not followed in several jurisdictions.[1]

§ 1264. Right to freight on land.

Freight due for land carriage under the common law, though it derives its name from maritime freight, is of a different nature.[2] There is no separate distinct interest, apart from the *chose in action* which the carrier has to recover his charges. It is, therefore, not quite literally accurate to speak of freight coming into being, under the common law, at the particular moment when the carriage begins. Freight which is due because of an express agreement or because of the provisions of the common law is not earned until delivery, by the carrier, as will be seen; but on the other hand the carrier obtains by the agreement or by the law a right to earn it by completing the carriage just as soon as delivery is made to him. After possession is given to the carrier, the owner cannot repossess himself of the goods without becoming liable to make payment. But there is a difference as to the amount due the carrier before the journey has begun and that due after the carrier has actually begun to carry. In the former case damages alone would be due. But in the latter case the carrier is entitled to the whole amount

---

[1] Cases which lay down a right to the entire amount of freight are: Tindall v. Taylor, 4 E. & B. (Eng.) 219 (1854); Bartlett v. Carnley, 6 Duer (N. Y.), 194 (1856); Van Buskirk v. Purinton, 2 Hall (N. Y.), 561 (1829); Collman v. Collins, 2 Hall (N. Y.), 569 (1829).

On the other hand, the following cases point out the possibility of reducing the amount of damages: Burgess v. Gun, 3 Har. & J. (Md.) 225 (1811); Bailey v. Damon, 3 Gray (Mass.), 92 (1854); Clemson v. Davidson, 5 Binn. (Pa.) 392 (1813).

[2] Shipton v. Thornton, 9 A. & E. (Eng.) 314 (1838), *semble*.

of freight. The owner who takes his goods before they have arrived at their destination, but after they have been put in transit, must pay the full amount of the freight. Full performance of the carriage is a condition precedent to liability; and by taking his goods during the journey the owner has waived further performance of the condition and must therefore fully perform on his side.[1]

§ 1265. **Effect of carriage over a portion of the journey.**
Where the carriage is interrupted when partly completed, since there is no delivery at the destination, the freight is not due; and since freight is an entirety there is nothing which can properly be recovered, in the absence of a new agreement. In the case of Luke v. Lyde,[2] to be sure, Lord Mansfield attempted to establish the doctrine that compensation proportioned to the distance the goods were carried, that is, freight *pro rata itineris*, might be recovered where the carrier was not at fault; but the attempt failed, and it is well settled that where the carriage is not completed, even though the carrier is not in fault and the owner receives a benefit, freight *pro rata itineris* cannot be recovered.[3] If, however, the owner voluntarily receives the goods short of destination by mutual consent of himself and the carrier, there is a novation, one term of which is the implied agreement to pay reasonable compensation, which is freight *pro rata itineris*.[4] Where the goods are offered for delivery by the carrier, but by the law of that place no delivery can be made, the carrier's obligation is

---

[1] Violett v. Stettinius, 5 Cr. C. C. (D. C.) 559 (1839); Braithwaite v. Power, 1 N. Dak. 455, 48 N. W. 354 (1891).

[2] 2 Burr. 882 (1759).

[3] Hunter v. Prinsep, 10 East (Eng.), 378 (1808); Vlierboom v. Chapman, 13 M. & W. (Eng.) 230 (1844); Caze v. Baltimore Ins. Co.,

7 Cr. (U. S.) 358, 3 L. ed. 370 (1813); Western Transp. Co. v. Hoyt, 69 N. Y. 230, 25 Am. Rep. 175, B. & W. 287 (1877).

[4] The Propeller Mohawk, 8 Wall. (U. S.) 153, 19 L. ed. 406 (1869); The Teutonia, L. R. 3 Adm. 394 (1871).

fulfilled and he is entitled to freight.[1] So where at the port of destination a vessel was not allowed to land part of her cargo, consisting of petroleum, but other goods were landed, it was held that freight was earned on the petroleum.[2]

§ 1266. No freight without delivery.

As the whole freight is an indivisible unit, it is obvious that without some new arrangement between the parties the carrier will not be entitled to any freight whatever for goods not delivered at the destination. No matter how little the carrier may lack of making the required delivery, only an absolute fulfilment of his obligation can entitle him to any freight whatever.[3] To quote from one case: [4] "The consignor is not bound to pay until the transportation is completed in accordance with the contract, but he may prevent the master's earning his freight. If he takes possession of the goods short of their destination, when the master, not in default, is willing and able to complete the transportation, he must pay full freight. He has prevented or waived the performance of the condition precedent. The law, therefore, regards it as performed."

§ 1267. Effect of partial delivery.

Where delivery is made of part of the goods only, it is sometimes possible to divide the shipment into separate units, and recover freight for as many such units as are delivered. This often happens where a large quantity of

[1] Cargo ex "Argos," L. R. 5 P. C. 134 (1873); Morgan v. Insurance Co., 4 Dallas (U. S.), 455, 1 L. ed. 907 (Pa., 1806).

[2] Cargo ex "Argos," *supra*.

[3] Brittan v. Barnaby, 21 How. (U. S.) 527, 16 L. ed. 177 (1858); McCullough v. Hellweg, 66 Md. 269 (1886); Lane v. Penniman, 4 Mass. 91 (1808); Harris v. Rand, 4 N. H. 259, 17 Am. Dec. 421 (1827); Western Transportation Co. v. Hoyt, 69 N. Y. 230, 25 Am. Rep. 175, B. & W. 287 (1877); Braithwaite v. Power, 1 No. Dak. 445, 48 N. W. 354 (1891).

[4] Braithwaite v. Power, *supra*.

similar things are shipped, or commodities are shipped in bulk, and a portion is lost. Thus where a cargo of fruit was shipped and part of it decayed, freight was recoverable on that portion of the cargo which was delivered *in specie*.[1] In fact, it may in such a case be the duty of the carrier to permit the consignee to treat the shipment as an aggregate of units. For instance, when such a cargo was being unloaded upon the wharf for delivery, and only part of it could be unloaded in a day, it was held that the consignee had a right to take that portion of the cargo so unloaded upon paying freight *pro rata*.[2]

§ 1268. Freight indivisible as a rule.

Where goods are shipped in a single shipment the freight cannot be broken up, and a *pro rata* amount charged for a part delivered. Thus the carrier, offering part, cannot libel it for freight,[3] and where part has been delivered, and the carrier fails to deliver the remainder, he is entitled to no freight.[4] Thus: "unless freight is wholly earned by a strict performance of the voyage, no freight is due or recoverable. The contract of the carrier is indivisible, and he can recover for no portion of the voyage that has been made, until the whole is finished and the goods have reached their destination."

§ 1269. Entire freight when goods arrive damaged.

If the goods arrive *in specie*, but have been damaged without fault of the carrier, entire freight is due.[5] If, however, the goods do not arrive *in specie*, though through

---

[1] The Brig Collenberg, 1 Black (U. S.) 170, 17 L. ed. 89 (1859).

[2] Brittan v. Barnaby, 21 How. (U. S.) 527, 16 L. ed. 177 (1858).

[3] In re Vitrified Pipes, 14 Blatch. 274, Fed. Cas. 10,536 (1877), reversing 5 Ben. 402, Fed. Cas. 14,280 (1871).

[4] Western Transportation Co. v. Hoyt, 69 N. Y. 230, 25 Am. Rep. 175, B. & W. 287 (1877).

[5] Lawrence v. Denbreens, 1 Black. (U. S.) 170, 17 L. ed. 89 (1862); The Cuba, 3 Ware, 260, Fed. Cas. 3,458 (1860); Seaman v. Adler, 37 Fed. 268 (1889).

no fault of the carrier, no freight whatever is earned.[1] If
they arrive damaged by fault of the carrier, so long as
they are still *in specie*, the owner cannot refuse to receive
them. In England he must pay the entire freight, and
recover damages for the injury as a separate matter.[2] In
the United States, however, he may if he chooses deduct
from the freight the damage to the goods.[3] As, however,
no excess of damage can be recovered in that way and if
recoupment is made no action will lie for the' excess of
the damage, this course is not wise unless the amount of
damage is less than the freight.

§ 1270. General principles as to additional charges.

The entire service of the carrier in connection with a
single shipment being conceived of as a unit, it should
follow that only one charge may be made, covering the
entire unit of service. Ordinarily this is true. The railroad company cannot make a variety of different charges
for the facilities it uses and the servants it employs; for
instance, it would be absurd for it to make a block signal
charge or an engineer charge. It would seem to be the
duty of the railroad to equip itself fully for the service it
undertakes, and then to make a single rate to the shipper
who wishes the transportation of certain goods to a certain
place.[4] This ought to hold true of all usual services which

[1] Ridyard v. Phillips, 4 Blatch.
443, Fed. Cas. 11,820 (1860).

[2] Meyer v. Dresser, 10 C. B. N. S.
646 (1864).

[3] *Connecticut.*—Relyea v. New Haven R. M. Co., 42 Conn. 579 (1873).

Illinois.—Edwards v. Todd, 2
Ill. 462 (1837).

Kentucky.—Boggs v. Martin, 13
B. Mon. (Ky.) 239 (1852).

Michigan.—Ward v. Fellers, 3

Mich. 281 (1854); Elwell v. Skiddy,
77 N. Y. 282 (1879).

Pennsylvania.—Leech v. Baldwin, 5 Watts (Pa.), 446 (1836).

[4] In Interstate Commerce Comm.
v. Stickney, 215 U. S. 98, 54 L. ed.
000, 30 Sup. Ct. 66 (1909), it was
held a carrier may charge and receive compensation for service that
it may render, or procure to be
rendered, off its own line, or outside of the mere transportation.

the carrier must render the shipper in the line of its duty, but as to services outside its obligation to the shipper it may render a separate bill if it pleases.   More than this, there are, it must be admitted, certain extraordinary services in special kinds of shipments which are not required by shippers generally, and for which, it seems, it is more convenient, if indeed not more just, to make a separate charge.[1]

[1] It was held in the 319½ Tons of Coal, 14 Blatch. 453 (1878), that a railroad could not justify charging a shipper for shoveling at a coal tipple more than the current rate for such service.

PART X. PREVENTION OF DISCRIMINATION

CHAPTER XXXVII

PROHIBITION OF DISCRIMINATION

§ 1280. The rule against discrimination.

Topic A. Development of the Rule

§ 1281. Evolution of the rule.
1282. No law originally against discrimination as such.
1283. Later rule against unreasonable differences.
1284. Special rates may not be discriminatory.
1285. Exclusiveness once held indispensable.
1286. Discrimination as evidence of unreasonable rates.
1287. Complainant charged more than regular rates.
1288. Others charged less than regular rates.
1289. Outright discrimination universally condemned.
1290. Modern law against all discrimination.
1291. Necessity for the rule against discrimination.
1292. Discrimination inconsistent with public duty.

Topic B. What Constitutes Illegal Discrimination

§ 1293. What amounts to a rebate.
1294. Sanctity of the schedule rate.
1295. Explanation of this policy.
1296. Decisions inconsistent with this policy.
1297. Continuing contracts no justification.
1298. Whether contracts are different.
1299. Rule not limited to discrimination between competitors.
1300. Rule universal in public service.
1301. Giving free passes discrimination.
1302. Statutory exceptions usually made.
1303. Reductions for charitable purposes.
1304. Concessions for government business.
1305. Reductions for general classes.
1306. No obligation to grant such concession.

[1122]

§ 1280. The rule against discrimination.

The term unjust discrimination has been in the public service law from the beginning, but it has never meant as much as it does to-day. When an innkeeper took in one traveler and turned the next away this would be called discrimination, when in reality the wrong to the second man is refusal to serve him, not discrimination against him. What would be discrimination in the modern sense would be if a carrier should, while accepting goods from two shippers willingly enough, charge one more than the other for the same transportation. So if a railroad in time of stress should give cars to earlier shippers and have none left for later applicants, this would sometimes be called discrimination; but in this case the default of the carrier is his failure to provide sufficient facilities for all. But although it is not discrimination for a carrier of passengers to assign separate cars to negro passengers it would be discrimination if these cars were not as well appointed as those assigned to white passengers.

Topic A. Development of the Rule

§ 1281. Evolution of the rule.

The fundamental limitation upon the charges of a common carrier, that they shall be in no respect unreasonable, has just been discussed with much detail. But a further requirement of the public service law governing the rates of the common carrier remains to be considered, and that is the more modern requisite that rates shall be in no respect unjustly discriminatory. It must be plain to all who have followed the course of events with the least attention that there has been distinct evolution in the law governing public employment during the last twenty-five years.[1] The rule against discrimination is the most recent

---

[1] Thus to protect himself against discrimination it was once necessary for a patron of a public service company to get the company to

development in the definition of public duty. A comparatively few years ago it was held that if a public service company served all at reasonable rates it performed its obligation,[1] but modern industrial conditions require the further law that it shall serve all with equality. The study of the general course of this development is well worth the space which will be devoted to it in this chapter. One cannot know exactly what the present law is upon this or any other subject without knowing its history.

§ 1282. No law originally against discrimination as such.

The state of the law as to this matter at the middle of the nineteenth century is well set forth in the important case of Fitchburg Railroad v. Gage.[2] The principal issue in this case was whether the railroad could charge one shipper a fifty cent rate on ice from one point on their route to another while it was charging another shipper a twenty cent rate on brick for the same transportation. It will be seen that this case really involves no question of personal discrimination since these are obviously very different goods which are being shipped over the route. Still the language of the court is often cited as expressing the opinion that there is no rule against discrimination as such; and this undoubtedly was its view, as it was of other courts at that time. Mr. Justice Merrick thus concluded his discussion of the general rights and duties of common carriers according to the common law as he conceived it to be: "The principle derived from that source is very plain and simple. It requires equal justice to all. But the equality which is to be observed in relation to the public and to

contract with him that it would not discriminate against him. See Pennsylvania Coal Co. v. Delaware & H. Canal Co., 31 N. Y. 91 (1865).

[1] Where there is a statute against discrimination it is sometimes thought by courts to-day that un-

less the case in hand comes within the statute there is no law against the discrimination. Bibber-White Co. v. White River Valley Electric Co., 175 Fed. 470 (1910).

[2] 12 Gray (Mass.), 393 (1859).

every individual consists in the restricted right to charge, in each particular case of service, a reasonable compensation, and no more. If the carrier confines himself to this, no wrong can be done, and no cause afforded for complaint If, for special reasons, in isolated cases, the carrier sees fit to stipulate for the carriage of goods or merchandise of any class for individuals for a certain time or in certain quantities for less compensation than what is the usual, necessary, and reasonable rate, he may undoubtedly do so without thereby entitling all other persons and parties to the same advantage and relief." [1]

[1] The principal cases which have held that there is no rule against all discrimination as such are collected in this note for the convenience of the reader:

United States.—Parsons v. Chicago & N. W. Ry. Co., 167 U. S. 447, 42 L. ed. 231, 17 Sup. Ct. 887 (1897), *semble;* De Bary Baya M. L. v. Jacksonville, T. & K. W. Ry. Co., 40 Fed. 392 (1889).

California.—Cowden v. Pacific C. S. S. Co., 94 Cal. 470, 29 Pac. 873, 28 Am. St. Rep. 142, 18 L. R. A. 221 (1892).

Colorado.—Bayles v. Kansas Pac. R. R. Co., 13 Colo. 181, 22 Pac. 341, 5 L. R. A. 480 (1889).

Florida.—Johnson v. Pensacola & P. R. R. Co., 16 Fla. 623, 26 Am. Rep. 731 (1878).

Illinois.—Chicago, B. & Q. R. R. Co. v. Parks, 18 Ill. 460, 68 Am. Dec. 562 (1857).

Iowa.—Cook v. Chicago, R. I. & Pac. Ry. Co., 81 Iowa, 551, 46 N. W. 1080, 25 Am. St. Rep. 512, 9 L. R. A. 764 (1890), *semble.*

Massachusetts.—Fitchburg R. R. Co. v. Gage, 12 Gray, 393 (1859).

Missouri.—Christie v. Missouri P. R. R. Co., 94 Mo. 453, 7 S. W. 567 (1888), *semble.*

New Hampshire.—Concord & P. R. R. v. Forsaith, 59 N. H. 122, 47 Am. Rep. 181 (1879), *semble.*

New York.—Killmer v. New York C. R. R. Co., 100 N. Y. 395, 3 N. E. 293, 53 Am. Rep. 194 (1885); Root v. Long I. R. R. Co., 114 N. Y. 300, 21 N. E. 403, 11 Am. St. Rep. 643, 4 L. R. A. 331 (1889); Lough v. Outerbridge, 143 N. Y. 271, 38 N. E. 292, 42 Am. St. Rep. 712, 25 L. R. A. 674 (1894); Parks v. Jacob Dold Packing Co., 6 N. Y. Misc. 570, 27 N. Y. Supp. 289 (1894).

Pennsylvania.—Audenried v. Philadelphia & R. R. R., 68 Pa. St. 370, 8 Am. Rep. 195 (1871), *semble.*

South Carolina.—Ex parte Benson & Co., 18 S. C. 38, 44 Am. Rep. 564 (1882); Avinger v. So. Car. R. R., 29 S. C. 265, 7 S. E. 493, 13 Am. St. Rep. 716 (1888).

Tennessee.—Ragan & B. v. Aiken, 9 Lea, 609 (1882).

Texas.—Houston & T. C. Ry. Co. v. Rust & D., 58 Tex. 98 (1882).

§ 1283. Later rule against unreasonable differences.

For a considerable time thereafter this remained the prevailing statement of the extent of the limitations which the law placed upon the charges of the carrier. Indeed as new cases arose the courts committed themselves to still more definite statements. Thus in the case of Johnson v. Pensacola and Perdido Railroad Company [1] the court refused to grant reparation to a complainant who showed that, while it was charging him one rate for transportation of lumber, it was charging another shipper one-third less for the same transportation under circumstances and conditions in all respects that were essential entirely similar. Mr. Justice Westcott in delivering the opinion of the court held this declaration demurrable by the weight of authority. "Our conclusions," he said, "are that, as against a common or public carrier, every person has the same right; that in all cases, where his common duty controls, he cannot refuse A and accommodate B; that all, the entire public, have the right to the same *carriage at a reasonable price, and at a reasonable charge for the service performed;* that the commonness of the duty to *carry for all* does not involve a commonness or equality of compensation or charge; that all the shipper can ask of a common carrier is, *that for the service performed he shall charge no more than a reasonable sum to him;* that whether the carrier charges another more or less than the price charged a particular individual, may be a matter of evidence in determining whether a charge is too much or too little for the service performed, and that the difference between the charges cannot be the measure of damages in any case, unless it is established by proof that the

---

Vermont.—State v. Central Vt. Ry. Co., 81 Vt. 463, 71 Atl. 194, 130 Am. St. Rep. 1065 (1908).

England.—Nicholson v. Gt. West-

ern R. R. Co., 5 C. B. (N. S.) 366 (1858).

[1] 16 Fla. 623, 26 Am. Rep. 731 (1878).

smaller charge is the true reasonable charge in view of the transportation furnished, and that the higher charge is excessive to that degree." [1]

§ 1284. Special rates may not be discriminatory.

In the case of Cleveland, Columbus, Cincinnati & Indianapolis Railroad Company v. Closser,[2] where suit was brought for a rebate promised by the railroad upon especial arrangement for a through shipment of grain, no other facts appearing, it was held that where a carrier agrees that he will carry goods at a certain rate and that after the shipment he will repay the shipper a rebate of part of such rate, this is only an agreement to carry the goods at a compensation ultimately agreed upon, and is not illegal in itself. The general attitude of the court may be seen from the following extract from the opinion of Mr. Justice Eliott, in which he states the extent of the law against discrimination as the Indiana court sees it. "It is by no means every favor shown a particular shipper, although it may constitute in some measure a discrimination favorable to him and unfavorable to other shippers that impresses upon a contract for the carriage of goods the seal of condemnation. The common-law authorities fully support the position here taken that reference always must be had to such circumstances as quantity, distance and kindred considerations. The hinge of the ques-

---

[1] To the same effect see:

Georgia.—Central of Ga. Ry. v. Augusta Brokerage Co., 122 Ga. 646, 50 S. E. 473 (1905).

Iowa.—Cook v. Chicago, R. I. & P. Ry. Co., 81 Iowa, 551, 46 N. W. 1080, 25 Am. St. Rep. 512, 9 L. R. A. 764 (1890).

Massachusetts.—Spofford v. Boston & M. R. R. Co., 128 Mass. 326 (1880).

South Carolina.—Ex parte Benson, 18 S. C. 38, 44 Am. St. Rep. 564 (1882).

Tennessee.—Ragan & B. v. Aiken, 9 Lea, 609 (1882).

Vermont.—State v. Central Vt. Ry. Co., 81 Vt. 463, 71 Atl. 194, 130 Am. St. Rep. 1065 (1908).

[2] 126 Ind. 348, 26 N. E. 159, 22 Am. St. Rep. 593, 9 L. R. A. 754 (1890).

tion is not found in the single fact of discrimination, for discrimination without partiality is inoffensive and partially exists only in cases where advantages are equal and one party is unduly favored at the expense of another who stands upon an equal footing." [1]

§ 1285. Exclusiveness once held indispensible.

In a similarly inconclusive case, Christie v. Missouri Pacific Railroad Company,[2] where a petition alleged that a contract was made with the agent of a railroad company regarding the shipment of grain at a reduced price, stating its terms, it was held that nothing appeared to show that the arrangement was against public policy, Chief Justice Norton saying: "A common carrier has the right to contract to ship freight at a lower rate than the published tariff rate, if he choose to do so; and such a contract is not against public policy unless the privilege to ship at such rate is granted exclusively to the shipper with whom it is made, or is denied to other shippers. It is the exclusiveness of the privilege granted to one and denied to another which makes the discrimination, and renders the contract void as against public policy. No such exclusiveness or discrimination appears in the contract sued upon, and the objection of defendant to the reception of any evidence was properly overruled." [3]

§ 1286. Discrimination as evidence of unreasonable rates.

How cautious many courts were in working the new rule out may be seen by an extract from the opinion of Judge Bruce in Samuels v. Louisville and Nashville Rail-

---

[1] The same doctrine appears prominently in Lough v. Outerbridge, 143 N. Y. 271, 38 N. E. 292, 42 Am. St. Rep. 712, 25 L. R. A. 674 (1894).

[2] 94 Mo. 453, 7 S. W. 567 (1888).

[3] The case of Toledo, W. & W. R. Co. v. Elliott, 76 Ill. 67 (1875), was relied upon by the court.

road Company,[1] where the court sustained on demurrer a complaint which stated discrimination, but did not allege unreasonable charge: "But the question in this case is to be determined upon the common law, and in the light of those principles as applied to railroad companies. In a case like the one at bar, can there be a reasonable charge which is not at the same time a substantially equal charge? And is not a charge unreasonable when it is unequal, and in breach of the obligation and duty of the common carrier to the public?"[2]

§ 1287. Complainant charged more than regular rates.

Thus in outrageous cases relief would be given in all jurisdictions by some one of these principles. In one of the most extreme cases in the books, Menacho v. Ward,[3] it was set forth by the shippers in their application for relief that the carrier in question had arbitrarily refused them equal terms, facilities and accommodations to those

[1] 31 Fed. 57 (1887).

[2] Discrimination was held evidence of unreasonable rates in the following cases, among others:

United States.—Union Pac. Ry. Co. v. Goodridge, 149 U. S. 680, 37 L. ed. 896, 13 Sup. Ct. 970 (1893); Parsons v. Chicago & N. W. Ry., 167 U. S. 447, 42 L. ed. 231, 17 Sup. Ct. 887 (1897); Hays v. Pennsylvania Co., 12 Fed. 309 (1882); Menacho v. Ward, 27 Fed. 529 (1886); Missouri Pac. R. R. Co. v. Texas & Pac. R. R. Co., 30 Fed. 2 (1887); Burlington C. R. & N. Ry. Co. v. N. W. Fuel Co., 31 Fed. 652 (1887); Bibber-White Co. v. White River V. El. Co., 175 Fed. 170 (1910).

Alabama.—Mobile & O. R. R. Co. v. Dismukes, 94 Ala. 135, 17 L. R. A. 113 (1891).

Colorado.—Bayles v. Kansas Pac. R. R. Co., 13 Colo. 181, 22 Pac. 341, 5 L. R. A. 480 (1889).

Illinois.—St. Louis, A. & T. H. R. R. Co. v. Hill, 14 Ill. App. 579 (1884).

Indiana.—Louisville, E. & St. L. C. R. Co. v. Wilson, 132 Ind. 517, 32 N. E. 311 (1892).

Iowa.—Cook v. Chicago, R. I. & P. Ry. Co., 81 Iowa, 551, 46 N. W. 1080, 25 Am. St. Rep. 512, 9 L. R. A. 764 (1890).

Missouri.—Christie v. Missouri, P. R. R. Co., 94 Mo. 453, 7 S. W. 567 (1888).

New Hampshire.—McDuffee v. Portland & R. R. R. Co., 52 N. H. 430, 13 Am. Rep. 72 (1873).

[3] 27 Fed. 529 (1886).

granted and allowed to other shippers, and had arbitrarily exacted from them a much greater rate of freight than he was at the same time charging to shippers of merchandise generally. It appeared that these shippers had thus been "blacklisted" because they maintained business relations with a rival carrier. But the court found this no excuse for charging the complainants more than the regular rates, Judge Baxter, although still believing as the majority of people then believed that the law did not require any greater equality than that no shipper should be charged an unreasonable rate, nevertheless finding upon the evidence that the complainants had been treated outrageously. "The fact that the carrier charges some less than others for the same service is merely evidence for the latter, tending to show that he charges them too much; but when it appears that the charges are greater than those ordinarily and uniformly made to others for similar services, the fact is not only competent evidence against the carrier, but cogent evidence, and shifts upon him the burden of justifying the exceptional charge." [1]

---

[1] This distinctive rule against unjustifiable discrimination was recognized in:

United States.—De Bary Baya M. L. v. Jacksonville, T. & K. W. Ry. Co., 40 Fed. 392 (1889); Samuels v. Louisville & N. R. R. Co., 31 Fed. 57 (1887); Postal Cable Telegraph Co. v. Cumberland Telephone & Telegraph Co., 177 Fed. 726 (1910).

Florida.—Johnson v. Pensacola & P. R. R., 16 Fla. 623, 26 Am. St. Rep. 731 (1878).

Illinois.—Chicago, B. & Q. R. R. v. Parks, 18 Ill. 460, 68 Am. Dec. 562 (1857).

Massachusetts.—Fitchburg Railroad Co. v. Gage, 12 Gray, 393 (1859).

Missouri.—Rothschild v. Wabash, St. L. & P. R. R., 92 Mo. 91, 4 S. W. 418 (1887); McNees v. Missouri Pacific R. R. Co., 22 Mo. App. 224 (1886).

New York.—Killmer v. New York Cent. & H. R. R. R. Co., 100 N. Y. 395, 3 N. E. 293, 53 Am. Rep. 194 (1885).

North Carolina.—Griffin v. Goldsboro Water Co., 122 N. C. 206, 30 S. E. 319, 41 L. R. A. 240 (1898).

England.—Steamship Co. v. McGregor, 21 Q. B. Div. 544, affirmed

§ 1288. Others charged less than regular rates.

It is not surprising that the distinction just discussed has fallen into disrepute. Whether the complainant is charged more than the regular rates which others are called upon to pay, or whether he is compelled to pay the regular rates while others are given reductions there is the same inequality in treatment and the same disadvantage in business. That this distinction is ignored in modern times is shown in several recent years in many cases but in none is it better set forth than in a water rates case where the complaint made by certain takers was that certain others were getting much lower rates. The company explained that these others had threatened to start a rival water company and that these concessions had been necessary to ward off this project; but the North Carolina court held this no justification.[1] Mr. Justice Clark wrote a striking opinion well worth full quotation to show the modern way of looking at the wrong of discrimination: "The acceptance by a water company of its franchise carries with it the duty of supplying all persons along the lines of its mains, without discrimination, with the commodity which it was organized to furnish. All persons are entitled to have the same service on equal terms and at uniform rates. If this were not so, and if corporations existing by the grant of public franchises and supplying the great conveniences and necessities of modern city life, as water, gas, electric light, street cars, and the like could charge any rates however unreasonable, and could at will favor certain individuals with low rates

23 Q. B. Div. 598 (1892), 17 App. Cas. 25; Evershed v. Railway Co., 3 Q. B. Div. 135, affirmed L. R. 3 App. Cas. 1029 (1878).

[1] Griffin v. Goldsboro Water Co., 122 N. C. 206, 30 S. E. 319, 41 L. R. A. 240 (1898).

Accord is Harris v. Cockemoutn Ry. Co., 3 C. B. (N. S.) 693 (lower rate to one threatening new railway not justified).

See further State v. Birmingham Water Works Co. (Ala.), 51 So. 354 (1910).

and charge others exorbitantly high or refuse service altogether, the business interests and the domestic comfort of every man would be at their mercy. They could kill the business of one and make alive that of another and instead of being a public agency created to promote the public comfort and welfare these corporations would be the masters of the cities they were established to serve. A few wealthy men might combine and, by threatening to establish competition, procure very low rates which the company might recoup by raising the price to others not financially able to resist— the very class which most needs the protection of the law —and that very condition is averred in this complaint. The law will not and cannot tolerate discrimination in the charges of these quasi-public corporations. There must be equality of rights to all and special privileges to none, and if this is violated, or unreasonable rates are charged, the humblest citizen has the right to invoke the protection of the laws equally with any other." [1]

§ 1289. Outright discrimination universally condemned.

Even in the earlier cases some qualifications were made; the power to discriminate as much as it pleased between shippers was not left to the railroads. For even then it was vaguely felt that equal service to all dealers upon fair terms was necessary for the maintenance of free industrial conditions. And the courts never went so far that they could not be continually more insistent that they had meant that reasonable rates to all must be equal rates to all unless the conditions were shown to be dissimilar. This is the position still taken in many jurisdictions; and

[1] According to two recent cases a gas company cannot legally give lower rates to its own stockholders.

Indiana.—Redkey C. Nat. Gas L., F. & P. Co. v. Orr (Ind. App.), 60 N. E. 716 (1901).

Pennsylvania.—Crescent Steel Co. v. Equitable Gas Co., 23 Pitts. L. J. (N. S.) 316 (1892).

it will be seen that to a large extent it prevents discriminatory rates as well as unreasonable charges. An elaborate case of the sort just described from a comparatively recent period is Cook v. Chicago, Rock Island and Pacific Railway Company.[1] In that case it appeared that the plaintiffs, who were shippers of cattle, were charged by the defendant from three to ten dollars per car load of cattle shipped more than the charges made to certain favored shippers who were given a secret rebate. The court held that the railroad must make reparation for this wrong by refunding these overpayments thus extorted. The opinion of Chief Justice Rothrock is too elaborate for full summarizing here. He comes to agreeing with the advanced view which had but recently been put forward by Hutchinson: where in section 243 after review of the various cases it was said: "Hence we may conclude that in this country, independently of statutory provisions, all common carriers will be held to the strictest impartiality in the conduct of their business, and that all privileges or preferences given to one customer, which are not extended to all, are in violation of public duty. An examination of the authorities cited by these learned authors leaves no doubt that a common carrier has no right to make unreasonable charges for his services, and that he cannot lawfully make unjust discrimination between his customers."[2]

[1] 81 Iowa, 551, 46 N. W. 1080, 25 Am. St. Rep. 512, 9 L. R. A. 764 (1890).

[2] The same way of looking at the problem may be seen in the following cases among others:

United States.—Hays v. Pennsylvania Co., 12 Fed. 309 (1882).

Georgia.—Savannah, F. & W. Ry. Co. v. Bundick, 94 Ga. 775, 21 S. E. 994 (1894).

Illinois.—Indianapolis, D. & S. R. R. Co. v. Ervin, 118 Ill. 250 (1886).

Maine.—New England Exp. Co. v. Maine Cent. R. R. Co., 57 Me. 188, 2 Am. Rep. 31 (1869).

New York.—Lough v. Outerbridge, 143 N. Y. 271, 38 N. E. 292, 42 Am. St. Rep. 712, 25 L. R. A. 674 (1894).

New Hampshire.—McDuffee v.

§ 1290. Modern law against all discrimination.

By the better view, it is submitted, the common law to-day forbids all discrimination between two applicants who ask the same service. This is the modern view reached after some bitter experiences with the results of discriminations by the railroads in disturbing the normal industrial order, in suppressing competition and fostering monopoly. But over thirty years ago this doctrine that there is a necessary common law rule against discrimination involved in the law defining the public duty of the common carrier was stated in a way which has never been improved upon. In the leading case of Messenger v. Pennsylvania Railroad Company,[1] Mr. Justice Beasley said in part: "Recognizing this as the settled doctrine, I am not able to see how it can be admissible for a common carrier to demand a different hire from various persons for an identical kind of service, under identical conditions. Such partiality is legitimate in private business, but how can it square with the obligations of a public employment? A person having a public duty to discharge, is undoubtedly bound to exercise such office for the equal benefit of all, and therefore to permit the common carrier to charge various prices, according to the person with whom he deals, for the same services, is to forget that he owes a duty to the community. If he exacts different rates for the carriage of goods of the same kind between the same points, he violates, as plainly, though it may be not in the same degree, the principle of public policy which, in his own despite, converts his business into a public employment. The law that forbids him to make any discrimination in favor of the goods of A over the goods of B, when

Portland & R. R. R. Co., 52 N. H. 430, 13 Am. Rep. 72 (1873).

Texas.—Dittmar v. New Braunfels, 20 Tex. Civ. App. 293 (1899).

[1] 7 Vroom (36 N. J. Law), 407, 13 Am. Rep. 457, 8 Vroom (37 N. J. L.), 531, 18 Am. Rep. 754 (1874).

the goods of both are tendered for carriage, must, it seems to me, necessarily forbid any discrimination with respect to the rate of pay for the carriage." [1]

§ 1291. Necessity for the rule against discrimination.

In last analysis therefore, it is public opinion which has dictated this rule, although it is not too much to claim that this rule is a logical development in the law of public

[1] The following cases among others hold discrimination to be illegal in itself if the conditions under which the service is rendered are similar:

United States.—American Express Co. v. United States, 212 U. S. 522, 53 L. ed. 635, 29 Sup. Ct. 315 (1908); Western U. T. Co. v. Call Pub. Co., 181 U. S. 92, 45 L. ed. 765, 21 Sup. Ct. 561 (1901); Hays v. Pennsylvania R. R. Co., 12 Fed. 309, B. & W. 368 (1882); Postal Cable Telegraph Co. v. Cumberland Telephone & Telegraph Co., 177 Fed. 726 (1910).

Alabama.—Mobile v. Bienville Water Supply Co., 130 Ala. 379, 30 So. 445 (1901).

Georgia.—Savannah, F. & W. Ry. Co. v. Burdick, 94 Ga. 775, 21 S. E. 994 (1894).

Illinois.—Snell v. Clinton Electric Light Co., 196 Ill. 626, 63 N. E. 1082, 89 Am. St. Rep. 341, 58 L. R. A. 284 (1902).

Indiana.—Indiana Nat. & I. Gas Co. v. State ex rel., 158 Ind. 516, 63 N. E. 220 (1902).

Kansas.—Missouri, K. & T. Ry. Co. v. New Era Milling Co. (Kan.), 100 Pac. 273 (1909).

Kentucky.—Owensboro Gaslight Co. v. Hildebrand, 19 Ky. L. Rep. 983, 42 S. W. 351 (1897).

New Jersey.—Steward v. Lehigh V. R. R. Co., 38 N. J. L. 505 (1875).

New York.—Armour Packing Co. v. Edison Electric Co., 115 N. Y. App. Div. 51, 100 N. Y. Supp. 605 (1906).

North Carolina.—Griffin v. Goldsboro Water Co., 122 N. C. 206, 30 S. E. 319, 41 L. R. A. 240 (1898).

Ohio.—Scofield v. Lake Shore & M. S. R. R., 43 Ohio St. 571, 3 N. E. 907, 54 Am. Rep. 846 (1885); State v. Cincinnati, N. O. & T. P. Ry. Co., 47 Ohio St. 130, 23 N. E. 928 (1890); Brundred v. Rice, 49 Ohio St. 640, 32 N. E. 169, 34 Am. St. Rep. 589 (1892); Baltimore & O. R. R. Co. v. Diamond Coal Co., 61 Ohio St. 242, 55 N. E. 616 (1899); Cincinnati, H. & P. R. R. Co. v. Bowling Green, 57 Ohio St. 336, 49 N. E. 129, 41 L. R. A. 122 (1897).

Pennsylvania.—Sandford v. Catawissa, W. & E. R. R., 24 Pa. St. 378, 64 Am. Dec. 667 (1885); Long v. Springfield Water Co., 8 Del. Co. 151 (1901).

Tennessee.—Crumley v. Watauga Water Co., 99 Tenn. 420, 41 S. W. 1058, 63 Am. St. Rep. 184 (1897).

Texas.—Dittmar v. New Braunfels, 20 Tex. Civ. App. 293 (1899).

Vermont.—Fitzgerald v. Grand Trunk Ry. Co., 63 Vt. 169, 22 Atl. 76, 13 L. R. A. 70 (1891).

duty. So involved are the services of the common carrier directly or indirectly in all modern businesses that it is already felt to be unbearable if transportation is not open to all upon equal terms. And the rule must be exact. It is not enough to say that all must be given rates which are not unreasonable, for by that principle in many cases unequal rates might be justified. What public opinion requires to-day is that the rates shall be equal; if they are different by a few cents upon a hundredweight it may mean the fortune of the shipper who gets the lower rate and the ruin of his competitor who pays the higher rate. As was said in one of the leading cases against personal discrimination, Schofield v. Lake Shore & Michigan Southern Railway Company,[1] of discrimination for benefits received: "The principle is opposed to a sound public policy. It would build and foster monopolies, add largely to the accumulated power of capital and money, and drive out all enterprise not backed by overshadowing wealth. With the doctrine as contended for by the defendant, recognized and enforced by the courts, what will prevent the great grain interests of the northwest, or the coal and iron interests of Pennsylvania, or any of the great commercial interests of the country, bound together by the power and influence of aggregate wealth, and in league with the railroads of the land, driving to the wall all private enterprises struggling for existence, and with an iron hand thrusting back all but themselves?" [2]

§ 1292. Discrimination inconsistent with public duty.

It is only within this last generation, therefore, that it has been appreciated that discrimination is truly inconsistent with public duty. Indeed, it was bitter experience

[1] 43 Ohio St. 571, 3 N. E. 907, 54 Am. Rep. 846 (1885).

[2] See particularly all of the opinions in Messenger v. Pennsylvania R. R. Co., 7 Vroom (36 N. J. L.), 407, 13 Am. Rep. 457, 8 Vroom (37 N. J. L.), 531, 18 Am. Rep. 754 (1874).

that forced the establishment of this law rather than any process of logical deduction. But now that our eyes have been opened it is seen that this rule against discrimination is involved in the general law of public service. And in many cases of recent date it is stated as a matter of course that the duty owed to all alike involves the obligation to treat all alike. The double aspect in which the duty of the common carrier in making rates is viewed by the more advanced courts is well stated by one Judge [1] thus: "The statement that one is a common carrier *ex vi termini*, imports a duty to the public, and a corresponding legal right in the public, a right common to all. One of the duties imposed upon the common carrier is, that he is bound to carry for a reasonable remuneration, and is not allowed to make unreasonable and excessive charges. He cannot, like a merchant or mechanic consult his pleasure or caprice in the conduct of his business, and cannot even by special agreement receive an excessive and extortionate price for his services. Another duty imposed upon him is to make no unjust, injurious or arbitrary discrimination between individuals in his dealings with the public. The right to the transportation services of the carrier is a common right belonging to every one alike." [2]

Topic B. What Constitutes Illegal Discrimination

§ 1293. What amounts to a rebate.

Not only are the outright discounts and the flimsy rebates of the earlier time illegal, but any device by which the charge to a shipper is made less than the schedule rate is now held discrimination. Thus free cartage for the collection and delivery of freight for certain shippers only

[1] Baker, J., in St. Louis, A. & T. H. R. R. Co. v. Hill, 14 Ill. App. 579 (1884).

[2] See the strong opinion of Judge

Grosscup in United States v. Michigan Central R. R. Co., 122 Fed. 544 (1903).

is an illegal rebate.[1] And the allowance to certain shippers of a certain sum for the use of their private sidings is another case of illegal reduction.[2] As such obvious devices have thus become too dangerous, more elaborate schemes have developed for getting an advantage in rates. Thus many large concerns have organized, often as a separate concern, an industrial railway from their premises to the trunk line. They may thus attempt to pose as a connecting carrier, and not only obtain from the trunk line a division of the rate to market but that disproportionately large share which the originating carrier gets.[3] Another late scheme is the organization of a dummy transportation company by a manufacturing company to carry its products to market, getting as payment not only the rental of their special cars at extraordinarily high rate but a virtual commission for furnishing the business.[4] It is needless to say that the courts have now become too sophisticated to be thus imposed upon. Indeed rebating in all its forms has now become a very smoky sin indeed, and anyone who is concerned in it will be smutted.

§ 1294. Sanctity of the scheduled rate.

The strict provisions against rebating in the recent legislation are based upon an ingenious and apparently effective plan. A schedule of rates prepared by the railroad must be filed with the commission, and duly published [5] as required. When this has been done, the rate so scheduled cannot be changed by the railroad without the

[1] Wight v. United States, 167 U. S. 512, 42 L. ed. 258, 17 Sup. Ct. 822 (1897). See also Evershed v. London & N. W. Ry., L. R. 2 Q. B. 254.

[2] Chicago & A. Ry. Co. v. United States (C. C. A.), 156 Fed. 558 (1907).

[3] See United States v. Atchison,

T. & S. F. R. R. Co., 142 Fed. 176 (1905).

[4] See United States v. Milwaukee Refrig. Transit Co. (C. C. A.), 145 Fed. 1007 (1906).

[5] Due publication of rates may be required by legislation. Stone et al. v. Yazoo & M. V. R. R. Co., 62 Miss. 607 (1885).

filing and sufficient publication of a new rate. The doctrine is carried to such an extent that even if a shipper is at first charged a lower rate quoted him by a freight agent, he can be compelled to pay the difference between this and the scheduled rate.[1] If the rate so published is unreasonable in itself or otherwise disproportionate, nevertheless the shipper cannot accept nor the railroad grant a departure from it.[2] The shipper's remedy is a complaint to the commission, which will result, if successful, in a reduction in the future and in damages for past unfair exactions. It follows that not only are rebates to favored individuals and even special rates for good reasons, if they have not been publicly offered, made criminal; but it is

[1] *United States.*—Texas & P. R. R. Co. v. Mugg, 202 U. S. 242, 50 L. ed. 1011, 26 Sup. Ct. 628 (1906), reversing 98 Tex. 352, 83 S. W. 800.

Alabama.—Southern Ry. Co. v. Harrison, 119 Ala. 539, 24 So. 55 (1898).

Arkansas.—St. Louis & S. F. R. R. v. Ostrander, 66 Ark. 567, 52 S. W. 435 (1899).

Connecticut.—Rowland v. New York, N. H. & H. R. R. Co., 61 Conn. 103, 23 Atl. 755, 29 Am. St. Rep. 175 (1891).

Georgia.—Savannah F. & W. Ry. Co. v. Bundick, 94 Ga. 775, 21 S. E. 995 (1898).

Louisiana.—Foster G. Co. v. Kansas City So. Ry. Co., 121 La. 1053, 40 So. 1014 (1908).

Montana.—Bullard v. Northern Pacific Ry. Co., 10 Mont. 168, 25 Pac. 120 (1890).

Nebraska.—Haurigan v. Chicago & N. W. Ry. Co., 80 Neb. 132, 117 N. W. 100 (1907).

Texas.—See Southern Pac. Ry.

Co. v. Redding (Tex. Civ. App.), 43 S. W. 1061 (1897).

[2] *United States.*—Texas & P. Ry. Co. v. Abilene Cotton Oil Co., 204 U. S. 426, 51 L. ed. 553, 27 Sup. Ct. 350 (1907); Southern Ry. Co. v. Tift, 206 U. S. 428, 51 L. ed. 1061, 27 Sup. Ct. 709 (1907), *semble,* American Union Coal Co. v. Pennsylvania R. R. Co., 159 Fed. 278 (1908); Van Patten v. Chicago, M. & St. P. Ry. Co., 81 Fed. 545 (1897).

Georgia.—Georgia R. R. Co. v. Creety, 5 Ga. App. 424, 63 S. E. 528 (1909).

Missouri.—Mires v. St. Louis & S. F. Ry. Co., 134 Mo. App. 379, 114 S. W. 1052 (1908).

Nebraska.—W e n t z-Bates Mercantile Co. v. Union Pacific Ry. Co., 85 Neb. 584, 123 N. W. 1085 (1909).

Oklahoma.—Atchison, T. & S. F. Ry. Co. v. Holmes, 18 Okla. 92, 90 Pac. 22 (1907).

West Virginia.—R o b i n s o n v. Baltimore & R. Co., 64 W. Va. 406, 63 S. E. 323 (1908).

also criminal for railroads or shippers to receive or give less than the published rates, even though both parties agree that the published rates are unreasonable and discriminatory. Indeed, it is easy to see that any power to the parties concerned to alter the published rates on the ground that they are illegal would put an end to the effectiveness of the whole act. The scheduled and published rate is a public record, back of which no party can go until it is altered in the way provided by the act. [1]

§ 1295. Explanation of this policy.

Thus the statute provides a complete system. It prevents rebating by making the published rate obligatory on all concerned, and it gives relief from unfair published rates by complaint to the commission. This policy is thus emphasized in a recent opinion: [2] "The object of the statutes relating to interstate commerce is to secure the transportation of person and property by common carriers for reasonable compensation. No rate can possibly be reasonable that is higher than anybody else has to pay. Recognizing this obvious truth, the law requires the carrier to adhere to the published rate as an absolute standard of uniformity. The requirement of publication is imposed in order that the man having freight to ship may

---

[1] How far shippers are affected with familiarity with schedules which they are invited to inspect may be seen in Mannheim Ins. Co. v. Erie & W. Tr. Co., 72 Minn. 357, 75 N. W. 602 (1898).

[2] State v. Chicago & A. Ry. Co., 148 Fed. 648.

The granting of a rebate contrary to the provision of the Interstate Commerce Act does not render the bill of lading void, so that no action can be maintained against the carrier for loss of the goods by negligence. Merchants' C. P. & S. Co. v. Insurance Co. of N. A., 151 U. S. 368, 38 L. ed. 195, 14 Sup. Ct. 367 (1894).

But it has been held that where a person riding on a free pass issued to him in violation of statute is injured in an accident he cannot recover from the railroad. McNeill v. Durham & C. R. R. Co., 132 N. C. 510, 44 S. E. 34 (1903).

ascertain by an inspection of the schedules exactly what will be the cost to him of the transportation of his property; and not only so, but the law gives him another and a very valuable right, namely, the right to know, by an inspection of the same schedule, exactly what will be the cost to his competitor of the transportation of his competitor's property." Still more emphatic is the language in the latest case:[1] "Effective railroad rate regulation must begin with publicity of rates. To be public the rates must be laid before the Interstate Commerce Commission, must be kept in the stations of the carriers for the information of the public, and must also be printed in such form that they shall be intelligible to the average shipper upon examination. All of this was perceived by the lawmakers 20 years ago, and the rules, based upon these considerations, then written into the law, have continued unchanged, except as they have been from time to time strengthened and amplified."

§ 1296. Decisions inconsistent with this policy.

Most of the decisions bear out this theory; there are, however two recent decisions which threaten its integrity. One of these is the latest decision in the notorious case of the Standard Oil Company of Indiana.[2] The dangerous thing in the recent decision of Judge Grosscup in the Cir-

[1] United States v. Illinois Terminal Ry. Co., 168 Fed. 546 (1909).

The effect of a violation of the Interstate Commerce Act is to make the contract of carriage including the rate named therein, invalid. The carrier therefore cannot be sued for breach of an executory term of the contract. Interstate Commerce Commission v. Chesapeake & O. Ry. Co., 128 Fed. 59 (1904).

When a railroad transports goods for a customer at less than the scheduled rates wrongfully intending to give him a rebate therefrom being in *pari delicto* it cannot recover the unpaid part of the scheduled rate. Illinois Central R. R. Co. v. Seitz, 214 Ill. 350, 73 N. E. 585 (1905).

[2] Standard Oil Co. of Ind. v. United States, 164 Fed. 376, 90 C. C. A. 364 (1908).

cuit Court of Appeals overruling Judge Landis was the suggestion thrown out that one cannot be found guilty of accepting a rebate by mere proof that he paid for transportation a less sum than the scheduled rate. This apparently makes it necessary in every prosecution for rebating to show beyond a reasonable doubt that the lower rate was accepted with actual knowledge of the higher rate and with the intention of taking an illegal rebate from that rate. If this guilty mind must be shown, the effectiveness of the act is very seriously impaired. Of what avail is the whole system for the publication of schedules if those who ship are not bound to take notice of what is on file at their disposal? The other decision referred to is that upon the so-called Olean indictments,[1] charging the Standard Oil Company with taking advantage of the rates by certain routing which were disproportionately low as compared with the rates by other routings. The company claimed that it paid the railroad its scheduled rate. So long as the rate remains in force one should be safe in paying it. On the facts both cases were probably rightly decided; but it is submitted that their dicta are dangerous.

§ 1297. Continuing contracts no justification.

A troublesome problem arises when the continuing to render service at certain rates fixed by a contract which was legal when it was made comes into conflict with new rates later scheduled by which the public generally are called upon to pay higher rates.[2] It once seems to have been thought that a continuing contract to take shipments must be respected when rates generally are raised. In those days it will be remembered any concession for which

---

[1] United States v. Standard Oil Co., 179 Fed. 614 (1910).

[2] Chicago & A. R. R. Co. v. Chicago V. & W. Coal Co., 79 Ill. 121 (1875).

anything could be said was held justifiable.[1]   But of late with the stringent law against all discrimination and the insistent enforcement of it, even a definite contract still continuing by its terms is held no justification for giving to the particular customer lower rates than those called for from all by the present schedule.[2]   Once the policy against discrimination is well established there is no difficulty in saying that for reasons of public policy no further obligation attaches to such a contract.   To the argument that the contract may have been valid when made if it fixed the rate then charged all and that therefore the subsequent action of the railroad in advancing rates generally could not invalidate it, the United States Supreme Court[3] replied recently: "This contention loses sight of the central and controlling purpose of the law, which is to require all shippers to be treated alike, and that the filed and published rate, shall be equally known by and available to every shipper."

§ 1298. Whether executed contracts are different.

It would of course be agreed that after a shipment was once made it would be too late to increase the rate on goods which have been actually received and they should go forward under the old rate.   This was said in a comparatively recent New York case,[4] where however, it was held that

[1] Houston & T. C. Ry. Co. v. Rust & D., 58 Tex. 98 (1882).

[2] *Missouri.*—Southern Wire Co. v. St. Louis, B. & T. R. R. Co., 38 Mo. App. 191 (1899).

Vermont.—Fitzgerald v. Grand Trunk Ry., 63 Vt. 169, 22 Atl. 76, 13 L. R. A. 70 (1891).

[3] Armour Packing Co. v. United States, 209 U. S. 56, 52 L. ed. 681, 28 Sup. Ct. 428 (1908).

See also Pennsylvania R. R. Co.

v. International Coal Mining Co., 173 Fed. 1, 97 C. C. A. 383 (1909).

[4] See Strough v. New York Central & H. R. R. R. Co., 92 App. Div. 584, 87 N. Y. Supp. 30 (1904).

See also People v. Green Island Water Co., 9 N. Y. Supp. 168 (1890).

See further Emerson v. Boston & M. R. R. Co., 75 N. H. 427, 75 Atl. 321 (1910).

the mere accumulation of freight for shipment, and even the ordering of cars was not enough to bring the case within the rule stated. Another class of cases is more difficult. Where the full consideration for subsequent transportation has been paid in advance the continued execution of this contract does not seem to be discrimination against those who must pay as they go the rates scheduled later. But it was held in the latest Federal case,[1] that a contract by a railroad upon consideration of a past release that the releasors should travel without charge for the remainder of their lives was not to be supported after stringent legislation against transportation at varying rates had been enacted.

§ 1299. Rule not limited to discrimination between competitors.

As has been seen what forced the development of the law against discrimination was the necessity of preventing discrimination between shippers who were competitors in business. This has already been seen from the language of many of the judges whose opinions have been quoted; but few of these judges limited the operation of this rule against discrimination to those cases in which the discrimination was between competitors, for almost all of them relied upon the legal argument that the common right of all involved the duty to give equal rates to all. A typical case in which the reasoning covers the whole field is Fitzgerald v. Grand Trunk Railway Company,[2] where Mr.

---

[1] Mottley v. Louisville & N. R. Co., decided Feb. 20, 1911, by the United States Supreme Court overruling the previous decisions. The same parties were involved in Louisville & N. R. Co. v. Mottley (Ky.), 118 S. W. 982 (1909).

See also Curry v. Kansas & Col.

Pacific R. R. Co., 58 Kans. 6, 48 , Pac. 583 (1897).

See, however, Hurley v. Big Sandy & C. Ry. Co. (Ky.), 125 S. W. 302 (1910).

[2] 63 Vt. 169, 22 Atl. 76, 13 L. R. A. 70 (1891).

Justice Powers in holding an agreement to give a rebate illegal said: "At common law, common carriers were held to be persons who exercised their calling for the public good, upon equal terms, and with the same facilities to all their customers. They could not lawfully exercise their calling by granting advantages to one customer which they denied to another, but were held to the duty of serving all alike."[1]

§ 1300. Rule universal in public service.

It should therefore be appreciated that the rule against discrimination has outgrown its original occasion to protect those in competition and become a universal rule to protect all who are being served. What makes this clear beyond question is that the rule against discrimination has been in late years applied throughout all the public services as an integral part of the public service law. Householders are not competitors and yet they must have water, for example, at equal rates. This conception, therefore, now dominates the law of all public services, although as has been seen the railroad situation gave it origin. Thus in Owensboro Gaslight Company v. Hildebrand,[2] Mr. Justice Hazelrigg said of the gas companies: "Their business, therefore, is affected with public interest, and they are

---

[1] However, when the party who got the rebate was not in competition with the other customers this fact was formerly made prominent by the courts which would not find anything illegal in discriminatory practices unless they were compelled to do so. See:

Alabama.—Louisville & N. R. R. v. Fulgham, 91 Ala. 555, 8 So. 803 (1890).

Colorado.—Bayles v. Kan. Pac. R. R., 13 Colo. 181, 22 Pac. 341, 5 L. R. A. 480 (1889).

Florida.—Johnson v. Pensacola & P. R. Ry., 16 Fla. 623, 26 Am. Rep. 731 (1878).

Illinois.—Louisville, E. & St. L. C. R. R. v. Crown Coal Co., 43 Ill. App. 228 (1891).

Pennsylvania.—Hoover v. Pennsylvania R. R. Co., 156 Pa. St. 220, 27 Atl. 282, 36 Am. St. Rep. 43, 22 L. R. A. 263 (1893).

Tennessee.—Ragan & Buffet v. Aiken, 9 Lea, 609 (1882).

[2] 19 Ky. L. Rep. 983, 42 S. W. 351 (1897).

quasi-public corporations, and practically they have a monopoly of the business of manufacturing and furnishing gas within the corporate limits of the city. It is therefore their duty to furnish the city's inhabitants with gas, and to do so upon terms and conditions common to all, and without discrimination. They cannot fix a variety of prices, or impose different terms and conditions, according to their caprice or whim." [1]

§ 1301. Giving free passes discrimination.

It was formerly customary to give free passes very freely to the families and acquaintances of those connected with the railroad management, and also to various gentlemen whose claim for the privilege of free transportation was

[1] The language in the following cases involving other public services than transportation systems is particularly strong against all discrimination:

United States.—Postal Cable-Telegraph Co. v. Cumberland Telephone & T. Co., 177 Fed. 726 (1910).

Alabama.—Mobile v. Bienville Water Supply Co., 130 Ala. 379, 30 So. 445 (1901).

Arkansas.—Danaher v. Southwestern Telephone & T. Co. (Ark.), 127 S. W. 963 (1910).

Illinois.—Snell v. Clinton Electric L. Co., 196 Ill. 626, 63 N. E. 1082, 89 Am. St. Rep. 341, 58 L. R. A. 284 (1902).

Indiana.—Redkey C. Nat. Gas L., F. & P. Co. v. Orr, 27 Ind. App. 1, 60 N. E. 716 (1901).

Iowa.—Phelan v. Boone Gas Co. (Iowa), 125 N. W. 208 (1910).

Michigan.—Bradford v. Citizens' Telephone Co. (Mich.), 126 N. W. 444 (1910).

Missouri.—Home Telephone Co. v. Granby & N. Telephone Co. (Mo. App.), 126 S. W. 773 (1910).

New York.—Armour Packing Co. v. Edison Electric Co., 115 N. Y. App. Div. 57, 100 N. Y. Supp. 609 (1906).

North Carolina.—Griffin v. Goldsboro Water Co., 122 N. C. 206, 30 S. E. 319, 41 L. R. A. 240 (1898).

Ohio.—Toledo v. North Western Ohio Gas Co., 8 Oh. Dec. 277 (1900).

Pennsylvania.—Long v. Springfield Water Co., 8 Del. Co. 151 (1901).

Tennessee.—Crumley v. Watauga Water Co., 99 Tenn. 420, 41 S. W. 1058, 63 Am. St. Rep. 184 (1897).

Texas.—Dittimar v. New Braunfels, 20 Tex. Civ. App. 293 (1899).

But see:

K e n t u c k y.—East Tenn. Telephone Co. v. Harrodsburg (Ky.), 122 S. W. 126 (1909).

New York.—People v. Albion Water Works Co., 121 N. Y. Supp. 660 (1910).

based upon the fact that they were long eminent in the public service, higher officers of the States, prominent officials of the United States, members of legislative railroad committees, and newspaper men, bankers, whose good will was claimed to be important to the railroad, and lawyers and doctors who might be of service.[1] Within the last few years the statute law and the interpretation of it based upon common law principles has become increasingly opposed to the issue of such passes. The temper of the courts under the new régime may be judged from the following language, often cited, used in a charge to the grand jury [2] by Morrow, district judge, when he said squarely: "In other words, one of the objects of Congress in this character of legislation was to do away with the pernicious practice of unjust discriminations in rates, and to break up the odious system of favoritism and special privileges, so contrary to the principles of our government, of which one of the fundamental ideas is that all men are equal in the eyes of the law, and should be so treated. It was designed by the act referred to, to compel common carriers of interstate commerce to discharge their public function impartially in charging for transportation; treating everybody alike, so far as that is practicable, whether in high or low station, whether public functionary or private citizen, whether rich or poor."

§ 1302. Statutory exceptions usually made.

Under the old régime many classes of people got free transportation or reduced rates. So far did this go that many decisions spoke of exceptional classes for which concessions were legally justifiable. In the original Inter-

---

[1] This list is largely made up from a description of the former situation in St. Louis & S. F. Ry. Co. v. Hadley, 168 Fed. 317 (1909). See also State v. Martyn, 82 Neb. 225, 117 N. W. 719, 23 L. R. A. (N. S.) 217 (1908).

[2] 66 Fed. 146 (1895). See, further, State v. Southern Ry. Co., 125 N. C. 666, 34 S. E. 527 (1900).

state Commerce Act there were express provisions as to
certain classes of reduced rates, but the statutory list omitted many usual concessions. When this was brought to the
attention of the Supreme Court it was held [1] that the list
was not exclusive, but indicated the sort of exceptions that
could be made. In other words, this section is rather illus-
trative than exclusive. "Indeed," said the court, "many,
if not all, the excepted classes named are those which, in
the absence of this section, would not necessarily be held
the subjects of an unjust discrimination, if more favorable
terms were extended to them than to ordinary passengers.
Such, for instance, are property of the United States, State
or municipal governments; destitute and homeless persons transported free of charge by charitable societies;
indigent persons transported at the expense of municipal
governments; inmates of soldiers' homes, and ministers
of religion." To remedy this indefinite condition one of
the amendments of 1906 contains a most elaborate list
of the instances where free transportation or reduced rates
may be given. It is now properly held that this list is exclusive. Thus in a recent case the Supreme Court held [2]
that an express company could no longer give franks to
their own officers or to those allied railroads as had been
their custom, a courtesy which had even included the families of these officers. The court spoke positively now saying that the legislation was not to be construed away:
"We think it was the intention of Congress to prevent a
departure from the published rates and schedules in any
manner whatsoever. If this be not so a wide door is

---

[1] The quotation is from the opinion of Mr. Justice Brown in Interstate Comm. Comm. v. Baltimore
& O. R. R. Co., 145 U. S. 163, 36
L. Ed. 699, 12 Sup. Ct. 844 (1892).

See Schuyler v. Southern Pacific
Co. (Utah), 109 Pac. 458 (1910).

[2] The quotation is from the opinion of Mr. Justice Day in American
Exp. Co. v. United States, 212 U. S.
522, 53 L. ed. 635, 29 Sup. Ct. 315
(1909).

See State v. Union Pacific Co.
(Neb.), 126 N. W. 859 (1910).

opened to favoritism in the carriage of property in the instances mentioned free of charge."

§ 1303. Reductions for charitable purposes.

The argument has been made in several cases, most of them early cases, that it could not be contrary to law for the carrier to make occasional concessions in particular cases, as no harm of any considerable sort would be done to others by the granting of such special favors. The example usually given of such occasional favors is that the railroad might carry for charity in particular instances. Is this be so, it must according to modern ideas be subject to the most strict limitations; and if this exception remains in modern common law it can only be with the qualification expressed by Chief Justice Doe in one of his great cases: [1] "This question may be made unnecessarily difficult by an indefiniteness, confusion, and obscurity of ideas that may arise when the public duty of a common carrier, and the correlative common right to his reasonable service for a reasonable price, are not clearly and broadly distinguished from a matter of private charity. If A receives, as a charity, transportation service without price, or for less than a reasonable price, from B, who is a common carrier, A does not receive it as his enjoyment of the common right; B does not give it as a performance of his public duty; C, who is required to pay a reasonable price for a reasonable service, is not injured; [2] and the public,

---

[1] McDuffee v. Portland & R. R. R., 52 N. H. 430, 13 Am. Rep. 72 (1873).

[2] See the following cases:

United States.—Interstate Comm. Comm. v. Baltimore & O. R. R. Co., 145 U. S. 163, 36 L. ed. 699, 12 Sup. Ct. 844 (1892), stating that upon common-law principles free transportation or reduced rates might be given to destitute or indigent persons, inmates of institutions, ministers of religion, etc.

Iowa.—Cook v. Chicago, R. I. & P. Ry. Co., 81 Iowa, 551, 46 N. W. 1080, 25 Am. St. Rep. 512, 9 L. R. A. 764 (1890), "alms-giving" permissible.

Michigan.—Preston v. Water Commissioners, 117 Mich. 589, 76

supplied with reasonable facilities and accommodations on reasonable terms, cannot complain that B is violating his public duty.   There is, in such a case, no discrimination, reasonable or unreasonable, in that reasonable service for a reasonable price which is the common right.   A person who is a common carrier may devote to the needy, in any necessary form of relief, all the reasonable profits of his business.   He has the same right that anyone else has to give money or goods or transportation to the poor.   But it is neither his legal duty to be charitable at his own expense, nor his legal right to be charitable at the expense of those whose servant he is."

§ 1304. Concessions for government business.

It is generally said that special reductions or even free service may be given a government, of whatever grade it may be, without its being considered undue preference or illegal discrimination.   Thus the Supreme Court of the United States has squarely said [1] that as a common law matter regardless of whether the exception was specifically made in the legislation the property of United States, State, county or municipal governments might be transported on more favorable terms than for other parties without its being illegal discrimination.   It is certainly true that a municipal government operating its own plant

N. W. 92 (1898), charitable institutions.

New York.—That a telephone company allowed a discount of 25% to clergymen, to charitable institutions, and to the city of New York, has been held not to amount to an unfair or unreasonable discrimination as against a department store service.   New York Telephone Co. v. Siegel-Cooper Co., 121 N. Y. Supp. 1033 (1910).

Washington.—Twitchell v. Spokane, 55 Wash. 86, 104 Pac. 150, 24 L. R. A. (N. S.) 290 (1909), charitable purposes.

[1] *United States.* — Interstate Comm. Comm. v. Baltimore & O. R. R. Co., 145 U. S. 163, 36 L. ed. 699, 12 Sup. Ct. 844 (1892).

New York.—New York Telephone Co. v. Siegel-Cooper Co., 121 N. Y. Supp. 1033 (1910).

may serve its own departments without making charges against itself without any taxpayer having any complaint.[1] It is, moreover, well established that in granting any legal privileges to a public service company, if the franchise conferred be no more than incorporation itself, the granting government, of whatever grade it may be, may stipulate for free service for its own public purposes.[2] And it may also be provided that certain public employees shall have transportation at special rates. It should be noted, however, that there is often special legislation forbidding public officers to accept free transportation.[3]

§ 1305. Reductions for general classes.

The suggestion is made in several cases that general reductions may be made to further certain policies, provided that the public interests are thereby promoted. It is urged that such concessions if permitted will turn out for the best interests of all concerned in the end. The weight of this line of argument may be judged by the following abstract of part of the opinion of Judge Baxter in Hays v. Pennsylvania Company.[4] He said in effect that it is only when the discrimination inures to the undue advantage of one man, in consequence of some injustice inflicted on another, that the law intervenes for the pro-

[1] *Michigan.*—Preston v. Water Commissioners, 117 Mich. 589, 76 N. W. 92 (1898).

Washington.—Twitchell v. Spokane, 55 Wash. 86, 104 Pac. 150, 24 L. R. A. (N. S.) 290 (1909).

[2] *United States.*—Waterworks Co. v. Kansas City, 4 McCreary, 198 (1882), public buildings.

Idaho.—City of Boise City v. Artesian Hot & Cold Water Co., 4 Idaho, 351, 39 Pac. 562 (1895), hydrant service.

[3] Dempsey v. New York Central & Hudson River Ry. Co., 146 N. Y. 290, 40 N. E. 867 (1895).

But in Oklahoma City v. Oklahoma Ry. Co., 20 Okla. 1, 93 Pac. 48 (1907), it was held that a municipality may stipulate for transportation free of policemen, firemen, mail carriers, and small children.

[4] 12 Fed. 309 (1882).

This principle is fully set forth in Lough v. Outerbridge, 143 N. Y. 271, 38 N. E. 292, 42 Am. St. Rep. 712, 25 L. R. A. 674 (1894).

tection of the latter. Harmless discrimination such as a concession to a general class might be indulged in. For instance, he said that the carrying of supplies at nominal rates to communities scourged by disease or rendered destitute by floods or other casualty would not entitle other communities to have their supplies carried at the same rate. Furthermore it is the custom as he pointed out for railroad companies to carry fertilizers and machinery for mining and manufacturing purposes to be employed along the lines of their respective roads to develop the country and stimulate productions, as a means of insuring a permanent increase of their business at lower rates than are charged on other classes of freight; and such discrimination while it tends to advance the interest of all worked no injustice, he thought, to anyone.[1]

§ 1306. No obligation to grant such concessions.

It should be noted however, here as throughout this whole discussion, that there is no common law obligation resting upon the company to give concesssions of any kind from the rates others pay for the same service. This makes one doubtful of the legal character of these exceptions; for were there imperative reasons dictating such exceptions a company could not refuse to make them in any case. But it is well agreed that the company need not make any such concessions. It may even refuse to the United States government a party rate ticket for soldiers which it usually sells to other managers of travelers in groups, as

---

[1] In Hoover v. Penna. R. R. Co., 156 Pa. St. 220, 27 Atl. 282, 36 Am. St. Rep. 43, 22 L. R. A. 263 (1893), discussed fully in § 1333, *infra*, it was held in accordance with these principles that a lower rate might be made for coal brought in by factories than for coal consigned to coal yards.

In Hilton Lumber Co. v. Atlantic C. L. Ry. Co., 136 N. C. 479, 48 S. E. 813 (1904), fully discussed in § 1334, *infra*, these concessions were held illegal in the case involving a lower rate on lumber made to a shipper of furniture.

one extreme case holds.[1]   Moreover it may discriminate in granting its favors, which is proof positive that this is no part of its legal obligation.   Thus a particular minister of the gospel whom a carrier refused to carry for the customary reduced fare charged such persons has no right of action against the carrier because of the discrimination.[2] The most that these exceptions amount to, therefore, is that there is a sufficient public policy in them to justify the proprietors of a public business in extending these special favors.

[1] United States v. Chicago & N. W. R. R. Co., 127 Fed. 785 (1904).

[2] Illinois C. R. Co. v. Dunnigan (Miss.), 50 So. 443, 24 L. R. A. (N. S.) 503 (1909).

In Carlisle v. Carlisle G. & Water Co. (Pa. St.), 4 Atl. 179 (1886), it was held that a water company which had been giving hydrant service to a community free might at any time begin to charge a proper rate for that service.

In People's Gaslight Co. v. Hale, 94 Ill. App. 406 (1900), it was held that a gas company which has formerly made a lower rate for gas used for fuel purposes might begin to charge the same price for gas used for any purpose.

CHAPTER XXXVIII

ILLEGAL DISCRIMINATION

§ 1310. What constitutes illegal discrimination.

In the preceding chapter the general principles as to discrimination were set forth, and it was seen that by the modern law that if two customers asked the same service under the same conditions they ought to be given the same rate. In this chapter it is proposed to describe with some detail what constitute substantially identical services. In most of the cases in this chapter it will be seen upon examination that the services are not dissimilar. Whenever a public service company initiates a policy which will get it more business, or enable it to hold the business that it has, it is prone to claim that the differing conditions in the particular case justify making a lower rate to one patron or class of patrons while maintaining higher rates for other customers. But in many such cases it will be found that what the company is doing is in the face of the fundamental rule forbidding personal discrimination. And no matter how advantageous these policies may appear from a business point of view they cannot stand in law if they are truly inconsistent with public duty.

Topic A. Concessions to Get Competitive Business

§ 1311. Concessions once allowed in competition.

The idea runs through some of the cases from the transition period in the evolution of the rule against discrimination that concessions made for a business purpose might be justified. Especially was this held to justify making a lower rate to induce a person to give up his present connections. Thus according to several of the earlier cases, one shipping by a rival route might be given a special rate to get his business. In ex parte Benson [1] for example, the court permitted the recovery of a rebate promised certain shippers to induce them to ship by rail rather than

[1] 18 S. C. 38, 44 Am. Rep. 564 (1882).

by river. The language of Chief Justice Simpson leaves no doubt as to his belief: "The extent of the common law rule seems to be, not that carriers shall transport for all parties at the same rate of compensation, otherwise their contracts are illegal and void, but that they shall transport at reasonable rates to all. A difference in the charge does not *per se* invalidate the contracts as inequitable and against public policy; but to have this effect, there must be an element of unreasonableness in the charge itself, as applied to the services rendered, between the parties to the contract and without comparison to the charges against others." [1]

§ 1312. Competitive conditions no justification.

It must be insisted upon at the outset that to-day competitive conditions in themselves do not justify the making of personal discriminations between shippers, giving a lower rate to those to whom it is necessary to make concessions. This is forbidden generally to-day both by common law and under the acts forbidding discrimination, while permitting reasonable concessions when the conditions are dissimilar. Thus in the important case of Interstate Commerce Commission v. Texas and Pacific Railroad Company,[2] it was said: "The Interstate Commerce Act would be emasculated in its remedial efficacy, if not practically nullified, if a carrier can justify a discrimination in rates merely upon the ground that unless it is given,

---

[1] Concessions to get competitive business have been justified in some cases even if they involve discrimination.

Florida.—Johnson v. Pensacola & P. R. R., 16 Fla. 623, 26 Am. Rep. 731 (1878).

Illinois.—Chicago & A. R. R. v. Coal Co., 79 Ill. 121 (1875).

New York.—Lough v. Outer-bridge, 143 N. Y. 271, 38 N. E. 292, 42 Am. St. Rep. 712, 25 L. R. A. 674 (1894).

South Carolina.—Avinger v. So. Carolina R. R., 29 S. C. 265, 7 S. E. 493, 13 Am. St. Rep. 716 (1888).

Tennessee.—Ragan & Buffet v. Aiken, 9 Lea, 609 (1882).

[2] 52 Fed. 187 (1892).

the traffic obtained by giving it would go to a competing carrier. A shipper having a choice between competing carriers would only have to refuse to send his goods by one of them unless given exceptional rates to justify that one in making a discrimination in his favor on the ground of the necessity of the situation." [1]

§ 1313. Concessions to get outside business.

It has been seen that some courts permitted any difference in the situation to be seized upon as a reason for making a discrimination. Thus in Ragan & Buffet v. Aiken, [2] where a bill in equity was filed by merchants at a station on the defendant's railway who were charged a twenty-five cent rate, who alleged that other shippers who brought their goods from an outlying district were charged only a fifteen cent rate, the court sustained a demurrer to the bill, taking the ground that there was a difference shown in the circumstances. The argument of Mr. Justice Cooper writing the opinion of the court was: "In determining whether or not a company has given undue preference to a particular person, the court may look to the interests of the company. [3] In other words, if the charge on the goods of the party complaining is reasonable, and such as the company would be required to adhere to as to all persons

---

[1] But by the better view such concessions are held unjustifiable when they involve discrimination.

United States.—Wight v. United States, 167 U. S. 512, 42 L. ed. 258, 17 Sup. Ct. 822 (1897); Menacho v. Ward, 27 Fed. 529 (1886).

New Jersey.—Messenger v. Pennsylvania R. R., 7 Vroom (36 N. J. L.), 407, 13 Am. Rep. 457, 8 Vroom (37 N. J. L.), 531, 18 Am. Rep. 754 (1874).

Ohio.—Brundred v. Rice, 49 Ohio St. 640, 32 N. E. 169, 34 Am. St. Rep. 589 (1892).

Vermont.—Fitzgerald v. Grand Trunk Ry. Co., 63 Vt. 169, 22 Atl. 76, 13 L. R. A. 70 (1891).

England.—London & N. W. R. R. Co. v. Evershed, L. R. 3 App. Cas. 1029 (1878).

[2] 9 Lea (77 Tenn.), 609 (1882).

[3] Citing Ransome v. Eastern Counties Ry., 1 C. B. (N. S.) 437 (1855).

in like condition, it may, nevertheless, lower the charge
to another person if it be to the advantage of the company,
not inconsistent with the public interest, and based on a
sufficient reason.   It is obvious that the intention of the
defendant, in this instance, was not to discriminate against
the complainants in favor of any person of the same place,
and in the same condition.   His object was to get business
for his road from persons at a distance from its terminus,
which otherwise would reach their destination by a different route."

§ 1314. Rebating to get business illegal.

Such reductions to get business from a rival line are
regarded as personal discrimination in most cases, however complicated the facts.   This is a matter upon which
the English cases have been particularly strong in holding that it is not sufficient that the railway company
merely desires to attract the traffic from another line to
itself, especially where the favor thus shown to a few is
prejudicial to many others in the same trade as the favored persons.[1]   Thus the fact that one shipper can go by
another route and will probably do so if charged as much
as the charge made to the complaining party, is not a
circumstance justifying an unequal charge; nor will the
fact that those charged a less rate are seeking to develop
a new trade.[2]   For the lowering of rates for the purpose
of developing business is an undue preference;[3] and so is
making a lower rate in consequence of a threat from the
owner of a colliery to construct another railway, by which
traffic would be diverted.[4]

[1] Thompson v. London, etc., R.
Co., 2 Nev. & Mac. 115.

[2] Denaby Main Colliery Co. v.
Manchester, S. & L. R. Co., L. R.
11 App. Cas. 97.

[3] Oxlade v. North Eastern R. Co.,

1 C. B. (N. S.) 454, 1 Nev. & Mac.
72.

[4] Harris v. Cockermouth & W. R.
Co., 1 C. B. N. S. 454, S. C., 26 L.
J. C. P. 129, 1 Nev. & Mac. 72.

§ 1315. Competitive rates for through business.

The recent American cases are equally clear. Thus in a fairly recent case, it was held that a lower rate could not be made for the transportation of goods from B to C which came from A, whence a competitive line to C ran.[1] And in a recent state case it was held that a lower rate could not be made for transportation from A to B of goods destined to be forwarded from B to C.[2] Although the law thus no longer permits such concessions to get business, because it is seen that these would constitute personal discrimination between two customers asking exactly the same service, yet these considerations are still held to justify making a lower rate from a more distant point. Where a competitive line exists at this point it will even justify this where the long haul includes the short haul within it. This means of course, that the general law against all discrimination has not as yet become as recognized as the particular law against personal discrimination, but in this relative discrimination the law is where it was as to personal discrimination some time ago.

§ 1316. Additional services performed for certain customers.

Upon the general principles now under discussion it will constitute discrimination to perform additional services for certain customers in order to get their business. For example, the issue has several times been raised whether it would be permissible for a railroad to make allowance for cartage to certain shippers distant from its station, but near to the station of a rival railroad while making no such allowance to other shippers, and the decision has

---

[1] Bigbee & W. R. P. Co. v. Mobile & O. R. Co., 60 Fed. 545 (1893). See also Brandt Milling Co. Case, 4 Can. Ry. Cas. 259 (1904).

[2] Alabama & V. R. R. Co. v. Railroad Comm., 86 Miss. 667, 38 So. 356 (1905). See also Hope Cotton Oil Co. v. Texas & P. R. R. Co., 10 I. C. C. Rep. 696 (1905).

always been that this would be illegal discrimination.[1] For the feeling has been universal that even the varying cost of shippers in delivering to the carrier for shipment can have no bearing on the case. Mr. Justice Brewer said: "Whatever the Baltimore & Ohio Company might lawfully do to draw business from a competing line, whatever inducements it might offer to the customers of that competing line to induce them to change their carrier, is not a question in this case. The wrong prohibited by the section is discrimination between shippers. It was designed to compel every carrier to give equal rights to all shippers over its own road and to forbid it by any device to enforce higher charges against one than another."[2]

§ 1317. Customers induced to make expensive preparations.

There are certain cases where a customer has been induced to make expensive preparations for giving his business by the promise of concessions. In Bundred v. Rice,[3] a shipper of oil set forth in his complaint a most extraordinary state of affairs—a contract whereby a railroad company bound itself to carry for one shipper crude petroleum at half the rate it agreed to charge all others, and to pay such favored shipper one half the amount collected

---

[1] Wight v. United States, 167 U. S. 512, 42 L. ed. 258, 17 Sup. Ct. 822 (1897). But it has been held that a railroad may give cartage without additional charge to all customers at a competitive station without making the same concession to its patrons at another station. Interstate Comm. Comm. v. Detroit, G. H. & M. Ry. Co., 167 U. S. 633, 42 L. ed. 306, 17 Sup. Ct. 986 (1897).

[2] Evershed v. London & N. W. Ry. Co., L. R. 3 App. Cas. 1029

(1878). Conversely if a railroad switches cars free for certain consignees at a given station it would be discrimination not to do this switching for all. Galesburg & G. E. R. R. Co. v. West, 108 Ill. App. 504 (1903).

[3] 49 Ohio St. 640, 32 N. E. 169, 34 Am. St. Rep. 589 (1892).

But see Willcox v. Durham & C. R. R. Co. (N. C.), 67 S. E. 758 (1910).

from others, in consideration of his agreeing to establish and maintain a system of pipe lines to its road. This was held wholly void and money so paid by a shipper in ignorance of the agreement, and received by the favored shipper was recovered back in an action for money had and received by the former against the latter. An extract from the *per curiam* opinion follows: "Whatever may have been the financial condition of the railroad company, it was not warranted in making a contract by which it bound itself to carry for one shipper at half the rate it agreed to charge all others for the same service, in consideration of his agreeing to establish a system of pipe lines to its road; at the same time and for the same consideration binding itself to charge all others double the amount as a fixed, open rate, and to pay to such favored shipper one half of it when collected." [1]

Topic B. Concessions to Large Customers

§ 1318. Whether concessions may be made to large customers.

It has not been uncommon for the managers of public service corporations to make lower proportionate rates to larger than to smaller customers. In the older times this was practiced openly as there was then no recognized rule against discrimination as such. But even in these later days it is often attempted to defend this practice on principle. For this policy is of great importance to the managers of public services who may often see the opportunity to get large amounts of valuable business, highly profitable in the aggregate even at lower proportionate rates, if

---

[1] In Gallagher v. Equitable Gaslight Co., 141 Cal. 699, 75 Pac. 329 (1904), no objection was raised to a contract by which a gas company gave unusually low rates to a hotel proprietor who had formerly lighted his premises by electricity on the ground that he had spent large sums in changing his fixtures from electricity to gas.

they can still maintain higher proportionate rates upon the regular business which they get from smaller customers who are not in a position to dictate their terms. That this policy may often be advantageous in public business, as it is in private business, may be admitted, but it has already been seen that public duty may conflict with business policies. If, therefore, these concessions to larger shippers are in conflict with the public duty which the common carrier owes to smaller shippers, they must be held illegal as unjust discriminations. And this will be the clearer when it is shown that the favoring of such large shippers will give them such commercial advantages that they may crush out their smaller competitors in the common markets. The prevalent rule forbidding the granting of special reductions to larger shippers, as such, on the ground that they furnish a greater aggregate of business to the common carrier, seems, therefore, a necessary part of the law forbidding all personal discrimination.

§ 1319. Unreasonable differences universally forbidden.

All courts now agree that if there is an unreasonable difference made between the rates given to the large patron and the rates charged a small patron, the schedule is illegal in that respect. The most recent case which brings out this test is Western Union Telegraph Company v. Call Publishing Company,[1] where the plaintiff complained of a $5 rate per 100 words daily per month charged it for news despatches while its contemporary was charged only $1.50. Mr. Justice Brewer pointed out that it could not be said even in this case that the apparent discrimination could not be justified; for the general principle as he pointed out has two sides. Of course, such equality of right does not prevent differences in the modes and kinds of serv-

---

[1] Western Union Telegraph Co. v. Call Publishing Co., 181 U. S. 92, 45 L. ed. 765, 21 Sup. Ct. 561 (1901).

ice and different charges based thereon. There is no cast iron line of uniformity which prevents a charge from being above or below a particular sum, or requires that the service shall be exactly along the same lines. But that principle of equality does forbid any difference in charge which is not based upon difference in service, and even when based upon difference of service, must have some reasonable relation to the amount of difference, and cannot be so great as to produce an unjust discrimination.[1]

§ 1320. Reasonable differences sometimes permitted.

In some jurisdictions it is still held that there is no legal objection to making a reasonable difference in the rates given to large shippers in comparison with the rates charged small shippers. The argument is that this is a business policy universally practiced; but the answer seems to be that this may nevertheless be opposed to the peculiar duties which the common carrier owes to the public as a whole. However, an extract is given from the opinion of Mr. Justice Allen in Concord and Portsmouth Railroad Company v. Forsaithe,[2] so that the weight of this argument may be felt. In holding that the complainant, a small shipper, had no case, even under a statute which forbade discriminations, he said: "The terms of the statute must receive the interpretation which long-established usage and the custom of the commercial world have given them. That custom in all branches of business always has been, and is, to move, care for, and sell a large

---

[1] It was against unreasonable differences of this sort that Mr. Justice Brewer, then upon circuit, declared himself in Burlington, C. R. & N. Ry. v. Northwestern Fuel Co., 31 Fed. 652 (1887), where there was a rate of $2.40 per ton to all persons shipping less than 100,000 tons of coal per annum over its road while $1.60 was charged to those who shipped over 100,000 tons.

[2] 59 N. H. 122 (1879).

This case was approved in State v. Central Vt. Ry. Co., 81 Vt. 463, 71 Atl. 194, 130 Am. St. Rep. 1065 (1908).

amount of a given commodity, in one parcel or in a given time, at a less price per pound, yard or ton, than a smaller quantity of the same commodity, distributed in many and smaller parcels at different times. The expense of handling, carrying, and storing the smaller amount is much greater, *pro rata*, than that of the same operations upon the larger amount in one body, and a discrimination in favor of the larger dealers is not inequality, but reasonable equality. By any other construction the statute would defeat itself; for taking into account the lessened expense *pro rata* for transporting the greater amount of property in a single body or in a given time, the carrier would, by absolute equality of rates for all cases, receive a greater price for carrying the larger quantity than the smaller, and thereby make an unjust discrimination against the person transporting the largest quantity of goods. Unreasonable equality is inequality." [1]

§ 1321. Authority for such differentials.

From the point of view of the company, thus it is an obvious business right to make lower proportionate rates to larger customers. And where the rule against discrimination is not recognized to its full extent, such concessions are freely admitted. Thus in a New York case [2] it was held that lower water rates might be given to large consumers than to small consumers, the court saying: "The objection made here is that the persons who consumed the large quantities of water were not charged

---

[1] See also:

Iowa.—Cook v. Chicago, R. I. & P. R. R. Co., 81 Iowa, 551, 46 N. W. 1080, 25 Am. St. Rep. 512, 9 L. R. A. 764 (1890).

Missouri.—Rothschild v. Wabash, St. L. & P. C. R. R. Co., 92 Mo. 91, 4 S. W. 418 (1887).

[2] *New York.*—Silkman v. Yonkers Water Commissioners, 152 N. Y. 327, 46 N. E. 612 (1897).

See also Metropolitan Electric Supply Co. v. Ginder (1901), 2 Ch. 799, holding lower rates for large users of electricity justifiable.

as much per hundred cubic feet as those who consumed a less amount. Under this statute the question of consumption was one of the elements to be considered in determining the rates. Surely, it cannot be said to be unreasonable to provide less rates where a large amount of water is used than where a small quantity is consumed. That principle is usually present in all contracts or established rents of that character. It will be found in contracts and charges relating to electric lights, gas, private water companies, and the like, and is a business principle of general application. We find in the rates as they were established nothing unreasonable, or that would in any way justify a court in interfering with them." [1]

§ 1322. Prevalent doctrine against such concessions.

It may be asserted with confidence, however, that it is opposed to fundamental principles to permit the giving of special concessions to the large shipper as such. In the leading case of Hays v. Pennsylvania Company,[2] this doctrine is well worked out. The plaintiffs in that case, had for several years been engaged in mining coal for sale in the Cleveland market. Their complaint was that the defendant discriminated against them and in favor of their competitors in business, in the rates charged for carrying coal from Salineville to Cleveland. It appeared in evidence that defendant's regular price for carrying coal between the points mentioned, in 1876, was $1.60 per ton, with a rebate of from 30 to 70 cents

---

[1] In St. Louis Brewing Assn. v. St. Louis, 140 Mo. 419, 37 S. W. 525, 41 S. W. 911 (1897), it was held that a water company could not only make lower rates to manufacturers than to other consumers, but also lower rates to large manufacturers than to small.

In Boeth v. Detroit City Gas Co., 152 Mich. 654, 116 N. W. 628, 18 L. R. A. (N. S.) 1197 (1908), it was held that a gas company might grant a lower rate to persons consuming large quantities for different purposes.

[2] Hays v. Pennsylvania Co., 12 Fed. 309 (1882).

per ton to all persons or companies shipping, 5,000 tons
or more during the year,—the amount of rebate being
graduated by the quantity of freight furnished by each
shipper. In an excellent opinion by Baxter, the United
States circuit judge, the various grounds upon which differences in rates have been justified by reason of differences in the cost of service by reason of economies of
handling the business were reviewed,[1] but he held very
properly that none of these applied to the exclusive
shipper as such, his conclusion being well worth quoting
at length. "In all particulars the plaintiffs occupied
common ground with the parties who obtained lower
rates. Each tendered coal for transportation in the same
condition and at such time as suited his or their convenience. The discrimination complained rested exclusively
on the amount of freight supplied by the respective shippers during the year. Ought a discrimination resting
exclusively on such a basis be sustained? If so, then the
business of the country is, in some degree, subject to the
will of railroad officials; for, if one man engaged in mining
coal, and dependent on the same railroad for transportation to the same market, can obtain transportation thereof
at from 25 to 50 cents per ton less than another competing
with him in business, solely on the ground that he is able
to furnish and does furnish the larger quantity for shipment, the small operator will sooner or later be forced
to abandon the unequal contest and surrender to his

---

[1] The following cases are strongly
to the same effect:

United States.—Western U. T.
Co. v. Call Pub. Co., 181 U. S. 92,
45 L. ed. 765, 21 Sup. Ct. 561
(1901); Kingsley v. Buffalo, N. Y.
& P. R. R. Co., 37 Fed. 18
(1888).

Indiana.—Louisville, E. & St. L.

C. R. Co. v. Wilson, 132 Ind. 517,
32 N. E. 311 (1892).

Ohio.—Scofield v. Lake Shore &
M. S. R. R. Co., 43 Ohio St. 571, 3
N. E. 907, 54 Am. St. Rep. 846
(1885).

Vermont.—Fitzgerald v. Grand
Trunk Ry. Co., 63 Vt. 169, 22 Atl
76, 13 L. R. A. 70 (1891).

more opulent rival. If the principle is sound in its application to rival parties engaged in mining coal, it is equally applicable to merchants, manufacturers, millers, dealers in lumber and grain, and to everybody else interested in any business requiring any considerable amount of transportation by rail; and it follows that the success of all such enterprises would depend as much on the favor of railroad officials as upon the energies and capacities of the parties prosecuting the same."

§ 1323. Services to large and small customers practically identical.

Moreover, the services to large shippers and to small shippers are practically identical. The large shipper sends more car loads in the aggregate than the small shipper, it is true; but it makes no real difference whether a railroad takes two cars from A or one car each from A and B. And it is plain that to carry two barrels of sugar for one person on a given date, and to carry one barrel of sugar for another person, between the same points, over the same route, two days later, are contemporaneous, and like services.[1] Moreover there is not from an operating point of view any real basis for making a lower price to customers who run up larger bills in the course of a stated period. Indeed, the person who has a large aggregate bill may have received a multitude of costly small services. There is nothing to differentiate the large shipper from the small shipper in such a case except that one may perhaps seem to be a more desirable customer than the other; but this is not enough in itself.[2]

§ 1324. Company need never grant such reductions.

It would probably be generally agreed that a public

[1] United States v. Tozer, 39 Fed. 369 (1889).

[2] Kingsley v. Buffalo, N. Y. & P. R. R. Co., 37 Fed. 181 (1888).

service company would not be acting unreasonably which
made a flat rate for all customers whether their bills be
large or small. Thus in one case where a city was charging
all customers large and small a flat meter rate of five cents
per thousand gallons it was held that the mere fact that
the complainant was a very large customer gave him no
ground for complaint.[1] Even those courts which permit
the making of a lower rate for larger consumption of
water require that it shall all be sold to one place; a large
real estate owner cannot get his bills added together
and get the lower rate.[2]

Topic C. Rebates to Exclusive Customers

§ 1325. Whether exclusive policies may be adopted.

Undoubtedly there is a commercial advantage in being
able to adopt the policy of promoting exclusive arrangements with desirable customers by offering reductions.
The essential illegality of this policy appears most plainly,
as has been seen in other connections, when there is an
outright refusal to serve those who deal with a rival. A
railroad cannot refuse to take freight from a shipper who
formerly shipped by it exclusively but has now made
arrangements to ship part of his freight by another line.
A telephone company cannot take out its instruments
from a customer who has subscribed to another system.[3]
It is no ground for refusing an application for gas that the
applicant is connected with another system.[4] If the

[1] St. Louis Brewing Assn. v. St.
Louis, 140 Mo. 419, 37 S. W. 525,
41 S. W. 911 (1897).

[2] Penn Iron Co. v. Lancaster, 17
Lanc. L. Rev. 161 (1900).

[3] State ex rel. Gynn v. Citizens'
Telephone Co., 61 S. C. 83, 39 S. E.
257, 85 Am. Rep. 870 (1901).

But see Bald Eagle Valley R. R.

Co. v. Nittany Valley R. R. Co., 171
Pa. St. 284, 33 Atl. 239 (1895).

[4] Portland Nat. Gas & I. Co. v.
State ex rel., 135 Ind. 54, 34 N. E.
818, 21 L. R. A. 639 (1893).

See also Sorraine v. Pittsburgh,
J., E. & E. R. R. Co., 205 Pa. St.
132, 54 Atl. 580, 61 L. R. A. 502
(1903).

companies cannot refuse to serve for the promotion of their business interests, no more can they discriminate to get the advantages which may accrue to the company if it may make lower rates to those who will deal exclusively with it, are plain and this policy would still prevail in making rates in competitive business doubtless as it once did were it not for the modern recognition of its essential illegality. That such a policy may be advantageous to the company which employs it may be granted, but it has already been seen that those who conduct a public employment must forego many methods of getting business and holding it which are permissible in private affairs.

§ 1326. Such discriminations foster monopolies.

The leading case against such personal discrimination is Schofield v. Lake Shore & Michigan Southern Railway Company.[1] In that case it appeared that the railway company, having tariff rates for the public generally, contracted with the Standard Oil Company that, in consideration of said company giving to the railway its entire freight business in the products of petroleum, they would transport such freight for the company at certain rates, about ten cents per barrel cheaper than for any other customers whatsoever. Plaintiffs, one Schofield and others, being also engaged in the manufacture and also dealers in refined and other products of petroleum, offered their products to the railway company for shipment on the same terms granted to the Standard Oil Company, and, on being refused shipment on the terms, brought their bill to enjoin the railway company from charging and collecting from them, for freight on said line, rates and amounts in excess of those charged to the Standard Company for like goods to the same points, or from dis-

[1] 43 Ohio St. 571, 3 N. E. 907, 54 Am. Rep. 846 (1885).

criminating against them in favor of the Standard Company. The prayer of the bill was granted in an elaborate opinion, the tenor of which may be judged from the following paragraph: "The principle is opposed to a sound public policy. It would build and foster monopolies, add largely to the accumulated power of capital and money, and drive out all enterprise not backed by overshadowing wealth. With the doctrine as contended for by the defendant, recognized and enforced by the courts, what will prevent the great grain interests of the northwest, or the coal and iron interests of Pennsylvania, or any of the great commercial interests of the country, bound together by the power and influence of aggregate wealth, and in league with the railroads of the land, driving to the wall all private enterprises struggling for existence, and with an iron hand thrusting back all but themselves?" [1]

§ 1327. Those who use rival line charged more than usual.

It would seem to be plainly contrary to public duty for a public service company to charge customers who at times employ a rival concern more than the usual rates which others are charged. Yet this sort of discrimination has been defended before the courts more than once even in its most extreme forms. The leading case on this point is undoubtedly Menacho v. Ward. [2] The complainants in that case were notified by the defendant steamship owners that they would be "placed upon the black-list" if they shipped goods by the steamers which had gone on the route in opposition to them and that their rates of freight would thereafter be advanced on all goods which they might have occasion to send by the defendants.

---

[1] See, further, Louisville, E. & St. L. C. R. R. Co. v. Wilson, 132 Ind. 517, 32 N. E. 311 (1892).

[2] 27 Fed. 529 (1886).

Since that time the defendants have habitually charged the complainants greater rates of freight than those merchants who shipped exclusively by the defendants. In disposing of this case Mr. Justice Wallace pointed out that there were various situations justifying different rates between shippers asking for the same transportation, and in enumerating them he was undoubtedly unduly liberal; but this particular case before him he rightly decided to go beyond all justification as the conclusion of his opinion which follows will show: "The vice of the discrimination here is that it is calculated to coerce all those who have occasion to employ common carriers between New York and Cuba from employing such agencies as may offer. Its tendency is to deprive the public of their legitimate opportunities to obtain carriage on the best terms they can. If it is tolerated it will result practically in giving the defendants a monopoly of the carrying trade between these places. Manifestly it is enforced by the defendants in order to discourage all others from attempting to serve the public as carriers between these places. Such discrimination is not only unreasonable, but is odious." [1]

§ 1328. Lower rates to exclusive customers sometimes permitted.

On the other hand it is maintained by some few courts that while higher than usual rates cannot be charged those who will not ship exclusively, yet lower rates may be given to exclusive shippers. That this is the view of the highest court in New York may be seen by an examination of the leading case of Lough v. Outerbridge.[2] In that case a

[1] *A fortiori* it is illegal to refuse altogether to accept goods from a shipper who persists in using a rival line. Chicago & A. R. R. Co. v. Suffern, 129 Ill. 274, 21 N. E. 824 (1889).

[2] 143 N. Y. 271, 38 N. E. 292, 42 Am. St. Rep. 712, 25 L. R. A. 416 (1894).

lower rate was given those who would agree to ship their freight exclusively by the established line when the rival boat ran. The Court of Appeals of New York, one justice dissenting, held for the defendant company. In writing the opinion of the court Mr. Justice O'Brien said: "The authorities cited seem to me to remove all doubt as to the right of a carrier, by special agreement, to give reduced rates to customers who stipulate to give them all their business, and to refuse these rates to others who are not able or willing to so stipulate, providing, always, that the charge exacted from such parties for the service is not excessive or unreasonable. The principle of equality to all, so earnestly contended for by the learned counsel for the plaintiffs, was not, therefore, violated by the defendants, since they were willing and offered to carry the plaintiffs' goods at the reduced rate, upon the same terms and conditions that these rates were granted to others; and, if the plaintiffs were unable to get the benefit of such rate, it was because, for some reason, they were unable or unwilling to comply with the conditions upon which it was given to their neighbors, and not because the carrier disregarded his duties or obligations to the public. The case of Menacho v. Ward does not apply, because the facts were radically different. That action was to restrain the carrier from exacting unreasonable charges habitually for services, the charges having been advanced as to the parties complaining, for the reason that they had at times employed another line. It decides nothing contrary to the general views here stated." [1]

[1] The cases principally relied upon by the court in reaching this opinion were: Fitchburg R. R. Co. v. Gage, 12 Gray, 393 (1859); Sargent v. R. R. Co., 115 Mass. 416 (1874); Mogul Steamship Co. v. McGregor, 21 Q. B. Div. 544, affirmed, 23 Q. B. Div. 598, and by H. L. 17 App. Cas. 25 (1892); Evershed v. Railway Co., 3 Q. B. Div. 135.

It seems that the important case of Mogul Steamship Co. v. McGregor, *supra*, cannot be cited, for

§ 1329. Comparison of these decisions.

Notwithstanding the weight to be given to this decision it is submitted that it is opposed to what are conceived to be fundamental principles. As between two shippers who offer the same goods for the same transportation it seems to be personal discrimination with all its accompanying evils to make one rate to one and another rate to another by reason of the fact that one ships exclusively and the other does not. And it ought to be plain that whether this is done as in Menacho v. Ward,[1] by charging the one who does not ship exclusively more than the usual rate or as in this case of Lough v. Outerbridge,[2] by giving exclusive shippers concessions from regular rates, the fact remains that in either case there is a personal discrimination against the shipper who will not enter into an exclusive arrangement.

§ 1330. Customers contracting for large amounts.

It would seem to follow, although this has appeared to some courts [3] more doubtful that shippers who agree to furnish large quantities of freight should have no better standing. It is true that the advantage to the railroad company may be proved, but the injustice to the small shipper who can make no such undertaking remains the controlling factor in the situation. This was well shown in an Indiana case,[4] where the court said: "It is contended by the appellant that, in view of the fact it secured by its contract with Dickason a certain income of $7,000

the proposition that in public business a rebate may be given exclusive shippers, the shipowners in that case may have been private carriers for all that appears; at all events the point that they were common carriers was not made by the courts or by counsel, so far as can be discovered.

[1] *Supra.*

[2] *Supra.*

[3] Chicago & A. R. R. Co. v. Chicago V. & W. Coal Co., 79 Ill. 121 (1875), upholding a concession based upon this fact in part.

[4] Louisville, E. & St. L. C. R. Co. v. Wilson, 132 Ind. 517, 32 N. E. 311 (1892).

per month, it could as well afford to carry ties for him at $14 per car as to carry them for the appellees at $24 per car. We find it unnecessary to inquire whether the appellant is correct or otherwise in this contention, for, as we understand the law, a railroad company engaged in the business of a common carrier is not permitted by the law to discriminate in favor of a shipper who is able to furnish a large amount of freight over one engaged in the same business who is unable to furnish the same quantity as that shipped by his more opulent rival. The reasons for prohibiting such discrimination are well stated in the case of Hays v. Pennsylvania Co. In our opinion, the fact that Dickason was able to furnish a larger number of car loads of ties for shipment than the appellees could constituted no sufficient reason for a discrimination in his favor over the rates charged to the appellees."

§ 1331. Customers under exclusive contract to give business.

The mere fact, therefore, that a shipper agrees to give all his business to the carrier does not justify a concession from regular rates. Such inducements seem once to have been held out to shippers commonly in England; but the decisions of the courts have been against them.[1] They have uniformly held it unlawful preference to give reduced rates in consideration of an agreement to employ other lines of the company for the carriage of other traffic or to employ the company in other distinct business. This is obviously good law, as the carriage of goods to other points does not affect the cost of carriage between the particular points.[2] Upon the same principles the rail-

---

[1] Baxendale v. Great Western R. Co., 5 C. B. (N. S.) 309 (1858); Diphwys Casson Slate Co. v. Festining R. Co., 2 Nev. & Mac. 73 (1860); Bellsdyke Coal Co. v. N. B. R. Co., 2 Nev. & Mac. 105 (1860).

[2] Baxendale v. Great Western R. Co., 5 C. B. (N. S.) 309 (1858);

ways have been forbidden to charge a higher wharfage rate on goods to be conveyed by another railway [1] or to grant a reduced rate in consideration of a contract to carry all of certain goods and to prevent their being carried by water or other means.[2] It seems plain that in all of these cases no other decisions would have been justifiable than those which were given, because the policies pursued by the railways in all of these cases seem opposed to the public duty which the common carrier owes the shipping public.

Topic D. Concessions for Special Kinds of Business

§ 1332. Different rates for service differently employed.

Notwithstanding the obvious analogy to the policies already generally condemned, it is still strongly urged at the present time by the managers of the public service companies that they should be allowed to make different rates for service which is to be differently employed. Railroad managers, for example, here point out again that in order to get more traffic, which by reason of the law of increasing returns is for the benefit of all concerned, it will often be necessary for them to make lower rates for goods which are going to be used for one purpose than for goods which are going to be used for another purpose. Moreover, the railroad managers take a higher plane of argument when they urge that to make different rates for different users they may further the development of the industries of the communities which they serve. But neither of these arguments can be pushed too far in a legal discussion because in so far as any railroad policy involves discrimination it is illegal; and to charge one of

Twellis v. Pa. R. R. Co., 3 Am. L. Reg. (N. S.) 728 (1863); Bellsdyke Coal Co. v. North British R. Co., 2 Nev. & Mac. 105 (1860).

[1] Toomer v. London R. Co., 3 Nev. & Mac. 79 (1865).

[2] Garton v. Bristol & E. R. R. Co., 1 Nev. & Mac. 218 (1856).

two shippers who want exactly the same transportation
of the same goods one rate while another shipper is charged
another rate is personal discrimination by definition. Not
only is this argument urged by the railroads, but in other
services such as gas supply for different purposes it is
claimed that economical operation is greatly hampered.

§ 1333. Such rates allowed by some cases.

And indeed, the argument for allowing the making of
different rates for the same commodities which are destined
to be used for different purposes is a strong one. How
strong it is from an economic point of view may be seen
by an examination of the leading case supporting this argument, Hoover v. Pennsylvania Railroad Company.[1] In
that case the court held that an agreement made in 1881 to
charge a uniform rate on shipment of coal to the Bellefonte
Nail Works for consumption in operating its machinery
could not be complained of as unjust discrimination against
a mere dealer, who received his coal over the same road
and was charged a higher rate. This was held not to be
unjust discrimination, the court relying upon the broadest
grounds of public policy to justify this result, Mr. Justice Green saying: "Such discrimination, as has thus far
transpired, has not been felt to be undue or unreasonable,
or contrary to legal warrant. In point of fact, it is perfectly well known and appreciated that the output of
freights from the great manufacturing centers upon our
lines of transportation constitutes one of the chief sources
of the revenues which sustain them financially. Yet no
part of this income is derived from those who are mere '

---

[1] 156 Pa. St. 220, 27 Atl. 282, 22
L. R. A. 263, 36 Am. St. Rep. 43
(1893). See also Louisville & W.
R. R. Co. v. Fulgam, 91 Ala. 555,
8 So. 803 (1890); holding that under a statute permitting reductions
designed to promote industries,
provided that these concessions are
duly published, a miller is entitled
to rank with other manufacturers
without discrimination.

buyers and sellers of coal. When the freight is paid upon the coal they buy, the revenue to be derived from that coal is at an end. Not so, however, with the revenue from the coal that is carried to the manufacturers. That coal is consumed on the premises in the creation of an endless variety of products, which must be put back upon the transporting lines, enhanced in bulk and weight by the other commodities which enter into the manufactured product, and is then distributed to the various markets where they are sold." [1]

§ 1334. Repudiation of this doctrine.

However, this doctrine is plainly inconsistent with the modern law against discrimination which in its latest development insistently forbids all discrimination. This is well brought out in the Railroad Discrimination Case [2] where it was held that a carrier may not give one customer a lower rate for the shipment of logs, than another, merely because the former ships the manufactured product over the carrier's line, Clark, C. J., saying: "The proposition is that a common carrier has a right to charge one person a lower rate of freight than another for shipping the same quantity the same distance, under the same conditions, provided the shipper give the company a consideration (shipping the manufactured lumber subsequently over its line), which its managers think will make good to it the

---

[1] In Missouri, K. & T. R. R. Co. v. Trinity C. L. Co., 1 Tex. Civ. App. 553, 21 S. W. 290 (1892), the court left the question open whether a lower rate might be given a connecting carrier on railway cars than to a logging railway.

See also, Fry v. Louisville & N. R., 103 Ind. 265, 2 N. E. 744 (1885), where a lower rate was quoted for commodities for "farm purposes,"

notwithstanding which the court enforced the bargain of the parties.

[2] Hilton Lumber Co. v. Atlantic Coast Line, 136 N. C. 479, 48 S. E. 813 (1904).

See the further discussion of this case in an eloquent opinion against all discrimination in Hilton Lumber Co. v. Atlantic C. L. Ry. Co., 141 N. C. 171, 53 S. E. 823 (1906).

abatement of rate given to such parties. But if this is equality as to the treasury of the company, it is none the less a discrimination against the plaintiff." [1]

§ 1335. Supply put to different uses.

There is also some authority on this point in regard to supplying services. Thus it has been held in Missouri [2] that lower rates for water supply could be made to the manufacturer than to all other takers notwithstanding that the city charter forbade exceptional discriminations in water rates, on the ground that as all manufacturers were included in the class the discrimination was not illegal. And in Michigan,[3] it was held that a consumer is not entitled to enjoin the enforcement against him by a gas company of a rate which the company is authorized to charge, because it grants a lower rate to persons consuming gas for other purposes in larger amounts, as it does not appear that any injury is inflicted upon the complainant by such rates.

§ 1336. Discrimination in such supply.

If other discrimination is involved in the arrangement it will all be declared illegal without question in all courts. Another Pennsylvanian case, Bailey v. Fayette Gas & Fuel Company,[4] decided since Hoover v. Pennsylvania Railroad Company [5] brings this out. In that case a higher price per cubic foot was charged to customers who used

[1] The railroad commissions are now generally set against such discriminations. See Capital City Gas Co. v. Central Vt. Ry. Co., 11 Int. Comm. Comm. Rep. 103 (1906), and Manufacturers' Coal Rates Case, 3 Can. Ry. Cas. 427 (1904).

[2] St. Louis Brewing Assn. v. St. Louis, 140 Mo. 419, 37 S. W. 525, 41 S. W. 911 (1897).

[3] Boerth v. Detroit City Gas Co., 152 Mich. 654, 116 N. W. 628, 18 L. R. A. (N. S.) 1197 (1907).

[4] 193 Pa. St. 175, 44 Atl. 451 (1899).

[5] 156 Pa. St. 220, 27 Atl. 282, 36 Am. St. Rep. 43, 22 L. R. A. 263 (1893).

gas simply for illuminating than was charged to such customers as used gas also for fuel. This was properly held to constitute discrimination; but the language of Mr. Justice Mitchell apparently goes much further than the immediate facts: "The gas is brought by the company through the same pipes for both purposes and delivered to the customers at the same point, the curb. Thence it goes into pipes put in by the consumer, and, after passing through a meter, is distributed by the customer through his premises according to his own convenience. The regulation in question seeks to differentiate the price according to the use for heating or for light. It is not claimed that there is any difference in the cost of the product to the company, the expense of supplying it at the point of delivery or its value to the company in the increase of business or other ways."

§ 1337. Commodities carried of different character.

Of course different rates may be given when the commodities are not of exactly the same sort. This is probably the explanation of a series of cases in Kentucky justifying a difference in rate between steam coal to manufacturers and domestic coal for dealers. Thus in Commonwealth v. Louisville & Nashville Railroad Company [1] the facts shown at the trial were that the electric light company which was getting the lower rate was bringing in a very low grade of coal, commonly known as "slack," used by it for steam purposes, while Wade, a coal dealer, was being charged a higher rate for the transportation of the highest grade of coal, known as "lump." Both kinds of coal were hauled in the same sort of cars, and unloaded in the same manner, but defendant's regular freight tariff on coal from Bevier to Franklin, was $1.50 per ton, while on the coal used for steam purposes by

[1] 68 S. W. 1103 (1902).

manufacturers, which term included gas, electric light, power, and ice companies, the rate was 30 per cent less than $1.50 per ton.   Upon a review of the authorities cited in the note [1] the court held that "it was allowable and proper for a railroad company to classify freight according to its quality or character and marketable value; and discrimination in charges for carrying different classes or kinds is not only universally recognized, but plainly authorized.   And that this settled the question since it was admitted in the pleadings and shown by proof that the respective car loads of coal upon which this action was founded were wholly different both as to quality and marketable value."

§ 1338. Supply under different conditions.

Similarly when the arrangement by which the service is devoted to a different use is such that there may be said to be a difference in the service rendered a different rate may be justified.   Thus gas supplied to manufacturers on the understanding that service may be curtailed in favor of other business in emergencies is obviously a different service from the domestic service which is being given priority; and a lower rate is perhaps justified.[2]   So when electric current is sold for power by day, as it costs less to so supply current at that part of the day when the equipment is largely idle than it would to take on new lighting contracts involving probably new equipment, it may be that the conditions of this service are so different as to justify a difference in rates.[3]

[1] Louisville & N. R. R. Co. v. Com., 105 Ky. 179, 48 S. W. 416 (1898); Louisville & N. R. R. Co. v. Com., 108 Ky. 628, 57 S. W. 508 (1900).

[2] Logansport & W. V. Gas Co. v. Ott, 30 Ind. App. 93, 65 N. E. 549 (1902).

[3] Metropolitan Electric Co. v. Guider, 2 Ch. Div. 799 (1901).

CHAPTER XXXIX

JUSTIFIABLE DIFFERENCES

§ 1340. Propriety of proportionate rates.

In the last chapter it was seen that what is forbidden is any difference in the rate charged when the service asked is identical. It follows logically that when services which are really different are asked it is entirely proper to make the rate charged proportionally different. Thus it has already been explained that the railway company may classify freights and passengers and charge different rates for the different classes, if there are reasonable grounds for such discrimination in the difference of the cost of service, risk of carriage, in the accommodations furnished or the like. But it will constitute discrimination if different classification is given to like goods without justification. As a general rule a railway company is justified in carrying goods for one person at a less rate than that at which it carries goods for another only where there are circumstances which make the cost of carrying the former less than the cost of carrying the latter. And, to be exact, the difference in the rates between the different classifications of like articles must be proportionate to this difference in cost to the carrier of performing the service.

Topic A. Actual Differences in Total Cost

§ 1341. Extent of the rule against discrimination.

When the services asked of the carrier are dissimilar, the rule against discrimination although apparently modified is in reality extended. It is rightly held that different rates may be made without discrimination when the cost of service is different. Indeed, to enforce equal rates under those circumstances would in reality be discriminatory under ordinary conditions. All this is seen even in the most extreme case against personal discrimination, Messenger v. Pennsylvania Railroad Company.[1] "It must not be inferred that a common carrier, in adjusting his price, cannot regard the peculiar circumstances of the particular transportation. Many considerations may properly enter into the agreement for carriage or the establishment of rates, such as the quantity carried, its nature, risks, the expense of carriage at different periods of time, and the like; but he has no right to give an exclusive advantage or preference, in that respect, to some over others, for carriage, in the course of his business. For a like service, the public are entitled to a like price.[2]

§ 1342. Differences in the cost.

There is no illegal discrimination unless the services compared are substantially the same. Thus a reasonable classification of commodities or passengers according to the nature of the goods or the accommodations furnished does not result in discrimination.[3] "And for a like reason an inferior class of freight may be carried at a less rate than first-class merchandise of greater value and requiring more labor, care, and responsibility in the handling. It has been held that 20 separate parcels done up in one package, and consigned to the same person may be carried at a less rate per parcel than 20 parcels

---

[1] 7 Vroom (36 N. J. L.), 407, 13 Am. Rep. 457, 8 Vroom (37 N. J. L.), 531, 18 Am. Rep. 754 (1874).

[2] For a late statement of the principle that the present law does not prohibit the giving of all preferences and advantages, but only those that are undue and unreasonable. See Gamble-Robinson Com. Co. v. Chicago & N. W. R. Co., 168 Fed. 161, 94 C. C. A. 217, n., 21 L. R. A. (N. S.) 982 (1899).

[3] For this general principle see among other cases:

United States.—Brewer v. Central of Ga. Ry. Co., 84 Fed. 258 (1897).

Illinois.—Wagner v. City of Rock Island, 146 Ill. 139 (1893).

Kentucky.—Louisville & N. Ry. Co. v. Com., 108 Ky. 628, 57 S. W. 508 (1900).

Pennsylvania.—Paine v. Pennsylvania Ry., 7 Kulp, 187.

of the same character consigned to as many different persons at the same destination, because it is supposed that it costs less to receive and deliver one package containing 20 parcels to one man, than it does to receive and deliver 20 different parcels to as many different consignees. Such are some of the numerous illustrations of the rule that might be given." [1]

§ 1343. Economies in passenger transportation.

That there are differences in the cost of service by reason of ways in which traffic is handled is of course obvious, and in so far as these economies in conducting the transportation are real a proportionate reduction may be made for the service in question. This is as true of passenger carriage as of freight transportation. Passengers may be divided into different classes, and the price regulated in accordance with the accommodations furnished to each, because it costs less to carry an emigrant with the accommodations furnished to that class, than it does to carry an occupant of a palace car. [2] It is justifiable to charge a higher rate when fare is paid upon the train than when tickets are bought at the office, the saving to the company thereby being sufficiently obvious. [3] These are but two examples of many cases which could be put.

§ 1344. Economies in freight transportation.

Upon the principles now under discussion it will be plain why it is permissible to make differences in the rating of the same goods based on the nature and size of the package, large packages being given relatively lower rates than small packages. [4] And likewise if the

[1] The quotation is from Hays v. Pennsylvania R. R. Co., 12 Fed. 309 (1882).

[2] See Hays v. Pennsylvania R. R. Co., 12 Fed. 309 (1882).

[3] See Nellis v. New York C. R. R. Co., 30 N. Y. 505 (1864).

[4] For the general principle involved, see: Nicholson v. Gt. Western R. R. Co., 5 C. B. (N. S.) 366 (1858).

shipment is in a form more convenient for handling, as in casks rather than in cases, or if the freight is tendered in a form permitting a greater car load, the difference between cotton in bulk and in tightly compressed bales for example, lower rates may be given proportionate to the difference in the cost of service. "We are not unmindful of the rule" said the Indiana court in a leading case, "which permits a common carrier to discriminate in favor of a shipper who transports large quantities of a given commodity in one parcel at a time, as against a shipper who transports the broken packages. Such discrimination is rendered necessary by the increased expense of handling, storing, and caring for the smaller quantities, and is not unreasonable." [1]

§ 1345. Different charges for different service.

Where a customer requires less service than usual a lower rate is justified in his case. On the other hand where a customer requires more service than usual, it is not unreasonable to charge him more than others. In neither case is it discrimination to recognize the differences in the cost of service in making the rates; indeed in extreme cases it would be unreasonable not to do so. Thus a telephone subscriber outside of usual limits may without discrimination be charged a higher rate than his fellow citizens generally. [2] A telegraph company may make an extra charge for the delivery of messages outside its usual limits. [3] Again a gas company can require a large taker to make a proportionally larger deposit. [4] And an electric

[1] Quoted from Louisville, E. & St. L. C. R. Co. v. Wilson, 132 Ind. 517, 32 N. E. 311 (1892).

Legislation compelling railroads to sell mileage tickets at a loss is unconstitutional. Lake Shore & M. S. Ry. Co. v. Smith, 173 U. S. 684, 43 L. ed. 858, 19 Sup. Ct. 565 (1899).

See further Philadelphia v. Philadelphia R. T. Co. (Pa. St.), 73 Atl. 923 (1909).

[2] Central Dist. & P. Telegraph Co. v. Com., 114 Pa. St. 592 (1886).

[3] Evans v. Western Union Telegraph Co., 56 S. W. 609 (1900).

[4] Williams v. Mutual Gas Co.,

company may make higher charges when asked to install a service wire for a taker whose premises are far from the established main.[1] These examples taken almost at random from various public services all illustrate the accepted principle, that when the cost of service plainly is different a different rate can be made.

§ 1346. Difference in the nature of the service.

Various other illustrations of this rule may be found in the public services other than transportation. Throughout public service a difference in charge based upon a difference in the service asked is justifiable. Thus a telephone company may make a lower rate to those who have a simple instrument of the ordinary type than those who have an elaborate installation involving special equipment.[2] So a telegraph company may make a lower rate for a night message which need not be handled with such dispatch as the day message for which the higher rate is paid.[3] A water company may sell unfiltered water for manufacturing purposes cheaper than filtered water for domestic uses.[4] And an electric company may sell high tension electricity for power purposes cheaper than it sells transformed electricity for household use.[5] Examples of difference of this sort in rates proportioned to the cost of service have already been seen in dealing with particular rates.

§ 1347. Both rates must be open to all.

But the modern fear of discrimination is such that it is

52 Mich. 449, 18 N. W. 236, 50 Am. Rep. 266 (1884).

[1] Gould v. Edison Electric Co., 29 N. Y. Misc. 241, 60 N. Y. Supp. 559 (1899).

[2] Gardner v. Providence Telephone Co., 23 R. I. 312, 50 Atl. 1014, 55 L. R. A. 113 (1901).

[3] Bartlett Western Union Telegraph Co., 62 Me. 209, 16 Am. Rep. 471 (1873).

[4] Wilkes-Barre v. Spring Brook Water Co., 4 Lack. Leg. News (Pa.), 367 (1899).

[5] See Moore v. Champlain Electric Co., 88 N. Y. App. Div. 289, 85 N. Y. Supp. 37 (1903).

not open to a company to make concessions to one customer who is asking a cheaper service without at the same time giving other customers the right to get the lower rate by conforming with the conditions under which it is offered. Thus in one recent successful prosecution by the government for giving or taking a rebate the gravamen of the charge was not that the allowance of $1.00 per car for the terminal facilities furnished by the guilty shipper was improper in itself, but that the railroad had not properly announced such allowances in its published schedules.[1] And if it be granted that a lower rate may be made for fuel gas than for illuminating gas, any householder who wants only fuel gas can insist that he gets the same rate as those who also use gas for illumination.[2]

Topic B. Service in More Convenient Units

§ 1348. Shipment in carloads.

The most obvious application of the principles under discussion is the relatively lower rate almost universally quoted for car load lots as compared with less than car load. Substantial reasons exist for making the rate lower per barrel in car load lots than in less than car load quantities. The cost of service is very considerably less in the case of shipments in car load lots than in less than car load quantities.[3] The shipment by the car load goes direct to destination. It is loaded by the shipper and is unloaded by the consignee. The freight in it does not stop at the way stations to be handled in parcels to dif-

[1] United States v. Chicago & A. Ry. Co., 148 Fed. 646 (1906).

[2] State v. New Orleans Gas Co., 108 La. 67, 32 So. 179 (1902).

[3] However, this concession to shippers of goods in car load lots need not be made by a railroad company; apparently if it chooses not to schedule a reduced car load rate shippers cannot complain. Railroad Commrs. v. Weld, 96 Tex. 394, 73 S. W. 529 (1902).

ferent consignees along the line. Only one bill of lading is made. It requires but one entry upon the waybill. The time occupied in transporting it to destination is far less than in the case of a shipment in less than car load quantities. There is but one collection of charges for freight. Where the shipment is made in less than car load quantities a separate receipt or bill of lading has to be given to every shipper for his parcel. A separate entry of every item has to be made on the way bill. The shipment is by a local freight train which stops at every station for which there is a package of freight. The freight has to be taken out in parcels and delivered at each of these stations. The freight is loaded and unloaded by the railroad company. There are as many collections of charges for freight as there are different parcels. The time occupied in transporting it is usually from two to three times as long as in the case of a car load shipment—according to distance. It occupies a whole car, and for the vacant space in that car the company is receiving no compensation. Altogether the economies of handling freight in car load lots are apparent. A rate per 100 pounds in less than car load lots may well be 100 per cent greater than the rate upon car load lots and is not unreasonable.[1]

§ 1349. Shipments made in bulk.

That there are often certain advantages to the carrier in shipments in bulk in car lots over shipments in packages in car lots cannot be denied. It is upon this basis that it is cheaper to handle the traffic that the railroads have felt justified in giving a lower rate per ton mile to those who ship oil in bulk in tank cars in comparison

---

[1] If, however, car load rates are granted all shippers may insist upon having them upon the same terms. New York, T. & M. R. R. Co. v. Gallaher, 79 Tex. 685, 15 S. W. 694 (1891).

with those who ship oil in barrels in car lots. It is urged in behalf of the right of the railroads to make such differences in the rates that the different circumstances and conditions about these two modes of carrying oil fully justify these differences in the rates, viz.: the carrier furnishes the car for transporting the barrel oil, while the shipper usually supplies car and tank for carriage of tank oil, and that at a less charge for mileage than actual cost of maintenance of the car; injury to the cars used for barrel oil unfitting them for general use; larger return-empty haul on box cars used for barrel oil than on tank cars; greater risk of such goods in transit and in depot, as well as greater danger to other freights in same train and in same depot in the case of barrel oil over that of tank oil, greater cost of service in loading and unloading barrel oil to and from the cars by the carrier, when tank oil is invariably loaded and unloaded by the shipper; inability of carrier to secure insurance on cars used for transporting barreled oil, while shipper of tank oil furnishes the car and assumes all risk. Such differences in the cost of the service should, it would seem, justify a carrier in making reasonable differences in its rates.

§ 1350. Comparison of bulk and package rates.

So different are the conditions under which freight is carried in packages and in bulk that it is not proper to institute comparisons as to particular factors connected with each. As the United States Supreme Court [1] said in a recent case: "Because circumstances existed which prevented the economical use of the tank car by plaintiffs (no demand being made for the use of a tank car) is no ground for finding discrimination in the charge for the weight of the barrel package (such charge being in itself

[1] Pennsylvania Refining Co. v. Western N. Y. & P. R. R. Co., 208   U. S. 208, 52 L. ed. 456, 28 Sup. Ct. 268 (1908).

not an unreasonable one), while none is made for the tank containing the oil." If, however, the railroad fails to provide tank cars for the use of its shippers it would be unfair discrimination to charge shippers of oil in packages for the additional weight. As the Supreme Court of Ohio [1] said in the leading case on this point: "It must either provide tank cars for all of its customers alike, or give such rates of freight in barrel packages by the car load, as will place its customers using that method on an equal footing with its customers adopting the other method.

§ 1351. Shipments in train loads.

It is urged with considerable force that a railroad is justified under the rules that are now under discussion in giving a lower rate for a train load consigned from one shipping point to one point of delivery, since it cannot be denied that there is at least a slight difference in the cost of handling the traffic in train loads. But such concessions are dangerous, as it would tend to concentrate the business of the country into very few hands if a lower rate could be given to the great operator who could ship in train lots. At all events the Interstate Commerce Commission is set against such special rates for train loads. In Paine Bros. & Co. v. Lehigh Valley Railroad,[2] it expressed itself thus: "We perceive no sufficient reason for different rates on carload than on cargo or train load shipments, whether the grain is carried for export or for domestic use. The principle involved in such a distinction violates the rule of equality and tends to defeat its just and wholesome purpose. That purpose is not fully accomplished if one scale of charges is applied to cargo

---

[1] State v. Cincinnati, N. O. & T.
P. R. R. Co., 47 Oh. St. 130, 23
N. E. 928 (1890).

[2] 7 Int. Comm. Rep. 218 (1897).

shipments and a higher rate is imposed for single carloads, even though all cargo shippers pay the same and all carload shippers are charged alike." But as there is a real though a slight difference in the cost of service there is no reason why a fair concession from the car load rate should not be made if the regulating authority were not so overborne by the fear of discrimination as to ignore it.[1]

§ 1352. Regular shipments in large units.

In some English cases concessions are permitted to shippers who agree to make regular shipments in large units. The leading case for this is Nicholson v. Great Western Railway Company.[2] There the court said that in considering the question of undue preference the fair interest of the railroad company ought to be taken into account; that the preference or prejudice, referred to by the statute, must be undue or unreasonable to be within the prohibition. Because it appeared that the cost of carrying coal in fully loaded trains, regularly furnished at the rate of seven trains per week, was less per ton to the railway company than coal delivered in the usual way, and at irregular intervals, and in unequal quantities, in connection with the coal company's undertaking to ship annually coal enough over defendant's road, for at least a distance of 100 miles, to produce a gross revenue to the railroad of £40,000, the court held that the discrimination complained of in the case was neither undue nor unreasonable, and therefore denied the application.[3]

§ 1353. Units in passenger service.

It has already been indicated that the unit principle is applicable to passenger service. Thus a lower rate for a limited ticket than for an unlimited ticket may be justi-

[1] But see Nicholson v. Great Western R. R. Co., 5 C. B. (N. S.) 366 (1858).

[2] 5 C. B. (N. S.) 366 (1858).

[3] But a difference in rates between an agreement to ship for

fied, since there will be more bother if the transportation is broken into several separate services by stop-overs instead of being taken as a whole.[1] A lower rate may be made to those who buy their tickets in lots instead of for the single trip, such as strip tickets and mileage tickets. And it has been held that a railroad may make a lower rate than twenty fares to twenty people traveling together under one transportation contract.[2] But another case probably states a general principle in its pertinent dictum that a railroad is not obliged to sell commutation tickets if it chooses not to; but if it does, any traveler may demand it.[3] Here again the necessity for establishing separate units is not sufficiently plain to imperatively demand recognition; if not, indeed, distinctly considerable, a company is not irrational which ignores it. Moreover, it seems to be well established that if the regulating authority attempts to order the issuance of mileages, for example, its interference will be held to be outrageously vexatious.[4]

§ 1354. Operating units in supplying service.

Chief attention has been given thus far in this topic to common carriage, because it is in this field that the law justifying various rates for various units has been worked out. It will have been noticed that even here the permission to make such different rates is grudgingly given by modern courts. Only if the operating cost in performing the service is plainly different can a different rate be made

thirty years and another for fourteen years was held an undue preference. Holland v. Festiniog Ry. Co., 2 Nev. & Mac. 278 (1876).

[1] Edson v. So. Pacific Ry. Co., 144 Cal. 182, 77 Pac. 894 (1904).

[2] Interstate Commerce Commission v. Baltimore & O. R. R. Co., 145 U. S. 263, 36 L. ed. 699, 12 Sup. Ct. 844 (1892).

[3] State ex rel. v. Delaware, L. & W. Ry. Co., 48 N. J. L. 55, 2 Atl. 803 (1887).

[4] Lake Shore & M. S. Ry. Co. v. Smith, 173 U. S. 684, 43 L. ed. 858, 19 Sup. Ct. 565 (1898).

nowadays. A shipper of a carload to be sure gets a lower rate than the shipper of a package; but one who ships two car loads simultaneously to the same consignee gets no lower rate. If this attitude is maintained in other branches of public service, it is difficult to see how a progressive scale of lower rates for large consumers of water for example can be justified. A minimum rate, as has been seen, doubtless may be justified, unless some explicit legislation stands in the way—because of the excessively large cost of such service in its earliest stages.[1] But the difference in cost of supplying a larger amount as compared with a smaller amount at any later stage, although it is not impossible to estimate it, perhaps, is certainly not so great as to imperatively demand recognition to prevent injustice to the larger taker. The authorities on this matter as has been seen already are somewhat conflicting,[1] but they may be reconciled if one wishes to

[1] *Alabama.*—In Montgomery Light & P. Co. v. Watts (Ala.), 51 So. 726 (1909), it was held that where the franchise limitation upon the gas company was clear it could not make a minimum rate.

California.—In Sheward v. Citizens' Water Co., 90 Cal. 635, 27 Pac. 4, 439 (1891), the court went so far as to justify a fixed charge on water bills for measured service as meter rent.

Kentucky.—In Louisville Gas Co. v. Dulaney, 100 Ky. 405, 38 S. W. 703, 36 L. R. A. 125 (1897), the court while admitting the propriety of minimum charges for gas supplied held the company in question was precluded by its charter from imposing them.

Missouri.—In State ex rel. v. Sedalia Gaslight Co., 34 Mo. App. 501 (1889), the court held that a

minimum charge for gas supplied was entirely justified on every ground.

[2] *Michigan.*—In Boerth v. Detroit City Gas Co., 152 Mich. 654, 116 N. W. 628, 18 L. R. A. (N. S.) 1197 (1908), it was held that a gas company might grant a lower rate to persons consuming large quantities for different purposes.

Missouri.—In St. Louis Brewing Assn. v. St. Louis, 140 Mo. 419, 37 S. W. 525, 41 S. W. 911 (1897), it was held a water company could not only make a lower rate to manufacturers than to other consumers but also lower rates to large manufacturers than to small; but it was intimated that there was no obligation to make such concessions.

New York.—In Silkman v. Yonkers Water Commissioners, 152 N. Y. 327, 46 N. E. 612, (1897), the

do so by recognizing that this problem is so close that the adoption of a graded schedule by a supply company is not irrational, but then again neither is the fixing of a flat rate.

§ 1355. Such reductions apparently discriminatory.

Naturally the advantage to the company if it may induce larger purchases is obvious; and indeed the theoretical advantage to all concerned by a general decrease in cost resulting therefrom may be admitted. But whether the decisions permitting lower rates for large consumption shall stand depends upon whether the general law against all discrimination engulfs everything. It is not enough to say that the same law against discrimination is not required in the supply services as in the transportation services; because the evil of favoring one competitor against another is not present. In the first place that factor is by no means absent; rival laundries, one larger, the other smaller, need water supply, for example. In the second place the law against discrimination is by no means confined to discrimination between competitors, giving a pass to a friend traveling for pleasure is forbidden as much as giving a lower rate to one iron founder which is refused to another.

Topic C. Facilities Furnished by Customers

§ 1356. Terminal facilities furnished by shippers.

By an important application of these general principles it is held permissible for a railroad to make a lower rate

court permitted the granting of lower rates per hundred cubic feet of water to those who take larger amounts; the court saying of this sort of schedule: "It will be found in contracts and charges relating to electric lights, gas, private water companies and the like, and is a business principle of general application.

Pennsylvania.—In Penn. Iron Co. v. Lancaster, 17 Lanc. L. Rev. 161 (1900), the court emphasized the point that water company need not make such gradations unless it chose.

to a shipper who furnishes a part of the facilities which the carrier must otherwise provide in order to serve him. One of the leading cases in establishing this particular rule is undoubtedly Root v. Long Island Railroad,[1] where a lower rate was given to a shipper who had built a pocket from which he loaded himself the cars in which he shipped. The court decided that there was no public policy opposed to the enforcement of this contract. "Had this provision stood alone, unqualified by other provisions, without the circumstances under which it was executed explaining the necessity therefor" said Mr. Justice Haight: "We should be inclined to the opinion that it did provide for an unjust discrimination; but, upon referring to the contract, we see that the rebate was agreed to be paid in consideration for the dock and coal pocket which was to be constructed upon the defendant's premises at an expense of $17,000, in part for the use and convenience of the defendant. Quintard was to load all the cars with the coal that was to be transported. It was understood that a large quantity of coal was to be shipped over defendant's line, thus increasing the business and income of the company. The facilities which Quintard was to provide for the loading of the coal, his services in loading the cars, the large quantities which he was to ship, in connection with the large sums of money that he had expended in the erection of the dock, in part for the use and accommodation of the defendant, are facts which tend to explain the provisions of the contract complained of, and render it a question of fact for the determination of the trial court as to whether or not the rebate, under the circumstances of this case, amounted to an unjust discrimination, to the injury and prejudice of others. Therefore, in this case, the question is one of fact, and not of law; and, inas-

[1] 114 N. Y. 330, 21 N. E. 403, 11   Am. St. Rep. 643, 4 L. R. A. 33
(1889).

much as the discrimination has not been found to be unjust or unreasonable, the judgment cannot be disturbed." [1]

§ 1357. Transportation expenses paid by shipper.

Whatever is done by the shipper which directly reduces to the railroad company the cost of serving him may be allowed for in the rate made to him without causing discrimination. One of the plainest cases of this sort before the Interstate Commerce Commission is Castle v. Baltimore & Ohio Railroad Company,[2] where complainant alleged that defendant had unjustly discriminated in rates and facilities for the transportation of sand against him and in favor of his competitors. Discussing the essential facts, the Commission said: "The only remaining point, and by far the most important one raised by this issue, is that involved in the alleged discriminations in favor of Brown, the complainant's competitor at Dock Siding. Brown, it appears, owned and at times leased other cars and equipment, paid the trainmen, conductors, and necessary telegraph operators, and relieved the defendant from all liability from either loss or damage to rolling stock or injury to employees; in consideration of which the defendant charged him for track service only. The complainant owned neither cars nor equipment, and when shipping in the defendant's cars was charged the published rate." [3]

§ 1358. Rental paid for shipper's cars.

If the shipper provides his own cars the railroad, it would seem clear, may allow him a reduction in his freight

---

[1] It is generally agreed at common law that a reduction may be made to such shippers as furnish a part of the facilities necessary to serve them. See Savitz v. Ohio & M. Ry., 150 Ill. 208, 27 N. E. 235, 27 L. R. A. 626 (1894), affirming 49 Ill. App. 315 (1892); Scofield v. Lake Shore & M. S. R. R., 43 Ohio St. 571, 3 N. E. 907, 54 Am. Rep. 846 (1885).

[2] 8 Int. Comm. Rep. 333 (1899).

[3] See Chicago & A. R. R. Co. v. Chicago V. & W. Coal Co., 79 Ill. 121 (1875), where a shipper furnishing the rolling stock was given an unusual concession from regular rates.

rate, equal to the rental value of his cars. It is properly the business of the railway companies, to be sure, to supply cars for their customers; but if they stand ready to do this, they may, nevertheless, at their option make an allowance to the shipper who furnishes his own cars, which is not disproportionate to the reduced cost of serving him. Even in the extreme case of State v. Cincinnati, New Orleans & Texas Pacific Railroad Company,[1] which is most opposed to special arrangements of this sort, this is admitted. "No doubt, a shipper who owns cars may be paid a reasonable compensation for their use, so that the compensation is not made a cover for discriminating rates, or other advantages to such owner as a shipper." [2]

§ 1359. Allowances for facilities closely scrutinized.

It must be realized, however, that a good deal of the law that has just been stated is obsolescent. With the rigorous enforcement of the law against all discrimination in late years, such arrangements as have been just described are being condemned, if not as virtual discrimination at least as a cover for discrimination. At all events, the whole facts will be gone into to discover whether too advantageous terms are being obtained. Thus in a recent case it was discovered that a car company was getting so much for the use of its cars that the reduction was being made the basis for reduced rates to those who shipped in those cars.[3] And in another recent case not charging certain shippers demurrage for cars upon an apparently private siding found to be public while others paid demurrage in regular yards was held plain discrimination.[4] However, the railroads are still allowed to make

[1] 47 Ohio St. 130, 23 N. E. 928 (1890).

[2] See also Brundred v. Rice, 49 Ohio St. 640, 32 N. E. 169, 34 Am. St. Rep. 589 (1892).

[3] Interstate Commerce Commission v. Reichman, 145 Fed. 235 (1905).

[4] Ohio Coal Co. v. Whitcomb, 123 Fed. 359 (1903).

arrangements with customers furnishing their own facilities. Some difficulty is inseparable from this situation, but probably not enough to justify the radical remedy of forbidding such arrangements altogether. Those who get allowances which are not scheduled will, however, fall foul of the modern statutes against discriminations, even if the allowance made is proper enough in itself.[1] Moreover, when the arrangement is in its nature an exclusive one of which other patrons cannot take advantage it would generally be condemned.[2]

§ 1360. Allowances for facilities still permissible.

It would, however, be outrageous if there was no way to give a proper allowance to shippers who employ their own property and devote their own labor to some of the work that the carrier must otherwise do for them. In the latest Federal case [3] this is vehemently insisted upon in setting aside a ruling of the Interstate Commerce Commission that no allowance should be made elevator men who supply their own grain from their own elevators. "Pecuniary advantages derived by shippers from the ownership or use of such facilities of trade are attributable to that ownership, and not to the transportation of the articles shipped, and the consideration and regulation of these advantages are without the scope of the commission's power. The truth is that trade advantages of this nature do not condition the questions of reasonableness of rates, or rebates, or of discrimination. The shipper who owns warehouses, tipples, spur tracks, cars, mills, and by their use derives greater profit from the dealing

---

[1] Thus an allowance for terminal facilities which is not scheduled cannot be properly paid. Chicago & A. Ry. Co. v. United States (C. C. A.), 156 Fed. 558 (1907).

[2] See Chesapeake & O. Ry. Co. v. Standard Lumber Co., 174 Fed. 107 (1910), where an allowance of 10% off all freight bills was allowed a shipper who had built a hoist to load his ties.

[3] Peavey & Co. v. Union Pac. R. Co., 176 Fed. 409 (1910).

in the articles which he ships over a railroad, is entitled to the same rate of charge for transportation and the same reasonable compensation for transportation services which he renders that the shipper who owns less or no such trade facilities and derived less profit is entitled to." [1]

Topic D. Independent Consideration for Reductions

§ 1361. When consideration is given for reduction.

Abstractly it is not discrimination if one shipper pays his freight rate in money and another pays the same rate, partly in money and partly in services. There was once no doubts expressed about the propriety of such an arrangement and this has been permitted in several cases, for example in Rothschild v. Wabash Railroad Company [2] where a certain reduction was allowed to certain shippers who acted as "eveners" in distributing the traffic to several railways. In permitting these facts to be shown in justification, Judge Lewis said: "Suppose a railway company, instead of paying its conductor a salary, should choose to compensate his services by a percentage of the receipts from passengers traveling on his train. Suppose the conductor to purchase tickets at regular rates, for the use of members of his family, as passengers, on his train. He claims and receives his percentage on such tickets, as upon all others. Would it not be strangely absurd to allege that, by reason of this percentage, there is an unjust discrimination in the conductor's favor, reducing the cost of transportation to him, below what others are compelled to pay for the same facilities? The principle involved would be exactly the same that appears in the present case." [3]

[1] Citing Harp v. Choctaw, O. & G. Ry. Co., 125 Fed. 445, 61 C. C. A. 405 (1903).

[2] 92 Mo. 91, 4 S. W. 418 (1887).

See further Sultan Ry. & T. Co. v. Gt. Northern Ry. Co. (Wash.), 109 Pac. 320, 1020 (1910).

[3] There are other cases in which

§ 1362. Indefinite considerations considered dangerous.

It may be conceded that it does not make any difference in what way the freight rate is paid, so that it appears plainly that the full rate is paid. But if some indefinite consideration on which no estimate can accurately be made to ascertain the amount of the charge is alleged, it will be dangerous to permit that to pass. Thus in the important case of Goodridge v. Union Pacific Railway Company,[1] the complainant demanded a refund of over-charges by reason of discrimination against him by giving a lower rate to the Marshall Coal Mining Company. The defendant railroad as part of its defense brought out that it was formerly liable to the Marshall Company to a suit for damages for an alleged trespass and to settle this suit it entered into this contract for giving this company these lower rates. But Judge Hallet said that to allow this would endanger the law forbidding discrimination. "This law cannot be controlled or defeated by any agreement between the railroad company and the favored shipper. It is true that when the consideration paid for reduced rates by the favored shipper is obviously equal to the discount allowed him, the law does not apply. Whenever that fact appears, since it matters not in what form the shipper pays the usual rates, the alleged discrimination disappears, and the contract is no longer obnoxious to the law. If, to illustrate, the damages due from the Denver & Western Company had been liquidated,[2] and the

various considerations inuring to the benefit of the carrier have been permitted to be shown. Thus that other business is thereby secured was once thought enough. See Johnson v. Pensacola & P. R. R. Co., 16 Fla. 623, 26 Am. Rep. 731 (1878).

[1] 73 Fed. 182 (1889), affirmed in 149 U. S. 680, 37 L. ed. 986, 13 Sup. Ct. 970 (1893). See further State v. Union Pacific R. R. Co. (Neb.), 126 N. W. 859 (1910).

Note that on Feb. 20, 1911, the Supreme Court of the United States held that advertisements could not be set off against transportation.

[2] The distinction made in the principal case above will reconcile two Federal cases of recent instance.

agreement was to carry a certain quantity of coal for the amount so fixed, the question would be different. As it stands, the agreement is to give to the Marshall Company a reduced rate for certain considerations which defendant says are sufficient to make up the discount from the schedule rate; and as to that matter, the fact cannot be ascertained from the contract or otherwise. So understood it is clear that the contract affords no protection to defendant for the discrimination in rates to which plaintiffs and other shippers of coal over defendant's road are subjected."

§ 1363. Reductions for services rendered.

Similarly there were formerly no doubts that persons who had rendered valuable services to a railroad company could be given transportation free or at reduced rates. Thus employees of the company itself may be given passes as part of their wages.[1] In one of the earlier cases it will be remembered the services of certain shippers as "eveners" in distributing traffic was held to be a fair consideration for a fixed percentage of reduction in their freight rates.[2] But the progress of the law may be shown by the latest cases in which it is held that passes issued for indefinite services are too likely to be in fact discrimination against those who pay the regular rates for their transportation. Thus a pass issued to a physician who contracts to per-

In one it was held that when a liquidated sum is owed a shipper by a carrier, the carrier can pay it off at regular rates. Interstate Comm. Comm. v. Cheaspeake & O. R. Co., 128 Fed. 59 (1904). In the other it was held to be no defense in a prosecution of a railroad company for granting concessions to a shipper from its published rates, in violation of the Elkins Act, that such con-cessions were granted in compromise of unliquidated claims against the company for loss of property in transit. United States v. Atchison, T. & S. F. Ry. Co., 163 Fed. 11 (1907).

[1] Dempsey v. New York C. & H. R. R. Co., 146 N. Y. 290, 40 N. E. 867 (1894).

[2] Rothschild v. Wabash R. R. Co., 92 Mo. 91, 4 S. W. 418 (1887).

form certain service for a railroad company is in contemplation of law, a free pass, if the services do not require a major portion of the physician's time.[1] So a pass issued to the proprietor of a newspaper in return for publicity of various sorts is within the prohibition of the stringent clauses against discrimination in recent statutes.[2] And indeed it would seem to be a necessary holding under these recent statutes directed against discrimination that money value should be the only standard of compensation receivable, otherwise it will be impossible to insure equal rates to all.

§ 1364. Continuing obligations for past consideration.

It was once common to give as consideration in various contracts made by the railroads promises to give free transportation. Thus it was not uncommon in buying land for the railroad to agree to transport free for life the grantors and sometimes their families also. The courts once had no hesitation in supporting such contracts both in favor of the promisee and of the beneficiary.[3] In late years the question has come up whether the passage of legislation against free transportation applies to this situation. Even in the present rage against discrimination it is felt that such transportation for executed consideration is a vested right which should not be destroyed.[4] But the latest case seems to be so radical as to ignore this right.

[1] State v. Martyn, 82 Neb. 225, 117 N. W. 719, 23 N. L. R. A. (N. S.) 217 (1908).

[2] McNeill v. Durham & C. R. R. Co., 132 N. C. 510, 44 S. E. 34 (1903); State v. Union Pacific Ry. Co. (Neb.), 126 N. W. 859 (1910), *accord.*

[3] *Minnesota.*—Grimes v. Minneapolis, L. & M. Ry. Co., 37 Minn. 66, 33 N. W. 34 (1887).

Pennsylvania.—Erie & P. Ry. Co. v. Douthet, 88 Pa. St. 245, 32 Am. Rep. 45 (1878).

[4] *United States.*—M o t t l e y v. Louisville & N. R. R. Co., 150 Fed. 406 (1907), overruled by the U. S. Supreme Ct. Feb. 20, 1911.

Kansas.—In re Curry v. Kansas C. & P. R. Co., 58 Kan. 6, 48 Pac. 579 (1897).

§ 1365. Concessions to those with whom it deals.

The dangers inherent in any permission to the common carrier to make different rates to different classes of customers requiring the same service is most apparent in a case like Louisville, Evansville & St. Louis Consolidated Railroad Company v. Wilson.[1] In that case it appeared that the railroad made high rates on cross-ties to all except one Dickason, with whom it entered into a contract giving him low rates in return for his agreement to sell it the ties it should wish at a specified price. When this scheme was brought before the court for examination in a suit by a shipper who had suffered by this discrimination, it appeared that while he was paying $24 per car from one point to another, this Dickason was paying only $14 per car for the same transportation. The highest court sustained the instructions given in behalf of the plaintiff: "If the contract was of such a character as to destroy the business of the appellees by reason of the discrimination in favor of Dickason, and thus enable Dickason to acquire a monopoly of the business of purchasing and shipping cross-ties on appellant's road, the discrimination was unjust, without regard to the consideration upon which it was based." [2]

§ 1366. Rates adopted to foster its interests.

Despite any policy which the carrier may have in mind it must be evident that all patrons of the road have a right to adequate service at fair rates. Every producer has a right to sell his product as he pleases in the best market available, and rates must not be adopted with the idea of compelling the product to be disposed of in a way

[1] 132 Ind. 517, 32 N. E. 311 (1892); American Tie & T. Co., Ltd., v. Kansas City So. Ry. Co., 175 Fed. 28 (1909), *accord.*

[2] See, to the same effect, Cedar Lumber Products Case, 3 Can. Ry. Cas. 312 (1903), and Paxton Tie Co. v. Detroit So. Ry. Co., 10 I. C. C. Rep. 422 (1905).

desired by the carrier.[1] In one extreme case of this sort
the railroad company refused to furnish cars for a coal
miner who would not sell his coal to a coal company which
was allied with the railroad.[2] In granting a mandamus in
that case Mr. Justice Dean said: "It is a refusal to carry
his coal because he will not sell it at a low price to the president's coal company. As the court below, in substance,
says, it was iniquitous. It, in effect, if kept up, would com-
pletely destroy his plant, with the consequent loss of his
invested capital; and even if now his wrong is, to some
extent, remedied, he has lost months of active business."

[1] See cases discussed in last paragraph.
[2] Loraine v. Pittsburg, J. E. & E.

R. R., 205 Pa. St. 132, 54 Atl. 580,
61 L. R. A. 502 (1903).

CHAPTER XL

RELATIVE DISCRIMINATION

§ 1370. Essential illegality of relative discrimination.

§ 1370. Essential illegality of relative discrimination.

It must now be apparent that the fundamental ques-

[1205]

tion under discussion is how far public duty must necessarily deprive those who conduct public employments from basing their business policies upon the elementary principle of the law of increasing returns. That net returns tend to increase with the volume of business in a normal case of an industrial enterprise is obvious; and the question is whether a public service company is to be permitted without hindrance to shape all things so as to hold its present business and to add to it. Some managers of public service companies assert this boldly, and a few say frankly, for example, that they base their classifications and their rates upon what the traffic will bear in view of the situation of the customer making high charges against business from which high rates can be got, conceding low rates in order to get competitive business which could not otherwise be obtained. Of course this consideration has some place in every philosophy of rate making, but it is submitted that it is a dangerous principle which may often operate to the disadvantage of the public. For example, if railway managers are left practically unrestrained by law, it is sufficiently plain that they will maintain a high schedule of rates between localities where they have control of the situation and for valuable goods which will bear high rates, while at the same time making disproportionate concessions from this standard to get business at competitive points or to induce the movement of low grade commodities. The modern law seems to be that while in private business nothing need be considered except the law of decreasing cost, in public business there is the law against discrimination to be reckoned with.

Topic A. Discrimination Between Localities Served

§ 1371. Unjust rates between localities.

At common law the public servant deals with the individual; except under a statute a community as such cannot complain of a discrimination against its inhabitants. Thus at common law it is the shipper who complains of a disproportionate rate, not the locality which complains of discrimination. Whatever may be the present law as to the right of a customer in one locality to complain that his rates are disproportionally high as compared with those charged other customers of the company on other localities, it is certain that such discrimination is in itself evidence that the higher charge is an unreasonable one. Thus, whenever a rate between two points is attacked by an individual shipper as unreasonable in itself, as evidence in support of the complaint he may show that rates are lower for a similar haul between other points.[1] But except so far as it has evidentiary bearing on the reasonableness of the rate in question, rates to and from other points were formerly not material.[2] This rate complained of may be so outrageously disproportionate that nothing can justify it.[3] But if a rational defense can be made for higher rate the courts have been inclined to permit it to stand.[4]

§ 1372. Evidence of disproportionate charging.

Such comparisons have always had an evidentiary bearing on the reasonableness of the rate complained of, even though it was thought that the showing that the rates to other places were disproportionate was not material at common law. How much weight shall be given to such evidence must, of course, depend on the facts of each case. In the Naval Stores case the Federal court in finding the rates unjust gave considerable weight to rates charged for

---

[1] State v. Minneapolis & St. L. Ry. Co., 80 Minn. 191, 83 N. W. 60 (1900).

[2] Interstate Comm. Comm. v. Louisville & N. R. R. Co., 73 Fed. 409 (1896).

[3] Tift v. Southern Ry. Co., 138 Fed. 753 (1905).

[4] Interstate Comm. Comm. v. Western & A. R. R. Co., 93 Fed. 38 (1899).

similar hauls.[1] And in the East Tennessee Railroad case
the Federal judge went so far as to hold that a less rate
for a longer haul tended to prove the higher rate unreasonable.[2] On the other hand in the Danville case[3] the Federal judge, after hearing evidence as to the rates charged
between various other localities in the South, felt that the
evidence presented did not show that the rates complained
of were improper. And in the Hampton case[4] the Federal
court held that there was not evidence enough that the
rates were unreasonable, notwithstanding that they compared somewhat unfavorably with other rates.

§ 1373. Railroad rates not upon a mileage basis.

Rate regulation upon legal principles, basing the rate
charged ultimately upon the cost of the service, will not
in the case of railroads, as many fear, mean an immediate
recourse to a mileage basis. The chief reason that it can
never come to that basis altogether is that mere mileage,
as all authorities recognize, never measures the cost of the
service. It is fundamental that a long haul is relatively
cheaper per ton than a short haul.[5] This is all the clearer

---

[1] Interstate Comm. Comm. v.
Louisville & N. Ry. Co., 118 Fed.
613 (1902).

[2] Interstate Comm. Comm. v.
East Tennessee, V. & G. Ry. Co., 85
Fed. 107 (1898).

[3] Interstate Comm. Comm. v.
Southern Ry. Co., 117 Fed. 741
(1902).

[4] Interstate Comm. Comm. v.
Nashville, C. & St. L. Ry. Co., 120
Fed. 934 (1903).

[5] In the Federal courts particularly there have never been any
doubts that this rule justified the
making of a lower rate per ton-mile
for a longer haul. See among many

others: Union Pacific Ry. Co. v.
United States, 117 U. S. 355, 29 L.
ed. 920, 6 Sup. Ct. 772 (1886); East
Tennessee, V. & G. Ry. Co. v. Inter-
state Comm. Comm., 181 U. S. 1, 45
L. ed. 719, 21 Sup. Ct. 516 (1901);
Tozer v. United States, 52 Fed. 917
(1890); Augusta S. R. Co. v.
Wrightsville & T. R. Co., 74 Fed.
522 (1896); Northern Pacific Ry.
Co. v. Keyes, 91 Fed. 47 (1899);
Southern Ry. Co. v. St. Louis, H. &
G. Co., 156 Fed. 728 (1906); St.
Louis & S. F. Ry. v. Hadley, 168
Fed. 317 (1909); Missouri, K. & T.
Ry. Co. v. Love, 177 Fed. 493
(1910).

if the shorter haul has unusual physical obstacles making it actually more expensive; it will then justify a lower rate for a longer haul.[1] Moreover the less expensive terminals may make the longer route the cheaper, so that sometimes business may be better handled if great volumes of low grade freights are diverted from congested points by differential rates. It is also often justifiable to group together various stations for convenience in making rates. These and many other considerations may be set aside the mere mileage involved. But undoubtedly rate regulation in the future will pay more attention to operating cost and mileage tables than in the past. Indeed what in the long run can prove to be a fundamental basis except the natural justice of dealing squarely with real conditions? The regulation of rates will henceforth inevitably tend to be determined by inquiry into costs.

§ 1374. Various systems of making distance rates.

In practice it must be admitted rates have been made by the railroads with but little reference to mileage. There are four principal methods of making freight rates: (1) mileage rates, never exactly followed in practice; (2) group rates, the same rate being made to all points within a certain zone; (3) basing points to which through rates are made, the local rates therefrom being added to get rates for tributary territory; (4) competitive rates, the rate to the competitive point plus the local rate. Each has its advantages and each is open to some objections. The remote parts of the country object to a mileage basis. The blanket rate finds objectors where an important point is

---

[1] The possibility that the actual cost of the shorter transportation between certain points may be greater than that of a longer transportation between other points is made much of in the English cases. See among many others: Bellsdyke Coal Co. v. North British Ry. Co., 2 Ry. & C. Tr. Cas. 105 (1875); Coal Co. v. Caledonia Ry. Co., 2 Ry. & C. Tr. Cas. 39 (1874).

ambitious to supply the surrounding territory. The basing point system arouses friction, in that rival center points demand like privileges. And no community which suffers by the competitive rate system can ever see anything but extortion in it.

§ 1375. Long and short haul.

The charge by a carrier of a less rate between two points than is charged for carriage from the same initial point to an intermediate point on the same route seems at first sight indefensible upon any legal basis. Nevertheless such rates have always been common in every railroad schedule and are still vigorously defended. Such discrimination flourished practically without any real check during the period when no rule against any discrimination was recognized. In the interstate commerce legislation of 1887 there were clauses against all kinds of discriminatory rates, specifying in a separate clause charging more for a short haul than for a long haul which included it. There is similar legislation, including the same specific clause, in many of the states as well. And consequently there is a large body of judicial construction of these prohibitions both general and special, which although really germane enough, it would be really beyond the scope of this work to discuss in the detail it demands.

§ 1376. The similar circumstances proviso.

This long and short haul clause in the Interstate Commerce Act expressly provided that exceptions to it must be by special dispensation from the commission.[1] But

---

[1] The philosophy of the act as expressed by Judge Shiras in Van Patten v. Chicago, M. & St. P. Ry., was that competition would reduce the rates to a fair amount at all competitive points, and that the fourth section would then keep the rates at noncompetitive points down to the level of the competitive rates. The courts, however, finally decided in view of the limitation of the section to cases where the conditions were substantially similar that competition with other rail-

tucked away in the section was the vague phrase, "under substantially similar circumstances," which proved its destruction. At first there was some disposition to enforce the act according to its obvious reading, and the Interstate Commerce Commission began to grant dispensations from its operation on petition of the railroad in proper cases. But it was finally held that wherever there was competition at the distant points, the conditions were dissimilar.[1] As a result of this the railroads were then freed from the operation of this particular clause in every case where there is any business reason why they should wish to act in violation of it. In the latest Federal legislation the power to prevent such discrimination is apparently restored to the commission. It is to be hoped that when the time comes for judicial action upon this new legislation, it will not be construed away.

§ 1377. Competition as a justification for disproportion.

It is now well settled in the Federal courts that competition with other carriers at a certain point justifies a lower rate at that point than at neighboring noncompetitive points.[2] But this is not admitted by a majority of the

roads would justify a lower rate for the longer haul, and as practically all cases of the sort before the passage of the act had been due to the competition of other railways, this decision in effect qualified the whole section.

[1] The first case to decide this was Texas & P. R. R. Co. v. Interstate Comm. Comm., 162 U. S. 197, 40 L. ed. 940, 16 Sup. Ct. 6 (C. C., 1896).

[2] Cincinnati, N. O. & T. P. Ry. Co. v. Interstate Comm. Comm., 162 U. S. 184, 16 Sup. Ct. 700, 40 L. ed. 935, B. & W. 424 (1896); Inter-

state Comm. Comm. v. Alabama Midland Ry. Co., 168 U. S. 144, 18 Sup. Ct. 45, 42 L. ed. 414 (1897); Louisville & N. R. R. Co. v. Behlmer, 175 U. S. 648, 20 Sup. Ct. 209, 44 L. ed. 309 (1900); East Tennessee, V. & G. Ry. Co. v. Interstate Comm. Comm., 181 U. S. 1, 21 Sup. Ct. 516, 45 L. ed. 719 (1901); Texas & P. Ry. Co. v. Interstate Comm. Comm., 162 U. S. 197, 16 Sup. Ct. 666, 40 L. ed. 940 (1896); Interstate Comm. Comm. v. Louisville & N. R. R. Co., 190 U. S. 273, 47 L. ed. 1047, 23 Sup. Ct. 687 (1903); Interstate Comm. Comm. v. Southern

State courts by any means.[1] It even has not been applied under all circumstances by the Federal courts. Under what circumstances the Federal doctrine has been applied is indeed interesting. Water competition was at first held an excuse for a lower rate for the longer haul. Then rail competition was recognized.[2] Next potential competition over existing routes was held enough.[3] But finally the courts refused to consider the mere possibility of new routes.[4] At the same time a competitive point might lose its preference by consolidation of existing routes, thus eliminating competition, and in this way the commerce of

Ry. Co., 105 Fed. 703 (1909); Interstate Comm. Comm. v. Nashville, C. & S. L. Ry. Co., 120 Fed. 934, 57 C. C. A. 224 (1903); Interstate Comm. Comm. v. Cincinnati, P. & V. R. R. Co., 124 Fed. 624 (1903); Interstate Comm. Comm. v. Chicago Gt. W. Ry. Co., 141 Fed. 1003 (1905).

The court was much influenced by the English cases, the language of the English act being similar. See Phipps v. London & N. W. R. R. Co. (1892), 2 Q. B. 229.

[1] State cases against relative discrimination are:

Illinois.—Illinois Central Ry. Co. v. People, 121 Ill. 304, 12 N. E. 670 (1887).

Iowa.—Blair v. Sioux City & P. Ry. Co., 109 Ia. 369, 80 N. W. 673 (1899).

Kentucky.—Louisville & N. Ry. Co. v. Com., 21 Ky. L. Rep. 232, 51 S. W. 164, 1012 (1899).

Massachusetts.—See Com. v. Worcester & N. R. R. Co., 124 Mass. 561 (1878).

Missouri.—Cohn v. St. Louis, I.

M. & S. Ry. Co., 181 Mo. 30, 79 S. W. 961 (1904).

New Hampshire.—Osgood v. Concord R. R. Co., 63 N. H. 255 (1884).

Oregon.—Portland Ry., L. & P. Co. v. Railroad Commission (Oreg.), 109 Pac. 273 (1909).

But see apparently *contra:*

Alabama.—Lotspeich v. Central Ry. & B. Co., 73 Ala. 306 (1882).

Minnesota.—State ex rel. Minneapolis & St. Louis Ry. Co., 80 Minn. 191, 83 N. W. 60, 89 Am. St. Rep. 514 (1900).

South Carolina.—Ex parte Benson & Co., 18 S. C. 38, 44 Am. Rep. 564 (1882).

T e n n e s s e e.—Ragan & B. v. Aiken, 9 Lea, 609 (1882).

[2] Texas & P. R. R. v. Interstate Comm. Comm., 162 U. S. 197, 40 L. ed. 940, 16 Sup. Ct. 666 (1896).

[3] Interstate Comm. Comm. v. Alabama Midland Ry. Co., 168 U. S. 144, 42 L. ed. 414, 18 Sup. Ct. 45 (1897).

[4] East Tennessee, V. & G. Ry. v. Interstate Comm. Comm., 181 U. S. 1, 45 L. ed. 719, 21 Sup. Ct. 516 (1901).

a flourishing town might pass to a rival, because its railways were consolidated and competition thus eliminated, while its rival still enjoyed the lower competitive rate.[1]

§ 1378. Undue preference.

The general clauses in these statutes, as has been said, cover undue and unjust preference or priority between localities or communities under substantially similar circumstances and conditions. So general is this language that it has not been invoked nearly so often as the more specific long and short haul clause from which it is usually distinguished. It can, therefore, hardly be discussed except in generalities. It is not enough under the act that freight charges to a certain place should be reasonable. Rates must be relatively reasonable as compared with those to other places in the same part of the country,[2] in order to prevent unjust discrimination. This discrimination may be made in other treatment as well as transportation charges; for instance, car distribution. The prejudice is not illegal unless it is undue, and whether this is true is a question of fact.[3] In passing upon the question, it is not only legitimate, but proper, to take into consideration, besides the mere differences in charges, various ele-

[1] Interstate Comm. Comm. v. Southern Ry., 117 Fed. 741 (1902).

[2] As to what constitutes relative discrimination, see:

United States.—Chicago, R. I. & P. Ry. Co. v. Interstate Comm. Comm., 171 Fed. 680 (1909).

Iowa.—Blair v. Sioux City & P. Ry. Co., 109 Iowa, 369, 80 N. W. 673 (1899).

Nebraska.—Chicago, B. & Q. R. R. Co. v. Anderson, 72 Neb. 856, 101 N. W. 1019 (1907).

Pennsylvania.—Central Iron Co. v. Pennsylvania R. R. Co., 17 Pa. Co. Ct. 651 (1895).

[3] As to what is not relative discrimination:

United States.—Interstate Comm. Comm. v. Detroit, G. H. & M. Ry. Co., 167 U. S. 633, 42 L. ed. 306, 17 Sup. Ct. 986 (1897).

Arkansas.—Little Rock Ry. Co. v. Oppenheimer, 64 Ark. 271, 43 S. W. 150, 44 L. R. A. 353 (1897).

Kentucky.—Louisville & N. R. R. Co. v. Walker, 23 Ky. L. Rep. 453, 63 S. W. 20 (1901).

Massachusetts.—Com. v. Worcester & N. R. R. Co., 124 Mass. 561 (1878).

ments, such as the convenience of the public, the fair interest of the carrier, the relative quantities or volume of the traffic involved, the relative cost of the services and profit to the company, and the situation and circumstances of the respective customers with reference to each other. In comparing rates from two points to a common destination, distance is the first factor to consider, though it is not controlling or always the most important. As has often been stated, rates are not made on a ton-mile basis, and they cannot be expected to bear an exact proportion to the distance. If, however, the localities are neighboring ones and the conditions substantially the same it seems that distance should govern.

§ 1379. Argument for competitive rates.

As a matter of reasonableness the charge has still to be justified at common law; but this may be done in some cases. If competition is met at one point and not at another, a competitive rate is established at the former point. A railroad whose line runs through the noncompetitive to the competitive point must at the latter point either meet the competitive rate or lose all business. It must of course give up the business rather than carry at a loss, and throw upon the remaining traffic the burden of supporting the road and also of making up the loss. But the competitive rate is ordinarily slightly remunerative; it yields a net income, though less than is necessary to pay its proportion of the fixed charges. If the business is given up, all the fixed charges must be paid by the traffic at the noncompetitive points; if the competitive rate is met and business obtained, the profit from the business will go to reduce the amount of fixed charges to be paid by the noncompetitive traffic. As the competitive traffic will not pay its share of the fixed charges, the noncompetitive traffic, having more than its share of the fixed charges to bear, will necessarily pay a rate higher than the competitive rate in proportion to the distance; and it may well be obliged to pay absolutely a higher rate than the competitive rate for a longer haul.[1] Nevertheless, the rate will be lower than it would be if the railroad did not meet the competitive rate and obtain its share of the business; and therefore, being the lowest rate which the carrier can charge and obtain fair compensation, it may be said to have some reason in it.[2]

§ 1380. Competitive rates must not be ruinous.

Every one agrees that there is at least this limitation upon this permission to reduce rates to meet competition, that rates must not be brought below the special expense of doing the business. This was clearly explained by Mr. Justice White in one of the leading cases[3] in the United States Supreme Court thus: "Take a case where the carrier cannot meet the competitive rate to a given point without transporting the merchandise at less than the cost of transportation, and therefore without bringing about a deficiency, which would have to be met by increased charges upon other business. Clearly, in such a case, the engaging in such competitive traffic would both bring about an unjust discrimination and a disregard of the public interest, since a tendency towards unreasonable rates on other business would arise from the carriage of traffic at less than the cost of transportation to particular places."[4]

[1] See the opinion of Bathca, J., in Interstate Commerce Commission v. Chicago Gt. Western R. R. Co., 141 Fed. 1003 (1906).

[2] See the opinion of Collins in State ex. rel. v. Minneapolis & St. L. Ry. Co., 80 Minn. 191, 83 N. W. 60 (1900).

[3] East Tennessee, V. & G. R. R. Co. v. Interstate Comm. Comm., 181 U. S. 1, 19, 45 L. ed. 719, 21 Sup. Ct. 516 (1901).

[4] See further the general talk of the court in Interstate Commerce Commission v. Alabama Midland Ry. Co., 168 U. S. 144, 42 L. ed. 414, 18 Sup. Ct. 45 (1907).

§ 1381. Reconsignment arrangements.

A very important feature in modern railroading is the permission given to the owners of goods in transit to have the advantages of the through rate upon paying a very small additional premium, although the transit is interrupted for a time to do something to the commodities in question at some intermediate point, to prepare them for market, or even to entirely change their form by manufacture of some sort. Thus the railroads not uncommonly grant the privilege of cleaning in transit, of bagging in transit, of compressing in transit and of milling in transit. Upon similar principles a through rate may be established, not by uniting on a single rate for one entire haul over two roads, but by charging the separate rate on the goods to the junction point, and then upon the goods being there reconsigned and reshipped over a second road, paying a rebate on the charges of the first or of the second road.[1] This is sometimes allowed when the goods are taken by the consignee at the junction point and there held for a considerable time, for the purpose of awaiting a favorable turn of the market. These privileges are only applicable to shipments intended from the outset to be through shipments.[2] Loose practice in giving rebates on reconsigned goods may lead to a state of affairs which results in discrimination.

---

[1] Railroads which have formerly allowed reconsignment without additional charge may make an extra charge for cars standing on a "hold track" awaiting reconsignment directions: State v. Atchison, T. & S. Ry. Co., 176 Mo. 687, 75 S. W. 776 (1903). See also State v. Atlantic C. L. Ry. Co. (Fla.), 52 So. 4 (1910).

[2] Although a true rebilling rate is permissible where the same goods are reconsigned at some point in transit, the granting of a special rate for the transportation of other goods from a certain point to those who show "expense bills" for an equal amount received over an associated line constitutes illegal discrimination. Alabama & V. Ry. Co. v. Railroad Commission, 86 Miss. 667, 38 So. 356 (1905), affirmed in 203 U. S. 496, 51 L. ed. 289, 27 Sup. Ct. 163 (1906).

§ 1382. Back freights.

There is no reason for requiring the same charge for carriage between the same points in opposite directions. Various factors which properly enter into the rate may be different in the two cases. One reason often given for justifying higher rate in one direction is the fact that the volume of traffic may be less. It is characteristic of the inexact character of the law of rate making that this fact might also justify a lower rate, if the railroad chose to make it. At all events where in the direction of lighter traffic a railroad is carrying many empty cars, it will be justified in lowering the rate in order to fill the cars.[1] When the preponderance of freight is so largely in one direction that the supply of empty cars exceeds the demand for return loads at full rates, it is held to be not unlawful to encourage business by affording transportation on less profitable terms. Of course this making of low "back freights" is subject to the limitation that the rate must not be so low as not to recoup the railroad for the additional expenses in hauling back loaded cars, which must receive due protection during transit.[2]

§ 1383. Equalization of economic advantage.

A theory of fixing rates which appeals to many economists, which is in fact a modification or special application of the rule for charging what the traffic will bear, is the theory that rates should be so fixed as to equalize

[1] Special circumstances, such as the flow of traffic, may show that a higher freight rate in one direction than in the opposite is not an overcharge. Scull v. Atlantic C. L. R. R. Co., 144 N. C. 180, 56 S. E. 876 (1907).

[2] But in testing the reasonableness of a freight charge for carriage in one direction the fact that the freight rate is lower in the opposite direction tends to show that the higher rate is unreasonable where the grades on the road and the expense of moving trains is substantially the same in both directions. Southern Ry. Co. v. Railroad Commission, 42 Ind. App. 88, 83 N. E. 721 (1908).

the advantage of its patrons for the good of the country.
And some of the State courts have given countenance to
these doctrines. Thus in a Minnesota case [1] Judge Collins justified the railroad commission in prescribing an
abnormally low rate for a long haul of coal as compared
with other commodities and other distances upon the
commercial considerations of the sort above described,
"namely, the application of principles when fixing rates
which are forced upon common carriers by various conditions and circumstances and are in common practice among
them,—a business policy which actuates and influences the
carriers themselves to disregard a rule of strict comparison
and strict equality as between bulk, or weight, or value
as well as distance of carriage." And in a recent Georgia
case [2] where the issue also was whether the railroad commission had acted irrationally in taking economic considerations into account in fixing the rate upon particular
commodities between stations, Judge Evans said: "We
do contend that the commission, in the discharge of its
duty to fix reasonable rates, is not precluded from the
consideration of economic conditions recognized by the
carriers in the conduct of their business. The full purpose
of the creation of the commission would be thwarted if it
could not consider and act on every economic or industrial
factor potentially influencing the operation of a railroad
and the transportation of freight. It cannot act arbitrarily
nor by edict produce abnormal conditions of trade; it cannot display favoritism by capriciously giving preferential
rates to one locality which are denied to another. It may,
however, recognize the traffic conditions between given
points, and adjust its schedule to meet these conditions."

[1] State v. Minneapolis & St.
Louis Ry. Co., 80 Minn. 191, 83
N. W. 60 (1900).

[2] Southern Ry. Co. v. Atlanta
Stove Wks., 128 Ga. 207, 57 S. E.
429 (1907).

§ 1384. Law against commerical equalization.

It has sometimes been urged that a carrier should so arrange its rates as to bring about some desirable commercial result, whether by equalizing commercial advantages between two localities or by otherwise affecting natural conditions. However much this theory may have appealed to some economists who have applied their theories of what is for the best interests of society to the railroad problem, it has very little weight with the lawyers who have had to do with the question. As was said in one of the earlier Federal cases: [1] "Shall government undertake the impossible, but injurious, task of making the commercial advantages of one place equal to those of another? It might as well attempt to equalize the intellectual powers of its people. There should be no attempt to deprive a community of its natural advantages, or those legitimate rewards which flow from large investments, business industries, and competing systems of transportation to facilitate and increase commerce." In the latest case [2] involving this problem it plainly appeared that the Interstate Commerce Commission had employed various economic policies in fixing the relative rates in question. The lower Federal court held that the Commission had no power to lower through rates between certain points, as between Atlantic seaboard points and Mississippi river points and Denver, so as to give, for example the Missouri river cities an artificial advantage over other points in shipments east of Denver, and Denver an advantage over Missouri river cities to points west of Denver. But the United States Supreme Court has just

[1] Brewer v. Central of Ga. Ry. Co., 84 Fed. 268 (1897). See also Interstate Commerce Commission v. Louisville & N. Ry. Co., 118 Fed. 613 (1902).

[2] Chicago, R. I. & P. R. R. Co. v. Interstate Commerce Commission, 171 Fed. 680 (1909); overruled by Interstate Commerce Commission v. Chicago, R. I. & P. R. R. Co., 218 U. S. 88, 54 L. ed. 000, 30 Sup. Ct. 65 (1910).

handed down a reversal of this decision setting forth this general principle: "The outlook of the Commission and its powers must be greater than the interest of the railroads or of that which may affect those interests. It must be as comprehensive as the interest of the whole country. If the problems which as presented to it, therefore, are complex and difficult, the means of solving them are as great and adequate as can be provided."

§ 1385. No obligation to make preferential rates.

How weak the argument is in favor of preferential rates of any kind is disclosed by one feature not perhaps as yet sufficiently emphasized. The utmost that these cases permitting preferential treatment have decided is that the company which adopts one of these policies to get business may perhaps be justified for making disproportionate rates. But it should be noted that no company receives any condemnation which ignores these policies altogether in fixing its rates. Even the most enthusiastic economists would not go so far as to argue that the railroads must make it their policy to equalize natural advantages, to the end that all regions shall have equal access to central markets.[1] Certainly legislation designed to enforce relative equality between rates is not outrageous; and surely no rate making body would compel the establishing of preferential rates.[2]

§ 1386. Due consideration of true differences.

But even if the general principle against every sort of discrimination is held to cover not only absolute discrim-

[1] A State may insist upon an equality of rates under equivalent conditions. Seaboard Air Line Co. v. Florida, 203 U. S. 261, 51 L. ed. 175, 27 Sup. Ct. 109 (1906).

[2] A State may enforce equality of local rates even if loss results. Alabama & V. Ry. Co. v. Mississippi R. R. Comm., 203 U. S. 496, 51 L. ed. 289, 27 Sup. Ct. 163 (1906).

ination when the conditions are the same, but also relative discrimination when the conditions are different, the difficult condition must be faced that while the rule against absolute discrimination is in its nature exact and will be seen to be violated if the slightest difference is made in the rates charged to patrons asking substantially the same service, the rule against relative discrimination, on the other hand, must in its nature be inexact, for there are many elements which go to make up the difference between services really unlike, all of which must be taken into account. Whether or not the different rates charged for different services are really disproportionate is not therefore to be settled by any simple computation. Thus in fixing the relative rates between different localities it is obvious that it is not a matter of mileage alone, for it is well known that the cost per ton per mile tends to diminish with the length of the haul; still other elements must be considered, such as the increase in the cost of haulage by heavy grades, of the decrease in the cost by handling a dense traffic. In determining whether there is clear disproportion between the varying rates charged to different localities, all these considerations and many more must be taken into account before a decision can be made.

Topic B. Discrimination Between Services Rendered

§ 1387. Disproportionate rates for different services.

Similar difficulties are encountered in reviewing different rates upon different commodities. Obviously this is not a question of the relative values of these commodities, although that is one element; other factors, such as the care required in handling, the speed necessary, the equipment requisite and the volume of business, must be taken into account before it can be said with any confidence that there is unreasonable disproportion in the relative rates. But although the rule has inherent difficulties in its application, it cannot be that in expert hands it is really impossible to give it sufficient enforcement to prevent gross injustice. And despite all outcry by railroad managers to the effect that it is practically impossible for others to determine the cost of service, it cannot be that these managers themselves in fixing their own rates have no principles for the determination of relative costs.

§ 1388. Charging what the traffic will bear.

Before the lawyers got control of the problem of the regulation of rates, the economists had developed a theory that rates should correspond with value, since the more valuable the commodity, the more it could afford to pay for its carriage. Of course those who are running railroads did not need to be taught the business advantage of charging "what the traffic will bear," but it was pleasing to them to hear the system defended by the economists. However, few lawyers have ever been able to see why a carrier should be allowed to constitute himself, as it were, a tax gatherer. Indeed it seems to most lawyers eminently unjust that a railroad with its virtual monopoly should be allowed to impose such charges as it may extort. The economist used to commend the railroads for making rates so as to create markets, praise which the railroad managers willingly accepted. But the general public led by the lawyers have always been restive under this immemorial justification of benevolent despotism; for the power is too great to be intrusted to private hands without legal standards for effective control.

§ 1389. Difference in rate between freight classes.

It has been pointed out that there are great differences between the rates payable for transportation for the same distances upon goods in different classes. There is no fixed percentage for fixing the differentiation even of the six classes usually established; still less is there any definite rule for the differences to be made between commodities with extra class rating. But it is matter of common knowledge that there are great differences between rates payable by the different classes, the highest class usually paying for the same transportation many times what is paid by the lowest class. All that can be said in general is that the principles as to rate making apply here as elsewhere and that the burden must be thrown upon the various classes without outrageous disproportion. The principles governing this matter have already been given. If the charge is excessive as compared with the charges of the same corporation for other commodities of like bulk and weight, value and risk it would seem to be improper. That such comparisons are generally resorted to is proof enough that the rule against disproportion is generally observed. To be sure the practice has been to make relatively very low rates below the class rates for commodities which would not move otherwise and very high rates, double first class for example, against valuable products which will bear the higher rates. It may be admitted that a great difference, although not so great a difference, may be made between these two extremes of the schedule, even by the theory which has chief regard to the comparative costs of service. But whether so great a gap as now exists will be permitted in the future is a question.

§ 1390. Differences should not be grossly disproportionate.

To go to one extreme it is held low grade commodities may be carried at rates relatively very low indeed. Provided that the rate is remunerative, the other classes cannot complain that the rate is disproportionately low, since unless such a rate were made the traffic would not be got and the higher classes would lose the benefit. On the other hand, just because high grade commodities will stand a rate relatively very much higher, it is not justifiable to charge them outrageously disproportionate rates. The principle to be deduced from all the cases which have just been discussed is plainly that the differences in rates between the classes in a classification should not be disproportionate.

§ 1391. Comparison the basis of the differential.

In a recent case in the United States Supreme Court [1] not only the question of the relation of car-load rates to less than car-load rates, but also the relation of less than car-load rates to each other was thus elaborately dealt with. "The question presented is not one involving only the proper relation of soap in less than carload lots, to soap in carload lots, but also its proper relation to other articles in less than carload lots. Freight is carried either in carload lots, or in less than carload lots. This division of freight necessarily attends transportation by rail. Classification, within the meaning of the act to regulate commerce, relates to these divisions separately. The classification of soap in less than carload lots is not controlled by the classification of soap in carload lots, nor is the reclassification of soap in less than carload lots controlled by the relation it bears to other articles in less than carload lots,—that relation is to be determined by the degree in which, in comparison with such other articles, its handling and carrying is, or may be, affected by the cost of the service, competitive and commercial con-

---

[1] Cincinnati, H. & D. R. R. Co. v. Interstate Commerce Commission, 206 U. S. 142, 51 L. ed. 995, 27 Sup. Ct. 648 (1907). See also Tucker v. Missouri Pac. Ry. Co. (Kan.), 108 Pac. 89 (1910).

ditions, volume, density, distance, value, and risk of loss or damage. It is true that these elements must also be considered in determining the classification of articles in carload lots, but from a different standpoint. A given article of traffic may be more or less desirable when shipped in less than carload lots, than when shipped in carload lots. Bulk, weight, form, manner of packing, etc., may materially affect the classification of different articles to be carried in the same car, when they might have little or no weight in the classification of a single article to be carried in carload lots." [1]

§ 1392. Difference in commodity rates.

As in the making of distance rates so in the making of commodity rates it is often urged that commercial equalization should be in the mind of the rate maker. But although such a policy may be employed to a certain extent here as elsewhere, it is also true that the rate maker may ignore it altogether. In a recent case a railroad was complained of for making its rate on live cattle higher than that on dressed beef. Making the rate on the raw material proportionately lower than on the finished product, seems to some economists most necessary; but the Supreme Court of the United States said: [2] "It is insisted that the making of the livestock rate higher than the product rate is violative of the almost universal rule that the rates on raw material shall not be higher than on the manufactured product. This may be conceded, but that the rule is not universal the proposition itself

---

[1] Until recently the Interstate Commerce Commission had no power to fix a rate by insisting upon a certain classification. Interstate Commerce Commission v. Lake Shore & M. S. Ry. Co., 134 Fed. 942 (1905). Sustained in 202 U. S.

613, 50 L. ed. 1171, 26 Sup. Ct. 776 (1906).

[2] Interstate Commerce Commission v. Chicago Gt. Western Ry. Co., 209 U. S. 108, 52 L. ed. 705, 28 Sup. Ct. 000 (1909), reversing 141 Fed. 1041 (1905).

recognizes, and the findings of the court give satisfactory reasons for the exception here shown. The cost of carriage, the risk of injury, the larger amount which the companies are called upon to pay out in damages make sufficient explanation. They do away with the idea that in the relation established between the two kinds of charges any undue or unreasonable preference was intended or secured."

§ 1393. Rates vary with values.

That rates may differ to a considerable extent as values differ is within this general theory that rates should be proportional. This was brought out clearly some time since by a ruling of the Interstate Commerce Commission that it was not reasonable for a railroad to make a higher rate for window shades than for the holland cloth from which they were made. But the Federal court refused to accede to this, Mr. Justice Wallace saying: [1] "The order of the interstate commerce commission which the court is now asked to enforce prohibits the railway carriers, the parties respondent, from charging any greater compensation for the transportation of window shades of any description—whether the cheap article worth $3 per dozen, or the hand-decorated article worth $10 per pair—than the third-class rate charged for the transportation of the materials used in making window shades. Such an order, in my judgment, ignores the element of the value of the service in fixing the reasonable compensation of the carrier, and denies him any remuneration for additional risk. I cannot regard it as justifiable upon principle, and must refuse to enforce it. The petition is dismissed."

§ 1394. Improper to equalize values.

To admit that a difference in rates may be made by

[1] Interstate Commerce Commission v. Delaware, L. & W. Ry. Co., 64 Fed. 723 (1894).

reason of difference in value is not to permit that difference to be made so great as to equalize the difference in
value in the ultimate market of the commodities carried.
The Interstate Commerce Commission having adopted
that policy, in a recent proceeding the Federal court set
aside their order saying: [1] "The similarity of circumstances and conditions under which a service of carriage
is rendered, which under the interstate commerce act,
requires an equality of rate, relates to the circumstances
and conditions which affect the service only, and, where
different coal mining localities are grouped into a district
for rate-making purposes a carrier is not justified in making a different rate for the same or substantially similar
service from a particular locality in such district or on
the product of a particular mine or vein, from that charged
others because the difference in the product from such
locality mine or vein and that from other mines in the
district is such that it can pay a higher rate and still compete in the market."

§ 1395. Policy against all discrimination.

As has been seen, the authorities upon these questions
are a seething mass. The various commissions which
are near to actual conditions seem to show a tendency to
condemn the fixing of the differing rates between localities
solely by economic principles of demand and supply, the
unequal and unjust results of which the courts are apparently too far removed from the vital facts to realize
or appreciate. But even in the courts a reaction seems
to be at hand. It is not enough to say that this power to
make preferential rates may be used for the benefit of its
territory as a whole, the fact remains that it is a power
which may be abused. So long as this power is left in

[1] Philadelphia & R. Ry. Co. v.   Interstate Commerce Commission,
174 Fed. 687 (1909).

the hands of the railway management without power of review by any authority upon any fundamental principle, it is in the hands of the railroad officials to build up an artificial market where the natural conditions are adverse, or to turn an industrious city into a wilderness again. It is believed that these are too great powers to intrust to private hands without governmental control based upon some recognized standards. Indeed the public law in this, as in the other cases, should put sufficient limitations upon any business policy, however profitable, which comes in conflict with the fundamental principle of equal service to all applicants. And it seems that there can be violation of this principle by disproportionate rates in different services as well as by discrimination in the same service.

§ 1396. Relative discrimination inconsistent with public duty.

It is submitted, therefore, that the public service law will not be satisfied in the end unless with some reasonable degree of certainty each applicant who requires a service is charged his proportion of the total cost, including in that cost, over and above all current and fixed charges a fair return upon proper capitalization. It must be admitted that the law relating to disproportion is still in the making; it is as indefinite as the law relating to discrimination was twenty-five years ago. A lawyer who saw no visions then would have relied upon the fact that by the weight of authority there was no law whatever against discrimination as such. Provided each applicant for the same service was quoted a rate reasonable in itself, all was then well; although outrageous differences even at that time might be evidence that the higher rate was unreasonable. In the same way to-day, very probably by the weight of authority, there is no law against disproportion as such. Provided each applicant for different service is quoted a rate which is reasonable in itself, it may be that there is no redress by established law, however outrageous the disproportion may be; although it seems to be agreed that outrageous differences may be evidence that the higher rate is unreasonable in itself. And yet it is quite in the line of the evolution of the public service law that a rule against disproportion as such may eventually be recognized, despite the fact that it might interfere with the business policies of the public companies even more than the present rule against outright discrimination has done. For it seems plain to the writer that the same principles which forbid any differences when the conditions are the same, should prohibit disproportionate differences when the conditions are different.

CHAPTER XLI

CONSTITUTIONAL SUMMARY

§ 1400. Control of public employment.

Topic A. Character of the Power to Regulate

§ 1401. Nature of the power to regulate.
  1402. Power to regulate not a judicial power.
  1403. Power to regulate not strictly legislative.
  1404. Power to regulate is administrative.
  1405. Regulating body presumably reasonable.
  1406. Duty of the courts to decide reasonableness.

Topic B. Method of Exercising the Power to Regulate

§ 1407. Fixing rules by legislation.
  1408. Delegation of regulating power.
  1409. Functions of administrative commissions.
  1410. Action by municipal, or other local government.
  1411. Function of the courts in declaring regulation void.
  1412. When suit is against State official.

Topic C. Division Between Federal and State Jurisdiction

§ 1413. What constitutes interstate commerce.
  1414. Continuous carriage under common control.
  1415. Continuity of interstate shipment.
  1416. Carriage wholly within the State.
  1417. State legislation burdening interstate commerce.
  1418. Scope for State police power.
  1419. Effect of action by Congress.
  1420. Power of Congress to regulate.

Topic D. Impairing Obligation of Contract

§ 1421. Contract character of charter privileges.
  1422. Express contractual provision necessary.
  1423. Conferring powers does not create contract.
  1424. Contracts made by municipal ordinance.

§ 1400. Control of public employment.

The basis of the right of the state to regulate the public service companies lies in the principle first clearly apprehended and expressed by Lord Hale in his treatise " De Portibus Maris," that when property is affected with a public interest it ceases to be *juris privati* only. "Property," as Mr. Chief Justice Waite has said, "does become clothed with a public interest when used in a manner to make it of public consequence and affect the community at large. When, therefore, one devotes his property to a use in which the public has an interest he, in effect, grants to the public an interest in that use, and must submit to be controlled by the public for the common good, to the extent of the interest he has thus created." This common law principle has come down to us from time immemorial; and therefore proper legislation regulating such business has always been considered by us as due process of law.

Topic A. Character of the Power to Regulate

§ 1401. Nature of the power to regulate.

The simplest form which the power to regulate the conduct of public service can take is that adopted by the common law, that is, the action of the courts, declaring the conduct of the proprietor improper or inexcusable upon suit of the party who has gained thereby. Such power has been exercised by the courts of common law from the beginning of their history.[1] It has always been recognized that if a carrier attempted to charge a shipper an unreasonable sum, the courts had jurisdiction to inquire into that matter, and to award to the shipper any amount exacted from him in excess of a reasonable rate.[2] This power, which has aptly been called a visitorial power of the State [3] is only one example of the general power of the State to oversee the acts of those who are engaged in its public service, and to make sure that they really serve the public interests. Thus the power to order the location of stations is within the general jurisdiction of the courts of law.[4] But the power of the State over public service employments is not limited to its power to pass on the reasonableness of their acts after they have been established; the power to initiate action, to lay down rules in the first instance by way of regulating action, is fully recognized at common law and by the general practice of all common law countries. Legislation of this sort has existed from time immemorial and is therefore always due process of law abstractly.[5] It is a special

[1] Waite, C. J., in Railroad Commission Cases, 116 U. S. 307, 29 L. ed. 636, 6 Sup. Ct. 334 (1886).

[2] Brewer, J., in Reagan v. Farmers' L. & T. Co., 154 U. S. 362, 38 L. ed. 1014, 14 Sup. Ct. 1047 (1893).

[3] Williams, J., in Brymer v. But-

ler Water Co., 179 Pa. St. 231, 36 Atl. 249, 36 L. R. A. 260 (1897).

[4] Doe, C. J., in Concord & M. R. R. Co. v. Boston & M. R. R. Co., 67 N. H. 464; 41 Atl. 463 (1893).

[5] Waite, C. J., in Munn v. Illinois, 94 U. S. 113, 24 L. ed. 77 (1876).

branch of the general police power inherent in the legislative branch.[1]

§ 1402. Power to regulate not a judicial power.

The earliest action of the State in dealing with rates was doubtless the action of the courts in passing upon the reasonableness of rates fixed by the carrier, and in Munn v. Illinois [2] it was insisted that the power over rates was a judicial power, and could not be exercised by the legislature. But the court held otherwise, the line of argument being somewhat as follows. In common law countries this power has been exercised from time immemorial by the legislature, which has fixed a maximum beyond which charges are unreasonable. Granting the power to regulate at all, the power to fix rates follows, since that is one means of regulation. The power of the common law to affect rates by providing that they must be reasonable is admitted; but this is itself a regulation. If, then, rates are and always have been regulated by law, that law, like any other, may be changed by the legislature, since no one has a vested interest in any rule of the common law. A legislative regulation of rates is therefore a mere instance of a change in the common law, which it is entirely within the power of the legislature to make; and in doing so it is not exercising judicial functions. This view of the question has been universally followed.[3] The distinction between legislative and judicial functions is a vital one, and cannot be altered either by legislative act or by judicial decree.[4] Legislation prescribes rules

[1] Blatchford, J., in Budd v. New York, 143 U. S. 517, 36 L. ed. 247, 12 Sup. Ct. 468 (1891).

[2] 94 U. S. 113, 133, 24 L. ed. 77 (1876).

[3] Interstate Commerce Commission v. Cincinnati, N. C. & T. P. R. Co., 167 U. S. 479, 42 L. ed. 243, 17 Sup. Ct. 896 (1897); Louisville & N. R. R. Co. v. Brown, 123 Fed. 946 (1903), State v. Wilson, 121 N. C. 650, 28 S. E. 553 (1897).

[4] Western Union Tel. Co. v. Myatt, 98 Fed. 335 (1899).

for the future; litigation determines rights and wrongs for the past. To prescribe a tariff of rates for the future is therefore not a judicial act; to determine whether existing or prescribed rates and charges are unreasonable, on the other hand, is a judicial act.[1]

§ 1403. Power to regulate not strictly legislative.

But while the power to fix rates may be exercised directly by the legislature, it is not, strictly speaking, a legislative power; but rather the so-called administrative function. Mr. Justice Brewer in the Circuit Court, in Chicago & N. W. Ry. v. Dey,[2] used on this point language which has often been quoted: "While, in a general sense, following the language of the Supreme Court, it must be conceded that the power to fix rates is legislative, yet the line of demarcation between legislative and administrative functions is not always easily discerned. The one runs into the other. The law books are full of statutes unquestionably valid, in which the legislature has been content to simply establish rules and principles, leaving execution and details to other officers. Here it has declared that rates shall be reasonable and just, and committed what is, partially at least, the mere administration of that law to the railroad commissioners." The difficulty felt in this passage in distinguishing legislative and administrative functions is a real one; but it is usually not necessary to make a sharp distinction, and for the present it is enough to point out that the function, while not judicial, is not in the strict sense legislative.[3]

[1] Reagan v. Farmers' L. & T. Co., 154 U. S. 362, 38 L. ed. 1014, 14 Sup. Ct. 1047 (1894); Smyth v. Ames, 169 U. S. 466, 42 L. ed. 819, 18 Sup. Ct. 418 (1898); Wheeler v. No. Col. Irr. Co., 10 Colo. 582, 17 Pac. 487 (1887); Brush E. I. Co. v. Consolidated T. & E. Co., 15 N. Y. Supp. 811 (1891).

[2] 35 Fed. 866, 874 (1888).

[3] See Chicago B. & Q. R. R. Co. v. Jones, 149 Ill. 361, 37 N. E. 247, 41 Am. St. Rep. 278, 24 L. R. A. 141 (1894).

§ 1404. Power to regulate is administrative.

If it is necessary to find a place for the regulating power in one of the three departments into which government is commonly divided, it undoubtedly forms part of the executive department. We have seen that the power is neither judicial nor legislative; it does not involve the power to make laws, or to interpret and apply them, but to aid in carrying the laws into effect.[1] The danger is that these distinctions will be forgotten and the attempt be made to create a body in which the powers of government are unjustifiably blended. This attempt was made in Kansas, where the legislature established a Court of Visitation, gave it the ordinary constitution and powers of a court, and conferred upon it the right to issue writs and injunctions, to summon witnesses, and to decide between parties, and finally granted to it the power to fix railroad rates. This legislation was held unconstitutional, as violating the constitutional separation of powers, since the body was to exercise both legislative and judicial functions. "Concisely stated," said District Judge Hook,[2] "the Court of Visitation may make laws, sit judicially upon their own acts, and then enforce their enactments which have received their judicial sanction. Can this be done? Can there be vested in one body such a union of powers of the different departments or branches of government, to be exercised respecting the same subject-matter and in the same proceeding?"

§ 1405. Regulating body presumptively reasonable.

It is often provided that the rate as fixed by regulating commission shall be taken as reasonable until the contrary is shown, or that the action of the commission shall

[1] In re Railroad Comrs., 15 Neb. 679, 50 N. W. 276 (1883); Nebraska Tel. Co. v. Cornell, 59 Neb. 737, 82 82 N. W. 1 (1900).

[2] Western Union Tel. Co. v. Myatt, 98 Fed. 335 (1899); State v. Johnson, 61 Kan. 803, 60 Pac. 1060, 49 L. R. A. 662 (1900).

be *prima facie* evidence of the reasonableness of the rate as found. This is not unconstitutional; the legislature has power over the weight of evidence, and this provision is merely an exercise of that power.[1] It is sometimes provided that the action of the regulating commission should be "sufficient evidence of the reasonableness of the rates established by them." In one case [2] it was claimed that this meant conclusive evidence and therefore that the action of the commission in establishing such a rate was unconstitutional. The court, however, held that this meant merely that the action of the commission constituted *prima facie* evidence of reasonableness, which in the absence of evidence to the contrary would be sufficient to justify a verdict to that effect.

§ 1406. Duty of the courts to decide reasonableness.

To whatever body the power of fixing rates may be confided, it is the function of the regular courts to pass upon the reasonableness of the rates thus established; and the courts cannot be deprived of this power. The question of reasonableness cannot be so conclusively determined by the legislature of the State, or by regulations adopted under its authority, that the matter may not become the subject of judicial inquiry.[3] And legislation imposing outrageous penalties for failing to conform to its provisions while appealing to the courts to set it aside as unconstitutional is altogether bad.[4]

[1] Chicago, B. & Q. R. R. Co. v. Jones, 149 Ill. 361, 37 N. E. 247, 41 Am. St. Rep. 278, 24 L. R. A. 141 (1894); Burlington, C. R. & M. R. R. Co. v. Dey, 82 Ia. 312, 48 N. W. 98, 31 Am. St. Rep. 477, 12 L. R. A. 436 (1891).

[2] Richmond & D. R. R. Co. v. Trammel, 53 Fed. 196 (1892). See also Minneapolis & St. Louis R. R. Co. v. Minnesota, 186 U. S. 257, 46 L. ed. 1151, 22 Sup Ct. 900 (1902).

[3] Reagan v. Farmers' L. & T. Co., 154 U. S. 362, 38 L. ed. 1014, 14 Sup. Ct. 1047 (1894).

[4] Ex parte Young, 209 U. S. 123, 52 L. ed. 715, 28 Sup. Ct. 441 (1908).

Topic B. Method of Exercising the Power to Regulate

§ 1407. Fixing rules by legislation.

In the United States, where the division of powers is strictly enforced, it is well settled that the legislature [1] has power to limit the amount of charges by railroad companies for the transportation of persons and property within its own jurisdiction, unless restrained by some contract or other in the charter of the railroad. But it is equally well settled that the action of the legislature in regulating the conduct of a public service may be attacked in the courts as outrageous in its application to the complainant. The general doctrine that a statute which is contrary to the Constitution is void is too well understood to be expatiated upon. If the statute which fixes or gives power to fix the rate is void, the rate does not exist in effect, and will be disregarded by the court. It is possible, however, to provide by statute that the rate shall be binding between the parties until declared void by the courts. [2]

§ 1408. Delegation of regulating power.

It has already been seen that the regulating power may be delegated to a subordinate body; and this is not unconstitutional as a delegation of legislative power. The

[1] *United States.*—Munn v. Illinois, 94 U. S. 113, 24 L. ed. 77 (1876), Chicago & G. T. Ry. Co. v. Wellman, 143 U. S. 339, 36 L. ed. 176, 12 Sup. Ct. 400 (1892); Budd v. New York, 143 U. S. 517, 36 L. ed. 247, 12 Sup. Ct. 468 (1892); Chesapeake & P. Tel. Co. v. Manning, 186 U. S. 238, 46 L. ed. 1144, 22 Sup. Ct. 881 (1902); Atlantic & P. Co. v. United States, 76 Fed. 186 (1896); Ball v. Rutland R. R. Co., 93 Fed. 513 (1889).

Arkansas.—Missouri Pac. Ry. v. Smith, 60 Ark. 221, 29 S. W. 752 (1895).

Indiana.—Hockett v. State, 105 Ind. 250, 5 N. E. 178 (1885).

Michigan.—Pingree v. Michigan Cent. R. R. Co., 118 Mich. 314, 76 N. W. 635 (1898).

[2] See especially Reagan v. Farmers' L. & T. Co., 154 U. S. 362, 38 L. ed. 1014, 14 Sup. Ct. 1047 (1894).

legislative act of requiring the rates to be reasonable is either the act of the common law or is part of the act by which the delegation of authority is conferred. The functions of such bodies in determining and fixing reasonable rates are administrative rather than legislative. The authority conferred on them relates merely to the administration in practice of the general rules laid down by the common law and by the legislature. So in the Railroad Commission Cases [1] the legality of the action of the Mississippi Legislature in creating a railroad commission with power to fix rates was justified. The rate so fixed would be enforced in the courts, unless the courts should find it unjust. The delegation of the rate fixing power to a commission in this way was held to be constitutional. [2]

§ 1409. Functions of administrative commissions.

It is much more convenient for the legislature to confer on a subordinate administrative body the power to regulate than to do so itself. This has been done in England by placing the power in the Board of Trade, one of the executive or rather administrative departments of the government. In this country, the power has, in the last quarter century, very generally been referred to an administrative commission. The reason for delegating the power of fixing rates in detail to a commission has never

[1] 116 U. S. 307, 29 L. ed. 636, 6 Sup. Ct. 334 (1886). See also Chicago & N. W. Ry Co. v. Dey, 35 Fed. 866 (1888).

[2] See Siler v. Louisville & N. R. R. Co., 213 U. S. 175, 53 L. ed. 753, 29 Sup. Ct. 451 (1909); and Gulf, C. & S. F. Ry. Co. v. State (Tex. Civ. App.), 120 S. W. 1028 (1909).

In a State where the division of powers is not strictly insisted upon in the constitution, the power to fix rates may be conferred upon an inferior court, as in Kentucky upon the county court, with appeal to the superior courts in regular series. Troutman v. Smith, 105 Ky. 231, 48 S. W. 1084 (1899); or as in Pennsylvania where the county court may fix water rates. Brymer v. Butler Water Co., 179 Pa. St. 231, 36 Atl. 249, 36 L. R. A. 260 (1897).

been better expressed than by Mr. Justice Brewer: [1] "The reasonableness of a rate changes with the changed condition of circumstances. That which would be fair and reasonable to-day, six months or a year hence may be either too high or too low. The legislature convenes only at stated periods; in this State once in two years. Justice will be more likely done if this power of fixing rates is vested in a body of continual session than if left with one meeting only at stated and long intervals. Such a power can change rates at any time, and thus meet the changing conditions of circumstances. While, of course, the argument from inconvenience cannot be pushed too far, yet it is certainly a matter of inquiry whether in the increasing complexity of our civilization and our social and business relations, the power of the legislature to give increased extent to administrative functions must not be recognized." [2]

[1] Chicago & N. W. Ry. Co. v. Dey, 35 Fed. 866, 875 (1888).

[2] *United States.*—Railroad Commission Cases, 116 U. S. 307, 29 L. ed. 636, 6 Sup. Ct. 334 (1886); Dinsmore v. So. Exp. Co., 183 U. S. 115, 46 L. ed. 111, 22 Sup. Ct. 46 (1901); Tilley v. Savannah, F. & M. R. R. Co., 5 Fed. 641, 4 Woods, 427 (1881); Chicago & N. W. Ry. Co. v. Dey, 35 Fed. 866 (1888); Southern Pacific R. R. Co. v. Railroad Commissioners, 76 Fed. 236 (1896); Chicago, M. & S. P. Ry. Co. v. Tompkins, 90 Fed. 363 (1898); Metropolitan Trust Co. v. Houston & T. C. R. R. Co., 90 Fed. 683 (1898); Haverhill G. L. Co. v. Barker, 109 Fed. 694 (1901); Wallace v. Arkansas Cent. R. R. Co., 118 Fed. 422, 55 C. C. A. 192 (1902).

Florida.—McWhorter v. Pensacola & A. R. R. Co., 24 Fla. 417, 5 So. 129, 12 Am. St. Rep. 220, 2 L. R. A. 504 (1888); Storrs v. Pensacola & A. R. R. Co., 29 Fla. 617, 11 So. 226 (1892).

Georgia.—Georgia R. R. & B. Co. v. Smith, 70 Ga. 694 (1883).

Illinois.—Chicago, B. & Q. R. R. Co. v. Jones, 149 Ill. 361, 37 N. E. 247, 41 Am. St. Rep. 278, 24 L. R. A. 141 (1894).

Iowa.—Hooper v. Chicago, M. & St. P. Ry. Co., 91 Ia. 639, 60 N. W. 487 (1894).

Minnesota.—State v. Chicago, M. & S. P. R. R. Co., 38 Minn. 281, 37 N. W. 782 (1888), reversed on another point, Chicago, M. & S. P. R. R. Co. v. Minnesota, 134 U. S. 418, 33 L. ed. 970, 10 Sup. Ct. 462.

Nebraska.—State v. Fremont & E. M. V. R. R. Co., 22 Neb. 313, 23 Neb. 117 (1887).

Texas.—Railroad Commission v.

§ 1410. Action by municipal or other local government.

The legislature may by statute confer the power of fixing rates upon counties, cities, or villages, or any such bodies as constitute local governments; and the power so conferred may be exercised by the body named in accordance with the terms of the statute.[1] The power is derived solely from the statute; and in the absence of such authority there is no power inherent in a municipal corporation to regulate the rates of public service companies.[2] Nor is the power involved in the police power, the licensing power, or the general power to regulate

---

Houston & T. C. R. R. Co., 90 Tex. 340, 38 S. W. 750 (1897).

Virginia.—Atlantic Coast Line Ry. Co. v. Commonwealth, 102 Va. 599, 46 S. E. 911 (1904).

[1] San Diego L. & T. Co. v. National City, 174 U. S. 739, 43 L. ed. 1154, 19 Sup. Ct. 804 (1899); San Diego, L. & T. Co. v. Jasper, 189 U. S. 439, 47 L. ed. 892, 23 Sup. Ct. 571 (1903); Cleveland G. & C. Co. v. Cleveland, 71 Fed. 610 (1896); Capital City Gas Co. v. Des Moines, 72 Fed. 818, 829 (1896); New Memphis G. & L. Co. v. Memphis, 72 Fed. 952 (1896); Milwaukee E. R. & L. Co. v. Milwaukee, 87 Fed. 577 (1898); Spring Valley Waterworks v. San Francisco, 124 Fed. 574 (1903); Palatka Waterworks v. Palatka, 127 Fed. 161 (1903); Cleveland City Ry. Co. v. Cleveland, 94 Fed. 385 (1899).

Alabama.—Crosby v. City Council, 108 Ala. 498, 18 So. 723 (1895).

California.—San Diego Water Co. v. San Diego, 118 Cal. 556, 50 Pac. 633, (1897); Redlands L. & C. D. Water Co. v. Redlands, 121 Cal. 365, 53 Pac. 843 (1898).

Florida.—Tampa v. Tampa Waterworks Co., 45 Fla. 600, 34 So. 631 (1903).

Illinois.—Chicago, P. & P. Co. v. Chicago, 88 Ill. 221, 30 Am. Rep. 545 (1878); Rogers Park Water Co. v. Fergus, 178 Ill. 571, 53 N. E. 363, 69 Am. St. Rep. 315 (1899); Chicago Union Traction Co. v. Chicago, 199 Ill. 484, 65 N. E. 451 (1902).

Iowa.—Des Moines v. Des Moines Waterworks Co., 95 Ia. 348, 64 N. W. 269 (1895); Cedar Rapids Water Co. v. Cedar Rapids, 118 Ia. 234, 91 N. W. 1081 (1902).

Maryland—Charles Simon's Sons Co. v. Maryland T. & T. Co., 99 Md. 141, 57 Atl. 193 (1904).

Missouri.—State v. Laclede Gas Light Co., 102 Mo. 472, 14 S. W. 974 (1890).

Tennessee.—Knoxville v. Knoxville Water Co., 107 Tenn. 647, 64 S. W. 1075 (1901).

[2] *Indiana.*—Louisville Nat. Gas Co. v. State, 135 Ind. 49, 34 N. E. 704 (1894).

Kansas.—In re Pryor, 55 Kan. 724, 41 Pac. 958 (1895).

corporations using the streets.[1] If, however, the right to fix rates by ordinance is granted to the city it will be construed as a permanent power, not exhausted by a single act of fixing rates, but capable of being exercised by revising the rates after they have been once fixed.[2]

§ 1411. Function of the courts in declaring regulation void.

But any action by any subordinate body may be attacked in any court in which the question may come up as unconstitutional. And as a practical matter in almost every case where such an attack is made, it may be based upon a provision of the constitution of the United States:[3] that against impairing the obligation of contracts, depriving of equal protection of the laws, or taking property without due process of law. A considerable number of cases have therefore been taken to the Supreme Court of the United States and an important body of doctrine has been developed by the decisions, which will be examined at large in this chapter.[4]

§ 1412. When suit is against State official.

If the rate order complained of in an unconstitutional

[1] Old Colony Trust Co. v. Atlanta, 83 Fed. 39 (1897).

[2] Freeport Water Co. v. Freeport, 180 U. S. 587, 45 L. ed. 679, 21 Sup. Ct. 493 (1901).

[3] The following are cases of this sort: Railroad Commission Cases, 116 U. S. 307, 29 L. ed. 636, 6 Sup. Ct. 334, 388, 1191 (1886); Dow v. Beidelman, 125 U. S. 680, 31 L. ed. 841, 8 Sup. Ct. 1028 (1888); Georgia R. & Bkg. Co. v. Smith, 128 U. S. 174, 32 L. ed. 377, 9 Sup. Ct. 47 (1888); Chicago, M. & St. P. Ry. Co. v. Minnesota, 134 U. S. 418, 33 L. ed. 970, 10 Sup. Ct. 462, 702 (1889); Chicago & G. T. Ry. Co. v.

Wellman, 143 U. S. 339, 36 L. ed. 176, 12 Sup. Ct. 400 (1892); Reagan v. Farmers' Loan & T. Co., 154 U. S. 362, 38 L. ed. 1014, 14 Sup. Ct. 1047 (1894); St. Louis & S. F. R. R. Co. v. Gill, 156 U. S. 649, 39 L. ed. 567, 15 Sup. Ct. 484 (1895); Covington & L. Turnp. Road Co. v. Sandford, 164 U. S. 578, 41 L. ed. 560, 17 Sup. Ct. 198 (1896); Smyth v. Ames, 169 U. S. 466, 42 L. ed. 819, 18 Sup. Ct. 418 (1898).

[4] See particularly Cleveland v. Cleveland City Ry. Co., 194 U. S. 517, 48 L. ed. 1102, 24 Sup. Ct. 756 (1904).

statute is void, a suit to restrain a State official from enforcing it is not a suit to restrain him in acting under a State law, nor is it a suit against a State. A Federal court may therefore entertain such a suit.[1] "It is the settled doctrine of this court that a suit against individuals for the purpose of preventing them as officers of a State from enforcing an unconstitutional enactment to the injury of the rights of the plaintiff, is not a suit against the State within the meaning of that amendment."[2]

Topic C. Division Between Federal and State Jurisdiction

§ 1413. What constitutes interstate commerce.

The question whether a certain transaction constitutes interstate commerce must be determined by ascertaining what the real transit is, and whether that traffic is or is not between separate States. Whenever a commodity has begun to move as an article of trade from one State to another, commerce in that commodity between the States has commenced. The fact that several different and independent agencies are employed in transporting the commodity, some acting entirely in one State and some acting through two or more States, in no respect affects the character of the transaction.[3] Even a train composed of empty coal cars, although destined for a point in another State to procure a load, has been held to be engaged in transporting articles of interstate commerce so as to be beyond the control of State laws.[4] However, it is now settled that even if the termini are within the same State it is interstate commerce if the goods are to move

[1] Reagan v. Farmers' L. & T. Co., 154 U. S. 362, 38 L. ed. 1014, 14 Sup. Ct. 1047 (1894).

[2] Harlan, J., in Smyth v. Ames, 169 U. S. 466, 42 L. ed. 819, 18 Sup. Ct. 418 (1898).

[3] The Daniel Ball, 10 Wall. 557, 19 L. ed. 999 (1871).

[4] Norfolk & W. R. R. Co. v. Com., 93 Va. 749, 24 S. E. 837, 34 L. R. A. 105 (1896).

See also Larrabee Flour Mills v.

through another State during the transit,[1] although at one time it seemed to be decided that such commerce did not involve interchange of commodities between States.[2] Anything may be the subject of interstate commerce, it seems. Thus Congress may forbid the interstate transportation of lottery tickets.[3] But diseased cattle are apparently held not the subject of interstate commerce.[4]

§ 1414. Continuous carriage under common control.

When goods are shipped under a through bill of lading from a point in one State to a point in another, and are taken by a State common carrier under a conventional division of the charges, such carrier must be deemed to have subjected its road to an arrangement for a continuous carriage or shipment within the meaning of the law.[5] The through billing and rating is the usual but by no means the only method of manifesting a common arrangement.[6] In the case of carriage of passengers a similar interpretation will be made; assent by a carrier to the

Missouri Pacific Ry Co., 74 Kan. 808, 88 Pac. 72 (1906).

[1] *United States.*—Hanley v. Kansas City So. Ry. Co., 187 U. S. 617, 47 L. ed. 333, 23 Sup. Ct. 214.

Minnesota.—State v. Chicago, S. P., M. & O. R. R. Co., 40 Minn. 267, 3 L. R. A. 238 (1889).

South Carolina.—Sternberger v. Cape Fear & Y. V. R. R. Co., 29 S. C. 510 (1888).

[2] *United States.*—Lehigh Valley R. R. Co. v. Pennsylvania, 145 U. S. 192, 36 L. ed. 672, 12 Sup. Ct. 806, (1892); United States v. Lehigh Valley R. R. Co., 115 Fed. 373 (1902).

Missouri.—Seawell v. Kansas City, F. S. & M. R. R. Co., 119 Mo. 222, 24 S. W. 1002 (1893).

New York.—Dillon v. Erie R. R.

Co., 19 N. Y. Misc. 116, 43 N. Y. Supp. 320 (1897).

[3] Lottery Case, 188 U. S. 321, 47 L. ed. 4921, 23 Sup. Ct. 321 (1903).

[4] Missouri, K. & T. Ry. Co. v. Haber, 169 U. S. 613, 42 L. ed. 878, 18 Sup. Ct. 488 (1898).

[5] Cincinnati, N. O. & T. P. Ry. Co. v. Interstate Commerce Commission, 162 U. S. 184, 40 L. ed. 935, 16 Sup. Ct. 700 (1896); Louisville & N. R. R. Co. v. Behlmer, 175 U. S. 648, 44 L. ed. 309, 20 Sup. Ct. 209 (1899); United States v. Seaboard Ry. Co., 82 Fed. 563 (1897); Interstate S. Y. Co. v. Indianapolis U. Ry. Co., 99 Fed. 472 (1900).

[6] State v. Gulf, C. & S. F. Ry. Co. (Tex. Civ. App.), 44 S. W. 542 (1898).

issue of a through ticket over several railroads constitutes an arrangement for continuous carriage.[1] Where, therefore, a local carrier takes part in the carriage of goods through to destination in another State, though its share of the carriage is entirely within the State, it is engaged in interstate commerce.[2] This is often shown to be the case by a through billing and rating of the goods assented to by the carrier in question.[3] In Texas it has been held that through billing is not enough, and a State carrier is not engaged in interstate commerce unless it takes part in a through rating.[4] But it is now certain that the rating need not be joint; the State carrier is none the less an interstate carrier, because its share of the total rate is equal to his entire local rate, if it takes part in or permits through billing.[5] And it does not seem necessary for the establishment of a through carriage to prove that a technical through rate has been named.

§ 1415. Continuity of interstate shipment.

If the transporting of goods or passengers to an ultimate destination in another State has begun, interstate commerce has begun, and no device to break up the transit into intrastate portions will affect its real nature. So where transportation of goods destined for a point without the State has been actually begun, temporary stoppage within the State without the intention of abandoning the

[1] Carrey v. Spencer, 36 N. Y. Supp. 886 (1895); Missouri, K. & T. R. R. Co. v. Fookes (Tex. Civ. App.), 40 S. W. 858 (1897).

[2] Norfolk & W. R. R. Co. v. Pennsylvania, 136 U. S. 114, 34 L. ed. 394, 10 Sup. Ct. 958 (1890); Ex parte Kochler, 30 Fed. 867 (1887); Augusta So. R. R. Co. v. Wrightsville & T. R. R. Co., 74 Fed. 522 (1896).

[3] Cincinnati, N. O. & T. P. Ry.

Co. v. Interstate Comm. Comm., 162 U. S. 184, 40 L. ed. 935, 16 Sup. Ct. 700 (1896).

[4] Gulf, C. & S. F. Ry. Co. v. Nelson, 4 Tex. Civ. App. 345, 23 S. W. 732 (1893); Houston & T. C. Ry. Co. v. Williams (Tex. Civ. App.), 31 S. W. 556 (1895); Houston & T. C. Ry. Co. v. Davis, 11 Tex. Civ. App. 24, 31 S. W. 308 (1895).

[5] United States v. Seaboard Ry. Co., 82 Fed. 563 (1897).

original movement (which movement is ultimately completed), will not deprive the transportation of the character of interstate commerce.[1]   And so if the goods are first billed to a point in the State of shipment, and at that point are rebilled to their ultimate destination in another State, without breaking of bulk, the whole constitutes a single carriage.[2]   The continuity of the carriage of freight over a line formed by two or more roads is not broken in fact merely by the declaration on the part of one or more of said carriers that as to the transportation over its road it is local and not a through carrier.   Neither is the continuity of the shipment broken by a sale of the goods *in transitu*.[3]   If, however, the goods are consigned to a dealer and he, selling them before arrival, rebills to the purchaser without breaking bulk, the two carriages are distinct.[4]   The transit is a single unit, continuing from the time of the original shipment to the ultimate end of the carriage; and where the beginning and end are in different States, the entire transit from beginning to end is interstate.   It does not cease to be interstate when the goods finally enter the State of destination; it continues an interstate shipment even within that State, until delivery.[5]   Therefore any attempt by the State to make orders in regard to the switching of such shipments to the consignee is a regulation of interstate commerce.[6]

[1] Cutting v. Florida Ry. & Nav. Co., 46 Fed. 641 (1891).

[2] Texas & P. Ry. Co. v. Avery (Tex. Civ. App.), 33 S. W. 704 (1895); Houston, D. & N. Co. v. Insurance Co., 89 Tex. 1, 32 S. W. 889, 30 L. R. A. 713, 59 Am. St. Rep. 17 (1895); Mexican Nat. R. R. Co. v. Savage (Tex. Civ. App.), 41 S. W. 663 (1897); State v. Gulf, C. & S. F. Ry. Co. (Tex. Civ. App.), 44 S. W. 542 (1898).

[3] Gulf, C. & S. F. Ry. Co. v. Fort Grain Co. (Tex. Civ. App.), 72 S. W. 419 (1903).

[4] Gulf, C. & S. F. Ry. Co. v. State, 97 Tex. 274, 78 S. W. 495 (1904), aff'd in Gulf, C. & S. F. Ry. Co. v. Texas, 204 U. S. 403, 51 L. ed. 540, 27 Sup. Ct. 360 (1907).

[5] State v. Southern Ry. Co. (Tex. Civ. App.), 49 S. W. 252 (1899).

[6] McNeill v. Southern Ry. Co.,

§ 1416. Carriage wholly within the State.

Even though passengers or goods are being carried between two States, a carrier transporting them may nevertheless not be engaged in interstate commerce. Though a carrier receives goods directed to a point outside the State, he is not an interstate carrier if he is only to carry within the State, and there deliver to an entirely independent succeeding carrier, with whom he has no common arrangement.[1] So if the carrier receives within the State of destination goods brought from without the State by an entirely independent carrier, the receiving carrier is not engaged in interstate commerce.[2] This is commonly the case where the intrastate carrier does not issue a through bill of lading, or receive freight upon through bills issued by an interstate carrier.[3] So where goods are shipped in one State, directed to a consignee in another, but carried only to the State line, and there received by the consignees, the shipment is not interstate.[4] A mere switching company which transfers goods from one carrier to another within the State, entirely without reference to their final destination, is not engaged in interstate commerce, whatever the destination of the goods.[5] This is true whether the switching is before or after loading.[6] And so the cab service of a railroad company at its New York terminus is wholly subject to local regulation.[7]

202 U. S. 543, 50 L. ed. 1142, 26 Sup. Ct. 722 (1906). See also Interstate S. Y. Co. v. Indianapolis U. Ry. Co., 99 Fed. 472 (1900).

[1] Ex parte Koehler, 30 Fed. 867 (1887).

[2] Fort Worth & D. C. Ry. Co. v. Whitehead, 6 Tex. Civ. App. 595, 26 S. W. 172 (1894).

[3] Interstate Comm. Comm. v. Bellaire, Z. & C. Ry. Co., 77 Fed. 942 (1897).

[4] United States v. Chicago, K. & S. R. R. Co., 81 Fed. 783 (1897).

[5] Kentucky & J. Bridge Co. v. Louisville & N. R. R. Co., 37 Fed. 567, 2 L. R. A. 289 (1889).

[6] Missouri Pacific R. R. Co. v. Larrabee Flour Mills, 211 U. S. 612, 53 L. ed. 352, 29 Sup. Ct. 696 (1909).

[7] New York ex rel. v. Knight, 192 U. S. 21, 48 L. ed. 325, 24 Sup. Ct. 202 (1904).

This is like the case where goods which had been consigned to one point within a State were afterwards sold and forwarded to another point.[1]

§ 1417. State legislation burdening interstate commerce.

If certain cases only are examined it would seem that State statutes which restrict the conduct of interstate transportation in any substantial degree are unconstitutional, the absence of congressional regulation on the subject being held equivalent to a declaration that the matter should be left undisturbed. Thus a State statute forbidding the separation of travelers has been held void as applied to interstate transportation.[2] But it follows that as the matter is to be left without legislative interference a carrier may make proper regulations separating white passengers from black, which may apply to interstate commerce.[3] A State statute directed against all discrimination in freight rates has been held unconstitutional, so far as its application to interstate shipments is concerned.[4] And of course a State statute cannot penalize the failure to deliver an interstate message promptly in another State.[5] There have been doubts as to the extent to which a State can regulate the stopping of interstate trains. It was at first said that the State could order this.[6] But it is now well established that this cannot be done, if the company provides an adequate

[1] Gulf, C. & S. F. Ry. Co. v. Texas, 204 U. S. 403, 51 L. ed. 540, 27 Sup. Ct. 360 (1907).

[2] Hall v. Decuir, 95 U. S. 485, 24 L. ed. 547 (1878).

[3] Chiles v. Chesapeake & O. R. R. Co., 218 U. S. 71, 30 Sup. Ct. 667 (1910).

[4] Wabash, St. L. & P. Ry. Co. v. Illinois, 118 U. S. 557, 30 L. ed. 244 (1886).

[5] Western Union Tel. Co. v. Pendleton, 122 U. S. 347, 30 L. ed. 1187 (1886).

[6] Lake Shore & M. S. Ry. Co. v. Ohio, 173 U. S. 285, 43 L. ed. 702, 19 Sup. Ct. 465 (1899). This case was virtually overruled by Cleveland, C., C. & St. L. R. R. Co. v. Illinois, 177 U. S. 514, 44 L. ed. 868, 20 Sup. Ct. 722 (1900).

local service.¹ It may be that a State can provide redress for failure to respond to a request for service even when the service refused is interstate.² But it is a question whether this is not going too far.³

§ 1418. Scope for State police power.

It will have been noticed that the problem is how far the conduct of interstate commerce should be left subject to the same law throughout the Union without disturbance by local law, and how far the police power of the State may be exercised by general legislation applying to the conduct of interstate commerce as well as to all things done within its borders. If the regulation is regarded as of vital importance to the State, the Federal courts may permit it to apply to interstate business, at least in the absence of congressional action. Thus a State may prohibit a railway from receiving even for interstate shipment hides not duly inspected to prevent fraudulent shipment of branded skins, because of the peculiar necessity for such policy in those regions.⁴ And a State may by general law prohibit running of freight trains interstate as well as intrastate on Sunday, this statute governing the conduct of all within the jurisdiction.⁵ To safeguard its citizens a State may require that all locomotive engineers operating trains within its borders shall be examined and licensed.⁶ And a State may es-

---

¹ See the latest cases on this point: Atlantic C. L. R. R. Co. v. Wharton et al., 207 U. S. 328, 52 L. ed. 230, 28 Sup. Ct. 121 (1907); Herndon v. Chicago, R. I. & P. R. R. Co., 218 U. S. 135, 30 Sup. Ct. 633 (1910).

² Western Union Tel. Co. v. James, 162 U. S. 650, 40 L. ed. 1105, 16 Sup. Ct. Rep. 934 (1895).

³ Houston & T. C. R. R. Co. v.

Mayes, 201 U. S. 321, 50 L. ed. 772, 26 Sup. Ct. 491 (1906).

⁴ New Mexico ex rel. v. Denver & R. G. R. R. Co., 203 U. S. 38, 51 L. ed. 78, 27 Sup. Ct. 1 (1906).

⁵ Hennington v. Georgia, 163 U. S. 299, 41 L. ed. 166, 16 Sup. Ct. 1086 (1896).

⁶ Smith v. Alabama, 124 U. S. 465, 31 L. ed. 508 (1888).

tablish quarantine against the introduction of diseases through interstate commerce.[1] But it may not unreasonably forbid the importation of all cattle whether diseased or not.[2] It is, however, established beyond question by many decisions that a State may not forbid, or even hamper the bringing in, of intoxicating liquors, the sale of which is forbidden within its borders in the belief that their consumption constitutes a danger to society.[3] The difference between diseased cattle and intoxicating liquor, one perceives, is, at best, a difference in degree. Perhaps the State may go further than this exercise of the police power strictly in regulating service, but it cannot go far without being told that it is hampering interstate commerce. Thus a State may regulate the heating of cars, those upon interstate trains as well as others.[4] But it may not require that cars shall be furnished for interstate shipments.[5] And so a State may require an interstate carrier to settle claims promptly.[6] But a State may not increase the liabilities of an initial carrier engaged in interstate commerce.[7]

§ 1419. Effect of action by Congress.

Whatever doubts there may be as to the extent to

[1] Kimmish v. Ball, 129 U. S. 217, 32 L. ed. 695 (1889).

[2] Railroad Co. v. Husen, 95 U. S. 465, 24 L. ed. 527 (1877).

[3] Bowman v. Chicago & N. W. Ry. Co., 125 U. S. 465, 31 L. ed. 700 (1881); Vance v. W. A. Vandercook Co., 170 U. S. 438, 42 L. ed. 1100, 18 Sup. Ct. 674 (1898); Adams Exp. Co. v. Kentucky, 206 U. S. 129, 51 L. ed. 987, 27 Sup. Ct. 606 (1907); Adams Express Co. v. Kentucky, 214 U. S. 218, 53 L. ed. 972, 29 Sup. Ct. 633 (1910).

[4] New York, N. H. & H. R. R. Co. v. New York, 165 U. S. 628, 41 L. ed. 853, 17 Sup. Ct. 418 (1897).

[5] Houston & T. C. Ry. Co. v. Mayes, 201 U. S. 321, 50 L. ed. 772, 26 Sup. Ct. 491 (1906).

[6] Atlantic C. L. Ry. Co. v. Mazursky, 216 U. S. 122, 30 Sup. Ct. 378 (1910).

[7] Central of Ga. Ry. Co. v. Murphey, 196 U. S. 194, 49 L. ed. 444, 25 Sup. Ct. 218 (1905).

which State regulation of interstate commerce may go
in the absence of Federal regulation, there is no doubt as
to the fate of State regulation of the conduct of interstate
commerce which comes in conflict with Federal regulation. Thus State legislation forbidding the charging of
more for a short haul than for a long haul can have no
application to interstate rates in view of the express provisions of the interstate commerce act as to this matter.[1]
So a State statute providing for redress for those charged
more than the scheduled rates is certainly without force
as to charges for interstate shipments in view of the
similar provision of the Interstate Commerce Act.[2] But
Congress cannot go so far in regulation of the conduct of
interstate commerce as to invade the general police jurisdiction of the States as to action within its borders. Thus
Congress cannot subject carriers hauling intrastate shipments to peculiar liabilities to their employés, so intermingled are the duties of these employés with both kinds
of commerce.[3] And Congress cannot empower a Secretary to fix a quarantine line beyond which cattle shall
not be moved by rail, so as to affect intrastate shipments.[4]

§ 1420. Power of Congress to regulate.

The regulation of interstate and foreign commerce is
one of the principal powers confided by the Constitution
to the Congress of the nation. That this power carries
with it the right to exercise it in all appropriate ways
would seem to be unquestionable.[5] In one of the first

---

[1] Louisville & N. Ry. Co. v.
Eubank, 184 U. S. 27, 46 L. ed. 416,
22 Sup. Ct. 277 (1902).

[2] Gulf, C. & S. F. Ry. Co. v.
Hefley, 158 U. S. 98, 39 L. ed. 910,
15 Sup. Ct. 802 (1895).

[3] The Employers' Liability Cases,
207 U. S. 463, 52 L. ed. 297, 28 Sup.
Ct. 141 (1908).

[4] Illinois Central R. R. Co. v.
McKendree, 203 U. S. 514, 51 L. ed.
298, 27 Sup. Ct. 153 (1906).

[5] Chesapeake & P. Telephone Co.
v. Manning, 186 U. S. 238, 46 L. ed.
1144, 22 Sup. Ct. 881 (1902).

cases [1] under the Interstate Commerce Act Mr. Justice Brewer said of the legislative power of Congress to regulate rates: "There were three obvious and dissimilar courses open for consideration. Congress might itself prescribe the rates; or it might commit to some subordinate tribunal this duty; or it might leave with the companies the right to fix rates subject to regulations and conditions." There would therefore seem to be no doubt that Congress possesses the inherent right which every legislature having power has, either to fix rates itself or give to its commission power in the premises. Thus far it has wisely refused to fix rates itself; and it has with equal wisdom withheld from the commission the power to make schedules of rates. By its persistent policy it has given the commission only power to give relief from unreasonable rates in particular cases where redress is asked. The first grant of power in this regard was held by the courts to go no further than to authorize the commission to declare the rate complained of improper.[2] But in the latest legislation the commission is given power in giving relief to designate what the proper rate shall be henceforth.[3]

Topic D. Impairing Obligation of Contract

§ 1421. Contract character of charter privileges.

A State may be disabled from fixing the rates of a railroad company by reason of some provision in its charter which constitutes a contract with the State.[4]   Such a

---

[1] Interstate Comm. Comm. v. Cincinnati, N. O. & T. P. Ry. Co., 167 U. S. 479, 42 L. ed. 243, 17 Sup. Ct. 896 (1897).

[2] Cincinnati, N. O. & T. P. Ry. Co. v. Interstate Comm. Comm., 162 U. S. 184, 40 L. ed. 935, 16 Sup. Ct. 700 (1896).

[3] See Railroad Commission Cases, 116 U. S. 307, 29 L. ed. 636 (1886).

[4] Stone v. New Orleans & N. E. R. R. Co., 116 U. S. 352. See also Stone v. Yazoo & Miss. R. R. Co., 62 Miss. 607, 52 Am. Rep. 193 (1883).

See, however, Georgia Ry. & Bk.

contract is made by a provision in a charter allowing a certain maximum charge to be made by the railroad. The charter having been accepted, the legislature cannot subsequently reduce the maximum rate.[1] So where the charter provided that rates should not be so reduced that the company should earn less than twelve per cent, this constituted a contract.[2] Later action impairs the obligation of earlier contracts.[3] But the contract must in reality be impaired by the later action.[4] And, perhaps it is needless to add, the action complained of must be subsequent to the contract pretended.[5]

§ 1422. Express contractual provision necessary.

A charter provision will not be construed as limiting the power of the legislature over rates unless there is an express provision to that effect. The presumption is against such limitations.[6] This was said in one case [7] where the charter provided that the charge for transportation should not exceed a certain amount. The court held that this provision did not constitute a contract limiting the power of the legislature to reduce rates. Mr. Justice Field said: "If the charter in this way provides that the charges

Co. v. Smith, 128 U. S. 174, 32 L. ed. 377, 9 Sup. Ct. 47 (1888), and see, contra, Laurel Fork R. R. Co. v. West Va. Transportation Co., 25 W. Va. 324 (1884).

[1] Detroit v. Detroit Citizens' St. Ry. Co., 184 U. S. 368, 46 L. ed. 592, 22 Sup. Ct. 410 (1902); Pingree v. Michigan Cent. R. R. Co., 118 Mich. 314, 76 N. W. 635 (1898).

[2] Ball v. Rutland R. R. Co., 93 Fed. 513 (1899).

[3] Minneapolis v. Minneapolis St. Ry. Co., 215 U. S. 417, 30 Sup. Ct. 118 (1910).

[4] People's Gaslight & Coke Co.

v. Chicago, 194 U. S. 1, 48 L. ed. 85, 24 Sup. Ct. 520 (1904).

[5] Oshkosh Waterworks Co. v. Oshkosh, 187 U. S. 437, 47 L. ed. 249, 23 Sup. Ct. 234 (1903).

[6] Chicago, M. & St. P. Ry. Co. v. Minnesota, 134 U. S. 418, 33 L. ed. 970, 10 Sup. Ct. 462 (1889).

See also Owensboro v. Owensboro Waterworks Co., 191 U. S. 358, 48 L. ed. 217, 24 Sup. Ct. 82 (1903).

[7] Georgia Ry. & B. Co. v. Smith, 128 U. S. 174, 32 L. ed. 377, 9 Sup. Ct. 47 (1888).

See also Helena Waterworks Co. v. Helena, 195 U. S. 383, 49 L. ed. 245, 25 Sup. Ct. 40 (1904).

which the company may make for its service in the transportation of persons and property shall be subject only to its own control up to the limit designated, exemption from legislative interference within that limit will be maintained. But to effect this result, the exemption must appear by such clear and unmistakable language that it cannot be reasonably construed consistently with the reservation of the power by the State. There is so such language in the present case."

§ 1423. Conferring powers does not create contract.

The ordinary clauses in railroad charters do not constitute a contract by the State not to regulate rates. Thus no such contract is created either by the grant of power to carry persons and property, or by the power to make by-laws, rules and regulations, or by the power to fix, regulate and receive the tolls and charges. This is merely conferring on the corporation the powers that an individual carrier would have, and it leaves the corporation, like the individual carrier, subject to the regulation of the State.[1] In Stanislaus County v. San Joaquin and King's River Canal and Irrigation Company,[2] the charter gave the company power to fix rates, subject to regulation by a board of supervisors, who, however, were not to reduce the rates below a certain maximum. It was held that this did not prevent the legislature itself from affecting the rates. "There is no promise made in the act that the legislature would not itself subsequently alter that authority."

§ 1424. Contracts made by municipal ordinance.

A contract limiting the power over rates may be made between a city and a public service company. Before

[1] Railroad Commission Cases, 116 U. S. 307, 29 L. ed. 636, 6 Sup. Ct. 334 (1886).

[2] 192 U. S. 201, 48 L. ed. 406, 24 Sup. Ct. 241 (1903).

holding that such a contract exists, a court must first determine whether the city has power to make such a contract.[1] Such power may be conferred on a city.[2] And thus a city ordinance, accepted by a public service company, which defines the duties of the company and names a maximum rate of compensation, constitutes a contract, and the rate named in such an ordinance cannot thereafter be diminished.[3] There is, however, a constant tendency to find that the ordinance did not constitute a contract and that the power over rates continues.[4]

§ 1425. Loss of the privilege.

The contractual exemption from regulation may, it would seem, be lost by a company by long-continued non-user as evidence of rescission of the contract, or by waiver. In San Joaquin Canal and Irrigation Company v. Stanislaus County,[5] it appeared that by a provision in its charter

[1] Walla Walla v. Walla Walla Water Co., 172 U. S. 1, 43 L. ed. 341, 19 Sup. Ct. 77 (1898); Los Angeles v. Los Angeles City Water Co., 177 U. S. 558, 44 L. ed. 886, 20 Sup. Ct. 736 (1900); Freeport Water Co. v. Freeport, 180 U. S. 587, 45 L. ed. 679, 21 Sup. Ct. 493 (1901); Rogers Park Water Co. v. Fergus, 180 U. S. 624, 45 L. ed. 702, 21 Sup. Ct. 493 (1901).

[2] Los Angeles v. Los Angeles City Water Co., 177 U. S. 558, 44 L. ed. 886, 20 Sup. Ct. 736 (1900); City of Cleveland v. Cleveland City Ry. Co., 194 U. S. 517, 48 L. ed. 1102, 24 Sup. Ct. 756 (1904); In re Pryor, 55 Kan. 724, 41 Pac. 958 (1895); Louisville Natural Gas Co. v. State, 135 Ind. 49, 34 N. E. 702 (1894).

[3] Detroit v. Detroit Citizens' St. Ry. Co., 184 U. S. 368, 46 L. ed. 592, 22 Sup. Ct. 410 (1902); Cleve-

land v. Cleveland City Ry. Co., 194 U. S. 517, 48 L. ed. 1102, 24 Sup. Ct. 756, 1904, aff'g 94 Fed. 385; Crosby v. City Council, 108 Ala. 498, 18 So. 723 (1895); State v. Laclede Gaslight Co., 102 Mo. 472, 14 S. W. 974 (1890); Columbus v. Columbus St. Ry. Co., 45 Ohio St. 98, 12 N. E. 651 (1886).

[4] Vicksburg Waterworks Co. v. Vicksburg, 185 U. S. 65, 46 L. ed. 808, 22 Sup. Ct. 585 (1902); Freeport Water Co. v. Freeport, 180 U. S. 587, 45 L. ed. 679, 21 Sup. Ct. 493 (1901); Rogers Park Water Co. v. Fergus, 180 U. S. 624, 45 L. ed. 702, 21 Sup. Ct. 490 (1901).

[5] 113 Fed. 930 (1902). On appeal the Supreme Court held that there was no contract. Stanislaus County v. San Joaquin & K. R. C. & I. Co., 192 U. S. 201, 48 L. ed. 406, 24 Sup. Ct. 241 (1903).

the company's revenues should not be reduced so as to yield a profit of less than 1½ per cent a month. This provision was made in 1862, and from that time until 1896 the company, fixing its own rates, never realized so much profit. In 1885 a statute was passed which provided that the rates of such companies should not be less than six nor more than eighteen per cent a year. In 1896 the proper board made rates which yielded revenue less than eighteen per cent a year. The court held the act legal, on the ground that the company having never for so long a period reduced its nominal right to possession had waived it.[1]

§ 1426. Assignment of the privilege.

The privilege of exemption is ordinarily personal with the grantee, and cannot be assigned in case of sale, lease or consolidation to another company which succeeds to its property and franchises.[2] So a statute dividing a turnpike company into two distinct corporations, controlling different portions of the road, and providing that each shall retain "all the powers, rights, and capacities" granted by the charter of the original company, does not pass to the new companies a right of exemption from legislative control of tolls which was reserved to the original company by its charter.[3] And so an exemption from State regulation of the price of gas, contained in the charter of a gas company, does not extend to the plants of,

---

[1] But where the waiver is by a municipal corporation, since the State is not a party to the contract, there seems to be no basis, in spite of intimations to the contrary for regarding the State's power to regulate as also waived in Minneapolis v. Minneapolis St. Ry. Co., 215 U. S. 417, 30 Sup. Ct. 118 (1910).

[2] St. Louis & S. F. Ry. Co. v. Gill, 156 U. S. 649, 39 L. ed. 567, 15 Sup. Ct. 484 (1895). But see Ball v. Rutland R. R. Co., 93 Fed. 513 (1899).

[3] Covington & L. T. Ry. Co. v. Sandford, 164 U. S. 578, 41 L. ed. 560, 17 Sup. Ct. 198 (1896).

and territory occupied by, certain other gas companies, not possessing such immunity in their own right, when absorbed by the former company under the general power of consolidation and merger conferred upon gas companies by an act which provided that the consolidated corporation should be subject to the legal obligations of the companies absorbed.[1] In Chicago Union Traction Company v. Chicago,[2] the question of violation of a contractual right of the company was involved. The company was lessee of two other street railways; both the latter had a right to charge a five-cent fare for each passenger carried, and this right in each case was alleged to have been assigned to the traction company. The court expressed the opinion that the grant of such a privilege was personal to the grantee, and could be assigned.

Topic E. Confiscation of Property

§ 1427. The doctrine of the " Granger Cases."

The question of rate regulation was first raised in the United States Supreme Court in the "Granger Cases," so called.[3] These were appeals from the State courts of Illinois, Wisconsin, and Minnesota, and from the Federal court in Iowa. In each of these States the legislature had

[1] People's Gaslight & Coke Co. v. Chicago, 194 U. S. 1, 48 L. ed. 851, 24 Sup. Ct. 520 (1904).

[2] 199 Ill. 484, 65 N. E. 451, 59 L. R. A. 631 (1902).

The court followed the decision in St. Louis & S. F. Ry. Co. v. Gill, 156 U. S. 649, 39 L. ed. 567, 15 Sup. Ct. 484 (1895), and distinguished the later case of Detroit v. Detroit Citizens' St. Ry. Co., 184 U. S. 368, 46 L. ed. 592, 22 Sup. Ct. 410 (1902), on the ground that in that case the question of the assigna-

bility of the exemption was not raised.

[3] Munn v. Illinois, 94 U. S. 113, 24 L. ed. 77 (1876); Chicago, B. & Q. R. R. Co. v. Iowa, 94 U. S. 155, 24 L. ed. 94 (1876); Peik v. Chicago & N. W. Ry. Co., 94 U. S. 164, 24 L. ed. 97 (1876); Chicago, M. & St. P. R. R. Co. v. Ackley, 94 U. S. 179, 24 L. ed. 99 (1876); Winona & St. P. R. R. Co. v. Blake, 94 U. S. 180, 24 L. ed. 99 (1876); Stone v. Wisconsin, 94 U. S. 181, 24 L. ed. 102 (1876).

regulated the rates of public service companies; in the first case a grain elevator, in the other cases a railroad. This legislation was attacked as unconstitutional, because a taking of the property without due process of law. The court, however, upheld the acts, on the ground that the property was affected with a public interest, and the rate for the use of it was therefore a subject of legislation. Mr. Chief Justice Waite went very far in supporting the power of the legislature. "We know," he said in Munn v. Illinois, "that this is a power which may be abused; but that is no argument against its existence. For protection against abuses by legislatures the people must resort to the polls, not to the courts." Again in Peik v. Chicago & Northwestern Railway he said: "Where property has been clothed with a public interest, the legislature may fix a limit to that which shall in law be reasonable for its use. This limit binds the courts as well as the people. If it has been improperly fixed, the legislature, not the courts, must be appealed to for the change."

§ 1428. Early modification of the doctrine.

There is no doubt of the meaning of the court in these cases. The action of the legislature was deemed binding at least as between private parties, without regard to the reasonableness of the rates. This extreme view was, however, soon abandoned. In Ruggles v. Illinois,[1] Mr. Justice Field in a concurring opinion, expressed the view that no unreasonable rate would be legal. And in Spring Valley Waterworks v. Schottler,[2] Mr. Chief Justice Waite spoke in a most conservative fashion, saying: "What may be done if the municipal authorities do not exercise an honest judgment, or if they fix upon a price which is manifestly unreasonable, need not now be considered." In

[1] 108 U. S. 526, 27 L. ed. 812, 2 Sup. Ct. 832 (1883).

[2] 110 U. S. 347, 28 L. ed. 173, 4 Sup. Ct. 48 (1884).

the Railroad Commission Cases [1] Mr. Chief Justice Waite, however, went further and said, in language which has formed the basis of the rule as it was finally established: "It is not inferred that this power of limitation or regulation is itself without limit. This power to regulate is not a power to destroy, and limitation is not the equivalent of confiscation." The rule was not yet finally settled, however. In Dow v. Beidelman [2] the court declined to enter upon the general question presented, Mr. Justice Gray saying that "the court has no means, if it would under any circumstances have the power, of determining that the rate of three cents a mile fixed by the legislature is unreasonable."

§ 1429. Fair return finally protected.

In Chicago, Milwaukee & St. Paul Railway v. Minnesota [3] the court held for the first time that after a rate is fixed by legislature or commission it is necessarily within the power of the courts to declare the rate illegal if it is unreasonable. "The question of the reasonableness of a rate of charge for transportation by a railroad company, involving, as it does, the element of reasonableness, both as regards the company and as regards the public, is eminently a question for judicial investigation, requiring the process of law for its determination. If the company is deprived of the power of charging reasonable rates for the use of its property, and such deprivation takes place in the absence of an investigation by judicial machinery, it is deprived of the lawful use of its property, and thus, in substance and effect, of the property itself, without due process of law, and in violation of the Constitution of the United States; and, in so far as it is thus deprived,

[1] 116 U. S. 307, 331, 29 L. ed. 636, 6 Sup. Ct. 334 (1886).

[2] 125 U. S. 680, 31 L. ed. 841, 8 Sup. Ct. 1028 (1888).

[3] 134 U. S. 418, 33 L. ed. 970, 10 Sup. Ct. 462 (1889).

while other persons are permitted to receive reasonable profits upon their invested capital, the company is deprived of the equal protection of the laws." In Reagan v. Farmers' Loan & Trust Company [1] the court reiterated this doctrine so strongly that it can no longer be regarded as open to question. Mr. Justice Brewer said: "There is nothing new or strange in this. It has always been a part of the judicial function to determine whether the act of one party (whether that party be a single individual, an organized body, or the public as a whole) operates to divest the other party of any rights of person or property."

§ 1430. When rates are confiscatory.

Ever since the leading case of Smyth v. Ames [2] it has been generally recognized that when a rate is fixed so low as to impair the earning power of the corporation and render it impossible to obtain a fair return upon its investment, the rate operates a confiscation of the property invested in the business, and is unconstitutional as depriving the company of its property without due process of law. As the rule is generally expressed, an unreasonably low rate is an illegal rate, whether it is fixed by the legislature itself,[3] or by a municipal corporation or board,

[1] 154 U. S. 362, 38 L. ed. 1014, 14 Sup. Ct. 1047 (1894).

[2] 169 U. S. 466, 42 L. ed. 819, 18 Sup. Ct. 418 (1898).

[3] In the following cases, among others, the new rates imposed by governmental authority were held confiscatory by the above principles on the showing made by the evidence adduced.

United States.—St. Louis & San Francisco Ry. Co. v. Gill, 156 U. S. 649, 39 L. ed. 567, 15 Sup. Ct. 484; Cotting v. Kansas City S. Y. Co., 183 U. S. 79, 46 L. ed. 92, 22 Sup. Ct. 30 (1901); Cleveland Gaslight Co. v. Cleveland, 71 Fed. 610 (1891); New Memphis Gaslight Co. v. Memphis, 72 Fed. 952 (1896); Southern Pac. Ry. Co. v. Railroad Commission, 78 Fed. 236 (1896); Northern Pac. Ry. Co. v. Keyes, 91 Fed. 47 (1898); Milwaukee Electric Ry. Co. v. Milwaukee, 87 Fed. 577 (1898); Spring Valley Waterworks v. San Francisco, 124 Fed. 574 (1903); Palatka Waterworks v. Palatka, 127 Fed. 161 (1903); Ozark

or by a commission.   On the other hand ever since the
leading case of San Joaquin Irrigation Co. v. Stanislaus
County [1] it has been recognized that when a fair return
is left the fact that the previous profits have been much
reduced is immaterial.[2]   It certainly is not confiscation

Bell Telephone Co. v. Springfield,
140 Fed. 666 (1905); Southern R.
R. Co. v. M'Neill, 155 Fed. 759
(1907); Seaboard Air Line Ry. Co.
v. Railroad Comm., 155 Fed. 792
(1907).

California.—Spring Valley Waterworks v. San Francisco, 82 Cal.
286, 22 Pac. 910 (1890).

Illinois.—Chicago v. Rogers Pk.
Co., 214 Ill. 212, 73 N. E. 375
(1905).

Maryland.—Maryland Tel. Co.
v. Simons Sons Co., 103 Md. 137,
63 Atl. 314 (1906).

Michigan.—Alpena Electric Co.
v. Alpena, 130 Mich. 413, 90 N. W.
36 (1902).

Nebraska.—Wabaska Electric Co.
v. City of Wymore, 60 Neb. 199,
82 N. W. 626 (1900).

New York.—Brooklyn Union Gas
Co. v. City of New York, 115 App.
Div. 69, 100 N. Y. Supp. 571 (1906).

Pennsylvania.—Pennsylvania R.
R. Co. v. Philadelphia County, 220
Pa. St. 100, 68 Atl. 676, 15 L. R. A.
(N. S.) 108 (1908).

Texas.—Texas & N. O. R. R. Co.
v. Sabine Tram. Co. (Tex. Civ.
App.), 121 S. W. 256 (1909).

Vermont.—State v. Central Vt.
Ry. Co., 81 Vt. 463, 71 Atl. 194, 130
Am. St. Rep. 1065 (1908).

[1] 192 U. S. 201, 48 L. ed. 406, 24
Sup. Ct. 241 (1903).

[2] In the following cases, among
others, the new rates imposed by

governmental authority were held
not to be confiscatory by the above
principles on the showing made by
the evidence adduced:

United States.—San Diego Land
& Town Co. v. National City,. 174
U. S. 739, 43 L. ed. 1154, 19 Sup.
Ct. 804 (1899); Minneapolis & St.
Louis R. R. Co. v. Minnesota, 186
U. S. 257, 46 L. ed. 1151, 22 Sup.
Ct. 900 (1902); San Diego Land &
Town Co. v. Jasper, 189 U. S. 439,
47 L. ed. 892, 23 Sup. Ct. 571
(1903); Prentice v. Atlantic C. L.
Ry. Co., 211 U. S. 210, 53 L. ed.
150, 29 Sup. Ct. 67 (1908); Will-
cox v. Consolidated Gas Co., 212 U.
S. 19, 53 L. ed. 382, 29 Sup. Ct.
192 (1909); Old Colony Trust Co.
v. City of Atlanta, 83 Fed. 39
(1897); Ball v. Rutland R. Co., 93
Fed. 513 (1899); Kimball v. City
of Cedar Rapids, 99 Fed. 130
(1900); Perkins v. Northern Pac.
Ry. Co., 155 Fed. 445 (1907); Home
Tel. & Tel. Co. v. Los Angeles, 155
Fed. 554 (1907), Central of Ga. Ry.
Co. v. M'Lendon, 157 Fed. 961
(1907).

Florida.—State v. Seaboard Air
Line Ry. Co., 48 Fla. 153, 37 So.
658 (1904).

Illinois.—Chicago v. Rogers Pk.
Co., 214 Ill. 212, 73 N. E. 375
(1905).

Indiana.—Chicago I. & L. Ry.
Co. v. Railroad Commission, 39
Ind. App. 358, 79 N. E. 520 (1907).

of the property if it is permitted to earn for its owners the current income on its actual value. All this has been so thoroughly discussed in the preceding chapters that this summary should be sufficient.

§ 1431. When fair net earnings left.

It is apparently now constitutional law that a rate may be fixed on a single class of freight though it would, if applied to all freight, produce less than a fair return to the railroad company. In the case of Minneapolis and St. Louis Railroad v. Minnesota [1] the plaintiff railroad attacked as unconstitutional a rate fixed by the railroad commission for the carriage of coal. The railroad did not claim that the reduction of this rate alone would deprive it of a fair return, but only that if the reduced rate

Iowa.—Cedar Rapids W. Co. v. Cedar Rapids, 118 Ia. 234, 91 N. W. 1081 (1902).

Kansas. — Tucker v. Missouri Pacific Ry. Co., 108 Pac. 89 (1910).

Maine.—Kennebec Water Dist. v. Waterville, 97 Me. 185, 54 Atl. 6, 60 L. R. A. 856 (1902).

Minnesota.—State ex rel. v. Minneapolis & St. Louis Ry. Co., 80 Minn. 191, 83 N. W. 60 (1900).

New York.—Richman v. Consolidated Gas Co., 114 App. Div. 216, 100 N. Y. Supp. 81 (1906).

Wisconsin.—Minneapolis, St. P. & S. S. M. R. R. Co. v. Railroad Commissioners, 137 Wis. 80, 116 N. W. 905 (1908).

[1] 186 U. S. 257, 46 L. ed. 1151, 22 Sup. Ct. 901 (1902), aff'g 80 Minn. 191, 83 N. W. 60 (1900).

See further in accord with the principal case:

United States.—Interstate Consolidated St. Ry. Co. v. Massachusetts, 207 U. S. 79, 28 Sup. Ct. 26 (1908); Willcox v. Consolidated Gas Co., 212 U. S. 19, 53 L. ed. 382, 29 Sup. Ct. 192 (1909); Southern R. R. Co. v. McNeill, 155 Fed. 756 (1907); Central of Ga. Ry. Co. v. McLendon, 157 Fed. 961 (1907).

Arkansas.—Missouri Pacific R. R. Co. v. Smith, 60 Ark. 221, 29 S. W. 752 (1895).

Minnesota.—State v. Minneapolis & St. L. Ry. Co., 80 Minn. 191, 83 N. W. 60 (1900).

Florida.—Pensacola & A. R. R. Co. v. Florida, 27 Fla. 403, 5 So. 833 (1889).

Georgia.—Southern Ry. Co. v. Atlanta Stove Wks., 128 Ga. 207, 57 S. E. 429 (1907).

North Dakota.—State ex rel. v. Northern Pacific Ry. Co. (N. D.), 120 N. W. 869, 25 L. R. A. (N. S.) 1001 (1909).

were applied to all freights the income of the road would be insufficient. The court held the rate legal, notwithstanding this fact; and there are many cases apparently to the same effect, both Federal and State. However, there are various cases both Federal and State which are plainly enough to the contrary.[1]

§ 1432. Reasonable rates not necessarily profitable.

In another case [2] of much the same sort, like language was used, Mr. Justice Carter of Florida saying: "The railroads have attempted to question the reasonableness of the rates established by the Railroad Commissioners. They will urge vehemently that the rates are not just and reasonable, and these general allegations are qualified by other statements that the rates, if enforced, will not afford a reasonable income, or in fact any net income over and above the reasonable cost of operating and maintaining them. The vice in this method lies in the fact that the question of reasonableness is made to depend upon the capacity of the rates to yield a net income over and above the cost of constructing and maintaining the road and the payment of fixed charges, whereas circumstances may exist under which rates are reasonable which do not afford a net income above the cost of operation and taxes, or the cost of operation, taxes and fixed charges. The returns set forth a few elements entering into the question as to what constitutes a reasonable rate, and attempt to make these elements controlling; whereas the conditions surrounding the operation of the road may deprive them of controlling force." [3]

[1] See particularly:

United States.—Lake Shore & M. S. Ry. Co. v. Smith, 173 U. S. 684, 43 L. ed. 858, 19 Sup. Ct. 565 (1899).

Pennsylvania.—Philadelphia R.

R. Co. v. Philadelphia Co., 220 Pa. St. 100, 68 Atl. 576, 15 L. R. A. (N. S.) 108 (1908).

[2] State v. Seaboard Air Line Ry. Co. (Fla.), 37 So. 314 (1901).

[3] The court seems to have com-

Topic F. Due Process of Law

§ 1433. Imposition of absolute liability.

Statutes may be passed defining further the obligations of those engaged in public employment to serve all that apply in accordance with their requirements. But if these statutes go so far as to impose an absolute liability upon the proprietors to act at all events, they ask more than a State can require in view of the Fourteenth Amendment. Thus a statute which made it the unqualified duty of a railroad to furnish cars within a certain number of days after request, has been held unconstitutional by the United States Supreme Court on the ground that it would unjustifiably subject to its penalties a railroad which had reasonable excuses for its failure to act in the particular case.[1] The only way in which the State courts can save a statute of this sort is to say that its general language is to be construed in view of the common law obligation which it reënforces, which is subject to many excuses recognized as inherent in the obligation.[2]

§ 1434. Requiring service outside employment.

Although one who devotes himself to public employment submits himself to regulation therein to the extent of the calling he has professed, it would be in reality depriving him of his liberty and property to force him into a service which is in fact outside the employment he has undertaken. This has come before the United States Supreme Court several times by the attempt of the States

mitted itself to this doctrine in St. Louis & S. F. R. R. Co. v. Gill, 156 U. S. 649, 39 L. ed. 567, 15 Sup. Ct. 484 (1895).

[1] Houston & T. C. R. R. Co. v. Mayes, 201 U. S. 321, 50 L. ed. 772, 26 Sup. Ct. 491 (1906).

[2] *Arkansas.*—St. Louis, I. M. & So. Ry. Co. v. Wynne H. & C. Co., 81 Ark. 373, 99 S. W. 375 (1907).

North Carolina.—Hardware Co. v. Railroad Co., 150 N. C. 703, 64 S. E. 873 (1908).

Texas.—Allen v. Texas & P. Ry. Co., 100 Tex. 525, 105 S. W. 792 (1907).

to make railroads perform service off their route. In one case it was held that a railroad could not be compelled to build sidings to manufacturing plants, at least at its own expense.[1] In another it was held that a railroad could not be compelled to furnish cars for foreign shipments, at least without many safeguards.[2] On the other hand a railroad can be compelled to perform its service in connecting with others to the full extent. It may be ordered to make its time tables conform with another's,[3] as one recent Supreme Case holds. And it may even be compelled to enter into joint through rates with a connection as another Supreme Court case holds.[4]

§ 1435. Police power unusually extensive.

It is universally agreed that the legislature may exercise over public service companies to an unusual extent, its general regulating power (which is commonly called its police power) for the benefit of all concerned. This was emphasized in one of the earliest of the leading cases[5] upon the police power where legislation requiring a railroad to maintain cattle guards was supported on this general reasoning. "Railways may be required so to conduct themselves, as to other persons, natural or corporate, as not unreasonably to injure them or their property. And if the business of railways is specially dangerous, they may be required to bear the expense of erecting such safeguards as will render it ordinarily safe to others, as is often required of natural persons under such circum-

---

[1] Missouri Pacific Ry. Co. v. Nebraska, 217 U. S. 196, 30 Sup. Ct. 461 (1910).

[2] Louisville & N. R. R. Co. v. Central S. Y. Co., 212 U. S. 132, 53 L. ed. 441, 29 Sup. Ct. 246 (1909).

[3] Atlantic C. L. Ry. Co. v. North Carolina Corp. Comm., 206 U. S.

1, 51 L. ed. 933, 27 Sup. Ct. 585 (1907).

[4] Wisconsin, M. & P. R. R. Co. v. Jacobson, 179 U. S. 287, 45 L. ed. 194, 21 Sup. Ct. 115 (1900).

[5] Thorpe v. Rutland & B. R. R. Co., 27 Vt. 140 (1855).

stances. There would be no end of illustrations upon this subject, which, in the detail are more familiar to others than to us. It may be extended to the supervision of the track, tending switches, running upon the time of other trains, running a road with a single track, using improper rails, not using proper precaution by way of safety beams in case of the breaking of axletrees, the number of brakemen upon a train with reference to the number of cars, employing intemperate or incompetent engineers and servants, running beyond a given rate of speed, and a thousand similar things, most of which have been made the subject of legislation or judicial determination, and all of which may be." [1]

§ 1436. Regulation must not be discriminatory.

It is usually stated as a general principle that in the regulation of public employment there must be no discrimination. But this is subject to the principle that all regulation should be appropriate to the object in view. To accommodate these two rules is not easy; but it may be done, in words at least, by saying that regulation should not be discriminatory, while it may be discriminating. The difficulty will be more apparent if two Supreme Court cases, both apparently in good standing, are contrasted. In the Stock Yards Case [2] the Supreme Court held unconstitutional a statute which regulated stock yards only of a certain size. In the Commodities Case [3] the Supreme Court held constitutional a statute which forbade the transportation of certain commodities produced by the railroad in question. If it is not possible

---

[1] See for a late case involving these points New York, N. H. & H. R. R. Co. v. New York, 165 U. S. 628, 41 L. ed. 853, 17 Sup. Ct. 418 (1897).

[2] Cotting v. Kansas City S. Y. Co., 183 U. S. 79, 46 L. ed. 92, 22 Sup. Ct. 30 (1901).

[3] United States v. Delaware & H. Co., 213 U. S. 366, 53 L. ed. 836, 29 Sup. Ct. 527 (1909).

to reconcile these cases, the latter seems to be preferable; for legislation should be appropriate to the matter in hand and designed to remedy actual conditions. Thus it has always been held that legislation may be properly made applicable only to railroad companies.[1] And in general, to require more of public service companies than of ordinary corporations is not improper in view of the difference in their nature.[2]

§ 1437. New limitations upon industrial liberty.

Liberty does not mean to men at the beginning of the twentieth century what it meant to men at the beginning of the nineteenth century. When the theory of *laissez faire* prevailed it meant liberty for the individual to do as he pleased with his own. To-day we know that in order that a man shall be free he must be protected from those who would do with him as they please. In order to protect the individual from the abuse of their power by others, we know that there can no longer be freedom of action for those who have gained undue power. We are beginning to appreciate that paradox which has come down to us from the sages of old, that liberty is not to be had without restraint. In a modern State we are no longer content in seeing that the weak are safe from the violence of the strong. Not until the people generally are protected from the oppression of those who control their destinies will there be real liberty.

§ 1438. Differentiation of the public services.

The truth is that so long as virtual competition yet prevails there is no necessity for coercive law since there is

---

[1] Missouri, K. & T. Ry. Co. v. May, 194 U. S. 267, 48 L. ed. 971, 24 Sup. Ct. 638 (1904) (note, however, the dissenting opinion).

[2] Seaboard A. L. Ry. Co. v. Seegers, 207 U. S. 73, 52 L. ed. 108, 28 Sup. Ct. 28 (1907). See also the cases cited.

then no power over the purchasing public. But where in any business virtual monopoly is permanently established the people will not be denied in their deliberate policy of effectual regulation for such public services for the common good. Only to this extent the individualistic ideal of society gives place to the collective policy. It is with true appreciation of the real issue that we are fighting for state control to gain individual liberty. It may once have been the ideal of industrial freedom that a man might do as he pleased with his own; in any event that is no longer our notion of social justice. It is believed now that with growth in power over the particular market comes increase in responsibility to the dependent public. No one who is inspired to any degree by the spirit of the times would entertain the suggestion that we ought to work to turn the law back to that time fifty years ago when those who had the control of public utilities were, by a failure to apply the law promptly, left to deal with their public or not as they pleased. Nor could anyone hope to bring the law of public service back to its imperfect state of twenty-five years ago when the railroads could treat one shipper differently from another. The most of us of this generation not only believe in the law of public employment, but in its enforcement to its utmost extent.

§ 1439. Ultimate regulation of all monopoly.

So far as one can judge the future holds no possibility of the coercive regulation of the conduct of all businesses which, it is apparent, would be one form of socialism. Regulation of this extreme sort will be confined to those businesses which are affected with a public interest. It is, however, certain that the other businesses than those now within this classification will be brought within it. Indeed, in reading the early chapters of this work the generalization must have occurred to one that all businesses which have a virtual monopoly firmly established in the nature of things, are so affected with a public interest as to be within the class of callings which are considered public employments. What branches of industry will eventually be considered of such public importance as to be included within the category of public callings it would be rash to predict. But no one can study the authorities on this subject without feeling their great potentialities. In private businesses, one may sell or not as one pleases, manufacture what qualities one chooses, demand any price that can be gotten, and give any rebates that are advantageous. It is because the modern trusts are carrying on a predatory competition under the cover of this law that we have the trust problem. All this time in public businesses one must serve all that apply without exclusive conditions, provide adequate facilities to meet all the demands of the consumer, exact only reasonable charges for the services that are rendered, and between customers under similar circumstances make no discriminations. If this law might be enforced against the trusts, it is believed that a solution of the problem would be found.

§ 1440. State control not socialism.

Regulation does not mean socialism. Belief in state control does not lead one to socialism; indeed, it saves one from socialism if truly understood. It is only in those few businesses where the conditions are monopolistic that dangerous power over their public has been attained by those who have the control. In most businesses the virtual competition which prevails puts the distributors at the mercy of their public. In current opinion the recognition of this distinction is manifest. Men are as eager for an open market as ever; but they wish the control of monopoly to insure it. The demand is for freer trade where competition prevails and stricter regulation where monopoly is found. In times of peril to our industrial organization faith in our common law may show the way out. It cannot be that this law has guided our destinies from age to age through the countless dangers of society, only to fail us now.

APPENDIX

APPENDIX A

THE INTERSTATE COMMERCE ACT

Be it enacted by the Senate and House of Representatives of the United States of America in Congress assembled,

§ 1. Regulation of transportation.[1]

SECTION 1. (*As amended June 29, 1906, April 13, 1908, and June 18, 1910.*)

That the provisions of this Act shall apply to any corporation or any person or persons engaged in the transportation of oil or other commodity, except water and except natural or artificial gas, by means of pipe lines, or partly by pipe lines and partly by railroad, or partly by pipe lines and partly by water, and to telegraph, telephone, and cable companies (whether wire or wireless) engaged in sending messages from one State, Territory, or District of the United States to any other State, Territory, or District of the United States or to any foreign country, who shall be considered and held to be common carriers within the meaning and purpose of this Act, and to any common carrier or carriers engaged in the transportation of passengers or property wholly by railroad (or partly by railroad and partly by water when both are used under a common control, management, or arrangement for a continuous carriage or shipment), from one State or Territory of the United States or the District of Columbia to any other State or Territory of the United States or the District of Columbia, or from one place in a Territory to another place in the same Territory, or from any place in the United States to an adjacent foreign country, or from any place in the United States through a foreign country to any other place in the United States, and also to the transportation

---

[1] This heading is not in the act.

in like manner of property shipped from any place in the United States to a foreign country and carried from such place to a port of transshipment, or shipped from a foreign country to any place in the United States and carried to such place from a port of entry either in the United States or an adjacent foreign country: *Provided, however,* That the provisions of this Act shall not apply to the transportation of passengers or property, or to the receiving, delivering, storage, or handling of property wholly within one State and not shipped to or from a foreign country from or to any State or Territory as aforesaid, nor shall they apply to the transmission of messages by telephone, telegraph, or cable wholly within one State and not transmitted to or from a foreign country from or to any State or Territory as aforesaid.

The term "common carrier" as used in this Act shall include express companies and sleeping car companies. The term "railroad" as used in this Act shall include all bridges and ferries used or operated in connection with any railroad, and also all the road in use by any corporation operating a railroad, whether owned or operated under a contract, agreement, or lease, and shall also include all switches, spurs, tracks, and terminal facilities of every kind used or necessary in the transportation of the persons or property designated herein, and also all freight depots, yards, and grounds used or necessary in the transportation or delivery of any of said property; and the term "transportation" shall include cars and other vehicles and all instrumentalities and facilities of shipment or carriage, irrespective of ownership or of any contract, express or implied, for the use thereof and all services in connection with the receipt, delivery, elevation, and transfer in transit, ventilation, refrigeration or icing, storage, and handling of property transported; and it shall be the duty of every carrier subject to the provisions of this Act to provide and furnish such transportation upon reasonable request therefor, and to establish through routes and just and reasonable rates applicable thereto; and to provide reasonable facilities for operating such through routes and to make reasonable rules and regulations with respect to the exchange, interchange, and return of cars used therein, and for the operation of such through routes, and providing for reasonable compensation to those entitled thereto.

All charges made for any service rendered or to be rendered in the transportation of passengers or property and for the transmission of messages by telegraph, telephone, or cable, as aforesaid, or in connection therewith, shall be just and reasonable; and every unjust and unreasonable charge for such service or any part thereof is prohibited and declared to be unlawful: *Provided,* That messages by telegraph, telephone, or cable, subject to the provisions of this Act, may be classified into day, night, repeated, unrepeated, letter, commercial, press, Government, and such other classes as are just and reasonable, and different rates may be charged for the different classes of messages: *And provided further,* That nothing in this Act shall be construed to prevent telephone, telegraph, and cable companies from entering into contracts with common carriers for the exchange of services.

And it is hereby made the duty of all common carriers subject to the provisions of this Act to establish, observe, and enforce just and reasonable classifications of property for transportation, with reference to which rates, tariffs, regulations, or practices are or may be made or prescribed, and just and reasonable regulations and practices affecting classifications, rates, or tariffs, the issuance, form, and substance of tickets, receipts, and bills of lading, the manner and method of presenting, marking, packing, and delivering property for transportation, the facilities for transportation, the carrying of personal, sample, and excess baggage, and all other matters relating to or connected with the receiving, handling, transporting, storing, and delivery of property subject to the provisions of this Act which may be necessary or proper to secure the safe and prompt receipt, handling, transportation, and delivery of property subject to the provisions of this Act upon just and reasonable terms, and every such unjust and unreasonable classification, regulation, and practice with reference to commerce between the States and with foreign countries is prohibited and declared to be unlawful.

No common carrier subject to the provisions of this Act

[1275]

shall, after January first, nineteen hundred and seven, directly
or indirectly, issue or give any interstate free ticket, free pass,
or free transportation for passengers, except to its employees
and their families, its officers, agents, surgeons, physicians, and
attorneys at law; to ministers of religion, traveling secretaries
of railroad Young Men's Christian Associations, inmates of
hospitals and charitable and eleemosynary institutions, and
persons exclusively engaged in charitable and eleemosynary
work; to indigent, destitute, and homeless persons, and to such
persons when transported by charitable societies or hospitals,
and the necessary agents employed in such transportation; to
inmates of the National Homes or State Homes for Disabled
Volunteer Soldiers, and of Soldiers' and Sailors' Homes, including those about to enter and those returning home after discharge; to necessary care takers of live stock, poultry, milk,
and fruit; to employees on sleeping cars, express cars, and to
linemen of telegraph and telephone companies; to Railway Mail
Service employees, post-office inspectors, customs inspectors,
and immigration inspectors; to newsboys on trains, baggage
agents, witnesses attending any legal investigation in which the
common carrier is interested, persons injured in wrecks and
physicians and nurses attending such persons: *Provided*, That
this provision shall not be construed to prohibit the interchange
of passes for the officers, agents, and employees of common carriers, and their families; nor to prohibit any common carrier
from carrying passengers free with the object of providing relief
in cases of general epidemic, pestilence, or other calamitous visitation: *And provided further*, That this provision shall not be
construed to prohibit the privilege of passes or franks, or the
exchange thereof with each other, for the officers, agents, employees, and their families of such telegraph, telephone, and
cable lines, and the officers, agents, employees and their families of other common carriers subject to the provisions of this
Act: *Provided further*, That the term "employees" as used in
this paragraph shall include furloughed, pensioned, and super-
annuated employees, persons who have become disabled or
infirm in the service of any such common carrier, and the remains of a person killed in the employment of a carrier and ex-

employees traveling for the purpose of entering the service of any such common carrier; and the term "families" as used in this paragraph shall include the families of those persons named in this proviso, also the families of persons killed, and the widows during widowhood and minor children during minority of persons who died while in the service of any such common carrier. Any common carrier violating this provision shall be deemed guilty of a misdemeanor, and for each offense, on conviction, shall pay to the United States a penalty of not less than one hundred dollars nor more than two thousand dollars, and any person, other than the persons excepted in this provision, who uses any such interstate free ticket, free pass, or free transportation shall be subject to a like penalty. Jurisdiction of offenses under this provision shall be the same as that provided for offenses in an Act entitled "An Act to further regulate commerce with foreign nations and among the States," approved February nineteenth, nineteen hundred and three, and any amendment thereof. (*See section 22.*)

From and after May first, nineteen hundred and eight, it shall be unlawful for any railroad company to transport from any State, Territory, or the District of Columbia, to any other State, Territory, or the District of Columbia, or to any foreign country, any article or commodity, other than timber and the manufactured products thereof, manufactured, mined, or produced by it, or under its authority, or which it may own in whole or in part, or in which it may have any interest, direct or indirect, except such articles or commodities as may be necessary and intended for its use in the conduct of its business as a common carrier.

Any common carrier subject to the provisions of this Act, upon application of any lateral, branch line of railroad, or of any shipper tendering interstate traffic for transportation, shall construct, maintain, and operate upon reasonable terms a switch connection with any such lateral, branch line of railroad, or private side track which may be constructed to connect with its railroad, where such connection is reasonably practicable and can be put in with safety and will furnish sufficient business to justify the construction and maintenance of the same; and shall

furnish cars for the movement of such traffic to the best of its
ability without discrimination in favor of or against any such
shipper. If any common carrier shall fail to install and operate
any such switch or connection as aforesaid, on application therefor in writing by any shipper or owner of such lateral, branch
line of railroad, such shipper or owner of such lateral, branch
line of railroad may make complaint to the Commission, as
provided in section thirteen of this Act, and the Commission
shall hear and investigate the same and shall determine as to
the safety and practicability thereof and justification and reasonable compensation therefor, and the Commission may make
an order, as provided in section fifteen of this Act, directing
the common carrier to comply with the provisions of this section in accordance with such order, and such order shall be enforced as hereinafter provided for the enforcement of all other
orders by the Commission, other than orders for the payment of
money.

§ 2. Unjust discrimination defined and forbidden.[1]

Sec. 2. That if any common carrier subject to the provisions
of this Act shall, directly or indirectly, by any special rate, rebate, drawback, or other device, charge, demand, collect, or
receive from any person or persons a greater or less compensation for any service rendered, or to be rendered, in the transportation of passengers or property, subject to the provisions of
this Act, than it charges, demands, collects, or receives from any
other person or persons for doing for him or them a like and contemporaneous service in the transportation of a like kind of
traffic under substantially similar circumstances and conditions,
such common carrier shall be deemed guilty of unjust discrimination, which is hereby prohibited and declared to be unlawful.

§ 3. Undue or unreasonable preference or advantage for-
bidden.[1]

Sec. 3. That it shall be unlawful for any common carrier subject to the provisions of this act to make or give any undue or
unreasonable preference or advantage to any particular person,

[1] This heading is not in the act.

company, firm, corporation, or locality, or any particular description of traffic, in any respect whatsoever, or to subject any particular person, company, firm, corporation, or locality, or any particular description of traffic, to any undue or unreasonable prejudice or disadvantage in any respect whatsoever.

Every common carrier subject to the provisions of this Act shall, according to their respective powers, afford all reasonable, proper, and equal facilities for the interchange of traffic between their respective lines, and for the receiving, forwarding, and delivering of passengers and property to and from their several lines and those connecting therewith, and shall not discriminate in their rates and charges between such connecting lines; but this shall not be construed as requiring any such common carrier to give the use of its tracks or terminal facilities to another carrier engaged in like business.

§ 4. Long and short haul provision.[1]

SEC. 4. (*As amended June 18, 1910.*)

That it shall be unlawful for any common carrier subject to the provisions of this Act to charge or receive any greater compensation in the aggregate for the transportation of passengers, or of like kind of property, for a shorter than for a longer distance over the same line or route in the same direction, the shorter being included within the longer distance, or to charge any greater compensation as a through route than the aggregate of the intermediate rates subject to the provisions of this Act; but this shall not be construed as authorizing any common carrier within the terms of this Act to charge or receive as great compensation for a shorter as for a longer distance: *Provided, however,* That upon application to the Interstate Commerce Commission such common carrier may in special cases, after investigation, be authorized by the Commission to charge less for longer than for shorter distances for the transportation of passengers or property; and the Commission may from time to time prescribe the extent to which such designated common carrier may be relieved from the operation of this section: *Provided, further,* That no rates or charges lawfully existing at the time of

---

[1] This heading is not in the act.

the passage of this amendatory Act shall be required to be changed by reason of the provisions of this section prior to the expiration of six months after the passage of this Act, nor in any case where application shall have been filed before the Commission, in accordance with the provisions of this section, until a determination of such application by the Commission.

Whenever a carrier by railroad shall in competition with a water route or routes reduce the rates on the carriage of any species of freight to or from competitive points, it shall not be permitted to increase such rates unless after hearing by the Interstate Commerce Commission it shall be found that such proposed increase rests upon changed conditions other than the elimination of water competition.

§ 5. Pooling of freights and division of earnings forbidden.[1]

SEC. 5. That it shall be unlawful for any common carrier subject to the provisions of this Act to enter into any contract, agreement, or combination with any other common carrier or carriers for the pooling of freights of different and competing railroads, or to divide between them the aggregate or net proceeds of the earnings of such railroads, or any portion thereof; and in any case of an agreement for the pooling of freights as aforesaid, each day of its continuance shall be deemed a separate offense.

§ 6. Printing and posting of schedules.[1]

SEC. 6. (*Amended March 2, 1889. Following section substituted June 29, 1906. Amended June 18, 1910.*)

That every common carrier subject to the provisions of this Act shall file with the Commission created by this Act and print and keep open to public inspection schedules showing all the rates, fares, and charges for transportation between different points on its own route and between points on its own route and points on the route of any other carrier by railroad, by pipe line, or by water when a through route and joint rate have been established. If no joint rate over the through route has been established, the several carriers in such through route shall file,

---

[1] This heading is not in the act.

print, and keep open to public inspection, as aforesaid, the separately established rates, fares and charges applied to the through transportation. The schedules printed as aforesaid by any such common carrier shall plainly state the places between which property and passengers will be carried, and shall contain the classification of freight in force, and shall also state separately all terminal charges, storage charges, icing charges, and all other charges which the Commission may require, all privileges or facilities granted or allowed and any rules or regulations which in any wise change, affect, or determine any part or the aggregate of such aforesaid rates, fares, and charges, or the value of the service rendered to the passenger, shipper, or consignee. Such schedules shall be plainly printed in large type, and copies for the use of the public shall be kept posted in two public and conspicuous places in every depot, station, or office of such carrier where passengers or freight, respectively, are received for transportation, in such form that they shall be accessible to the public and can be conveniently inspected. The provisions of this section shall apply to all traffic, transportation, and facilities defined in this Act.

Any common carrier subject to the provisions of this Act receiving freight in the United States to be carried through a foreign country to any place in the United States shall also in like manner print and keep open to public inspection, at every depot or office where such freight is received for shipment, schedules showing the through rates established and charged by such common carrier to all points in the United States beyond the foreign country to which it accepts freight for shipment; and any freight shipped from the United States through a foreign country into the United States the through rate on which shall not have been made public, as required by this Act, shall, before it is admitted into the United States from said foreign country, be subject to customs duties as if said freight were of foreign production.

No change shall be made in the rates, fares, and charges or joint rates, fares, and charges which have been filed and published by any common carrier in compliance with the requirements of this section, except after thirty days' notice to the

Commission and to the public published as aforesaid, which shall plainly state the changes proposed to be made in the schedule then in force and the time when the changed rates, fares, or charges will go into effect; and the proposed changes shall be shown by printing new schedules, or shall be plainly indicated upon the schedules in force at the time and kept open to public inspection: *Provided,* That the Commission may, in its discretion and for good cause shown, allow changes upon less than the notice herein specified, or modify the requirements of this section in respect to publishing, posting, and filing of tariffs, either in particular instances or by a general order applicable to special or peculiar circumstances or conditions.

The names of the several carriers which are parties to any joint tariff shall be specified therein, and each of the parties thereto, other than the one filing the same, shall file with the Commission such evidence of concurrence therein or acceptance thereof as may be required or approved by the Commission, and where such evidence of concurrence or acceptance is filed it shall not be necessary for the carriers filing the same to also file copies of the tariffs in which they are named as parties.

Every common carrier subject to this Act shall also file with said Commission copies of all contracts, agreements, or arrangements with other common carriers in relation to any traffic affected by the provisions of this Act to which it may be a party.

The Commission may determine and prescribe the form in which the schedules required by this section to be kept open to public inspection shall be prepared and arranged and may change the form from time to time as shall be found expedient.

No carrier, unless otherwise provided by this Act, shall engage or participate in the transportation of passengers or property, as defined in this Act, unless the rates, fares, and charges upon which the same are transported by said carrier have been filed and published in accordance with the provisions of this Act; nor shall any carrier charge or demand or collect or receive a greater or less or different compensation for such transportation of passengers or property, or for any service in connection therewith, between the points named in such tariffs than the rates, fares, and charges which are specified in the tariff filed and in effect at the time; nor shall any carrier refund or remit in any manner or by any device any portion of the rates, fares, and charges so specified, nor extend to any shipper or person any privileges or facilities in the transportation of passengers or property, except such as are specified in such tariffs: *Provided,* That wherever the word "carrier" occurs in this Act it shall be held to mean "common carrier."

That in time of war or threatened war preference and precedence shall, upon the demand of the President of the United States, be given, over all other traffic, to the transportation of troops and material of war, and carriers shall adopt every means within their control to facilitate and expedite the military traffic.

The Commission may reject and refuse to file any schedule that is tendered for filing which does not provide and give lawful notice of its effective date, and any schedule so rejected by the Commission shall be void and its use shall be unlawful.

In case of failure or refusal on the part of any carrier, receiver, or trustee to comply with the terms of any regulation adopted and promulgated or any order made by the Commission under the provisions of this section, such carrier, receiver, or trustee shall be liable to a penalty of five hundred dollars for each such offense, and twenty-five dollars for each and every day of the continuance of such offense, which shall accrue to the United States and may be recovered in a civil action brought by the United States.

If any common carrier subject to the provisions of this Act, after written request made upon the agent of such carrier hereinafter in this section referred to, by any person or company for a written statement of the rate or charge applicable to a described shipment between stated places under the schedules or tariffs to which such carrier is a party, shall refuse or omit to give such written statement within a reasonable time, or shall misstate in writing the applicable rate, and if the person or company making such request suffers damage in consequence of such refusal or omission or in consequence of the misstatement of the rate, either through making the shipment over a line or route for which the proper rate is higher than the rate over another available line or route, or through entering into any sale or other contract whereunder such person or company obligates himself or itself to make such shipment of freight at his or its cost, then the said carrier shall be liable to a penalty of two hundred and fifty dollars, which shall accrue to the United States and may be recovered in a civil action brought by the United States.

It shall be the duty of every carrier by railroad to keep at all times conspicuously posted in every station where freight is received for transportation the name of an agent resident in the city, village, or town where such station is located, to whom application may be made for the information by this section required to be furnished on written request; and in case any carrier shall fail at any time to have such name so posted in any station, it shall be sufficient to address such request in substantially the following form: "The Station Agent of the —— Company at —— Station," together with the name of the proper post-office, inserting the name of the carrier company and of the station in the blanks, and to serve the same by depositing the request so addressed, with postage thereon prepaid, in any post-office.

§ 7. Continuous carriage of freights.[1]

Sec. 7. That it shall be unlawful for any common carrier subject to the provisions of this Act to enter into any combination, contract, or agreement, expressed or implied, to prevent, by change of time schedule, carriage in different cars, or by other means or devices, the carriage of freights from being continuous from the place of shipment to the place of destination; and no break of bulk, stoppage, or interruption made by such common carrier shall prevent the carriage of freights from being and being treated as one continuous carriage from the place of shipment to the place of destination, unless such break, stoppage, or interruption was made in good faith for some necessary purpose, and without any intent to avoid or unnecessarily interrupt such continuous carriage or to evade any of the provisions of this Act.

§ 8. Liability of common carriers for damages.[1]

Sec. 8. That in case any common carrier subject to the

[1] This heading is not in the act.

provisions of this Act shall do, cause to be done, or permit to be done any act, matter, or thing in this Act prohibited or declared to be unlawful, or shall omit to do any act, matter, or thing in this Act required to be done, such common carrier shall be liable to the person or persons injured thereby for the full amount of damages sustained in consequence of any such violation of the provisions of this Act, together with a reasonable counsel or attorney's fee, to be fixed by the court in every case of recovery, which attorney's fee shall be taxed and collected as part of the costs in the case.

§ 9. Election whether to complain to the Commission or bring suit.[1]

SEC. 9. That any person or persons claiming to be damaged by any common carrier subject to the provisions of this Act may either make complaint to the Commission as hereinafter provided for, or may bring suit in his or their own behalf for the recovery of the damages for which such common carrier may be liable under the provisions of this Act, in any district or circuit court of the United States of competent jurisdiction; but such person or persons shall not have the right to pursue both of said remedies, and must in each case elect which one of the two methods of procedure herein provided for he or they will adopt. In any such action brought for the recovery of damages, the court before which the same shall be pending may compel any director, officer, receiver, trustee, or agent of the corporation or company defendant in such suit to attend, appear, and testify in such case, and may compel the production of the books and papers of such corporation or company party to any such suit; the claim that any such testimony or evidence may tend to criminate the person giving such evidence shall not excuse such witness from testifying, but such evidence or testimony shall not be used against such person on the trial of any criminal proceeding.

§ 10. Penalties for violations of Act by carriers.[1]

SEC. 10. (*As amended March 2, 1889, and June 18, 1910.*)

That any common carrier subject to the provisions of this

[1] This heading is not in the act.

Act, or, whenever such common carrier is a corporation, any
director or officer thereof, or any receiver, trustee, lessee, agent,
or person acting for or employed by such corporation, who,
alone or with any other corporation, company, person, or party,
shall willfully do or cause to be done, or shall willingly suffer or
permit to be done, any act, matter, or thing in this Act prohibited or declared to be unlawful, or who shall aid or abet
therein, or shall willfully omit or fail to do any act, matter, or
thing in this Act required to be done, or shall cause or willingly
suffer or permit any act, matter, or thing so directed or required
by this Act to be done not to be so done, or shall aid or abet any
such omission or failure, or shall be guilty of any infraction of
this Act for which no penalty is otherwise provided, or who shall
aid or abet therein, shall be deemed guilty of a misdemeanor,
and shall, upon conviction thereof in any district court of the
United States within the jurisdiction of which such offense was
committed, be subject to a fine of not to exceed five thousand
dollars for each offense: *Provided*, That if the offense for which
any person shall be convicted as aforesaid shall be an unlawful
discrimination in rates, fares, or charges for the transportation
of passengers or property, such person shall, in addition to the
fine hereinbefore provided for, be liable to imprisonment in the
penitentiary for a term of not exceeding two years, or both such
fine and imprisonment, in the discretion of the court.

Any common carrier subject to the provisions of this Act, or,
whenever such common carrier is a corporation, any officer or
agent thereof, or any person acting for or employed by such corporation, who, by means of false billing, false classification, false
weighing, or false report of weight, or by any other device or
means, shall knowingly and willfully assist, or shall willingly
suffer or permit, any person or persons to obtain transportation
for property at less than the regular rates then established and
in force on the line of transportation of such common carrier,
shall be deemed guilty of a misdemeanor, and shall, upon conviction thereof in any court of the United States of competent
jurisdiction within the district in which such offense was committed, be subject to a fine of not exceeding five thousand dollars, or imprisonment in the penitentiary for a term of not ex-

ceeding two years, or both, in the discretion of the court, for each offense.

Any person, corporation, or company, or any agent or officer thereof, who shall deliver property for transportation to any common carrier subject to the provisions of this Act, or for whom, as consignor or consignee, any such carrier shall transport property, who shall knowingly and willfully, directly or indirectly, himself or by employee, agent, officer, or otherwise, by false billing, false classification, false weighing, false representation of the contents of the package or the substance of the property, false report of weight, false statement, or by any other device or means, whether with or without the consent or connivance of the carrier, its agent, or officer, obtain or attempt to obtain transportation for such property at less than the regular rates then established and in force on the line of transportation; or who shall knowingly and willfully, directly or indirectly, himself or by employee, agent, officer, or otherwise, by false statement or representation as to cost, value, nature, or extent of injury, or by the use of any false bill, bill of lading, receipt, voucher, roll, account, claim, certificate, affidavit, or deposition, knowing the same to be false, fictitious, or fraudulent, or to contain any false, fictitious, or fraudulent statement or entry, obtain or attempt to obtain any allowance, refund, or payment for damage or otherwise in connection with or growing out of the transportation of or agreement to transport such property, whether with or without the consent or connivance of the carrier, whereby the compensation of such carrier for such transportation, either before or after payment, shall in fact be made less than the regular rates then established and in force on the line of transportation, shall be deemed guilty of fraud, which is hereby declared to be a misdemeanor, and shall, upon conviction thereof in any court of the United States of competent jurisdiction, within the district in which such offense was wholly or in part committed, be subject for each offense to a fine of not exceeding five thousand dollars or imprisonment in the penitentiary for a term of not exceeding two years, or both, in the discretion of the court: *Provided*, That the penalty of imprisonment shall not apply to artificial persons.

If any such person, or any officer or agent of any such corporation or company, shall, by payment of money or other thing of value, solicitation, or otherwise, induce or attempt to induce any common carrier subject to the provisions of this Act, or any of its officers or agents, to discriminate unjustly in his, its, or their favor as against any other consignor or consignee in the transportation of property, or shall aid or abet any common carrier in any such unjust discrimination, such person or such officer or agent of such corporation or company shall be deemed guilty of a misdemeanor, and shall, upon conviction thereof in any court of the United States of competent jurisdiction within the district in which such offense was committed, be subject to a fine of not exceeding five thousand dollars, or imprisonment in the penitentiary for a term of not exceeding two years, or both, in the discretion of the court, for each offense; and such person, corporation, or company shall also, together with said common carrier, be liable, jointly or severally, in an action to be brought by any consignor or consignee discriminated against in any court of the United States of competent jurisdiction for all damages caused by or resulting therefrom.

§ 11. The Interstate Commerce Commission.[1]

SEC. 11. That a Commission is hereby created and established to be known as the Interstate Commerce Commission, which shall be composed of five Commissioners, who shall be appointed by the President, by and with the advice and consent of the Senate. The Commissioners first appointed under this Act shall continue in office for the term of two, three, four, five, and six years, respectively, from the first day of January, Anno Domini eighteen hundred and eighty-seven, the term of each to be designated by the President; but their successors shall be appointed for terms of six years, except that any person chosen to fill a vacancy shall be appointed only for the unexpired time of the Commissioner whom he shall succeed. Any Commissioner may be removed by the President for inefficiency, neglect of duty, or malfeasance in office. Not more than three of the Commissioners shall be appointed from the same political party.

[1] This heading is not in the act.

No person in the employ of or holding any official relation to any common carrier subject to the provisions of this act, or owning stock or bonds thereof, or who is in any manner pecuniarily interested therein, shall enter upon the duties of or hold such office. Said Commissioners shall not engage in any other business, vocation, or employment. No vacancy in the Commission shall impair the right of the remaining Commissioners to exercise all the powers of the Commission. (*See section 24, enlarging Commission and increasing salaries.*)

§ 12. Powers and duties of the Commission.[1]

SEC. 12. (*As amended March 2, 1889, and February 10, 1891.*)

That the Commission hereby created shall have authority to inquire into the management of the business of all common carriers subject to the provisions of this Act, and shall keep itself informed as to the manner and method in which the same is conducted, and shall have the right to obtain from such common carriers full and complete information necessary to enable the Commission to perform the duties and carry out the objects for which it was created; and the Commission is hereby authorized and required to execute and enforce the provisions of this Act; and, upon the request of the Commission, it shall be the duty of any district attorney of the United States to whom the Commission may apply to institute in the proper court and to prosecute under the direction of the Attorney-General of the United States all necessary proceedings for the enforcement of the provisions of this Act and for the punishment of all violations thereof, and the costs and expenses of such prosecution shall be paid out of the appropriation for the expenses of the courts of the United States; and for the purposes of this Act the Commission shall have power to require, by subpœna, the attendance and testimony of witnesses and the production of all books, papers, tariffs, contracts, agreements, and documents relating to any matter under investigation.

Such attendance of witnesses, and the production of such documentary evidence, may be required from any place in the United States, at any designated place of hearing. And in case

---

[1] This heading is not in the act.

of disobedience to a subpœna the Commission, or any party to a proceeding before the Commission, may invoke the aid of any court of the United States in requiring the attendance and testimony of witnesses and the production of books, papers, and documents under the provisions of this section.

And any of the circuit courts of the United States within the jurisdiction of which such inquiry is carried on may, in case of contumacy or refusal to obey a subpœna issued to any common carrier subject to the provisions of this Act, or other person, issue an order requiring such common carrier or other person to appear before said Commission (and produce books and papers if so ordered) and give evidence touching the matter in question; and any failure to obey such order of the court may be punished by such court as a contempt thereof. The claim that any such testimony or evidence may tend to criminate the person giving such evidence shall not excuse such witness from testifying; but such evidence or testimony shall not be used against such person on the trial of any criminal proceeding.

The testimony of any witness may be taken, at the instance of a party in any proceeding or investigation pending before the Commission, by deposition, at any time after a cause or proceeding is at issue on petition and answer. The Commission may also order testimony to be taken by deposition in any proceeding or investigation pending before it, at any stage of such proceeding or investigation. Such depositions may be taken before any judge of any court of the United States, or any commissioner of a circuit, or any clerk of a district or circuit court, or any chancellor, justice, or judge of a supreme or superior court, mayor or chief magistrate of a city, judge of a county court, or court of common pleas of any of the United States, or any notary public, not being of counsel or attorney to either of the parties, nor interested in the event of the proceeding or investigation. Reasonable notice must first be given in writing by the party, or his attorney, proposing to take such deposition to the opposite party or his attorney of record, as either may be nearest, which notice shall state the name of the witness and the time and place of the taking of his deposition. Any person may be compelled to appear and depose, and to produce documentary evidence, in the same manner as witnesses may be compelled to appear and testify and produce documentary evidence before the Commission as hereinbefore provided.

Every person deposing as herein provided shall be cautioned and sworn (or affirm, if he so request) to testify the whole truth, and shall be carefully examined. His testimony shall be reduced to writing by the magistrate taking the deposition, or under his direction, and shall, after it has been reduced to writing, be subscribed by the deponent.

If a witness whose testimony may be desired to be taken by deposition be in a foreign country, the deposition may be taken before an officer or person designated by the Commission, or agreed upon by the parties by stipulation in writing to be filed with the Commission. All depositions must be promptly filed with the Commission.

Witnesses whose depositions are taken pursuant to this Act, and the magistrate or other officer taking the same, shall severally be entitled to the same fees as are paid for like services in the courts of the United States.

§ 13. Complaints to Commission.[1]

SEC. 13. (*As amended June 18, 1910.*)

That any person, firm, corporation, company, or association, or any mercantile, agricultural, or manufacturing society or other organization, or any body politic or municipal organization, or any common carrier, complaining of anything done or omitted to be done by any common carrier subject to the provisions of this Act, in contravention of the provisions thereof, may apply to said Commission by petition, which shall briefly state the facts; whereupon a statement of the complaint thus made shall be forwarded by the Commission to such common carrier, who shall be called upon to satisfy the complaint, or to answer the same in writing, within a reasonable time, to be specified by the Commission. If such common carrier within the time specified shall make reparation for the injury alleged to have been done, the common carrier shall be relieved of liability to the complainant only for the particular violation of

[1] This heading is not in the act.

law thus complained of. If such carrier or carriers shall not satisfy the complaint within the time specified, or there shall appear to be any reasonable ground for investigating said complaint, it shall be the duty of the Commission to investigate the matters complained of in such manner and by such means as it shall deem proper.

Said Commission shall, in like manner and with the same authority and powers, investigate any complaint forwarded by the railroad commissioner or railroad commission of any State or Territory at the request of such commissioner or commission, and the Interstate Commerce Commission shall have full authority and power at any time to institute an inquiry, on its own motion, in any case and as to any matter or thing concerning which a complaint is authorized to be made, to or before said Commission by any provision of this Act, or concerning which any question may arise under any of the provisions of this Act, or relating to the enforcement of any of the provisions of this Act. And the said Commission shall have the same powers and authority to proceed with any inquiry instituted on its own motion as though it had been appealed to by complaint or petition under any of the provisions of this Act, including the power to make and enforce any order or orders in the case, or relating to the matter or thing concerning which the inquiry is had excepting orders for the payment of money. No complaint shall at any time be dismissed because of the absence of direct damage to the complainant.

§ 14. Commission must make reports.[1]

Sec. 14. (*Amended March 2, 1889, and June 20, 1906.*)

That whenever an investigation shall be made by said Commission, it shall be its duty to make a report in writing in respect thereto, which shall state the conclusions of the Commission, together with its decision, order, or requirement in the premises; and in case damages are awarded such report shall include the findings of fact on which the award is made.

All reports of investigations made by the Commission shall be entered of record, and a copy thereof shall be furnished to the

---

[1] This heading is not in the act.

party who may have complained, and to any common carrier that may have been complained of.

The Commission may provide for the publication of its reports and decisions in such form and manner as may be best adapted for public information and use, and such authorized publications shall be competent evidence of the reports and decisions of the Commission therein contained in all courts of the United States and of the several States without any further proof or authentication thereof. The Commission may also cause to be printed for early distribution its annual reports.

§ 15. Commission may prescribe rates and classifications.[1]

SEC. 15. (*As amended June 29, 1906, and June 18, 1910.*)

That whenever, after full hearing upon a complaint made as provided in section thirteen of this Act, or after full hearing under an order for investigation and hearing made by the Commission on its own initiative (either in extension of any pending complaint or without any complaint whatever), the Commission shall be of opinion that any individual or joint rates or charges whatsoever demanded, charged, or collected by any common carrier or carriers subject to the provisions of this Act for the transportation of persons or property or for the transmission of messages by telegraph or telephone as defined in the first section of this Act, or that any individual or joint classifications, regulations, or practices whatsoever of such carrier or carriers subject to the provisions of this Act are unjust or unreasonable or unjustly discriminatory, or unduly preferential or prejudicial or otherwise in violation of any of the provisions of this Act, the Commission is hereby authorized and empowered to determine and prescribe what will be the just and reasonable individual or joint rate or rates, charge or charges, to be thereafter observed in such case as the maximum to be charged, and what individual or joint classification, regulation, or practice is just, fair, and reasonable, to be thereafter followed, and to make an order that the carrier or carriers shall cease and desist from such violation to the extent to which the Commission finds the same to exist, and shall not thereafter publish, demand, or collect any

---

[1] This heading is not in the act.

rate or charge for such transportation or transmission in excess of the maximum rate or charge so prescribed, and shall adopt the classification and shall conform to and observe the regulation or practice so prescribed. All orders of the Commission, except orders for the payment of money, shall take effect within such reasonable time, not less then thirty days, and shall continue in force for such period of time, not exceeding two years, as shall be prescribed in the order of the Commission, unless the same shall be suspended or modified or set aside by the Commission, or be suspended or set aside by a court of competent jurisdiction. Whenever the carrier or carriers, in obedience to such order of the Commission or otherwise, in respect to joint rates, fares, or charges, shall fail to agree among themselves upon the apportionment or division thereof, the Commission may, after hearing, make a supplemental order prescribing the just and reasonable proportion of such joint rate to be received by each carrier party thereto, which order shall take effect as a part of the original order.

Whenever there shall be filed with the Commission any schedule stating a new individual or joint rate, fare, or charge, or any new individual or joint classification, or any new individual or joint regulation or practice affecting any rate, fare, or charge, the Commission shall have, and it is hereby given, authority, either upon complaint or upon its own initiative without complaint, at once, and if it so orders, without answer or other formal pleading by the interested carrier or carriers, but upon reasonable notice, to enter upon a hearing concerning the propriety of such rate, fare, charge, classification, regulation, or practice; and pending such hearing and the decision thereon the Commission upon filing with such schedule and delivering to the carrier or carriers affected thereby a statement in writing of its reasons for such suspension may suspend the operation of such schedule and defer the use of such rate, fare, charge, classification, regulation, or practice, but not for a longer period than one hundred and twenty days beyond the time when such rate, fare, charge, classification, regulation, or practice would otherwise go into effect; and after full hearing, whether completed before or after the rate, fare, charge, classification, regulation, or practice goes into effect, the Commission may make such order in reference to such rate, fare, charge, classification, regulation, or practice as would be proper in a proceeding initiated after the rate, fare, charge, classification, regulation, or practice had become effective: *Provided*, That if any such hearing cannot be concluded within the period of suspension, as above stated, the Interstate Commerce Commission may, in its discretion, extend the time of suspension for a further period not exceeding six months. At any hearing involving a rate increased after January first, nineteen hundred and ten, or of a rate sought to be increased after the passage of this Act, the burden of proof to show that the increased rate or proposed increased rate is just and reasonable shall be upon the common carrier, and the Commission shall give to the hearing and decision of such questions preference over all other questions pending before it and decide the same as speedily as possible.

The Commission may also, after hearing, on a complaint or upon its own initiative without complaint, establish through routes and joint classifications, and may establish joint rates as the maximum to be charged and may prescribe the division of such rates as hereinbefore provided and the terms and conditions under which such through routes shall be operated, whenever the carriers themselves shall have refused or neglected to establish voluntarily such through routes or joint classifications or joint rates; and this provision shall apply when one of the connecting carriers is a water line. The Commission shall not, however, establish any through route, classification, or rate between street electric passenger railways not engaged in the general business of transporting freight in addition to their passenger and express business and railroads of a different character, nor shall the Commission have the right to establish any route, classification, rate, fare, or charge when the transportation is wholly by water, and any transportation by water affected by this Act shall be subject to the laws and regulations applicable to transportation by water.

And in establishing such through route, the Commission shall not require any company, without its consent, to embrace in such route substantially less than the entire length of its railroad and of any intermediate railroad operated in conjunction and under a common management or control therewith which lies between the termini of such proposed through route, unless to do so would make such through route unreasonably long as compared with another practicable through route which could otherwise be established.

In all cases where at the time of delivery of property to any railroad corporation being a common carrier, for transportation subject to the provisions of this Act to any point of destination, between which and the point of such delivery for shipment two or more through routes and through rates shall have been established as in this Act provided to which through routes and through rates such carrier is a party, the person, firm, or corporation making such shipment, subject to such reasonable exceptions and regulations as the Interstate Commerce Commission shall from time to time prescribe, shall have the right to designate in writing by which of such through routes such property shall be transported to destination, and it shall thereupon be the duty of the initial carrier to route said property and issue a through bill of lading therefor as so directed, and to transport said property over its own line or lines and deliver the same to a connecting line or lines according to such through route, and it shall be the duty of each of said connecting carriers to receive said property and transport it over the said line or lines and deliver the same to the next succeeding carrier or consignee according to the routing instructions in said bill of lading: *Provided, however*, That the shipper shall in all instances have the right to determine, where competing lines of railroad constitute portions of a through line or route, over which of said competing lines so constituting a portion of said through line or route his freight shall be transported.

It shall be unlawful for any common carrier subject to the provisions of this Act, or any officer, agent, or employee of such common carrier, or for any other person or corporation lawfully authorized by such common carrier to receive information therefrom, knowingly to disclose to or permit to be acquired by any person or corporation other than the shipper or consignee, without the consent of such shipper or consignee, any information concerning the nature, kind, quantity, destination, consignee, or routing of any property tendered or delivered to such common carrier for interstate transportation, which information may be used to the detriment or prejudice of such shipper or consignee, or which may improperly disclose his business transactions to a competitor; and it shall also be unlawful for any person or corporation to solicit or knowingly receive any such information which may be so used: *Provided*, That nothing in this Act shall be construed to prevent the giving of such information in response to any legal process issued under the authority of any state or federal court, or to any officer or agent of the Government of the United States, or of any State or Territory, in the exercise of his powers, or to any officer or other duly authorized person seeking such information for the prosecution of persons charged with or suspected of crime; or information given by a common carrier to another carrier or its duly authorized agent, for the purpose of adjusting mutual traffic accounts in the ordinary course of business of such carriers.

Any person, corporation, or association violating any of the provisions of the next preceding paragraph of this section shall be deemed guilty of a misdemeanor, and for each offense, on conviction, shall pay to the United States a penalty of not more than one thousand dollars.

If the owner of property transported under this Act directly or indirectly renders any service connected with such transportation, or furnishes any instrumentality used therein, the charge and allowance therefor shall be no more than is just and reasonable, and the Commission may, after hearing on a complaint or on its own initiative, determine what is a reasonable charge as the maximum to be paid by the carrier or carriers for the services so rendered or for the use of the instrumentality so furnished, and fix the same by appropriate order, which order shall have the same force and effect and be enforced in like manner as the orders above provided for under this section.

The foregoing enumeration of powers shall not exclude any power which the Commission would otherwise have in the making of an order under the provisions of this Act.

§ 16. Award of damages by Commission.[1]

Sec. 16. (*Amended March 2, 1889, June 29, 1906, and June 18, 1910.*)

That if, after hearing on a complaint made as provided in section thirteen of this Act, the Commission shall determine that any party complainant is entitled to an award of damages under the provisions of this Act for a violation thereof, the Commission shall make an order directing the carrier to pay to the complainant the sum to which he is entitled on or before a day named.

If a carrier does not comply with an order for the payment of money within the time limit in such order, the complainant, or any person for whose benefit such order was made, may file in the circuit court of the United States for the district in which he resides or in which is located the principal operating office of the carrier, or through which the road of the carrier runs, or in any state court of general jurisdiction having jurisdiction of the parties, a petition setting forth briefly the causes for which he claims damages, and the order of the Commission in the premises. Such suit in the circuit court of the United States shall proceed in all respects like other civil suits for damages, except that on the trial of such suit the findings and order of the Commission shall be prima facie evidence of the facts therein stated, and except that the petitioner shall not be liable for costs in the circuit court nor for costs at any subsequent stage of the proceedings unless they accrue upon his appeal. If the petitioner shall finally prevail he shall be allowed a reasonable attorney's fee, to be taxed and collected as a part of the costs of the suit. All complaints for the recovery of damages shall be filed with the Commission within two years from the time the cause of action accrues, and not after, and a petition for the enforcement of an order for the payment of money shall be filed in the circuit court or state court within one year from the date of the order, and not after.

In such suits all parties in whose favor the Commission may have made an award for damages by a single order may be joined as plaintiffs, and all of the carriers parties to such order awarding such damages may be joined as defendants, and such suit

---

[1] This heading is not in the act.

may be maintained by such joint plaintiffs and against such joint defendants in any district where any one of such joint plaintiffs could maintain such suit against any one of such joint defendants; and service of process against any one of such defendants as may not be found in the district where the suit is brought may be made in any district where such defendant carrier has its principal operating office. In case of such joint suit the recovery, if any, may be by judgment in favor of any one of such plaintiffs against the defendant found to be liable to such plaintiff.

Every order of the Commission shall be forthwith served upon the designated agent of the carrier in the city of Washington or in such other manner as may be provided by law.

The Commission shall be authorized to suspend or modify its orders upon such notice and in such manner as it shall deem proper.

It shall be the duty of every common carrier, its agents and employees, to observe and comply with such orders so long as the same shall remain in effect.

Any carrier, any officer, representative, or agent of a carrier, or any receiver, trustee, lessee, or agent of either of them, who knowingly fails or neglects to obey any order made under the provisions of section fifteen of this Act shall forfeit to the United States the sum of five thousand dollars for each offense. Every distinct violation shall be a separate offense, and in case of a continuing violation each day shall be deemed a separate offense.

The forfeiture provided for in this Act shall be payable into the Treasury of the United States, and shall be recoverable in a civil suit in the name of the United States, brought in the district where the carrier has its principal operating office, or in any district through which the road of the carrier runs.

It shall be the duty of the various district attorneys, under the direction of the Attorney-General of the United States, to prosecute for the recovery of forfeitures. The costs and expenses of such prosecution shall be paid out of the appropriation for the expenses of the courts of the United States.

The Commission may employ such attorneys as it finds necessary for proper legal aid and service of the Commission or its members in the conduct of their work or for proper representation of the public interests in investigations made by it or cases or proceedings pending before it, whether at the Commission's own instance or upon complaint, or to appear for and represent the Commission in any case pending in the Commerce Court; and the expenses of such employment shall be paid out of the appropriation for the Commission.

If any carrier fails or neglects to obey any order of the Commission other than for the payment of money, while the same is in effect, the Interstate Commerce Commission or any party injured thereby, or the United States, by its Attorney-General, may apply to the Commerce Court for the enforcement of such order. If, after hearing, that Court determines that the order was regularly made and duly served, and that the carrier is in disobedience of the same, the Court shall enforce obedience to such order by a writ of injunction or other proper process, mandatory or otherwise, to restrain such carrier, its officers, agents, or representatives, from further disobedience of such order, or to enjoin upon it or them obedience to the same.

The copies of schedules and classifications and tariffs of rates, fares, and charges, and of all contracts, agreements, and arrangements between common carriers filed with the Commission as herein provided, and the statistics, tables, and figures contained in the annual or other reports of carriers made to the Commission as required under the provisions of this Act shall be preserved as public records in the custody of the secretary of the Commission, and shall be received as prima facie evidence of what they purport to be for the purpose of investigations by the Commission and in all judicial proceedings; and copies of and extracts from any of said schedules, classifications, tariffs, contracts, agreements, arrangements, or reports, made public records as aforesaid, certified by the secretary, under the Commission's seal, shall be received in evidence with like effect as the originals.

§ 16*a*. Commission may grant rehearings.[1]

SEC. 16*a*. (*Added June 29, 1906.*)

That after a decision, order, or requirement has been made by

[1] This heading is not in the act.

the Commission in any proceeding any party thereto may at any time make application for rehearing of the same, or any matter determined therein, and it shall be lawful for the Commission in its discretion to grant such a rehearing if sufficient reason therefor be made to appear. Applications for rehearing shall be governed by such general rules as the Commission may establish. No such application shall excuse any carrier from complying with or obeying any decision, order, or requirement of the Commission, or operate in any manner to stay or postpone the enforcement thereof, without the special order of the Commission. In case a rehearing is granted the proceedings thereupon shall conform as nearly as may be to the proceedings in an original hearing, except as the Commission may otherwise direct; and if, in its judgment, after such rehearing and the consideration of all facts, including those arising since the former hearing, it shall appear that the original decision, order, or requirement is in any respect unjust or unwarranted, the Commission may reverse, change, or modify the same accordingly. Any decision, order, or requirement made after such rehearing, reversing, changing, or modifying the original determination shall be subject to the same provisions as an original order.

§ 17. Form of procedure.[1]
SEC. 17. (*As amended March 2, 1889.*)

That the Commission may conduct its proceedings in such manner as will best conduce to the proper dispatch of business and to the ends of justice. A majority of the Commission shall constitute a quorum for the transaction of business, but no Commissioner shall participate in any hearing or proceeding in which he has any pecuniary interest. Said Commission may, from time to time, make or amend such general rules or orders as may be requisite for the order and regulation of proceedings before it, including forms of notices and the service thereof, which shall conform, as nearly as may be, to those in use in the courts of the United States. Any party may appear before said Commission and be heard in person or by attorney. Every vote and official act of the Commission shall be entered of record,

---

[1] This heading is not in the act.

and its proceedings shall be public upon the request of either party interested. Said Commission shall have an official seal, which shall be judicially noticed. Either of the members of the Commission may administer oaths and affirmations and sign subpœnas.

§ 18. Organization of the Commission.[1]

Sec. 18. (*As amended March 2, 1889.*) [*See Section 24, increasing salaries of Commissioners.*]

That each Commissioner shall receive an annual salary of seven thousand five hundred dollars, payable in the same manner as the judges of the courts of the United States. The Commission shall appoint a secretary, who shall receive an annual salary of three thousand five hundred dollars, [now $5,000] payable in like manner. The Commission shall have authority to employ and fix the compensation of such other employees as it may find necessary to the proper performance of its duties. Until otherwise provided by law, the Commission may hire suitable offices for its use, and shall have authority to procure all necessary office supplies. Witnesses summoned before the Commission shall be paid the same fees and mileage that are paid witnesses in the courts of the United States.

All of the expenses of the Commission, including all necessary expenses for transportation incurred by the Commissioners, or by their employees under their orders, in making any investigation, or upon official business in any other places than in the city of Washington, shall be allowed and paid on the presentation of itemized vouchers therefor approved by the chairman of the Commission.

§ 19. Office of the Commission.[1]

Sec. 19. That the principal office of the Commission shall be in the city of Washington, where its general sessions shall be held; but whenever the convenience of the public or the parties may be promoted, or delay or expense prevented thereby, the Commission may hold special sessions in any part of the United States. It may, by one or more of the Commissioners, prosecute

[1] This heading is not in the act.

any inquiry necessary to its duties, in any part of the United States, into any matter or question of fact pertaining to the business of any common carrier subject to the provisions of this Act.

§ 20. Annual reports to Commission. [1]

SEC. 20. (*As amended June 29, 1906, February 25, 1909, and June 18, 1910.*)

That the Commission is hereby authorized to require annual reports from all common carriers subject to the provisions of this Act, and from the owners of all railroads engaged in interstate commerce as defined in this Act; to prescribe the manner in which such reports shall be made, and to require from such carriers specific answers to all questions upon which the Commission may need information. Such annual reports shall show in detail the amount of capital stock issued, the amounts paid therefor, and the manner of payment for the same; the dividends paid, the surplus fund, if any, and the number of stockholders; the funded and floating debts and the interest paid thereon; the cost and value of the carrier's property, franchises, and equipments; the number of employees and the salaries paid each class; the accidents to passengers, employees, and other persons, and the causes thereof; the amounts expended for improvements each year, how expended, and the character of such improvements; the earnings and receipts from each branch of business and from all sources; the operating and other expenses; the balances of profit and loss; and a complete exhibit of the financial operations of the carrier each year, including an annual balance sheet. Such reports shall also contain such information in relation to rates or regulations concerning fares or freights, or agreements, arrangements, or contracts affecting the same as the Commission may require; and the Commission may, in its discretion, for the purpose of enabling it the better to carry out the purposes of this Act, prescribe a period of time within which all common carriers subject to the provisions of this Act shall have, as near as may be, a uniform system of accounts, and the manner in which such accounts shall be kept.

[1] This heading is not in the act.

Said detailed reports shall contain all the required statistics for the period of twelve months ending on the thirtieth day of June in each year, or on the thirty-first day of December in each year if the Commission by order substitute that period for the year ending June thirtieth, and shall be made out under oath and filed with the Commission at its office in Washington within three months after the close of the year for which the report is made, unless additional time be granted in any case by the Commission; and if any carrier, person, or corporation subject to the provisions of this Act shall fail to make and file said annual reports within the time above specified, or within the time extended by the Commission, for making and filing the same, or shall fail to make specific answer to any question authorized by the provisions of this section within thirty days from the time it is lawfully required so to do, such party shall forfeit to the United States the sum of one hundred dollars for each and every day it shall continue to be in default with respect thereto. The Commission shall also have authority by general or special orders to require said carriers, or any of them, to file monthly reports of earnings and expenses, and to file periodical or special, or both periodical and special, reports concerning any matters about which the Commission is authorized or required by this or any other law to inquire or to keep itself informed or which it is required to enforce; and such periodical or special reports shall be under oath whenever the Commission so requires; and if any such carrier shall fail to make and file any such periodical or special report within the time fixed by the Commission, it shall be subject to the forfeitures last above provided.

Said forfeitures shall be recovered in the manner provided for the recovery of forfeitures under the provisions of this Act.

The oath required by this section may be taken before any person authorized to administer an oath by the laws of the State in which the same is taken.

The Commission may, in its discretion, prescribe the forms of any and all accounts, records, and memoranda to be kept by carriers subject to the provisions of this Act, including the accounts, records, and memoranda of the movement of traffic as well as the receipts and expenditures of moneys. The Commission shall at all times have access to all accounts, records, and memoranda kept by carriers subject to this Act, and it shall be unlawful for such carriers to keep any other accounts, records, or memoranda than those prescribed or approved by the Commission, and it may employ special agents or examiners, who shall have authority under the order of the Commission to inspect and examine any and all accounts, records, and memoranda kept by such carriers. This provision shall apply to receivers of carriers and operating trustees.

In case of failure or refusal on the part of any such carrier, receiver, or trustee to keep such accounts, records, and memoranda on the books and in the manner prescribed by the Commission, or to submit such accounts, records, and memoranda as are kept to the inspection of the Commission or any of its authorized agents or examiners, such carrier, receiver, or trustee shall forfeit to the United States the sum of five hundred dollars for each such offense and for each and every day of the continuance of such offense, such forfeitures to be recoverable in the same manner as other forfeitures provided for in this Act.

Any person who shall willfully make any false entry in the accounts of any book of accounts or in any record or memoranda kept by a carrier, or who shall willfully destroy, mutilate, alter, or by any other means or device falsify the record of any such account, record, or memoranda, or who shall willfully neglect or fail to make full, true, and correct entries in such accounts, records, or memoranda of all facts and transactions appertaining to the carrier's business, or shall keep any other accounts, records, or memoranda than those prescribed or approved by the Commission, shall be deemed· guilty of a misdemeanor, and shall be subject, upon conviction in any court of the United States of competent jurisdiction, to a fine of not less than one thousand dollars nor more than five thousand dollars or imprisonment for a term not less than one year nor more than three years, or both such fine and imprisonment: *Provided,* That the Commission may in its discretion issue orders specifying such operating, accounting, or financial papers, records, books, blanks, tickets, stubs, or documents of carriers which may, after a reasonable time, be destroyed, and prescribing the length of time such books, papers, or documents shall be preserved.

Any examiner who divulges any fact or information which may come to his knowledge during the course of such examination, except in so far as he may be directed by the Commission or by a court or judge thereof, shall be subject, upon conviction in any court of the United States of competent jurisdiction, to a fine of not more than five thousand dollars or imprisonment for a term not exceeding two years, or both.

That the circuit and district courts of the United States shall have jurisdiction, upon the application of the Attorney-General of the United States at the request of the Commission, alleging a failure to comply with or a violation of any of the provisions of said Act to regulate commerce or of any Act supplementary thereto or amendatory thereof by any common carrier, to issue a writ or writs of mandamus commanding such common carrier to comply with the provisions of said Acts, or any of them.

And to carry out and give effect to the provisions of said Acts, or any of them, the Commission is hereby authorized to employ special agents or examiners who shall have power to administer oaths, examine witnesses, and receive evidence.

That any common carrier, railroad, or transportation company receiving property for transportation from a point in one State to a point in another State shall issue a receipt or bill of lading therefor and shall be liable to the lawful holder thereof for any loss, damage, or injury to such property caused by it or by any common carrier, railroad, or transportation company to which such property may be delivered or over whose line or lines such property may pass, and no contract, receipt, rule, or regulation shall exempt such common carrier, railroad, or transportation company from the liability hereby imposed: *Provided*, That nothing in this section shall deprive any holder of such receipt or bill of lading of any remedy or right of action which he has under existing law.

That the common carrier, railroad, or transportation company issuing such receipt or bill of lading shall be entitled to recover from the common carrier, railroad, or transportation company on whose line the loss, damage, or injury shall have been sustained the amount of such loss, damage, or injury as it may be required to pay to the owners of such property, as may be evidenced by any receipt, judgment, or transcript thereof.

§ 21. Annual reports of the Commission.[1]

SEC. 21. (*As amended March 2, 1889.*)

That the Commission shall, on or before the first day of December in each year, make a report, which shall be transmitted to Congress, and copies of which shall be distributed as are the other reports transmitted to Congress. This report shall contain such information and data collected by the Commission as may be considered of value in the determination of questions connected with the regulation of commerce, together with such recommendations as to additional legislation relating thereto as the Commission may deem necessary; and the names and compensation of the persons employed by said Commission.

§ 22. Persons and property that may be carried free or at reduced rates.[1]

SEC. 22. (*As amended March 2, 1889, and February 8, 1895.*) [*See section 1, 4th par.*]

That nothing in this Act shall prevent the carriage, storage, or handling of property free or at reduced rates for the United States, State, or municipal governments, or for charitable purposes, or to or from fairs and expositions for exhibition thereat, or the free carriage of destitute and homeless persons transported by charitable societies, and the necessary agents employed in such transportation, or the issuance of mileage, excursion, or commutation passenger tickets; nothing in this Act shall be construed to prohibit any common carrier from giving reduced rates to ministers of religion, or to municipal governments for the transportation of indigent persons, or to inmates of the National Homes or State Homes for Disabled Volunteer Soldiers, and of Soldiers' and Sailors' Orphan Homes, including those about to enter and those returning home after discharge, under arrange-

---

[1] This heading is not in the act.

ments with the boards of managers of said homes; nothing in this Act shall be construed to prevent railroads from giving free carriage to their own officers and employees, or to prevent the principal officers of any railroad company or companies from exchanging passes or tickets with other railroad companies for their officers and employees; and nothing in this Act contained shall in any way abridge or alter the remedies now existing at common law or by statute, but the provisions of this Act are in addition to such remedies: *Provided*, That no pending litigation shall in any way be affected by this Act: *Provided further*, That nothing in this Act shall prevent the issuance of joint interchangeable five-thousand-mile tickets, with special privileges as to the amount of free baggage that may be carried under mileage tickets of one thousand or more miles. But before any common carrier, subject to the provisions of this Act, shall issue any such joint interchangeable mileage tickets with special privileges, as aforesaid, it shall file with the Interstate Commerce Commission copies of the joint tariffs of rates, fares, or charges on which such joint interchangeable mileage tickets are to be based, together with specifications of the amount of free baggage permitted to be carried under such tickets, in the same manner as common carriers are required to do with regard to other joint rates by section six of this Act; and all the provisions of said section six relating to joint rates, fares, and charges shall be observed by said common carriers and enforced by the Interstate Commerce Commission as fully with regard to such joint interchangeable mileage tickets as with regard to other joint rates, fares, and charges referred to in said section six. It shall be unlawful for any common carrier that has issued or authorized to be issued any such joint interchangeable mileage tickets to demand, collect, or receive from any person or persons a greater or less compensation for transportation of persons or baggage under such joint interchangeable mileage tickets than that required by the rate, fare, or charge specified in the copies of the joint tariff of rates, fares, or charges filed with the Commission in force at the time. The provisions of section ten of this Act shall apply to any violation of the requirements of this proviso.

§ 23. Jurisdiction of United States courts.[1]

SEC. 23. (*Added March 2, 1889.*)

That the circuit and district courts of the United States shall have jurisdiction upon the relation of any person or persons, firm, or corporation, alleging such violation by a common carrier, of any of the provisions of the Act to which this is a supplement and all Acts amendatory thereof, as prevents the relator from having interstate traffic moved by said common carrier at the same rates as are charged, or upon terms or conditions as favorable as those given by said common carrier for like traffic under similar conditions to any other shipper, to issue a writ or writs of mandamus against said common carrier, commanding such common carrier to move and transport the traffic, or to furnish cars or other facilities for transportation for the party applying for the writ: *Provided*, That if any question of fact as to the proper compensation to the common carrier for the service to be enforced by the writ is raised by the pleadings, the writ of peremptory mandamus may issue, notwithstanding such question of fact is undetermined, upon such terms as to security, payment of money into the court, or otherwise, as the court may think proper, pending the determination of the question of fact: *Provided*, That the remedy hereby given by writ of mandamus shall be cumulative, and shall not be held to exclude or interfere with other remedies provided by this Act or the Act to which it is a supplement.

§ 24. Constitution of the Commission.[1]

SEC. 24. (*Added June 29, 1906.*)

That the Interstate Commerce Commission is hereby enlarged so as to consist of seven members with terms of seven years, and each shall receive ten thousand dollars compensation annually. The qualifications of the Commissioners and the manner of the payment of their salaries shall be as already provided by law. Such enlargement of the Commission shall be accomplished through appointment by the President, by and with the advice and consent of the Senate, of two additional Interstate Commerce Commissioners, one for a term expiring De-

---

[1] This heading is not in the act.

cember thirty-first, nineteen hundred and eleven, one for a term expiring December thirty-first, nineteen hundred and eleven, one for a term expiring December thirty-first, nineteen hundred and twelve. The terms of the present Commissioners, or of any successor appointed to fill a vacancy caused by the death or resignation of any of the present Commissioners, shall expire as heretofore provided by law. Their successors and the successors of the additional Commissioners herein provided for shall be appointed for the full term of seven years, except that any person appointed to fill a vacancy shall be appointed only for the unexpired term of the Commissioner whom he shall succeed. Not more than four Commissioners shall be appointed from the same political party.

(*Additional provisions in Act of June 29, 1906.*) (SEC. 9.) That all existing laws relating to the attendance of witnesses and the production of evidence and the compelling of testimony under the Act to regulate commerce and all Acts amendatory thereof shall apply to any and all proceedings and hearings under this Act.

(SEC. 10.) That all laws and parts of laws in conflict with the provisions of this Act are hereby repealed; but the amendments herein provided for shall not affect causes now pending in courts of the United States, but such causes shall be prosecuted to a conclusion in the manner heretofore provided by law.

(SEC. 11.) That this Act shall take effect and be in force from and after its passage.

Joint resolution of June 30, 1906, provides: "That the Act entitled 'An Act to amend an Act entitled "An Act to regulate commerce," approved February 4, 1887, and all Acts amendatory thereof, and to enlarge the powers of the Interstate Commerce Commission,' shall take effect and be in force sixty days after its approval by the President of the United States."

APPENDIX B

THE COMMERCE COURT ACT

§ 1. Creation and jurisdiction of Commerce Court.[1]

(Commerce Court and other additional provisions in the Act of June 18, 1910.)

(SEC. 1.) That a court of the United States is hereby created which shall be known as the Commerce Court and shall have the jurisdiction now possessed by circuit courts of the United States and the judges thereof over all cases of the following kinds:

First. All cases for the enforcement, otherwise than by adjudication and collection of a forfeiture or penalty or by infliction of criminal punishment, of any order of the Interstate Commerce Commission other than for the payment of money.

Second. Cases brought to enjoin, set aside, annul, or suspend in whole or in part any order of the Interstate Commerce Commission.

Third. Such cases as by section three of the Act entitled "An Act to further regulate commerce with foreign nations and among the States," approved February nineteenth, nineteen hundred and three, are authorized to be maintained in a circuit court of the United States.

Fourth. All such mandamus proceedings as under the provisions of section twenty or section twenty-three of the Act entitled "An Act to regulate commerce," approved February fourth, eighteen hundred and eighty-seven, as amended, are authorized to be maintained in a circuit court of the United States.

Nothing contained in this Act shall be construed as enlarging the jurisdiction now possessed by the circuit courts of the United

[1] This heading is not in the act.

States or the judges thereof, that is hereby transferred to and vested in the Commerce Court.

The jurisdiction of the Commerce Court over cases of the foregoing classes shall be exclusive; but this Act shall not affect the jurisdiction now possessed by any circuit or district court of the United States over cases or proceedings of a kind not within the above-enumerated classes.

The Commerce Court shall be a court of record, and shall have a seal of such form and style as the court may prescribe. The said Court shall be composed of five judges, to be from time to time designated and assigned thereto by the Chief Justice of the United States, from among the circuit judges of the United States, for the period of five years, except that in the first instance the Court shall be composed of the five additional circuit judges to be appointed as hereinafter provided, who shall be designated by the President to serve for one, two, three, four, and five years, respectively, in order that the period of designation of one of the said judges shall expire in each year thereafter. In case of the death, resignation, or termination of assignment of any judge so designated, the Chief Justice shall designate a circuit judge to fill the vacancy so caused and to serve during the unexpired period for which the original designation was made. After the year nineteen hundred and fourteen no circuit judge shall be redesignated to serve in the Commerce Court until the expiration of at least one year after the expiration of the period of his last previous designation. The judge first designated for the five-year period shall be the presiding judge of said Court, and thereafter the judge senior in designation shall be the presiding judge.

Each of the judges during the period of his service in the Commerce Court shall, on account of the regular sessions of the court being held in the city of Washington, receive in addition to his salary as circuit judge an expense allowance at the rate of one thousand five hundred dollars per annum.

The President shall, by and with the advice and consent of the Senate, appoint five additional circuit judges no two of whom shall be from the same judicial circuit, who shall hold office during good behavior and who shall be from time to time designated and assigned by the Chief Justice of the United States for service in the circuit court for any district, or the circuit court of appeals for any circuit, or in the Commerce Court.

The associate judges shall have precedence and shall succeed to the place and powers of the presiding judge whenever he may be absent or incapable of acting in the order of the date of their designations. Four of said judges shall constitute a quorum, and at least a majority of the Court shall concur in all decisions.

The Court shall also have a clerk and a marshal, with the same duties and powers, so far as they may be appropriate and are not altered by rule of the Court, as are now possessed by the clerk and marshal, respectively, of the Supreme Court of the United States. The offices of the clerk and marshal of the Court shall be in the city of Washington, in the District of Columbia. The judges of the Court shall appoint the clerk and marshal, and may also appoint, if they find it necessary, a deputy clerk and deputy marshal; and such clerk, marshal, deputy clerk, and deputy marshal shall hold office during the pleasure of the Court. The salary of the clerk shall be four thousand dollars per annum; the salary of the marshal three thousand dollars per annum; the salary of the deputy clerk two thousand five hundred dollars per annum; and the salary of the deputy marshal two thousand five hundred dollars per annum. The said clerk and marshal may, with the approval of the Court, employ all requisite assistance. The costs and fees in said Court shall be established by the Court in a table thereof, approved by the Supreme Court of the United States, within four months after the organization of the Court; but such costs and fees shall in no case exceed those charged in the Supreme Court of the United States, and shall be accounted for and paid into the Treasury of the United States.

The Commerce Court shall always be open for the transaction of business. Its regular sessions shall be held in the city of Washington, in the District of Columbia; but the powers of the Court or of any judge thereof, or of the clerk, marshal, deputy clerk, or deputy marshal may be exercised anywhere in the United States; and for expedition of the work of the Court and the avoidance of undue expense or inconvenience to suitors the Court shall hold sessions in different parts of the United States as may be found desirable. The actual and necessary expenses of the judges, clerk, marshal, deputy clerk, and deputy marshal of the Court incurred for travel and attendance elsewhere than in the city of Washington shall be paid upon the written and itemized certificate of such judge, clerk, marshal, deputy clerk, or deputy marshal by the marshal of the Court, and shall be allowed to him in the statement of his accounts with the United States.

The United States marshals of the several districts outside of the city of Washington in which the Commerce Court may hold its sessions shall provide, under the direction and with the approval of the Attorney-General of the United States, such rooms in the public buildings of the United States as may be necessary for the Court's use; but in case proper rooms cannot be provided in such public buildings, said marshals, with the approval of the Attorney-General of the United States, may then lease from time to time other necessary rooms for the Court.

If, at any time, the business of the Commerce Court does not require the services of all the judges, the Chief Justice of the United States may, by writing, signed by him and filed in the Department of Justice, terminate the assignment of any of the judges or temporarily assign him for service in any circuit court or circuit court of appeals. In case of illness or other disability of any judge assigned to the Commerce Court the Chief Justice of the United States may assign any other circuit judge of the United States to act in his place, and may terminate such assignment when the exigence therefor shall cease; and any circuit judge so assigned to act in place of such judge shall, during his assignment, exercise all the powers and perform all the functions of such judge.

In all cases within its jurisdiction the Commerce Court, and each of the judges assigned thereto, shall, respectively, have and may exercise any and all of the powers of a circuit court of the United States and of the judges of said Court, respectively, so far as the same may be appropriate to the effective exercise of the jurisdiction hereby conferred. The Commerce Court may issue all writs and process appropriate to the full exercise of its jurisdiction and powers and may prescribe the form thereof. It may also, from time to time, establish such rules and regulations concerning pleading, practice, or procedure in cases or matters within its jurisdiction as to the Court shall seem wise and proper. Its orders, writs, and process may run, be served, and be returnable anywhere in the United States; and the marshal and deputy marshal of said Court and also the United States marshals and deputy marshals in the several districts of the United States shall have like powers and be under like duties to act for and in behalf of said Court as pertain to United States marshals and deputy marshals generally when acting under like conditions concerning suits or matters in the circuits of the United States.

The jurisdiction of the Commerce Court shall be invoked by filing in the office of the clerk of the Court a written petition setting forth briefly and succinctly the facts constituting the petitioner's cause of action, and specifying the relief sought. A copy of such petition shall be forthwith served by the marshal or a deputy marshal of the Commerce Court or by the proper United States marshal or deputy marshal upon every defendant therein named, and when the United States is a party defendant, the service shall be made by filing a copy of said petition in the office of the secretary of the Interstate Commerce Commission and in the Department of Justice. Within thirty days after the petition is served, unless that time is extended by order of the court or a judge thereof, an answer to the petition shall be filed in the clerk's office, and a copy thereof mailed to the petitioner's attorney, which answer shall briefly and categorically respond to the allegations of the petition. No replication need be filed to the answer, and objections to the sufficiency of the petition or answer as not setting forth a cause of action or defense must be taken at the final hearing or by motion to dismiss the petition based on said grounds, which motion may be made at any time before answer is filed. In case no answer shall be filed as provided herein the petitioner may apply to the Court on notice for such relief as may be proper upon the facts alleged in the petition. The Court may, by rule, prescribe the method of taking evidence in cases pending in said court; and may prescribe that the evidence be taken before a single judge of the court, with power to rule upon the admission of evidence. Except as may be otherwise provided in this Act, or by rule of the Court, the practice and procedure in the Commerce Court shall conform as nearly as may be to that in like cases in a circuit court of the United States.

The Commerce Court shall be opened for the transaction of business at a date to be fixed by order of the said Court, which shall be not later than thirty days after the judges thereof shall have been designated.

§ 2. Appeals to Supreme Court.[1]

(SEC. 2.) That a final judgment or decree of the Commerce Court may be reviewed by the Supreme Court of the United States if appeal to the Supreme Court be taken by an aggrieved party within sixty days after the entry of said final judgment or decree. Such appeal may be taken in like manner as appeals from a circuit court of the United States to the Supreme Court, and the Commerce Court may direct the original record to be transmitted on appeal instead of a transcript thereof. The Supreme Court may affirm, reverse, or modify the final judgment or decree of the Commerce Court as the case may require.

Appeal to the Supreme Court, however, shall in no case supersede or stay the judgment or decree of the Commerce Court appealed from, unless the Supreme Court or a justice thereof shall so direct, and appellant shall give bond in such form and of such amount as the Supreme Court, or the justice of that court allowing the stay, may require.

An appeal may also be taken to the Supreme Court of the United States from an interlocutory order or decree of the Commerce Court granting or continuing an injunction restraining the enforcement of an order of the Interstate Commerce Commission, provided such appeal be taken within thirty days from the entry of such order or decree.

Appeals to the Supreme Court under this section shall have

---

[1] This heading is not in the act.

priority in hearing and determination over all other causes except criminal causes in that court.

§ 3. Suits to enjoin orders of Commission.[1]

(SEC. 3.) That suits to enjoin, set aside, annul, or suspend any order of the Interstate Commerce Commission shall be brought in the Commerce Court against the United States. The pendency of such suit shall not of itself stay or suspend the operation of the order of the Interstate Commerce Commission; but the Commerce Court, in its discretion, may restrain or suspend, in whole or in part, the operation of the Commission's order pending the final hearing and determination of the suit. No order or injunction so restraining or suspending an order of the Interstate Commerce Commission shall be made by the Commerce Court otherwise than upon notice and after hearing, except that in cases where irreparable damage would otherwise ensue to the petitioner, said Court, or a judge thereof, may, on hearing, after not less than three days' notice to the Interstate Commerce Commission and the Attorney-General, allow a temporary stay or suspension in whole or in part of the operation of the order of the Interstate Commerce Commission for not more than sixty days from the date of the order of such Court or judge, pending application to the Court for its order or injunction, in which case the said order shall contain a specific finding, based upon evidence submitted to the judge making the order and identified by reference thereto, that such irreparable damage would result to the petitioner and specifying the nature of the damage. The Court may, at the time of hearing such application, upon a like finding, continue the temporary stay or suspension in whole or in part until its decision upon the application.

§ 4. Suits to be brought by or against United States.[1]

(SEC. 4.) That all cases and proceedings in the Commerce Court which but for this Act would be brought by or against the Interstate Commerce Commission shall be brought by or against the United States, and the United States may intervene in

---

[1] This heading is not in the act.

any case or proceeding in the Commerce Court whenever,
though it has not been made a party, public interests are involved.

§ 5. Control of such suits.[1]

(Sec. 5.) That the Attorney-General shall have charge and
control of the interests of the Government in all cases and proceedings in the Commerce Court, and in the Supreme Court of
the United States upon appeal from the Commerce Court; and
if in his opinion the public interest requires it, he may retain
and employ in the name of the United States, within the appro-
priations from time to time made by the Congress for such
purposes, such special attorneys and counselors at law as he
may think necessary to assist in the discharge of any of the
duties incumbent upon him and his subordinate attorneys; and
the Attorney-General shall stipulate with such special attorneys and counsel the amount of their compensation, which shall
not be in excess of the sums appropriated therefor by Congress
for such purposes, and shall have supervision of their action:
Provided, That the Interstate Commerce Commission and any
party or parties in interest to the proceeding before the Commission, in which an order or requirement is made, may appear
as parties thereto of their own motion and as of right, and be
represented by their counsel, in any suit wherein is involved the
validity of such order or requirement or any part thereof, and
the interest of such party; and the Court wherein is pending such
suit may make all such rules and orders as to such appearances
and representations, the number of counsel, and all matters of
procedure, and otherwise, as to subserve the ends of justice and
speed the determination of such suits: *Provided further,* That
communities, associations, corporations, firms, and individuals
who are interested in the controversy or question before the
Interstate Commerce Commission, or in any suit which may be
brought by anyone under the terms of this Act, or the Acts
of which it is amendatory or which are amendatory of it, relating to action of the Interstate Commerce Commission, may
intervene in said suit or proceedings at any time after the in-

[1] This heading is not in the act.

stitution thereof, and the Attorney-General shall not dispose of or discontinue said suit or proceeding over the objection of such party or intervenor aforesaid, but said intervenor or intervenors may prosecute, defend, or continue said suit or proceeding unaffected by the action or nonaction of the Attorney-General of the United States therein.

Complainants before the Interstate Commerce Commission interested in a case shall have the right to appear and be made parties to the case and be represented before the courts by counsel under such regulations as are now permitted in similar circumstances under the rules and practice of equity courts of the United States.

§ 6. Pending and other proceedings.[1]

(SEC. 6.) That until the opening of the Commerce Court as in section one hereof provided, all cases and proceedings of which from that time the Commerce Court is hereby given exclusive jurisdiction may be brought in the same courts and conducted in like manner and with like effect as is now provided by law; and if any such case or proceeding shall have gone to final judgment or decree before the opening of the Commerce Court, appeal may be taken from such final judgment or decree in like manner and with like effect as is now provided by law. Any such case or proceeding within the jurisdiction of the Commerce Court which may have been begun in any other court as hereby allowed before the said date shall be forthwith transferred to the Commerce Court, if it has not yet proceeded to final judgment or decree in such other court unless it has been finally submitted for the decision of such Court, in which case the cause shall proceed in such Court to final judgment or decree and further proceeding thereafter, and appeal may be taken direct to the Supreme Court, and if remanded such cause may be sent back to the Court from which the appeal was taken or to the Commerce Court for further proceeding as the Supreme Court shall direct; and all previous proceedings in such transferred case shall stand and operate notwithstanding the transfer, subject to the same control over them by the Commerce Court

[1] This heading is not in the act.

and to the same right of subsequent action in the case or proceeding as if the transferred case or proceeding had been originally begun in the Commerce Court. The clerk of the Court from which any case or proceeding is so transferred to the Commerce Court shall transmit to and file in the Commerce Court the originals of all papers filed in such case or proceeding and a certified transcript of all record entries in the case or proceeding up to the time of transfer.

It shall be the duty of every common carrier subject to the provisions of this Act, within sixty days after the taking effect of this Act, to designate in writing an agent in the city of Washington, District of Columbia, upon whom service of all notices and processes may be made for and on behalf of said common carrier in any proceeding or suit pending before the Interstate Commerce Commission or before said Commerce Court, and to file such designation in the office of the secretary of the Interstate Commerce Commission, which designation may from time to time be changed by like writing similarly filed; and thereupon service of all notices and processes may be made upon such common carrier by leaving a copy thereof with such designated agent at his office or usual place of residence in the city of Washington, with like effect as if made personally upon such common carrier, and in default of such designation of such agent, service of any notice or other process in any proceeding before said Interstate Commerce Commission or Commerce Court may be made by posting such notice or process in the office of the secretary of the Interstate Commerce Commission.

§ 7. Pending cases.[1]

(SEC. 15.) That nothing in this Act contained shall undo or impair any proceedings heretofore taken by or before the Interstate Commerce Commission or any of the Acts of said Commission; and in any cases, proceedings, or matters now pending before it, the Commission may exercise any of the powers hereby conferred upon it, as would be proper in cases, proceedings, or matters hereafter initiated; and nothing in this Act contained shall operate to release or affect any obligation, liability, pen-

---

[1] This heading is not in the act.

alty, or forfeiture heretofore existing against or incurred by any person, corporation, or association.

§ 8. Special commission to investigate securities.[1]

(SEC. 16.) That the President is hereby authorized to appoint a commission to investigate questions pertaining to the issuance of stocks and bonds by railroad corporations, subject to the provisions of the Act to regulate commerce, and the power of Congress to regulate or affect the same, and to fix the compensation of the members of such commission. Said commission shall be and is hereby authorized to employ experts to aid in the work of inquiry and examination, and such clerks, stenographers, and other assistants as may be necessary, which employees shall be paid such compensation as the commission may deem just and reasonable, upon a certificate to be issued by the chairman of the commission. The several departments and bureaus of the Government shall detail from time to time such officials and employees and furnish such information to the commission as may be directed by the President. For the purposes of its investigations the commission shall be authorized to incur and have paid upon the certificate of its chairman such expenses as the commission shall deem necessary: *Provided, however,* That the total expenses authorized or incurred under the provisions of this section for compensation, employees, or otherwise, shall not exceed the sum of twenty-five thousand dollars.

§ 9. Interlocutory injunctions restraining enforcement of State statutes.[1]

(SEC. 17.) That no interlocutory injunction suspending or restraining the enforcement, operation, or execution of any statute of a State by restraining the action of any officer of such State in the enforcement or execution of such statute shall be issued or granted by any justice of the supreme court, or by any circuit court of the United States, or by any judge thereof, or by any district judge acting as circuit judge, upon the ground of the unconstitutionality of such statute, unless the application for the same shall be presented to a justice of the Supreme Court

¹ This heading is not in the act.

of the United States, or to a circuit judge, or to a district judge
acting as circuit judge, and shall be heard and determined by
three judges, of whom at least one shall be a justice of the Supreme Court of the United States or a circuit judge, and the
other two may be either circuit or district judges, and unless a
majority of said three judges shall concur in granting such application. Whenever such application as aforesaid is presented
to a justice of the Supreme Court of the United States, or to a
judge, he shall immediately call to his assistance to hear and
determine the application two other judges: *Provided, however,*
That one of such three judges shall be a justice of the Supreme
Court of the United States or a circuit judge. Said application
shall not be heard or determined before at least five days' notice
of the hearing has been given to the governor and to the attorney-
general of the State, and to such other persons as may be defendants in the suit: *Provided,* That if of opinion that irreparable
loss or damage would result to the complainant unless a temporary restraining order is granted, any justice of the Supreme
Court of the United States, or any circuit or district judge, may
grant such temporary restraining order at any time before such
hearing and determination of the application for an interlocutory
injunction, but such temporary restraining order shall only remain in force until the hearing and determination of the application for an interlocutory injunction upon notice as aforesaid.
The hearing upon such application for an interlocutory injunction shall be given precedence and shall be in every way expedited and be assigned for a hearing at the earliest practicable
day after the expiration of the notice hereinbefore provided for.
An appeal may be taken directly to the Supreme Court of the
United States from the order granting or denying, after notice
and hearing, an interlocutory injunction in such case.

§ 10. When act effective.[1]

(SEC. 18.) That this act shall take effect and be in force from
and after the expiration of sixty days after its passage, except
as to sections twelve [sec. 15 of Act to regulate commerce, p. 23
herein] and sixteen [sec. 16 of Commerce Court Act, p. 47

---

[1] This heading is not in the act.

herein], which sections shall take effect and be in force immediately.

Public, No. 41, approved February 4, 1887, as amended by Public, No. 125, approved March 2, 1889, and Public, No. 72, approved February 10, 1891. Public, No. 38, approved February 8, 1895. Public, No. 337, approved June 29, 1906. Public Res., No. 47, approved June 30, 1906. Public, No. 95, approved April 13, 1908. Public, No. 262, approved February 25, 1909. Public, No. 218, approved June 18, 1910.

APPENDIX C

THE ELKINS ACT

§ 1. Carrier corporation as well as officer liable to conviction.[1]

Be it enacted by the Senate and House of Representatives of the United States of America in Congress assembled, SEC. 1. (*As amended June 29, 1906.*)

That anything done or omitted to be done by a corporation common carrier, subject to the Act to regulate commerce and the Acts amendatory thereof, which, if done or omitted to be done by any director or officer thereof, or any receiver, trustee, lessee, agent, or person acting for or employed by such corporation, would constitute a misdemeanor under said Acts or under this Act, shall also be held to be a misdemeanor committed by such corporation, and upon conviction thereof it shall be subject to like penalties as are prescribed in said Acts or by this Act with reference to such persons, except as such penalties are herein changed. The willful failure upon the part of any carrier subject to said Acts to file and publish the tariffs or rates and charges as required by said Acts, or strictly to observe such tariffs until changed according to law, shall be a misdemeanor, and upon conviction thereof the corporation offending shall be subject to a fine of not less than one thousand dollars nor more than twenty thousand dollars for each offense; and it shall be unlawful for any person, persons, or corporation to offer, grant, or give, or to solicit, accept or receive any rebate, concession, or discrimination in respect to the transportation of any property in interstate or foreign commerce by any common carrier subject to said Act to regulate commerce and the Acts amendatory thereof whereby any such property shall by any device

[1] This heading is not in the act.

[1324]

whatever be transported at a less rate than that named in the tariffs published and filed by such carrier, as is required by said Act to regulate commerce and the Acts amendatory thereof, or whereby any other advantage is given or discrimination is practiced. Every person or corporation, whether carrier or shipper, who shall, knowingly, offer, grant, or give, or solicit, accept, or receive any such rebates, concession, or discrimination shall be deemed guilty of a misdemeanor, and on conviction thereof shall be punished by a fine of not less than one thousand dollars nor more than twenty thousand dollars: *Provided,* That any person, or any officer or director of any corporation subject to the provisions of this Act, or the Act to regulate commerce and the Acts amendatory thereof, or any receiver, trustee, lessee, agent, or person acting for or employed by any such corporation, who shall be convicted as aforesaid, shall, in addition to the fine herein provided for, be liable to imprisonment in the penitentiary for a term of not exceeding two years, or both such fine and imprisonment, in the discretion of the court. Every violation of this section shall be prosecuted in any court of the United States having jurisdiction of crimes within the district in which such violation was committed, or through which the transportation may have been conducted; and whenever the offense is begun in one jurisdiction and completed in another it may be dealt with, inquired of, tried, determined, and punished in either jurisdiction in the same manner as if the offense had been actually and wholly committed therein.

In construing and enforcing the provisions of this section, the act, omission, or failure of any officer, agent, or other person acting for or employed by any common carrier, or shipper, acting within the scope of his employment, shall in every case be also deemed to be the act, omission, or failure of such carrier or shipper as well as that of the person. Whenever any carrier files with the Interstate Commerce Commission or publishes a particular rate under the provisions of the Act to regulate commerce or Acts amendatory thereof, or participates in any rate so filed or published, that rate as against such carrier, its officers or agents, in any prosecution begun under this Act shall be conclusively deemed to be the legal rate, and any departure from such rate, or any offer to depart therefrom, shall be deemed to be an offense under this section of this Act.

Any person, corporation, or company who shall deliver property for interstate transportation to any common carrier, subject to the provisions of this Act, or for whom, as consignor or consignee, any such carrier shall transport property from one State, Territory, or the District of Columbia to any other State, Territory, or the District of Columbia, or foreign country, who shall knowingly by employee, agent, officer, or otherwise, directly or indirectly, by or through any means or device whatsoever, receive or accept from such common carrier any sum of money or any other valuable consideration as a rebate or offset against the regular charges for transportation of such property, as fixed by the schedules of rates provided for in this Act, shall in addition to any penalty provided by this Act forfeit to the United States a sum of money three times the amount of money so received or accepted and three times the value of any other consideration so received or accepted, to be ascertained by the trial court; and the Attorney-General of the United States is authorized and directed, whenever he has reasonable grounds to believe that any such person, corporation, or company has knowingly received or accepted from any such common carrier any sum of money or other valuable consideration as a rebate or offset as aforesaid, to institute in any court of the United States of competent jurisdiction a civil action to collect the said sum or sums so forfeited as aforesaid; and in the trial of said action all such rebates or other considerations so received or accepted for a period of six years prior to the commencement of the action may be included therein, and the amount recovered shall be three times the total amount of money, or three times the total value of such consideration, so received or accepted, or both, as the case may be.

§ 2. Persons interested may be made parties.[1]

SEC. 2. That in any proceeding for the enforcement of the provisions of the statutes relating to interstate commerce, whether such proceedings be instituted before the Interstate

---

[1] This heading is not in the act.

Commerce Commission or be begun originally in any circuit court of the United States, it shall be lawful to include as parties, in addition to the carrier, all persons interested in or affected by the rate, regulation, or practice under consideration, and inquiries, investigations, orders, and decrees may be made with reference to and against such additional parties in the same manner, to the same extent, and subject to the same provisions as are or shall be authorized by law with respect to carriers.

§ 3. Proceedings to enjoin or restrain departures from published rates or any discrimination.[1]

SEC. 3. That whenever the Interstate Commerce Commission shall have reasonable ground for belief that any common carrier is engaged in the carriage of passengers or freight traffic between given points at less than the published rates on file, or is committing any discriminations forbidden by law, a petition may be presented alleging such facts to the circuit court of the United States sitting in equity having jurisdiction; and when the act complained of is alleged to have been committed or as being committed in part in more than one judicial district or State, it may be dealt with, inquired of, tried, and determined in either such judicial district or State, whereupon it shall be the duty of the court summarily to inquire into the circumstances, upon such notice and in such manner as the court shall direct and without the formal pleadings and proceedings applicable to ordinary suits in equity, and to make such other persons or corporations parties thereto as the court may deem necessary, and upon being satisfied of the truth of the allegations of said petition said court shall enforce an observance of the published tariffs or direct and require a discontinuance of such discrimination by proper orders, writs, and process, which said orders, writs, and process may be enforceable as well against the parties interested in the traffic as against the carrier, subject to the right of appeal as now provided by law. It shall be the duty of the several district attorneys of the United States, whenever the Attorney-General shall direct, either of his own motion

[1] This heading is not in the act.

or upon the request of the Interstate Commerce Commission, to institute and prosecute such proceedings, and the proceedings provided for by this Act shall not preclude the bringing of suit for the recovery of damages by any party injured, or any other action provided by said Act approved February fourth, eighteen hundred and eighty-seven, entitled "An Act to regulate commerce" and the Acts amendatory thereof. And in proceedings under this Act and the Acts to regulate commerce the said courts shall have the power to compel the attendance of witnesses, both upon the part of the carrier and the shipper, who shall be required to answer on all subjects relating directly or indirectly to the matter in controversy, and to compel the production of all books and papers, both of the carrier and the shipper, which relate directly or indirectly to such transaction; the claim that such testimony or evidence may tend to criminate the person giving such evidence shall not excuse such person from testifying or such corporation producing its books and papers, but no person shall be prosecuted or subjected to any penalty or forfeiture for or on account of any transaction, matter, or thing concerning which he may testify or produce evidence, documentary or otherwise, in such proceeding: *Provided*, That the provisions of an Act entitled "An Act to expedite the hearing and determination of suits in equity pending or hereafter brought under the Act of July second, eighteen hundred and ninety, entitled 'An Act to protect trade and commerce against unlawful restraints and monopolies,' 'An Act to regulate commerce,' approved February fourth, eighteen hundred and eighty-seven, or any other acts having a like purpose that may be hereafter enacted, approved February eleventh, nineteen hundred and three," shall apply to any case prosecuted under the direction of the Attorney-General in the name of the Interstate Commerce Commission.

§ 4. Conflicting laws repealed.[1]

SEC. 4. That all Acts and parts of Acts in conflict with the provisions of this Act are hereby repealed, but such repeal shall not affect causes now pending, nor rights which have already ac-

[1] This heading is not in the act.

crued, but such causes shall be prosecuted to a conclusion and such rights enforced in a manner heretofore provided by law and as modified by the provisions of this Act.

Sec. 5. That this Act shall take effect from its passage.

Public, No. 103, approved February 19, 1903.

APPENDIX D

THE EXPEDITING ACT

§ 1. Expedition of cases.[1]

Be it enacted by the Senate and House of Representatives of the United States of America in Congress assembled, Sec. 1. (*As amended June 25, 1910.*)

That in any suit in equity pending or hereafter brought in any circuit court of the United States under the Act entitled " An Act to protect trade and commerce against unlawful restraints and monopolies," approved July second, eighteen hundred and ninety, "An Act to regulate commerce," approved February fourth, eighteen hundred and eighty-seven, or any other Acts having a like purpose that hereafter may be enacted, wherein the United States is complainant, the Attorney General may file with the clerk of such court a certificate that, in his opinion, the case is of general public importance, a copy of which shall be immediately furnished by such clerk to each of the circuit judges of the circuit in which the case is pending. Thereupon such case shall be given precedence over others and in every way expedited, and be assigned for hearing at the earliest practicable day, before not less than three of the circuit judges of said court, if there be three or more; and if there be not more than two circuit judges, then before them and such district judge as they may select or, in case the full court shall not at any time be made up by reason of the necessary absence or disqualification of one or more of the said circuit judges, the justice of the Supreme Court assigned to that circuit or the other circuit judge or judges may designate a district judge or judges within the circuit who shall be competent to sit in said court at the hearing of said suit. In the event the judges sit-

---

[1] This heading is not in the act.

[1330]

ting in such case shall be equally divided in opinion as to the decision or disposition of said cause, or in the event that a majority of said judges shall be unable to agree upon the judgment, order, or decree finally disposing of said case in said court which should be entered in said cause, then they shall immediately certify that fact to the Chief Justice of the United States, who shall at once designate and appoint some circuit judge to sit with said judges and to assist in determining said cause. Such order of the Chief Justice shall be immediately transmitted to the clerk of the circuit court in which said cause is pending, and shall be entered upon the minutes of said court. Thereupon said cause shall at once be set down for reargument and the parties thereto notified in writing by the clerk of said court of the action of the court and the date fixed for the reargument thereof. The provisions of this section shall apply to all causes and proceedings in all courts now pending, or which may hereafter be brought.

§ 2. Appeal to Supreme Court.[1]

SEC. 2. That in every suit in equity pending or hereafter brought in any circuit court of the United States under any of said Acts, wherein the United States is complainant, including cases submitted but not yet decided, an appeal from the final decree of the circuit court will lie only to the Supreme Court and must be taken within sixty days from the entry thereof: *Provided*, That in any case where an appeal may have been taken from the final decree of a circuit court to the circuit court of appeals before this Act takes effect, the case shall proceed to a final decree therein, and an appeal may be taken from such decree to the Supreme Court in the manner now provided by law.

Public, No. 82, approved February 11, 1903; Public, No. 310, approved June 25, 1910.

---

[1] This heading is not in the act.

APPENDIX E

FORMS FOR PROCEEDINGS BEFORE COMMISSIONS

§ 1. Complaint of unreasonable charges.

INTERSTATE COMMERCE COMMISSION

McCLAIN, WADE & CO.
     against
OREGON RAILWAY &
  NAVIGATION CO.

The petition of the above-named complainants respectfully shows:

I. Your petitioners complain of the Oregon Railway & Navigation Company and respectfully represent: That on the 13th day of June, D. A. 1887, your petitioners shipped from the City of Colfax, in the Territory of Washington, to the City of Portland, in the State of Oregon, two car loads of wheat, to wit: 122 sacks of wheat of the weight of 20,000 pounds on one car, and 230 sacks of wheat of the weight of 30,000 pounds on the other car. That the said two car loads of wheat were loaded on said cars at your petitioners' sole expense, and were delivered to said Oregon Railway & Navigation Company for transportation to Portland, Oregon, as aforesaid, on said 30th day of June, A. D. 1887. That the distance from the said City of Colfax, in Washington Territory, to Portland, Oregon, does not exceed 320 miles. That the said Oregon Railway & Navigation Company, against the protests of your petitioners, have charged your petitioners for transporting the said two cars loads of wheat the said 320 miles, the full sum of $175, or at the rate of $7 for each ton of 2,000 pounds.

II. Your petitioners further aver that it is stated in the annual report of the said Oregon Railway & Navigation Company for 1886, that the total cost of all property of every description owned by said company, including ocean steamers, river and sound boats, barges and wharves, is $32,924,433.72; while its net income from railroad earnings alone was, as appears by the same report, $2,256,589.78, or 6 8/10 per

[1332]

cent on the whole nominal investment of that company, without counting its earnings from other sources. That during the same year that company transported over its railroad lines 123,413,669 tons of freight and merchandise, and that the average price it received for transporting merchandise from Portland, Oregon, to Colfax, Washington Territory, was in excess of $30 per ton.

III. Your petitioners further allege that the rates recommended by the railroad commissioners of the State of Oregon, for the transportation of wheat from points in the State of Oregon, equidistant from said Portland, Oregon, with the city of Colfax, in Washington Territory, and reached by the line of the Oregon Railway & Navigation Company, is $4 per ton, or $3 per ton less than the said company has charged your petitioners.

IV. Your petitioners further allege that the said Oregon Railway & Navigation Company has agreed to make a rate from points in Columbia county, Washington Territory, as far from Portland, Oregon, as is the city of Colfax, for the transportation of wheat and other grains over the line of said railroad to said Portland, Oregon, of $5 per ton, while still continuing the rate from said Colfax at $7 per ton, thus charging your petitioners, and all other handlers of grain in Colfax, $2 per ton more for transporting their wheat the same distance than is charged the wheat raisers and buyers shipping from said points in Columbia county.

V. And your petitioners further allege that the sum of $7 per ton for the transportation of wheat as aforesaid from Colfax, Washington Territory, to Portland, Oregon, is unjust and unreasonable; and that a just and reasonable charge for such transportation is $3.50 per ton, which is approximately the rate fixed for a haul of the same distance by the Illinois State law.

VI. Wherefore, your petitioners pray that you may direct the said Oregon Railway & Navigation Company to reimburse to your petitioners the sum of $87.50, the sum paid by your petitioners to the said Oregon Railway & Navigation Company for the transportation of said two car loads of wheat to Portland, Oregon, in excess of a just and reasonable freight charge. And your petitioners further pray that the said Oregon Railway & Navigation Company may be required to establish a rate for the transportation of grain from Colfax, Washington Territory, to Portland, Oregon, not in excess of $3.50 per ton.

McClaine, Wade & Co.,
By Alfred Coolidge,
Member of Firm.

§ 2. Complaint of wrong classification.

INTERSTATE COMMERCE COMMISSION

NATIONAL MACHINERY &
WRECKING CO.
      against
PITTSBURG, CINCINNATI, CHICAGO
& ST. LOUIS RY. CO. ET AL.

The petition of the above-named complainant respectfully shows:

I. That the complainant is a partnership composed of Jacob W. and Milton S. Kohn, in the State of Ohio, having its principal office and place of business in the city of Cleveland in said State and is a dealer in boilers, generators, motors and other machines, shipping the same, new and secondhand, between points lying in different States of the United States, particularly in those States lying in Official Classification territory, which is generally described as that territory lying north of the Potomac and Ohio and east of the Mississippi rivers.

II. The above-named defendants are common carriers engaged in the transportation of property by continuous carriage or shipment by railroad between points in different States of the United States and largely in said Official Classification territory, and as such common carriers are subject to the provisions of the Act to Regulate Commerce approved February 4, 1887, and acts amendatory thereof or supplementary thereto.

III. That complainant, in the course of its business, ships over defendants' lines of railroad old and secondhand dynamos from points in other States to Cleveland, where they are converted into junk. That in Official Classification No. 26, dated January 2, 1905, adopted by defendants and now enforced upon their lines, dynamos, new and secondhand, boxed or on skids, crated, are classified at first class and take first-class rates over defendants' lines. That by such classification and rating defendants compel complainant to pay on its shipments of old and secondhand dynamos, which are practically worthless, the first-class rate, which is the same as is charged on new and valuable dynamos. That said rating of secondhand dynamos in the same class as new dynamos is unreasonable, unduly discriminatory, and should be changed. That the classification of secondhand or defective dynamos should be the same as that applied to junk in Official Classification, to wit, sixth class, which affords sufficient compensation for the transportation service performed, because such second-hand dynamos have no more value than the metal contained in them.

IV. That the wrongful classification and rating above set forth results in unreasonable and unjust transportation charges on complainant's shipments of secondhand dynamos in Official Classification territory, in violation of section one of said Act to Regulate Commerce, and subjects complainant and other shippers of secondhand dynamos, and their traffic, within the Official Classification territory, to unjust discrimination and undue and unreasonable prejudice and disadvantage, in violation of sections two and three of said Act to Regulate Commerce.

V. That on or about the 5th day of October, 1905, complainant had shipped to it from Marietta, Georgia, one secondhand dynamo, weighing 6,300 pounds, and costing complainant $85.00, which was delivered by connections to the defendant, the Pittsburg, Cincinnati, Chicago & St. Louis Railway Company, at Cincinnati, Ohio, and transported thence by said defendant to Columbus, Ohio, thence via the Cleveland, Akron & Columbus Railway Company to Hudson, Ohio, and thence via the Pennsylvania Company to complainant at Cleveland, Ohio. That said shipment was billed out as "one box of scrap iron" and complainant expected it to take the scrap-iron rate of 65 cents per 100 pounds; but before delivery the rate was advanced to the rate on new dynamos of $1.33 per 100 pounds. That complainant was compelled to pay the unjust and unreasonable rate of $1.33 per 100 pounds for the transportation of such shipment, aggregating the sum of $83.79, instead of the just and reasonable rate of 65 cents per 100 pounds, aggregating the sum of $40.95. That by reason of said unjust classification complainant was compelled to pay an excess charge of $42.84, for which reparation is claimed.

Wherefore, complainant prays that defendants may be required to answer the charges herein; that after due hearing and investigation an order be made requiring the defendants, the Pittsburg, Cincinnati, Chicago & St. Louis Railway Company, the Cleveland, Akron & Columbus Railway Company, and the Pennsylvania Company, to pay to complainant the sum of $42.84, or such other sum as, upon the proof to be adduced, the Commission may find complainant entitled to; and requiring all the defendants herein mentioned to wholly cease and desist from the aforesaid violation of said Act to Regulate Commerce; and that such other and further order or orders may be entered as the

Commission may deem necessary in the premises and complainant's cause may appear to require.

Dated at Cleveland, Ohio.

NATIONAL MACHINERY & WRECKING COMPANY,

By...........................

Secretary.

§ 3. Answer on the merits.

INTERSTATE COMMERCE COMMISSION

[Caption as above.]

The Pennsylvania Railroad Company, for answer to the said petition, or so much thereof as it is advised it is necessary for it to make answer unto, saith:

First. That it admits that a through route between the various companies respondent exists, substantially as alleged in said petition, and that the rate of charges for lumber from the points indicated in said petition, that is to say, from Macon and Atlanta in the State of Georgia, and from Johnson City, in the State of Tennessee, to Boston, are, as per their tariffs filed, the same as set out in the said petition.

Second. That whether the petitioners have a large amount of money invested in business in Johnson City, which they cannot withdraw without severe loss, is a fact as to which this respondent cannot be advised, and asks that the petitioners be held to proof thereof. This respondent, however, denies that the rate which the tariff describes for lumber on said through line from Johnson City to Boston is unjust or unreasonable, or that it greatly unjures or unjustly restricts the business of the petitioners.

Third. That the rates from Macon of 36 cents and from Atlanta of 34 cents per 100 pounds upon lumber, as well as the rate of 36 cents per 100 pounds from Johnson City, were fixed by the East Tennessee, Virginia & Georgia Railway Company, the initial company; and that the reasons justifying the said rates of 36 cents and 34 cents per 100 pounds respectively from Macon and Atlanta, respectively 1328 miles and 1240 miles from Boston, as compared with the rate of 36 cents per 100 pounds for the shorter distance from Johnson City, in the State of Tennessee, to Boston, are as follows:

(a) That the rates in the State of Georgia are fixed and controlled by the Railroad Commissioners of that State, that Commission fixing the charges for transportation to coast cities from mills in the State of Georgia.

[1336]

(b) The fact of water competition from Brunswick, Georgia, on the Atlantic Ocean, to Boston and other North Atlantic points; that adding the rate from the mills to Brunswick, as fixed by the Railroad Commissioners of Georgia, to the rate given by the coast line water carriers to Boston, the aggregate is less than the amount charged, as aforesaid, upon the tariffs of the respondents on their through railroad carriage from Macon and Atlanta to Boston.

(c) A large amount of freight is received at Altanta and Macon from eastern cities, including Boston, vessels containing which would have to return empty in large part, but for the fact that they can be returned loaded with lumber.

(d) The reason why the Atlanta charge is the same as that from Macon arises from the fact that the lumber shipped from Atlanta is manufactured at mills a considerable distance from that city, and transported there over local roads before being marketed.

(e) That the lumber shipped from Johnson City is for the most part poplar lumber, while that which goes from Georgia territory is exclusively Georgia pine; and that the rate per 100 pounds per mile for hauling poplar, by reason of its greater bulk, should reasonably be greater than that for hauling pine.

As to all of which matters reference is made for fuller details, to the answer of the East Tennessee, Virginia & Georgia Railway Company.

Wherefore this respondent prays that the said petition be dismissed.

THE PENNSYLVANIA RAILROAD COMPANY,

By..............................

General Freight Agent.

§ 4. Answer denying the jurisdiction.

INTERSTATE COMMERCE COMMISSION

[Caption as above.]

The New York & New England Railroad Company, one of the respondents in the above-entitled cause, separately answering such portions of the complainants' petition as it is advised it is important and necessary to make answer unto, says:

That it is not true, as averred in the first paragraph of the said complaint, that the respondent with the other companies named therein form one connecting through line under joint traffic arrangements; that the respondent has no contract or contracts or traffic arrangements with the East Tennessee, Virginia & Georgia Railway Company nor the Norfolk & Western Railway Company, nor with the Shenandoah Valley Railroad Company; that it has no contract or contracts or traffic arrangements with the respondents named herein whose railroads are located south of the Cumberland Valley Railroad Company; the lumber received by the respondent from points south of the Cumberland Valley Railroad is rebilled by said Cumberland Valley Railroad Company and again rebilled by the New York, New Haven & Hartford Railroad Company at Harlem River.

It admits that it has carried lumber at the rate of 36 cents per 100 pounds in full car-load lots, which it is informed has come from Johnson City, in the State of Tennessee, to Boston as aforesaid; but the respondent denies that it has carried any lumber from Atlanta, Georgia, or any other point south of Hagerstown at a rate of 34 cents per 100 pounds from such initial point to Boston; and it denies that it has charged or received any greater compensation in the aggregate for the transportation of like kind of property under substantially similar circumstances and conditions for a shorter than for a longer distance over the same line, in the same direction, the shorter being included within the longer distance.

It admits that it has carried lumber over this road which it is informed has come from Macon, in the State of Georgia, to Boston, at a rate of 36 cents per 100 pounds, and says that this rate was made by the initial road without consultation with this respondent.

And the respondent, further answering, says the rate of 36 cents per 100 pounds for transportation of lumber from Johnson City to Boston, a distance of 915 miles, which rate of 36 cents is less than eight mills per ton per mile, and which is divided among seven railroad companies, for which service this respondent is required to furnish expensive terminal facilities is not in itself an unreasonably high rate, and that said rate should not be reduced.

This respondent denies each and all of the allegations of the petitioners' complaint not hereinbefore admitted or denied.

New York & New England R. R. Company,

By.........................

Vice-President.

APPENDIX F

FORMS FOR PROCEEDINGS INVOLVING COMMISSIONS

§ 1. Bill to enforce order of the Commission.

BILL OF COMPLAINT

INTERSTATE COMMERCE COMMISSION against ILLINOIS CENTRAL RAILROAD COMPANY ET AL.	IN THE CIRCUIT COURT OF THE UNITED STATES. IN EQUITY.

To the Circuit Court of the United States sitting in equity, etc. [*hereafter these bills will be brought in the Commerce Court sitting*].

Your petitioner the Interstate Commerce Commission, which was created and established and now exists under and by virtue of an act of the Congress of the United States, entitled an Act to Regulate Commerce, approved February 4, 1887, as amended, etc. (here follow dates of amendatory acts), humbly complaining showeth:

I. That the Illinois Central Railroad Company is, etc. (here follow the names of the various railroad corporations made defendants with the usual descriptions).

II. That the defendants above named were on the 24th day of July, 1903, and ever since have been and still are common carriers engaged in the transportation of persons and property by railroad under joint through rates and as members of continuous through lines between points in different States of the United States, and particularly in the transportation of lumber from lumber-shipping points on their respective lines, [etc.] to "Ohio River points" [etc.], and to points north of the Ohio River and on and east of the Mississippi River, and as such common carriers and in respect to such transportation were and

[1339]

are subject to the provisions of the said act to regulate commerce and the amendments thereto.

III. That on the said 24th day of July, 1903, the Central Yellow Pine Association, composed of persons, firms and corporations engaged in the business of handling yellow pine lumber in the States of [etc.] filed, under section 13 of said Act to Regulate Commerce, a petition or complaint alleging violations on the part of the defendants of certain provisions of said act, as at large and more fully appears in and by the said complaint or petition on file in the office of the complainant herein, a copy whereof is hereunto annexed and made a part of this bill of complaint as Exhibit A; and that a copy of said Exhibit A, attested by the secretary of the complainant under the seal of the complainant was duly forwarded by the complainant to each of said defendants, as required by section 13 of said act.

IV. That on August 15, 1903, the defendants filed answers to said complaint, Exhibit A hereto, as at large and more fully appears in and by said answers on file in the office of the complainant herein, copies of which are hereto annexed and made parts of this petition as Exhibits from B to F, both inclusive.

V. That thereafterwards the said cause being at issue upon the pleadings aforesaid, duly came on for investigation and hearing before the complainant herein, the said Interstate Commerce Commission at [etc.] on [etc.] at which times and places the parties complainant and defendant appeared by their attorneys, or had due notice to appear, and testimony was taken on behalf of said parties.

VI. That on February 7, 1905, the complainant herein duly determined the matter in controversy between the said parties before it and made a report in writing in respect thereof setting forth its findings of fact and its conclusions based on said findings, namely, that an advance made April 15, 1903, by all the defendants from, etc. [the shipping points named] to, etc. [the Ohio River points named], of 2 cents in the rate on lumber in car loads was not warranted and that the resultant increased rates were unreasonable and unjust, in violation of the Act to Regulate Commerce, as at large and more fully appears in and by the said report of the complainant, a copy whereof is hereunto annexed and made part of this petition or bill of complaint as Exhibit G.

VII. That forthwith upon the determination of said cause as aforesaid on, to wit: said 7th day of February, 1905, the complainant duly formulated an order and notice in the premises based upon its findings and conclusions, requiring the defendants to cease and desist on or before April 1, 1905, from further maintaining or enforcing the said unlawful advance of 2 cents per 100 pounds, or the said unlawful rates resulting therefrom as aforesaid, which said order now remains in full force and effect, and a copy whereof is hereunto annexed and made part of this bill of complaint as Exhibit H, etc.

VIII. That the complainant agreeably to the provisions of the law in this regard duly caused a properly authenticated copy of its said report, Exhibit G hereunto, together with its said order Exhibit H hereunto, to be delivered to said defendants herein, and complainant shows that the said defendants, unmindful of their duty in that regard, have, through their officers, servants and attorneys, wholly disregarded and set at naught said order of the complainant, Exhibit H hereto, and have willfully and knowingly violated and disobeyed the same, and still do neglect and refuse to comply with the same or any part thereof.

IX. And the complainant charges that the said advance of 2 cents in the said lumber rates was and is unwarranted and has resulted in rates excessive, unreasonable and unjust in violation of the act to regulate commerce.

X. Wherefore the complainant prays:

1. That a subpœna or other suitable process may issue according to the course of equity [etc.].

2. That an order be made by this honorable court directing the method of service of notice [etc.].

3. That proper orders may be passed pending the cause as will secure a speedy hearing [etc.].

4. That proper orders to facilitate inquiries be made [etc.].

5. That upon the final hearing hereof a decree may be entered granting to complainant a writ of injunction or other proper process, mandatory or otherwise, to restrain the said defendants, and each of them, and their respective officers, servants and agents, from further continuing in their violation of and disobedience to the said order of the Commission.

6. That a decree may be entered fixing a sum not exceeding $500 per day, for every day of disobedience to the injunction [etc.].

7. That a decree may be entered requiring the said defendants to pay the costs of this proceeding and reasonable counsel fees.

8. For such other and further relief in the premises as to the court may seem meet and justice and the equities of the case may require.

THE INTERSTATE COMMERCE COMMISSION,
by Edw. A. Moseley,
The Secretary thereof, thereto duly authorized.

[1341]

§ 2. Abstract of answer to the above complaint.

[Caption as above.   Beginning as is usual in answer in equity.]

I. Admit organization of the Commission, and existence of the defendant.

II. Admit that they are common carriers engaged in interstate transportation as described.

III. Admit proceedings duly begun by the Central Yellow Pine Association; and service thereof upon the defendants.

IV. Admit the filing of the answers as alleged.

V. Admit the hearings as described.

VI. Admit that the Commission determined the matter in controversy; but deny that the complainant "duly" determined it.

VII. Admit the formulation of the determination, but deny that the rates were properly found to be "unlawful."

VIII. Admit the service of the authenticated copy of the determination upon the defendants; and that the defendants conceiving said order to be unlawful have disregarded the same.

IX. Deny that the advance in the rate was unwarranted, deny that the resulting rate is excessive.

Respondents having fully answered pray to be hence dismissed with their reasonable cost.

§ 3. Bill to enjoin order of the Commission.

BILL OF COMPLAINT

THE CHICAGO & ALTON RAILROAD COM-
PANY, COMPLAINANT,
    against   ⎫
                                               ⎬ IN EQUITY.
THE INTERSTATE COMMERCE COMMIS-   ⎭
SION, DEFENDANT.

To the Honorable the Judges of the Circuit Court of the United States within and for the Northern District of Illinois:

The Chicago & Alton Railroad Company, a corporation organized and existing under and by virtue of the laws of the State of Illinois, brings this its bill against the Interstate Commerce Commission, established and existing under and by virtue of an act of the Congress of the United States, and thereupon your orator complains and says:

That the Chicago & Alton Railroad Company is a corporation duly organized under the laws of the State of Illinois; that the defendant, the Interstate Commerce Commission, had been created and exists, and during all the time herein mentioned, has existed, under and by virtue of an act of the Congress of the United States, entitled, "An Act to Regulate Commerce," approved February 4, 1887, and the acts amendatory thereof.

Your orator further avers that it has its principal operating office in the city of Chicago, Northern District of Illinois, Eastern Division.

Your orator further avers that the Chicago & Alton Railroad Company, is a common carrier, engaged in the transportation of property by railroad from and to points in various States and Territories of these United States to and from points within the States of Illinois and Missouri; that your orator is engaged and has been so engaged since the 29th day of April, 1908, in the transportation of commercial coal from the points within the States of Illinois and Missouri to points to the same States and beyond; that numerous coal mines are located on and along your orator's line, within the States of Illinois and Missouri, and principally within the State of Illinois; that these mines ship large quantities of commercial coal by your orator's line to consignees at different points upon the lines of other common carriers; that your orator for the accommodation of this commercial coal traffic, owns and operates 3,037 gondola coal cars; that when requested by the consignor or consignee, it furnishes in addition box cars for the transportation of coal; that its said 3,037 gondola cars and such box car equipment as may be desired by the shippers are sufficient at all ordinary times to transport all commercial coal tendered to your orator for shipment from the mines to consignees at various points upon your orator's line and beyond.

Your orator further avers (here it is stated that the railroad has 360 special fuel cars of its own which it utilizes exclusively to get its necessary fuel from the mines on its line).

Your orator further avers (here it is stated that the coal thus taken in fuel cars is not put into the course of commerce at all).

Your orator further avers (that at certain periods of the year, to wit, in the early winter months, there is a shortage of equipment for hauling commercial shipments of coal from mines along your orator's railroad; that at times of such car shortage your orator furnishes various mines along its line with commercial equipment pro rata in accordance with a certain circular bearing date October 17, 1906, effective November 1, 1906, and now in full force upon your orator's line, said circular being in words and figures as follows—here the rules governing the distribution of cars to coal mines contained in said circular are set forth in full, providing among other things that fuel cars will not be computed in assigning the quota of system cars).

Your orator further avers (that on, to wit, the 27th day of April, 1908, the Interstate Commerce Commission entered an order requiring your orator to cease and exist on or before the first day of July, 1908, and during a period of at least two years thereafter from maintaining and enforcing the present practice of coal car distribution along its line of railroad, said order being in words and figures as follows:—to wit,—here follows the order of the Interstate Commerce Commission directing that fuel cars shall be taken into consideration in making the allotment).

Your orator further avers (that a copy of said order was duly served upon a principal officer of your orator at his usual place of business).

Your orator further avers (that the said order of the said defendant the Interstate Commerce Commission was made upon a complaint filed with said body by the Illinois Collieries Company; that subsequent to the filing of said complaint, an answer was filed by your orator and testimony adduced by the said parties).

Your orator further avers (that, in requiring your orator to take into consideration its own fuel cars in determining the distribution of coal cars among the various mines along its line and to count as a part of the proportion of the mine, such cars as are consigned for your orator's own fuel, is unreasonable, unjust, oppressive and unlawful in that, etc.).

Your orator further avers (here it is claimed that the practice of car distribution is not subject to regulation by the Interstate Commerce Commission).

Your orator further avers (here it is claimed that the practice sought to be established by the Interstate Commerce Commission is not within its jurisdiction).

Your orator further avers (here it is claimed that there is no unreasonable discrimination by the non-counting of the orator's fuel cars).

Your orator further avers (here it is claimed that the fuel cars are not part of its commercial equipment).

Your orator further avers (here it is claimed that the order of the Interstate Commerce Commission is an unreasonable discrimination against mine supplying it with coal).

Your orator further avers (that the order limits the amount of coal to be mined, a matter outside the jurisdiction of the Commission).

Your orator further avers (here it is pointed out that the orator's own fuel supply does not enter into commerce).

Your orator further avers (that if the said order of the said defendant, the Interstate Commerce Commission, is allowed to become effective a multiplicity of suits against it will be caused).

Your orator further avers (that the acts of the Interstate Commerce Commission in which it intends to persist are contrary to equity and tend to the manifest injury of the orator.)

Your orator therefore prays that upon the filing of this bill a temporary or interlocutory order may be entered herein suspending the said order of the said Interstate Commerce Commission, and restraining the said Commission from taking any steps or instituting any proceedings to enforce said order, and that upon a final hearing of this cause a decree may be entered herein enjoining, setting aside, annulling or suspending, the said order of the said Interstate Commerce Commission, and perpetually enjoining the enforcement of said order, and perpetually enjoining to the said defendants and its members their agents, servants, and representatives from the enforcing of the said order, and from taking any steps or taking any proceedings towards the enforcement of the said order. Your orator further prays that such other and further relief may be granted in the premises as justice and equity may require.

Your orator prays that your honors may grant under your orator the writ of subpœna of the United States of America directed to the said Interstate Commerce Commissiom, commanding it on a certain day and under a certain penalty herein to be specified, personally to be and appear before your honors in this honorable court, and then and there full, true and complete answer to make to all and singular the premises, but not under oath, the answer under oath, hereby being expressly waived, and to stand to and abide by such order of decree herein as to your honors shall seem meet, and agreeable to equity and good conscience.

And your orator will ever pray, etc.

THE CHICAGO & ALTON RAILROAD COMPANY,

By...........................

Its Solicitors.

[1345]

State of Illinois,
County of Cook.

George H. Ross, being duly sworn says that he is vice-president of
the Chicago & Alton Railroad Company, complainant in the above-
entitled cause; that he knows the facts stated above and foregoing bill
of complaint and that the said facts are true.

Subscribed and sworn.

§ 4. Abstract of answer to this bill.

[Begins as is usual with an answer in equity.]

I. Sets forth the establishment of the Commission under the Interstate Commerce Act.

II. Sets forth its powers under section 12 of the act.

III. Sets forth its powers under section 13 of the act.

IV. Sets forth its powers under section 15 of the act.

V. Admits the defendant's fulfillment of its duties as an interstate
carrier except in time of car shortage.

VI. Relates to private cars.

VII. Admits the necessity of private fuel cars.

VIII. Admits defendant's car rules.

IX. Admits defendant's readiness generally.

X. Admits defendant's proper management.

XI. Sets forth the proceedings before the Commission.

XII. States that they were in due form.

XIII. Denies that its order was discriminatory.

XIV. Shows how the railroad distribution operated as a discrimination.

XV. Shows how the assignment of fuel cars worked undue preference.

XVI. Claims that as an expert body thus empowered its conclusions
should be held *prima facie* correct, and should not be set aside by the
courts except in a clear case of error.

XVII. Shows that the burden is upon the complainant to show why
its order should not be enforced, especially as the railroad is producing
no further evidence.

XVIII. Concludes as is usual in an answer in equity.

www.ingramcontent.com/pod-product-compliance
Lightning Source LLC
Chambersburg PA
CBHW021938220326
41599CB00010BA/281